Money,
Sound and Unsound

Money,
Sound and Unsound

Joseph T. Salerno

LvMI
MISES INSTITUTE

2nd printing

Published 2015 by the Mises Institute. This work is licensed under a
Creative Commons Attribution-NonCommercial-NoDerivs 4.0
International License.
http://creativecommons.org/license/by-nc-nd/4.0/

Ludwig von Mises Institute
518 West Magnolia Avenue
Auburn, Alabama 36832
mises.org

ISBN:978-1-61016-655-3

CONTENTS

Part One:
Foundations of Monetary Theory

Part Two:
Inflation, Deflation and Depression

Part Three:
The Gold Standard

Part Four:
Applications

Part Five:
Commentary

ACKNOWLEDGEMENTS

I wish to thank Douglas French and Jeffrey Tucker, President and Editorial Vice President of the Ludwig von Mises Institute, respectively, for originally suggesting the idea for this book and for their moral support and encouragement—and forbearance—during its preparation. I am especially thankful to the donors of the Mises Institute whose generous support has made the publication of this volume a reality. My greatest intellectual debt is to my dear friend and mentor Murray Rothbard. Throughout his brilliant career he was an articulate, courageous, and intransigent proponent of sound money. Of course, Mises and Hayek also profoundly influenced my thinking, and I learned much from the works of William H. Hutt, Henry Hazlitt, Hans Sennholz, Jacques Rueff, Michael Heilperin, Wilhelm Röpke, and Benjamin Anderson. All were fearless and outspoken advocates of sound money during the high tide of Keynesianism.

I am indebted to my many colleagues who have read and commented on various drafts of these essays and whose articles and books in the sound money paradigm have taught and inspired me over the years. Although far too numerous for me to properly acknowledge here, they include Walter Block, William Butos, John Cochran, Roger Garrison, Jeffrey Herbener, Hans-Hermann Hoppe, Jesús Huerta de Soto, Jörg Guido Hülsmann, Antony Mueller, Gary North, George Reisman, Pascal Salin, the late Larry Sechrest, the late Sudha Shenoy, Frank Shostak, Mark Thornton, Lawrence H. White, and, of course, the polymathic David Gordon. I am especially grateful to Llewellyn H. Rockwell, Jr. founder and Chairman of the Mises Institute who has steadfastly supported and encouraged all of my writing projects and has provided an institutional home for the modern sound money movement. Several of the essays collected in this book were presented as papers at New York University Colloquium on Market Institutions and Economic Processes (formerly, the Austrian Economics Colloquium), and I thank its members for their cogent suggestions and criticisms. Last but not least, I owe a great debt of gratitude to Helen and Michael Salerno, who suffered through my long absences, periods of distraction, and occasional irritability while these essays were being written. This is a debt that cannot easily be repaid.

INTRODUCTION

The twenty-six essays collected in this book were published over the last three decades in a variety of academic journals, scholarly books, policy report series, and periodicals aimed at the non-specialist. Several were originally published in electronic periodicals. They share a common theme despite the fact that they were written at different times and for disparate audiences. This theme may be broadly summed up in the term "sound money" as defined by Ludwig von Mises. According to Mises:

> [T]he sound money principle has two aspects. It is affirmative in approving the market's choice of a commonly used medium of exchange. It is negative in obstructing the government's propensity to meddle with the currency system.... Sound money meant a metallic standard.... The excellence of the gold standard is to be seen in the fact that it renders the determination of the monetary unit's purchasing power independent of governments and political parties.[1]

The idea of sound money was present from the very beginning of modern monetary theory in the works of the sixteenth-century Spanish Scholastics who argued against debasement of the coinage by the king on ethical and economic grounds.[2] The concept of sound

---

[1] Ludwig von Mises, *The Theory of Money and Credit*, 2nd ed. (Irvington-on-Hudson, New York: Foundation for Economic Education, 1971), pp. 414–16.

[2] Jesús Huerta de Soto, "New Light on the Prehistory of the Theory of Banking and the School of Salamanca," *Review of Austrian Economics*, 9, no. 2 (1996): pp. 59–81; idem, "Juan de Mariana: The Influence if the Spanish Scholastics," in Randall G. Holcombe, ed., *15 Great Austrian Economists* (Auburn, Ala.: Ludwig von Mises Institute, 1999), pp. 1–12; and Jörg Guido Hülsmann, *The Ethics of Money Production* (Auburn, Ala.: Ludwig von Mises Institute, 2008); and Alejandro Chafuen, *Faith and*

money, or "sound currency" as it was then called, was central to the writings of David Ricardo and his fellow "bullionists" in the early nineteenth century who argued that the price inflation observed in Great Britain during and after the Napoleonic Wars was caused by the suspension of the convertibility of bank notes into gold and silver mandated by the British government.[3] The ideal of the bullionists was "a self-regulating currency"[4] whose quantity, value and distribution among nations were governed exclusively by market forces of supply and demand.

The sound money doctrine reached the peak of its influence in the mid-nineteenth century after another great debate in Great Britain between the "currency" school and the "banking" school. Supporters of the "currency principle" favored a monetary system in which the money supply of a nation varied rigidly with the quantity of metallic money (gold or silver) in the possession of its residents and on deposit at its banks. Their banking school opponents upheld the "banking principle," according to which the national money supply would be adjusted by the banking system to accommodate the ever fluctuating "needs of trade." The currency school prevailed in the short run with the passage of Peel's Act of 1844. But although the currency principle was basically sound, its policy application was considerably weakened by two serious errors committed by its proponents. First, they failed to include demand deposits in the money supply, along with metallic coins and bank notes. Thus while they insisted that every new issue of bank notes was to be backed 100 percent by gold, they did not apply the same principle to the creation of new checking deposits. The result was that the money supply was still free to vary beyond the limits imposed by international gold flows thus subjecting the economy to continued recurrence of the inflation-depression cycle.

Liberty: The Economic Thought of the Late Scholastics, 2nd ed. (New York: Lexington Books, 2003).

[3] On the bullionist controversy, see Murray N. Rothbard, *Classical Economics: An Austrian Perspective on the History of Economic Thought Volume II*, pp. 157–224 and the literature cited therein.

[4] David Ricardo, 1838, p. 22.

This error in the currency school program was compounded by a second one that further undermined its ultimate goal of sound money and rendered the economy even more susceptible to cyclical fluctuations. Thus the currency school proposed that the Bank of England, a governmentally privileged bank with a quasi-monopoly of the note issue, oversee the application and enforcement of the currency principle. Of course a monopoly bank with such close ties to government would have both the incentive and influence to engineer departures from the principle during a financial panic in order to prevent a widespread bank run that would threaten its own gold reserves. To avoid a general loss of confidence in the banking system, it needed to expand its own supply of notes in order to lend to shaky private banks that did not have sufficient reserves to meet their own depositors' demands for redemption. This is exactly what occurred as Peel's Act was routinely suspended during panics, effectively guaranteeing an inflationary bailout of the banks in future crises and intensifying their inflationary propensity. Peel's Act thus did not moderate or abolish the business cycle and, indeed, came to be viewed as an impediment to the Bank of England operating as a lender of last resort during crises. As a result, the currency principle was thoroughly discredited and the ideal of sound money was badly tarnished.

The early opponents of the sound money principle, such as the anti-bullionists and the banking school, were nearly all naïve and unsophisticated inflationists who either confused money with wealth or believed that real economic activity was being stifled by a chronic scarcity of money. But in the late nineteenth century a new and much more sophisticated opposition to sound money began to develop during the debate over the bimetallic standard, a monetary system in which both gold and silver served as money with their exchange rate fixed by legal mandate. The bimetallic standard had functioned as the legal (if not always the de facto) standard for most major countries except Great Britain from the beginning of the nineteenth century until the 1870s, when silver was officially demonetized by the U.S., France, Italy, Switzerland, Belgium, the Scandinavian countries, and the newly created German Empire.

The proponents of the bimetallic standard argued for remonetization of silver on the grounds that this measure would increase the money supply and thus arrest the decline in prices under the monometallic gold standard that had begun in the late 1870s. The quantity theory of money was the foundation of the arguments put forward by the bimetallists. The theoretical counter-arguments of the advocates of the monometallic gold standard were completely inadequate to meet the challenge posed by the quantity theorists. They were based on the view that the costs of production of mining gold directly determined the price level, a distortion of classical monetary theory developed by Ricardo and the currency school.[5] Paradoxically, although the gold standard remained intact, at least for the short run, the seeds for its eventual abolition had been sown because the classical sound money doctrine had been discredited among economists.

As David Laidler, a modern proponent of the quantity theory, commented:

> [T]he refinement of the quantity theory after 1870 did not strengthen the intellectual foundations of the Gold Standard. On the contrary, it was an important element in bringing about its eventual destruction.... [T]he notion of a managed money, available to be deployed in the cause of macroeconomic stability and capable of producing a better economic environment than one tied to gold, was not an intellectual response to the monetary instability of the post-war period. The idea appeared in a variety of guises in the pre-war literature as a corollary of the quantity theory there expounded.[6]

Thus by the end of the nineteenth century the view that money should ideally be "stable" in value had fully displaced the classical ideal of "sound" money, meaning a commodity chosen by the market whose value was strictly governed by market forces and immune to

---

[5] On the error of the late nineteenth-century monometallists of interpreting classical monetary theory as involving strictly a cost-of-production theory of the value of money, see Will E. Mason, *Classical Versus Neoclassical Monetary Theories: The Roots, Ruts, and Resilience of Monetarism—and Keynesianism*, ed. William E. Butos (Boston: Kluwer Academic Publishers, 1996).

[6] David Laidler, *The Golden Age of the Quantity Theory* (Princeton: Princeton University Press, 1991), p. 2.

manipulation by governments. This new view culminated in the work of Irving Fisher, who in 1911 formalized the quantity theory in mathematical terms and proposed it as a formula for use by politicians and bureaucrats charged with the task of managing money in the interests of stability of the price level.[7] Indeed, it was Fisher and not Keynes who was the true founder of modern macroeconomics with its aggregative reasoning and its central notion of politically managed fiat money.[8] As the modern monetary theorist and historian of thought, Jürg Niehans wrote:

> Fisher's reformulation of the quantity theory of money ... has successfully survived seventy-five years of monetary debate without a need for major revision; its analytical content is accepted today by economists of all persuasions, and in the present world of fiat money it is actually more relevant than it was in Fisher's gold standard world.[9]

Such was the state of monetary economics when Mises published his seminal work on *The Theory of Money and Credit*, in 1912.[10] In writing this book, Mises achieved two aims. The first was to reconstruct monetary theory by integrating it with the subjective-value theory of price which had been developed by the early Austrian economists, most notably Carl Menger and Eugen Böhm-Bawerk. By doing this Mises was able to resolve the so-called "Austrian Circle," according to which the value of money could not be explained in terms of marginal utility because any such explanation involved circular reasoning. It was this misconception that opened the door to Fisher's analysis of money in terms of aggregative variables such as the national money supply, velocity of circulation of money, the average price level, and so

---

[7] Irving Fisher, *The Purchasing Power of Money, Its Determination and Relation to Credit, Interest, and Cycles*, 2nd ed. (New York: Macmillan, 1922); also idem, *The Money Illusion* (New York: Adelphi Company, 1928).

[8] Cf. Mark Thornton, "Mises vs. Fisher on Money, Method, and Prediction: The Case of the Great Depression," *Quarterly Journal of Economics* 11 (2008): 230–41.

[9] Jürg Niehans, *A History of Economic Theory: Classic Contributions, 1720–1980* (Baltimore, Md.: The Johns Hopkins University Press, 1994), p. 278.

[10] Ludwig von Mises, *The Theory of Money and Credit*, trans. H.E. Batson, 3rd ed. (Auburn Ala.: Ludwig von Mises Institute, 2009).

on, eventually leading to the unquestioned predominance of the macroeconomic quantity theory of money.

Mises's second accomplishment was to revive the currency school's sound money doctrine and correct its shortcomings by severing its ties with the classical cost-of-production theory of value and grounding it in modern monetary theory. Friedrich A. Hayek, Mises's protégé, further developed the theoretical foundations of the sound money doctrine in works published in the 1920s and early 1930s.[11]

Unfortunately, Mises's and Hayek's ideas on sound money were ignored, and the stable money doctrine continued in ascendancy after World War One. The Federal Reserve and other central banks instituted a regime of managed money and central bank "cooperation" during 1920s that stifled the natural operation of the gold standard. In the U.S., in particular, the Fed engineered a rapid and prolonged expansion of the money supply through the fractional-reserve banking system driving interest rates below the "natural" or equilibrium rate and precipitating bubbles in stock and real estate markets. However the inflationary monetary policy was not recognized by most of the American economics profession who were quantity theorists and stabilizers like Fisher. They focused almost solely on movements in wholesale or consumer prices, which remained basically unchanged during the 1920s. Under a sound money regime these prices would have dropped dramatically to reflect the increased abundance of goods that resulted from the extremely rapid growth in productivity and real output that occurred during the decade.[12]

The ultimate effect of the central banks' manipulation of the money supply and interest rates was the onset of the Great Depression. Mises and Hayek had been led by their analyses to anticipate such an

---

[11] The most important of these works are collected in F.A. Hayek, *Prices and Production and Other Works: F.A. Hayek on Money, the Business Cycle, and the Gold Standard*, ed. Joseph T. Salerno (Auburn, Ala.: Ludwig von Mises Institute, 2008).

[12] On the inflation of the 1920s and the remarkably profound and widespread influence of the stabilizationist idea on Anglo-American economists, bankers, monetary policymakers, and politicians during this period, see Murray N. Rothbard, *America's Great Depression*, 5th ed. (Auburn, Ala.: Ludwig von Mises Institute, 2000), pp. 85–135, 165–81.

occurrence.[13] Writing in 1932, the eminent Harvard economist and international monetary expert John H. Williams summarized the Austrians' position and noted their forecast of the depression:

> It can be argued but that for credit expansion prices would have fallen, and that they should have done so. It was on such grounds that the Austrian economists predicted the depression.[14]

In contrast to the Austrians, the stabilizers, especially Fisher, were surprised and totally befuddled by the event. But Hayek knew exactly where to place the blame, writing in 1932:

> We must not forget that, for the last six or eight years, monetary policy all over the world has followed the advice of the stabilizers. It is high time that their influence, which has already done harm enough, should be overthrown.[15]

The stable money doctrine was soon discredited, only to be replaced by the vastly more inflationary spending doctrine propounded by John Maynard Keynes, himself a former advocate of stable money. In its essentials, Keynes's doctrine harked back to John Law and the so-called "monetary cranks" of the nineteenth century. Keynes maintained that depression was simply the result of a deficiency of total spending or "aggregate demand," which was a chronic condition of the market economy. The only remedy for this problem, he argued, was government budget deficits that directly injected money spending into the economy combined with an expansionary monetary policy to lower interest rates and stimulate private investment spending. The Keynesian spending doctrine achieved unchallenged dominance in academic economics in the U.S. and Great Britain shortly after World War Two and by the 1960s was settled

---

[13] See Mark Thornton, "Mises vs. Fisher on Money, Method, and Prediction"; and idem, "Uncomfortable Parallels," www.LewRockwell.com (April 18, 2004). Also see, Mark Skousen, *The Making of Modern Economics: The Lives and Ideas of the Great Thinkers* (Armonk, N.Y.: M.E. Sharpe, 2001), pp. 291–93.

[14] John H. Williams, "Monetary Stabilization and the Gold Standard," in Quincy Wright, ed., *Gold and Monetary Stabilization* (Chicago: University Press, 1932), p. 149.

[15] Hayek, *Prices and Production and Other Works*, p. 7.

doctrine among economic policymakers, who eagerly implemented cheap-money and deficit-spending policies.

These policies eventually resulted in the accelerating inflation of the 1960s followed by the chronic stagflation of the 1970s. Like the earlier stable-money policies, aggregate demand policies led to consequences that were completely unexpected by their advocates and could not be explained within the Keynesian framework. By the late 1970s, Keynesianism as a policy program had lost its credibility and it was supplanted by monetarism, a movement led by Milton Friedman which had been growing in influence in academic economics since the early 1960s. But monetarism was nothing more than Fisher's stable money principle supported by a seemingly more sophisticated version of the quantity theory of money restated in Keynesian terminology. Instead of aiming directly at a stable price level, Friedman and the monetarists advocated that the central bank aim at stabilizing the growth of the money supply at a rate consistent with a zero or low long-run rate of inflation. Events soon falsified monetarist predictions of price and output movements during the mid-1980s, and orthodox monetarism rapidly declined in influence in academia and, especially, in the policy arena.

By the early 1990s, a new theoretical consensus in macroeconomics had emerged known as New Keynesian economics, which synthesized elements of Keynesianism, monetarism, and New Classical economics, an offshoot of monetarism.[16] The policy goal of this consensus remained stable money, or at least a low and stable rate of inflation. Although the Greenspan Fed did not articulate this goal explicitly, the central bank operated in a way consistent with it throughout the 1990s and consumer price inflation remained moderate and remarkably stable as growth of real output accelerated.

Beginning in 1995, a financial boom developed centered on technology stocks. Financial writers, media commentators, economists on

---

[16] N. Gregory Mankiw and David Romer, eds., New *Keynesian Economics,* 2 vols. (Cambridge, Mass.: MIT Press, 1991). For a short description, see N. Gregory Mankiw, "New Keynesian Economics," in David R. Henderson, ed., *The Concise Encyclopedia of Economics*, 2nd ed., available at http://www.econlib.org/library/CEETitles.html.

Wall Street and in academia, and even Alan Greenspan himself began to refer to the "New Economy" to designate the combination of low inflation, rapid productivity and output growth and a booming stock market that marked the latter half of the 1990s. Blinded by the fallacious stable money doctrine which focused narrowly on consumer price indexes, they all ignored the huge increase in the money supply that had fueled the boom. But once again the goal of stable money proved to be chimerical as the Dot-com bubble burst and the economy plunged into a short-lived recession in 2001. The Fed quickly pumped the economy out of the slump with a new burst of monetary expansion driving the Fed Funds rate down to 1 percent from 6.5 percent by mid-2003 and maintaining it at that level for a year. The recovery of financial markets and the speed up in economic growth by 2003 along with a continuing moderation of consumer price inflation allayed most doubts about the inflationary thrust of Fed policy and restored confidence in the stable money program. Still there were a handful of critics who warned that a massive housing bubble was forming as early as 2003, but they were ignored or ridiculed as "doomsayers" or "gold bugs." Most were either Austrian economists or bankers and financial commentators who had discovered and were influenced by the sound money tradition of Mises, Hayek and Rothbard.[17]

Despite their recent experience with the meltdown of the 1990s New Economy, the stable money enthusiasts inside and outside the economics profession were incorrigible and proclaimed that the economy had passed into a new era of long-run stability in the economy beginning in the mid-1980s. This new era they dubbed "The Great Moderation." The term was even used as the title of a speech delivered in 2004 by then Federal Reserve Board Governor and leading macroeconomist Ben Bernanke.[18] Another leading light of macroeconomics

---

[17] On Austrians who forecast a housing bubble in 2003–2004, see Mark Thornton, "The Economics of Housing Bubbles," in Randall G. Holcombe and Benjamin Powell, eds., *Housing America: Building Out of a Crisis* (New Brunswick, N.J.: Transaction Publishers, 2009), pp. 237–62.

[18] Ben S. Bernanke, "The Great Moderation," speech delivered at the meetings of the Eastern Economic Association, Washington, D.C. (February 20, 2004), available at http://www.federalreserve.gov/BOARDDOCS/SPEECHES/2004/20040220/default.htm.

Robert Lucas declared in 2003, "[the] central problem of depression-prevention has been solved, for all practical purposes." [19]

The whole notion of the Great Moderation trumpeted by establishment macroeconomists was uncannily reminiscent of the "New Era" of permanent prosperity proclaimed by Fisher and other stable money economists in the 1920s. The dawning of both eras was attributed to the adoption of new and improved money management techniques by the Fed. As was the case in the 1920s and the 1990s, however, the relative stability of the price level misled the stabilizers into ignoring or denying the growth of dangerous asset bubbles. Thus the Great Moderation ended in the spectacular deflation of the stock market and real estate bubbles followed by the financial crisis and stunning collapse of several iconic financial institutions. In the U.S., the crisis culminated in the longest recession since World War Two.

After the latest debacle caused by the stable money program, almost all mainstream macroeconomists were compelled to abandon the mathematical models and policy prescriptions of New Keynesianism in their search for an explanation and a remedy. They beat a headlong retreat straight back to old-fashioned Keynesianism with its emphasis on investor irrationality, wayward financial markets and the pervasive tendency of the public to "hoard." The recovery polices that they now recommended were designed to pump up spending through deficit financing and a zero interest rate. Several eminent macroeconomists even advocated the deliberate creation of inflationary expectations among the public as a legitimate tool of monetary policy.[20] They argued that spending would be stimulated if people

---

[19] Robert E. Lucas, "Macroeconomic Priorities," Presidential Address to the American Economic Association (January 10, 2003), p. 1. Available at http://home.uchicago.edu/~sogrodow/homepage/paddress03.pdf.

[20] See for example Paul Krugman, *The Return of Depression Economics and the Crisis of 2008* (New York: W.W. Norton & Company, Inc., 2009); N. Gregory Mankiw, "The Next Round of Ammunition," Greg Mankiw's Blog: Random Observations for Students of Economics (December 16, 2008), available at http://gregmankiw.blogspot.com/2008/12/next-round-of-ammunition.html; Kenneth Rogoff quoted in Rich Miller, "U.S. Needs More Inflation to Speed Recovery, Say Mankiw, Rogoff," *Bloomberg.Com* (May 19, 2009) available at http://www.bloomberg.com/apps/news?pid=20601109&sid=auyuQlA1lRV8.

were convinced that the value of their money "would melt away over time."[21] Others have put forward bizarre schemes, such as a tax on holding money, for forcing the nominal interest rate below zero and thereby stimulating investment spending.[22] The Keynesian spending doctrine is back with a vengeance!

Fortunately, there is a sound money alternative whose influence has grown prodigiously in the past decade. It is based on the works of Mises, Hayek and especially Murray Rothbard. By the end of World War Two, the Austrian School had been forgotten and the sound money doctrine was in danger of falling into oblivion until it was revived in the early 1960s by Rothbard, Mises's leading American follower. Rothbard made notable advances in the doctrine and sustained and promoted it in his copious writings. By the mid-1970s, Rothbard's efforts started to bear fruit as a growing number of young Austrian economists in academia began to publish articles and books on money and business cycles from an Austrian perspective. Despite Rothbard's untimely death in 1995, the new millennium dawned with the Austrian sound money paradigm thriving—but still ignored by the mainstream.

The bursting of the housing bubble and the meltdown of financial markets changed all this. A small number of economists and participants in financial markets forecast these events using the Austrian theory of the business cycle, which gives the only coherent explanation of booms, bubbles, and depressions. Word spread quickly through the banking and financial sector and among the general public via the Internet. Soon several high-profile financial pundits and other members of the official media were publically recognizing and

---

[21] Krugman, *The Return of Depression Economics*, p. 75.

[22] See N. Greg Mankiw, "Reloading the Weapons of Monetary Policy," Greg Mankiw's Blog: Random Observations for Students of Economics (March 19, 2009), available at http://gregmankiw.blogspot.com/2009/03/reloading-weapons-of-monetary-policy.html. For a deeper theoretical analysis of this scheme, see Marvin Goodfriend, "Overcoming the Zero Bound on Interest Rate Policy," Federal Reserve Bank of Richmond Working Paper Series (August 2000) available at http://www.richmondfed.org/publications/research/working_papers/2000/wp_00–3.cfm.

embracing the Austrian analysis. Even a few mainstream financial economists were stimulated to give it a sympathetic hearing.[23]

Prominent (and not-so-prominent) mainstream economists were nonplussed, if not alarmed, by this spreading challenge to their authority and attempted to respond to it by engaging Austrian business cycle theory on blogs and in popular periodicals.[24] But these attempts were little more than hysterical diatribes based on a very inadequate knowledge of the literature and a profound misconception of the nature and claims of the theory.[25] In the meantime, the doctrine of sound money, with Austrian monetary and business cycle theory at its core, has continued to flourish and grow and has emerged as the main challenger to the collapsing Keynesian spending paradigm. This book is intended as a contribution both to the theory of sound money and to the eventual restoration of a free and unhampered market in money.

The book comprises essays that were written for different purposes and with different audiences in mind and that therefore cannot be separated into neat categories. Nevertheless, for expository purposes a division of the book into five parts suggests itself. Part One

---

[23] For instance, Jerry H. Tempelman, "Austrian Business Cycle Theory and the Global Financial Crisis: Confessions of a Mainstream Economist," *Quarterly Journal of Economics*, 13, no. 1 (2010): pp. 3–15.

[24] See, for example, J. Brad DeLong, "The Financial Crisis of 2007–2009—Understanding Its Causes, Consequences—and Possible Cures," presented at MTI-CSC Economics Speaker Series Lecture, Singapore, September 5, 2009, available at http://www.scribd.com/doc/9719227/Paul-Krugman; idem, "What Is Austrian Economics," Grasping Reality with Both Hands (April 6, 2010), available at http://delong.typepad.com/sdj/2010/04/what-is-austrian-economics.html; John Quiggin, "Austrian Business Cycle Theory," Commentary on Australian and World Events from a Social Democratic Perspective (May 3, 2009), available at http://johnquiggin.com/index.php/archives/2009/05/03/austrian-business-cycle-theory. Another uncomprehending critique of Austrian business cycle theory written by a leading Keynesian macroeconomist during the Dot-Com bubble is Paul Krugman, "The Hangover Theory: Are Recessions the Inevitable Payback for Good Times?" *Slate* (December 4, 1998), available at http://www.slate.com/id/9593.

[25] For a thorough demolition of these mainstream critiques see Roger Garrison, "Mainstream Macro in a Nutshell," *Freeman: Ideas on Liberty*, 59 (May 2009), available at http://www.thefreemanonline.org/featured/mainstream-macro-in-an-austrian-nutshell/; idem, "A Rejoinder to Brad DeLong," *Mises Daily* (May, 11, 2009), available at http://mises.org/daily/3463; idem, "Contra Krugman," *Mises Daily* (December 2, 1998), available at http://mises.org/daily/103.

consists of six essays pertaining to the Foundations of Monetary Theory. These are the most technical essays in the book and focus on the
Austrian theory of money, which underlies the doctrine of sound
money. These essays set the Austrian theory in historical perspective,
elaborate and extend several of its characteristic doctrines, and contrast it with modern mainstream monetary theory on a number of
central issues. One essay in this part builds on the work of Murray
Rothbard identifying the empirical components of the money supply that correspond to the Austrian theoretical definition of money as
the general medium of exchange. This essay was published four years
before Robert Poole's memo formulating MZM (for "money of zero
maturity"), which has since become a well-known monetary aggregate calculated and reported by the Federal Reserve Bank of St Louis.[26]
MZM is very similar in conception and content to the "true money
supply" (TMS) aggregate that I proposed in my essay.[27] The five chapters in Part Two deal with Inflation, Deflation and Depression, mainly
within the context of an unsound fiat-money regime controlled by
a central bank. The first essay in this part elaborates William Hutt's
seminal concept of "price coordination," distinguishes it from F. A.
Hayek's concept of "plan coordination" and demonstrates its central
importance to Austrian macroeconomics. A second essay develops a
distinctively Austrian approach to expectations based on Mises's process analysis of inflation.

Part Three consists of essays on the gold standard. Here the term
"gold" should be construed as representing any commodity chosen
by the free market as the general medium of exchange. The essays in
this part taken together have three purposes. The first is to explore

---

[26] William Poole (1991). Statement before the Subcommittee on Domestic Monetary
Policy of the Committee on Banking, Finance and Urban Affairs, U.S. House of Representatives, November 6, 1991, Government Printing Office, Serial No. 102–82; John
B. Carlson & Benjamin D. Keen, "MZM: a monetary aggregate for the 1990s?" *Economic Review*, Federal Reserve Bank of Cleveland (2nd Quarter, 1996): pp. 15–23.

[27] The term "true" here is used in the sense of true to the theoretical definition of
money as the medium of exchange. For more recent articles on TMS, see Frank
Shostak, "The Mystery of the Money Supply Definition," *Quarterly Journal of Austrian Economics*, 3, no. 4 (2000): pp. 69–76; and Michael Pollaro, "Money Supply-
Metrics, the Austrian Take," *Mises Daily* (May 3, 2010), available at http://mises.org/
daily/4297.

the nature and operation of the Misesian neo-currency school ideal of a pure commodity money governed exclusively by market forces and unhampered by government intervention, including and especially the existence of a central bank. The second aim is to assess and respond to claims by mainstream monetary theorists and macroeconomists alleging various defects of the gold standard relative to an ideal monetary system based on fiat money issued by a central bank. Such an "ideal" is based on a fanciful notion of money as a government policy tool deliberately designed to stabilize the economy rather than on what it actually is: a general medium of exchange chosen by the market participants themselves as the most efficient means of carrying on their daily transactions.

During the past three decades, recurring crises throughout the world economy have provoked a general revival of interest in the gold standard as a possible alternative to our current monetary arrangements. A number of economists and media commentators have proposed restoring one or another historical variant of the gold standard or even implementing a modernized version. The third aim is thus to critically evaluate these proposals and to show that most of them contemplate watered-down or "false" versions of the gold standard that would result in unsound and disorderly monetary systems.

Since these essays on the gold standard were published my view has changed on one issue of some importance. I am much more sympathetic now than I was when I wrote my essay on "The Gold Standard: An Analysis of Some Recent Proposals" (Chapter 14) to the parallel private gold standard proposed independently by Professor Richard Timberlake and Henry Hazlitt. Their respective proposals now strike me as the most feasible route forward to sound money, because I have become much more skeptical about whether the U.S., or any other, government can competently and honestly manage a transition to a genuine gold standard. It is also appropriate to point out here that, in addition to minor revisions to improve style and clarity, there were deletions and some rewriting to eliminate repetition in a few of the essays in the book. But in some cases the elimination of the overlap between essays was not possible without disrupting the flow of the exposition. This is the case in Chapters 13 and 14 where a section of the later chapter substantially repeats, although in a little more detail, my critique of the supply-siders' gold price-rule proposal of the earlier chapter.

Part Four on Applications contains essays that apply the Austrian theories of money and the business cycle to analysis of historical episodes and events and to an evaluation of alternative monetary policies for emerging-market and small-open economies. Two of the essays elaborate and defend the Austrian position that the 1920s was an inflationary decade and that the Fed did aggressively attempt to reflate the money supply for most of the 1930s. The Austrian position was expounded in great detail by Murray Rothbard and sharply contradicts the monetarist explanation of the Great Depression formulated by Milton Friedman and Anna Schwartz, which is now widely accepted by macroeconomists.[28] Rothbard argued that the boom-bust cycle that culminated in the Great Depression was initiated by the inflationary policy pursued by the Fed during the 1920s.[29] He attributed the length and severity of the Depression to the unprecedented interventions by the Hoover and Roosevelt administrations designed to maintain nominal prices and especially wages above market-clearing levels. According to the Friedman-Schwartz story the 1920s was a halcyon decade of economic stability that was interrupted by a routine, "garden variety" recession that was rapidly transformed into a catastrophic depression by the Fed's error of permitting and even inducing a contraction of the U.S. money supply. Recently, the monetarist explanation of the depth of the Great Depression was challenged on essentially Rothbardian grounds by UCLA macroeconomist Lee Ohanian in a leading mainstream economics journal. [30]

Another essay in Part Four analyzes the causes of the October Stock Market Crash of 1987. Appended to this essay is an excerpt from a later article published in September of 1988. By that time the consensus among both academic and Wall Street economists was that

---

[28] Milton Friedman and Anna J. Schwartz, *A Monetary History of the United States, 1867–1960* (Princeton, N.J.: Princeton University Press, 1971).

[29] Rothbard, *America's Great Depression*.

[30] Lee E. Ohanian, "What—or Who—Started the Great Depression?" *Journal of Economic Theory* 144, no. 6 (November 2009): pp. 2310–2335.

the crisis had passed and a recession had been averted because the Greenspan Fed had taken decisive action in flooding the financial markets with liquidity. I dissented and, based on Austrian business cycle theory, forecast a recession "in late 1989 or early 1990, which should strike the U.S. economy with a particularly heavy impact on the thrift and banking industries." The recession struck in 1990 when the S&L crisis was already well under way. Of the remaining two essays in this part, the first outlines a sound money policy for a typical transition economy in Eastern Europe and the second critically evaluates the institution of the currency board as an alternative to a central bank in light of the two Hong Kong currency crises of the late 1990s.

Part 5 contains reviews, comments and less technical essays on contemporary economic events and controversies.

CHAPTER 1

Two Traditions in Modern Monetary Theory: John Law and A.R.J. Turgot

1. Introduction

John Law (1671–1729) is a prominent character both in the history of monetary events and in the development of monetary doctrines. As the founder and head of what, in effect, was one of the first national central banks in history,[1] the *Banque Générale Privée* (later, the *Banque Royale)* of France, Law almost singlehandedly destroyed the French monetary system in the course of four short years (1716–1720).[2] As a monetary theorist, Law has been called the "ancestor of

From "Two Traditions in Modern Monetary Theory: John Law and A.R.J. Turgot," *Journal des Economistes et Etudes Humaines* 2 (June/September 1991): pp. 337–39.

[1] The Bank of England, established in 1692, had been granted an effective legal monopoly of the note issue by the Act of 1709 and was well on its way to evolving into a full-blown central bank by the time Law's system was implemented in France. See Michael Andreades, *History of the Bank of England* (London: P.S. King and Son, 1909), pp. 72–85, 121–24.

[2] For the story well told, see Adolphe Thiers, *The Mississippi Bubble: A Memoir of John Law* (New York: Greenwood Press, [1859] 1969) and Joseph S. Nicholson, *A Treatise on Money and Essays on Monetary Problems* (Edinburgh: Blackwood, 1888).

the idea of a managed currency" by no less an authority on economic doctrine than Joseph Schumpeter.[3]

This paper will explore the surprising degree to which Law's fundamental ideas on money pervade monetary theorizing and policy advocacy in the U.S. today.

This endeavor is not without precedent. In 1951, a leading French economist and monetary theorist Charles Rist published an article in a major French economic journal, *Revue d'Economie Politique,* pointing out the surprising persistence of Law's doctrines among English-speaking economists.[4]

Rist introduced this article with the following statements[5]

> It is said that history repeats itself. One can say the same thing about economists. At the present time there is a writer whose ideas have been repeated since Keynes, without ever being cited by name. He is called John Law. I would be curious to know how many, among the Anglo-Saxon authors who have found again, all by themselves, his principal arguments, have taken the trouble to read him.

The balance of Rist's article is devoted to detailing the numerous parallels between the monetary ideas of Keynes and those of Law, who was born a little more than two centuries before Keynes. Moreover, Law's ideas did not enjoy a sudden recrudescence with the overthrow of classical monetary theory by the Keynesian revolution, for, as Rist[6] noted in an earlier treatise on the history of monetary and banking theory, there are significant similarities between Law's approach to

---

[3] Joseph A. Schumpeter, *History of Economic Analysis* (New York: Oxford University Press, 1954), p. 321.

[4] The article was reprinted in English as "Old Ideas on Money Which Have Become New," in Charles Rist, *The Triumph of Gold* (New York: Philosophical Library, 1961), pp. 144–70. L. Albert Hahn, another leading Continental monetary theorist, published an article with a similar theme a few years earlier: see L. Albert Hahn, *The Economics of Illusion: A Critical Analysis of Contemporary Economic Theory and Policy* (New York: Squirer Publishing Co., 1949), pp. 106–18.

[5] Rist, *The Triumph of Gold,* p. 144.

[6] Charles Rist, *History of Monetary and Credit Theory: From John Law to the Present Day,* trans. Jane Degras (New York: Augustus M. Kelley, [1940] 1966).

money and the approach of various Anglo-American quantity theorists, from David Hume and David Ricardo to Alfred Marshall and Irving Fisher. Thus, academic economists have not moved away from Law's ideas in their headlong flight from Keynesian economics and back toward classical monetary doctrines in recent years.

In the following section, I set out Law's basic monetary doctrines. I then show how these ideas are embodied in the monetary doctrines of three schools of economists which are currently prominent in macroeconomic policy debates in the U.S., namely, the neo-Keynesian, the monetarist, and the supply-side schools. Finally, I contrast the Law tradition of monetary analysis with an alternative tradition, which derives from one of Law's eighteenth-century critics, the French statesman and economist Anne Robert Jacques Turgot, and which includes the modern Austrian school of economics.

2. John Law's Monetary Doctrines

In 1705, Law[7] published his principal work on money, entitled *Money and Trade Considered: With a Proposal for Supplying the Nation with Money.* Law's "proposal" was intended to provide his native Scotland with a plentiful supply of money endowed with a long-run stability of value. The institutional centerpiece envisioned in Law's scheme resembles a modern central bank, empowered to supply paper fiat money via the purchases and sales of securities and other assets on the open market. Also strikingly modern are the theoretical propositions with which Law supports his policy goals and prescriptions.

Law initiates his monetary theorizing with two fundamental assumptions about the nature and function of money. The first is that if money is not exactly an original creation of political authority, it ideally functions as a tool to be molded and wielded by government. Law believes that the State, as incarnated in the King, is the *de facto* "owner" of the money supply and that it therefore possesses the right

---

[7] John Law, *Money and Trade Considered: With a Proposal for Supplying the Nation with Money* (New York: Augustus M. Kelley, [1705] 1966).

and the power to determine the composition and quantity of money in light of the "public interest." Writes Law:[8]

> All the coin of the Kingdom belongs to the State, represented in France by the King: it belongs to him in precisely the same way as the high roads do, not that he may appropriate them as his own property, but in order to prevent others doing so; and as it is one of the rights of the King, and of the King alone, to make changes in the highways for the benefit of the public, of which he (or his officers) is the sole judge, so it is also one of his rights to change the gold or silver coin into other exchange tokens, of greater benefit to the public....

Translating Law's statement into modern terms, money is an "instrument" that is or should be deliberately designed to achieve the "policy goals" considered desirable by political money managers and other government planners.

Law's second basic assumption is that money serves solely as a "voucher for buying goods" or an "exchange token." Thus, for Law,[9] "Money is not the value for which goods are exchanged, but the value by which they are exchanged: The use of money is to buy goods and silver, while money is of no other use." In other words, money is a dematerialized claim to goods having no valuable use in itself.

From these two premises, Law draws out a number of theoretical propositions regarding the functioning of money and of a monetary exchange economy.

First, if money functions solely as an exchange voucher, then it should be promptly spent by its recipient on goods. "Hoarding" or holding an unspent balance of money income for any extended period of time serves no purpose and causes severe damage to the economy in the bargain. It therefore behooves the political authority to suppress or discourage hoarding by all the means at its disposal, including and especially the substitution of paper currency for metallic currency.

---

[8] Quoted in Rist, *History of Monetary and Credit Theory*, pp. 59–60.

[9] Law, *Money and Trade Considered*, p. 100.

Law argues vehemently on this point:[10]

> ... as the coin of gold or silver bears the image of the prince
> or some other public mark, and as those who keep this coin
> under lock and key regard it as exchange tokens, the prince
> has every right to compel them to surrender it, as failing to
> put this good to its proper use. The prince has this right even
> over goods which are your own property, and he can com-
> pel you to sow your land and repair your houses on pain of
> losing them; because, at bottom, your goods are yours only
> on condition that you use them in a manner advantageous
> to the community. But, in order to avoid the searches and the
> confiscations of money, it would be better to go at once to
> the source of evil, and to give men only that kind of money
> which they will not be tempted to hoard [i.e., paper money].

But what is the nature of the economic harm caused by hoarding? According to Law, hoarding creates a deficiency of circulating
money and spending, resulting in a reduction of trade and employment. Under such conditions, an increase in the money supply raises
spending, employment, and real output :

> ... trade depends on money. A greater quantity employs
> more people than a lesser quantity. A limited sum can only
> set a number of people to work proportioned to it, and 'tis
> with little success laws are made for employing the poor or
> idle in countries where money is scarce; good laws may bring
> money to full circulation 'tis capable of, and force it to those
> employments that are most profitable to the country: But no
> laws can make it go further, nor can more people be set to
> work, without more money to circulate so as to pay the wages
> of a greater number.[11]

It is important to note that Law does not fall victim to the naive
mercantilist fallacy of confusing money with wealth. Law, in fact,
upholds the modern view that money is merely the means or "policy
tool" by which the goal of increasing national income and wealth is
achieved. That Law does not consider a plentiful supply of money to
be the ultimate aim of policy is evident from the following passage:

---

[10] Quoted in Rist, *History of Monetary and Credit Theory*, p. 60.
[11] Law, *Money and Trade Considered*, p. 13.

> National power and wealth consists in numbers of people,
> and magazines of home and foreign goods. These depend
> on trade, and trade depends on money. So to be powerful
> and wealthy in proportion to other nations, we should have
> money in proportion with them....[12]

The belief that if left to their own devices, market participants
are prone to stop up the monetary circulation by hoarding leads
Law to conclude that the market economy is inherently unstable
and likely to generate chronic unemployment of labor and other
resources. Underlying and supporting this line of reasoning is
Law's implicit assumption, which was reintroduced into modern economics by Keynes, that for most goods it is quantities and
not prices that normally respond to variations in total spending,
as well as to shifts in relative demands. For example, Law[13] writes
that "Perishable goods, as corns, etc. increase or decrease in quantity as the demand for them increases or decreases; so their value
continues equal or near the same.... Goods will continue equal in
quantity as they are now to demand, or won't differ much: For the
increase of most goods depends on the demand. If the quantity of
oats be greater than the demand for consumption and magazines,
what is over is a drug, so that product will be lessen'd...."[14]

In addition to his assumption that the prices of most goods are
"sticky downward," Law further anticipates Keynes and modern macroeconomists by positing a causal chain that runs from the supply
of and demand for money through the interest rate to the volume of
business investment and employment. Thus Law[15] argues that "As the
quantity of money has increased ... much more than the demand for
it ... so of consequence money is of lesser value: A lesser interest is
given for it ... if the demand had increased in the same proportion
with the quantity ... the same interest would be given now as then...."

---

[12] Ibid., pp. 59–60.

[13] Ibid., pp. 63, 69–70.

[14] Douglas Vickers, *Studies in the Theory of Money, 1690–1776* (New York: Augustus M. Kelley, [1959] 1968), pp. 113–19, discusses Law's "implicit assumption" regarding the "elasticity of supply of commodities produced."

[15] Law, *Money and Trade Considered*, pp. 67, 71–72.

Furthermore, the lowered interest rates produced by the expansion of a deficient money stock, according to Law, serve as a stimulus to investment in the import and export trades and in domestic manufacturing and thus bring about an expansion of employment. Writes Law:[16] "... if lowness of interest were the consequence of a greater quantity of money, the stock [of capital] applied to trade would be greater, and merchants would trade cheaper, from the easiness of borrowing and the lower interest of money ... [and] all imported goods would be cheaper, money being easier borrowed, merchants would deal for a greater value, and men of estates would be capacitate to trade, and able to sell at less profit."

Conversely, if the shortage of money is not alleviated, high interest rates will persist, preventing investment opportunities from being exploited and causing price deflation and depression of the trade and manufacturing sectors. Thus Law[17] argues that, although profit opportunities may exist in the export trade "... money being scarce [export merchants] cannot get any to borrow, tho their security may be good.... So for want of money to Exchange by, Goods fall in value, and Manufacture decays."

A further implication of the assumption that money is merely a claim ticket for goods is that, ideally, its value should remain perfectly stable. Stability of the purchasing power of money is necessary to insure that an individual who sells goods for money is reasonably certain of purchasing goods of equivalent value at a later time. Gold and silver, however, are not suited to serve as such a "voucher to buy," precisely because they are tangible and useful commodities whose value naturally fluctuates according to changing market conditions. On these grounds alone, Law[18] advocates the replacement of market-chosen specie money by a government-issued paper money "backed" by land, a commodity with an allegedly more stable market value:

> Money is ... a value payed, or contracted to be payed, with which 'tis supposed, the receiver may, as his occasions require,

---

[16] Ibid., pp. 20, 75.

[17] Ibid., p. 116.

[18] Ibid., pp. 61–62, 64, 84, 102.

buy an equal quantity of the same goods he has sold, or other goods equal in value to them: And that money is the most secure value, either to receive, to contract for, or to value goods by; which is least liable to a change in its value.

Silver money is more uncertain in its value than other goods, so less qualified for the use of money.... Silver in bullion or money changes its value, from any change in its quantity, or in the demand for it.... And the receiver is doubly uncertain whether the money he receives or contracts for, will, when he has occasion, buy him the same goods he has sold, or the goods he is to buy.... Land is what in all appearance will keep its value best, it may rise in value, but cannot well fall: Gold and silver are liable to many accidents whereby their value may lessen, but cannot well rise in value.

From whence it is evident, that land is more qualified for the use of money than silver ... being more certain in its value, and having the qualities necessary in money, in a greater degree: With other qualities silver has not, so more capable of being the general measure by which goods are valued, the value by which goods are exchanged, and in which contracts are taken.

Now, the reference to land aside, the foregoing is a remarkable statement of the modern argument in favor of a political price-level stabilization scheme and against a free-market commodity money such as gold. Law also argues that paper money is cheaper than metallic money, and that, as a consequence, the substitution of the former for the latter for use as exchange tokens facilitates an increase of national income and wealth. Once again, Law's argument strongly anticipates modern criticisms of the gold standard based on considerations of its high "resource costs" :

Gold and silver are of course commodities like any other. The part of them used for money has always been affected by this use, and goldsmiths have always been forbidden to buy gold and silver louis [i.e., French coins] and use them for their craft. Thus all this part has been withdrawn from ordinary commerce by a law for which there were reasons ... but which is a disadvantage in itself. It is as if a part of the wool or silk in the kingdom were set aside to make exchange tokens: would it not be more commodious if these were given over to their natural use, and the exchange tokens made of materials which in themselves serve no useful purpose?[19]

Finally, Law clearly recognizes that the best route to the establishment of a paper money which can be inflated *ad libitum* by the political authorities is through the institution of banking. Law understood as early as 1705 what was only to be generally understood by the economics profession over two centuries later: that the expansion of loans by fractional-reserve banks leads to the creation of new money and thereby increases the aggregate quantity of money in the economy. According to Law:[20] "The use of banks has been the best method yet practised for the increase of money.... So far as they lend they add to the money, which brings a profit to the country by employing more people, and extending trade; they add to the money to be lent, whereby it is easier borrowed, and at less use [i.e., interest]...."

Law's modern insight into the money-creating powers of fractional-reserve banks was supplemented by his forthright recognition of the potential instability of these institutions, due to the temporal mismatching between their loan assets and their deposit liabilities. The result of this inherent "term-structure risk," Law accurately foretold, would be repeated suspensions of cash payments to depositors, but he argued that this disadvantage was far outweighed by the benefits yielded by these institutions as instruments for the attainment of macroeconomic policy goals, such as high employment, low interest rates, and stability of the price level. As Law[21] states the argument, when a bank lends out a part of its cash deposits,

> ... the bank is less sure, and tho none suffer by it, or are apprehensive of danger, its credit being good; yet if the whole demands were made, or demands greater than the remaining money, they could not all be satisfied, till the banks had called in what sums were lent.

> The certain good it does, will more than balance the hazard, tho once in two or three years it failed in payment; providing the sums lent be well secured: Merchants who had money

---

[19] Quoted in Rist, *History of Monetary and Credit Theory*, p. 59.

[20] Law, *Money and Trade Considered*, pp. 36–37.

[21] Ibid., pp. 37–38.

there, might be disappointed of it at demand, but security
being good and interest allowed; money would be had on a
small discount, perhaps at par.

Based on his theory of money and banking, Law[22] elaborates a
scheme for monetary reform. A commission, appointed and super-
vised by Parliament, would be set up to issue notes against the security of land. The commission would be authorized to issue its notes in
three ways:

(1) by lending notes at a market rate of interest, the total loan not
to exceed two-thirds of the market value of lands offered as collateral
by the borrower;

(2) by making loans equal to the full price of lands which were
temporarily ceded to the commission until the loan was repaid and
the lands redeemed;

(3) by purchasing lands outright in exchange for its notes.

The commission would also be authorized to sell the mortgages
and lands in its possession on the market in exchange for its notes.
With the commission's notes convertible into mortgages and lands,
Law believed, the supply of and demand for money would always
tend to match, causing the value of money as expressed in the general level of prices to remain stable. He reasoned that if the supply of
money were in excess, people would quickly rid themselves of the
surplus notes by redeeming them for productive lands and interest-bearing mortgages. In the opposite case of an excess demand or
shortage of money, people would rush to acquire additional cash balances by selling mortgages and lands to the note-issuing commission.
In this way, significant fluctuations in the value of money would be
done away with and, at the same time, there would always exist the
optimum quantity of money in circulation to facilitate the needs of
real economic activity.

Writes Law:[23]

---

[22] Ibid., pp. 84–100.
[23] Ibid., pp. 89, 102.

This paper money will not fall in value as silver money has fallen or may fall.... But the commission giving out what sums are demanded, and taking back what sums are offered to be returned; this paper money will keep its value, and there will always be as much money as there is occasion, or employment for, and no more.... The paper money proposed being always equal in quantity to the demand, the people will be employed, the country improved, manufacture advanced, trade domestic and foreign will be carried on, and wealth and power attained.

Now, at first blush, Law's bizarre scheme appears totally unrelated to modern monetary institutions and arrangements. However, as I shall argue below, a closer study reveals that the fundamental ideas underlying this proposal are strikingly similar to assumptions and propositions widely accepted by most modern monetary theorists and policymakers. As for the institutional framework of Law's proposal—the peculiar role of land notwithstanding—it defines the basic blueprint for the modern central bank.

In the nineteenth century, the monetary theorist and gold-standard advocate Henry Dunning MacLeod, graphically drew attention to the similarity between Law's plan and the standard practice of the Bank of England (and of modern central banks) of "monetizing government debt." With reference to the latter procedure, MacLeod[24] wrote:

... it is perfectly clear that its *principle* is utterly vicious. There is nothing so wild or absurd in John Law's *Theory of Money* as this. His scheme of basing a paper currency upon land is sober sense compared to it. If for every debt the government incurs an equal amount of money is to be created, why, here we have the philosopher's stone at once.... But let us coolly consider the principle involved in this plan of issuing notes upon the security of the public debts. Stated in simple language, it is this: *That the way to CREATE money is for the Government to BORROW money.* That is to say, A lends B money on mortgage, *and, on the security of the mortgage is allowed to create an equal amount of money to what he has already lent* !! Granting that to an extent this may be done

---

[24] Henry Dunning MacLeod, *The Theory and Practice of Banking,* 5th ed. (London; New York : Longmans, Green, 1892–1893), vol. 1, pp. 487–88.

without any practical mischief, yet, as a general principle, what can be more palpably absurd?

Today, instead of manipulating the supply of money by printing up and exchanging notes for lands and mortgages, the Federal Reserve System, for example, creates additional bank reserves and checkable deposits in the economy by purchasing Treasury securities from the public and the banks.

These then are Law's main ideas on money and monetary policy. They have been critically summarized by Rist:[25]

> Law's writings ... already contain all the ideas which constitute the equipment of currency cranks—fluctuations in the value of the precious metals as an obstacle to their use as a standard ... the ease with which they can be replaced by paper money, money defined simply as an instrument of circulation (its function of serving as a store of value being ignored), and the conclusion drawn from this definition that any object can be used for such an instrument, the hoarding of money as an offence on the part of the citizens, the right of the government to take legal action against such an offence, and to take charge of the money reserves of individuals as they do of the main roads, the costliness of the precious metals compared with the cheapness of paper money....

3. Law's Ideas in the Modern World

The neo-Keynesians, monetarists, and supply-siders, differ among themselves in important areas of theory and policy,[26] but all share most of Law's fundamental ideas about money.

---

[25] Rist, *History of Monetary and Credit Theory*, p. 65.

[26] Good nontechnical discussions of the differences between Keynesianism and monetarism, by a Keynesian and a monetarist respectively, can be found in Charles P. Kindleberger, "Keynesianism vs. Monetarism in Eighteenth- and Nineteenth-Century France," *History of Political Economy* 12, no. 4 (Winter 1980), and Brunner, "Has Monetarism Failed?," in *The Search for Stable Money: Essays on Monetary Reform*, eds. J.A. Dorn and A.J. Schwartz (Chicago: University of Chicago Press, 1987), pp. 163–71.

3.1. Money as a Policy Tool

All three schools predicate their monetary theories and policy prescriptions on Law's fundamental assumption that money is a means or "tool" to be used by government planners in pursuing certain objectives, usually referred to as "policy goals". In modern welfare states, these goals are typically formulated in terms of statistical aggregates and averages which are presumed to gauge the performance of the overall national, or "macro," economy, e.g., the CPI, the unemployment rate, the rate of growth of real GNP, and so forth.[27]

Specifically, neo-Keynesians treat money creation as a policy tool which complements government taxing, spending, and borrowing. Together, these tools of monetary and fiscal policy are supposed to enable the national government to manage total spending or "aggregate demand" in the economy so as to achieve some optimal trade-off between the twin ills of inflation and unemployment, which are allegedly permanent features of a free-market economy.

A typical expression of the Keynesian view is given by G.L. Bach:[28]

> Effective use of monetary and fiscal policy is necessary if we are to achieve stable economic growth with high-level employment of men and machines over the years ahead. History shows the unfortunate tendency of the largely private enterprise economic system in the United States to swing between recession and inflation. And there is little reason to suppose that in the future the system will automatically generate stable growth with high employment unless monetary and fiscal policies help to keep aggregate money demand growing roughly apace with the economy's capacity to produce.... The two [i.e., monetary and fiscal policy] are the major instruments for regulating the level of aggregate demand.

---

[27] For an enumeration of these goals, see George Leland Bach, *Making Monetary and Fiscal Policy* (Washington, D.C.: The Brookings Institution, 1971), pp. 24, 38.

[28] George Leland Bach, *Making Monetary and Fiscal Policy*, p. 3.

Modern monetarists are the intellectual descendants of the pre-World War Two Chicago School, which included extreme monetary interventionists such as Henry Simons, Lloyd Mints, and Jacob Viner. This school viewed the money supply as the most important policy variable available to the political authorities for stabilizing the national price level and thus minimizing or eradicating business fluctuations caused by erratic swings in private spending. According to Mints[29] "... the case for attempting to stabilize the price level by monetary means lies in the fact that the quantity of money is the one easily and deliberately controllable factor and in the belief that variations in the stock of money can be so managed as largely to offset disturbing fluctuations in other factors, particularly the velocity of circulation."

So convinced was Viner[30] that money is the ideal macro-policy variable that he formulated the quantity theory of money as a technical recipe for government monetary policy. This theory, he argued, "... is understood as holding only: (1) that an authority powerful enough to make the quantity of money what it pleases can so regulate that quantity as to make the price level approximate to what it pleases, and (2) that the possibility of existence of such power is not inconceivable a priori."

The most extreme in his views, however, was Simons, who regarded regulation of the quantity of money as "a fundamental function of government" and therefore advocated that complete and absolute control of the supply of money be vested in an agency of the central government. According to Simons,[31] "In the past, governments have grossly neglected their positive responsibility of controlling the currency; private initiative has been allowed too much freedom in determining the character of our financial structure and in directing changes in the quantity of money and money substitutes ... if the stability of [a price] index is to be maintained

---

[29] Lloyd W. Mints, *A History of Banking Theory in Great Britain and the United States* (Chicago: University of Chicago Press, 1945), p. 275.

[30] Jacob Viner, *The Long View and the Short: Studies in Economic Theory and Policy* (Glencoe, Ill.: The Free Press, 1958), p. 365.

[31] Henry C. Simons, *Economic Policy for a Free Society* (Chicago: University of Chicago Press, 1948), pp. 161–62, 180.

with the least resistance and the minimum of disturbing administrative measures, it is essential that the power to issue money and near-money should increasingly be concentrated in the hands of the central government." In order to insure that the State's monopoly control over the supply of money remains forever unchallenged and that the opportunity for the private market to create near-moneys is minimized, Simons[32] went as far as to call for "drastic limitation on the formal borrowing power of all private corporations and especially upon borrowing at short term." For the same reasons, Simons[33] even contemplated limitations on "financing via the open account (book credit) and installment sales."

Whereas the earlier Chicago economists desired to directly stabilize a price index, modern monetarists tout the merits of a monetary policy or "rule," which would stabilize the rate of growth of the quantity of (fiat) money. The monetarists argue that the "quantity" rule would insure a relatively stable price level, an outcome tending to dampen rather than to amplify the mild business fluctuations which, they believe, inevitably attend the operation of the dynamic market economy. The monetarists would charge a central government agency, such as the central bank or the treasury department, with the responsibility of administering their preferred rule. For the purpose of carrying out its charge, the agency in question, of course, would be endowed with the "natural" monopoly of issuing a paper fiat currency.

It is noteworthy that, in one important respect, the monetarists are actually closer in spirit to Law than are their generally more interventionist Keynesian opponents. Keynes and his followers generally decry the gold standard because the "inelasticity" of the supply of gold affords little or no scope for the operation of a "discretionary" monetary policy. Monetarists and their forerunners, on the other hand, are even reluctant to admit that a monetary system can exist and function without some degree of political control and management. It is their contention that all practicable monetary regimes necessarily

---

[32] Ibid., p. 182.
[33] Ibid., p. 171.

involve the explicit or implicit choice of a particular policy rule by the State to guide its inevitable manipulations of the money supply. This view accounts for the peculiarly monetarist characterization of the gold standard as a system in which the monetary authority follows the rule of intervening in the market to "fix" the price of gold in terms of the national currency unit, say for instance, at thirty-five dollars per ounce. Accordingly, the monetarists condemn the gold standard, not because it leaves no scope for discretionary management but because it involves the choice of a suboptimal policy rule.

For example, Simons[34] declares that "the utter inadequacy of the old gold standard ... as a definite system of rules ... seems beyond intelligent dispute." In the same vein, David I. Meiselman,[35] a current monetarist, writes that "The proponents of a gold standard and of a fixed nominal price of gold have an excellent point in proposing an explicit rule. The main problem of fixing the gold price is that *it is the wrong rule*—we can do better."

The supply-siders, at first glance, appear to represent an exception to the prevailing belief that economic stability requires political control and manipulation of the money supply. Indeed, they advocate the gold standard on the basis of its ability to "automatically" adapt the supply of money to changes in the demand for money. However, a closer look at the monetary reform proposals of prominent supply-siders, like Arthur Laffer, Robert Mundell, and HUD Secretary Jack Kemp reveals that what is actually being proposed is a governmental price-fixing scheme or a "price rule" involving gold and not a genuine gold standard.[36] Under the gold price rule, money remains a politically manipulated paper fiat currency and gold becomes merely an "external standard," whose price is pegged by the central bank as a

---

[34] Ibid., p. 169.

[35] David I. Meiselman, "Comment: Is Gold the Answer?" in *The Search for Stable Money: Essays on Monetary Reform*, eds. James A. Dorn and Anna Jacobson Schwartz (Chicago: University of Chicago Press, 1987), p. 260.

[36] For a critique of the proposal for a gold price see Joseph T. Salerno, "Gold Standards: True and False," in *The Search for Stable Money: Essays on Monetary Reform*, eds. James A Dorn and Anna Jacobson Schwartz (Chicago: University of Chicago press, 1987), pp. 249–52 [reprinted here as Chapter 13].

means of achieving general price stability. Thus, the "gold standard" as it is understood by supply-siders represents not an unmanaged market-chosen money but a more efficient policy rule than the quantity rule prescribed by monetarists.

3.2. Money as an Exchange Token

As I noted above, the second flawed premise underlying Law's monetary theory is that money functions solely as an "exchange token" or a "voucher to buy." This misconception led Law to single out hoarding as the main culprit in economy-wide disruption of trade and depression of economic activity. While modern macroeconomists do not view the function of money quite as one-sidedly as Law did, most regard hoarding and the related shrinkage of the money-spending stream as a source of potentially serious macroeconomic instability.

For example, despite Keynes's well-known discussion of the different motives for holding money, the primary analytical and policy focus of Keynesians has always been the level of aggregate demand in the economy. They emphasize that the piling up of "idle balances," due to irrationally heightened "liquidity preferences" of the public, raises interest rates and constricts investment spending and aggregate demand, thereby depressing overall economic activity. As a result, real output is reduced and there is chronic unemployment of labor and other productive resources.

Earlier Keynesians expressed themselves emphatically and simplistically on the role of money-spending in determining the level of economic activity and employment, and they exhorted government to aggressively wield the instruments of fiscal and monetary policy to insure a full-employment level of aggregate demand. For example, Lord Beveridge[37] wrote: "Employment depends on outlay [i.e., spending]. Full employment cannot be attained unless outlay in total is sufficient to set up a demand for the whole of the labor that is available for employment. Where should the responsibility be placed for

---

[37] William H. Beveridge, *Full Employment in a Free Society* (New York: W.W. Norton & Company, Inc., 1945), pp. 134–35.

insuring adequate total outlay?.... The central proposition of this Report is that responsibility of ensuring at all times outlay sufficient in total to employ all available man-power ... should formally be placed ... upon the State."

It was their Law-like emphasis on the spending-output connection, coupled with their dread of private individuals' unruly and antisocial propensities to hoard, that caused early Keynesians to belittle the importance of the actual *stock* of money in existence and to emphasize the *flow* of money payments. In the words of one early and radical disciple of Keynes, Abba Lerner:[38] "The level of employment depends on the *flow* of acts of *payment* involved in the spending, not on the *stock* or amount of *money* in existence.... The only thing that matters is the *flow* of money spending. The stock of money can be of significance only to the degree that it may influence the flow of spending...."

Lerner[39] argues, as Law did earlier, that the total spending stream must be stabilized, because the inflexibility of wage rates and other prices in the free market make depression and unemployment the likely outcome of any shrinkage of aggregate demand. Unfortunately, even individuals enlightened by Keynesian doctrine respond "perversely" to the anticipated variations in aggregate demand generated by their own erratic spending habits. Thus Lerner[40] concludes, "It is the government, therefore, that must accept the responsibility for keeping total spending at the level that gives us full employment without inflation. By making use of the fiscal instruments at its disposal it can [keep] spending from going too high or too low and thus [assure] permanent prosperity and stability."

For Lerner,[41] then, money is a purely political element whose quantity is to be determined solely by the needs of a government fiscal policy designed to manipulate the overall spending stream in the

---

[38] Abba P. Lerner, *Economics of Employment* (New York: McGraw-Hill Book Company, Inc., 1951), pp. 51, 53.

[39] Ibid., pp. 203–06.

[40] Ibid., p. 141.

[41] Ibid., p. 133.

economy: "The use of the [fiscal] instrument should never be hampered just because there may not be enough money stock in the treasury at the moment. To sacrifice the prevention of deflation because of shortage of money which could be printed is no more sensible than to refrain from carrying out any other important government action because the necessary paper forms or stationery would have to be printed."

Chastened by the manifest failure of this earlier Keynesian analysis to make good on Lerner's promise to insure "permanent prosperity and stability" or even to come to grips with the possibility of the stagnation that has ravaged Western mixed economies in the last two decades, modern Keynesians have been forced to retreat to the drawing board. But while they may now differ from the earlier followers of Keynes on various points of high theory, they still firmly adhere to Keynes's and Law's central message that the aggregate flow of money-spending determines overall employment and output, at least in the short run, and that this flow of spending can and should be managed by the political authorities. As one prominent neo-Keynesian, Allan Blinder,[42] recently declared:

> In [many] respects, 1980s Keynesianism differs from its 1960s counterpart. But many of the central tenets of Keynesian economics remain much as they were twenty-five years ago. The private economy is not a giant auction hall [i.e., wage rates and prices tend to be rigid] and will not regulate itself smoothly and reliably. Recessions are economic maladies, not vacations. The government has both monetary and fiscal tools that it can and should use to limit recessions and fight inflations; but it cannot do both at once.

Now let us consider the monetarist approach to the function of money. In the realm of high theory, it is true, money is treated as a "temporary abode of purchasing power," as one among a spectrum of assets of varying degrees of liquidity held in investment portfolios by private individuals. Nonetheless, following the quantity-theorist Irving Fisher, monetarists believe that a key element in the practical understanding and control of monetary phenomena is the "velocity of

---

[42] Alan S. Blinder, *Hard Heads, Soft Hearts: Tough-Minded Economics for a Just Society* (New York: Addison-Wesley, 1987), p. 108.

circulation of money." This concept refers to the average rate at which a unit of money is "turned over" or spent in the economy.

Although monetarists generally contend that the velocity of money (or, sometimes, its growth rate) is stable and predictable over the long run, they do entertain the theoretical possibility that a sudden and sharp decline in velocity and spending, due, for example, to an increase in people's demand to hold money, can lead to a recession, unless offset by a timely injection of new money into the economy. As one proponent of the monetarist quantity rule argues:

> The k in the money equation [i.e., the reciprocal of the velocity of money] is stable in longer periods, not seasonally and not cyclically. Business recession is initiated by an increase in k.... Demand for money rises at the expense of demand for goods. Excess demand for money is eventually satisfied, but its costs mount up in the forms of falling prices, falling output, and falling employment.... The sensible solution for the shortage of money balances is simply creation of more money balances, in nominal amount, by the monetary system.[43]

Some monetarists even consider the possibility that a "self-generating deflation," which is precipitated by a reduction of private spending, could lead to a "runaway deflation."[44] Interestingly, the spectre of a self-generating "hyperdeflation" was first raised by radical Keynesians such as Lerner.[45]

Generally, however, monetarists do not expect such sudden and severe declines in velocity and spending to be spontaneously generated by the market economy. The focus of their policy recommendations is on insuring that the spending stream is kept growing at a rate sufficient to accommodate the secular growth of real output in the economy. For monetarists, then, the primary concern is a deficiency of money and spending, which can emerge when the growth rate of

---

[43] Edward S. Shaw, "The Case for an Automatic Monetary Pilot," in *The Battle against Unemployment: An Introduction to a Current Issue of Public Policy*, ed. Arthur M. Okun (New York: W.W. Norton and Company, Inc., 1965), p. 195.

[44] J. Huston McCulloch, *Money and Inflation: A Monetarist Approach,* 2nd ed. (New York: Academic Press, 1982), pp. 53–54.

[45] Lerner, *Economics of Employment*, pp. 205–06.

the velocity of money lags behind the growth rate of real output. This is a long-run development which can stunt economic growth and possibly lead to recessionary declines in output and employment.

Supply-side monetary theorists quibble with the peculiar monetarist contention that the long-run or "trend" growth rate of velocity is stable and predictable and that short run deviations from trend are quickly reversed. If, as supply-siders claim, the demand for money, or its velocity, are subject to large and unpredictable fluctuations from one moment to the next, then aggregate demand, the price level, and real output will be unstable. The supply-side plan for a gold price rule, therefore, is designed to provide the political authorities with the information and wherewithal necessary to make the rapid adjustments in the supply of money which are necessary to offset the potentially volatile and destructive fluctuations of private spending in the economy. As supply-sider Marc Miles[46] argues in defense of a general price rule:

> The important point is that under the price rule, the Fed does not have to worry about whether or why money demand has risen or whether velocity is stable. If the private sector wants more money, for whatever reason, the Fed finds out soon enough. The dollar price of spot silver falls, as people try to become liquid, and the Fed must react. The Fed provides the market with dollars, in exchange for spot deliveries of silver, and the desired additional money becomes available. The Fed maintains the stable price between silver and the basic dollar, and the market tells the Fed when to adjust liquidity. The Fed no longer concerns itself with the imprecise, indirect policy barometer, the money supply.

Interestingly, the supply-side school's preoccupation with unpredictable velocity movements and its corresponding support for a price rule harks back to the earlier Chicago School. For instance, Simons[47] was led to withhold his recommendation of the quantity rule, because of its "obvious weakness," which "... lies in the danger of sharp

---

[46] Marc A. Miles, *Beyond Monetarism: Finding the Road to Stable Money* (New York: Basic Books, Inc., 1984), pp. 187–88.

[47] Simons, *Economic Policy*, p. 164.

changes on the velocity side, for no monetary system can function effectively or survive politically in the face of extreme alternations of hoarding and dishoarding." Conversely, Simons[48] contended that "one great advantage of a price-index rule [is] that it defines, within a definite long-term rule, appropriate measures for dealing with velocity changes."

3.3. Stabilization of the Price Level

As a result of his narrow focus on money's function as an exchange token, Law considered a stable value of money to be of primary importance to the functioning of the market economy. Neo-Keynesians, monetarists, and supply-siders likewise regard stabilization of the price level as one of the most important goals of macroeconomic policy. Since none of the three schools advocates actually freezing the level of each particular price, what they seek in practice is constancy of a selected statistical average or index of prices.

Keynes and his early followers preferred that policy aim at a "stable general level of money-wages," at least in the short run.[49] The attainment of this policy goal was at first thought to be compatible with and, indeed, a necessary precondition of, full employment. When it was later found that, despite the implementation of Keynesian policies, unemployment coexisted with a rising level of prices, Keynesian economists posited a stable "Phillips-curve tradeoff" or inverse relationship between inflation and unemployment.

Keynesians then advised that policymakers choose from this "menu of policy choices" the attainable combination of unemployment and inflation rates which would "optimize" society's welfare. During the 1970s and 1980s, however, it became painfully obvious that the Phillips relationship was not stable, as inflation and unemployment rates spiralled upward in tandem.

---

[48] Ibid., p. 331, fn. 16.

[49] John Maynard Keynes, *The General Theory of Employment, Interest, and Money* (New York: Harcourt, Brace and World, [1936] 1964), pp. 270–71; Lerner, *Economics of Employment*, pp. 228–29.

Today, while neo-Keynesians have been forced to admit that the Phillips curve is stable and yields an "exploitable tradeoff" only in the short run, they still urge that policymakers use fiscal policy and monetary policy to "make the best of a bad situation" and to "strike a balance" in pursuing the two desirable goals of price-level stability and full employment. For Keynesians, however, the right balance for macroeconomic policy has always been and still remains heavily biased toward the attainment of "full employment," even at the cost of substantial inflation. The neo-Keynesian position on these matters is summed up by Blinder:[50]

> ... the fact that unemployment and inflation can, and sometimes do, rise together does not mean that the makers of national economic policy no longer face a trade-off between inflation and unemployment. The same unpleasant choices must be made. It is just that they may be a good deal nastier than we came to believe in the halcyon days of the 1960s....
>
> The damage that high unemployment does to economic efficiency is enormous and inadequately appreciated. By contrast, the harm that inflation inflicts on the economy is often exaggerated.... Hard-headed devotion to the principle of efficiency thus argues for worrying less about inflation and running a high-pressure economy in which jobs are plentiful. This prescription, of course, is precisely the opposite of what the Western world has been doing for more than a decade.

In contrast to the Keynesians, monetarists do not believe that the achievement of full employment requires the sacrifice of price stability. In fact, monetarists argue that a stable price level is the *sine qua non* of an efficiently functioning market economy. Underlying the monetarist concern with a stable price level is the view, prominently featured in Law's work, that money is not only the general medium of exchange, and therefore an indispensable "micro" tool for calculating profits and losses and orienting individual economic action, but that it is a measure of value. Thus Law[51] repeatedly referred to money as "the measure by which goods are valued."

---

[50] Blinder, *Hard Heads, Soft Hearts*, pp. 43, 65.
[51] Law, *Money and Trade Considered*, pp. 52, 61, 92, 102.

By treating money as some sort of social measuring rod for value, what Law and the monetarists ignore is the fact that money's use as a medium of exchange is precisely what precludes it from possessing an invariant market value. The reason is that the medium of exchange, by its very nature, is a commodity which is routinely exchanged and held throughout the market, and thus its value is necessarily determined by the ever-changing conditions of supply and demand. A medium of exchange possessing a fixed purchasing power is therefore a self-contradictory concept.

It is not surprising, then, that those who treat money as a measure of value tend to conceptually isolate it from real-world market processes, attributing the origination of money and of its purchasing power to some vague extra-market "convention." Thus, for example, Friedman[52] declares, "the existence of a common and widely accepted medium of exchange rests on a convention" and "the value of money rests on a fiction." Following classical monetary theorists like John Stuart Mill, Friedman[53] argues that money is a "veil," which is neutral to and does not influence the underlying "'real' forces that determine the wealth of a nation." The only time that money impinges on the real economy, according to Friedman, is when it "gets out of order" and the "fiction" supporting money's common acceptance and market value threatens to completely dissolve. For Friedman and the monetarists, disorderly money is characterized by an unstable price level. From this position it is a short jump to the policy conclusion that the value of money should not be subject to determination by changeable and unpredictable market forces, but should be controlled and stabilized by an extra-market organization, which in practice can only be the State.

Earlier writers in the tradition of monetary analysis represented by Friedman and the monetarists were emphatic regarding the necessity of price stabilization to insure a well-functioning market economy. According to these writers, although the market automatically and efficiently adapts to changes in the relative prices of goods and

---

[52] Milton Friedman and Rose Friedman, *Free to Choose: A Personal Statement* (New York: Harcourt Brace Jovanovich, 1980), p. 249.
[53] Ibid.

services, it is inherently incapable of smoothly adjusting to significant changes in the overall price level. Thus, Simons[54] argued that the economy "... could be trusted systematically and automatically to correct disturbances in *relative* prices and *relative* outputs of goods and services.... General price (price-level) movements, however, served quite as systematically to set in motion forces which served, not to correct but to aggravate the initial disturbance."

The main reason given by Simons[55] for the inability of the market economy to adapt to price-level fluctuations without significant effects on output and employment is the fact that costs are "extremely inflexible downward." While Simons[56] places part of the blame for such cost rigidities on government price controls and political toleration of union violence in the fixing of some wage rates, a large share of the blame is attributed to the exercise of private monopoly power, which is alleged to pervade the unregulated market economy and to permit monopolistic firms to cut quantities rather than prices in response to a fall in demand. But even if all goods and services were supplied in "highly competitive markets," so that overall prices could adjust relatively rapidly to changes in the relationship between the demand for and supply of money, Simons[57] argues, "... such price-level instability is undesirable and disturbing in other decisive respects; and the degree of price and wage flexibility necessary to assure reasonable stability of production and employment in the face of great monetary instability is utterly unattainable." Simons, like Law, therefore denies that free-market prices and wage rates can ever be flexible enough to permit the smooth operation of a monetary system based on a commodity money originated and supplied strictly by market forces. Accordingly, Simons[58] concludes that "If a free-market system is to function effectively ... it must operate within a framework of monetary stability which it cannot create for itself and which only government can provide."

---

[54] Simons, *Economic Policy*, pp. 108–09.

[55] Ibid., p. 55.

[56] Ibid., pp. 53–54.

[57] Ibid., p. 108.

[58] Ibid., p. 109.

A similar position was taken by Mints,[59] who declared that "It is only under conditions of a stable general level of prices and some minimum amount of flexibility in the price system that an equilibrium level of relative prices can be maintained.... The truth is that the need for some given system of relative prices for the purpose of maintaining optimum employment and output is a strong argument in defense of stabilizing the price level."

The Law-Simons-Mints position remains one of the key tenets of modern monetarist doctrine. According to Friedman,[60] "What is seriously disturbing to economic stability are rapid and sizable fluctuations in prices, not mild and steady secular movements in either direction." For Friedman,[61] therefore, the "ultimate end" of monetary policy is "achieving a reasonably stable price level." As the most effective means for pursuing this desideratum, Friedman and the monetarists prescribe the aforementioned quantity rule, which dictates a slow and steady growth rate of one of the monetary aggregates, more or less under the direct control of the monetary authority.

Supply-siders emphasize money's function as a measure of value and the corollary importance of an invariant price level for macroeconomic stability even more strongly than do the monetarists. The case is argued by Miles[62] in the following terms:

> A dollar bill is like a yardstick. It is a common guide for comparing the worth of different commodities today, and a single commodity over time.... So the money yardstick is a system for conveying information about value. It is analogous to yardsticks used in specific industries. Take, for example, shoe sizes. Like the dollar, shoe sizes are a yardstick or information system; they provide a way to compare different pairs of shoes.... Money is like shoe sizes. The monetary system provides information that people use to make plans for today and for the future. It is only going to be used as long as it continues

---

[59] Mints, *A History of Banking Theory*, p. 275.

[60] Milton Friedman, *A Program for Monetary Stability* (New York: Fordham University Press, 1960), p. 92.

[61] Ibid., p. 88.

[62] Miles, *Beyond Monetarism*, pp. 189–91.

> to provide reasonably accurate and dependable information. As the system becomes more volatile, people turn away from it, employing the best alternatives.... [T]he economy experiences a period of turmoil, uncertainty, and slow growth.

In contrast to the monetarist policy prescription, however, supply-siders advocate a price rule, which would constrain the monetary authority to fix the price of a single commodity or the combined price of a group of commodities. As we have seen, the supply-siders do not believe that the steady growth of aggregate demand that is necessary to stabilize the price level can be secured by fixing the growth rate of the money stock via a quantity rule, because they reject the monetarists' claim that the velocity is stable.

Under the supply-siders' preferred alternative, the Fed is obliged to target the price of a commodity, say gold, whose market value is believed to be a sensitive indicator of impending changes in the overall price level. For example, if the target price of gold is established at $400 per ounce and it starts to exhibit a tendency to decline below this level on the open market, it indicates to the Fed that there is a developing shortage of money and spending, which threatens to reduce prices throughout the economy. By purchasing gold or even Treasury securities from the public in exchange for newly-created dollars until the price of gold returns to its target level, the Fed automatically remedies the monetary shortage and thereby offsets the tendency of the price level to decline. On the other hand, a surfeit of cash balances in the economy is indicated by upward pressure on the market price of gold. The Fed relieves this pressure by selling gold or securities to the public and, in the process, absorbs and extinguishes the excess dollars before the general price level can be driven up.

3.4. The Resource Costs of a Commodity Money

As we saw above, Law counted the high costs of supplying commodity money relative to the costs of supplying paper fiat money as a serious defect of metallic monetary standards. "Resource costs" also bulk large in the monetarist case against the gold standard. For example, Friedman[63] writes: "The fundamental defect of a commodity standard, from the point of view of the society as a whole, is that it requires the use of real resources to add to the stock of money. People must work hard to dig gold out of the ground in South Africa—in order to rebury it in Fort Knox or some similar place." But why is it necessary for additions to the nominal money stock ever to occur?

Underlying Friedman's reasoning on this point is the assumption, shared with Law, that, since money is a measure of value, an efficient monetary standard must insure a stable price level. Thus, Friedman[64] argues that the achievement of a stable price level under a 100 percent gold standard requires that the annual production of gold be sufficient to increase the money supply at the same rate as the annual increase of real output in the economy (assuming a constant velocity of circulation of money). According to his estimates for the U.S. economy in the 1950s, the production of the necessary yearly increment to the supply of gold money would "cost" approximately 50 percent of the average annual increase in real GNP.[65] By comparison, the cost of achieving a stable price level under a paper fiat standard is virtually nil, because the resource costs of adding to the money supply under such a standard are negligible.

Setting aside the unsupported and heroic assumption that a paper fiat currency monopolized by the State will be managed so as to yield a constant price level, this accounting of the alternative costs of the two monetary standards is meaningless. The reason is that the criterion which Friedman and the monetarists apply in judging the efficiency of competing monetary standards—that is, the expenditure of resources which each requires to deliver stability in the value of money—is

---

[63] Milton Friedman, *Essays in Positive Economics* (Chicago: University of Chicago Press, 1953), pp. 209–10; Friedman, *A Program for Monetary Stability*, p. 5.

[64] Friedman, *Essays in Positive Economics*, pp. 209–10; Friedman, *A Program for Monetary Stability*, p. 5.

[65] Friedman, *A Program for Monetary Stability*, p. 5. For the U.S. economy in the 1980s, Meltzer (Allan H. Meltzer, "Monetary Reform in an Uncertain Environment," in *The Search for Stable Money: Essays in Monetary Reform*, eds. James A. Dorn and Anna Jacobson Schwartz [Chicago: University of Chicago Press, 1987], p. 213), estimates the annual cost of a commodity money to equal 16 percent of the average annual increase in real GNP.

singularly inapplicable to the commodity employed as the universal medium of exchange in a dynamic market economy. According to the anti-Law tradition of monetary analysis outlined below, the value of money, like that of any other commodity, can and does fluctuate in response to unceasing changes in supply and demand. Thus, if general growth in productivity and real output in the economy results in an increase in the overall demand for money, there is no need for an increase in the production of the monetary commodity.

In fact, gold is chosen as money precisely because it is a commodity which maintains its extreme scarcity relative to human wants despite the progressive intensification of the division of labor and the ongoing capital accumulation and technological innovation that mark the evolving market economy. This inelasticity of supply means that, under the gold standard, the increased demand for money resulting from economic growth is satisfied mainly by a rise in the purchasing power of the monetary unit, which involves a general fall in prices and requires little or no expenditure of real resources for mining additional gold. This is the reason why the spectacular growth of the industrialized market economy operating under the nineteenth-century gold standard was characteristically accompanied by a gently declining price level.[66]

But what of the monetarist objection that the secular decline in prices operates to undermine money's function as a measure of value? The response of the anti-Law monetary theorist is that money is not an eternally fixed "measure" in any sense, but a tool of economic calculation which permits capitalist-entrepreneurs to appraise the profitability of prospective investments and production processes. The latter function is not in the least thwarted by the secular tendency of prices to decline under the gold standard. As Ludwig von Mises[67] writes:

---

[66] For example, the phenomenal growth of the U.S. economy between 1879 and 1896 occurred against a backdrop of declining prices. See Ron Paul and Lewis Lehrman, *The Case for Gold: A Minority Report of the U.S. Gold Commission* (Washington, D.C.: Cato Institute, 1982), pp. 102–10.

[67] Ludwig von Mises, *Human Action: A Treatise on Economics,* 3rd rev. ed. (Chicago: Henry Regnery Company, 1966), pp. 469–70.

In the conduct of business, reflections concerning the secular trend of prices do not play any role whatever. Entrepreneurs and investors do not bother about secular trends. What
guides their actions is their opinion about the movement of
prices in the coming weeks, months, or at most years. They
do not heed the general movement of all prices. What matters for them is the existence of discrepancies between the
prices of the complementary factors of production and the
anticipated prices of the products. No businessman embarks
upon a definite production project because he believes that
the prices, i.e., the prices of all goods and services, will rise.
He engages himself if he believes that he can profit from a
difference between the prices of goods of various orders. In
a world with a secular tendency toward falling prices, such
opportunities for earning profit will appear in the same way
in which they appear in a world with a secular trend toward
rising prices....

A secular tendency toward a rise in the monetary unit's purchasing power would require rules of thumb on the part of
businessmen and investors other than those developed under
the secular tendency toward a fall in its purchasing power.
But it would certainly not influence substantially the course
of economic affairs.

3.5. The Supply of Money as a Political Monopoly

The cornerstone of Law's scheme for monetary reform is a
monopolistic money-issuing institution which resembles a modern central bank. Needless to say, the three modern macroeconomic
schools under examination all staunchly support the idea that supply
of money needs to be centralized under a political monopoly.

This position requires explanation in the case of the monetarists,
who generally are insightful and vigorous exponents of the virtues of
the free market. To justify their support for a monopoly central bank,
most monetarists fall back on the peculiar idea, mentioned above,
that every viable monetary standard presupposes that the political
authorities follow a policy rule of some type. Under the gold standard, for example, some agency of government must peg the price of

gold in terms of the national currency unit.[68] Hence, in the monetarist view, the practical choice is between a monopoly central bank supplying a nearly costless fiat money and a governmental price-fixing
scheme which involves gold or some other commodity and entails
high resource costs. As one leading monetarist, Allan Meltzer,[69] for-
mulates the choice:

> A gold standard or commodity money standard requires the
> government to control a price. A monetary rule gives the power
> to control money to a government monopolist, but limits the
> monopolist's freedom to set a price or choose a quantity other
> than the prescribed quantity or growth rate.... Economic effi-
> ciency is rarely compatible with either price-fixing or monop-
> oly arrangements. Yet, in the case of money, a monopoly central
> bank can be the most efficient method of producing money.

> The principal reasons are that a monopoly central bank low-
> ers the resource cost of the standard by substituting incon-
> vertible paper money for commodity money, by reducing
> some monitoring or enforcement costs, and by lowering the
> levels of risk and uncertainty that society bears.

4. Turgot and the Anti-Law Tradition

Turgot was a brilliant eighteenth-century French statesman
and economist, and a trenchant critic of Law's monetary thought.[70]
In his brief contributions to monetary theory, Turgot set out for the
first time the basic outlines of a tradition of monetary analysis which
is represented in the U.S. today by the resurgent Austrian school of
economics.

---

[68] However, lately monetarists have become more willing to contemplate wholly private monetary systems, including specie-based "free" banking arrangements and
schemes for competition among private issuers of inconvertible paper currencies.
See, for example, Meltzer, "Monetary Reform," pp. 214–17, and Milton Friedman,
"Monetary Policy: Tactics Versus Strategy," in *The Search for Stable Money: Essays
on Monetary Reform*, eds. James A. Dorn and Anna Jacobson Schwartz (Chicago:
University of Chicago Press, 1987), pp. 373–76.

[69] Meltzer, "Monetary Reform," pp. 214–18.

[70] For the best discussion of Turgot's contributions to economic science, see Murray N.
Rothbard, *The Brilliance of Turgot* (Auburn, Ala.: Ludwig von Mises Institute, 1986).

Turgot flatly rejects Law's primary contention that money is merely an exchange token, whose supply must be manipulated by the political authorities in order to achieve selected policy goals. According to Turgot[71] money is essentially a medium of exchange and the unit in which relative prices are expressed: "These two properties, of serving as a common measure of all values [i.e., the unit in which all prices are expressed] and of being a representative pledge of all commodities of a like value [i.e., the medium of exchange], include all that constitutes the essence and utility of what is called money...."

As Turgot[72] points out, however, these two functions of money can only be performed by an article which is already widely used, valued, and exchanged under barter: "... all money is essentially merchandise. We can take for a common measure of values only that which has a value, and which is received in Commerce in exchange for other values: and there is no pledge universally representative of a value save another equal value." Since money thus necessarily originates as a useful commodity from within the market economy itself, Turgot[73] emphatically denies the possibility that "a purely conventional money" without a pre-existing purchasing power can be imposed from outside the market. According to Turgot,[74] "It is not in virtue of a *convention* that money is exchanged against all other values; it is because money itself is an object of commerce, a part of wealth, because it itself has a value, and in trade all values are exchanged against equal values."

Turgot[75] argues further that, while almost all commodities may more or less conveniently serve as money, gold and silver have been chosen as the "universal money" because they possess in the greatest degree the various physical properties which peculiarly suit them to that role. Anticipating early twentieth-century textbook writers,

---

[71] A.R.J. Turgot, *Reflections on the Formation and the Distribution of Riches* (New York: Augustus M. Kelley, [1770] 1971), p. 36.

[72] Ibid.

[73] Ibid.

[74] Quoted in Rist, *History of Monetary and Credit Theory*, p. 106, fn. 3.

[75] Turgot, *Reflections*, pp. 31–32, 36, 38.

Turgot[76] gives the following comprehensive list of these properties: a general demand under barter; natural rarity or high inelasticity of supply; a high value to weight ratio; divisibility; durability, homogeneity of supply; and the ease with which their genuineness and purity may be verified.

As people come to recognize the superior suitability of the precious metals to serve as media of exchange, their individual actions generate a "spontaneous" and self-reinforcing market process by which gold and silver evolve into money. According to Turgot,[77] as market participants become increasingly eager to acquire and hold ready stocks of gold and silver for use in future exchanges, the demands for and market values of these metals are augmented and this very development further enhances their usefulness as media of exchange. In addition, once gold and silver become the universally preferred exchange media and are therefore traded against every other good in the market, the weights of the metals naturally become the units in which all market values or prices are expressed.[78] Contrary to the contention of the monetarists, then, a metallic standard does not require that the political authorities arbitrarily proclaim and fix an exchange rate between some disembodied monetary unit and the standard metal, because the monetary unit itself always evolves on the market as a specific weight of gold or silver.

Turgot[79] thus concludes that money is not a creation of law or of human convention, but is the product of a natural market process:

> Thus, then, we come to the constitution of gold and silver as money and universal money, and that without any arbitrary convention among men, without the intervention of any law, but by the nature of things. They are not, as many people have imagined, signs of values; they have themselves a value. If they are susceptible of being the measure and pledge of other values, they have a value in Commerce....

---

[76] Turgot, *Reflections*, pp. 37–39; A.R.J. Turgot, *The Life and Writings of Turgot*, ed. W. Walker Stephens (London: Longmans, Green and Co., 1895), p. 207.

[77] Turgot, *Reflections*, p. 40.

[78] Ibid., p. 38.

[79] Turgot, *Reflections*, p. 39; *Life and Writings*, p. 207.

> It is then as merchandise that coined money is (not the sign)
> but the common measure of other merchandise, and that
> not by an arbitrary convention, founded on the glamour of
> that metal, but because, being fit to be employed in different
> shapes as merchandise, and having on account of this prop-
> erty a saleable value, a little increased by the use made of it
> as money, and being besides suitable of reduction to a given
> standard and of being equally divided, we always know the
> value of it.

In thus denying that money is merely a "sign of values," which
itself possesses only a fictional or representative value, Turgot is challenging Law's contention that money is essentially an exchange token,
which is designed to be promptly spent. With his focus on money
as the most marketable among all exchangeable goods, Turgot conceives the demand for money in the modern sense of the demand
to acquire and hold a stock of cash to employ in future exchanges.
Writes Turgot:[80] "Everyone who has a surplus commodity, and has
not at the moment any need of another commodity for use, will hasten to exchange it for money; with which he is more sure, than with
anything else, to be able to procure the commodity he shall wish for
at the moment he is in want of it." Elsewhere, Turgot[81] writes that men
"[exchange] all their superfluity for money, and [exchange] money
only for the things which are useful or agreeable to them at the
moment...."

Moreover, since the same causes, i.e., supply and demand, which
determine relative prices among the general array of goods also determine the "price" or purchasing power of money in terms of goods,
Turgot flatly rejects Law's central conclusion that there is a tendency
for the stock of metallic money to become deficient:

> But has it been left to Law to remain ignorant that gold falls
> in value like everything else by becoming more plentiful? If
> he had read and studied Locke ... he would have known that
> all the commodities of a country are balanced between them-
> selves, and with gold and silver, according to the proportion
> of their quantity and the demand for them; he would have

---

[80] Turgot, *Reflections*, p. 39.
[81] Ibid., p. 42.

learned that gold has not a value which corresponds always to a certain quantity of merchandise, but when there is more gold it is cheaper, and one gives more of it for a determinate quantity of merchandise; that thus gold, when it circulates freely suffices always to the need of the State, and that it becomes a matter indifferent to have one hundred millions of marks or one million, if we are to buy all commodities dearer in the same proportion.

In this passage Turgot enunciates one of the most important policy implications of sound monetary theory, namely, that any quantity of money always provides the full utility of a medium of exchange to society, and, therefore, an increase in the nominal quantity of money can yield no increase in social welfare. As Turgot points out, all that results from inflating the supply of money is a fall in the purchasing power of the monetary unit and a corresponding rise of the scale of prices in the economy.

Turgot's emphasis on the medium of exchange as the universally demanded and supplied "merchandise" leads him to a dual critique of price stabilization schemes of the kind championed by Law, and later by the Simons-Friedman Chicago School. First, Turgot argues that money as the most saleable commodity naturally possesses a market value which is not constant but varies in response to changes in market conditions. Writes Turgot:[82]

This value [of money] is susceptible of change, and in fact does change continually; so that the same quantity of metal which corresponded to a certain quantity of such or such a commodity ceases to correspond to it, and more or less money is needed to represent the same commodity....

A thousand different causes concur to fix at each moment the value of commodities when compared either with one another or with money, and to cause them to change incessantly. The same causes determine the value of money, and cause it to vary when compared, either with the value of each particular commodity, or with the totality of the other values which are actually in Commerce.

---

[82] Ibid., pp. 40–41.

Second, not only are fluctuations in the "price level" a natural outcome of a free market in money, but, according to Turgot, such fluctuations are the indispensable means by which the market continually adjusts the purchasing power of the monetary unit to avoid an excess demand or supply of money. Any increase in the overall demand for money is costlessly accommodated by the market via a general fall in prices and the attendant increase in the total purchasing power of the existing supply of money; there is no need for an increase the "nominal" supply of money. Thus, as Turgot[83] points out, Law raises a false issue when he argues (as do the Friedmanites in our own day) that the resource costs of adding to the supply of metallic money far exceed the costs of increasing a paper fiat currency. It is in fact the policy of price stabilization itself that frustrates and incapacitates the market's efficient means of equilibrating the supply of money and the demand for it and, in the process, imposes on society the high costs of the economic distortions that political manipulation of the money supply invariably brings about.

This brings us to another flaw which Turgot identifies in schemes to issue paper money. With brilliant insight, Turgot[84] argues that the very issuance of paper money would interfere with and distort the sensitive market process by which the existing money stock is allocated among the public according to their individual demands to hold cash. These demands are by their very nature subjective, ever-changing, and therefore unknown to the money issuers. In the words of Turgot:[85] "Gold and silver themselves, regarding them only as signs [i.e., media of exchange], are, by the fact of their very circulation, actually distributed among the public according to the proportion of the commodities, of the industry, lands, and real wealth of every kind existing. Now this proportion can never be primarily known, because it is hidden, and because it varies continually by a new circulation. The king will not proceed to distribute his paper-money to each person in the proportion that he holds gold and silver money...."

---

[83] Turgot, *Life and Writings*, pp. 206–07.
[84] Ibid., p. 208.
[85] Ibid.

In the language of modern monetary theory, Turgot is arguing in this passage that money is "nonneutral" and that every injection of new money into the economy is inevitably accompanied by "distribution effects" or redistributions of income and wealth among individual economic agents. This insight of Turgot's is the starting point of the tradition of monetary process analysis which eventually culminated in the development of the Austrian theory of the business cycle. One of the most important implications of this theory is that any attempt by central banks to stabilize prices by adding to the quantity of money through the expansion of commercial bank reserves and business loans will invariably cause distortions of interest rates and relative prices, malinvestment of capital, and, ultimately, economy-wide recession or depression. Thus for Turgot and modern Austrians it is not the mild fluctuations in the price level which would occur under a full-bodied gold standard but the attempt to endow money with a chimerical neutrality that leads to disorderly money and a discoordinated economy.

Accordingly, in sharp contrast to Law and modern proponents of managed money, Turgot is an implacable foe of fractional-reserve banking. He argues that note-issuing and deposit-taking by fractional-reserve banks are fundamentally unsound and are not just another species of free-market credit relations. There exists a qualitative difference between the credit granted by lenders to private business and the "credit" granted by depositors or note holders to fractional-reserve banks, because inherent in the operation of the latter institutions is the temporal mismatching of assets and liabilities. According to Turgot:[86]

> [Business credit] necessarily supposes an exchange at the term foreseen and fixed in advance; for if the [merchant's] bills were payable at sight, the merchant would not be free to turn to use the money he had borrowed. Thus it is a contradiction of terms for a bill at sight to bear interest, and such a credit cannot exceed the capital of the borrower.... In a word, every credit is a borrowing, and has an essential relation to its repayment.... A merchant who would buy goods to tenfold

---

[86] Ibid., pp. 204–06.

his capital and who would pay for them by notes, payable to
the bearer, would soon be ruined....[87]

Finally, Turgot's emphasis on money's function as a "common
measure of all values," and therefore as a tool of economic calculation,
combined with his profound insight into the vital role of monetary
calculation and money capital in orienting and driving the social production process, suggests a criterion that is relevant to the modern
search for sound money.

According to Turgot,[88] "all labours, whether for agriculture or for
industry, require advances [of capital] ... capitals are the indispensable
foundation of every undertaking...." In other words, capitalist-entrepreneurs must save and accumulate a fund of capital in order to pay in
advance for the resources necessary to promote and sustain an enterprise whose output emerges only after a lapse of time from the initial
investment of resources in the production process. The introduction
of money has enormously simplified and facilitated the task of saving
and accumulating capital. Anyone—landowner, laborer, or entrepreneur—can undertake the accumulation of capital by saving out of his
monetary income. As the generally acceptable medium of exchange,
money may be invested in agriculture or any other type of production

----

[87] Turgot's staunch opposition to fractional-reserve banking places him squarely in
the mainstream of eighteenth-century monetary thought, which can be interpreted
as a reaction against Law's writings and schemes. Theorists such as Isaac Gervaise,
Jacob Vanderlint, David Hume, and Joseph Harris argued that the extension of credit
by fractional-reserve banks was economically destructive, while Richard Cantillon
deeply distrusted banks and held that they added negligibly to aggregate real income.
See Joseph T. Salerno, *The Doctrinal Antecedents of the Monetary Approach to
the Balance of Payments* (Ann Arbor, Mich.: University Microfilms International,
1980), pp. 71–193, passim. In sharp contrast to these writers, Adam Smith sought
to rehabilitate some aspects of Law's thought. He lauded Law's "splendid, but vision-
ary ideas" while complaining of the "excess of banking" to which they contributed
(Adam Smith, *An Inquiry into the Nature and Causes of the Wealth of Nations* [New
York: Random House, Inc., [1776] 1965], p. 302). For Smith, "the judicious operations of banking," which would substitute the notes and deposits of competitive "free"
banks for specie money, would "very considerably" increase resource productivity
and output by providing a metaphorical "waggon-way through the air" to replace the
costly highway made of gold and silver (p. 305). For a discussion of Law's influence
on Smith and its deleterious effect on later British monetary theory, see Rist, *History
of Monetary and Credit Theory*, pp. 84–85, 323.

[88] Turgot, *Reflections*, pp. 51, 64.

process. Capital of any kind thus comes to be universally evaluated and calculated in terms of money. As Turgot[89] states "… it is absolutely indifferent whether this sum of values or this capital consists in a mass of metal or anything else, since the money represents every kind of value, just as every kind of value represents money."

It is the competitive bidding among entrepreneurs to acquire the means of production via what Turgot calls "advances" of money capital that establishes the current money prices for the various kinds of resources. Thus, for example, the prices of land resources "… are always easily determined in the same manner as the price of all other commodities; that is … in accordance with the current price established by the competition of those who wished to exchange lands for cattle and of those who wished to part with cattle in order to get lands."[90]

In the case of land rents, Turgot[91] theorizes that "The competition of rich Undertakers in agriculture fixes the current price of leases…." Consistent with his analysis of the determination of the price of consumer goods,[92] Turgot[93] views catallactic competition among entrepreneurs as the driving force leading to the emergence of a market-clearing price for land services, with "the Proprietor only letting his land to him who offers the highest rent." Finally, in the labor market, although sellers' competition establishes a market-clearing wage rate "less than [the laborer] would like," the competition is never so intense as to prevent the more "active" and "expert" worker, who is "above all, more economical" in his personal consumption, from earning a price for his labor in excess of subsistence for himself and his family enabling him to accumulate wealth.[94] These resource prices, of course, ultimately reflect entrepreneurial appraisements of the future

---

[89] Ibid., p. 51.

[90] Ibid., p. 48. In this example, Turgot uses cattle to represent what he calls "moveable wealth," which functioned as a quasi-money during the era preceding the emergence of a universal medium of exchange. In this form, capital was accumulated and advanced to resource owners.

[91] Ibid., p. 56.

[92] Ibid., pp. 29–30.

[93] Ibid., p. 56.

[94] Ibid., p. 44.

sale prices of the array of consumer products, because, as Turgot[95] points out, "The Undertakers [*i.e.,* the capitalist-entrepreneurs or promoters], either in the cultivation of land or in Manufactures, get back their advances and their profits only from the sale of the fruits of the earth or of the manufactured commodities. It is always the wants and the means of the Consumer that set the price at sale...." We may thus reasonably infer from Turgot's discussion that the competitive process yields a structure of market-clearing input prices that is coordinated with respect to entrepreneurial expectations of future output prices, and thereby insures full utilization of scarce productive resources.

Current resource prices, although established by the competitive bidding of all entrepreneurs, are taken as data in the monetary cost and profit calculations that inform the production decisions of the individual entrepreneur in any branch of production. Turgot[96] gives explicit recognition to the all-important role of monetary calculation in guiding production decisions. The decision to lease land and undertake an agricultural enterprise, for example, is made "... according to the calculation the Farmers make, both of their expenses and of the profits they ought to draw from their advances...." Likewise, the commercial entrepreneur ascertains the money prices of merchandise at various locations and "... directs his speculations accordingly; he sends the commodities from the place where they bear a low price to those where they are sold for a higher; it being understood, of course, that the expense of carriage enters into the calculation of the advances which have to return to him."

Furthermore, as Turgot[97] continually reiterates, in calculating the prospective profitability of a given enterprise, all entrepreneurs count as costs, in addition to their money expenditures on the factors of production, the forgone money revenue based on the rate of return on capital investment, or, in Wicksellian terminology, "the natural rate of interest" which can be earned in alternative branches of production.

---

[95] Ibid., p. 58.
[96] Ibid., pp. 56, 62.
[97] Ibid., pp. 53, 55–56, 57, 61.

Turgot[98] recognizes, moreover, that, in the long run, the natural rate of interest on investment in various processes of production and the rate of interest on loans "preserve a kind of equilibrium."

In a stroke of methodological genius, Turgot concludes his analysis of the monetary aspects of the production process by focusing on an economy in the fictional state of long-run equilibrium and identifying the vital role played by the regularly recurring accumulation and investment of capital guided by monetary calculation. Writes Turgot:[99]

> We see … how that the cultivation of land, manufactures of all kinds, and all branches of commerce depend upon a mass of capitals, or of moveable accumulated riches, which having been at first advanced by the Undertakers in each of these different classes of labours, must return to them every year with a steady profit; that is, the capital to be again invested and advanced anew in the continuation of the same enterprises, and the profit to provide for the more or less comfortable subsistence of the Undertakers. It is this advance and this continual return of capitals which constitute *what one must call the circulation of money;* that useful and fruitful circulation which gives life to all the labours of the society, which maintains movement and life in the body politic, and which is with great reason compared to the circulation of blood in the animal body.

Thus, in Turgot's view, monetary calculation tends to insure that capital investment and productive resources are allocated among the various branches of production strictly in accord with consumer preferences as expressed in the pattern of expenditures on the array of consumer products. In appropriating from Law the term "circulation of money" and emphatically redefining it to signify the process of monetary saving and investment that initiates and sustains round after endless round of productive activity in the evenly rotating economy, Turgot seeks to depict the complex and unique link between money and capitalistic production.

---

[98] Ibid., pp. 83–85.
[99] Ibid., pp. 62–63.

According to Turgot:[100]

> … before the introduction of gold and silver in commerce …
> it was almost impossible to accumulate considerable capitals,
> and still more difficult to multiply and divide payments, as
> much as is necessary to facilitate and multiply exchanges to
> the extent which is demanded by a thriving commerce and
> circulation [of capital].… In fact, almost all savings are made
> in nothing but money; it is in money that the revenues come
> to the proprietors, that the advances and the profits return to
> undertakers of every kind; it is, therefore, from money that
> they save, and the annual increase of capitals take place in
> money: but none of the undertakers make any other use of
> it than to convert *it immediately* into the different kinds of
> effects upon which their undertaking depends; and thus this
> money returns to circulation, and the greater part of capitals
> exists only in effects of different kinds.…

Thus, although Turgot recognizes, indeed emphasizes, the link
between money and production, he quite clearly avoids the error,
common to Law and his latter-day followers, of supposing that what
drives production is the brute fact of spending money. For Turgot[101] it
is the finely-balanced order in which expenditures take place (*"l'ordre
des dépenses"*) which coordinates and maintains the social structure
of capital and production. Once allow "disorder" or discoordination
"in the sequence of expenditures" and the result is the disappearance
of profits and the reduction of business enterprises, employment, consumption, production, and income.

The criterion for sound money that is derived from Turgot's
work, therefore, centers upon money's role as a tool of economic
calculation which serves the entrepreneurial function of allocating
capital and coordinating the uses of productive resources in light of
anticipated consumer preferences.

In the period since the second world war, Turgot's insights and
ideas about money and banking have been developed most fully by
monetary theorists associated with the Austrian School of economics.

------

[100] Ibid., pp. 64, 98.

[101] Ibid., p. 63.

These include most notably Ludwig von Mises and Murray N. Rothbard.[102]

Turgot's influence was transmitted to modern Austrians primarily via Carl Menger, the nineteenth-century co-discoverer of marginal utility theory and founder of the Austrian School of economics. Menger's knowledge of early economic literature was encyclopedic,[103] and he was especially familiar with, and influenced by, the eighteenth century Franco-Italian tradition that began with Richard Cantillon and included, along with Turgot, the Abbé Condillac and Ferdinando Galiani. This tradition culminated in the work of J.B. Say, which exercised an enormous influence on Continental economics throughout the nineteenth century. Menger absorbed the Cantillon-Turgot-Say tradition directly, as we can see from the footnotes and appendices to his *Principles of Economics*,[104] and also indirectly, through his study of early nineteenth century German economists, such as Karl Heinrich Rau and Friedrich B.W. Hermann, whose theoretical approach was derived from Say.

Menger's most important contribution to monetary theory was the development of a rigorous theoretical explanation of the catallactic origin of money, the germ of which is to be found in Turgot's brilliant insight, noted above, that money is not created from outside the market by "an arbitrary convention" but evolves as "merchandise" with a

---

[102] Friedrich Hayek's stream of brilliant contributions to Austrian business-cycle theory and international monetary theory, for which he was awarded a share of the Nobel Prize in Economics in 1974, began to flow forth in 1925 but had come to an end by 1940. Hayek's contributions are contained in the following works: F.A. Hayek, *Monetary Theory and the Trade Cycle* (New York: Augustus M. Kelley, [1933] 1966); *Prices and Production*, 2nd. ed. (New York: Augustus M. Kelley, [1935] 1967); *Monetary Nationalism and International Stability* (New York: Augustus M. Kelley, [1937] 1971); *Profits, Interest, and Investment, and Other Essays on the Theory of Industrial Fluctuations* (New York: Augustus M. Kelley, [1939] 1969); *Money, Capital, and Fluctuations: Early Essays*, ed. Roy McCloughry (Chicago: The University of Chicago Press, 1984).

[103] F.A. Hayek, "Introduction: Carl Menger," introduction to Carl Menger, *Principles of Economics*, trans. James Dingwall and Bert F. Hoselitz (New York/London: New York University Press, 1981), p. 14.

[104] Carl Menger, *Principles of Economics*, trans. James Dingwall and Bert F. Hoselitz (New York: New York University Press, [1950] 1981).

"saleable value" that is originally determined under the preexisting state of barter. In fact, Menger[105] cites Turgot as one of three eighteenth-century writers who decisively rejected the long-held theory of Aristotle which ". . . traces the origin of money to a contract between men."

Menger's second contribution to Austrian monetary theory is his formulation of the demand for money as the sum of individual demands to hold a stock of cash in order to finance anticipated transactions. Moreover, among the three economists—Menger, Léon Walras, and Alfred Marshall—who are generally credited with priority in independently and fully articulating the cash balance approach to the demand for money, Menger alone seems to have possessed the depth of insight to explicitly reject the concept of the velocity of circulation of money and to avoid the error of treating velocity as the inverse of the demand for money.[106] Despite the fact that he was familiar with Cantillon's much-praised discussion of the "rapidity of circulation of money,"[107] Turgot, as we saw above, had also eschewed any reference to velocity as a factor in determining the value of money, instead suggesting an analysis that runs strictly in terms of the individual's desire to maintain a reserve of the exchange medium.

Also like Turgot, Menger emphasizes that no exchangeable good, including money, can ever possess a stable purchasing power, and he proceeds to demonstrate the fallacy of supposing that money is a measure of value and that it is possible to devise a theoretically unexceptionable statistical index of the general price level.[108] Finally, Menger seeks to rehabilitate the Turgotian concept of capital as the monetary appraisement of the aggregate of goods an individual

---

[105] Ibid., p. 318.

[106] Arthur W. Marget, *The Theory of Prices: A Re-examination of the Central Problems of Monetary Theory*, 2 vols. (New York: Augustus M. Kelley, [1938–1942] 1966), Vol. 1: p. 297; Vol. 2, p. 59; Hans F. Sennholz, "The Monetary Writings of Carl Menger," in *The Gold Standard: An Austrian Perspective*, ed. Llewellyn H. Rockwell, Jr. (Lexington, Mass.: D.C. Heath and Company, 1985), p. 22.

[107] Richard Cantillon, *Essai sur la Nature du Commerce en Général*, ed. and trans. Henry Higgs (New York: Augustus M. Kelley, Bookseller, [1931] 1964), pp. 127–49.

[108] Erich Roll, "Menger on Money," *Economica* 3, no. 12 (November 1936): pp. 457–58.

devotes to producing with the aim of acquiring a monetary income.[109] For Menger, then, the concept of capital is inextricably entwined with the concept of monetary calculation; it is "the productive property, whatever technical nature it may have, so far as its money value is the subject of economic calculation, that is, if it appears in our accounting as a productive sum of money."[110]

Eugen von Böhm-Bawerk is generally not credited with any contribution to monetary economics. In fact, Böhm-Bawerk[111] even criticized Menger's identification of capital with the monetary valuation of an individual's income-producing property as prescientific and "a leaning toward the mercantilistically colored speech of everyday life."[112]

Nevertheless, Böhm-Bawerk initiated the development of the modern Austrian emphasis on the central role of monetary calculation in guiding the social production process. Böhm-Bawerk's exposition of the "law of costs," in which he presents a causal explanation of the determination of the prices of the factors of production, is based on the explicit recognition that money functions as "the neutral common denominator for the otherwise noncomparable needs and emotions of different individuals."[113] Like Turgot, with whose work he was intimately familiar,[114] Böhm-Bawerk stressed the pivotal role of competition among capitalist-entrepreneurs in appraising the monetary value of productive factors in light of the prices of consumer goods.

---

[109] Hayek, "Carl Menger," p. 28.

[110] Ibid.

[111] Eugen von Böhm-Bawerk, *Capital and Interest*, 3 vols., trans. George D. Huncke and Hans F. Sennholz (South Holland, Ill.: Libertarian Press, 1959), pp. 50–53.

[112] It was left to Mises (*Human Action*, pp. 259–64) to demonstrate that the Mengerian concept of capital as the correlative of monetary income for calculation purposes and the Böhm-Bawerkian concept of capital goods as the produced means of production are both indispensable to the elaboration of economic theory.

[113] Eugen von Böhm-Bawerk, "The Ultimate Standard of Value," in *Shorter Classics of Eugen von Böhm-Bawerk*, trans. Charles W. Macfarlane (South Holland, Ill.: Libertarian Press, 1962), p. 250.

[114] In the first volume of *Capital and Interest*, Böhm-Bawerk devoted a chapter of critical analysis to Turgot's theory of interest, dismissing it as involving circular reasoning (Böhm-Bawerk, *Capital and Interest*, pp. 39–45). Nonetheless an earlier, and as yet unpublished, seminar paper written by Böhm-Bawerk indicates that Turgot had an "enormous influence" on him (Rothbard, *The Brilliance of Turgot*, p. 21).

The establishment of an integrated structure of money prices for all consumer and producer goods, which results from this competitive process, enables entrepreneurs to calculate and compare the expected costs and revenues of alternative productive ventures, and the prospect of maximum profit leads them to rationally allocate resources in the service of the most urgent of future consumer demands.

Thus, for Böhm-Bawerk,[115] it is monetary calculation which insures that the causal processes described by the "law of costs" are "in strictest conformity with" the law of marginal utility. Accordingly, Böhm-Bawerk[116] emphasizes: "*Even the originary productive powers of the nation* [*i.e.,* land and labor] *are forced into uses in the order of profitability and receive their value and their price from the last of them.*... [I]n the end every want will attract the productive powers it requires, directly or indirectly, and in proportion to the powers of attraction inherent in its [monetary] 'valuation figures'".

Elsewhere, Böhm-Bawerk[117] writes:

> To meet ... practically unlimited demand we have a labor power which in comparison with this demand is always limited. It is never sufficient to satisfy all our desire ... we must, therefore, always choose which of our desires we will gratify. Under the influence of self-interest we will satisfy them according to the height or the amount of the fee which we are willing to pay for their satisfaction.... The existing productive power is ... fully employed in the satisfying of those wants, for whose satisfaction we are willing and able to pay [the equilibrium money wage rate].... The fact that there are always a number of laborers out of employment tells in no way against my contention; it is a result, not of an excess of labor force, but of those never-failing disturbances of the organization of the entire, yet insufficient, supply of labor forces.

The foregoing passages contain the seeds of the concept of "price coordination" which undergirds the macroeconomic theorizing of

---

[115] Böhm-Bawerk, *Capital and Interest*, p. 255.

[116] Ibid., pp. 253–54.

[117] Böhm-Bawerk, "The Ultimate Standard of Value," pp. 355–56.

the modern Austrian school.[118] According to this concept, the competitive market process, guided by monetary calculation and unhampered by political interventions, *always* appraises and prices scarce resources so as to insure that they are fully employed in those uses anticipated by entrepreneurs to be most value-productive from the point of view of consumers.

Böhm-Bawerk, in fact, went far beyond Menger and Wieser and other contemporary marginal-utility theorists in explaining the catallactic phenomena of money costs and of the allocation of resources according to monetary calculation.[119] Böhm-Bawerk's great concern to elucidate the causal link between individuals' subjective value rankings and the social, objective, and cardinal phenomena of money prices and costs has left an indelible imprint on the efforts of later Austrians to develop a criterion for sound money which highlights money's role as a tool of economic calculation.

Mises,[120] the acknowledged founder of modern Austrian monetary theory, surely had Böhm-Bawerk[121] foremost in mind when he wrote:

---

[118] Joseph T. Salerno, "The Concept of Coordination in Austrian Macroeconomics," in *Austrian Economics: Perspectives on the Past and Prospects for the Future*, ed. Richard M. Ebeling (Hillsdale, Mich.: Hillsdale College Press, 1991) [reprinted here as Chapter 7].

[119] In Menger's work, "... the role that cost of production plays in determining the relative value of different commodities is not explicitly explained" (Hayek, "Carl Menger," p. 19). Wieser's work is marred by a peculiar and fruitless attempt to derive the principles of value and cost imputation from the analysis of a nonmonetary, communist economy (Friedrich von Wieser, *Natural Value*, ed. William Smart [New York: Augustus M. Kelley, [1893] 1971). For this among other reasons, Mises writes concerning Wieser: "His imputation theory is untenable. His ideas on value calculation justify the conclusion that he could not be called a member of the Austrian School, but rather was a member of the Lausanne school...." (Ludwig von Mises, *Notes and Recollections* [South Holland, Ill.: Libertarian Press, 1978], p. 36).

[120] Ludwig von Mises, *Epistemological Problems of Economics,* trans. George Reisman (New York: New York University Press, [1960] 1981), p. 165.

[121] Although Menger's *Principles of Economics* had an admittedly formative influence on Mises (Mises, *Notes and Recollections*, p. 33), Mises considers Böhm-Bawerk's three-volume *Capital and Interest* to be "no doubt ... the most eminent contribution to modern economic theory" (Ludwig von Mises, "Capital and Interest: Eugen von Böhm-Bawerk and the Discriminating Reader," in idem, *Economic Freedom and Interventionism: An Anthology of Articles and Essays,* ed. Bettina Bien Greaves [Irvington-on-Hudson, N.Y.: Foundation for Economic Education, 1990]

Only the reduction of the concept of cost to its ultimate basis, as carried out by the theory of marginal utility, brings the social aspect of economic action entirely into view.

Within the field of modern economics the Austrian School has shown its superiority to the School of Lausanne and the schools related to the latter, which favor mathematical formulations, by clarifying the causal relationship between value and cost, while at the same time eschewing the concept of function, which in our science is misleading. The Austrian School must also be credited with not having stopped at the concept of cost, but, on the contrary, with carrying on its investigations to the point where it is able to trace back even this concept to subjective value judgments.

Mises's discovery that the intellectual operation of monetary calculation based on market prices is the indispensable precondition for the existence of the social division of labor, which underlies his famous critique of socialism,[122] takes as its point of departure the Böhm-Bawerkian elaboration of the law of costs. In his development of monetary theory proper, as opposed to the theory of monetary calculation, Mises's work can be characterized as "the direct continuation of Menger's work."[123] Mises's student Rothbard has

---

p. 133). "Especially important" according to Mises (p. 134) is the third book of the second volume, which contains Böhm-Bawerk's exposition of value and price theory, including the law of costs. Schumpeter who was a student of Wieser's and exhibited a general methodological stance more reflective of Lausanne than of Vienna, concurs with Mises in his appraisal of Böhm-Bawerk's contribution: "His theory of price is still the best we possess [as of 1914], the one that best answers all fundamental problems and all basic difficulties.... [The] 'theory of imputation' ... owes to Böhm-Bawerk one of its most perfect formulations" (Joseph A. Schumpeter, "Eugen von Böhm-Bawerk: 1851–1914," in *Ten Great Economists: from Marx to Keynes*, trans. H.K. Zassenhaus [New York: Oxford University Press, 1965], pp. 159, 171). Finally, Hayek notes that the Austrian formulation of the subjective value doctrine "... including the theory of cost, was largely the result of Böhm-Bawerk's brilliant exposition," which went beyond Menger and Wieser "in matters relating to price" (F.A. Hayek, "Hayek on Wieser," in *The Development of Economic Thought: Great Economists in Perspective*, ed. H.W. Spiegel [New York: John Wiley and Sons, 1952], p. 558.).

[122] Ludwig von Mises, *Economic Calculation in the Socialist Commonwealth*, trans. S. Adler (Auburn, Ala.: Ludwig von Mises Institute, Praxeology Press, 1990).

[123] Hayek, "Carl Menger," p. 31.

made original contributions to the theories of money and monetary calculation,[124] which also lie squarely within the Turgot-Menger tradition.

It is in the writings of Mises and Rothbard, therefore, that we find the most sophisticated and complete rejection of the Law tradition. In his regression theorem, Mises[125] takes Menger's explanation of the emergence of money to its logical conclusion, demonstrating the utter impossibility of the origination of money by government fiat or explicit social contract. Money can never spring into existence as a product of convention or as a ready-made tool of government policy; it always evolves as a catallactic institution.

Rothbard[126] builds on the work of Mises and Menger in formulating what may be called a "progression theorem" of fiat money, a historico-logical account of how paper fiat money can and does come into being only as the result of a long series of government interventions which progressively undermines the market-evolved commodity

---

[124] Rothbard makes three contributions of the first rank to the theory of monetary calculation. He definitively demonstrates that the social appraisement process operative in an unhampered market economy cannot give rise to a monopolistic misallocation of resources that contradicts Böhm-Bawerk's law of costs (Murray N. Rothbard, *Man, Economy, and State: A Treatise on Economic Principles,* 2 vols. [Los Angeles: Nash Publishing, [1962] 1970], pp. 604–15). He shows that a free-market cartel is strictly limited in size by the necessity that every one of its capital-good inputs possess a market price for use in economic calculation. Thus, according to Rothbard no cartel can sustain expansion to the point at which it subsumes the entire market for a particular capital good—let alone the entire economy—because the result would be calculational chaos and economic inefficiency, which is inconsistent with the cartel's goal of maximum profit (Murray N. Rothbard, "Ludwig von Mises and Economic Calculation under Socialism," in *The Economics of Ludwig von Mises: A Critical Reappraisal,* ed. Laurence S. Moss [Kansas City, Mo.: Sheed and Ward, Inc., 1976], pp. 75–76. Finally, Rothbard establishes that under a pure commodity money, changes in the supply of money are incapable of falsifying monetary calculation and creating the intertemporal discoordination in the production structure that typifies an Austrian-type business cycle (Murray N. Rothbard, *America's Great Depression,* 3rd ed. [Kansas City, Mo.: Sheed and Ward, 1975], pp. 37–38).

[125] Ludwig von Mises, *The Theory of Money and Credit,* trans. H.E. Batson (Indianapolis: Liberty Classics, [1952] 1981), pp. 129–36.

[126] Murray N. Rothbard, *What Has Government Done to Our Money?* 4th ed. (Auburn, Ala.: Ludwig von Mises Institute, Praxeology Press, [1963] 1990).

standard.[127] One important implication of Rothbard's theorem for monetary reform is that there is no possibility of replacing a government monopolized fiat money with schemes for competing private inconvertible paper currencies. The reason is that the established fiat money, barring a hyperinflationary crackup, retains an indissoluble evolutionary link with the original commodity money by virtue of its position as the universally employed unit of price appraisement. For Mises[128] and Rothbard,[129] then, the only sure route to eventually denationalizing the money supply is to redefine the existing fiat monetary unit as a specific weight of gold, the market-chosen medium of exchange.

Mises[130] and Rothbard,[131] like Menger, are consistent adherents of the cash-balance approach, which builds up the market demand for money directly from the subjective valuations of money holdings by individual economic agents. They explicitly reject the common emphasis that neo-Keynesians, monetarists, and supply-siders place on the spending of money when they explain overall price and output variations. In their view, the value or purchasing power of money is determined by the same market process that generates the array of goods' prices—it is in fact the reciprocal of this array. Moreover, this process is driven by individuals' subjective valuations and

---

[127] Early Austrians such as Menger and Wicksteed implied that the existence of a pure fiat money is impossible on theoretical grounds (Menger, *Principles of Economics*, p. 320; Philip H. Wicksteed, *The Common Sense of Political Economy and Selected Papers and Reviews on Economic Theory*, ed. Lionel Robbins [New York: Augustus M. Kelley, [1932] 1967], vol. 2, pp. 618–23). Wieser attempted to establish the possibility of a paper fiat money "for which the mass habit of acceptance has been historically formed," arguing by analogy that a historically evolved commodity money that had ceased to be used for industrial purposes would continue to function as a medium of exchange (Friedrich von Wieser, *Social Economics*, trans. A. Ford Hinrichs [New York: Augustus M. Kelley, (1927) 1967], pp. 270–72). Mises's regression theorem finally and rigorously established the logical possibility of a fiat money. However, even as late as 1966 in the third edition of *Human Action*, Mises (p. 429) expresses uncertainty as to whether conditions giving rise to a pure fiat money ever existed historically.

[128] Mises, *Theory of Money and Credit*, pp. 477–500.

[129] Murray N. Rothbard, "The Case for a Genuine Gold Dollar," in Llewellyn H. Rockwell, Jr., ed., *The Gold Standard: An Austrian Perspective* (Lexington, Mass.: D.C. Heath, 1985), pp. 1–17.

[130] Mises, *Human Action*, pp. 398–478.

[131] Rothbard, *Man, Economy, and State*, pp. 661–764.

entrepreneurial expectations. Therefore, Mises and Rothbard argue, the objectified, acatallactic, and holistic concept of velocity of circulation of money, which is the defining concept of the monetarist theoretical approach, is superflous at best, and misleading at worst, in analyzing the determination of the value of money.

Nor is there room in modern Austrian monetary theory for the neo-Keynesian postulate of a Phillips curve trade-off between inflation and unemployment. Such a trade-off can only be alleged if one ignores the price-coordinating feature of the social appraisement process by which resource prices are derived from and adapted to entrepreneurial forecasts of future output prices. In the Austrian view, a price deflation, far from being an antisocial event to be feared and fought via the printing of monopoly fiat money, is the market's response to an increase in the social demand for money, due, for example, to a growth in real output or to greater uncertainty of the future. Such a change in preferences to acquire and hold money, no less than any other type of alteration in consumer preferences, precipitates a market adjustment process which tends to reappraise and reallocate productive resources according to the Böhm-Bawerkian law of costs. Barring laws mandating minimum wage rates or collective bargaining privileges for labor unions, there is no reason for the operation of this process to produce "involuntary" unemployment of the Keynesian type.[132]

Austrian economists emphasize the central role of monetary calculation in guiding entrepreneurial production decisions in a world marked by ceaseless flux in the constellation of consumer preferences, production techniques, and resource availabilities. Modern Austrians are therefore reluctant to enshrine "stability," whether it be of monetary growth rates, selected commodity prices, the rate of growth of total spending, or some other economic index, as the goal of the monetary system. In the Austrian view, the market economy owes its existence and success not to money's alleged role in insuring macro-stability, but to its usefulness as a tool enabling market participants to interpret and adjust to the change that pervades human life and action.

---

[132] Salerno, "The Concept of Coordination in Austrian Macroeconomics," pp. 335–40 [reprinted here as Chapter 7].

Mises[133] says that "[t]he market economy is real because it can calculate." The market economy offers the only means by which individual human beings, cooperating in the social division of labor, are enabled, through calculated action, to continually alter the anticipated course of future events in a way which they judge will improve their satisfaction or welfare. Thus, for example, money is a tool of economic calculation for entrepreneurs seeking to profit by constantly readjusting production to expected changes in consumer wants, in technical know-how, and in the quantities and qualities of the available resources. It is the ever-changing structure of money prices that provides the data for entrepreneurs' calculations of profit and loss and, thereby, gives meaning and direction to their plans and efforts.

The market-clearing property of these prices, moreover, insures that, at every moment of time, the monetary calculations of independent and competing entrepreneurs are capable of producing an integrated structure of resource uses strictly and deftly governed by the expected demands of consumers. This is the meaning of Mises's statement that "[t]he coordination of the autonomous actions of all individuals is accomplished by the operation of the market." [134]

As a creation of and aid to human reason and action, therefore, monetary calculation always and everywhere aims to alter the future to achieve greater satisfaction. As a never-ending sequence of calculated and coordinated actions, the evolution of the market economy represents an irreversible historical process which, at every point, originates change at the same time that it seeks to adapt to it. Monetary calculation, then, as the lodestar of the dynamic market process, is the conceptual antipode of monetary stability. There is no possibility of ever truly "stabilizing" any economic quantity, without falsifying or abolishing monetary calculation and undermining or destroying the market economy.

In questing for sound money, the modern Austrian, then, is not seeking "macroeconomic stability," however that is to be interpreted; he is seeking a money that will optimally serve the purpose of economic

---

[133] Mises, *Human Action*, p. 259.
[134] Ibid., p. 725.

calculation. In the Austrian view, hyperinflation exemplifies the extreme case of unsound money, because when prices rise at astronomical and unforeseeably changing rates, there is no prospect of making reasonable appraisements of future output prices. Consequently, the time horizon of entrepreneurial forecasts is artificially and severely foreshortened and the resulting competitive price bids for resources come to reflect only the value of resource uses in production processes geared to serving consumer demand in the immediate future, for example, in consumer services, in the wholesale and retail trades, and in various speculative enterprises. Since the social appraisement process is incapable of taking account of the monetary value of resource contributions to relatively lengthy processes, the economy's structure of production cannot be coordinated with the pattern of consumer preferences for satisfaction in the present and future. Under these conditions, industrial processes, especially those involving the production of business structures and durable capital equipment, grind to a halt.

When the hyperinflation reaches its final stage, the public refuses to accept the depreciated money on any terms in exchange for "real" goods, monetary exchange disappears, and the economy collapses into a state of barter in which the very possibility of a unitary price appraisement process and economic calculation is precluded. Rational allocation of resources to production for the market becomes impossible and, therefore, the social division of labor is practically abolished.

A less extreme but much more insidious instance of unsound money distorting the social appraisement process and temporarily nullifying the conditions of operation of Böhm-Bawerk's law of costs occurs whenever new money in the form of "fiduciary media," i.e., checkable deposits and, in an earlier era, banknotes unbacked by cash reserves, is injected into the economy via the institution of fractional-reserve banking. This species of unsound money is a universal characteristic of modern monetary regimes, in which central banks routinely inflate their national money supplies through the creation of additional bank reserves, inducing the fractional-reserve banking system to engage in a multiple expansion of their loans and deposits.[135]

---

[135] Murray N. Rothbard, *The Mystery of Banking* (New York: Richardson and Snyder, 1983), pp. 127–77.

In fact, the Austrian theory of the business cycle is the explication of the process by which the creation of fiduciary media inevitably distorts the social appraisement process and leads to a situation in which the entrepreneurial allocation of resources among production processes spanning different time periods systematically diverges from society's intertemporal consumption preferences.[136]

It is their overriding concern with the twin issues of economic calculation and coordination which leads modern Austrians to prescribe the abolition of a politically monopolized fiat money. They recognize that the potential for hyperinflation inherent in such a money threatens the calculational basis and, hence, the very existence of market society. Austrians are not only opposed to the central bank qua monopoly issuer of fiat currency, however; they also object to a commodity money standard which is dominated by a central bank, for example, the classical gold standard as it operated in Great Britain before 1914. The Austrian case against the latter type of monetary arrangement rests, to a great extent, on Rothbard's progression theorem, which identifies the central bank as the prime institutional means for effecting the progressive transformation of the monetary unit from a fixed weight of a market-supplied commodity to a pure name. The disembodied monetary unit then can be affixed to an almost worthless object and multiplied, practically without cost and limit, by political fiat.

While modern Austrians tend to be of one mind in their evaluation of central banks and state-issued fiat money, they are divided in their attitude toward private fractional-reserve or "free" banking. Some adopt the Smithian position in support of a purely private and unregulated banking system based on gold reserves and featuring competitively determined reserve ratios. Others follow Turgot in advocating the total suppression of fiduciary media via the one hundred percent gold standard. Mises[137] himself presented a vigorous defense of gold-based free banking in 1949, arguing that it is "the only method available" for preventing the economic discoordination

---

[136] Mises, *Human Action*, pp. 538–86; Rothbard, *America's Great Depression*, pp. 11–38.

[137] Mises, *Human Action*, p. 443.

attendant upon the creation of fiduciary media. Only three years later, however, Mises[138] was recommending "a rigid 100 percent [gold] reserve for all future deposits" as a means of permanently eliminating any further bank credit expansion.

Building on the ideas of Mises and on the nineteenth-century American anti-bank tradition, which was linked to Turgot via the French philosopher and economist Count Destutt de Tracy,[139] Rothbard[140] presents the most sophisticated case for one hundred percent-reserve banking based on gold.

Lately, a number of younger Austrians, particularly George Selgin and Lawrence White, have elaborated the Misesian case for free banking in greater detail. However, one can detect in their work a significant shift of orientation away from Mises's original goal of preserving the integrity of monetary calculation by stanching as much as possible the outpouring of fiduciary media onto credit markets. For Selgin and White, the desirability of free banking rests on its alleged usefulness as a means for sensitively regulating the creation of fiduciary media in a manner which is consistent with the preservation of "stability," of the aggregate spending flow[141] and, above all else, of the fractional-reserve banking industry itself.[142]

---

[138] Ludwig von Mises, *The Theory of Money and Credit*, trans. Harold E. Batson (Indianapolis: Liberty Fund, [1952] 1981), p. 491.

[139] For a discussion of the French roots of the tradition of hostility to fractional-reserve banking in nineteenth-century American economic thought, see Salerno, "Gold Standards: True and False," pp. 140–43 [reprinted here as Chapter 13].

[140] Murray N. Rothbard, *The Case for a 100 Per Cent Gold Dollar* (Washington, D.C.: Libertarian Review Press, [1962] 1974).

[141] George A. Selgin, *The Theory of Free Banking: Money Supply under Competitive Note Issue* (Totowa, N.J.: Rowman and Littlefield, 1988), pp. 52–69; George A. Selgin, "The Implications of Freedom in Banking and Note Issue," (first of two parts) *Austrian Economics Newsletter* 10, no. 2 (Winter 1989): p. 4; Lawrence H. White, *Competition and Currency: Essays on Free Banking and Money* (New York: New York University Press, 1989), pp. 158–59.

[142] Selgin, *Theory of Free Banking*, pp. 133–39; Lawrence H. White, *Free Banking in Britain: Theory, Experience, and Debate, 1800–1845* (New York: Cambridge University Press, 1984), pp. 137–50. Selgin (*Theory of Free Banking*, pp. 60–63) rejects the central implication of Austrian business-cycle theory that any creation of new fiduciary media must, without fail, precipitate an inflationary discoordination of the economy which must culminate in crisis and depression. In Selgin's view, the credit

In conclusion, modern Austrian monetary thought, with its roots in the Turgot tradition and emphasis on the macroeconomic phenomena of entrepreneurial calculation and price coodination, stands in radical opposition to the modern macroeconomic schools of thought, whose monetary doctrines have been molded within the Law tradition.

Bibliography

Andreades, A. 1909. *History of the Bank of England.* London : P.S. King and Son.

Bach, G.L. 1971. *Making Monetary and Fiscal Policy,* Washington, D.C. The Brookings Institution.

Beveridge, William H. 1945. *Full Employment in a Free Society.* New York: W.W. Norton & Company, Inc.

Blinder, A.S. 1987. *Hard Heads, Soft Hearts: Tough-Minded Economics for a Just Society.* New York: Addison-Wesley Publishing Company, Inc.

Böhm-Bawerk, E. von. 1959. *Capital and Interest,* 3 vols., G.D. Huncke and H. Sennholz, trans. South Holland, Ill.: Libertarian Press.

_____. 1962. "The Ultimate Standard of Value." In idem, *Shorter Classics of Eugen von Böhm-Bawerk,* C.W. Mcfarlane, trans., pp. 303–70. South Holland, Ill.: Libertarian Press.

Brunner, K. 1987. "Has Monetarism Failed?" In *The Search for Stable Money: Essays on Monetary Reform,* J.A. Dorn and A.J. Schwartz, eds., pp. 163–99. Chicago: University of Chicago Press.

Cantillon, R. [1931] 1964. *Essai sur la nature du Commerce en Général,* H. Higgs, ed. and trans. New York: Augustus M. Kelley, Bookseller.

Endres, A.M. 1987. "The Origins of Böhm-Bawerk's 'Greatest Error': Theoretical Points of Separation from Menger." *Journal of Institutional and Theoretical Economics,* no. 143 (June): pp. 291–309.

Friedman, M. 1953. *Essays in Positive Economics.* Chicago: University of Chicago Press.

_____. 1960. *A Program for Monetary Stability.* New York: Fordham University Press.

_____. 1962. *Capitalism and Friedman.* Chicago: University of Chicago Press.

---

and deposit expansion which would occur under free banking in response to an increased demand for cash balances is perfectly consistent with the preservation of "monetary equilibrium," defined as an unchanged flow of aggregate spending. Selgin's position on this matter serves to accent the shift of focus from economic calculation to stability among current Austrian-oriented proponents of free banking.

_____. 1987. "Monetary Policy: Tactics Versus Strategy." In *The Search for Stable Money: Essays on Monetary Reform*, J.A. Dorn and A.J. Schwartz, eds., pp. 361–82. Chicago: University of Chicago Press.

Friedman, M., and R. Friedman. 1980. *Free to Choose: A Personal Statement*. New York: Harcourt Brace Jovanovich.

Hahn, L.A. 1949. *The Economics of Illusion: A Critical Analysis of Contemporary Economic Theory and Policy*. New York: Squirer Publishing Co., Inc.

Hayek, F.A. 1952. "Hayek on Wieser." In *The Development of Economic Thought: Great Economist in Perspective*, H.W. Spiegel, ed., pp. 554–67. New York: John Wiley and Sons, Inc.

_____. [1933] 1966. *Monetary Theory and the Trade Cycle*. New York: Augustus M. Kelley, Publishers.

_____. [1935] 1967. *Prices and Production*, 2nd. ed. New York: Augustus M. Kelley, Publishers.

_____. [1939] 1969. *Profits, Interest and Investment: And Other Essays on the Theory of Industrial Fluctuations*. New York: Augustus M. Kelley, Publishers.

_____ [1937] 1971. *Monetary Nationalism and International Stability*. New York: Augustus M. Kelley, Publishers.

_____. 1981. "Carl Menger." Introduction to *Principles of Economics* by Carl Menger., J. Dingwall and B.F. Hoselitz, trans., pp. 11–36. New York: New York University Press.

_____. 1984. *Money, Capital, and Fluctuations: Early Essays*, R. McCloughry, ed. Chicago: The University of Chicago Press.

Keynes, J.M. 1964. *The General Theory of Employment, Interest, and Money*. New York: Harcourt, Brace & World, Inc.

Kindleberger, C.P. 1980. "Keynesianism Vs. Monetarism in Eighteenth and Nineteenth-Century France." *History of Political Economy*, no. 12 (Winter): pp. 499–523.

Laffer, A.B. and M.A. Miles. 1982. *International Economics in an Integrated World*. Oakland, N.J.: Scott, Foresman and Company.

Law, J. [1705] 1966. *Money and Trade Considered: With a Proposal for Supplying the Nation with Money*. New York: Augustus M. Kelley.

Lerner, A.P. 1951. *Economics of Employment*, New York: McGraw-Hill Book Company, Inc.

McCulloch, J.H. 1982. *Money and Inflation: A Monetarist Approach*, 2nd ed. New York: Academic Press.

MacLeod, H.D. [1892] 1893. *Theory and Practice of Banking*, 5th ed. London.

Marget, A.W. [1938–1942] 1966. *The Theory of Prices: A Re-examination of the Central Problems of monetary Theory*. 2 vols. New York: Augustus M. Kelley Publishers.

Meiselman, D.I. 1987. "Comment: Is Gold the Answer?" In *The Search for Stable Money: Essays on Monetary Reform*, J.A. Dorn and A.J. Schwartz, eds., pp. 257–60. Chicago: University of Chicago Press.

Meltzer, A.H. 1987. "Monetary Reform in an Uncertain Environment." In *The Search for Stable Money: Essays on Monetary Reform*, J.A. Dorn and A.J. Schwartz, eds., pp. 201–20. Chicago: University of Chicago Press.

Menger, C. [1950] 1981. *Principles of Economics*, J. Dingwall and B.F. Hoselitz, trans. New York: New York University Press.

Miles, M.A. 1984. *Beyond Monetarism: Finding the Road to Stable Money*. New York: Basic Books, Inc.

Mints, L.W. 1945. *A History of Banking Theory in Great Britain and the United States*. Chicago: University of Chicago Press.

Mises, L. v. 1966. *Human Action: A Treatise on Economics*. 3rd ed. Chicago: Henry Regnery Company.

_____. 1978. *Notes and Recollections*. South Holland, Ill.: Libertarian Press.

_____. [1952] 1981. *The Theory of Money and Credit*, H.E. Batson, trans. Indianapolis: Liberty Classics.

_____. [1960] 1981. *Epistemological Problems of Economics*, G. Reisman, trans. New York: New York University Press.

_____. 1990a. "Capital and Interest: Eugen von Böhm-Bawerk and the Discriminating Reader." In idem, *Economic Freedom and Interventionism: An Anthology of Articles and Essays*, Bettina Bien Greaves, ed., pp. 133–35. Irvington-on-Hudson, N.Y.: Foundation for Economic Education.

_____. 1990b. *Economic Calculation in the Socialist Commonwealth*, S. Adler, trans. Auburn, Ala.: Praxeology Press.

Nicholson, J.S. 1888. *A Treatise on Money and Essays on Monetary Problems*. Edinburgh: Blackwood.

Paul, R., and L. Lehrman. 1982. *The Case for Gold: A Minority Report of the U.S. Gold Commission*. Washington, D.C.: Cato Institute.

Rist, C. [1940] 1966. *History of Monetary and Credit Theory: From John Law to the Present Day*. New York: Augustus M. Kelley Publishers.

_____. 1961. *The Triumph of Gold*. New York: Philosophical Library.

Roll, E. 1936. "Menger on Money." *Economica* (November): pp. 455–60.

Rothbard, M.N. [1962] 1970. *Man, Economy, and State: A Treatise on Economic Principles*. 2 vols. Los Angeles: Nash Publishing.

_____. [1962] 1974. *The Case for a 100 Percent Gold Dollar*. Washington, D.C.: Libertarian Review Press.

_____. 1975. *America's Great Depression*. 3rd ed. Kansas City, Mo. Sheed and Ward, Inc.

_____. 1976. "Ludwig von Mises and Economic Calculation under Socialism." In *The Economics of Ludwig von Mises: A Critical Reappraisal*, L.S. Moss, ed., pp. 67–77. Kansas City, Mo.: Sheed and Ward, Inc.

_____. 1983. *The Mystery of Banking*. New York: Richardson and Snyder.

_____. 1985. "The Case for a Genuine Gold Dollar." In *The Gold Standard: An Austrian Perspective*, L.H. Rockwell, Jr., ed., pp. 1–17. Lexington, Mass.: D.C. Heath and Company.

_____. 1986. *The Brilliance of Turgot*. Auburn, Ala.: Ludwig von Mises Institute.

_____. [1963] 1990. *What Has Government Done to Our Money?* Auburn, Ala.: Praxeology Press.

Salerno, J.T. 1980. *The Doctrinal Antecedents of the Monetary Approach to the Balance of Payments*. Ann Arbor, Mich.: University Microfilms International.

_____. 1987. "Gold Standards: True and False." In *The Search for Stable Money: Essays on Monetary Reform*, J.A. Dorn and A.J. Schwartz, eds., pp. 241–55. Chicago: University of Chicago Press.

_____. J.T. 1988. "The Neglect of the French Liberal School in Anglo-American Economics: A Critique of Received Explanations." *The Review of Austrian Economics*, no. 2: pp. 113–56.

_____. 1991. "The Concept of Coordination in Austrian Macroeconomics." In *Austrian Economics: Perspectives on the Past and Prospects for the Future*, R.M. Ebeling, ed., pp. 325–43. Hillsdale, Mich.: Hillsdale College Press.

Schumpeter, J.A. 1954. *History of Economic Analysis*. New York: Oxford University Press.

_____. 1965. "Eugen von Böhm-Bawerk: 1851–1914." In idem, *Ten Great Economists: From Marx to Keynes*, H.K. Zassenhaus, trans., pp. 143–90. New York: Oxford University Press.

Selgin, G.A. 1988. *The Theory of Free Banking: Money Supply under Competitive Note Issue*. Totowa, N.J.: Rowman & Littlefield.

_____. 1989. "The Implications of Freedom in Banking and Note Issue – Part I." *Austrian Economics Newsletter*, no. 10 (Winter): pp. 4–7.

Sennholz, H.F. 1985. "The Monetary Writings of Carl Menger." In *The Gold Standard: An Austrian Perspective*, L.H. Rockwell, Jr., ed., pp. 19–34. Lexington, Mass.: D.C. Heath and Company.

Shaw, E.S. 1965. "The Case for an Automatic Monetary Pilot." In *The Battle against Unemployment: An Introduction to a Current Issue of Public Policy*, A.M. Okun, ed., pp. 192–200. New York: W.W. Norton & Company, Inc.

Smith, A. [1776] 1965. *An Inquiry into the Nature and Causes of the Wealth of Nations*. New York: Random House, Inc.

Simons, H.C. 1948. *Economic Policy for a Free Society*. Chicago: University of Chicago Press.

Thiers, A. [1859] 1969. *The Mississippi Bubble: A Memoir of John Law*. New York: Greenwood Press, Publishers.

Turgot, A.R.J. 1895. *The Life and Writings of Turgot*. W.W. Stephens, ed. London: Longmans, Green and Co.

_____. [1770] 1971. *Reflections on the Formation and the Distribution of Riches*. New York: Augustus M. Kelley Publishers.

Vickers, Douglas. [1959] 1968. *Studies in the Theory of Money 1690–1776.* New York: Augustus M. Kelley, Publishers.

Viner, J. 1958. *The Long View and the Short: Studies in Economic Theory and Policy.* Glencoe, Ill. : The Free Press.

White, L.H. 1984. *Free Banking in Britain: Theory, Experience, and Debate, 1800–1845.* New York: Cambridge University Press.

____. 1989. *Competition and Currency: Essays on Free Banking and Money.* New York: New York University Press.

Wicksteed, P.H. [1932] 1967. *The Common Sense of Political Economy and Selected Papers and Reviews on Economic Theory,* 2 vols. New York: Augustus M. Kelley, Publishers.

Wieser, F.v. [1927] 1967. *Social Economics,* A.F. Hinrichs, trans. New York: Augustus M. Kelley, Publishers.

____. [1893] 1971. *Natural Value,* New York: Augustus M. Kelley, Publishers.

CHAPTER 2

Ludwig von Mises's Monetary Theory in Light of Modern Monetary Thought

L udwig von Mises's contributions to the development of the technical methods and apparatus of monetary theory continue to be
neglected today, despite the fact that Mises succeeded exactly
eight decades ago, while barely out of his twenties, in a task that still
admittedly defies the best efforts of the most eminent of modern
monetary theorists: integrating monetary and value theory. Such a
unified and truly general theory is necessary to satisfactorily explain
the functioning of the market economy, because the market economy,
or any economy based on social cooperation under the division of
labor, cannot exist without monetary exchange and calculation.[1]

From "Ludwig von Mises's Monetary Theory in Light of Modern Monetary Thought,"
The Review of Austrian Economics 8, no. 1 (1994): pp. 71–115.

[1] The first to make this point was Ludwig von Mises (1990) in his classic article dem-
onstrating the impossibility of economic calculation under socialist central planning.
For recent reviews and elucidations of the socialist calculation debate from a Mise-
sian perspective which emphasize the same point, see Murray N. Rothbard, "The
End of Socialism and the Calculation Debate Revisited," *The Review of Austrian
Economics* 5, no. 2 (1991); Joseph T. Salerno, "Ludwig von Mises as Social Ratio-
nalist," *The Review of Austrian Economics* 4, no. 1 (1990), pp. 45–49; and Joseph T.
Salerno, "Why a Socialist Economy Is 'Impossible,'" postscript to Ludwig von Mises,
Economic Calculation in the Socialist Commonwealth, trans. S. Adler (Auburn,
Ala.: Ludwig von Mises Institute, Praxeology Press, 1990).

Mises's work on monetary economics is not only ignored by mainstream neo- and "new" Keynesians, monetarists, and new classicists, it is also considered passé by many Austrian-oriented economists and policy analysts, especially those whose primary influence is the post-World War II writings of Mises's former student F. A. Hayek. A typical example of this flippant and uncomprehending dismissal of Mises's monetary thought is provided by a review of *The Gold Standard: An Austrian Perspective* that appeared in a publication of a freemarket think tank.[2] In commenting on this edited volume of mainly Misesian papers on the gold standard, the anonymous reviewer opined that "large parts of the book are unsatisfactory when considered as contributions to modern economic theory. Many of the essays have a strongly anachronistic flavor and do not succeed in integrating their arguments with the (often relevant) debates in modern monetary theory." *Mirabile dictu,* the reviewer then goes on to endorse as superior to the gold standard bizarre "laissez-faire" schemes such as the issuance of private fiat moneys and the separation of the unit of account from the medium of exchange, which have been resurrected under the rubric of the "New Monetary Economics" but which still emit the unmistakable musk of their association with obscure and long-dead monetary cranks.[3] Had the reviewer enjoyed even passing familiarity with Mises's regression theorem, he would have instantly realized the untenability of these schemes.[4]

But the problem goes beyond Hayekian epigones laboring as policy analysts in think tanks. Prominent economists, too, in the wake of the collapse in rapid succession of the Keynesian and then the monetarist paradigms, have been casting around recently for non-gold, "laissez-faire" alternatives to central bank manipulations of the money supply. There is, of course, Hayek's proposal for the issue of private fiat

---

[2] Review of *The Gold Standard: An Austrian Perspective,* ed. Llewellyn H. Rockwell, Jr., *Cato Policy Report* 8 (November/December 1986), pp. 14–15.

[3] For an overview of the forerunners of the New Monetary Economics by two of its proponents, see Tyler Cowen and Randy Kroszner, "The Development of the New Monetary Economics," *Journal of Political Economy* 95, no. 3 (1987).

[4] A critique of Hayek's scheme for privately issued paper fiat currencies is provided by Murray N. Rothbard, *The Gold Standard: Perspectives in the Austrian School* (Auburn, Ala.: Ludwig von Mises Institute, 1992), pp. 2–5.

currencies, and recently Milton Friedman has endorsed bimetallism as superior to a monometallic gold standard.[5] The plan coauthored by Yeager and Greenfield to dissolve the link between the monetary unit of account and the medium of exchange has recently been endorsed by another former monetarist, Richard Timberlake, who formerly advocated a parallel gold standard.[6] Even Lawrence White and George Selgin, supporters of a gold-based free-banking system who drew their initial inspiration from Mises, now argue that such a system would give rise to an "invisible-hand" maturation process that would eventually culminate in the complete and "spontaneous" withering away of the monetary gold base to yield a fiat bank money. (Mises advocated gold-based free banking because he believed it would severely restrain the issue of fiduciary media.)

All such schemes are based on the unfortunate failure of their authors to perceive money as an outgrowth and driving force of "micro" market processes. This perception can only be gained from Mises's monetary theory, with its unification of real and monetary analysis. What is urgently needed, then, and what I will attempt to supply in this paper, is a fresh evaluation of Mises's monetary theory and a clarification of its relationship to modern monetary thought.

I hope to demonstrate that Misesian theory provides fresh and relevant answers to the seemingly intractable problems that still confront modern monetary economics.

In 1985, James Rolph Edwards published *The Economist of the Country: Ludwig von Mises in the History of Monetary Thought,*[7]

---

[5] Milton Friedman, *Money Mischief: Episodes in Monetary History* (New York: Harcourt Brace Jovanovich, 1992).

[6] Robert L. Greenfield and Leland B. Yeager, "A Laissez-Faire Approach to Monetary Stability," *Journal of Money, Credit, and Banking* 15 (August 1983); Richard H. Timberlake, Jr., *Gold, Greenbacks, and the Constitution* (Berryville, Va.: George Edward Durrell Foundation, 1991). For a critique of the Timberlake twist on the Greenfield-Yeager proposal, see Murray N. Rothbard, "Aurophobia: or, Free Banking on What Standard?" *Review of Austrian Economics* 6, no. 1 (1992). Timberlake's earlier, and much sounder, proposal is evaluated by Joseph T. Salerno, "The Gold Standard: An Analysis of Some Recent Proposals." *Policy Analysis*, 16 (September 9, 1982), Washington, D.C.: Cato Institute, pp. 16–18 [reprinted here as Chapter 14].

[7] James Rolph Edwards, *The Economist of the Country: Ludwig von Mises in the History of Monetary Thought* (New York: Carlton Press, 1985).

an insightful and stimulating work in which he attempted a doctrinal assessment of Mises's contributions to monetary theory. As I shall indicate in detail below, Edwards shed important light on Mises's originality as a monetary theorist and brilliantly defended him against some modern detractors. He failed, however, in his misconceived project to portray Mises as the prototypical modern monetary economist, with an analytical tool kit that included an asset demand for money, the natural-rate hypothesis, the accelerationist view of lagged adjustment of nominal wages during inflation, a consistent modern monetary approach to the balance of payments and the exchange rate and rational expectations. Nonetheless, Edwards's book does provide a useful framework, which I will employ for comparing Misesian with modem monetary theory. I will use Edwards's order of topics to organize my own paper and also use some of his comments on Mises's theory as points of departure for my own evaluation.

In the next section, "The Nature, Development, and Supply of Money," I address Mises's approach to defining money, to classifying its different forms and components, and to measuring the money supply. I also briefly discuss Mises's development of a consistent ordinalist approach to value theory as a foundation for his monetary theory. The following section, "The Regression Theorem and the Demand for Money," deals with Mises's formulation of a cash-balance demand for money and of a supply-and-demand explanation of the determination of money's purchasing power, and also with his arguments in favor of the nonneutrality of money. The section concludes with a consideration of Mises's regression theorem and a defense of it against criticism by Don Patinkin and others. In the concluding section, "The Monetary Adjustment Process: The Interspatial Equalization of the Value of Money, and the Determination of Exchange Rates," I focus on Mises's approach to the interspatial equalization of the purchasing power of a single money and to the determination of the exchange rate between independent moneys. In the case of the former, I significantly elaborate on Mises's view that the market's arbitrage processes rapidly re-establish monetary equilibrium after it has been disturbed, and I demonstrate the importance to monetary analysis of Mises's methodological devices of the plain and final states of rest. I also draw attention to important methodological contributions by Philip Wicksteed and Arthur Marget which facilitate a better understanding of the monetary adjustment process. In discussing exchange rate determination I carefully distinguish between the Misesian version of the purchasing power parity theory and the Casselian version adopted by modern economists, and I explain why the former version is immune to many of the criticisms commonly raised against the latter.

The Nature, Development, and Supply of Money

In chapter two of *The Economist of the Country*, Edwards reviews Mises's seminal, though unhappily neglected, achievements in preparing the conceptual groundwork necessary to a full statement of the theory of money. These include the development of a purely ordinal theory of subjective value and of marginal utility more than two decades before the celebrated "ordinalist revolution" of the 1930s (which ended up totally and erroneously expunging the very concept of marginal utility from economics). As Edwards points out, compared to the equilibrium condition yielded by the indifference curve analysis based on infinitely divisible goods developed later by Anglo-American ordinalists, the equilibrium condition derived from Mises's value theory is "more general and correct," because "real trade more often than not [I would say "always"] involves discrete goods."[8] Despite Mises's clear priority in formulating a purely and consistently ordinal theory of value and in completely eliminating the notion of measurable utility from economics, "To this day the major historians of economic thought appear unaware of Mises's contributions here."[9]

As Edwards points out, Mises built on Carl Menger's work to develop a theory of the nature and origin of money.[10] As the

---

[8] Edwards, *The Economist of the Country*, p. 34.

[9] This oversight is just beginning to be redressed in the mainstream economic literature. See, for example, Jack High and Howard Bloch, "On the History of Ordinal Utility Theory: 1890–1932," *History of Political Economy* 21, no. 2 (1989) for recognition of Mises and other neglected Austrian forerunners of the ordinalist revolution of the 1930s.

[10] Edwards, *The Economist of the Country*, pp. 31–32.

most generally saleable good in society or "the general medium of exchange," money emerges step by step from an evolutionary market process driven by the actions of individuals consciously striving to obtain the maximum benefit from their cooperation in exchange and the division of labor. All other functions of money, e.g., as a "store of value," "unit of account," "standard of deferred payments," are and must remain subsidiary to money's primary function as a medium of exchange. As we will see below, Mises's regression theorem goes beyond Menger in demonstrating that, logically, money can only come into being as a product of voluntary catallactic processes.

Under the rubric of "Definitions and Components of the Money Stock,"[11] Edwards draws attention to Mises's original and indispensable taxonomy of money, which yields a statistical definition of money that is consistent with the one used by modem economists. Before Mises wrote *The Theory of Money and Credit*,[12] economists generally distinguished between bank notes and token coins on the one hand and demand deposits or checking account balances on the other.[13] Only the former were included along with specie in the category of money. Mises rejected this distinction as useless for the

---

[11] Ibid., pp. 36–38.

[12] Ludwig von Mises, *The Theory of Money and Credit*, New enl. ed., trans. Harold E. Batson (Irvington-on-Hudson, N.Y.: The Foundation for Economic Education, [1953] 1971).

[13] This is true even of such allegedly revolutionary monetary theorists as Irving Fisher, hailed by Milton Friedman as the "greatest economist that America has ever produced." While Fischer identified bank deposits as an "excellent substitute" for money, he insisted that they "are not money." See, Irving Fisher (*The Purchasing Power of Money: Its Determination and Relation to Credit, Interest and Prices*, 2nd ed. [Fairfield, N.J.: Augustus M. Kelley, [1913] 1985], pp. 47, 53). Even Edwin Cannan, who was one of the pioneers in formulating the demand for money as an asset or stock demand and whom Mises referred to more than once as "the great British economist," (see Ludwig von Mises, *Economic Freedom and Intervention: An Anthology of Articles and Essays*, ed. Bettina Bien Greaves (Irvington-on-Hudson, N.Y.: Foundation for Economic Education, 1990), pp. 23, 172) maintained a rigid distinction between bank deposits and money. See, for example, Edwin Cannan, *Money: Its Connexion with Rising and Falling Prices*, 6th ed. (Westminster, England: P.S. King and Son, 1929), pp. 64–85. A good survey of Cannan's contributions to monetary theory can be found in T.E. Gregory, "Professor Cannan and Contemporary Monetary Theory," in *London Essays in Economics: In Honor of Edwin Cannan*, eds. T.E. Gregory and Hugh Dalton (London: George Routledge and Sons, 1927).

purposes of economic science. Mises's repudiation of the older classification accords with his staunchly Mengerian "essentialist" approach
to economics, which finds expression in his dictum that "The greatest
mistake that can be made in economic investigation is to fix attention
on mere appearances, and to fail to perceive the fundamental difference between things whose externals alone are similar, or to discrimi-
nate between fundamentally similar things whose externals alone are
different."[14]

In formulating a new and more useful classificatory framework,
Mises draws a distinction between standard money—whether of the
"commodity," "credit," or "fiat" variety—and "money substitutes,"
defined as perfectly secure and immediately convertible claims to
money, such as bank notes and demand deposits, which substitute
for money in individuals' cash balances. Within the class of money
substitutes, Mises further distinguishes between "money certificates,"
which are notes and deposits fully covered by reserves of the standard
money, and "fiduciary media," which are uncovered money substitutes. Mises employs the term "money in the narrow sense" to denote
the aggregate stock of standard money in the economy, corresponding to what is today called "the monetary base." "Money in the broad
sense" is Mises's term for the monetary aggregate equal to standard
money plus money substitutes minus bank reserves or, alternatively,
equal to standard money (including reserves) plus fiduciary media.
This latter aggregate is roughly approximated by the current definition of M1.[15]

---

[14] Mises, *Theory of Money and Credit*, p. 62.

[15] Lawrence H. White criticizes Mises's use of the term "money substitutes" to designate secure and instantaneously redeemable claims to money, i.e., money certificates plus fiduciary media, as "confusing" because the term suggests "nonmoneyness"
(Lawrence H. White, "A Subjectivist Perspective on the Definition and Identification of Money," in *Subjectivism, Intelligibility and Economic Understanding: Essays
in Honor of Ludwig M. Lachmann on His Eightieth Birthday* ed. Israel M. Kirzner
[London: Macmillan Press, 1986], p. 314 n. 23). But Mises's point in using such a
term is precisely to indicate that claims to the standard money, e.g., gold, whether
fully backed by gold or not, as long as they are perceived by the issuing institution's
clients as instantaneously redeemable for gold at face value, are *not* money in themselves, because their value is not determined by a valuation process independent of
that which determines the value of gold. In contrast, in suggesting as replacements

In noting the similarity between Mises's broader definition
of money and modern Ml, Edwards commits an error of commission and an error of omission. Although both of these errors are
minor, they are worth noting because they elucidate Mises's essentialist approach to defining money. The error of commission occurs
when Edwards states that "in modern times, money consists of fiat
currency, token coins, and credit money with fractional reserves."[16]
Now the phrase "credit money with fractional reserves" clearly refers
to checkable deposits; however, Mises does not consider checkable
deposits to be credit money. He classifies them as fiduciary media, a
subclass of money substitutes. Credit money, on the other hand, as
noted above, is one of Mises's three categories of standard money,
which also includes fiat and commodity money. In *The Theory of
Money and Credit*, Mises defines credit money as "a claim against any
physical or legal person [which] must not be both payable on demand
and absolutely secure.... Credit money ... is a claim falling due in

---

for Mises's "money substitutes" and "money-in-the-narrower sense" the terms
"inside money" and "outside money," respectively, White himself might be charged
with sowing confusion for implying that the instantaneously redeemable bank notes
and deposits he denotes by "inside money" constitute a separate money whose value
is determined independently of the value of the money commodity. But if we look
more closely at White's free-banking position, we discover that this is precisely what
he intends to imply. For the free bankers, convertible bank notes and deposits, from
the moment of their first issue, are considered a fiat money in embryo. The "invisible-hand process" by which these former fiduciary media mature into an independent money also brings about the full and final expulsion of gold from its monetary
role. Thus, the contractual suspension of specie payments and option clauses that free
banks allegedly will negotiate with their clients, when they are implemented or even if
they are widely expected to be, will establish "bank money" (another favored term) as
an independently valued credit money. Eventually, in the "mature free-banking system," according to White and Selgin, there would emerge a situation in which, "[a]t
the limit, if inter-clearing-house settlements were made entirely with other assets ...
and if the public were completely weaned from holding commodity money, the active
demand for the old-fashioned money commodity would be wholly nonmonetary,"
and the public would presumably be finally freed from its shackles of gold to enjoy the
virtues of a private fiat money generated purely by the "invisible hand." See Lawrence
H. White and George A. Selgin, "The Evolution of a Free Banking System," [1987], in
Lawrence H. White, *Competition and Currency: Essays on Free Banking and Money*
(New York: New York University Press, 1989), p. 235.

16 Edwards, *The Economist of the Country*, p. 38.

the future that is used as a general medium of exchange."[17] Generally, credit money emerges when an issuer of fiduciary media suspends redemption of these media for a definite or indefinite period of time.

The essential economic difference between the two is that the value of a money substitute, considered as a perfectly secure and instantaneously redeemable claim to money, is completely dependent upon and always equal to the value of the sum of standard money to which it entitles its holder. In contrast, the value of credit money is established by an "independent process of valuation."[18] For example, Bank of England notes denominated in gold pounds were money substitutes during the periods of their unqualified convertibility prior to 1797 and after 1821; they circulated as credit money for the duration of suspended specie payments from 1797 to 1821. As we would expect of credit money, during the latter period the purchasing power of the paper pound fluctuated independently of the purchasing power of the quantity of gold which corresponded to its original definition. The fact that the prospects and timing of future redeemability influenced these fluctuations marked the currently inconvertible notes as credit rather than fiat money.

A proper understanding of the concept of credit money is important, because Mises seems inclined to classify most historical instances of noncommodity money as credit rather than fiat money. For example, in *The Theory of Money and Credit*, which was translated from the second German edition published in 1924, after the German hyperinflation had run its course, Mises writes: "It can hardly be contested that fiat money in the strict sense of the word is theoretically conceivable....Whether fiat money has ever actually existed is, of course, another question, and one that cannot offhand be answered affirmatively. It can hardly be doubted that most of those kinds of money that are not commodity money must be classified as credit money. But only detailed historical investigation could clear this matter up."[19] Even as late as 1966, in the third edition of *Human*

---

[17] Mises, *The Theory of Money and Credit*, pp. 61–62.

[18] Ibid., p. 61.

[19] Ibid.

Action, Mises stops short of categorically affirming the historical existence of fiat money, declaring that "It is not the task of catallactics but of economic history to investigate whether there appeared in the past specimens of fiat money or whether all sorts of money which were not commodity money were credit money."[20]

The error of omission in Edwards's discussion—partly explained by his narrow focus on *The Theory of Money and Credit*—is his failure to recognize Mises's ambivalent attitude toward the inclusion of saving deposits in his broader definition of money. A strong case can and has been made for the view that saving deposits in the contemporary U.S. economy constitute "perfectly secure and immediately convertible claims to money" and therefore, according to Mises's own criterion, are to be identified among the components of money in the broad sense.[21]

---

[20] Ludwig von Mises, *Human Action: A Treatise on Economics,* 3rd ed. (Chicago: Henry Regnery, 1966), p. 429.

[21] This case has been made by Rothbard and Salerno, who argue for including in the money supply all currently spendable dollars in the economy, i.e., those immediately obtainable without penalty or risk of capital loss. See Murray N. Rothbard, "Austrian Definitions of the Supply of Money," in *New Directions in Austrian Economics,* ed. Louis M. Spadaro (Kansas City: Sheed Andrews and McMeel, 1978); and Joseph T. Salerno, "The 'True' Money Supply: A Measure of the Supply of the Medium of Exchange in the U.S. Economy," *Austrian Economics Newsletter* 6 (Spring 1987) (available at http://www.mises.org) [reprinted here as Chapter 3]. As reported by the Federal Reserve Bank of Cleveland *Economic Trends,* July 1992, p. 3, Shadow Open Market Committee member William Poole has endorsed a monetary aggregate, MZM, (for "money of zero maturity") which seeks to identify and capture those dollars "immediately available without penalty or risk of capital loss" and which comes close to the TMS (for "true money supply") aggregate developed by Rothbard and Salerno. The main difference between the two is that TMS excludes, while MZM includes, all money market mutual fund shares. Both include, in addition to items in M1, savings deposits and money market deposit accounts, at the same time excluding small time deposits. On the other hand, White, in "Subjectivist Perspective on the Definition and Identification of Money," beginning from a Misesian medium-of-exchange definition of money similar to Rothbard and Salerno's, arrives at a much narrower empirical measure of the money supply which excludes noncheckable demand deposits, such as passbook savings accounts, on the grounds that the passbooks themselves do not literally pass from hand to hand in the payments process. Israel M. Kirzner, in a critique of Rothbard, raises the same objection as White to the inclusion of noncheckable deposits in the money supply, and then goes further to express skepticism of any attempts to produce a statistically unweighted aggregate of the nominal stock of money (Israel M. Kirzner, "Discussion of M. Rothbard, 'Austrian Definitions of the

As early as 1924, Mises recognized that institutional developments had led banks "to undertake the obligation to pay out small
sums of savings deposits at any time without notice."[22] This circumstance, according to Mises induced some people, for example, "small
business people and not very well-to-do private individuals," to utilize
these deposits as "current accounts" notwithstanding their technical
status as "investment deposits." Thus Mises implies that at least some
portion of saving deposits function economically as money substitutes and warrant inclusion in his broad category of money.

During the 1920s and into the 1930s, there was tremendous
growth in the volume and economic significance of savings deposits both in the U.S., due to Federal Reserve policies, and throughout
the world economy.[23] In an important but neglected article written in
1933, Mises places much of the blame for the financial and exchange-
rate instability of the early 1930s on the pandemic treatment of savings deposits as money substitutes, a development actively sought and
encouraged by the banks:

> The bank which receives [saving deposits] has to lend it to
> business. A withdrawal of the money entrusted to it by the
> saver can only take place in the same measure as the bank is
> able to get back the money it has lent. As the total amount
> of the saving deposits is working in the country's business, a
> total withdrawal is not possible. The individual saver can get
> back his money from the bank, but not all savers at the same
> time.... Since the saver does not need the deposited sum at
> call or short notice it is not necessary that the savings banks

Money Supply," paper presented at the Symposium on Austrian Economics, Windsor
Castle, England, August 1976). It is ironic that Kirzner's thoroughgoing commitment
to subjectivism should lead to his rediscovery of and support for a Divisia-type monetary aggregate in advance of its modern reintroduction into mainstream monetary
economics in the 1980s. For a brief critique of the White-Kirzner position on excluding noncheckable demand deposits from a monetary aggregate based on the medium-
of-exchange definition of money, see Salerno, "The 'True' Money Supply," pp. 2–3.

[22] Mises, *Theory of Money and Credit*, p. 270.

[23] See C.A. Phillips, T.F. McManus, and R.W. Nelson, *Banking and the Business
Cycle: A Study of the Great Depression in the United States* (New York: Arno Press
and *The New York Times*, [1937] 1972), pp. 29, 95–103; and Murray N. Rothbard,
America's Great Depression, 3rd ed. (Kansas City: Sheed & Ward, 1975), pp. 92–94.

or the other banks which take over such deposits should promise repayment at call or at short notice. Nevertheless, this is what they did. And so they became exposed to the dangers of a panic. They would not have run this danger, if they had accepted the saving deposits only on condition that withdrawal must be notified some months ahead.[24]

Mises also demonstrates that the root cause of the destructive exchange-rate gyrations of the 1930s was not the spontaneous and generalized "capital flight" that is usually alleged, rather it was the egregiously inflationary and foredoomed attempt made by central banks to insure the instantaneous redeemability of saving deposits promised by the commercial banks:

Capital invested in real estate or industrial plants or in shares of companies holding property of this nature cannot fly. You can sell such property and leave the country with the proceeds. But—unless there is no [sic] expansion of credit—the buyer simply replaces you.... One person or another can withdraw his capital from a country; but this can never be a mass movement. There is only one apparent exception, *i.e.*, the saving deposit which can be withdrawn from the bank at once or at short notice. When the saving deposits are subject to instant withdrawal and the bank of issue renders the immediate withdrawal possible by advancing credits for these savings to be withdrawn, then credit expansion and inflation cause the exchange ratio to rise [the domestic currency to depreciate]. It is obvious that not the flight of capital but the credit expansion in favor of the savings banks is the root of the evil.... If the Central Bank were to leave [the banks] to their fate, their peculiar embarrassment would not have any effect on the foreign exchanges. That the additional issue of great amounts of bank notes for the sake of the repayment of the total amount or of a great portion of a country's saving deposits makes the foreign exchange go up is easy to understand. It is not simply the wish of the capitalists to fly with

---

[24] Ludwig von Mises, "Senior's Lectures on Monetary Problems," in idem, *Money, Method, and the Market Process: Essays by Ludwig von Mises,* ed. Richard M. Ebeling (Norwell, Mass.: Kluwer Academic Publishers, [1933] 1990), pp. 107–08.

their capital, but the expansion of the circulation, that imperils monetary stability.[25]

Despite his brilliant and pathbreaking analysis of the causes and effects of the progressive transformation of saving deposits into de facto money substitutes, Mises was still unprepared in 1966, in the third edition of *Human Action*, to include these deposits in his broader definition of money. There[26] Mises refers to them as "demand deposits not subject to check," but then inconsistently denies that they are money substitutes. Instead, he identifies saving deposits as foremost among "secondary media of exchange," a category encompassing highly marketable financial assets, such as government bonds and blue chip stocks, which permit their owners to economize on the holding of cash balances. Unlike money substitutes, secondary media of exchange "must first be exchanged against money or money substitutes if one wants to use them—in a roundabout way—for paying or for increasing cash holdings."[27] Uncharacteristically, Mises does not address the momentous institutional fact, clearly recognized in his 1933 article, that, unlike stocks and bonds, whose exchange values in terms of money fluctuate according to market forces, saving deposits are "exchanged" on a market in which their money "price" is virtually fixed (at par value) and guaranteed by the practically inexhaustible resources of the central bank.

The Regression Theorem and the Demand for Money

Murray N. Rothbard has characterized the regression theorem as the *"pons asinorum"* for critics of Mises's monetary theory and as the "keystone of monetary theory" in general.[28] And, as Edwards points

---

[25] Ibid., pp. 108–09.

[26] Ludwig von Mises, *Human Action: A Treatise on Economics*, 3rd rev. ed. (Chicago: Henry Regnery Company, 1966), p. 460, n. 23.

[27] Ibid., p. 461.

[28] Murray N. Rothbard, "Timberlake on the Austrian Theory of Money: A Comment," *Review of Austrian Economics* 2 (1988): p. 179; and Murray N. Rothbard, private correspondence, September 1977.

out, Mises himself "considered the integration of monetary and value theory by the application of marginal analysis to be the central problem, and his solution to be the most important contribution, of [*The Theory of Money and Credit*]."[29] In this spirit, Edwards refers to the third chapter of his own book, which comprises trenchant defenses against critics of Mises's regression theorem and approach to the demand for money, as "perhaps the heart of the study."[30]

Against the allegation made by Don Patinkin and, later, Laurence S. Moss that Mises confused the marginal utility of holding money with the marginal utility attaching to the goods for which it exchanges, Edwards definitively demonstrates that the confusion is the critics' and that "The entire context of Mises's discussion unequivocally bears on the derivation of the individual and market demands for money to *hold* as *stock*."[31] Although Edwards affirms that Patinkin and Moss are "respectful in their treatment of Mises's contributions,"[32] one would surely be hard pressed to identify a single instance in the history of economic thought in which an eminent economist's position was interpreted less sympathetically, especially when one considers Patinkin's unsurpassed scholarship in the history of monetary theory.

Edwards also neatly disposes of the absurd charge by "real balance" theorists such as Howard S. Ellis and Moss that Mises conceives the demand for money as a demand for nominal units of money without regard to the purchasing power or exchange value of these units.[33] As Edwards argues, "If a unit of money has a value, then the individual can, for an additional unit of money income, compare the

---

[29] Edwards, *The Economist of the Country*, p. 49.

[30] Ibid., p. 24.

[31] Don Patinkin, *Money, Interest, and Prices: An Integration of Monetary and Value Theory*, 2nd ed. (New York: Harper & Row, 1965), p. 79; Laurence S. Moss, "The Monetary Economics of Ludwig von Mises," in idem, *The Economics of Ludwig von Mises: Toward a Critical Appraisal* (New York: New York University Press, 1976), pp. 13–49; Edwards, *The Economist of the Country*, p. 53.

[32] Edwards, *The Economist of the Country*, p. 65, fn. 35.

[33] Howard S. Ellis, *German Monetary Theory, 1905–1933* (Cambridge, Mass.: Harvard University Press, 1934), p. 163; Moss, "The Monetary Economics of Ludwig von Mises," p. 32.

marginal utilities of the additional present or future goods obtainable with that of adding that unit's worth of purchasing power to his/her cash balance, and it is precisely the magnitude of *real* balances that Mises is talking about determining by such a marginal calculation. The individual simply expresses that demand by demanding nominal units of money with a given purchasing power each."[34]

Indeed we may go further than Edwards and turn the tables on those who insist that money demand analysis must proceed via a "real value calculus" and in terms of the utility of "resources held in the form of money." In his outstanding but neglected tome on monetary theory, which includes an encyclopedic review of the development of the cash-balance approach to the demand for money, Arthur W. Marget conducts a remarkable running defense of the Menger-Mises-Cannan "money balance" variant against the claims of the Walras-Pigou-Keynes "real balance" variant.[35] First, Marget argues that the real balance approach is unrealistic, because it rests on the assumption that the holders of cash explicitly utilize an index number to "deflate" their money balances. According to Marget, "The real issue, so far as the question of realism is concerned, is whether the element of price change enters the 'calculations' of the cash balance administrator as a matter affecting 'his prospective receipts and payments in monetary units,' as Hawtrey [as well as Mises] holds, or whether it enters as part of a kind of 'deflation' process—in the statistical sense of 'deflation'—represented by the division of a cash balance by a price index. The question … is whether, from the standpoint of realism, it is helpful to think of cash-balance administrators as taking 'express account of any index number relating their cash to its equivalent in products.'"[36]

Marget's second objection to the real balance approach stems from the fact that "demand for 'resources in the form of currency' which is held to determine the price level, needs, in order that a given amount of 'money' may be translated into 'real' terms, a 'price level'

---

[34] Edwards, *The Economist of the Country*, pp. 53–54.

[35] Arthur W. Marget, *The Theory of Prices: A Re-Examination of the Central Problem of Monetary Theory* (New York: Augustus M. Kelley, [1938–42] 1966), vol. 1, pp. 414–83.

[36] Ibid., p. 446, fn. 88.

which assigns to 'resources in the form of currency' a given 'real' value."[37] Without dated price levels, *à la* Mises's regression theorem, however, exponents of this approach, which was developed as a means of escaping the so called "Austrian circle," are themselves trapped in a logical circle. Finally, Marget contends that, in deflating money balances to their "real" equivalent in terms of products, many real-balance theorists equate "the utility of a cash balance" to "the utility of the goods that might be purchased by the expenditure of the cash balance."[38] The result is that these theorists are unable to explain why anyone should ever choose to hold cash instead of other forms of wealth, given that equal utilities generate indifference among alternatives.

Edwards successfully counters the criticism, which has been advanced both by Ellis and Moss, that Mises's theory of the demand for money yields a demand curve that is drawn as a rectangular hyperbola in nominal cash balance space.[39] A demand curve of this shape, they note, is logically inconsistent with Mises's repeated and vigorous denials that an addition to the stock of money—even when this increment is distributed so as to equi-proportionally increase all individual cash balances—causes an equi-proportional increase of all prices. Edwards thoroughly demolishes this criticism by demonstrating that it rests on a clearly erroneous interpretation of Mises's theory "as saying that the individual values units of money only with a view to maintaining a predecided and given level of purchasing power, and that utility calculation is not applied to the level of real balances. From this perspective they [Ellis and Moss] find his non-proportionality argument contradictory. It does not occur to them that his non-proportionality argument is evidence *against* their interpretation of his theory of the demand for money."[40]

Edwards himself falls into error, however, when he charges Mises with "a failure to step from a non-rectangularly-hyperbolic

---

[37] Ibid., pp. 450–51 n. 99.

[38] Ibid., p. 451.

[39] Ellis, *German Monetary Theory, 1905–1933*, p. 164; Moss, "The Monetary Economics of Ludwig von Mises," p. 32.

[40] Edwards, *The Economist of the Country*, p. 55.

demand for nominal balances to the rectangularly-hyperbolic market equilibrium curve."[41] Edwards initiates his criticism by concurring with Mises that an equi-proportional addition to cash balances, let us say a doubling, will not lead *initially*, i.e., immediately prior to the first round of spending of the excess balances, to an inversely proportional variation (a halving) of marginal utilities of money on individual value scales. Thus, as Edwards recognizes, the overall elasticity of Mises's "instantaneous" demand curve for nominal balances, which is derived from instantaneous marginal utility schedules for goods and money, may properly take on (absolute) values less than, greater than, or equal to unity. Or, in other words, the instantaneous demand curve for money only fortuitously traces out a rectangular hyperbola.[42]

Edwards proceeds to argue, however, that Mises erred "in assuming that it followed that prices would not rise proportionately with M. This would occur because, as prices increased, real balances would decline, reversing all of the initial wealth effects, until equilibrium was attained at the initial level of real balances, *ceteris paribus*." Edwards is here contending, *à la* Patinkin, that, notwithstanding the nonunitary elasticity of the "instantaneous" demand curve for money, real balance effects generated by an increase of money will initiate a dynamic adjustment process that culminates in an equi-proportional increase in overall prices. But Patinkin's demonstration that an increase in money accomplished via an equi-proportional increase in everyone's cash balances brings forth an increase of all prices in the same proportion rests

---

[41] Ibid., p. 56.

[42] Rothbard's analysis of the demand for money implies that it tends to be basically inelastic due to the high inelasticity of what he calls the "exchange" or "pre-income" component of monetary demand, which is distinguished from the "reservation," "cash balance," or "post-income" component. The former is expressed in the exchange for money of the services of the original productive factors, land, and labor, and of existing inventories of capital and consumer goods, for which the reservation demands of their producers are usually highly inelastic. See Rothbard, *Man, Economy, and State*, vol. 1, pp. 662–67; vol. 2, pp. 350–56. The inelasticity of the exchange demand for money is similarly accounted for by Herbert J. Davenport (*The Economics of Enterprise* [New York: Augustus M. Kelley, [1913] 1968], pp. 267–73). Davenport (ibid., pp. 301–03, 316–21) also provides a surprisingly modern account of the reservation demand for money, as a short-run, speculative phenomenon, but he does not integrate the two components into a satisfactory overall theory of the demand for money.

either on his arbitrary assumption of the constancy of the real data, i.e., relative prices and real wealth, during the transition from one Walrasian equilibrium position to the next, or on his equivalent simplifying assumption that "prices rise during the *tatonnement* in an equiproportionate manner."[43]

In contrast, the time-spanning "step-by-step" method which Mises consistently applies in analyzing monetary phenomena leads inevitably to a denial that the real data of the system could, under any conceivable initial set of circumstances, remain unaltered during a disequilibrium adjustment or *tatonnement* process.[44] For Mises, "The process is always uneven and by steps, disproportionate and asymmetrical."[45] In fact, Mises rigorously demonstrates the long-run non-neutrality of money even under the most stringent and highly unrealistic assumption that new money is injected into the economic system in a way that does not disturb the preexisting relative distribution of total wealth among individuals.[46] In *Human Action,* Mises concludes that

> Changes in the supply of money must necessarily alter the disposition of vendible goods as owned by various individuals and firms.... We may, if we like, assume that every member gets a share of the additional money right at the moment of its inflow into the system, or shares in the reduction of the quantity of money. But whether we assume this or not, the final result of our demonstration will remain the same. This result will be that changes in the structure of prices brought about by changes in the supply of money available in the economic system never affect the prices of the various commodities and services to the same extent and at the same time. . . .

The main fault of the old quantity theory as well as the mathematical economists' equation of exchange is that they have ignored

---

[43] Patinkin, *Money, Interest, and Prices,* p. 44. On the key role of the assumption of constant relative prices in deriving the neutrality of money in Patinkin's system, see Stephen W. Rousseas, *Monetary Theory* (New York: Alfred A. Knopf, 1972), pp. 53, 72.

[44] See Ludwig von Mises, *Notes and Recollections* (South Holland, Ill.: Libertarian Press, 1978), p. 59.

[45] Mises, *Human Action,* p. 414.

[46] Mises, *Theory of Money and Credit,* pp. 141–42.

this fundamental issue. *Changes in the supply of money must bring about changes in other data too.* The market system before and after the inflow or outflow of a quantity of money is not merely changed in that cash holdings of the individuals and prices have increased or decreased. There have been affected also changes in the reciprocal exchange ratios between the various commodities and services which, if one wants to resort to metaphors, are more adequately described by the image of price revolution than by the misleading figure of an elevation or a sinking of a "price level."[47] [Emphasis added]

Thus for Mises, "real balance effects" are inextricably bound together with "distribution effects." The very process by which the market adjusts the (positive or negative) excess demands for money of individuals necessarily "revolutionizes" wealth positions and the price structure. And this is the case even if these (nonzero) individual excess demands sum to zero in the aggregate. Writes Mises:

> Every change in the money relation alters—apart from the effects on deferred payments—the conditions of the individual members of society. Some become richer, some poorer. It may happen that the effects of a change in the demand for or supply of money encounter the effects of opposite changes occurring by and large at the same time and to the same extent; it may happen that the resultant of the two opposite movements is such that no conspicuous changes in the price structure emerge. But even then the effects on the conditions of the various individuals are not absent. Each change in the money relation takes its own course and produces its own particular effects. If an inflationary movement and a deflationary one occur at the same time or if an inflation is temporally followed by a deflation in such a way that prices finally are not very much changed the social consequences of each of the two movements do not cancel each other. To the social consequences of an inflation those of a deflation are added. There is no reason to assume that all or even most of those favored by one movement will be hurt by the second one, or vice versa.[48]

---

[47] Mises, *Human Action*, pp. 412–13.

[48] Ibid., pp. 417–18.

Edwards also argues that Mises's "non-proportionality argument" contradicts Mises's own no less vigorously stated position that an increase in the aggregate money stock would leave human welfare unchanged, because "a change in M would result in a proportional change in P."[49] Edwards here implies that Mises derives his proposition that money always yields to society its full utility as a medium of exchange from a "process" analysis of the effects of a change in the quantity of money on a given economic system. For Mises, however, the proposition regarding the welfare effects of additions to the money stock is derived from a purely "comparative static" analysis of two unconnected economic systems which are based on identical real data and are assumed to differ only in the magnitudes of their nominal money stocks. The discussion by Mises which Edwards cites to support his interpretation is arguably ambiguous on this point,[50] but elsewhere in the same work Mises draws a clear-cut distinction between the two forms of analysis:

> the level of the total stock of money and of the value of the money unit are matters of complete indifference as far as the utility obtained from the use of the money is concerned. Society is always in enjoyment of the maximum utility obtainable from the use of money. Half of the money at the disposal of the community would yield the same utility as the whole stock, even if the variation in the value of the monetary unit was not proportioned to the variation in the stock of money. But it is important to note that it by no means follows from this that doubling the quantity of money means halving the objective exchange-value of money....

If we compare two static economic systems, which differ in no way from one another except that in one there is twice as much money as in the other, it appears that the purchasing power of the monetary unit in the one system must be equal to half that of the monetary unit in the other. Nevertheless, we may not conclude from this that a doubling of the quantity of money must lead to a halving of the purchasing power of the monetary unit; for every variation in the quantity of money introduces a dynamic factor into the static economic system.

---

[49] Edwards, *The Economist of the Country*, 1985, p. 56.
[50] Mises, *The Theory of Money and Credit*, p. 85.

The new position of static equilibrium that is established when the effects of the fluctuations thus set in motion are completed cannot be the same as that which existed before the introduction of the additional quantity of money.[51]

In the course of rebutting Moss's astounding contention that Mises "saw the demand for real balances as constant and given by the state of the world ... [and] did not apply subjective cost and benefit considerations to the demand for real balances," Edwards himself seriously misconstrues Mises's position on the relationship between the demand for money and the interest rate. Edwards correctly characterizes Mises's overall approach to the problem as "the classic one of long-run interest rate neutrality, based on a view that the rate of interest and the demand for money had essentially different determinants."[52] He then concludes that Mises "did not generally regard interest forgone as the cost of holding money."[53] This conclusion is incorrect on both exegetical and logical grounds.

Mises identified three basic categories of opportunity costs which may be incurred in the decision to hold cash balances. These include "interest forgone" as well as the forgoing of "instantaneous consumption" and of "plain saving" i.e., the accumulation of stocks of durable consumers goods.[54] That the forgoing of an interest return is one of the potential "costs" of holding money is logically implied in the very application of marginal utility theory to the explanation of the purchasing power of money. In this approach, the opportunity cost of allocating a sum of money to cash balance is the renunciation of the marginal utility of the most highly valued alternative use of this money, which may or may not be the investment of the sum in interest-bearing securities.

---

[51] Ibid., pp. 142, 145.

[52] For a recent, vigorously-argued vindication of this position, see Hans-Hermann Hoppe, "The Theory of Employment, Money, Interest, and the Capitalist Process: The Misesian Case against Keynes," in *Dissent on Keynes: A Critical Appraisal of Keynesian Economics,* ed. Mark Skousen (New York: Praeger, 1992).

[53] Edwards, *The Economist of the Country*, p. 57.

[54] On the nature of plain saving as distinguished from capitalist saving, see Mises, *Human Action*, pp. 530–31.

The assertion by Edwards to the contrary,[55] this is readily deducible
from Mises's analysis in *Theory of Money and Credit* of the manner in
which individuals adjust to a dis-equilibrating influx of newly-created
money into their cash balances:

> For these persons, the ratio between the demand for money
> and the stock of it is altered; they have a relative superfluity
> of money and a relative shortage of other economic goods.
> The immediate consequence of both circumstances is that
> the marginal utility to them of the monetary unit diminishes.
> This necessarily influences their behavior in the market....
> He who has more money on hand than he thinks he needs,
> will buy, in order to dispose of the superfluous stock of money
> that lies useless on his hands. If he is an entrepreneur, he will
> possibly enlarge his business. If this use of the money is not
> open to him, he may purchase interest-bearing securities; or
> possibly he may decide to purchase consumption goods.[56]

If we assume that one of the individuals in Mises's example
does in fact allocate his increment of new money to the purchase of
interest-bearing securities—assuming that his value rankings of the
utilities derived from the various uses of the money have remained
constant—it is to be inferred from this purchase that the forgone
interest on these securities constituted the opportunity cost of holding
an equal-sized unit of money *prior* to the infusion of new money into
his cash balance.

Mises is even more explicit on this point in *Human Action*,
where he states that:

> The keeping of cash holding requires sacrifices. To the extent
> that a man keeps money in his pockets or in his balance with
> a bank, he forsakes the instantaneous acquisition of goods he
> could consume or employ for production. In the market econ-
> omy these sacrifices can be precisely determined by calculation.
> They are equal to the amount of originary [or pure] interest he
> would have earned by investing the sum. The fact that a man

---

[55] Edwards, *The Economist of the Country*, p. 57.
[56] Mises, *Theory of Money and Credit*, pp. 139, 134–35.

takes this falling off into account is proof that he prefers the advantages of cash holding to the loss in interest yield.[57]

Not only does Mises conceive the interest rate as a potential cost of holding money, he also recognizes that it is a monetary phenomenon in a real and important sense. That is, in a barter economy, where monetary calculation does not exist, it would be impossible to even conceive the difference in value between present and future goods as a unitary rate. The reason, as Mises points out, is that "Only within a money economy can this value difference be comprehended in the abstract and separated from changes in the valuation of individual concrete economic goods. In a barter economy, the phenomenon of interest could never be isolated from the evaluation of future price movements of individual goods."[58]

Of course, recognizing that the interest rate is an outgrowth of monetary exchange and calculation expressible only in monetary terms and that, as an element determined within the system of interdependent money prices, it functions as an opportunity cost of holding money does not imply that "real balances [are] a function of wealth and the interest rate." That Edwards does not fully comprehend this point is attributable to his failure to appreciate that Mises's methodological approach is worlds apart from the neoclassical methodology of mutual determination that Edwards himself apparently espouses. The analytical framework of Mises's monetary theory is the general interrelationships and interdependencies of the system of market prices. Within this framework, there are multifarious opportunities for money expenditures on consumer goods which, in addition to the opportunity to hold ready cash, compete with opportunities to invest money at interest. Thus it might be argued that a fall in the interest rate, *ceteris paribus*, lowers a given individual's cost of currently consuming, let us say, apples. But it is an impermissible leap of logic from this unexceptionable statement to the conclusion that

---

[57] Mises, *Human Action*, p. 430. Also see pp. 404, 463 for similar statements.

[58] Ludwig von Mises, "The Position of Money among Economic Goods," in idem *Money, Method, and the Market Process*, trans. Alfred Zlabinger, ed. Richard M. Ebeling (Norwell, Mass.: Kluwer Academic Publishers, 1990), p. 65.

the interest rate is one of the functional determinants of the demand for apples.

Edwards does make an important contribution, however, in defending Mises's regression theorem against Patinkin and demolishing Patinkin's alternative "Walrasian solution" to the circularity problem in monetary analysis. Employing the methodology of simultaneous mutual determinism, Patinkin is able to formally demonstrate that no specific prior value of money need be assumed in deriving a market demand schedule or "excess demand function" for money. Moreover, Patinkin's demonstration implies that if economic agents form their subjective valuations of cash balances on day two with reference to the unique purchasing power of money prevailing on day one, as Mises assumes, then the outcome is not a schedule of quantities of money demanded at varying purchasing powers but a single quantity demanded. Thus Patinkin concludes that writers such as Mises who believe that there is a circularity problem in explaining the determination of the purchasing power of money fall victim to a "basic misunderstanding of the theory of price determination" and to an elementary "confusion of 'demand' with 'amount demanded.'"[59]

In defending Mises, Edwards argues that, before Patinkin's "individual-experiment" can proceed, i.e., before each individual can establish his indifference map for goods and (nominal) money balances, money itself must have utility and therefore a known and pre-existing purchasing power, because the very existence of indifference curves implies that the individual is able to maintain a given level of utility by substituting at the margin determinate quantities of goods for determinate quantities of money. Edwards's insightful argument on this point is worth quoting at length:

> note that [Patinkin's] method of generating a demand curve
> for money assumes the indifference curves to exist and have
> the normal properties. Yet, translating into modern terms,
> the whole essence of the problem, as recognized by all parties
> to the [circularity] debate at the time, was precisely that without some specific value of money *no* such indifference curves
> could even *exist*. Consider: we have goods on one axis, with

---

[59] Patinkin, *Money, interest, and Prices*, pp. 115–16.

a given intercept (the endowment), and money on the other. But money is only money when it is a medium of exchange, that is, when it has a value (purchasing power) in terms of other goods. Then it can be valued for storage purposes and the utility curves can exist.

We might place pieces of paper with a number on them on the axis, but if they have no nonmonetary utility and no purchasing power they would have no utility. The indifference curves can only exist when we place a budget line on the graph, that is, postulate a goods price of money, and that is precisely Mises's point. Mises would argue that since the indifference curves cannot exist until the budget line does, the latter is logically prior. His interpretation of such a graph would be that the budget used is yesterday's exchange value of money, while the indifference curves embody today's subjective valuations of money.[60]

Presumably, Patinkin would counter this critique by arguing that Mises's temporal and causal approach to explaining the demand for money, referring as it does to a particular value of money, would be incapable of generating more than a single point on a demand curve in nominal money space. Edwards's reply to this objection points us in the right direction, but it is not completely satisfactory. He argues, somewhat tentatively, that Patinkin's charge "is not quite correct," because, while the formation of an individual's subjective valuations for money with reference to "some *particular* prior value of money" yields only a single quantity demanded, "there is an infinite number of such possible prior values, and if their tangencies with individual's [sic] existing indifference curves were plotted, demand functions of the normal shapes would result."[61]

The point that Edwards should have made is this: in deciding upon the size of their cash balances, market participants are interested in the future purchasing power of money. In attempting to forecast the future structure of prices, which is the inverse of the purchasing power of money, they resort to the prices of the immediate past, let us

---

[60] Edwards, *The Economist of the Country*, pp. 59–60.

[61] Ibid., p. 66 fn. 47.

say, yesterday. They do not mechanically project the realized prices of yesterday into the future, but use them as the basis for appraising the structure of prices which will emerge and prevail today as a result of the anticipated changes intervening in yesterday's economic data.

Based on their appraisements of money's prospective purchasing power and their anticipated uses for a general medium of exchange today, market participants rank units of money on their subjective value scales and thus establish the marginal utilities that underlie today's market demand for money. For each individual, the marginal utility of money will decline as successive units of a given purchasing power are added to his cash balance. Consequently, an increase in the total stock of money, ceteris paribus, will lead to a decline in individual marginal utilities of money. Demand curves in goods markets will shift rightward and higher money prices will be offered and paid; that is, the purchasing power of money will decline. Thus, the instantaneous demand curve for money that emerges from Mises's analysis is multi-valued and negatively-sloped, and its intersection with the *vertical* line representing the current stock of money determines today's purchasing power of money.

Contrary to Patinkin's assertion, then, in Mises's analysis the demand for money is not logically constrained to a single quantity dependent on a specific realized purchasing power, but describes a schedule of quantities that responds inversely to variations in the current purchasing power of money. To illustrate this, if we assume that the total quantity of money that market participants desire to acquire and hold, based on their forecasts of the future purchasing power of money, is insufficient to completely absorb the current stock of money, then there will result a temporal process involving variations in total money expenditures on goods and services, i.e., "real balance effects," that drive the price structure and therefore the purchasing power of money to the level at which the stock of money and the demand for money are equated. Abstracting from distribution effects, the inverse response of the amount of money demanded to the alterations in its purchasing power, which occurs during this adjustment process, will trace out a segment of the instantaneous demand curve.

Summing up the differences between the methods of Mises and Patinkin for solving the circularity problem, Edwards sees a distinct advantage in the Misesian method, because it allows for the possibility of disequilibrium occurring between the actual and desired stock of cash balances and the operation of an adjustment process that eventually restores equilibrium. In contrast, the Walrasian solution offered by Patinkin effectively precludes the emergence of monetary disequilibrium and a dynamic adjustment process.[62] As Edwards argues: "Where demand and excess demand functions are derived using given preferences and hypothetical alternative values of money, and the value of money determined by the market demand and supply functions determines the actual quantities demanded simultaneously, the individual is always at equilibrium.... The solution to a simultaneous equation set never yields anything but equilibrium values."[63]

The Monetary Adjustment Process: The Interspatial Equalization of the Value of Money, and the Determination of Exchange Rates

In chapter four, Edwards examines Mises's contributions to international monetary theory, and, in the process, goes a long way towards establishing that Mises anticipated "every major element of the modern monetary approach to international adjustment (MAIA)." Indeed, Edwards argues that "This is true to such an extent that Mises might justly be designated the founding father of the MAIA in the twentieth century."[64]

The central proposition of the modern monetary approach is that "the balance of payments and currency exchange rate changes are essentially monetary phenomena equilibrating the stock demands for and supplies of national currencies."[65] Proponents of this approach

---

[62] Edwards, *The Economist of the Country*, p. 60.

[63] Ibid., p. 61.

[64] Ibid., p. 133.

[65] Ibid., pp. 69–70.

have traced the roots of the MAIA back to the writings of classical monetary theorists, including David Hume and British "bullionist" pamphleteers John Wheatley and David Ricardo. Edwards argues, however, that in their eagerness to identify and credit the classical forebears of the monetary approach, doctrinal historians have given a partly distorted account of its development, which completely overlooks Mises's unquestioned precedence in formulating important elements of the uniquely "modern" version.

As Edwards points out, before Mises, proponents of the monetary-oriented classical and neoclassical approaches to balance-of-payments adjustment, including prominent cash-balance theorists such as Alfred Marshall and Knut Wicksell, explained the international distribution of the money commodity using a macro expenditure flow concept of the demand for money.[66] According to this conception, each nation's equilibrium share in a given global stock of money is determined, given the payment habits of its population, by the relative volume of business it transacts at the exogenously given level of world prices. Or, in terms of the Fisherian Equation of Exchange, a nation's demand for money is conceived as a demand for a flow of money payments ($M \times V$) needed to support an aggregate expenditure flow ($P \times T$).

In contrast, Mises builds up his explanation of the distribution of the stock of money among nations from the Mengerian (and modern) conception of the individual's demand to hold a *stock* of the general medium of exchange. For Mises, individuals' subjective value rankings of money and goods hold the ultimate explanation for the allocation of the global stock of money among individual cash holders and thus among nations, obviating any reference to disembodied averages and aggregates such as a nation's velocity of circulation of money or total volume of business transactions. Thus in Mises's view, as in the modern MAIA, "international monetary *flows* (that is, deficits and surpluses in the balance of payments) act to equilibrate the stock demands and supplies of money" and, therefore, assuming a fixed global monetary stock, "only changes in the *demands* for money (resulting in

---

[66] Ibid., pp. 77–78.

net excess demand, positive or negative) can produce a surplus or deficit."[67] Conversely, "If the state of the balance of payments were such that international movements of money were required *independent of any altered estimation of money on the part of those involved* (that is, in the absence of change in the stock demands), operations would be induced to restore equilibrium."[68]

Unfortunately, in his own eagerness to establish Mises's rightful and preeminent position in the MAIA tradition, Edwards glosses over several significant differences between the Misesian and the rational-expectations-based modern approaches. These differences are important enough to warrant critical comment.

Edwards[69] points out that Mises, like the modern proponents of the monetary approach, holds that "the law of one price" applies to money as well as to commodities. In other words, in the case of a single money, the purchasing power of the monetary unit tends to be geographically uniform. For adherents of the modern monetary approach, such as Laffer and Miles,[70] this means that, assuming profit maximization and no barriers to trade, "Ml commodities' prices should be fully arbitraged in each and every numeraire at each and every moment in time." This concept of instantaneous arbitrage for an individual good then "can be extended to the overall price indexes of two countries by taking a weighted average of the prices of goods consumed in both countries."[71]

But the rational-expectationist conception of instantaneous arbitrage is inconsistent with the step-by-step method employed by Mises in his analysis of the monetary adjustment process. As Mises[72] emphasizes, "The step-by-step analysis must consider the lapse of

---

[67] Ibid., p. 77.

[68] Ibid., p. 76.

[69] Ibid., pp. 70–71, 73–74.

[70] Arthur B. Laffer and Marc A. Miles, *International Economics in an Integrated World* (Glenview, Ill.: Scott, Foresman, 1982), p. 232.

[71] Ibid.

[72] Ludwig von Mises, *Notes and Recollections* (South Holland, Ill.: Libertarian Press, 1978a), p. 59.

time." Moreover, Mises[73] criticizes and deliberately eschews the use of price indexes to measure changes in the purchasing power of money, except for rough historical estimates.[74] Therefore, when Mises[75] states that "The purchasing power of money is the same everywhere," he is *not* referring to a tendency to equalization of national price indexes, as Edwards[76] seems to imply at one point. For Mises, interspatial equalization of the value of money refers to an equilibration of the vast and unaveraged array of alternative quantities of goods which are purchasable by a unit of money.

Furthermore, from Mises's perspective, equilibration of money's purchasing power array cannot necessarily be expected to yield equality between the prices of physically identical goods available in different locations, let alone between the arbitrarily selected and weighted price indexes of different nations or regions. The reason is to be found in Mises's pathbreaking subjectivist insight that the situation of a good in space may affect its perceived usefulness and thus its subjective value in satisfying human wants.[77]

---

[73] Ludwig von Mises, *The Theory of Money and Credit*, 2nd ed. (Irvington-on-Hudson, N.Y.: Foundation for Economic Education, [1953] 1971), pp. 187–94; *Human Action*, pp. 219–23.

[74] Even the practical usefulness of index numbers for judging day-to-day variations in the purchasing power of money is severely limited. As Mises points out (*Human Action*, pp. 222–23), "A judicious housewife knows much more about price changes as far as they affect her own household than the statistical average can tell. She has little use for computations disregarding changes both in quality and in the amount of goods which she is able or permitted to buy at the prices entering into the computation. If she 'measures' the changes for her personal appreciation by taking the prices of only two or three commodities as a yardstick, she is no less 'scientific' and no more arbitrary that the sophisticated mathematicians in choosing their methods for the manipulation of the data of the market."

[75] Mises, *Theory of Money and Credit*, p. 176.

[76] Edwards, *The Economist of the Country*, p. 77.

[77] Mises arrived at this insight independently of Nassau Senior, whose work containing the treatment of this problem was not published until 1928. On this point and for a discussion of Senior's contribution, see Chi-Yuen Wu, *An Outline of International Price Theories* (London: George Routledge and Sons, 1939), pp. 126–28; also see Marian Bowley, *Nassau Senior and Classical Economics* (New York: Octagon Books), pp. 205–08.

Edwards[78] properly recognizes the implication of this insight for the case in which a "good has a subjective value as *consumption* good where it is, and a different one as *production* good in those places to which it may be transported." The good available at its place of production, for example, coffee-in-Brazil, is evaluated by coffee drinkers in New York City as a capital good which must be combined with further complementary capital goods, that is, the means of transportation, before it can attain the (higher) subjective value of the consumption good, coffee-in-New York. As Edwards[79] also notes, Mises distinguishes money from non-monetary commodities in this respect, because, in the case of the former, the use of money substitutes and clearing systems operates to render its position in space indifferent to economic agents. For Mises, then, stocks of money, wherever they may be situated within the unitary market area, for all practical purposes comprise a perfectly fungible commodity whose transference between market participants is virtually costless. Thus the Law of One Price fully applies to money, and Edwards[80] concurs with Mises's conclusion that "the purchasing power of money is the same everywhere, only the commodities offered are not the same."

Edwards defends Mises against Ellis's criticism that Mises has only proved the international equalization of "utility flows per unit of purchasing power" rather than of the purchasing power of money itself.[81] However, Edwards's defense itself rests on a failure to comprehend the full scope of Mises's insight regarding the influence of the spatial element on the quality of (nonmonetary) goods. Thus, in response to Ellis's critique, Edwards[82] upholds Mises's proposition that the objective value of money tends to equality and supports this position with the following example: "Consider a good sold in any number of locations in different directions from the factory, and at distances and elevations such that their transportation costs are the same. On Mises's assumptions it is clear that though such physically

---

[78] Edwards, *The Economist of the Country*, p. 74.

[79] Ibid.

[80] Ibid.

[81] Ellis, *German Monetary Theory, 1905–1933*, p. 224.

[82] Edwards, *The Economist of the Country*, p. 74.

identical goods are at different locations they are *economically* the same and their prices would not differ in equilibrium."

Edwards's conclusion is not fully consistent with Mises's conception of the spatial quality of goods, because this conception does not merely embrace the pure distance between the location of the consumer and the location of the good, but also the consumer's positive or negative psychic response to the very location of purchase or consumption. For example, the same brand of men's shirt may simultaneously sell for a significantly higher price at a mall boutique than at a downtown clothing store, because, at the margin, consumers are prepared to offer a higher price for the good purchasable at the more accessible and pleasant location. Or consider that alcoholic beverages consumed in a restaurant situated atop one of the towers of the World Trade Center, which offers a breathtaking view of Manhattan and its surroundings, command much higher prices than drinks mixed with the same ingredients and imbibed in a street-level pub located a few blocks away. Surely, we do not expect would-be bar patrons at the World Trade Center to react to knowledge of such price discrepancies by a mad scramble to the elevators in order to take advantage of the higher purchasing power of money at ground level. This is not to deny, of course, that whenever consumers are neutral between stocks of a technologically identical good ready for consumption or purchase at two different locations, the spatial equilibration of the purchasing power of money will imply the complete eradication of inter-local price differences.

The proper response to Ellis's critique is to point out that, for Mises, the equilibration of the purchasing power of money is accomplished within the same process that gives rise to the structure of relative prices. This process culminates in a state in which, barring further change in the data, mutual gains from further exchange between any two market participants are impossible, because the ordinal value rankings of equal units of the various goods and money are identical for all those possessing them. This state also reflects the *absolute* equalization of the objective exchange value of money between any two locations, because it implies both that inter-local differences between prices of technologically identical goods do not exceed their costs of transportation (abstracting from time in transit) between their consumption and production centers, and, more generally, that no individual can achieve a more desirable outcome from the exchange process by diminishing his expenditures on goods available at one location and substituting expenditures on goods, whether physically indistinguishable or not, offered at alternative locations. Thus, contrary to Ellis, interspatial equalization of the *objective* value of money can only exist when there also exist common *utility* rankings for goods and money on the individual value scales of all market participants or, less accurately, when "utility flows per unit of purchasing power" are equalized.

It is instructive to analyze in more detail the market adjustment process which produces the tendency to the interspatial equilibration of the purchasing power of money, because it elucidates the reasons for Mises's insistence, as against Wieser, that such a tendency strongly and rapidly reasserts itself amid the ceaseless fluctuations of the underlying economic data.[83] Or, more loosely speaking, it explains why monetary equilibrium is much more quickly established than the final equilibrium position of the real sector of the economy. This analysis also permits us to answer the question of whether the occasional unqualified statements by Mises[84] to the effect that "the purchasing power of money is the same everywhere" are intended as merely polemical flourishes or represent what Mises believed to be a close approximation to the actual moment-to-moment situation in the economy, as when we speak of "the" market price for wheat or for oil.

Mises's analysis of the market process is predicated on the indisputable premise that the process has an unavoidable spatial, as well as temporal, dimension, because the individual sellers and buyers whose actions constitute it are spatially diffuse and possess different capacities for forecasting, learning of, and adapting to the ceaseless change that characterizes human life.[85] At each moment in time, the unitary market process produces a structure of money prices which is determined

---

[83] Mises, *Theory of Money and Credit*, pp. 173–75.

[84] Ibid., pp. 201, 210.

[85] Mises, *Human Action*, p. 328.

by consumer valuations (including valuations of leisure and of present versus future goods) and entrepreneurial price appraisements interacting with the current stocks of goods of various orders. The exchanges which take place as a result of these subjective valuations and appraisements produce a situation in which no individual perceives that he can improve his situation by further exchange at prevailing prices, because the marginal utility of any good he might offer exceeds the marginal utility of the good he will receive in exchange. On every market in the economy, therefore, the situation is the same as it is at the close of Böhm-Bawerk's famed horse market.[86] This "momentary equilibrium," as Böhm-Bawerk[87] refers to it, or "plain state of rest" (PSR), as it is designated by Mises,[88] will persist only so long as the prevailing state of valuations of the marginal pairs in each market remain constant. But these valuations are bound to change precisely because, in many cases, they are formulated on the basis of inaccurate forecasts and incomplete information regarding market opportunities. The result is that the actual market prices which we observe are always in disequilibrium in two related but logically distinct senses. First, the array of realized prices embodies inter-local discrepancies in the exchange value of goods and money, which present the opportunity for arbitrage profits, whether in terms of money or of enhanced consumer surplus.[89] Second, for many of the goods exchanged, the prices that clear the market exceed or fall short of their respective monetary costs of production, including an interest return to time preference, thereby generating pure or entrepreneurial profits and losses.

In analyzing adjustment of the first type of disequilibrium, we must abstract from the inevitable changes in production decisions that will be initiated by capitalist-entrepreneurs consequent upon their experience of pure profits and losses. The analytical device which is ready-made for our purpose is Wicksteed's country fruit

---

[86] Böhm-Bawerk, *Capital and Interest*, pp. 217–30.

[87] Ibid., p. 231.

[88] Mises, *Human Action*, p. 244.

[89] I am using the term "consumer surplus" in a purely psychic sense to denote the ordinal difference in value ranking between a good and its monetary purchase price. This is the sense in which Mises uses the term in *Human Action*, p. 388.

market in which the stocks of the various (perishable) commodities as well as consumer valuations are fixed for the duration of the "market day," during the course of which buyers exercise their demands. This market is assumed to be "imperfect" in two senses. First, buyers and sellers are spatially constrained and, hence, neither group is instantaneously and fully informed of current transaction prices at all locations or "stalls." And second, neither buyers nor sellers have perfect knowledge of what Wicksteed calls the "ideal market" or "equilibrating" price for any commodity, which, when once established, will not vary for the remainder of the market day.[90]

In the absence of these imperfections of knowledge about the current and future state of the market, the prices established for the first set of transactions of the market day would invariably result in a PSR characterized by spatial equality in the purchasing power of money: the same commodity would have the same price at different stalls and each and every buyer would allocate his income among the different commodities available at different locations so that, at prevailing prices, no alteration in his spatial pattern of expenditures would result in an increase in his "total utility" or the utility-ranking of the aggregate collection of goods he purchases. Until sellers' stocks were completely exhausted and the market came to a close, this identical "Wicksteedian state of rest"[91] (WSR) would be repeatedly disrupted and then re-established as each new group of perfectly informed buy-

---

[90] The classic discussion of the country fruit market can be found in Philip H. Wicksteed, *The Common Sense of Political Economy and Selected Papers and Reviews on Economic Theory,* ed. Lionel Robbins, 2 vols. (New York: Augustus M. Kelley, [1932] 1967) vol. 1, pp. 219–28. A very good analysis of a pure exchange economy can also be found in Kirzner (1963, pp. 105–35). In contrast to Wicksteed's methodological focus on an isolated "market day" in a full production-and-exchange economy, however, Kirzner (Ibid., p. 106) begins his analysis with an "imaginary economy" in which he assumes *"no production is possible";* all commodities are obtained costlessly by natural endowment. Unfortunately, Kirzner's methodological construct is inferior to Wicksteed's, because it diverts attention from the vitally important point that the analysis applies just as fully to the real-world economy of continuing and costly production, since the market's pricing process always proceeds on the basis of stocks of goods that have already been produced and are therefore fixed or in inventory for the given moment.

[91] Although this construction of a fully arbitraged, but not final, state of rest is implicit in much of Mises's monetary theorizing, he never formally analyzes it, as he does the PSR.

ers arrived and undertook transactions at the prevailing equilibrium set of prices.

However, in Wicksteed's country fruit market the inescapable spatial and temporal constraints on market participants prevent the initial pricing process from culminating in a WSR. Aware of the deficiencies of their information and foresight, both buyers and sellers arrange the temporal pattern of their exchanges according to speculative anticipations of the course of actual market prices. Buyers seeking psychic arbitrage profits devote time to comparison shopping and forgo purchases offering a consumer surplus in one location while speculating on the availability at another location either of a higher-ranked good for an equal monetary expenditure or of the same good for a lower price. On their side, sellers may exercise a speculative reservation demand for their own commodities. Thus, the constellation of actual market prices that emerges at any moment early on in the market day will diverge from the equilibrating constellation as a result of ignorance and speculative errors. During the PSR which succeeds each set of transactions undertaken at "false" prices during the early going, market participants begin to discover spatial inequalities in the purchasing power of money and to exploit these opportunities for arbitrage profits. (For analytical convenience we are assuming, as Wicksteed did, that trading at false prices does not alter the structure of market demand.) As their experience of the market grows during the course of the day, buyers and sellers continually revise their transaction plans. These plans come to reflect more accurate and complete information and eventually give rise to the equilibrium set of prices. The lull or WSR which succeeds this latter set of transactions describes a situation in which the spatial divergences in the purchasing power of money have been completely eradicated and the prices of all goods fully arbitraged. For the rest of the market day, each successive set of transactions takes place at equilibrium prices and thus generates a momentary WSR until the arrival of the next group of buyers on the scene.

Wicksteed's analysis, with its assumptions of given consumer value scales and fixed stocks of goods and money, thus allows us to disentangle the complex phenomena of entrepreneurship and production from those of arbitrage. It also serves to emphasize that the determination of money's purchasing-power array is a pure exchange phenomenon: since everyone is a "dealer" in money and money is always "in inventory," a perfectly adequate explanation of the actual exchange ratio between money and goods may be made without reference to problems of production. In the same way, the Böhm-Bawerkian and Wicksteedian explanation of actual, moment-to-moment market prices of individual nonmonetary goods completely and correctly abstracts from production phenomena, due to the fact that the exchanges taking place at any moment in time are determined exclusively by the stocks of goods in existence and prevailing subjective valuations. As Böhm-Bawerk[92] has written: "I do really believe we have here hit upon the simplest and most natural, and indeed the most productive manner of conceiving exchange and price. I refer to the pricing process as a resultant derived from all the valuations that are present in society. I do not advance this as a metaphorical analogy but as living reality." And, as Mises[93] himself stresses, "The theorems implied in the notion of the plain state of rest are valid with regard to all transactions without exception.... The notion of the plain state of rest is not an imaginary construction but the adequate description of what happens again and again on every market."

Perhaps the most powerful defense of the analysis of momentary positions of rest and of their relevance for monetary analysis was presented by Marget. According to Marget.[94]

> The ultimate goal of any theory of prices [theory of indirect exchange], like that of any part of economics which undertakes to explain economic reality, is to explain why *realized* prices are what they are. "Quoted prices," the prices which are included in the *"ex ante"* schedule of the general theory of value [theory of direct exchange], "expected" prices, "equilibrium" prices (in most of the senses of the concept of equilibrium), or any kind of prices other than *realized* prices are to be introduced into the argument only insofar as they help to

---

[92] Böhm-Bawerk, *Capital and Interest*, p. 229.

[93] Mises, *Human Action*, p. 245.

[94] Marget, *Theory of Prices*, vol. 2, pp. 22, 240.

explain why prices actually realized on the market are what they are....

In a fully developed monetary economy, a realized price represents the passage of money for an article sold for money. And the "passage of money for articles sold for money" is precisely what constitutes the subject matter of those aspects of the theory of money and prices which undertake to explain why the dimensions of the stream of money which "passes" for a given commodity or group of commodities is relatively large at one time and relatively small at another....

But it also constitutes the subject matter of that part of the "general" theory of value which is built upon the proposition that any realized price is what it is as a result of the conformation and position of the market demand curve and market supply curve prevailing at the moment the price is realized.

Or, as Marget[95] summarizes it, "the prices which we must ultimately explain are the prices 'realized' at specific moments in clock time [and] the only demand and supply schedules which are directly relevant to the determination of these 'realized' prices are market demand and supply schedules prevailing at the moment the prices are 'realized.'" The only sense in which Margetian "realized" prices may be characterized as "equilibrium" prices is in the sense of an "equality between demand price and supply price for a given quantity of a commodity *in all cases in which prices are actually realized in the market for this quantity of the commodity.*"[96]

With respect to the "market" demand curves, whose variations account for "changes in realized money prices," Marget[97] conceives them as instantaneous curves, whose shape and position are influenced by forecasting errors and incomplete knowledge of arbitrage opportunities. Thus, each such curve represents "a set of 'plans' by prospective purchasers of a given commodity at the time that they reach the decision to purchase or refrain from purchasing that commodity at a given price. [And] the mere fact that these plans may themselves change

---

[95] Ibid., pp. 239–40.

[96] Ibid., p. 253.

[97] Ibid., p. 176.

between successive realized decisions to purchase or not to purchase does not alter the further fact that *the actual purchases themselves may be assumed to be based on calculations whose results are embodied in 'plans' the resultant of which is the decision to purchase a given amount if the price is at one level and another amount if the price is at another level.*[98]

Analogously, Marget[99] construes the "market" supply curve, which interacts with the market demand curve to yield realized prices, as the momentary Wicksteedian "curve of reserve prices," which is the reversed portion of the general demand curve representing sellers' reservation demand for the existing stock of the good. As Marget[100] points out, the concept of sellers' reserve prices embodies recognition of the element of expectation and of the all-important distinction between "amount supplied" and "amount produced," which is necessary when "accounting for prices *realized and the amount of sales realized* within a given historical ('clock-time') period."

The analytical significance which Marget assigns to momentary (disequilibrium) positions of rest is not intended to belittle the usefulness of equilibrium analysis, nor does it imply a lack of interest in market adjustment processes unfolding over time. To the contrary, it is precisely because the experienced outcomes of the market process do not coincide with expected outcomes that the participants are induced to revise their expectations and plans during each succeeding lull in the market process, thereby precipitating another round of realized transactions. Assuming the underlying data are unchanged, the Wicksteed-Mises-Marget approach yields a coherent explanation of how, as information becomes more complete and speculation more accurate, PSRs succeed one another until the intermediate equilibrium situation represented by a fully-arbitraged state of rest (or WSR) is brought into being. Thus as Marget[101] argues:

---

[98] Ibid., p. 177.

[99] Ibid., pp. 255–56, 553–56.

[100] Ibid., pp. 554, 556.

[101] Ibid., pp. 235–36.

without the use of [instantaneous] market demand and supply curves ... it is impossible to explain either (1) why, of
a given range of *possible* "ex ante" prices, only one is "realized" in a given market situation; or (2) how the *goals* of dealers and consumers, even when these goals are short-period
goals, are approached (if they are approached at all) through
successive realized market transactions. And without a conception of an "equilibrium" price, even over a period as short
as [Marshall's market day], it is in many cases impossible to
understand what these goals are, and therefore why the successive market demand and supply schedules show the direction and the type of change that they do, and therefore lead to
the successive realized prices actually registered in successive
market transactions.

It should be added that the "short-period" equilibrium implied
in Marget's dealer-consumer market is the WSR, which, as I argued
above, is appropriate to analyzing the short-period arbitrage processes
and nonproduction speculative activities involved in the adjustment
of the purchasing-power array of money. The WSR must not be confused with the concept of what Mises[102] calls the "final state of rest"
(FSR), which is an imaginary construction of the position of the economy when prices and production have been completely and finally
adjusted to a given alteration in the economic data, including a change
in the quantity of money. Any account of the economy's approach to
the FSR must refer to the specific function of the capitalist-entrepreneur or "promoter" who actively seeks to profit by allocating factors of
production among time-consuming, capitalist production processes,
a function which is ignored in the pure exchange analysis of the WSR,
dealing as it does with fixed stocks of goods. But, as Marget teaches,
the analysis of the temporal path to the FSR must also refer to the successive realized price structures that emerge momentarily and then
are displaced by a successor as the equilibrating changes occurring in
production continually alter the available stocks and marginal utilities
of goods until production has been fully adjusted and the structure of
"final" prices emerges.

---

[102] Mises, *Human Action*, pp. 246–47.

The usefulness of the imaginary construct of the FSR in monetary theorizing and its relationship to the concepts of the PSR and WSR is illustrated when we trace out the consequences of a change in the quantity of money. To fully analyze this adjustment process, we must completely abstract from all other exogenous changes and processes of adjustment, and so we must begin our analysis from an FSR in which not only the distribution of cash balances and the value of money but also relative prices and production have been fully adjusted to the existing economic data. An unanticipated increase in the total stock of money will disrupt the prevailing FSR as the initial recipients of the new money suddenly discover their cash balances to be in excess of their needs. On the very next market day, they begin to disgorge the excess money balances by increasing their demands for various goods and services according to their subjective marginal utility rankings of additional units of money and goods. If we maintain our assumption that arbitrage processes work themselves out over the course of the Wicksteedian market day, the final set of transactions of the day yields a fully arbitraged purchasing power of money. Not only will this purchasing-power array be lower than that existing at the end of the previous market day, it will also embody a different relative price structure, which reflects the altered pattern of relative demands caused by money's nonneutrality and which, to the extent that it has not been anticipated, results in entrepreneurial profits and losses.

Thus, while the purchasing power of money has been inter-spatially equalized, it is far from being fully equilibrated by the end of the first market day. The second-round recipients of the additional money—those sellers who were the first to be favored by the inflation-fueled increase in the demand for products and services—seeking to rid themselves of their excess cash balances, return to market the next day with their own increased demands for goods, and this brings about another revolution in the price structure, with yet a new WSR emerging by the end of the day. Each succeeding market day likewise will dawn with a revised structure of demands for goods and will terminate in a WSR featuring an altered purchasing power of money, until all prices and incomes have been affected to a greater or lesser extent by the injection of the new money. As noted above, however, the permanent redistributions of income and wealth brought about by the sequential nature of the monetary adjustment process, constituting what Mises[103] calls money's "driving force," will result in a permanently altered structure of relative demands for consumer goods as well as permanent alterations in the structure of individual time, liquidity, and leisure preferences. But even after the newly-injected money has percolated throughout the economy and exhausted its driving force in a general but uneven increase of prices, the adjustment process will not be complete, because it will take additional time for the production processes and capital structure of the "real" economy to be fully adapted by capitalist-entrepreneurs to the money-induced changes in consumer demands, time preferences, etc. It is only after the complete adaptation of production that the monetary adjustment process comes to an end and the "final" price structure and purchasing power of money emerges.

A Misesian analysis of the monetary adjustment process thus depends upon a number of concepts of rest or equilibrium. The PSR explains the purchasing power of money prevailing at any moment and embedded in the structure of "realized prices." The WSR is an imaginary construct which serves to isolate and illuminate the arbitrage and speculative forces that are constantly propelling the market to rapid convergence upon a single price for each and every commodity (taking into account differences in spatial quality) and a geographically uniform value of money. While the overall economy is unlikely to ever come to rest in a fully-arbitraged state, historical insight leads to the conclusion that arbitrage processes run their course relatively rapidly, especially where there exist professional arbitrageurs and commodity speculators, organized commodity and retail markets, sophisticated communications and transportation, and consumer advertising. Thus, the interspatial equalization of the purchasing power of money does not wait upon the culmination of the overall monetary adjustment process, which may take years, but is a powerful tendency exhibiting itself at every step of the process. For Mises[104] not only is such a tendency deduced "from

---

[103] Mises, *Human Action*, pp. 416–19.
[104] Mises, *Theory of Money and Credit*, p. 174.

the principles of the theory of prices," it is "clearly demonstrated day by day in the market." Therefore, it is a historical judgment and not polemics which prompts Mises[105] to declare that "the exchange ratios between money and economic goods of completely similar constitution in all parts of a unitary market area ... are at any time equal to one another." Wicksteed,[106] in fact, reaches a similar conclusion, stating that "this ideal state of equilibrium [i.e., the WSR] never exists; but a sense of mutual advantage is perpetually bringing about approximations to it."

However, as I argued above, the monetary adjustment process cannot be completely accounted for without reference to the FSR, because variations in the monetary data inevitably modify relative income and wealth positions and hence bring about an alteration in relative prices. These money-driven changes in the structure of relative prices account for the profits and losses realized in the transactions that establish the PSR at any point in the uncompleted adjustment process. The emergence of profits and losses impels entrepreneurs to immediately begin revising purchase, sale, and production decisions and so to drive the economy through a series of temporary states of rest toward a final position of full adjustment and zero profits. Unlike the geographically uniform value of money of the WSR, which is closely approximated in actually prevailing market conditions, at any point of historical time, the economy is always far from reaching the FSR. The FSR only indicates the direction of movement of the historical market process at any moment. As Mises[107] writes: "the final state of rest will never be attained. New disturbing factors will emerge before it will be realized ... the market at every instant is moving toward a final state of rest. Every later new instant can create new facts altering this final state of rest."

In addition to this pathbreaking analysis of the international adjustment process and his formulation of the law of one price under the conditions of a single money, Mises also pioneered in the early

---

[105] Ibid., p. 176.

[106] Wicksteed, *The Common Sense of Political Economy,* vol. 1, p. 144.

[107] Mises, *Human Action,* p. 245.

twentieth-century revival of the purchasing-power-parity (PPP) theory of exchange rates and in the formulation of what is now known as the "asset market" view of the influence of expectations on the formation of the exchange rate, two key elements of the MAIA when applied to the case of independent but co-existing moneys.

Edwards[108] points out that Mises rediscovered the PPP theorem four years before Cassel published the first of his many statements of it.[109] Edwards, unfortunately, does not perceive the fundamental difference between the Casselian and Misesian formulations of the theorem, which is crucial to explaining why Mises continued to rigorously maintain the "absolute" version of the theorem long after Cassel and almost all other economists abandoned it for the empirically testable "relative" version. Nor does he remark on the fact that Mises never vitiated the explanatory significance of the theorem by restricting it to a situation in which "real shocks" to the economy and therefore alterations in relative prices are assumed absent, as Cassel apparently did.[110]

For Mises, the equilibrium exchange rate, or what he initially called the "static" and later the "final" exchange rate, between two currencies exactly equals the inverse of the ratio between the purchasing powers of the two currencies. In the Misesian version of the theorem, moreover, a given depreciation of the overall purchasing power of currency A relative to currency B effects an increase of the final price of B in terms of A in precisely the same proportion, despite the permanent revolution in relative prices that is invariably produced by the depreciation process.

The differences between Mises and Cassel ultimately stem from Mises's analytical coup in perceiving the artificiality of the distinction long maintained in classical monetary analysis between the case of a

---

[108] Edwards, *The Economist of the Country*, p. 73.

[109] According to Officer ("The Relationship between the Absolute and the Relative PPP Theory of Cassel," p. 251 n. 1) Cassel devoted at least parts of twenty-five English-language publications to expounding the PPP theorem. Officer (ibid., p. 252) reports that Cassel claims to have perceived the main point of the theorem in 1904 and to have incorporated its main ideas into his classroom lectures as early as 1905.

[110] Lawrence H. Officer, "The Relationship between the Absolute and the Relative PPP Theory of Cassel," *History of Political Economy* 14 (Summer): p. 254.

parallel standard, i.e., two different moneys circulating side by side in domestic use, and the case in which there is only one kind of money employed in domestic transactions while another kind is in use abroad. According to Mises,[111] although "prevailing opinion" treats the two cases separately, "there is no theoretical difference between them as far as the determination of the exchange-ratio between the two sorts of money is concerned." Where economic relations exist between a gold-standard country and a silver-standard country, "from the economic point of view, both metals must be regarded as money for each area."[112] Furthermore, according to Mises,[113] whether traders utilize both moneys or the "foreign" money alone in carrying out an international transaction, "the only important point is that the existence of international trade relations results in the consequence that the money of each of the single areas concerned is money also for all other areas."

One of the few economists who appreciated Mises's theoretical breakthrough in this area was Lord Robbins[114] who wrote: "As von Mises pointed out years ago, the theory of the foreign exchanges can be viewed simply as a special case of the theory of parallel currencies."[115]

As simple and compelling as Mises's insight is, it has revolutionary implications for the analysis of exchange-rate determination. Most importantly, the exchange rate between two different national currencies is no longer determined, as it was for Cassel,[116] by the "quotient between the general levels of prices in the two countries." National price levels, each of which includes purely domestic goods, e.g., houses and haircuts, whose spatial quality components render

---

[111] Mises, *Theory of Money and Credit*, p. 179.

[112] Ibid., p. 180.

[113] Ibid.

[114] Lionel Robbins, *Money, Trade and International Relations* (New York: St. Martin's Press, 1971), p. 22.

[115] Rothbard (*Man, Economy and State*, p. 725) also follows the Misesian approach in theorizing about exchange rates.

[116] Quoted in Officer "The Relationship Between the Absolute and the Relative PPP Theory of Cassel," p. 252.

their prices interlocally, and, *a fortiori*, internationally incommensurable, are wholly irrelevant to the issue, because there is no longer a reason to distinguish between internationally "tradable" goods and domestically produced and consumed "nontradable" goods. As in the case of domestically co-existing parallel currencies, every spatially-differentiated good finds expression in the purchasing-power array of each of the two national currencies.

The Misesian exchange-rate theorist would thus reject out of hand the claim of modem macroeconomists such as Jeffrey D. Sachs and Felipe B. Larrain[117] that the presence of nontradable goods "affects every important feature of an economy, from price determination, to the structure of output, to the effects of macroeconomic policy [and] undermine[s] the case for purchasing power parity." In fact, all goods can be and are traded internationally, even though many are "immovable" or "nontransportable." Certainly, one of the lessons learned from the exchange-rate gyrations of the 1980s was that American real estate and consumer services, when rendered sufficiently cheap by a depreciated dollar, are purchasable by foreign speculators and tourists. For the Misesian, the apparent problem presented to the PPP theorem by the existence of goods whose position in space is fixed is easily soluble when the spatial dimension of quality is taken into account.

Thus, for example, if the final or PPP exchange rate between the U.S. dollar and the British pound is two-to-one, then the pound price of a house located in London must be exactly one-half the dollar price of this same house. Of course, due to consumer perceptions of the difference in quality between the two cities as residential locations, the final price in dollars (pounds) of an identically constructed house situated in Manhattan may be triple that of the London house also expressed in dollars (pounds). To maintain purchasing power parity, therefore, it is not necessary that technologically identical but immovable goods available in different locations maintain equal prices in the same currency, but only that the ratio of the prices in two different currencies of an immovable good in the same location equal the inverse of the exchange rate between these two currencies. If the

---

[117] Jeffrey D. Sachs and Felipe B. Larrain, *Macroeconomics in the Global Economy* (Englewood Cliffs, N.J.: Prentice-Hall, 1993), pp. 657–58.

ratio of currency prices for any given commodity diverges from the prevailing exchange rate, then the final state of rest has not yet been attained, and profit opportunities will exist for selling goods for the relatively overvalued currency, purchasing the undervalued currency, and using it to repurchase the original good. These arbitrage operations will drive the exchange rate and the ratio of currency purchasing powers toward a mutual and final adjustment.[118]

Another feature which significantly distinguishes Mises's formulation of the PPP theorem from Cassel's involves the question of whether the exchange rate is exclusively a monetary phenomenon, or whether changes in the nonmonetary data are capable of bringing about a permanent departure of the equilibrium exchange rate from the rate which maintains strict PPP between the two currencies. As noted above, Cassel himself, especially in his later writings, seemed to hint at what might be termed an "inclusive" approach to exchange-rate determination, i.e., one which includes references to non-monetary factors as codeterminants of the exchange rate.[119]

More recently, proponents of the modern MAIA have been sharply criticized for writing out models of exchange-rate determination that embody an absolute version of the PPP theorem along Casselian lines and that exclude any reference to the influence of real factors on the formation of the exchange rate. Thus, for example, Thomas M. Humphrey[120] has argued that "The main shortcoming of the monetary approach is that it ignores the effect of real relative price changes on the exchange rate. In particular, it ignores the influence of changes in the *real terms of trade* (i.e., the relative price of imports and exports) and

---

[118] A good explanation of this arbitrage process is given by Rothbard (*Man, Economy, and State*, pp. 725–26).

[119] Officer ("The Purchasing-Power Parity Theory of Exchange Rates," *IMF Staff Papers* 23, no. 1: p. 9) has argued this, while Paul Samuelson ("Theoretical Notes on Trade Problems," in *Collected Scientific Papers of Paul A. Samuelson*, ed. Joseph E. Stiglitz (Cambridge, Mass.: M.I.T. Press), vol. 2, pp. 821–30) has denied it. For a brief description of this "milder approach," see Anne O. Krueger (*Exchange-Rate Determination* New York: Cambridge University Press, 1983, p. 68).

[120] Thomas M. Humphrey, "Dennis H. Robertson and the Monetary Approach to Exchange Rates," in idem *Essays on Inflation*, 4th ed. (Richmond, Va.: Federal Reserve Bank of Richmond, [1980] 1983), pp. 195, 200.

internal relative prices (i.e., the relative price of exports and domestic nontradeable goods).... [R]eal structural changes in tastes, technology, and market structure ... operating through real relative prices ... necessitate real equilibrium changes in the exchange rate and thereby produce systematic divergences from purchasing power parity."

Whatever the validity of this criticism of the PPP theorem formulated in terms of relative national price levels, it has no bearing whatever on a theorem relating to the relative purchasing powers of independent currencies coexisting in a unitary market area. The Misesian version of the PPP theorem remains intact in its absolute and exclusively monetary formulation.

To illustrate, let us consider the case of a monopolistically-induced increase in the price of oil, the U.S. import, relative to the U.S. export, wheat. While the "terms of trade" turn against the U.S., *ceteris paribus,* i.e., in the (unlikely) absence of any induced changes in the monetary data, there will be no long-run depreciation of the U.S. dollar against the Saudi riyal, because both currencies experience an equal reduction of their purchasing powers in terms of oil and, assuming the demand for oil is inelastic along the relevant segment of the global demand curve, equal increases of their purchasing powers in terms of wheat. Of course, this is not to deny that short-run and self-reversing fluctuations in the exchange rate may accompany the market's adjustment to the alteration in relative prices. Thus U.S. consumers may initially respond to the increased price of oil by increased expenditures on oil without a corresponding reduction in their spending on wheat, allowing their cash balances to temporarily run down.[121] This

---

[121] Hayek (*Monetary Nationalism and International Stability*, p. 18) in his earlier incarnation as a Misesian monetary and business-cycle theorist discusses cash balances as cushions permitting market participants to soften and delay the adaptation of their real incomes to their altered money incomes. This function of cash balances has recently been rediscovered in the literature on the "buffer" or "shock-absorption" approach to the demand for money. See, for example, Vesa Kannianinen and Juha Tarkka, "The Demand for Money: Micro-foundations for the Shock-Absorption Approach," Department of Economics, University of Helsinki Working Paper No. 210, 1984; Anthonie Knoester, "Theoretical Principles of the Buffer Mechanism, Monetary Quasi-Equilibrium and Its Spillover Effects," Institute for Economic Research Discussion Paper Series No. 7908/G/M. Rotterdam, Netherlands: Erasmus University, n.d.; and David Laidler, "The Buffer Stock Notion in Monetary

will cause an "overabsorption" of output relative to their shrunken real income by U.S. residents, creating an excess demand for riyals in the foreign-exchange market and necessitating a temporary rise in the exchange rate and a depreciation of the dollar. The movement in the exchange rate will thus assist in clearing excess demands in output markets and adjusting the terms of trade to prevent overabsorption and preserve balance of payments equilibrium, but only until U.S. residents' expenditures adjust, cash balances are reestablished at their former equilibrium levels, and the exchange rate floats back down to its unchanged PPP level.

Moreover, other things are not likely to remain equal; in particular, we can expect a change in the relative demands for the two currencies which results from the redistribution of income and wealth from U.S. entrepreneurs and laborers to their Saudi counterparts and leads to a long-run depreciation of the dollar. But it is the relative decline in the cash-balance demand for the dollar and therefore in its purchasing power vis-à-vis the riyal, and not the deterioration of the U.S. terms of trade, which is the direct cause of the change in the *final* exchange rate.

There remains to be noted Mises's status as a forerunner of the modern explanation of the effect of expectations on the exchange rate. The modern "asset market view," as it is called, treats foreign exchange markets as efficient asset markets in which current prices and exchange rates adjust promptly to changing expectations regarding the prospective development of the relative purchasing powers of the various currencies. Modern writers in the MAIA tradition, who have been responsible for reviving this view, generally give credit for its origination to such writers as Cassel, Keynes, and Dennis Robertson, and to German-speaking writers, including Walter Eucken, Fritz Machlup , and Melchior Palyi.[122]

Economics," *Economic Journal,* Supplement 1984 (*The Economic Journal* 94, Supplement: Conference Papers (1984): pp. 17–34).

[122] Mordechai E. Kreinin and Lawrence H. Officer, *The Monetary Approach to the Balance of Payment: A Survey* (Princeton: Princeton University Press, 1978), pp. 28–31; Humphrey, "Dennis H. Robertson and the Monetary Approach to Exchange Rates," in *Essays on Inflation,* idem 4th ed. (Richmond, Va.: Federal Rserve Bank of Richmond, [1980] 1983); Edwards, *The Economist of the Country,* p. 79.

These economists writing in the 1920s arrived at this view while seeking to explain the significant discrepancy that they observed between the rates of price inflation and exchange-rate depreciation toward the end of the German hyperinflation. While Mises has been recognized as meriting inclusion in the group who pioneered the asset market view, and even as "perhaps its strongest proponent"[123] Edwards[124] discovers a sophisticated statement of the view presented by Mises in the first German edition of the *Theory of Money and Credit* published in 1912, two years before the inception of the German war inflation. Amazingly, while Mises thus enjoyed a temporal advantage over the other expositors of the asset market view, he suffered the distinct disadvantage *vis-à-vis* those writing in the 1920s of not having had the direct and stark experience of the hyperinflation available to guide his inquiry.

In re-evaluating the main elements of Mises's monetary theory, one thing especially stands out. Mises took great pains to establish his theory of money on the bedrock of value and price theory. However, the value-theoretic concepts that Mises relied upon in pursuing his monetary analysis were not derived from Walras, Pareto, or Marshall but from Menger, Böhm-Bawerk, and Wicksteed. This fact goes a long way toward explaining the lack of comprehension that Mises's monetary theory has generally met with among mainstream monetary economists. While it represents an added burden to those who seek to present the Misesian approach to a wider audience, it also offers an opportunity to acquaint neoclassical economists with the fruitfulness of an alternative, but not unrelated, tradition in value and price theory.

Bibliography

Böhm-Bawerk, Eugen von. 1959. *Capital and Interest.* Vol. 1: *The Positive Theory of Capital.* George D. Huncke, trans. South Holland, Ill.: Libertarian Press.

Bowley, Marian. [1937] 1967. *Nassau Senior and Classical Economics.* New York: Octagon Books.

---

123 Humphrey, "Dennis H. Robertson and the Monetary Approach to Exchange Rates," p. 192.
124 Edwards, *The Economist of the Country*, pp. 80–81.

Cannan, Edwin. 1929. *Money: Its Connexion with Rising and Falling Prices*, 6th ed. Westminster, England: P.S. King & Son.

Cowan, Tyler and Randy Kroszner. 1987. "The Development of the New Monetary Economics." *Journal of Political Economy* 95, no. 3: pp. 567–90.

Davenport, Herbert J. [1913] 1968. *The Economics of Enterprise*. New York: Augustus M. Kelley.

Edwards, James Rolph. 1985. *The Economist of the Country: Ludwig von Mises in the History of Monetary Thought*. New York: Carlton Press.

Ellis, Howard S. 1934. *German Monetary Theory 1905–1933*. Cambridge, Mass.: Harvard University Press.

Federal Reserve Bank of Cleveland. 1992. *Economic Trends* (July).

Fisher, Irving. [1913] 1985. *The Purchasing Power of Money: Its Determination and Relation to Credit, Interest and Prices*, 2nd ed. Fairfield, N.J.: Augustus M. Kelley.

Friedman, Milton. 1992. *Money Mischief: Episodes in Monetary History*. New York: Harcourt Brace Jovanovich,

Greenfield, Robert L., and Leland B. Yeager. 1983. "A Laissez-Faire Approach to Monetary Stability." *Journal of Money, Credit, and Banking* 15 (August): pp. 301–15.

Gregory, T.E. 1927. "Professor Cannan and Contemporary Monetary Theory." In *London Essays in Economics: In Honor of Edwin Cannan,* T.E. Gregory and Hugh Dalton, eds., pp. 31–65. London: George Routledge and Sons.

Hayek, F.A. [1937] 1971. *Monetary Nationalism and International Stability*. New York: Augustus M. Kelley.

High, Jack and Howard Bloch. 1989. "On the History of Ordinal Utility Theory: 1890–1932." *History of Political Economy* 21 no. 2: pp. 351–65.

Hoppe, Hans-Hermann. 1992. "The Theory of Employment, Money, Interest, and the Capitalist Process: The Misesian Case against Keynes." In *Dissent on Keynes: A Critical Appraisal of Keynesian Economics,* Mark Skousen, ed. New York: Praeger.

_____. and Robert E. Keleher. 1982. *The Monetary Approach to the Balance of Payments, Exchange Rates, and World Inflation*. New York: Praeger.

Humphrey, Thomas M. [1980] 1983. "Dennis H. Robertson and the Monetary Approach to Exchange Rates." In idem, *Essays on Inflation*, 4th ed. Richmond, Va.: Federal Reserve Bank of Richmond.

Kannianinen, Vesa, and Juha Tarkka. 1984. "The Demand for Money: Micro-foundations for the Shock-Absorption Approach." Department of Economics. University of Helsinki Working Paper No. 210.

Kirzner, Israel M. [1963] 1976. *Market Theory and the Price System*. Princeton: D. Van Nostrand. 1976.

_____. Discussion of M. Rothbard, "Austrian Definitions of the Money Supply." Presented at a Symposium on Austrian Economics. Windsor Castle, England. Unpub. Manuscript.

Knoester, Anthonie. N.D. "Theoretical Principles of the Buffer Mechanism, Monetary Quasi-Equilibrium and Its Spillover Effects." Institute for Economic Research Discussion Paper Series No. 7908/G/M. Rotterdam, Netherlands: Erasmus University.

Kreinin, Mordechai E., and Lawrence H. Officer. 1978. *The Monetary Approach to the Balance of Payments: A Survey.* Princeton Studies in International Finance No. 43. Princeton: Princeton University Press.

Krueger, Anne O. 1983. *Exchange-Rate Determination.* New York: Cambridge University Press.

Laffer, Arthur B., and Marc A. Miles. 1982. *International Economics in an Integrated World.* Glenview, Ill.: Scott, Foresman.

Laidler, David. 1984. "The Buffer Stock Notion in Monetary Economics." *Economic Journal,* Supplement 1984: pp. 17–33.

Marget, Arthur W. [1938–42] 1966. *The Theory of Prices: A Re-Examination of the Central Problem of Monetary Theory,* 2 vols. New York: Augustus M. Kelley.

Mises, Ludwig von. 1966. *Human Action: A Treatise on Economics,* 3rd ed. Chicago: Henry Regnery.

_____. [1953] 1971. *The Theory of Money and Credit,* 2nd ed. Irvington-on-Hudson, N.Y.: Foundation for Economic Education.

_____. 1978a. *Notes and Recollections.* South Holland, Ill.: Libertarian Press.

_____. 1978b. *On the Manipulation of Money and Credit,* Percy L. Greaves, ed., Bettina Bien Greaves, trans. Dobbs Ferry, N.Y.: Free Market Books.

_____. [1919] 1983. *Nation, State, and Economy: Contributions to the Politics and History of Our Time,* Leland B. Yeager, trans. New York: New York University Press.

_____. [1933] 1990. "Senior's Lectures on Monetary Problems." In idem, *Money, Method, and the Market Process,* Richard M. Ebeling, ed., pp. 104–9. Norwell, Mass.: Kluwer Academic Publishers.

_____. 1990a. *Economic Freedom and Intervention: An Anthology of Articles and Essays,* Bettina Bien Greaves, ed. Irvington-on-Hudson, N.Y.: Foundation for Economic Education.

_____. 1990b. "The Position of Money among Economic Goods." In idem, *Money, Method, and the Market Process,* Alfred Zlabinger, trans., Richard M. Ebeling, ed., pp. 55–68. Norwell, Mass.: Kluwer Academic Publishers.

_____. 1990c. *Economic Calculation in the Socialist Commonwealth.* Auburn, Ala.: Ludwig von Mises Institute.

Moss, Laurence S. 1976. "the Monetary Economics of Ludwig von Mises." In idem, *The Economics of Ludwig von Mises: Toward a Critical Appraisal,* pp. 13–49. New York: New York University Press.

Officer, Lawrence H. 1976. "The Purchasing-Power Parity Theory of Exchange Rates: A Review Article." *IMF Staff Papers* 23, no. 1: pp. 1–60.

_____. 1982. "The Relationship between the Absolute and the Relative PPP Theory of Cassel." *History of Political Economy* 14 (Summer): pp. 251–55.

Patinkin, Don. 1965. *Money, Interest, and Prices: An Integration of Monetary and Value Theory*, 2nd ed. New York: Harper & Row.

Phillips, C.A., T.F. McManus, and R.W. Nelson. [1937] 1972. *Banking and the Business Cycle: A Study of the Great Depression in the United States*. New York: Arno Press.

_____. 1986. Review of *The Gold Standard: An Austrian Perspective*, Llewellyn H. Rockwell, Jr., ed. *Cato Policy Report* 8 (November/December): pp. 14–15.

Robbins, Lionel. 1971. *Money, Trade and international Relations*. New York: St. Martin's Press.

Rothbard, Murray N. [1962] 1970. *Man, Economy, and State: A Treatise on Economic Principles*, 2 vols. Los Angeles: Nash.

_____. 1975. *America's Great Depression*, 3rd ed. Kansas City: Sheed & Ward.

_____. 1977. Private Correspondence (September).

_____. 1978. "Austrian Definitions of the Supply of Money." In *New Directions in Austrian Economics*, Louis M. Spadaro, ed. Kansas City: Sheed Andrews and McMeel.

_____. 1988. "Timberlake on the Austrian Theory of Money: A Comment." *Review of Austrian Economics* 2: pp. 179–87.

_____. 1991. "The End of Socialism and the Calculation Debate Revisited." *Review of Austrian Economics* 5, no. 2: pp. 51–76.

_____. 1992a. "Aurophobia: or, Free Banking on What Standard?" *Review of Austrian Economics* 6, no. 1: pp. 97–108.

_____. 1992b. "The Case for a Genuine Gold Dollar." In *The Gold Standard: Perspectives in the Austrian School*, Llewellyn H. Rockwell, Jr., ed., pp. 1–17. Auburn, Ala.: Ludwig von Mises Institute.

Rousseas, Stephen W. 1972. *Monetary Theory*. New York: Alfred A. Knopf.

Sachs, Jeffrey D., and Felipe B. Larrain. 1993. *Macroeconomics in the Global Economy*. Englewood Cliffs, N.J.: Prentice-Hall.

Salerno, Joseph T. 1982. *The Gold Standard: An Analysis of Some Recent Proposals*. Cato Institute Policy Analysis (September 9). Washington, D.C.: Cato Institute.

Salerno, Joseph T. 1987. "The 'True' Money Supply: A Measure of the Supply of the Medium of Exchange in the U. S. Economy." *Austrian Economics Newsletter* 6 (September): pp. 1–6.

Salerno, Joseph T. 1990a. "Ludwig von Mises as Social Rationalist." *Review of Austrian Economics* 4: pp. 26–54.

Salerno, Joseph T. 1990b. "Postscript: Why a Socialist Economy Is 'Impossible.'" In Ludwig von Mises, *Economic Calculation in the Socialist Commonwealth*, pp. 51–71. Auburn, Ala.: Ludwig von Mises Institute.

Samuelson, Paul A. 1966. "Theoretical Notes on Trade Problems." In *Collected Scientific Papers of Paul A. Samuelson*, vol. 2, Joseph E. Stiglitz, ed., pp. 821–30. Cambridge, Mass.: M.I.T. Press.

Timberlake, Richard H. 1991. *Gold, Greenbacks, and the Constitution*. Berryville, Va.: George Edward Durrell Foundation.

White, Lawrence H. [1986] 1989. "Subjectivist Perspective on the Definition and Identification of Money." In idem, *Competition and Currency: Essays on Free Banking and Money*, pp. 203–17. New York: New York University Press.

White, Lawrence H., and George A. Selgin. [1987] 1989. "The Evolution of a Free Banking System." In *Competition and Currency: Essays on Free Banking and Money*, Lawrence H. White, ed., pp. 218–42. New York: New York University Press.

Wicksteed, Philip H. [1932] 1967. *The Common Sense of Political Economy and Selected Papers and Reviews on Economic Theory*, 2 vols., Lionel Robbins, ed. New York: Augustus M. Kelley.

Wu, Chi-Yuen. 1939. *An Outline of International Price Theories*. London: George Routledge and Sons.

CHAPTER 3

The "True" Money Supply:
A Measure of the Supply of
the Medium of Exchange in the
U.S. Economy

T he "True" Money Supply (TMS), developed by Professor Murray Rothbard and the present author,[1] is an admittedly imperfect attempt to provide a statistical measure of money that is consistent with the theoretical definition of money as the general medium of exchange in society.[2]

From: "The 'True' Money Supply: A Measure of the Supply of the Medium of Exchange in the U.S. Economy," *Austrian Economics Newsletter* 6 (Spring 1987): pp. 1–6.

[1] Professor Rothbard presents the theoretical framework for this statistic in the following: Murray N. Rothbard, *America's Great Depression* (Princeton, N.J.: Van Nostrand, 1963), pp. 83–86; idem, "Austrian Definitions of the Supply of Money," in Louis M. Spadaro, ed., *New Directions in Austrian Economics* (Kansas City: Sheed Andrews and McMeel, 1978), pp. 143–56; and idem, *The Mystery of Banking* (New York: Richardson and Snyder, 1983), pp. 254–62.

[2] For a sample of recent contributions that have emphasized general acceptability in exchange as the defining characteristic of money, see: Lawrence H. White, "A Subjectivist Perspective on the Definition and Identification of Money," in Israel M. Kirzner, ed., *Subjectivism, Intelligibility and Economic Understanding: Essays in Honor of Ludwig M. Lachmann on His Eightieth Birthday* (London: Macmillan, 1986), pp. 301–14; Dale K. Osborne, "What Is Money Today?" *Federal Reserve Bank of Dallas Economic Review* (January 1985), pp. 1–15; idem, "Ten Approaches to the Definition of Money," *Federal Reserve Bank of Dallas Economic Review*

Measures of the U.S. money stock that are used in economic and business forecasting and in applied economics and historical research are flawed precisely because they are not based on an explicit and coherent theoretical conception of the essential nature of money. Given the pervasive role of money in the modern market economy, existing money-supply measures therefore tend to impede, rather than facilitate, understanding of economic events. Each of the familiar M's calculated by the Federal Reserve System, for example, both excludes some items that are identifiable as money by our definition and includes other items that lack the essential properties of a general medium of exchange.

As the general medium of exchange, money is a good that is universally and routinely accepted in exchange by market participants; or, put another way, it is the one good that is traded for all other goods on the market. One important implication of this fact—and an important empirical test of whether or not a thing can be counted as money—is that money serves *as the final means of payment in all* transactions. For instance, credit cards are not counted as part of the TMS, because use of a credit card in the purchase of a good does not finally discharge the debt created in the current transaction. Instead, it gives rise to a second credit transaction that involves present and future monetary payments. Thus the issuer of the card or lender is now bound to pay the seller of the good immediately with money on behalf of the card-holder or borrower. The latter, in turn, is obliged to make a monetary repayment of the loan to the issuer at the end of the month or at a later date, at which time the transaction is finally completed.[3]

In the case of a paper fiat money, such as the current U.S. dollar, there is a second test that can be applied to determine whether

---

(March 1984), pp. 1–23; Leland Yeager, "What Are Banks?" *Atlantic Economic Journal* 6 (December 1978): 1–14. Also see the classic article, Leland Yeager, "The Medium of Exchange," in R.W. Clower, ed., *Monetary Theory: Selected Readings* (Baltimore: Penguin Books, 1970), pp. 37–60.

[3] For a similar view of credit cards, see Paul A. Meyer, *Monetary Economics and Financial Markets* (Homewood, Ill.: Richard D. Irwin, 1982), p. 34; and White, "Definition and Identification of Money," pp. 310–11.

a particular item should be counted in money supply statistics. Unlike any good that is produced in the market, including a commodity money, whose quantities are ultimately determined by the interaction of supply and demand,[4] the quantity of government fiat money (but not its purchasing power) at any time is determined solely by decisions of suppliers of the good, i.e., government central banks, without respect to the desires and actions of the demanders. The fact that money is routinely accepted as the final means of payment by all participants in the market means that fiat money can be literally lent and spent into existence regardless of the public's existing demand for it. For example, if an additional quantity of Fed notes is printed up and spent by government on various goods and services, an excess supply of money will temporarily be created in the economy. The initial recipients of the new money will quickly get rid of the excess cash simply by increasing their own spending on goods; those who eagerly receive the new money as payments in the second or later rounds of spending will do likewise, in the process bidding up the prices of goods, reducing the purchasing power of the dollar, and, consequently, increasing the quantities of dollars that each individual desires to keep on hand to meet expected future payments or for other purposes. In summary, any excess supply of fiat money does not go out of existence, but is spent and respent and continually passed on like a "hot potato" throughout the economy until the surplus money is finally and fully absorbed by the resulting increase in general prices and in desired dollar holdings.[5] It is this criterion which is applied below in resolving the apparent inconsistency of including demand deposits and money market deposit accounts (MMDAs) in the TMS, while excluding checkable money market mutual fund (MMMF) equity shares.

In what follows, I explain briefly why various items have been included in or excluded from the TMS. To simplify the exposition,

---

[4] On this property of a pure commodity money, see, for example, Milton Friedman, "Commodity-Reserve Currency," in idem, *Essays in Positive Economics* (Chicago: University of Chicago Press, 1953), pp. 206–10.

[5] For a description of the unique process by which, in nominal terms, "the supply of money creates its own demand," see Yeager, "The Medium of Exchange," pp. 42–43; and idem, "What Are Banks?" pp. 6–7.

I organize my explanation around the several Fed definitions of the money supply and of total liquid assets.

Components of M1

Currency in the hands of the nonbank public, i.e., excluding currency held by the U.S. Treasury, the Fed, and in the vaults of commercial banks, is counted in the TMS, precisely because it is the physical embodiment of the generally accepted medium of exchange in the U.S. economy. Federal Reserve notes of various dollar denominations (as well as token coins and paper notes issued by the U.S. Treasury) are the "standard money" or ultimate "cash" of the U.S. monetary system, having replaced gold in this function, at least for American citizens, in 1933.

Demand deposits or checking account balances at commercial banks and other checkable deposits, such as Negotiable Order of Withdrawal (NOW) accounts held at savings and loan associations, are included in the TMS by virtue of the fact that they are claims to the standard money redeemable at par on demand by the depositor or by a third party designated by the depositor. Despite the fact that these deposits are only fractionally backed by cash or immediately cashable reserve deposits at the Fed, their instantaneous redemption at par value is effectively guaranteed by two factors. First there is federal deposit insurance, which legally insures up to $100,000 of each and every depositor at a given bank or thrift against loss, but which, in practice, has almost always guaranteed the full worth of all deposits, usually by subsidizing the merger of an ailing institution with a healthy one.[6] Second and more important, there is the Fed itself,

---

[6] As a former FDIC Chairman has recently written: "The pendulum has swung once again toward 100 percent protection of depositors and creditors. Despite the fact that Congress made it clear in the 1950 Act that FDIC was not created to insure all deposits in all banks, in the years since Congress has gradually increased the insured amount to $100,000. In addition, the regulators have devised solutions that protect even the uninsured in the preponderance of cases." (Irvine H. Sprague, *Bailout: An Insider's Account of Bank Failures and Rescues* [New York: Basic Books, 1986], p. 32.) Moreover, the uninsured depositors who incurred losses in a handful of recent bank failures were mainly holders of deposits in the category of "large time deposits," which, for the reasons stated below, are not included in TMS. The FDIC's

which, in its much publicized function as the "lender of last resort," always stands ready to head off a banking panic by simply printing up and lending the needed quantities of Fed notes to banks or thrifts unable to meet their demand liabilities.[7] For these reasons, checkable deposits held at federally-insured banks and thrifts are readily acceptable in exchange as perfect substitutes, dollar for dollar, for Federal Reserve notes.[8]

In contrast, travelers' checks issued by nonbank financial institutions, such as American Express, are excluded from the TMS because they neither are risk-free claims to immediate cash nor serve as final means of payment in transactions. What a travelers' check represents from an economic point of view is a credit claim on the investment portfolio of the issuing company. The purchase of travelers' checks from American Express involves, in effect, a "call" loan by the purchaser to American Express, which the latter pledges to repay to the purchaser or to a designated third party at an unspecified date

---

recent attempt to enforce market discipline on the banking industry by leaving the uninsured holders of large time deposits in small (but not large) banks unprotected appears to have had little effect. On this, see R. Alton Gilbert, "Recent Changes in Handling Bank Failures and Their Effects on the Banking Industry," Federal Reserve Bank of St. Louis *Review* 67 (June/July 1985): pp. 21–28.

[7] In his refusal to include "transactions balances," including demand deposits, in his statistical definition of the U.S. money supply, because they allegedly all cannot be spent simultaneously in any conceivable pattern of payments, Osborne ignores these institutional considerations. Thus, contrary to Osborne's contention, demand deposits in the U.S. today are indeed "means of simultaneous payment," precisely because, as the lender of last resort, the Fed is empowered to create base money ad libitum and would exercise this power to prevent a wholesale collapse of the fractional-reserve, multibank system. Because Osborne neglects this momentous institutional factor, the strict application of Shackle's "simultaneity" criterion to the empirical identification of the money stock leaves him with only the monetary base as the "generally acceptable means of exchange," i.e., money, in the U.S. See Osborne, "What Is Money Today?" pp. 3–5.

[8] As Barger observes, ". . . it is the bank deposit which is money—not the check which transfers the deposit. Bank deposits are always acceptable: checks may not be, for sometimes they turn out to be made of rubber. If your creditor refuses your check, it's no doubt because he's not convinced he's getting title to a bank deposit." (Harold Barger, *Money, Banking and Public Policy,* 2nd ed. [Chicago: Rand McNally, 1968], pp. 16–17.) This is an obvious point, but White appears to overlook it by attaching significance to the limited "sphere of acceptance" of "ordinary bank checks." (White, "Definition and Identification of Money," p. 305).

in the future. In the meantime, most of the proceeds of such loans are invested by American Express on its own account in interest bearing assets, while a fraction is held in the form of demand deposits to meet anticipated payments of its travelers' check liabilities as they "mature." In exchange for the foregone interest (and a small fee) the purchaser receives access to an alternative payment system which avoids the risk of loss associated with carrying cash payments and the potential delay or nonacceptance involved with payment by personal check drawn on a distant bank. But the travelers' checks themselves are not the final means of payment in a transaction;[9] the sellers who receive travelers' checks in exchange quickly and routinely present them for final payment at a bank and obtain either cash or a credit to their demand deposit accounts, with the sums paid out ultimately being debited to the demand deposit account of American Express. Moreover, in the highly unlikely event that financial reverses force the issuing company into institutional liquidation, the holders of its outstanding stock of travelers' checks would be, economically and legally, in the same boat as debtholders of any insolvent business firm, having no political guarantee of a dollar-for-dollar payoff of their debt claims, such as that provided by federal deposit insurance and privileged access to the lender of last resort.

Components of M2 Not Included in M1

Savings deposits, whether at commercial banks or thrift institutions, are economically indistinguishable from demand deposits and, are therefore included in the TMS. Both demand and savings deposits are federally insured under the same conditions and, consequently, both represent instantly cashable, par value claims to the general medium of exchange. The objection that claims on dollars

---

[9] Meyer is inconsistent in counting nonbank travelers' checks as part of the money supply merely because they are "means of payment." As Meyer recognizes in his discussion of credit cards, however, it is not enough that an item be able to serve as a means of payment in most transactions for it to be considered money; it must also serve, in his words, "to extinguish obligations between two parties," that is, serve as the final means of payment, to deserve the classification of money. See Meyer, *Monetary Economics*, pp. 33–34.

held in savings deposits typically do not circulate in exchange[10] (although certified or cashier's checks may be readily drawn against such deposits and are certainly generally acceptable in exchange), while not unimportant for some purposes of analysis, is here beside the point. The essential, economic point is that some or all of the dollars accumulated in, e.g., passbook savings accounts are effectively withdrawable on demand by depositors in the form of cash.[11] In addition, savings deposits are at all times transferrable,[12] dollar for dollar, into "transactions" accounts such as demand deposits or NOW accounts.[13]

---

[10] For example, White argues that because time deposits are not directly transferable, they do not serve as media of exchange, let alone as generally accepted media." (White, "Definition and Identification of Money," p. 310.) Yeager holds that the liabilities of nonbank financial intermediaries, such as deposits at savings and loan associations, are not money because they are not "routinely exchanged." (Yeager, "The Medium of Exchange," pp. 40–46, 53–56).

[11] As Rothbard pertinently remarks, the 30-day notice [of withdrawal of savings deposits] is a dead letter; it is practically never imposed, and, if it were, there would be a prompt and devastating run on the bank. Everyone acts as if his time deposits were redeemable on demand, and the banks pay out their deposits in the same way they redeem demand deposits. The necessity for personal withdrawal is merely a technicality; it may take a little longer to go down to the bank and withdraw the cash than to pay by check, but the essence of the process is the same. In both cases, a deposit at the bank is the source of monetary payment." (Rothbard, *America's Great Depression,* p. 84).

[12] Today, many institutions permit such transfer to be effected by telephone. Interestingly, one weighted aggregate of "transactions assets," the "MQ" measure, includes "savings deposits subject to telephone transfer" while excluding conventional savings deposits. See Dallas S. Batten and Daniel L. Thornton, "Are Weighted Monetary Aggregates Better Than Simple-Sum M1?" Federal Reserve Bank of St. Louis *Review* 67 (June/July 1985): pp. 29–40.

[13] In an early, and unfortunately neglected, contribution, Lin clearly recognized the economic equivalence of currency, demand deposits, and savings deposits, based on their "interchangeability" within the modern banking system. Thus, according to Lin,
   The term 'means of payment' describes but one phase of the meaning of money. It indicates only in what form money is 'spent,' but not in what form it may be 'kept.' In the modern banking and monetary system money may be kept in one form and spent in another. This is possible and is always done today [1937] because all forms of money issued either by banks or by the state must be interchangeable to maintain parity.... Money in whatever form it is kept and spent must be of general acceptability and of free interchangeability. By these criteria, all other credit devices are automatically eliminated because they are not generally acceptable and cannot be freely interchanged into one

The common-sense case for the inclusion of savings deposits in the stock of general media of exchange was cogently presented by the eminent German banker and economist, Melchior Palyi:

> In their own minds, *money is what people consider as purchasing power*, available at once or shortly. People's "Liquidity" status and financial disposition are not affected by juristic subtleties and technicalities. One kind of deposit is as good as another, provided it is promptly redeemable into legal tender at virtual face value and is accepted in settling debts. The volume of total demand for goods and services is not affected by the distribution of purchasing power among the diverse reservoirs into which that purchasing power is placed. As long as free transferability obtains from one reservoir to the other, the deposits cannot differ in function or value....

A source of confusion is the identification of savings deposits with savings. The former are no more and no less "saved" than are the funds put in a checking account or the currency held in stockings. In all three cases, someone is refraining from consumption (for the time being); in all three, the funds constitute actual purchasing power. And it makes no difference in this context how the purchasing power is generated originally: dug out of a gold mine, 'printed' by a government agency, or 'created' by a bank loan. As a matter of fact, savings banks and associations do exactly what commercial banks do: they build a credit structure on fractional reserves.[14]

Overnight repurchase agreements or "RPs" were devised in the mid-1970s as a means of evading the legal prohibition against the payment of interest on demand deposits. They are, in essence, interest bearing demand deposits held by business firms at commercial banks and therefore are included in the TMS. In a repurchase agreement, a

---

another. Treasury currency, bank notes, time and demand deposits are ... constantly interchanging into one another unit per unit without altering the total supply of money. (Lin Lin, "Are Time Deposits Money?" *American Economic Review* 27 [March 1937]: p. 85)

For one of the earliest hints of recognition of the monetary function of time deposits, see Frank A. Fetter, *Economics*, vol. 2: *Modern Economic Problems*, 2nd ed. (New York: Century, 1923), pp. 102–03.

[14] Melchior Palyi. *An Inflation Primer* (Chicago: Henry Regnery, 1961), pp. 137–38.

firm, in effect, makes a loan to a bank which is collateralized by government securities. The bank "sells" government securities to the firm with an agreement to "repurchase" them the following day at a slightly higher price, i.e., to repay the loan plus interest. When the purchase or loan is initially made, the bank debits the firm's demand deposit balance and credits its RP account by the amount of the loan. On the following day, the bank repays the loan with interest by reversing the process and crediting the firm's demand deposit with a sum that exceeds the previous day's debit by the amount of the interest payment. Since the loans are maturing daily, the firm has virtually instant access to the full amount of its dollars on deposit with the bank.[15]

Overnight Eurodollars are counted in the TMS for the same reason as overnight RPs: they are basically an accounting fiction that permits U.S. banks to pay interest on their business demand deposits and are therefore virtually redeemable on demand. In the case of overnight Eurodollars, deposits are made by U.S. firms in interest-bearing accounts at the Caribbean bank of a U.S. bank, where U.S. interest-rate regulations have no legal force. The dollars thus deposited plus interest earned are credited daily to the firms' demand deposit accounts held at the parent bank.[16]

Money market deposit accounts, as a hybrid of demand and savings deposits, are considered part of the TMS. MMDAs are federally insured up to $100,000[17] per account, they feature limited checking privileges, and they offer par value cashability upon demand of the depositor.

Although MMMF share accounts at first glance look like MMDAs, they are clearly excludable from the TMS, because they are neither instantly redeemable, par value claims to cash, nor final means of payment in exchange. This requires a brief explanation of the nature of MMMFs.[18]

---

[15] For a discussion of overnight RPs, see Meyer, *Monetary Economics*, p. 28.

[16] On overnight Eurodollars, see ibid., pp. 28–29.

[17] The federally insured limit has increased since this essay was written.

[18] The next three paragraphs, with some alterations, are drawn from Joseph T. Salerno, "What Investors and Depositors Should Know about Banks and the

Each MMMF share represents a claim to a pro rata share of a managed investment portfolio containing short-term financial assets, such as high-grade commercial paper, certificates of deposit, and U.S. Treasury notes. Although the value of a share is nominally fixed, usually, at one dollar, the total number of shares owned by an investor (abstracting from reinvested dividends) fluctuates according to market conditions affecting the overall value of the fund's portfolio.[19] Under extreme circumstances, such as a stratospheric rise in short-term interest rates or the bankruptcy of a corporation whose paper the fund has heavily invested in, the fund's investors may well suffer a capital loss in the form of an actual reduction of the number of fixed-value shares they own. Unlike a check drawn on a demand deposit or MMDA, therefore, an MMMF draft does not simply represent a direct transfer of current claims to currency, but a dual order to the fund's manager to sell a specified portion of the shareowner's asset holdings and then to transfer the monetary proceeds to a third party named on the check.[20] Note that the payment process is not finally completed until the payee receives money, typically in the form of a credit to his demand deposit.[21]

Another feature that distinguishes checkable MMMF shares from demand deposits and MMDAs is the fact that the former cannot

---

Financial Services Revolution," *Jerome Smith's Investment Perspectives* 2 (June 1984): pp. 3–4. A more detailed analysis of the nature of MMMFs and of their relationship to the supply of and demand for money under the gold standard may be found in Joseph T. Salerno, "Gold Standards: True and False," *The Cato Journal* 3 (Spring 1983): pp. 255–58 [reprinted here as Chapter 13].

[19] For a similar characterization of MMMFs, see Meyer, *Monetary Economics*, p. 29; and White, "Definition and Identification of Money," p. 310.

[20] "Typically, the funds establish a central clearing account at a bank. When checks, really drafts, written by individuals are presented to the bank, it notifies the mutual fund of the number of fund shares that must be liquidated to cover the check," (Monica Langley, "Holds on Checks Annoy Investors in Money Funds," *The Wall Street Journal* [November 11, 1986], p. 39).

[21] As White points out, "… the item that the check-writing MMMF customer relinquishes (ownership of shares in a portfolio of assets) is not what the payee accepts (ownership of an inside-money claim to bank reserves). Because the actual MMMF shares are not what the second party accepts (or intends to accept), MMMF shares cannot be considered a generally accepted medium of exchange; hence, they are not money." (White, "Definition and Identification of Money," p. 310).

be permanently expanded beyond the limit set by the public's willingness to hold such assets. If an excess supply of fund shares happens to emerge, the consequence would not be the general rise in prices occasioned by people's attempts to rid themselves of surplus dollars through increased spending.[22] Unwanted MMMF shares simply go out of existence, as fund investors directly redeem them for money or use MMMF drafts to purchase alternative investment assets or consumers' goods. In the extreme case, if the public suddenly preferred to invest directly in the short-term credit market, without the intermediation of managed mutual funds, then checkable MMMF shares would simply disappear from existence.

The existence of MMMFs does have an effect on overall prices in the economy, but not because checkable fund shares constitute an addition to the money supply. Rather, the liquidity and checkability features of these assets permit their holders to reduce the amount of money they need to keep on hand to meet anticipated payments and to insure against future contingencies. This is also true, as we saw, of credit cards, which similarly provide their holders with access to an alternative payments system that economizes on money. By thus reducing the overall demand for money, MMMFs and credit cards encourage a higher rate of aggregate spending in the economy and thus bring about a general rise in prices. However, the price increase associated with a given expansion of MMMFs is a "one-shot" phenomenon, whose magnitude is strictly governed by the corresponding reduction in the aggregate desired money balances of market participants. This sharply contrasts with inflation, which typically is a money-supply phenomenon involving a persistent decline in the purchasing power of the monetary unit that results from the creation of additional quantities of government fiat money, which, in theory, is limited only by the onset of a hyperinflationary currency breakdown.

The term "small-denomination time deposits" denotes mainly federally insured certificates of deposit (CDs) in denominations of less than $100,000. These are excluded from the TMS because they

---

[22] See White, "Definition and Identification of Money," pp. 2–3, for the description of this process.

involve loans by the public to banks and thrifts.[23] As time deposits, CDs nominally are not cashable on demand, but are payable in dollars only after a contractually fixed period of time ranging from thirty days to a number of years. However, the fact that the issuing institutions stand ready to redeem these liabilities in current dollars at any time prior to maturity does constitute a theoretical argument for their inclusion in the TMS at their current redemption value. On the other hand, depositors do have a strong incentive to abstain from cashing small CDs before their maturity dates, because the issuing institutions typically assess heavy penalties—varying from forfeiture of accrued interest to loss of part of the original principal—in the event of premature redemption. The ultimate decision to exclude this item was also heavily influenced by the practical problem of obtaining the data necessary to permit a reasonable estimate of its value in current dollars, i.e., net of penalty assessments.

Components of M3 Not Included in M2

Large-denomination time deposits, such as CDs issued in denominations of at least $100,000, are bona fide time liabilities, because they are not payable by the issuing institution before maturity.[24] Since they are not par value claims to immediately available dollars, they are excluded from the TMS. The same reasoning requires that term RPs and term Eurodollars be excluded from the TMS. The shares of "institution-only" MMMFs are excluded from the TMS for the same reasons as the shares of the "general purpose and broker/dealer" MMMFs included in M2.

Components of L Not Included in M3

U.S. Savings Bonds are instantly cashable at the U.S. Treasury (or at banks and thrifts acting in its behalf) at a fixed discount from their

---

[23] For details on institutional features of CDs, see Lester V. Chandler and Stephen M. Goldfeld, *The Economics of Money and Banking*, 7th ed. (New York: Harper and Row, 1977), pp. 148–49; also see Meyer, *Monetary Economics*, p. 88.

[24] Chandler and Goldfeld, *Money and Banking*, pp. 148–49.

face value.[25] As U.S. Treasury liabilities, moreover, their redeemability is "insured" by the full faith and credit of the Federal government. U.S. Savings Bonds are therefore included in the TMS at their redemption value, because they represent secure and current claims against the Treasury for contractually fixed quantities of the general medium of exchange.[26] In fact, U.S. Savings Bonds may usefully be treated as specific claims against "Treasury Cash," since this provides a rationale for the conventional omission of the latter item from money-supply statistics.[27]

In contrast to savings bonds, short-term Treasury securities are not payable before maturity and are therefore excluded from the TMS.

Memorandum Items

Three items which are not included in any Fed measure of the money supply (MI, M2, M3) or even of overall "liquidity" (L) find a

---

[25] Meyer, *Monetary Economics*, p. 152.

[26] In 1946, Fetter recognized savings bonds as "immediate purchasing power," and, as part of a comprehensive anti-inflation package, recommended absorbing savings bonds "redeemable on demand" by exchanging them for long-term bonds and life annuities. (Frank A. Fetter, "Inflation's Basic Cause: Too Much Money," *Saturday Evening Post* [July 13, 1946], p. 124). Palyi adopts a definition of the U.S. money supply that includes U.S. Savings Bonds at redemption value. However, from our medium-of-exchange perspective, Palyi goes too far by including in the money supply "highly liquid" assets such as Treasury securities of less than one year's maturity, commercial paper and bankers' acceptances. On the other hand, we sympathize with Palyi's apparent support for the inclusion of the cash surrender value of life insurance policies in money-supply figures. See Melchior Palyi, *The Twilight of Gold, 1914–1936: Myths and Realities* (Chicago: Henry Regnery, 1972), pp. 301–15. Albert G. Hart and Peter B. Kenen present a statistical definition of "liquid assets of the nonbank public," including U.S. Savings Bonds and the "net cash values of life insurance," that is very close to the TMS. There are no significant omissions, and the only clearly objectionable item is short-term government securities. See Albert G. Hart and Peter B. Kenen, *Money, Debt and Economic Activity*, 3rd ed. (Englewood Cliffs, N.J.: Prentice-Hall, 1969), pp. 3–6.

[27] Actually, the term "Treasury cash" denotes the small amount of Treasury-held gold which has not been monetized by the issue of gold certificates to the Fed in exchange for Treasury deposits. Nonetheless, since this "nonmonetized" gold stock may be converted into a stock of dollars at any time, via the issue of gold certificates to the Fed, it may be considered a monetary reserve for the redemption of savings bonds. On Treasury cash, see John G. Ranlett, *Money and Banking: An Introduction to Analysis and Policy*, 3rd ed. (New York: John Wiley, 1977), pp. 60–67.

place in the TMS. These are the demand deposits and other deposits held by the U.S. government, foreign official institutions, and foreign commercial banks at U.S. commercial and Fed banks.

The somewhat mysterious exclusion of these items from money-supply measures is typically justified by one recent writer who claims that the deposits of these institutions "… serve an entirely different purpose than the holdings of the general public" or are "… viewed as being held for peculiar reasons."[28] This overemphasis on the particular "motives" for holding money, as opposed to the importance of the quantity of money itself, is one of the modern legacies of the Keynesian revolution.[29]

Moreover, there is nothing at all "peculiar" about the reasons for which such deposits are held. As one modern advocate of their inclusion in money-supply statistics points out:

> The Treasury's deposits are not part of its reserve against money that it has issued, but are rather part of the general fund of the Treasury available for meeting general expenditures. Output is purchased and taxes are collected with the help of these deposits, and they would seem to be as much a part of the money stock with which the economy operates as are the deposits of state and local governments, which are included in adjusted demand deposits. Much the same may be said of Treasury deposits at Federal Reserve Banks. Also foreign-owned deposits at commercial banks are included, so why not foreign-owned deposits at the Federal Reserve?[30]

---

[28] Meyer, *Monetary Economics*, pp. 26–27.

[29] In analyzing the Keynesian motives for holding money, Hart and Kenen cogently argue that "We cannot divide the cash balance of a given holder into definite parts representing each of these motives…. If, for example, he also has accumulated cash for speculative purposes, he also has a margin of safety, so that his needs under the [precautionary] motive are swallowed up in those under the [speculative motive]. Besides, the different motives shade into one another. In analyzing them, it is less important to keep them distinct than to keep track of the common element that binds them all together—*the adaptation of business dealings to uncertainty.*" (Hart and Kenen, *Money, Debt and Economic Activity,* pp. 223–34).

[30] Barger, *Money, Banking and Public Policy,* p. 53.

Finally, pre-Keynesian monetary theorists routinely and properly counted "U.S. Government Deposits" in the "Total Deposits" component of the money supply.[31] This was and is the proper procedure, because it is variations of the total stock of money owned by all economic agents that are of vital importance in analyzing and attempting to forecast inflation and business-cycle phenomena.

Bibliography

Anderson, Benjamin M. [1949] 1979. *Economics and the Public Welfare: A Financial and Economic History of the United States, 1914–1946*, 2nd ed. Indianapolis: Liberty Press.

Barger, Harold. 1968. *Money, Banking and Public Policy*, 2nd ed. Chicago: Rand McNally.

Batten, Dallas S. and Daniel L. Thornton. 1985. "Are Weighted Monetary Aggregates Better Than Simple-Sum M1?" Federal Reserve Bank of St. Louis *Review* 67 (June/July 1985): pp. 29–40.

Chandler, Lester V., and Stephen M. Goldfeld. 1977. *The Economics of Money and Banking*, 7th ed. New York: Harper and Row.

Fetter, Frank A. 1923. *Economics*, vol. 2: *Modern Economic Problems*, 2nd ed. New York: Century.

_____. 1946. "Inflation's Basic Cause: Too Much Money." *Saturday Evening Post* (July 13): p. 124.

Friedman, Milton. 1953. "Commodity-Reserve Currency." In *Essays in Positive Economics*. Chicago: University of Chicago Press.

Gilbert, R. Alton. 1985. "Recent changes in Handling Bank Failures and Their Effects on the Banking Industry." Federal Reserve Bank of St. Louis *Review* 67 (June/July 1985): pp. 21–28.

Hart, Albert G., and Peter B. Kenen. 1969. *Money, Debt and Economic Activity*, 3rd ed. Englewood Cliffs, N.J.: Prentice-Hall.

Kemmerer, Edwin Walter. 1920. *High Prices and Deflation*. Princeton, N.J.: Princton University Press.

Langley, Monica. 1986. "Holds on Checks Annoy Investors in Money Funds." *The Wall Street Journal* (November 11, 1986), p. 39.

---

[31] See, for example: Edwin Walter Kemmerer, *High Prices and Deflation* (Princeton, N.J.: Princeton University Press, 1920), p. 27; Benjamin M. Anderson, *Economics and the Public Welfare A Financial and Economic History of the United States, 1914–1946*, 2nd ed. (Indianapolis: Liberty Press, 1979), pp. 98, 183, 265; and Palyi, *The Twilight of Gold*, p. 36.

Lin, Lin. 1937. "Are Time Deposits Money?" *American Economic Review* 27 (March 1937): p. 85.

Meyer, Paul A. 1982. *Monetary Economics and Financial Markets*. Homewood, Ill.: Richard D. Irwin.

Osborne, Dale K. 1984. "Ten Approaches to the Definition of Money." Federal Reserve Bank of Dallas *Economic Review* (March): pp. 1–23.

_____. 1985. "What Is Money Today?" Federal Reserve Bank of Dallas *Economic Review* (January): pp. 1–15.

Palyi, Melchior. 1961. *An Inflation Primer*. Chicago: Henry Regnery.

_____. 1972. *The Twilight of Gold, 1914–1936: Myths and Realities*. Chicago: Henry Regnery.

Ranlett, John G. 1977. *Money and Banking: An Introduction to Analysis and Policy*, 3rd ed. New York: John Wiley.

Rothbard, Murray N. 1963. *America's Great Depression*. Princeton, N.J.: D. Van Nostrand.

_____. 1978. "Austrian Definitions of the Supply of Money." In *New Directions in Austrian Economics*, Louis M. Spadaro, ed., pp. 143–56. Kansas City: Sheed Andrews and McMeel.

_____. 1983. *The Mystery of Banking*. New York: Richardson and Snyder.

Salerno, Joseph T. 1983. "Gold Standards: True and False." *The Cato Journal* 3 (Spring 1983): pp. 255–58.

_____. 1984. "What Investors and Depositors Should Know about Banks and the Financial Services Revolution." *Jerome Smith's Investment Perspectives* 2 (June 1984): pp. 3–4.

Sprague, Irvine H. 1986. *Bailout: an Insider's Account of Bank Failures and Rescues*. New York: Basic Books.

White, Lawrence H. 1986. "A Subjectivist Perspective on the Definition and Identification of Money." In *Subjectivism, Intelligibility and Economic Understanding: Essays in Honor of Ludwig M. Lachmann on His Eightieth Birthday*, Israel M. Kirzner, ed., pp. 301–14. London: Macmillan.

Yeager, Leland. 1970. "The Medium of Exchange." In *Monetary Theory: Selected Readings*, pp. 37–60. Baltimore: Penguin Books.

_____. 1978. "What Are Banks?" *Atlantic Economic Journal* 6 (December 1978): pp. 1–14.

CHAPTER 4

A Simple Model of
the Theory of Money Prices

1. Introduction

Ludwig von Mises[1] is generally and properly credited by economists of the contemporary Austrian school with having reintegrated monetary theory with general economic theory, from which it had been severed by the neoclassical quantity theory.[2] However, broader recognition of Mises's contribution in merging monetary and value theory has been hindered by certain deficiencies in the organization of his exposition and by the absence of a straightforward heuristic for conveying his achievement.[3] Indeed, it is questionable

From: "A Simple Model of the Theory of Money Prices," *Quarterly Journal of Austrian Economics*, vol. 9, no. 4 (2006), pp. 39–55.

[1] Ludwig von Mises, *The Theory of Money and Credit*, 3rd ed., trans. H.E. Batson (Indianapolis, Ind.: Liberty Classics, 1981); idem, *Human Action: A Treatise on Economics*, Scholar's Edition, Introduction by Jeffrey M Herbener, Hans-Hermann Hoppe, and Joseph T. Salerno (Auburn, Ala.: Ludwig von Mises Institute, 1998).

[2] In a neglected work, Will Mason argued compellingly that the unity of monetary and value theory in classical economics was sundered by early neoclassical quantity theorists such as Francis A. Walker and Joseph S. Nicholson (Will Mason, *Clarification of the Monetary Standard: The Concept and Its Relations to Monetary Policies and Objectives* [University Park: Pennsylvania State University Press, 1963], pp. 41–63).

[3] For example, in *Human Action* Mises placed the chapters that dealt with entrepreneurial profit and loss, the general pricing process, and the pricing of the factors of

whether Mises himself was completely aware of what he had accomplished in this area. He had in fact implicitly demonstrated that there is no theory of money properly speaking, but only a theory of money prices. It was left to Mises's leading follower in monetary theory, Murray N. Rothbard,[4] to formulate a mode of exposition that facilitated the clear delineation of economics as a unified theory of money prices.

In this paper a simple model is constructed that epitomizes Rothbard's contribution and captures the essential elements and relationships that constitute the theory of money prices. This model hopefully will also serve as a useful pedagogical device for those who are interested in introducing the unique Austrian view of the central role of money in the economy to their intermediate macroeconomics classes.

Section 2 presents Rothbard's formulation of the theory, including his innovative conceptualization of the demand for money, in the form of an equation. Section 3 shows the implications of the theory within a simple exchange economy. In Section 4 the restrictive assumptions of this model are dropped and the analysis is applied to the real-world economy. The implications of the theory for the meaning of Say's Law and of the quantity theory of money are briefly indicated in Section 5.

2. Rothbard's Equation

The exchange demand for each good—the amount of money that will be spent in exchange for the good—equals the stock of money in the society minus the following: the exchange demands for all other goods and the reservation demand for money. In short, the amount

---

production before the chapter on "Indirect Exchange," in which he discussed the origin and subjective valuation of money, pp. 286–311, 324–36). This unfortunate order of topics tended to obscure the central role of money prices in entrepreneurial appraisement and allocation on factor markets. Also, Mises's discussion of the demand for money (ibid., pp. 398–402) is very sketchy and cannot bear the full weight of a theory of money prices.

[4] Murray N. Rothbard, *Man, Economy, and State: A Treatise on Economic Principles* (Auburn, Ala.: Ludwig von Mises Institute, [1962] 1993).

spent on X good equals the total money supply minus the amount spent on other goods and the amount kept in cash balances.... Now, when all goods are considered, the exchange demand for goods equals the stock of money minus the reservation demand for money.... The exchange demand for money equals the stock of all goods minus the reservation demand for goods.[5]

Now the equation implicit in the above quotation from Rothbard[6] may be written as follows:

1. $(P_1 \times Q_1) + (P_2 \times Q_2) + \ldots + (P_N \times Q_N) = MS - MD_R$

Since the exchange demand for money is the obverse of the exchange demand for all goods and therefore equal to the total receipts of money for the sale of goods:

2. $MD_E = (P_1 \times Q_1) + (P_2 \times Q_2) + \ldots + (P_N \times Q_N)$

Substituting equation 2 into equation 1 gives us

3. $MD_E = MS - MD_R$

Rearranging terms, we get the statement that the supply of money equals the total demand for money, the familiar condition of equilibrium in the market for cash balances:

4. $MS = MD_E + MD_R = MD$

For purposes of our analysis, we substitute equation 2 and the equilibrium condition becomes

5. $MS = (P_1 \times Q_1) + (P_2 \times Q_2) + \ldots + (P_N \times Q_N) + MD_R$

where:

---

[5] Murray Rothbard was the first to analyze the demand for money in terms of its exchange demand and reservation demand components (Murray N. Rothbard, *Man, Economy, and State: A Treatise on Economic Principles* [Auburn, Ala.: Ludwig von Mises Institute, [1962] 1993], pp. 350–56, 662–67). In 1913, Herbert J. Davenport also clearly identified these two partial demands for money but ultimately failed to integrate them into an overall theory of the demand for money (Herbert J. Davenport, *The Economics of Enterprise* [New York: Augustus M. Kelley, [1913] 1968], pp. 267–73). The exchange demand for money bears no relation to the Keynesian transactions demand for money, which is an attempt to classify the motives for holding cash balances, i.e., "transactions," "precautionary," and "speculative."

[6] Rothbard, *Man, Economy and State*, p. 713.

MS = Money Supply

MD = Total Demand for Money

MD_E = Exchange Demand for Money

MD_R = Reservation Demand for Money

$P_1 \ldots N$ = Market-clearing price of nonmonetary
commodities 1 to N

$Q_1 \ldots N$ = Market-clearing quantity of nonmonetary
commodities 1 to N[7]

3. The Analytical Framework
In A Simple Model

What we might call Rothbard's Equation defines simultaneous equilibrium in all goods markets and the market for cash balances, yielding a set of money prices that embodies both relative prices and the purchasing power of money. We illustrate the application of Rothbard's Equation with the four graphs below, which represent an economy comprising three commodities (A, B, and C) and a general medium of exchange. The commodities are directly produced by the households in the economy so that there are no factor markets or payments. In addition we assume that leisure is not a consumer's good, although each individual's labor is absolutely limited by total exhaustion after a fixed number of hours per day. It is also assumed that each good is produced by labor and a completely specific land factor

---

[7] It is important to be clear about the precise sense in which the term "market-clearing price" is used in the theory of money prices, and about what this use of the term implies for the formulation of supply and demand schedules. The theory of money prices deals with quantities of money that are actually transferred in exchange. Mises called them "actual market prices" (*Human Action*, p. 327). Marget called them "realized prices" (Arthur W. Marget, *The Theory of Prices: A Re-examination of the Central Problems of Monetary Theory* [New York: Augustus M. Kelley, [1938–1942] 1966], vol. 2, p. 222). Therefore the demand and supply curves that are relevant to the determination of money prices are instantaneous curves whose shape and position inevitably embody speculative forecasts and incomplete knowledge of arbitrage opportunities. For a deep analysis of this issue see Marget, *Theory of Prices*, vol. 2, pp. 221–318. For a summary of Marget's analysis see Joseph T. Salerno, "Ludwig von Mises's Monetary Theory in Light of Modern Monetary Thought," *Review of Austrian Economics* 8, no. 1 (1994): pp. 100–03 [reprinted here as Chapter 2].

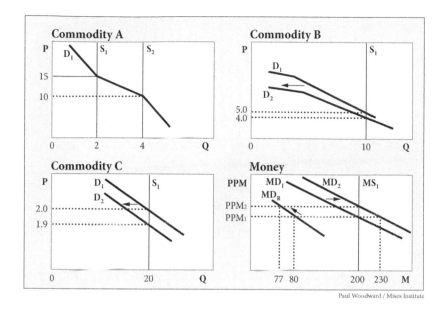

Paul Woodward / Mises Institute

owned by the household and that none of the producing households consumes any of the good it produces. These assumptions ensure that production is costless and the supply curve of each good is perfectly inelastic with respect to its price.

We further assume that the money commodity is permanently fixed in supply and has no use as an input in any production process. The markets for the three commodities run simultaneously on Sunday of every week, when all exchanges are made, and the commodities purchased are then consumed over the course of the week. All markets clear over the course of the market day and there is no false trading. There are no credit transactions; all payments are made in money. Finally, household consumption and liquidity preferences, resource endowments, and technical knowledge are liable to change from week to week resulting in uncertainty regarding future commodity prices and the purchasing power of money.

In the initial equilibrium position of our simple economy, determined by the intersection of demand and supply curves D_1 and S_1 respectively in the goods' markets and MD_1 and MS_1 in the market for cash balances:

$P_A = \$15.00; Q_A = 2$ units

$P_B = \$5.00; Q_B = 10$ units

$P_C = \$2.00; Q_C = 20$ units

$MS = \$200$

And therefore:

$MD_E = (\$15 \times 2) + (\$5 \times 10) + (\$2 \times 20) =$
$\qquad \$30 + \$50 + \$40 = \$120.$

This represents the total amount of money demanded by household-producers in exchange for commodities each week.

Subtracting the exchange demand from the existing money stock yields:

$MD_R = MS - MD_E = \$200 - \$120 = \$80.$

This is the total amount of money that households reserve in cash balances each week.[8]

Thus Rothbard's Equation is satisfied, the entire stock of money is demanded in exchange or reserved in cash balances and the money market clears along with all commodity markets:

$MS = MD_E + MD_R$ or $\$200 = \$120 + \$80$

Now let us assume that there is an increase of productivity in industry A due, e.g., to discovery of more accessible sources of the specific land input, and the supply curve of commodity A shifts out to 4 per week or S_2 and its market-clearing price falls from \$15 to \$10. We further assume that the demand curve for A is elastic over this range of prices and that the total expenditure on A therefore rises. This implies that in the new equilibrium position there must be a net reduction in total expenditure on commodities B and C or a reduction in dollars reserved in cash holdings or a combination of both.

---

[8] A positive reservation demand for cash balances is motivated by general uncertainty associated with the possibility of exogenous changes in the data, i.e., technological advances that increase goods or result in the availability of new ones, organizational innovations, changing availabilities of original resources, autonomous changes in consumer tastes and preferences including time preferences, all of which result in unforeseeable alterations in money prices, incomes, and wealth.

On the market for money, the increase in the overall stock of goods offered in exchange at the initially existing money prices represents an increase in the exchange demand for money, causing the total demand curve for money to shift to the right to MD_2 and a temporary excess demand for money to develop equal to $30, the current total price of the two additional units of A. Given the fixed supply of money, the purchasing power of money (PPM) must rise: i.e., commodity prices must fall, to accommodate the increased total demand.

In our example, the demands for B and C both decline to D_2 on the relevant market. Note also that, as the PPM rises, the nominal quantity of dollars reserved in cash balances is decreased along the reservation demand curve (MD_R) from $80 to $77, and the release of these dollars moderates the fall in money prices. This latter effect permits total spending on commodities, that is, the exchange demand for money, to increase from $120 to $123.

The new overall market equilibrium is as follows:

P_A = $10.00; Q_A = 4 units

P_B = $4.50; Q_B = 10 units

P_C = $1.90; Q_C = 20 units

MS = $200

And therefore:

MD_E = ($10 x 4) + ($4.50 x 10) + ($1.90 x 20) = $40 + $45 + $38 = $123 (the total amount of money demanded by household-producers in exchange for commodities each week) and

MD_R = MS − MD_E = $200 − $123 = $77 (the total amount of money that households reserve in cash balances each week)

Thus Rothbard's Equation is once again satisfied and the money market clears along with all commodity markets:

MS = MD_E + MD_R (= $200 = $123 + $77)

Interestingly, although the reservation demand for money has fallen in nominal terms, as pointed out above, it has increased in

terms of all three commodities, i.e., in real terms, as shown by the calculations below:

Equilibrium 1	Equilibrium 2
$MD_R / P_A = \$80 / \$15 / A = 5.33A$	$MD_R / P_A = \$77 / \$10 / A = 7A$
$MD_R / P_B = \$80 / \$5 / B = 16B$	$MD_R / P_B = \$77 / \$4.50 / B = 17.11B$
$MD_R / P_C = \$80 / \$2 / C = 40C$	$MD_R / P_C = \$77 / \$1.90 / C = 40.53C$

Since the nominal money supply has remained fixed at $200, these calculations imply that the total real money supply in the economy has increased. Thus, in our example, real cash balances and commodity A are complements, while commodities A and B and A and C are substitutes. The example could easily have been constructed to show different patterns of relationships between A and the other commodities and real cash balances while still satisfying Rothbard's Equation. We could have assumed, for example, that the range of the demand curve for A from 2 to 4 units was inelastic, resulting in a decreased expenditure on A and an increased demand and price for B while the demands for C and cash balances remained unchanged. In this case A and B would be complements, the cross price elasticity between A and C would equal zero, and the nominal reservation demand for cash balances would be unaffected.

The analytical framework provided by Rothbard's Equation makes it clear that the own price and cross price elasticities of demand for and between the various commodities and money are not exogenous and objective determinants of market outcomes but are themselves the product of the interaction of subjective value scales that constitute the dynamic market process. This allows us to finally recognize precisely where the strict marginal utility foundations of Austro-Wicksteedian theory of supply and demand clash with the Hicksian-neoclassical theory based on income and substitution effects. In our original example, the raw fact is that there appear on the market 2 more units of good A. The structure of people's value scales determines that the demand curve for A is elastic below the former equilibrium price, resulting in a greater expenditure on A and less on B and C and fewer dollars reserved in cash balances. Had value scales of market participants been structured differently so that the marginal utilities of additional units of A had declined more rapidly relative to those of B, C, and money balances, then the new equilibrium price of A might have settled at $2 per unit. In this case, total spending on A would have dropped dramatically from $30 to $8 (rather than increasing to $40) and the outcomes on the other markets would have been radically different. Any attempt to decompose the changes on these various markets into "substitution" and "income" effects are meaningless and irrelevant to our understanding of how the market process determines actual money prices. Prices at any moment are determined by the existing stocks of the various goods and money and existing value scales of buyers and sellers (which incorporate available though imperfect knowledge and speculative and fallible anticipations of future market conditions).

Lastly, we note that at the end of the market day equilibrium prevails in the market, in the sense that a different pattern of allocation of the existing stocks of commodities and money would not be mutually beneficial to any pair of market participants. This Mengerian exchange equilibrium is a real state of affairs that comes into being again and again in particular markets. This state was referred to as "momentary equilibrium" by Böhm-Bawerk[9] and "the plain state of rest" by Mises.[10] The analysis based on Rothbard's Equation thus reveals that the plain state of rest is a recurrent condition that punctuates the pricing process in the overall market.[11]

----

[9] Eugen von Böhm-Bawerk, *Value and Price: An Abstract*, 2nd ed. trans. George D. Huncke (Grove City, Penn.: Libertarian Press, 1973).

[10] See Mises, *Human Action*, p. 245. Menger was perhaps the first to recognize exchange equilibrium, or "rest," as a real condition of the market: "[W]e therefore observe the phenomenon of a perpetual succession of exchange transactions. But even in this chain of transactions we can, by observing closely, find points of rest at particular times, for particular persons, and with particular kinds of goods. At these points of rest, no exchange of goods takes place because an economic limit to exchange has already been reached." (Carl Menger, *Principles of Economics*, trans. James Dingwall and Bert F. Hoselitz [New York: New York University Press, [1950, 1976], p. 188).

[11] Of course, in the real-world economy with continuous and costly production, this state of rest is ephemeral, not merely because of recurring exogenous changes in the

4. From the Simple Model to the Real World

For purposes of pedagogical clarity we have formulated the analytical framework of Rothbard's Equation in the context of an extremely simple model. We can now drop the model's restrictive assumptions and show that the analysis applies to the real-world pricing process in a market economy with continuous markets for a multitude of consumer goods, factor services, capital assets, and credit instruments. At any moment there are buyers and sellers consummating exchanges across all markets in the economy. As noted above, the prices and quantities that define the momentary exchange equilibria in these markets are rigidly governed by Rothbard's Equation. That is, at any moment, the total stock of money in the economy must equal the exchange demand for money, or the total money expenditure on all goods, plus the reservation demand for money, or the portion of his money assets that everyone retains in his cash balance rather than exchanges on the market. Moreover, since at a given time there is always a stock of previously produced goods in inventory and ready for sale, the assumption of costless production in our model may be dispensed with without altering our analytical conclusions. (We will deal with the assumption of a vertical market-day supply curve below.)

For instance, on October 31, 2005, the total money supply as defined by M2 was $6,631 billion.[12] Assuming for the sake of argument that this aggregate correctly identifies the stock of money in the U.S. economy, if $500 billion of transactions took place between 1:00 pm and 1:05 pm that day, then the stock of money retained in cash balances was $6,131 billion (= $6,631 billion minus $500 billion). The prices paid times the quantities exchanged in all markets sum to $500 billion, thus satisfying Rothbard's Equation. Note that this equation is not a mere tautological accounting identity that somehow exogenously constrains prices and quantities in market transactions. Rather it is the result of the moment-to-moment interaction of subjective rankings of goods and money on individual

---

data but also because the pattern of prices that the plain state of rest defines invariably results in profits and losses, which in turn reshape the supply and demand schedules.

[12] Federal Reserve Bank of St. Louis, *U.S. Financial Data* (November 10, 2005), p. 15.

value scales in the unitary market process that coordinates all elements of supply and demand.

If we suppose that, during this historical interval, the marginal utilities of cash balances ranked lower on people's value scales because of, for example, a general fear of an imminent rise in the inflation rate, then, all other things equal, the reservation demand, and therefore the total demand for money would have been lower. Total spending on goods would have been higher, say $800 billion instead of $500 billion, as people disgorged an additional $300 billion from cash balances during that five minute period and caused a higher level of overall prices. At a lower PPM, the exchange demand for money would thus have been higher—in a quantity and not a schedule sense[13]—and exactly equal to $800 billion since it is the obverse of total spending on goods. Rothbard's Equation would be satisfied as the $300 billion decline in the reserved money supply corresponded to an upward shift in the demand schedules in commodity markets that raised market-clearing prices and expanded the exchange demand for money by precisely the amount of the actual transfer of newly released cash balances necessary to pay these higher prices.

Of course the foregoing example does not imply that the full adjustment of commodity prices to a change in the demand for money occurs immediately. Rather it is meant to lead us to conceive of the monetary adjustment process as a sequence of momentary states of rest that, ceteris paribus, will reach a final state of rest only after a definite lapse of time in which all prices and incomes have been affected.[14] It is important to reiterate, however, that every succeeding step of the adjustment process following the initial step discussed above is defined by a specific pattern of commodity prices and

---

[13] As illustrated in our simple model, Rothbard's Equation implies that an increase in the exchange demand schedule for money occurs only as a result of the increase in the total stock of goods available net of the reservation demand for goods and results in a decrease of overall prices.

[14] For the classic exposition of the monetary adjustment process, see F.A. Hayek, *Monetary Nationalism and International Stability* (New York: Augustus M. Kelley, [1937] 1971), pp. 17–25. The monetary adjustment process is delineated in terms of plain and final states of rest in Salerno, "Ludwig von Mises's Monetary Theory," pp. 96–106.

quantities and money transfers and holdings that culminates in an exchange equilibrium and is fully described by Rothbard's Equation.

Let us now examine the effect on our analysis of dropping the other main assumptions of our simple model. Introducing capitalist ownership of production processes and corresponding markets for both original (land and labor) and intermediate (capital goods) factors would increase the exchange demand for money as laborers and land owners supply their factor services in exchange for money rents. Likewise, in a structure of production consisting of multiple stages, the capitalist-producers of intermediate goods will exert a positive influence on the exchange demand for money as they sell or rent their assets to capitalists in immediately lower stages.[15] Capitalist-entrepreneurs will also reserve some of their money earnings in cash balance for business uses due to the unavoidably uncertain nature of production for the market, especially uncertainty regarding the amount and timing of their monetary revenues and expenditures. This will raise the overall reservation demand for money.

What about our assumption of the vertical market supply curve for all goods? In reality, producers and other owners (e.g., wholesalers, retailers, second-hand dealers, etc.) of more or less durable goods generally exercise a short-run speculative inventory or reservation demand for their own products, most commonly by setting minimum reservation prices.[16] This means that a portion of the total stock of goods that are technologically finished and ready for sale or rent at any moment to lower-order capitalists or consumers may be retained in inventory and therefore does not have an effect on the exchange demand for money. Using Wicksteedian analysis of the goods side of the economy, this reservation demand for a given good raises the total demand curve along the vertical total stock curve of the good, thereby

---

[15] On the effect that a transition to a more "capitalistic" structure of production has on the exchange demand for money, see F.A. Hayek, *Prices and Production*, 2nd ed. (New York: Augustus M. Kelley, [1935] 1967), pp. 53–54, 66–68; and Rothbard, *Man, Economy, and State*, pp. 478–79, 891–92 fn. 11, 12.

[16] In the case of labor, the reservation demand may also, or even mainly, be driven by considerations of leisure, which is desired as a consumer's good in the real world, contrary to the assumption of our model.

increasing its price.[17] Economy-wide, the phenomenon of inventory demand by owners of existing goods tends to lower the exchange demand for money and exert upward pressure on overall prices. Thus, as Rothbard[18] reminds us, "The exchange demand for money equals the total stock of all goods minus the reservation demand for all goods."[19]

Jettisoning the assumption of the absence of credit transactions leads to a decrease in the reservation demand for money. With ready access to credit markets provided, for example, by credit cards and overdraft facilities, households and businesses do not need to retain as much of their income in cash balances to meet both anticipated and unforeseen events. Also, highly liquid securities, including high-grade debt instruments with a short maturity, function as what Rothbard[20] calls "quasi money" that permit their owners to economize on the holding of cash balances. The emergence and growth of a credit market thus results in a decline in the PPM and a corresponding increase in overall spending on goods and services per period. The higher total expenditure on goods resulting from the increase in prices constitutes a greater exchange demand for money whose total when summed together with the reduced reservation demand will equal the total money supply.

It should be noted that credit transactions themselves, e.g., the sale of a bond for present money, do not directly affect the overall demand for money during the period in which they occur, because

---

[17] Wicksteed's total demand-stock analysis of price determination can be found in: Philip H. Wicksteed, *The Common Sense of Political Economy and Selected Papers and Reviews on Economic Theory*, ed. Lionel Robbins (New York: Augustus M. Kelley, [1932] 1967), vol. 1, pp. 213–38; vol. 2, pp. 493–526, 784–88; Kenneth E. Boulding, *Economic Analysis* (New York: Harper and Brothers, 1941), pp. 52–79; and Rothbard, *Man, Economy, and State*, pp. 118–40.

[18] Rothbard, *Man, Economy, and State*, p. 713.

[19] Strictly speaking, the exchange demand for money is calculated by summing up the series of products of the price of each good multiplied by the amount of the existing stock of that good and then subtracting the sum of the series of products of the price of each good multiplied by the number of units of that good retained in sellers' inventories.

[20] Rothbard, *Man, Economy, and State*, p. 723.

they constitute the transfer of money from one person's cash balance to another's so that any effects on the reservation demand for money cancel out. The seller of a security accumulates the proceeds of the sale in his cash balance until a later time when he spends it on productive factors or on consumers' goods, while the buyer of a security necessarily reserved the sale price of the security from income earned in an earlier period. Thus there is no net effect on the exchange or reservation demand for money in the current period, although the transaction does influence the current rate of interest.

5. Some Implications

The analytical framework based on Rothbard's Equation has implications for a number of central issues of macroeconomic theory. We now briefly consider two of these.

A. Rothbard's Equation and Say's Law

Rothbard's Equation facilitates a clarification of the precise meaning of Say's Law. The postwar controversy over this law, which involved Oskar Lange and Don Patinkin among other notables, revolved around the conditions under which "absolute prices" (i.e., money prices) as opposed to "relative prices" are determinate.[21] In their classic article summarizing the debate, Becker and Baumol[22] concluded:

> The Cambridge [quantity] equation implies that for every relative price structure there exists a unique absolute price level at which the money market will be in equilibrium (Say's Equality). This is equivalent to stating that for every set of relative prices there exists a price level which brings about over-all equilibrium in the commodity markets, i.e., the total quantity of money offered for commodities is equal to the

---

[21] A very clear textbook exposition of the meaning of this controversy for Austrian-oriented macroeconomic analysis can be found in Charles W. Baird, *Elements of Macroeconomics*, 2nd ed. (New York: West Publishing, 1981), pp. 63–78. I am indebted to John Egger for bringing this source to my attention.

[22] Gary S. Becker and William J. Baumol, in *Essays in Economic Thought: Aristotle to Marshall*, eds. Joseph J. Spengler and William R. Allen (Chicago: Rand McNally, [1952] 1960), p. 758.

total value of commodities supplied. Thus it is clear that his version of Say's Law is compatible with determinacy of an absolute price level.

The problem with the formulation of Say's Law as Say's Equality is that it relies on a meaningless concept, the absolute price level, and an unnecessary equation ($M = kPQ$) that effectively dichotomizes the pricing process. As our simple model above indicates, Rothbard's equation is based on an analysis that treats the structure of money prices as the real and elemental outcome of an ongoing pricing process. The pattern of "relative" prices is embedded in the constellation of actual money prices and only becomes meaningful as subjective inferences by participants during this process. The supply of and demand for money are thus co-determinants equally with the respective supplies of and demands for commodities of an integrated structure of money prices. A price that exists in absolute isolation from other prices is inconceivable; every price is meaningful only in its relation to all other prices.[23] Money prices are simply pieces of property that are exchanged for other kinds of property and, as such, their purely abstract interrelations are meaningless to human actors. The entrepreneur is guided in his choices by the actual quantities of money he expects to pay out and receive for alternative combinations of goods and never by an immaterial pattern of relative prices. The distinction between absolute and relative prices is redundant at best and grossly misleading at worst. It is completely irrelevant to Say's Law.

Using Becker and Baumol's terminology, let us assume that "the demand for money flow" (or the overall supply of commodities at given prices) exceeds "the supply of money flow" (or the overall demand for commodities at given prices). Expressing this glut in commodity markets in terms of Rothbard's Equation,

---

[23] Mises, *Human Action*, p. 389:

It would be absurd to look upon a definite price as if it were an isolated object in itself. A price ... does not indicate a relationship to something unchanging, but merely the instantaneous position in a kaleidoscopically changing assemblage. In this collection of things considered valuable by the value judgments of acting man each particle's place is interrelated with those of all other particles. What is called a price is always a relationship within an integrated system which is the composite of human valuations.

$$(P_1 \times Q_1) + (P_2 \times Q_2) + \ldots + (P_N \times Q_N) = MD_E > MS - MD_R,$$

reveals that the total demand for money is greater than the stock of money and thus,

$$MD_E + MD_R > MS.$$

Given that the marginal utilities of money and commodities are intertwined on unitary individual value scales, then, "commodity demand functions" are not "homogeneous of degree zero in prices alone." This means that the demand schedules for individual goods must inevitably be influenced by an "excess demand" for cash balances. Thus any insufficiency of cash balances will manifest instantaneously as a surplus of particular commodities, resulting in a fall in commodity prices and a corresponding increase in the purchasing power of money until exchange equilibrium is simultaneously re-established in the money and commodity markets. This is illustrated in the simple model in section 3 above, where "an increase in the supply of goods creates its own demand" by precipitating adjustments in the commodity and money markets that result in the actual flow demand for money (MD_E) being brought into equilibrium with the flow supply of money ($MD_E = MS - MD_R$), while the stock of money and the total demand for money are likewise equilibrated ($MS = MD$).

B. The Vacuousness of the Quantity Theory

Now that we have gained the analytical vantage point of Rothbard's Equation, we can see that the Quantity Theory of Money as expounded in terms of the Quantity Equation gets matters exactly wrong: it is not the flow of spending that determines the price level, given a level of output that is exogenously determined in some separate and mysterious real process. Rather the money prices and quantities of goods exchanged, which are codetermined in the overall market process, are the causal determinants of the spending flow. This bears elaboration.

Let's begin with the Quantity Equation as conventionally stated: $MV = PQ$. Our simple model above reveals that the real action is on the right side of the equation. Individuals' utility rankings of money and the various kinds of commodities give rise to schedules of monetary bids and offers in commodity markets. The interaction of these momentary supply and demand schedules determines a system of money prices and, simultaneously, the value of the monetary unit, since, as we saw, the latter is nothing more or less then the array of exchange ratios obtained by inverting money prices. The mechanical passing of a specific sum of money from one hand to the next in exchange, that is, "spending," is completely governed by the money price that has been antecedently established by the exchanging parties. Thus the money spent is merely an outcome of the pricing process and in no sense a causal factor. In other words, the aggregate flow of money spending is determined by the value of money and not the other way around.

The argument may be restated mathematically. Let P represent a vector whose elements, the lower case p's, are the money prices of all goods in the economy, and let Q represent a vector whose elements, the lower case q's, consist of the simultaneously determined quantities of goods exchanged at each of those prices. The multiplication of these two vectors yields an inner product. This product is equal to the total money spent by all buyers and received as income by all sellers in the economy during a given period of time.[24] As I noted above, the total amount of money spent cannot be said to be a causal influence on the value of money, because the value of money is already completely embedded in the structure of money prices, i.e., the elements of P, which were previously determined in exchanges on goods markets. Now, we may, if we like, divide total spending, the inner product PQ, by the existing stock of money, M, and label the resulting quotient "V." Then, by transposing the terms of our equation, we will have MV = PQ. But this will not alter the fact that the variations of the product on the left side of the equation, MV, are never independent of changes originating in the price and quantity vectors. More fundamentally, MV is not even knowable until these vectors have been determined.

---

[24] Contemporary monetary theorists interpret P as some kind of statistical construct. However, Clark Warburton, an influential forerunner of modern monetarism, defined the right side of the equation in a manner similar to Rothbard's, as "the summation of a series of arithmetic products obtained by multiplying the price of each type of product by the quantity sold at that price." (Clark Warburton, *Depression, Inflation, and Monetary Policy: Selected Papers, 1945–1953* [Baltimore: Johns Hopkins University Press, 1966], pp. 106–07) .

Note carefully that this does not mean that the quantity of money is "endogenous" or that it is irrelevant to the pricing process. To the contrary, as Rothbard's Equation has made clear, the stock of money is one of the immediate determinants of the structure of money prices and the purchasing power of money, in conjunction with its immediately past purchasing power, the existing stocks of goods, and the distribution of ownership and the relative rankings of goods and of money among market participants. In other words, the effect of a change in the stock of money on its purchasing power is direct and unmediated by a change in spending, because valuing and pricing are the logical and temporal antecedents of spending. Thus, to refer to a specific magnitude of total spending without first having specified the value of money is completely vacuous.

This argument can be illustrated with two examples. First assume that there occurs an increase in the stock of money. All other things equal, this will lower the marginal utility of money relative to the marginal utilities of goods on the value scales of the immediate recipients of the new money. The immediate result will be a shift of demand curves to the right and a corresponding rise in prices.[25] Now, by definition, this depreciation of the money unit means that a greater amount of money than before will be given in exchange for particular goods. We may

---

[25] Perhaps it is better to speak of a "rise" of demand curves instead of a "shift to the right," because this older terminology directs attention to the correct causal relation between the increase in money and increased spending. On the individual level, the rise in his demand curve for a particular good reflects the fact that the individual is now prepared to offer greater sums of money than previously for each successive unit of the good. Ceteris paribus, the increased monetary bids for the good by those experiencing a rising demand for it will result in a higher market price and this, in turn, will cause greater aggregate spending by all who wish to obtain units of the good. On the other hand, "a shift to the right in the demand curve" is often misinterpreted to mean that it is the increased spending on the good at the previous equilibrium price that "drives" its price up. Earlier Mengerian price theorists employed the terminology of rising and falling demand (and supply) curves. See, for example, Frank A. Fetter, "Markets and Prices," in *Economic Principles and Problems*, 3rd ed., ed. Walter E. Spahr (New York: Farrer and Rinehart, 1937), vol. 1, p. 492; and Davenport, *The Economics of Enterprise*, p. 49. Even as late as 1959, Henry Hazlitt (*The Failure of the "New Economics": An Analysis of the Keynesian Fallacies* [Princeton, N.J.: D. Van Nostrand, 1959], p. 271) clung to the terminology of rising and falling demand curves in preference to "the fashionable technical jargon, 'moved to the right' or 'to the left.'"

express this fact by saying that total spending has increased, but this is a trivial implication of the general rise of money prices, which, in turn, was directly caused by the lowered marginal utilities for money.[26]

The second example that undermines the quantity theorists' emphasis on spending as the proximate cause of fluctuations in the value of money is the case of a large redistribution of cash balances between groups in the economy, let us say laborers and capitalist-entrepreneurs, which leaves the overall demand for money unchanged. Assume laborers place higher valuations on money and choose to build up their cash balances by restricting their demands for goods, while capitalist-entrepreneurs seek to run down theirs by increasing reservation demand for their own products. These changed dispositions would be manifested in a sharp leftward shift of supply and demand curves on all goods' markets. Assuming that both supply and demand are reduced proportionally in each market, the final outcome would be a sharp decrease in the number of exchanges with no alteration in the value of money. In Rothbard's Equation this would be expressed as a reduction in the exchange demand for money on the part of business firms that is simultaneously and exactly offset by an increase in the reservation demand for money by households. The outcome would be that less money changed hands or was "spent" during the market day.

In terms of the Quantity Equation, all elements of Q would decline precipitously while the elements of P remained unchanged,

---

[26] Although Eugen von Böhm-Bawerk wrote little on money, he was one of the first to emphasize that the "subjective value of the medium of exchange" for buyers and for sellers were two of the direct determinants of money prices and that aggregate spending was an outcome of the pricing process. See Eugen von Böhm-Bawerk, *Basic Principles of Economic Value*, trans. Hans F. Sennholz (Grove City, Penn.: Libertarian Press, 2005), pp. 136–37, 143, 145, 153–54. He wrote, for example:

> At such moments [of crisis], [sellers] place especially high value on the medium of exchange, money, and for that reason are compelled to reconcile themselves to accepting small amounts of money for the goods they offer for sale. Herein lies part of the explanation of inordinately low prices at forced sales or in economic crises. (*Basic Principles of Economic Value*, p. 145)

For an enlightening treatment of Böhm-Bawerk's remarks on the determination of money prices, see Tjardus Greidanus, *The Value of Money: A Discussion of Various Monetary Theories, and an Exposition of the Yield Theory of the Value of Money* (London: P.S. King and Son, 1932), pp. 137–44.

causing a severe constriction of total spending MV. Now, presumably, quantity theorists would respond that a fall in spending does not affect the value of money if real output declines proportionally. But this is beside the point, for in this example real output did not change at all. Q declined because there was a revolution of the relative positions of money and goods on various individuals' value scales that was expressed in a reduction of the number of monetary transactions. The fall in Q implies, but was not caused by, the fall in spending.

6. Conclusion

The goal of this paper is not to present a comprehensive restatement of the theory of money prices as it developed in the Austrian tradition from Menger to Mises and Rothbard. Rather it is to formulate a heuristic device that facilitates a concise delineation of the theory's main points and helps in illustrating a few of its major implications. This endeavor is crucial to disseminating the theory to a broader audience and stimulating further interest in refining and advancing it.

Bibliography

Baird, Charles W. 1981. *Elements of Macroeconomics*. 2nd ed. New York: West Publishing.

Becker, Gary S., and William J. Baumol. [1952] 1960. In *Essays in Economic Thought: Aristotle to Marshall*. Joseph J. Spengler and William R. Allen, eds. Chicago: Rand McNally. pp. 753–71.

Böhm-Bawerk, Eugen von. 1973. *Value and Price: An Abstract*. 2nd ed. George D. Huncke, trans. Grove City, Penn.: Libertarian Press.

_____. 2005. *Basic Principles of Economic Value*. Hans F. Sennholz, trans. Grove City, Penn.: Libertarian Press.

Boulding, Kenneth E. 1941. *Economic Analysis*. New York: Harper and Brothers.

Davenport, Herbert J. [1913] 1968. *The Economics of Enterprise*. New York: Augustus M. Kelley.

Federal Reserve Bank of St. Louis. 2005. *U.S. Financial Data* (November 10, 2005). Available at http://research.stlouisfed.org.

Greidanus, Tjardus. 1932. *The Value of Money: A Discussion of Various Monetary Theories, and an Exposition of the Yield Theory of the Value of Money*. London: P.S. King and Son.

Fetter, Frank A. 1937. "Markets and Prices." In *Economic Principles and Problems*, 3rd ed., vol. 1, Walter E. Spahr, ed., pp. 478–502. New York: Farrar and Rinehart.

Hayek, F.A. [1937] 1971. *Monetary Nationalism and International Stability*. New York: Augustus M. Kelley.

———. [1935] 1967. *Prices and Production*. 2nd ed. New York: Augustus M. Kelley.

Hazlitt, Henry 1959. *The Failure of the "New Economics": An Analysis of the Keynesian Fallacies*. Princeton, N.J.: D. Van Nostrand.

Marget, Arthur W. [1938–42] 1966. *The Theory of Prices: A Re-Examination of the Central Problems of Monetary Theory*. 2 vols. New York: Augustus M. Kelley.

Mason, Will. 1963. *Clarification of the Monetary Standard: The Concept and Its Relations to Monetary Policies and Objectives*. University Park: Pennsylvania State University Press.

Menger, Carl. 1976. *Principles of Economics*. James Dingwall and Bert F. Hoselitz, trans. New York: New York University Press.

Mises, Ludwig von. 1998. *Human Action: A Treatise on Economics*. Scholar's Edition. Introduction by Jeffrey M. Herbener, Hans-Hermann Hoppe, and Joseph T. Salerno, Auburn, Ala.: Ludwig von Mises Institute.

———. 1981. *The Theory of Money and Credit*. 3rd ed. H.E. Batson, trans. Indianapolis, Ind.: Liberty Classics.

Rothbard, Murray N. [1962] 1993. *Man, Economy, and State: A Treatise on Economic Principles*. Auburn, Ala.: Ludwig von Mises Institute.

Salerno, Joseph T. 1994. "Ludwig von Mises's Monetary Theory in Light of Modern Monetary Thought." *Review of Austrian Economics* 8 (1): pp. 71–115.

Warburton, Clark. 1966. *Depression, Inflation, and Monetary Policy: Selected Papers, 1945–1953*. Baltimore: The Johns Hopkins Press.

Wicksteed, Philip H. [1932] 1967. *The Common Sense of Political Economy and Selected Papers and Reviews on Economic Theory*. 2 vols. Lionel Robbins, ed. New York: Augustus M. Kelley.

CHAPTER 5

International Monetary Theory

ustrian analysis of the balance of payments and the exchange rate originated in Ludwig von Mises's *Theory of Money and Credit*,[1] first published in German in 1912. In formulating his theories, Mises built on the analysis of the monetary adjustment process under a specie standard pioneered by eighteenth-century writers, most notably David Hume and Richard Cantillon, and on the extensions of their analysis to the case of an inconvertible paper money by the British bullionists of the early nineteenth century, especially David Ricardo. Important elaborations and applications of Mises's theoretical framework were subsequently undertaken by Mises[2] himself, writing during the German hyperinflation, and, later, by his student F.A. Hayek[3] and other economists associated with the London School of Economics during the 1930s, notably Lionel Robbins[4] and Frank Paish.[5]

From: "International Monetary Theory," in *The Edward Elgar Companion to Austrian Economics,* ed. Peter J. Boettke (Brookfield, Vt.: Edward Elgar, 1994), pp. 249–57.

[1] Ludwig von Mises, *The Theory of Money and Credit*, 3rd ed. (Indianapolis: Liberty Classics, [1953] 1981), pp. 195–213.

[2] Ludwig von Mises, *On the Manipulation of Money and Credit*, ed. Percy L. Greaves, Jr., trans. Bettina Bien Greaves (Dobbs Ferry, N.Y.: Free Market Books, 1978), pp. 1–55.

[3] F.A. Hayek, *Monetary Nationalism and International Stability* (New York: Augustus M. Kelley, [1937] 1971).

[4] Lionel Charles Robbins, *Economic Planning and International* Order (London: Macmillan, 1937); idem, *Money, Trade and International Relations* (London: Macmillan, 1971).

[5] Frank W. Paish, "Causes of Changes in Gold Supply," in *The Post-War Financial Problem and Other* Essays (London: Macmillan, 1950): pp. 149–86; idem, "Banking

Among Continental economists, the Polish-born Michael A. Heilperin, who was Mises's colleague at the Geneva Institute of International Studies in the 1930s, is especially noteworthy for following a basically Austrian approach in his writings on a broad range of international monetary issues.[6] In German-language publications of the 1920s and 1930s, Misesian monetary theorists such as the early Fritz Machlup,[7] the early Gottfried Haberler[8] and Wilhelm Röpke[9] developed the implications of the Austrian approach for the solution of the so-called "transfer problem" of unilateral payments and capital movements. More recently, Murray N. Rothbard[10] has criticized the case for fluctuating exchange rates and analysed twentieth-century international monetary experience, particularly the workings of the gold exchange standard, from an Austrian perspective; and Joseph T.

Policy and the Balance of International Payments," in *Readings in the Theory of International Trade*, eds. Howard S. Ellis and Lloyd A. Metzler (Homewood, Ill.: Richard D. Irwin, [1936] 1966): pp. 35–55.

[6] Joseph T. Salerno, "Gold and the International Monetary System: The Contribution of Michael A. Heilperin," in *The Gold Standard: Perspectives in the Austrian School*, ed. Llewellyn H. Rockwell (Auburn, Ala.: Ludwig von Mises Institute, 1992), pp. 81–111; Michael A. Heilperin, *Aspects of the Pathology of Money: Monetary Essays from Four Decades* (London: Michael Joseph, 1968); idem, *International Monetary Economics* (Philadephia: Porcupine Press, 1978).

[7] Fritz Machlup, "Foreign Debts, Reparations, and the Transfer Problem," in *International Payments, Debts and Gold: Collected Essays by Fritz Machlup* (New York: Charles Scribner's Sons, 1964a), pp. 396–416; idem, "Transfer and Price Effects," in *International Payments, Debts, and Gold: Collected Essays by Fritz Machlup* (New York: Charles Scribner's Sons, 1964b), pp. 417–24.

[8] Gottfried Haberler, "Transfer and Price Movements," in *Selected Essays of Gottfried Haberler*, ed. Anthony Y.C. Woo (Cambridge, Mass.: MIT Press, 1985), pp. 133–42.

[9] Wilhelm Röpke, "On the Transfer Problem in International Capital Movements," in *Against the Tide*, trans. Elizabeth Henderson (Chicago: Henry Regnery, [1930] 1969), pp. 1–23.

[10] Murray N. Rothbard, "Gold vs. Fluctuating Fiat Exchange Rates," in *Gold Is Money*, ed. Hans F. Sennholz (Westport, Conn.: Greenwood Press, 1975), pp. 24–40; idem, *What Has Government Done to Our Money?*, 4th ed. (Auburn, Ala.: Praxeology Press, 1990); idem, "The Gold Exchange Standard in the Interwar Years," in *Money and the Nation States,* eds. Devin Dowd and Richard Timberlake (Oakland, Calif.: Independent Institute, 1994).

Salerno[11] has restated the Austrian analysis in the light of the modern monetary approach and used it to evaluate the performance of the classical gold standard.

Austrian analysis of the balance of payments begins with the insight that disequilibria in payments balances between exchanging parties can never arise in a system of barter and that money in its role as the general medium of exchange is therefore the active element that determines the balance of payments. Money does not merely move to and fro in passive response to discrepancies that arise in the trade of commodities, services, and assets.[12] Balance-of-payments phenomena are thus treated, as they were by Cantillon, Hume, and the bullionists, as an integral part of the market process by which the purchasing power of money and its distribution among regions and nations sharing a common currency are adjusted to variations in the relationship between the demand for and supply of money. For example, under an international gold standard, an increase in the supply of money in a gold-mining nation that disrupts a pre-existing monetary equilibrium by furnishing some residents with excess cash balances leads to excess demands in goods and asset markets, and this results—sooner or later, depending on the concrete data of the case—in a net outflow of money through the nation's current and capital accounts and, hence, a deficit in its "money account" or overall balance of payments. When residents have succeeded in ridding themselves of their excess cash, equilibrium is restored in the domestic "money market" and subsequently in the balance of payments as the net outflow of money ceases.

In thus analyzing the balance of payments as a phase in the monetary adjustment process, the Austrian theory focuses on the actions of individual money holders linked to one another in a sequence of monetary exchanges. The steps in this sequential adjustment process

---

[11] Joseph T. Salerno, "Ludwig von Mises and the Monetary Approach to the Balance of Payments: Comment on Yeager," in *Method, Process, and Austrian Economics: Essays in Honor of Ludwig von Mises*, ed. Israel M. Kirzner (Lexington, Mass.: D.C. Heath, 1982), pp. 247–56 [reprinted here as Chapter 6]; idem, "The International Gold Standard: A New Perspective," *Eastern Economic Journal* 10 (October/December): pp. 488–98 [reprinted here as Chapter 15].

[12] Mises, *The Theory of Money and Credit*, p. 208; Salerno, "Monetary Approach to the Balance of Payments," p. 248.

are then accounted for by examining the causes and effects of the decisions to equilibrate their cash balance positions undertaken by individuals who constitute different links in the macroeconomic income and spending chains that reach back to the originating cause of the monetary disequilibrium. As Hayek[13] and Salerno[14] in particular have shown, it is therefore the interrelated variations in the complex of individual cash balances, incomes, and prices—and not brute up-and-down movements in national money supplies, nominal GDPs, and price levels—that drive this equilibrating process.

One of the more significant implications of this analysis is that a balance of payments adjustment under a common international money such as gold does not require or promote monetary inflation and deflation, as it is commonly said to do in the textbook characterization of the "price-specie-flow mechanism."[15] Under the international gold standard, the transfer of money from one nation to the rest of the world as a result of, say, a decline in world demand for that nation's exports, will be quickly reversed unless, as is likely to happen, it is accompanied by a relative decrease in the demand for cash balances on the part of workers and entrepreneurs experiencing falling real incomes in the contracting export industry. And even if demand for cash balances does fall the reduction in the nation's money supply does not represent a "deflation," properly defined as a reduction in the money supply of a closed system or "currency area," but merely the same type of redistribution of cash balances between individuals, industries and regions that regularly occurs when demand shifts from the product of one domestic industry to that of another within, for example, the present-day U.S. fiat dollar area.

According to Austrian theory, the monetary and balance of payments equilibrium that the market is continually driving towards can be described as one in which the purchasing power of money (the "PPM" for short) is everywhere absolutely equal. Interspatial equalization of the PPM is not taken to mean, however, that national price

---

[13] Hayek, *Monetary Nationalism and International Stability*, pp. 19–24.

[14] Salerno, "Monetary Approach to the Balance of Payments," pp. 490–91.

[15] Robbins, *Economic Planning and International Order*, pp. 280–90; Salerno, "Monetary Approach to the Balance of Payments," pp. 491–92.

indexes ever tend towards equality. Indeed, Austrians eschew the use of such statistical constructs when they theorize about changes in the PPM, using them only to obtain rough historical estimates of variations in the PPM.[16] For Austrian theorists the phrase "geographical equalization of the value of money" refers to an equilibration of the unaveraged and heterogeneous array of alternative quantities of goods that are exchangeable for a unit of money.

Thus conceived, equilibration of money's purchasing power array cannot be expected to yield equality between the prices of physically identical goods available in different locations, let alone between the arbitrarily selected and weighted price indexes of different nations or regions. The reason is to be found in Mises's subjectivist insight that the situation of a good in space may affect its perceived usefulness and thus its subjective value in satisfying human wants.[17] For example, coffee in Brazil is evaluated by coffee drinkers in New York City as a capital good which must be combined with additional labor and complementary capital goods—, that is, the means of transportation—before it can attain the (higher) subjective value of the consumption good, coffee in New York. Indeed, an important respect in which the money commodity differs from non-monetary commodities is that money's position in space is a matter of indifference to economic agents. The reason is that there exist "money substitutes" such as checkable deposits and bank notes which are routinely accepted as substitutes for the money commodity in exchange. With the use of clearing systems, money substitutes are virtually costless to transfer. Thus stocks of money, wherever they may be situated within the unitary market area, for all practical purposes constitute parts of a supply of a perfectly fungible commodity, subject to the operation of the Jevonian Law of Indifference, also known as the Law of One Price.

But the Austrian insight regarding the influence of the spatial element on the quality of (non-monetary) goods does not embrace merely the pure distance between the location of the consumer and the

---

[16] Ludwig von Mises, *The Theory of Money and Credit*, 2nd ed. (Irvington-on-Hudson, N.Y.: Foundation for Economic Education, [1953] 1971), pp. 187–94; Heilperin, *International Monetary Economics*, pp. 259–69.

[17] Mises, *The Theory of Money and Credit*, 3rd ed., pp. 195–203.

location of the capital good, but also the consumer's positive or negative psychic response to the very site of purchase or consumption. For
example, even in equilibrium, the same brand of men's shirt may simultaneously sell for different prices at a mall boutique and at a downtown
clothing store, because, at the margin, consumers are prepared to offer
a higher price for the shirt purchasable at the mall location, which is
perceived to be more easily accessible and more pleasant. Or consider
that a glass of beer consumed in a restaurant situated on top of a sky-
scraper and offering a breathtaking view of Manhattan commands a
much higher price than a glass of the same beer imbibed in a pub a
few blocks away at street-level. Surely we do not expect would-be bar
patrons at the former establishment to react to knowledge of such a
price discrepancy by a mad scramble to the elevators, precisely because
such a discrepancy does not represent a genuine interlocal disequilibrium in the PPM. Taking into account their spatial quality components,
the two glasses of beer represent different goods. This is not to deny,
of course, that, whenever consumers are neutral with respect to alternative locations of stocks of a technologically identical good ready for
consumption or purchase, the spatial equilibration of the PPM implies
the complete eradication of interlocal price differences.

Thus, from the Austrian point of view, the equilibration of the
PPM is accomplished as part of the same macroeconomic process
that gives rise to the structure of relative prices. As Phillip H. Wicksteed[18] has shown us, this process culminates in a state in which, barring further change in the data, no mutual gains can be obtained from
further exchange between any two market participants, because the
ordinal value rankings of equal-sized units of each of the various
goods and of money are identical for all those possessing them. This
state also reflects the *absolute* equalization of the objective exchange
value of money between any two locations, because it implies that
interlocal differences between prices of physically homogeneous
goods exactly equal their costs of transportation (abstracting from
time in transit) between their consumption and production centers

---

[18] Phillip H. Wicksteed, *The Common Sense of Political Economy and Selected
Papers and Reviews on Economic Theory*, 2 vols., ed. Lionel Robbins (New York:
Augustus M. Kelley, [1932] 1967), vol. 1, pp. 140–45.

and, more generally, that no individual can achieve a more desirable outcome, that is, an increase in total utility, from the exchange process by diminishing his expenditures on consumer goods available at one location and substituting expenditures on goods, whether physically homogeneous or not, offered at alternative locations.

The reference to Wicksteed suggests why Austrian balance of payments theorists, like their bullionist forerunners, consider monetary equilibrium to be relatively rapidly established. Wicksteed[19] begins his analysis by assuming that consumer value scales and the stocks of all goods (including money) remain constant over the course of a logically stipulated "market day" that dawns in disequilibrium and terminates in a pure exchange equilibrium. This procedure permits him to analyze the short-run arbitrage and speculative processes that lead to the equilibrium structure of relative prices (the inverse of the equilibrium PPM array) in isolation from the complex phenomena of entrepreneurship and production. It also serves to emphasize the point that the geographical equalization of the PPM is a pure exchange phenomenon which is constantly being approximated by real-world market processes and does not await the time-consuming adjustment of the production structure that characterizes the long-run equilibration of the overall economy. Austrians are thus inclined to speak of 'the' purchasing power of money only a little less confidently than they and other economists refer to "the" market prices of oil, steel, wheat and other broadly traded commodities.

Austrian analysis of the determination of the exchange rate between two independent moneys is based on the purchasing power parity (PPP) theory as it was first formulated by Mises in 1912,[20] four years before Gustav Cassel published the first of his many statements of it. In Mises's version of the theory—which, unlike Cassel's later version, is "absolute" and exclusively monetary—the long-run equilibrium or "final" exchange rate between two currencies is always exactly equal to the inverse of the ratio between the purchasing powers of the

---

[19] Wicksteed, *The Common Sense of Political Economy*, vol. 1, pp. 218–28.

[20] Mises, *Theory of Money and Credit*, 3rd ed., pp. 205–13; Chi-Yuen Wu, *An Outline of International Price Theories* (London: George Routledge & Sons, 1939), pp. 115–16, 233–35.

two currencies. This implies that a given depreciation of the overall purchasing power of currency A relative to that of currency B brings about an increase of the final price of *B* in terms of A in precisely the same proportion, regardless of the inevitable changes in relative prices that are produced by the nonneutral depreciation process.

The marked differences between the Misesian and Casselian versions of the PPP theory can be traced back to Mises's analytical coup in perceiving the artificiality of the distinction long maintained in classical monetary theory between the case of a parallel standard, that is, two different moneys circulating side by side in domestic use, and the case in which there is only one kind of money employed in domestic transactions while another kind is in use abroad.[21] According to Mises, as long as exchange relations exist between two different currency areas, economically, the money of one area necessarily functions as the money of the other area, since both moneys must be utilized in effecting an exchange between the two areas.

Most importantly, in the Misesian version of the theory the exchange rate between two different national currencies is not determined, as it is for Cassel, by the "quotient between the general levels of prices in the two countries." National price indexes, which generally include purely domestic goods, for example the "houses and haircuts" of textbook fame, whose spatial quality components render their prices interlocally and, a fortiori, internationally incommensurable, are wholly irrelevant to the issue, because there is no longer a reason to distinguish between internationally "tradeable" goods and domestically produced and consumed "non-tradeable" goods. As in the case of domestically coexisting parallel currencies, all goods entering into the exchange nexus, (and here we distinguish between spatially differentiated goods) find expression in the purchasing power array of each of the two national currencies, because all goods are potential objects of international trade, even though many may be "immovable" or "non-transportable." Certainly, one of the lessons learned from the exchange rate gyrations of the 1980s was that American real estate

---

[21] Mises, *Theory of Money and Credit*, 3rd ed., pp. 206–07; Lord Lionel Robbins, *Money, Trade and International Relations* (London: Macmillan, 1971), p. 22.

and consumer services, when rendered sufficiently cheap by a depreciated dollar, are purchasable by foreign speculators and tourists.

Thus the apparent problem for the PPP theory that is raised by the existence of goods having a fixed position in space is easily solved by taking the spatial dimension of quality into account. For example, if the final or PPP exchange rate between the U.S. dollar and the British pound is two to one, then the pound price of a house located in London must be exactly one-half the dollar price of this same house. Of course, owing to consumer perceptions of the difference in quality between the two cities as residential locations, the final price in dollars (pounds) of an identically constructed house situated in Manhattan may be three times the price of the London house also expressed in dollars (pounds). To maintain purchasing power parity, therefore, it is not necessary that technologically identical but immovable goods available in *different* locations maintain equal prices in the same currency, but only that the ratio of the prices in two different currencies of an immovable good in the *same* location equal the inverse of the exchange rate between these two currencies. If the ratio of currency prices for any given commodity diverges from the prevailing exchange rate, equilibrium has not yet been attained and profit opportunities will exist for selling the good for the relatively overvalued currency, employing the sale receipts to purchase the undervalued currency, and then using the latter to repurchase the original good. These arbitrage operations will drive the exchange rate and the ratio of currency purchasing powers towards a mutual and final adjustment.[22]

For the Austrian, then, the problems arising from "fixed" or "pegged" exchange rates between national fiat currencies are the same as the problems confronting a domestic bimetallic standard. Gresham's Law, which, as Mises[23] first recognized, is merely the application of the general theory of price controls to the monetary sphere, operates to cause a chronic shortage on foreign exchange markets or disappearance from domestic monetary circulation of the artificially undervalued national currency or metal.

---

[22] Rothbard, "What Has Government Done to Our Money," p. 42.
[23] Mises, *Theory of Money and Credit*, 3rd ed., pp. 90–93, 282–86.

Another feature which significantly distinguishes Mises's formulation of the PPP theory from Cassel's involves the question of whether the exchange rate is exclusively a monetary phenomenon or whether changes in the real data via movements in relative prices are capable of bringing about a permanent departure of the equilibrium exchange rate from the rate which maintains strict PPP between the two currencies. Like Cassel, especially in his later writings, most modern writers pursue what might be termed an "inclusive" approach to exchange rate determination, that is, one which includes references to non-monetary factors as codeterminants of the exchange rate. They therefore reject the absolute version of the PPP theory, on the grounds that it cannot account for the influence on the equilibrium exchange rate of variations in the nation's "real terms of trade," that is, the relative price between the nation's imports and exports.

Whatever the validity of this criticism against the PPP theory expressed in terms of relative national price levels, it has no bearing whatever on a theory referring to the relative purchasing powers of parallel currencies coexisting in a unitary market area. The Misesian version of the PPP theory remains intact in its absolute and exclusively monetary formulation. To illustrate, let us consider the case of a monopolistically induced increase in the price of oil, the U.S. import, relative to the U.S. export, wheat. While the terms of trade turn against the USA, *ceteris paribus,* that is, in the (unlikely) absence of any induced changes in the monetary data, there will be no long-run depreciation of the U.S. dollar against the Saudi riyal, because both currencies experience an equal reduction of their purchasing powers in terms of oil and, assuming the demand for oil is inelastic along the relevant segment of the global demand curve, equal increases of their purchasing powers in terms of wheat. Of course, this is not to deny that short-run and self-reversing fluctuations in the exchange rate may accompany the market's adjustment to the alteration in relative prices. Thus U.S. consumers may initially respond to the increased price of oil with increased expenditures on oil without a corresponding reduction in their spending on wheat, allowing their cash balances to run down temporarily. This response implies a planned "overabsorption" of output relative to their shrunken real income by U.S. residents, creating an excess demand for riyals in the foreign exchange market and necessitating a temporary rise in the exchange rate and a depreciation of the dollar. The movement in the exchange rate will thus assist in clearing excess demands in output markets and adjusting the terms of trade to prevent overabsorption and preserve balance of payments equilibrium, but only until U.S. residents' expenditures adjust, cash balances are re-established at their former equilibrium levels, and the exchange rate floats back down to its unchanged PPP level.

Moreover, other things are not likely to remain equal. In particular, the redistribution of income and wealth from U.S. entrepreneurs and laborers to their Saudi counterparts can be expected to result in a change in the relative demands for the two currencies and a depreciation of the dollar in the long run. But it is the relative decline in the cash balance demand for the dollar and therefore in its purchasing power *vis-à-vis* the riyal, and not the deterioration of the U.S. terms of trade, which is the direct cause of the change in the final exchange rate.

The foregoing analysis, of course, implies that Austrians conceive purchasing power parity between currencies as a condition which fully holds only in equilibrium, and they recognize that real factors do play a role, albeit subordinate and transient, in the determination of the spot exchange rate that is actually realized at each moment on the foreign exchange markets. With regard to the spot exchange rate, Austrians, taking their cue from Mises,[24] also emphasize its responsiveness to expectations of future variations in currency purchasing powers and in national money supplies. In recognizing that movements of the exchange rate generally anticipate adjustments forthcoming on the domestic money market, however, the Austrian approach must be distinguished from the rational expectations approach. While adherents of both approaches view the foreign exchange market as an asset market characterized by instantaneous market clearing and the participants' orientation to new information, Austrian theorists do not accept the "efficient market hypothesis" as a realistic description of the operation of this market. Rather, they consider the behavior of the exchange rate to be governed by the conflicting forecasts of ever-shifting aggregations of bears and bulls, who

---

[24] Mises, *Theory of Money and Credit*, 3rd ed., pp. 27–28, 51.

differ in their experiences and market situations and in their abilities
to predict future market conditions.

Bibliography

Haberler, Gottfried. 1985. "Transfer and Price Movements." In *Selected Essays of
    Gottfried Haberler*, Anthony Y.C. Woo, ed., pp. 133–42. Cambridge, Mass.:
    MIT Press.

Hayek, F.A. [1937] 1971. *Monetary Nationalism and International Stability*. New
    York: Augustus M. Kelley.

Heilperin, Michael A. 1968. *Aspects of the Pathology of Money: Monetary Essays
    from Four Decades*. London: Michael Joseph.

_____. [1939] 1978. *International Monetary Economics*. Philadelphia: Porcupine
    Press.

Machlup, Fritz. 1964a. "Foreign Debts, Reparations, and the Transfer Problem." In
    International Payments, Debts, and Gold: Collected Essays by Fritz Machlup,
    pp. 396–416. New York: Charles Scribner's Sons.

_____. 1964b. "Transfer and Price Effects." In *International Payments, Debts, and
    Gold: Collected Essays by Fritz Machlup*, pp. 417–24. New York: Charles
    Scribner's Sons.

Mises, Ludwig von. [1953] 1971. *The Theory of Money and Credit*. 2nd ed. Irving-
    ton-on-Hudson, N.Y.: Foundation for Economic Education.

_____. 1978. *On the Manipulation of Money and Credit*, Percy L. Greaves, Jr., ed.,
    Bettina Bien Greaves, trans. Dobbs Ferry, N.Y.: Free Market Books.

_____. [1953] 1981. *The Theory of Money and Credit*, 3rd ed. H.E. Batson, trans.
    Indianapolis: Liberty Classics.

Paish, F.W. 1950. "Causes of Changes in Gold Supply." In *The Post-War Financial
    Problem and Other Essays*, pp. 149–86. London: Macmillan.

_____. [1936] 1966. "Banking Policy and the Balance of International Payments."
    In *Readings in the Theory of International Trade*, Howard S. Ellis and Lloyd
    A. Metzler, eds., pp. 35–55. Homewood, Ill.: Richard D. Irwin.

Robbins, Lionel Charles. 1937. *Economic Planning and International Order*. Lon-
    don: Macmillan.

_____. 1971. *Money, Trade and International Relations*. London: Macmillan.

Röpke, Wilhelm. [1930] 1969. "On the Transfer Problem in International Capital
    Movements." In *Against the Tide*, Elizabeth Henderson, trans., pp. 1–23. Chi-
    cago: Henry Regnery.

Rothbard, Murray N. 1975. "Gold vs. Fluctuating Fiat Exchange Rates." In *Gold Is
    Money*, Hans F. Sennholz, ed., pp. 24–40. Westport, Conn.: Greenwood Press.

_____. 1990. *What Has Government Done to Our Money?*, 4th ed. Auburn, Ala.:
    Praxeology Press.

_____. 1994. "The Gold Exchange Standard in the Interwar Years." In *Money and the Nation States*, Kevin Dowd and Richard Timberlake, eds. Oakland, Calif.: Independent Institute.

Salerno, Joseph T. 1982. "Ludwig von Mises and the Monetary Approach to the Balance of Payments: Comment on Yeager." In *Method, Process, and Austrian Economics: Essays in honor of Ludwig von Mises*, Israel M. Kirzner, ed., pp. 247–56. Lexington, Mass.: D.C. Heath.

_____. 1984. "The International Gold Standard: A New Perspective." *Eastern Economic Journal* 10, October/December: pp. 488–98.

_____. 1992. "Gold and the International Monetary System: The Contribution of Michael A. Heilperin." In *The Gold Standard: Perspectives in the Austrian School*, Llewellyn H. Rockwell, Jr., ed., pp. 81–111. Auburn, Ala.: Ludwig von Mises Institute.

Wicksteed, Phillip H. [1932] 1967. *The Common Sense of Political Economy and Selected Papers and Reviews on Economic Theory*, 2 vols., Lionel Robbins, ed. New York: Augustus M. Kelley.

Wu, Chi-Yuen. 1939. *An Outline of International Price Theories*. London: George Routledge & Sons.

CHAPTER 6

Ludwig von Mises and the Monetary Approach to the Balance of Payments: Comment on Yeager

Leland Yeager offers an illuminating discussion of a serious problem that has historically plagued monetary theory and continues to do so to this day: the failure to clearly distinguish between the individual and the overall viewpoints when analyzing monetary phenomena. I wish to emphasize particularly Yeager's insight that the source of this problem lies in the failure of monetary theorists to heed "the sound precept of methodological individualism," which dictates that bridges be constructed between the two viewpoints ". . . by relating propositions about all economic phenomena, including the behavior of macroeconomic aggregates, to the perceptions and decisions of individuals." In detailing and critically analyzing the errors engendered by this confusion of viewpoints in monetary theory, Yeager has taught an elementary, yet much needed, lesson in the principles of economic reasoning and the dire consequences of neglecting them. I daresay this lesson would have been wholly unnecessary had economists attended more closely to the earlier lessons taught by Ludwig von Mises, certainly the foremost exponent and practitioner of methodological individualism in twentieth-century monetary theory.

From: "Ludwig von Mises and the Monetary Approach to the Balance of Payments: Comment on Yeager," in *Method, Process, and Austrian Economics: Essays in Honor of Ludwig von Mises,* ed. Israel M. Kirzner (New York: D.C. Heath and Company, 1982), pp. 247–56.

Since I am in fundamental agreement with the thrust of Yeager's argument, I shall utilize one illustration in his discussion to elucidate an especially neglected contribution to monetary theory made by Mises in his consistent application of methodological individualism to the explanation of monetary phenomena. In this connection, I wish to focus attention on Yeager's treatment of the modern monetary approach to the balance of payments. I propose to show, first, that the valid and vitally important insight upon which the monetary approach rests forms the basis of Mises's own elaboration of balance-of-payments theory and, second, that Mises's approach is not open to the objection that Yeager raises against the monetary approach, precisely because Mises firmly adheres to the precept of methodological individualism. This enterprise, it may be noted, has important implications for the contemporary formulation of the monetary approach as well as for doctrinal research into its historical antecedents. On the doctrinal side, it is a matter of setting the record straight. Several studies have appeared recently of the doctrinal roots of the monetary approach. With one minor exception,[1] all of them have completely neglected Mises's contribution. Hopefully, greater familiarity with Mises's approach to the balance of payments, which so strongly anticipates the monetary approach, will spark a rethinking of the latter approach and lead to its reformulation on sounder methodological foundations.

The fundamental insight of the monetary approach is that the balance of payments is essentially a monetary phenomenon. The very concept of a balance of payments implies the existence of money; as one writer puts it, "Indeed, it would be impossible to have a balance-of-payments surplus or deficit in a barter economy."[2] This being the case, any endeavor to explain balance-of-payments phenomena must naturally focus on the supply of and demand for the money commodity. The monetary approach consists in the rigorous delineation of the

---

[1] The exception is Thomas M. Humphrey, "Dennis H. Robertson and the Monetary Approach to Exchange Rates," *Federal Reserve Bank of Richmond Economic Review* 66 (May/June 1980), p. 24, wherein Mises is briefly mentioned as one whose contributions to the monetary approach have been largely overlooked.

[2] M.A. Akhtar, "Some Common Misconceptions about the Monetary Approach to International Adjustment," in *The Monetary Approach to International Adjustment*, eds. Bluford H. Putnam and D. Sykes Wilford (New York: Praeger, 1978), p. 121.

implications of this simple yet powerful insight for the analysis of balance-of-payments disequilibrium, adjustment, and policy. As I shall
attempt to demonstrate, Mises fully anticipated the modern monetary
approach by explicitly recognizing these implications.

Mises grounds his balance-of-payments analysis on the insight
that the balance of payments is a monetary concept. He states that, "If
no other relations than those of barter exist between the inhabitants
of two areas, then balances in favor of one party or the other cannot
arise."[3] Mises thus conceives of money as the active element in the balance of payments and not as a residual or accommodating item that
passively adjusts to the "real" flows of goods and capital:

> The surplus of the balance of payments that is not settled by
> the consignment of goods and services but by the transmission
> of money was long regarded as merely a consequence of the
> state of international trade. It is one of the great achievements
> of Classical political economy to have exposed the fundamen-
> tal error in this view. It demonstrated that international move-
> ments of money are not consequences of the state of trade; that
> they constitute not the effect, but the cause, of a favorable or
> unfavorable trade balance. The precious metals are distributed
> among individuals and hence among nations according to the
> extent and intensity of their demand for money.[4]

Mises uses his marginal-utility theory of money to explain
the "natural" or equilibrium distribution of the world money stock
among the various nations. Regarding the case of a 100 percent specie
standard, he writes that:

> the proposition is as true of money as of every other eco-
> nomic good, that its distribution among individual economic
> agents depends on its marginal utility ... all economic goods,
> including of course money, tend to be distributed in such
> a way that a position of equilibrium among individuals is
> reached, when no further act of exchange that any individual
> could undertake would bring him any gain, any increase of
> subjective utility. In such a position of equilibrium, the total

---

[3] Ludwig von Mises, *The Theory of Money and Credit*, new enl. ed., trans. H.E. Batson (Irvington-on-Hudson, N.Y.: Foundation for Economic Education, 1971), p. 182.
[4] Ibid.

stock of money, just like the total stocks of commodities, is distributed among individuals according to the intensity with which they are able to express their demand for it in the market. Every displacement of the forces affecting the exchange-ratio between money and other economic goods [i.e., the supply and demand for money] brings about a corresponding change in this distribution, until a new position of equilibrium is reached.[5]

Mises goes on to conclude that the same principles that determine the distribution of money balances among persons also determine the distribution of money stocks among nations, since the national money stock is merely the sum of the money balances of the nation's residents.[6] In thus building up his explanation of the international distribution of money from his analysis of the interpersonal distribution of money balances, Mises sets the stage for an analysis of balance-of-payments phenomena that conforms to the precept of methodological individualism.

Like the later proponents of the monetary approach, Mises envisages balance-of-payments disequilibrium as an integral phase in the process by which individual and hence national money holdings are adjusted to desired levels. Thus, for example, the development of an excess demand for money in a nation will result in a balance-of-payments surplus as market participants seek to augment their money balances by increasing their sales of goods and securities on the world market. The surplus and the corresponding inflow of the money commodity will automatically terminate when domestic money balances have reached desired levels and the excess demand has been satisfied. Conversely, a balance-of-payments deficit is part of the mechanism by which an excess supply of money is adjusted.

The role played by the balance of payments in the monetary-adjustment process is clearly spelled out by Mises in the following passage.

In a society in which commodity transactions are monetary transactions, every individual enterprise must always take care

---

[5] Ibid., pp. 183–84.
[6] Ibid., p. 184.

to have on hand a certain quantity of money. It must not permit its cash holding to fall below the definite sum considered
necessary for carrying out its transactions. On the other hand,
an enterprise will not permit its cash holding to exceed the
necessary amount, for allowing that quantity of money to be
idle will lead to loss of interest. If it has too little money, it must
reduce purchases or sell some wares. If it has too much money,
then it must buy goods.

… In this way, every individual sees to it that he is not without money. Because everyone pursues his own interest in
doing this, it is impossible for the free play of market forces
to cause a drain of all money out of the city, a province or an
entire country.…

If we had a pure gold standard, therefore, the government need
not be the least concerned about the balance of payments. It could
safely let the market take care of maintaining a sufficient quantity of
gold within the country. Under the influence of free trade forces, gold
would leave the country only if a surplus of cash balances were on
hand. Coversely it would always flow into the country if cash balances
were insufficient. Thus, for Mises, the monetary-adjustment process ensures that gold money, like all other commodities, is imported
when in short supply and exported when in surplus.[7]

An implication of this view of the balance of payments as a
phase in the monetary adjustment process is that international movements of money that do not reflect changes in the underlying monetary data can only be temporary phenomena. "Thus," writes Mises,
"international movements of money, so far as they are not of a transient nature and consequently soon rendered ineffective by movements in the contrary direction, are always called forth by variations
in demand for money."[8]

Although Mises therefore does regard the long-run causes of balance-of-payments disequilibrium as exclusively monetary in nature, he

---

[7] Ludwig von Mises, *On the Manipulation of Money and Credit*, ed. Percy L.
Greaves, trans. Bettina Bien Greaves (Dobbs Ferry, N.Y.: Free Market Books, 1978),
pp. 53–54.

[8] Mises, *Theory of Money and Credit*, p. 185.

does not make the error, which Yeager attributes to the more radical, global-monetarist proponents of the monetary approach, of identifying a balance-of-payments surplus with the process of satisfying an excess demand for domestic money or a deficit with the process of working off an excess supply of domestic money. Mises explicitly recognizes that changes occurring on the "real" side of the economy, for example, a decline in the foreign demand for a nation's exports, may well have a disequilibrating impact on the balance of payments, even in the absence of a change in the underlying conditions of monetary supply and demand. However, in Mises's view, such nonmonetary disturbances of balance-of-payments equilibrium are merely short-run phenomena. It is one of the functions of the balance-of-payments adjustment mechanism to reverse the disequilibrating flows of money that attend these disturbances and to restore thereby the equilibrium distribution of the world money stock, which is determined solely by the configuration of individual demands for money holdings.

> If the state of the balance of payments is such that movements of money would have to occur from one country to the other, independently of any altered estimation of money on the part of their respective inhabitants, then operations are induced which re-establish equilibrium. Those persons who receive more money than they will need hasten to spend the surplus again as soon as possible, whether they buy production goods or consumption goods. On the other hand, those persons whose stock of money falls below the amount they will need will be obliged to increase their stock of money, either by restricting their purchases or by disposing of commodities in their possession. The price variations, in the markets of the countries in question, that occur for these reasons give rise to transactions which must always re-establish the equilibrium of the balance of payments. A debit or credit balance of payments that is not dependent upon an alteration in the conditions of demand for money can only be transient.[9]

The foregoing passage illustrates the difference between Mises and the global monetarists, who deny the possibility that international flows of money can proceed from nonmonetary causes. Their

---

[9] Ibid., pp. 184–85.

denial is tantamount to claiming that all international movements of money are necessarily equilibrating, since they are undertaken solely in response to disequilibrium between national supplies of and demands for money. As Yeager has pointed out, this line of reasoning leads to the outright and fallacious identification of balance-of-payments surpluses and deficits with the process of adjusting national money stocks to desired levels.

It is not difficult to pinpoint the source from which this erroneous line of reasoning stems: it is the tendency of the monetary approach to depart from the sound precept of methodological individualism and to focus on the nation rather than the individual as the basic unit of analysis. In so doing, it has naturally, although quite illegitimately, applied to the nation analytical concepts and constructs that are appropriate only to the analysis of individual action. In particular, the monetary approach attempts to explain balance-of-payments phenomena by conceiving the nation in the manner of a household or firm that is consciously aiming at acquiring and maintaining an optimum level of money balances. The concept of what Ludwig Lachmann has called "the equilibrium of the household and of the firm" is then invoked to describe the actions which the nation-household must and will undertake in the service of this goal.[10] As Lachmann explains, the concept of household-firm equilibrium is implied in the very logic of choice.[11] An economic agent will always choose the course of action consistent with his goals and their ranking given his knowledge of available resources and of technology. His actions are, therefore, always equilibrating in the sense that they are always aimed at bringing about a (possibly only momentarily) preferred state of affairs.

In the context of the issues dealt with by the monetary approach, the implication of this analytical concept is that the nation will never alter the level of its stock of money unless it is dissatisfied with it, that is, unless there is an excess supply of or demand for domestic money. A further implication is that all international movements of money will

---

[10] Ludwig M. Lachmann, *Capital, Expectations, and the Market Process: Essays on the Theory of the Market Economy,* ed. Walter E. Grinder (Kansas City: Sheed Andrews and McMeel, 1977), p. 117.

[11] Ibid., pp. 117, 189.

be equilibrating, the result of deliberate steps undertaken by nations to adjust their actual money balances to desired levels. National payments, surpluses and deficits, then, are logically always associated with the adjustment of monetary disequilibrium. To argue that balance-of-payments disequilibria may arise, even temporarily, for reasons unrelated to monetary disequilibrium is to argue that the economic agent, in this case the nation, has taken leave of economic rationality. Why else acquire or rid oneself of money balances, if not as a deliberate act of choice aimed at securing a more preferred position? Thus the global monetarists are prepared to deny, for example, that a shift in relative demands from domestic to foreign products would create even a temporary deficit in the balance of payments in the absence of the development of an excess supply of domestic money.

This clearly illustrates the confusion that results when monetary theorists lapse into methodological holism and apply to hypostasized entities such as the nation concepts whose use is inappropriate outside the realm of individual action. The concept of household-firm equilibrium has meaning only within the framework of the logic of choice. And the logic of choice itself is meaningful only within the context of individual action.

By virtue of his thoroughgoing methodological individualism, Mises maintains a firm grasp on the all-important distinction between the equilibrium of the individual actor and interindividual equilibrium in his balance-of-payments analysis. This difference between Mises's approach and the monetary approach may be seen in their divergent analyses of the effects on the balance of payments of a change emanating from the "real" or "goods" side of the economy. Assuming an international pure specie currency and starting from a situation of monetary and balance-of-payments equilibrium, let us suppose that domestic consumers increase their expenditures on foreign imports and that this increase reflects increased valuations of foreign products relative to domestic products. Let us further assume that the overall demand for money balances remains unchanged and that no other changes in the real or monetary data occur elsewhere in the system.

Under these conditions, those proponents of the monetary approach who are inclined to identify balance-of-payments surpluses and deficits with the process of adjusting monetary disequilibrium would naturally deny any disequilibrating effect on the balance of payments, since the nation, by hypothesis, does not wish to alter its level of money balances but merely its mix of consumers' goods. The adjustment will thus proceed entirely in the goods sphere, with the nation simply increasing its exports of domestic products, which it now demands less urgently, to pay for the increased imports of the now more highly esteemed foreign products, while the level of its money balances remains unchanged.

For Mises, however, things are not simple, since the adjustment process does not consist of the mutually consistent choices and actions of a single macroeconomic agent. Rather, it involves a succession of configurations of mutually inconsistent individual equilibria representing numerous microeconomic agents who are induced by the price system to bring their individual actions into closer and closer coordination until a final interindividual equilibrium is effected.

As a consequence, in Mises's analysis there will indeed emerge an initial balance-of-payments deficit and corresponding outflow of money from the nation as domestic consumers shift their expenditures from domestic products to foreign imports. Now, from the point of view of these individual domestic consumers, this outflow of money is certainly "equilibrating" in the logic-of-choice sense, because it demonstrably facilitates their attainment of a more preferred position. Nevertheless, from the point of view of the economic system as a whole, far from serving to adjust a preexisting monetary disequilibrium, this flow of money disrupts the prevailing equilibrium in the interindividual distribution of money balances and is therefore ultimately self-reversing. Thus, the domestic producers of those goods for which demand has declined experience a shrinkage of their incomes, which threatens to leave them with insufficient money balances. On the other hand, the foreign producers, the demand for whose products have increased, experience an augmentation of their incomes and a consequent buildup of excess money balances. Without going into detail, suffice it to say that the steps undertaken by both groups to readjust their money balances to desired levels will initiate a balance-of-payments adjustment process that will reestablish the original, equilibrium distribution of money holdings among individuals, and hence among nations.

Mises thus arrives at the same long-run, comparative-static conclusion as the proponents of the monetary approach do, to the effect that the change in question will not result in any alteration in national money stocks. However, his focus on the individual economic agent leads him to analyze the dynamic macroeconomic process by which the comparative-static, macroeconomic result emerges.

Before concluding, I wish to briefly note two other important ways in which Mises anticipated the monetary approach. The first involves the global perspective of the monetary approach, which contrasts so sharply with the narrowly national focus of closed-economy macro-models typical of the various Keynesian approaches to the balance of payments. The monetary approach views the world economy as a unitary market with the various national commodity and capital submarkets fully integrated with one another and subject to the rule of the law of one price. As a consequence, arbitrage insures that a particular nation's prices and interest rates are rigidly determined by the forces of supply and demand prevailing on the world market.

The analytical importance of the global perspective, which has revolutionized modern balance-of-payments analysis, was grasped completely by Mises:

> The mobility of capital goods, which nowadays is but little restricted by legislative provisions such as customs duties, or by other obstacles, has led to the formation of a homogeneous world capital market. In the loan markets of the countries that take part in international trade, the net rate of interest is no longer determined according to national, but according to international, considerations. Its level is settled, not by the natural rate of interest in the country, but by the natural rate of interest *anywhere.*... So long and in so far ... as a nation participates in international trade, its market is

only a part of the world market; prices are determined not nationally but internationally.[12]

I might add that Mises's individualist and subjectivist analytical focus enables him to deal more trenchantly than the writers on the monetary approach with the objection that the existence of internationally nontraded goods and services, for example, houses, haircuts, ice cream cones, severely limits the operation of the law of one price and thus undermines the unity of the world price level. The response of the proponents of the monetary approach, such as Jacob Frankel and Harry Johnson, is the empirical assertion that the elasticities of substitution between the classes of traded and nontraded goods approaches infinity in both consumption and production, a condition that places extremely narrow limits on the range of relative price changes between the two classes of goods.[13]

Mises, on the other hand, disposes of the objection theoretically.[14] His argument is based on the important insight that the location of a good in space is a factor conditioning its usefulness and, therefore, its subjective value to the individual economic agent. For this reason, technologically identical goods that occupy different positions in space are, in fact, different goods. To the extent that the overall valuations and demands of market participants for such physically identical goods differ according to their locations, there will naturally be no tendency for their prices to be equalized. Mises is able to conclude logically, therefore, that the existence of so-called nontraded goods whose prices tend to diverge internationally does not constitute a valid objection to the worldwide operation of the law of one price in the case of each and every good and the corollary tendency to complete equalization of the purchasing power of a unit of the world money.

---

[12] Mises, *Theory of Money and Credit*, pp. 374–75.

[13] Jacob A. Frenkel and Harry G. Johnson, "The Monetary Approach to the Balance of Payments: Essential Concepts and Historical Origins," in *The Monetary Approach to the Balance of Payments*, eds. Jacob A. Frenkel and Harry G. Johnson (Toronto: University of Toronto, 1976), pp. 27–28.

[14] Mises, *Theory of Money and Credit*, pp. 170–78.

A final respect in which Mises can be considered as a forerunner of the monetary approach is in his analysis of the causes and cures of a persistent balance-of-payments disequilibrium. For Mises and for the monetary approach, a chronic balance-of-payments deficit can only result from an inflationary monetary policy that continuously introduces excess money balances into the domestic economy via bank-credit creation. The deficit and the corresponding efflux of gold reflects the repeated attempts of domestic money holders to rid themselves of these excess balances, which are being re-created over and over again by the inflationary intervention of the monetary authority. The deficits will only be terminated when the inflationary monetary policy is brought to a halt or the stock of gold reserves is exhausted. Tariffs and other protectionist measures will fail to rectify the situation, since they do not address the fundamental cause of monetary disequilibrium.

The connection between inflationist, interventionist monetary policies and chronic balance-of-payments disequilibrium is delineated by Mises in the following passage:

> If the government introduces into trade quantities of inconvertible banknotes or government notes, then this must lead to a monetary depreciation. The value of the monetary unit declines. However, this depreciation in value can affect only the inconvertible notes. Gold money retains all, or almost all, of its value internationally. However, since the state—with its power to use the force of the law—declares the lower-valued monetary notes equal in purchasing power to the higher-valued gold money and forbids the gold money from being traded at a higher value than the paper notes, the gold coins must vanish from the market. They may disappear abroad. They may be melted down for use in domestic industry. Or they may be hoarded....
>
> No special government intervention is needed to retain the precious metals in circulation within a country. It is enough for the state to renounce all attempts to relieve financial distress by resorting to the printing press. To uphold the currency, it need do no more than that. And it need do *only* that to accomplish this goal. All orders and prohibitions, all

measures to limit foreign exchange transactions, etc., are completely useless and purposeless.[15]

In conclusion, Mises's contribution to balance-of-payments analysis should be hailed not only as a doctrinal milestone in the development of the monetary approach but, much more importantly, as a shining exemplar of methodological individualism in monetary theory.[16]

Bibliography

Akhtar, M.A. 1978. "Some Common Misconceptions about the Monetary Approach to International Adjustment." In *The Monetary Approach to International Adjustment*, Bluford H. Putnam and D. Sykes Wilford, eds. New York: Praeger.

Frenkel, Jacob A., and Harry G. Johnson. 1976. "The Monetary Approach to the Balance of Payments: Essential Concepts and Historical Origins." In *The Monetary Approach to the Balance of Payments*, Jacob A. Frenkel and Harry G. Johnson, eds. Toronto: University of Toronto.

Humphrey, Thomas M. 1980. "Dennis H. Robertson and the Monetary Approach to Exchange Rates." Federal Reserve Bank of Richmond *Economic Review* 66 (May/June).

Lachmann, Ludwig M. 1977. *Capital, Expectations, and the Market Process: Essays on the Theory of the Market Economy*, Walter E. Grinder, ed. Kansas City: Sheed Andrews and McMeel.

Mises, Ludwig von. 1971. *The Theory of Money and Credit*, new enl. ed. H.E. Batson, trans. Irvington-on-Hudson, N.Y.: Foundation for Economic Education.

_____. 1978. *On the Manipulation of Money and Credit*, Percy L. Greaves, Jr., ed. Bettina Bien Greaves, trans. Dobbs Ferry, N.Y.: Free Market Books.

---

[15] Mises, *Manipulation of Money and Credit*, p. 55.

[16] Limitation of space has precluded a discussion of Mises's analysis of the exchange rate. Suffice it to say that Mises anticipated the monetary approach to the exchange rate, both in his pathbreaking explanation of the purchasing-power-parity theory (which predated Cassel) and also in his integration of expectations into the explanation of short-run exchange-rate movements. Moreover, Mises brought his global perspective to bear in his insight that the exchange rate between national currencies is to be explained on the same principles as the exchange rate between parallel currencies circulating in the same nation.

CHAPTER 7

The Concept of Coordination in Austrian Macroeconomics[1]

In the conclusion of his paper, Roger Garrison suggests that the concept of coordination "can serve as the organizing principle" in a unified macroeconomics, just as it now "provides the macroeconomic foundation for macroeconomics." It is specifically the Austrian concept of intertemporal coordination that Garrison offers as the "organizing theme" to reconstruct and unify the currently compartmentalized standard theories of macroeconomics, growth, and business cycles.

In view of the importance which Garrison and other modern Austrian economists assign to the notion of coordination, it is important to clarify the meaning and uses of the concept. The focus of Garrison's paper is on the usefulness of intertemporal coordination as a device for broadening standard macroeconomics to encompass both the Keynesian and Austrian visions of the market forces at work at various levels of resource idleness. As Garrison uses the term, intertemporal coordination refers to the market forces which lead

From: "The Concept of Coordination in Austrian Macroeconomics," in *Austrian Economics: Perspectives on the Past and Prospects for the Future,* ed. Richard M. Ebeling (Hillsdale College Press, 1991), pp. 325–43.

[1] This is a comment on Roger Garrison ("Austrian Capital Theory and the Future of Macroeconomics," Paper presented at Conference on Austrian Economics: Perspectives on the Past and Prospects for the Future, Hillsdale College, Hillsdale, Mich., April 1990), but can be read as a self-contained article.

entrepreneurs to construct and maintain an integrated time structure of investment activities which corresponds to the intertemporal consumption preferences, or "time preferences," expressed by market participants. I intend to focus on the broader concept of what may be termed "price coordination," which encompasses intertemporal coordination and which I maintain is the starting point of the uniquely Austrian approach to macroeconomic theory.

Price coordination must not be confused with *plan* coordination, a concept originally formulated by Friedrich von Hayek. In his article "Economics and Knowledge," which has heavily influenced modern Austrian writers, Hayek suggested a concept of equilibrium based on "coordination of plans"[2] as a substitute for the concept of equilibrium based on "constancy of the data." In contrast, price coordination, as I elaborate the concept below, is the indispensable complement to the concept of an evenly rotating economy based on constant data. As Ludwig von Mises has repeatedly emphasized, the evenly rotating economy, although an imaginary state which can never be realized in the unfolding of the historical market process, is yet indispensable to the identification and analysis of the entrepreneurial function of the real world.[3] Entrepreneurs, however, can formulate and execute production plans only in a world in which economic calculation is possible, that is, in which catallactic competition generates market-clearing prices which, at every moment of calendar time and without fail, reflect, promote, and coordinate those uses of the available scarce resources that are expected to be the most highly valued by consumers. Price coordination, therefore, is not a phenomenon associated with an unrealizable state of equilibrium, however the latter is conceived; rather, price coordination is the essential characteristic of the plain state of rest, which, as Mises tells us, "... is not an

---

[2] In fact, Hayek never used this term in the article, but at several places in the article referred to the "mutual compatibility" or "intercompatibility" of plans in denoting his concept.

[3] For an insightful analysis and defense of Mises's view of the nature and uses of the evenly rotating economy, see J. Patrick Gunning, "Mises on the Evenly Rotating Economy," *The Review of Austrian Economics* 3: pp. 123–35.

imaginary construction but the adequate description of what happens again and again on every market."[4]

The concept of price coordination emerges out of a particular view of the market process, which is most fully developed in the works of William H. Hutt,[5] Mises,[6] Phillip H. Wicksteed,[7] and economists of the American psychological school, especially Herbert J. Davenport.[8]

According to these economists, the market is to be understood as a social appraisement process,[9] in which the money prices for the economy's available means of production are determined in light of their importance for achieving the ends of the economic system, that is, consumer preferences.[10] As Mises's contribution to the socialist calculation debate has taught us, price appraisement of the means of production is the specifically social function of the market, because, in the absence of prices determined by the competitive bidding of entrepreneurs for stocks of privately owned resources, economic calculation

---

[4] Ludwig von Mises, *Human Action: A Treatise on Economics*, 3rd ed. (Chicago: Henry Regnery Company, 1966), p. 245.

[5] William H. Hutt, *Keynesianism-Retrospect and Prospect: A Critical Restatement of Basic Economic Principles* (Chicago: Henry Regnery Company, 1963); idem, *A Rehabilitation of Say's Law* (Athens, Ohio: Ohio University Press, 1974); idem, *The Keynesian Episode* (Indianapolis: Liberty Press, 1977).

[6] Mises, *Human Action*.

[7] Phillip E. Wicksteed, *The Common Sense of Political Economy and Selected Papers and Reviews on Economic Theory* (New York: Augustus M. Kelley, 1967).

[8] Herbert J. Davenport, *The Economics of Enterprise* (New York: Augustus M. Kelley, 1968).

[9] Mises employs the term "appraisement" in two different senses. In the first sense, it refers to a speculative judgment exercised by an individual entrepreneur. This is Mises's use of the term when he states that "Appraisement is the anticipation of an expected fact. It aims at establishing what prices will be paid on the market for a particular commodity...." (Mises, *Human Action*, p. 332). The second sense in which Mises uses the term refers to a social market process. Thus Mises (*Human Action*, p. 333) writes, "The factors of production are appraised with regard to the prices of the products, and from this appraisement their prices emerge." In what follows, it will be clear from the context in what sense the term is being used.

[10] Following Hutt (*Keynesian Episode*, p. 300), I use the term "consumer preferences" to include leisure preferences, risk preferences, time preferences, and liquidity preferences.

and, therefore, rational allocation of resources under the social division of labor are impossible.[11]

In analyzing the social appraisement process, we find that it is inherently entrepreneurial, competitive, and coordinative. Let us consider these qualities each in turn.

Since all production processes take time to complete, and are therefore oriented to an uncertain future, any act of production undertaken for the market presupposes entrepreneurial bidding for productive inputs based on a speculative appraisement of the price of the planned output. In forecasting future market conditions, the entrepreneur has only his experience and his understanding to rely upon.[12] His starting point is his experience of the present (actually immediately past) structure of market prices and of the pattern of the economic data engendering this structure. Based on this experience, the entrepreneur employs his faculty of understanding to forecast the successive changes that will occur in the qualitative economic data over the course of the contemplated production period and to appraise the future structure of quantitative price ratios that will be determined by these estimated data changes.

It is thus clear that production decisions cannot be made based only on knowledge of realized, and therefore past, market prices. As shapers of future-oriented production processes, entrepreneurs require detailed information about the qualitative or nonprice data to fulfill their dynamic function as forecasters and future price appraisers.

Hutt, in particular, recognizes the importance of entrepreneurial forecasting and appraisement to the production process, emphasizing that, "[P]roduction ... is *the response to the forecast expression of economic ends*.... Entrepreneurial decision-making is dominated by

---

[11] For review and analysis of Mises's contribution to the socialist calculation debate, see Joseph T. Salerno, "Ludwig von Mises as Social Rationalist," *The Review of Austrian Economics* 4: pp. 26–54; idem, "Why a Socialist Economy Is 'Impossible,'" A postscript to *Economic Calculation in the Socialist Commonwealth* by Ludwig von Mises (Auburn, Ala.: Praxeology Press, 1990b) pp. 53–71.

[12] On the role played by experience and understanding in forecasting the uncertain future, see Mises, *Human Action*, pp. 112, 118, 337–38, 678.

perpetual forecasting. [Unless otherwise noted, all emphases are those of the author cited.]"[13]

Hutt also understands the crucial role that detailed information about past configurations of the qualitative economic data play in entrepreneurial forecasting, arguing that "... *the crucial decisions are made in the light of detailed as well as generalized knowledge* ... 'planning' under free enterprise is ... deliberate, purposeful and based upon detailed, specialized, local knowledge of means to ends, as well as careful observation of ends themselves."[14] In the same vein, Hutt favorably cites Wicksteed's emphasis on what he calls "the 'planning aspect' of business management, that is, the conscious purposive actions of *those entrepreneurs who can be aware of the detailed facts about changing ends and means.*" [15]

Mises, too, stresses the importance of detailed nonprice information for the formulation of business forecasts, stating that: "No businessman may safely neglect any available source of information. Thus no businessman can refuse to pay close attention to newspaper reports."[16] Indeed, for Mises, the accuracy of a judgment regarding the future state of the market depends upon a close reading of many details of catallactic experience, and, therefore, the entrepreneur "... takes information about the past state of affairs from experts in the fields of law, statistics, and technology...."[17]

Finally, Wicksteed makes the point that even after a stock of goods has been produced and lies in inventory ready to be sold at the dawn of a new market day, the producer cannot mechanically extrapolate today's equilibrium price from the price in yesterday's market, but must make a speculative appraisement of today's price based on detailed information regarding existing market conditions. Using the example of a country market, Wicksteed writes:

---

[13] Hutt, *The Keynesian Episode,* p. 300.

[14] Ibid., p. 76.

[15] Ibid., p. 74.

[16] Ludwig von Mises, *On the Manipulation of Money and Credit* (Dobbs Ferry, N.Y.: Free Market Books, 1978), p. 165.

[17] Mises, *Human Action,* p. 307.

... the stall-keepers will form a general estimate, based partly on actual inspection of the market, partly on a variety of sources of information and grounds of conjecture which they commanded before entering it, as to the amount, say, of some particular fruit and the most obvious substitutes for it that are in the market that day. And further, they will form an estimate, based on the experiences of previous days or years, of the equilibrium price corresponding to that amount....

An interesting indication that the seller is thus guided in naming the price by a series of inferences and speculations as to the ultimate facts that must determine it, is to be found in the circumstance that a seller cannot always answer the question what the price is. It often happens in small country markets that when a customer asks the price of something early in the day the stallkeeper will answer that she does not know. She feels herself unequal to forming an intelligent estimate of the amount of stock in the market, the scale of preferences of possible purchasers, and the resultant price which will ultimately reign.[18]

In the Wicksteedian account of the price equilibration process, then, sellers actively seek the detailed information needed to formulate appraisements of the prospective equilibrium price. This account of the process contrasts with the account given by those who view the price system as a device for economizing on information, in which it is held that sellers, innocent of knowledge of the underlying economic data, revise their expectations and plans in passive response to the surpluses and shortages associated with realized market prices.

It is thus clear that, in contrast, for example, to Friedrich von Hayek[19] and Israel M. Kirzner,[20] the social appraisement economists cited above do not view the discovery of knowledge as the social outcome of competition but as its necessary precondition. That is, before the commencement of the competitive process in which entrepreneurs

---

[18] Wicksteed, *The Common Sense of Political Economy*, p. 22.

[19] Friedrich von Hayek, "Competition as a Discovery Procedure," in *Individualism and Economic Order* (Chicago: Henry Regnery, 1972), pp. 179–90.

[20] Israel Kirzner, "The Primacy of Entrepreneurial Discovery," in *Discovery and the Capitalist Process* (Chicago: University of Chicago Press, 1985) and "The Economic Calculation Debate," *The Review of Austrian Economics* (1987).

bid against one another to acquire the scarce resources needed to carry out future-oriented production plans, it is necessary for each participant in the process to already have obtained information regarding what Wicksteed, in the quotation above, refers to as "the ultimate facts." The "discovery" of such nonprice knowledge pertaining to past and future states of the market underlies and conditions entrepreneurial appraisement of future output prices and, therefore, the resulting catallactic competition for productive resources. Hence, the knowledge discovery process must be characterized as the nonsocial prerequisite for competition, since it depends crucially on the exercise of interpretive understanding by individual human minds.

The *outcome* of competition, on the other hand, is the price appraisement of the factors of production and the concomitant creation of a unified price structure, in which goods and services of every type and order are assigned a cardinal number that can be meaningfully employed in the processes of economic calculation. The market's price structure thus may be termed a "social" phenomenon, because, although it is generated by the mental operations of every member of society in his dual role as consumer and producer, it remains impossible to replicate by an process operative within the individual human mind.[21]

We come at last to the concept of coordination and its relationship to the social appraisement process. The coordinative functioning of this process has received the most explicit treatment in the works of Hutt.[22]

In Hutt's view, the price structure established by the social appraisement process coordinates, at every moment of time, the multitude of resource uses and combinations and integrates them into a unitary structure of production designed and tending to optimally serve consumer preferences. This result is insured by the fact that the

---

[21] The best summary and description of the social appraisement process in its competitive and entrepreneurial aspects is provided by Mises, *Human Action*, pp. 335–38. A remarkably similar description can be found in Davenport, *Economics of Enterprise*, pp. 109–13.

[22] Hutt, *Keynesianism*; idem, *A Rehabilitation of Say's Law*; and idem, *The Keynesian Episode*.

prices bid by entrepreneurs for inputs into their planned production processes are necessarily adjusted to their appraisements of the future prices of the outputs expected to emerge from these processes. Thus, the prices of all resources, including all orders of intermediate or capital goods, are ultimately coordinated with the expected prices of consumer goods and therefore with consumer preferences. According to Hutt, therefore, the pricing process is "… the process through which the heterogeneous economic aims which people are seeking are brought into consistency, and through which a synchronized cooperation in response to those aims is achieved."[23]

The market-clearing nature of these prices insures at the same time that entrepreneurial production plans are carried out with full utilization of scarce resources, since the price that clears each resource market represents the resource's expected marginal revenue product in the production structure. Under these circumstances, the only resources that remain unutilized by entrepreneurs are those which have no value, for example, submarginal land, or those whose direct use to the resource owner yields a higher utility than that yielded by its marginal revenue product, which is the case, for example, when an individual chooses leisure over his most preferred employment opportunity. Of course, an individual who, under a regime of market-clearing prices, is currently without a job but actively seeking work, is not idle in the economic sense but is self-employed in what Hutt calls "job prospecting."[24] In rejecting known employment opportunities at prevailing wage rates in favor of exploring for a more remunerative opportunity, this individual "… is really investing in himself by working on his own account without immediate remuneration."[25]

Hutt describes the importance of market-clearing prices to the coordinative functioning of the social appraisement process in the following terms:

---

[23] Hutt, *The Keynesian Episode*, p.151.
[24] Hutt, *The Theory of Idle Resources: A Study in Definition*, 2nd ed. (Indianapolis: Liberty Press, 1979), p. 83.
[25] Ibid.

> If the rate of production of any particular final commodity is perfectly coordinated with the system as a whole, the market price will be such that consumers are *able* and *willing* to buy the full flow coming forward.... If, at any stage, the price of a material or intermediate product is reduced, the rate of flow at that stage will, *ceteris paribus,* tend to increase because, demand remaining the same, *final output is likely to increase;* and if the price is raised, the rate of flow will tend to decline.... It follows that the rate of flow of directly consumed services and work in progress, through all the stages of production and into consumption as final products, is determined by the prices asked being fixed at market-clearing levels.... But if every particular price is adjusted to all other current and expected prices, and provided services offered are not for any reason *valueless,* the rate of flow of any one needed thing *can* be synchronized, through pricing, with the rates of flow of all complementary things.... For unless services *are* valueless there must be a demand for them and, in the absence of restraint, the potential products into which they are embodied will move through the stages of production toward and into consumption.

When prices are coordinatively determined, then, not only are final prices fixed in relation to money income and consumer preference, but the prices of services and intermediate products at all stages of production are fixed in relation to expectations of demand at the next stage. Prospective prices at the next stage of demand are in turn derived from predictions of demand at subsequent stages, including the ultimate demand for the final product.[26]

The importance of entrepreneurial forecasting to the social appraisement process thus cannot be overstated. But what if production plans are based on forecasts and price appraisements which are proved false by market conditions as they subsequently emerge (which is frequently the case in the real world)? Is discoordination and "involuntary" unemployment of valuable resources not the result of such entrepreneurial error? The answer is "no"; the social appraisement process is at every point in time and under all circumstances effectively coordinating as long as price flexibility is maintained. The

---

[26] Hutt, *The Keynesian Episode,* pp. 137–38.

social appraisement of resources which is embodied in the structure of market-clearing prices, in fact, *always* reflects the speculative judgments of entrepreneurs regarding a pattern of consumer preferences that is of necessity temporally remote. The inevitable imperfection of entrepreneurial understanding of the future which results, ex post, in the misappraisement of resources, to use Hutt's words "… does not explain *non-use* of valuable (i.e., potentially demanded) services. It explains *wrong-use.*"[27]

Even in the face of the most grievous errors of entrepreneurial forecasting, full employment and effective coordination of scarce productive resources are insured by the market-clearing prices that result when access to markets for all participants in the social division of labor is unobstructed by the threat of legal or illegal coercion. As Hutt remarks: "What is essential in a coordinated economy is the *right of access* to markets for all resources and services; and in a money economy, this requires *pricing* to satisfy both buyer and seller. 'Markets' can be 'assured' for *producers as a whole* in no other way."[28]

Indeed, it is the losses that emerge when resources are priced to fully reflect erroneous forecasts which are the most accurate indicator to entrepreneurs of the direction in which their expectations need to be revised. Thus, Hutt emphasizes "… the importance of the principle that the *path* to the creation of *justified* entrepreneurial expectations is wage-rates (and other prices constituting costs) which are sensitively adjusted to entrepreneurial forecasts, *however unjustifiably pessimistic those forecasts may happen to be at the outset.*"[29]

The ex post discovery by some entrepreneurs that their courses of action have led to pecuniary losses therefore does not impede coordination. To the contrary, the experience of losses, if they are expected to continue to result from present resource combinations, stimulates a revision of entrepreneurial forecasts, production plans, and bids for productive inputs, leading to a restructuring of price relationships among higher-order goods. The full and coordinated employment

---

[27] Hutt, *A Rehabilitation,* p. 96 fn.

[28] Ibid., p. 150.

[29] Ibid., p. 97.

of productive resources then continues uninterrupted on the basis of this revised, but still speculative, social appraisement.

Nor is the coordinative functioning of the appraisement process obstructed in the slightest by the existence of contractually fixed prices for inputs or outputs which, it may turn out, are negotiated on the basis of mistaken expectations. Such prices, as Hutt emphasizes, do not constitute rigid market prices that distort the allocation of resources.[30] In fact, in the instant after they are contractually established, prices governing future transactions lose the character and function of market prices and begin to operate merely as terms upon which speculative gains and losses resulting from fluctuations of spot prices are distributed between buyers and sellers in the structure of production, for example, laborers and employers, materials suppliers and materials users, retailers and wholesalers, and so on.

Perhaps the most widespread and persistent doubt concerning the coordinative capacity of the social appraisement process, expressed even in the writings of some Austrian economists, arises from a consideration of the effects of a rise in the liquidity preferences of the public.[31] According to the conventional view, the process by which the purchasing power of the monetary unit rises in response to an attempt by market participants to increase their cash balances can involve serious discoordination of economic activity, including "involuntary" unemployment of resources.[32] Those who propound this view, however, never come to grips with the crucial point made by Hutt that the structure of resource prices generated by the social appraisement process is determined in light of the full set of consumer

---

[30] Hutt, *The Keynesian Episode*, p. 144.

[31] A rise in liquidity preference is tantamount to an increase in what Murray N. Rothbard (*Man, Economy, and State: A Treatise on Economic Principles*, 2 vols. [Los Angeles: Nash Publishing, 1970], p. 662) calls the "reservation demand" for money and may be loosely equated with a decline in the velocity term in the Fisherian equation of exchange. Rothbard distinguishes the reservation demand from the "exchange demand" for money, which is represented by the transactions term in the Fisherian equation.

[32] One Austrian who takes this view is George A. Selgin (*The Theory of Free Banking: Money Supply under Competitive Note Issue* [Totowa, N.J.: Rowman & Littlefield, 1988], p. 55).

preferences.[33] As a subset of consumer preferences, therefore, liquidity and time preferences do not stand athwart the appraisement process, as is frequently supposed, but help to give it direction and meaning. The fact that competitive bidding for productive resources in every stage of the production structure is ultimately limited by the height of expected money prices for consumer goods, in conjunction with the aggregate flow of saved funds into the hands of entrepreneurs insures that the overall scale and interstage relationships of resource prices are jointly and naturally adjusted to liquidity and time preferences.

Thus, to the extent that an increase in the cash-balance demand for money is anticipated beforehand by entrepreneurs, there will arise a potentially discoordinating divergence between the spot and (expected) future values of money, creating what Hutt refers to as "unstable price rigidities."[34] Present input prices will momentarily exceed forecast output prices, thereby rendering production at present rates unprofitable. However, those entrepreneurs who perceive the intertemporal divergence in the value of money will immediately react by lowering their current bids for resources and investing in speculative cash balances.

Such speculative "hoarding" will precipitate a reduction in current input prices and will continue until these prices have been fully coordinated with entrepreneurial appraisements of future output prices. Far from disrupting the coordinative functioning of the social appraisement process, changes in the demand for money due to speculative motives are indispensable for maintaining price coordination in the face of discrepancies between the spot and future values of money, which continually recur in a world in which agents are unequally endowed with entrepreneurial foresight.

As long as market-clearing prices prevail in resource markets, then, the economy remains fully coordinated during the adjustment to a change in liquidity preferences. This is not to deny that an upsurge in quits, layoffs, and even business bankruptcies may occur during the process as a result of the refusal of laborers who do not

---

[33] Hutt, *The Keynesian Episode*, p. 300.

[34] Ibid., p. 147.

foresee the imminent increase in the value of money to accept low-ered nominal wage rates. Nonetheless, such an occurrence is not evi-dence of nonuse of valuable resources attributable to a coordination failure; rather, it represents—what in retrospect is revealed to be—an uneconomic diversion of resources to job prospecting as a conse-quence of entrepreneurial error in forecasting the effects of a change in liquidity preferences. Such forecasting errors and resulting resource misallocations, of course, are not specifically associated with changes in liquidity preferences, but are part and parcel of the process of adjustment to any alteration in consumer preferences.

To convince ourselves of the hardiness of the coordinative forces of the market's appraisement process, let us now consider the adjustment to a change in the demand for cash balances under much less favorable conditions. Let us assume that both entre-preneurs and resource-owners are caught totally unawares by the change and that each entrepreneur misinterprets the decline in his selling price as evidence of a permanent reduction in the relative demand for his product. Reasoning from these unrealistic assump-tions, most economists conclude that an increase in liquidity pref-erences among the public, if not fully offset by a timely injection of new money into the economy, is likely to cause discoordination of economic activity that results in a more or less prolonged slump in employment and real output.

Thus, for example, in discussing the effects of an unanticipated increase in the demand for money on the part of wage earners which is unmatched by an increase in the supply of money, George Selgin writes:

> Businesses' nominal revenues become deficient relative to outlays for factors of production—the difference represent-ing money that wage earners have withdrawn from circula-tion. Since each entrepreneur notices a deficiency of his own revenues only, without perceiving it as a mere prelude to a general fall in prices *including factor prices,* he views the fall-ing off of demand for his product as symbolizing (at least in part) a lasting decline in the profitability of his particular line of business. If all entrepreneurs reduce their output, the result

is a general downturn, which ends only once a general fall in prices raises the real supply of money to its desired level.[35]

Granting Selgin's dubious assumptions that entrepreneurs are inexplicably unable to forecast changes emanating from the money side of the economy and, then, when such changes do occur, routinely misinterpret the variations in expenditure and revenue flows which accompany them, it still can be demonstrated that the social appraisement process is capable of maintaining a full and coordinated use of scarce resources as it adjusts to an increase in liquidity preferences.

The initial impact of a rise in liquidity preferences is a shrinkage of the revenues and cash balances of those firms which sell directly to the individuals who have decided to build up their inventories of cash. In response to what they mistakenly believe is a permanent decline in the relative demand for their output, these firms immediately restrict their demand for inputs. In consequence, temporary surpluses appear on labor and other resource markets at prevailing prices. Owners of land and capital resources that are specific to the production processes of the revenue-losing firms, despite their erroneous expectations of the future value of money, have no alternative but to accept market equilibrating cuts in the prices of their resources. However, things are different on the markets for nonspecific resources, such as labor. If laborers do not foresee the imminent increase in the purchasing power of money, as we assume, they refuse to acquiesce in the reduction of their nominal wage rate to a level consonant with their current employer's forecast of their marginal revenue product, and they accordingly seek alternative employment opportunities. Thus the excess supply on the labor market initially is cleared by a reduction of supply as labor services are withdrawn from the market and diverted to self-employment in job prospecting.

These early job prospectors sooner or later discover that their best employment opportunities are with those firms whose selling prices have not yet been altered by the monetary adjustment process and which, therefore, are in a position to absorb a small amount of additional labor at nominal wage rates only slightly below previously ruling

[35] Selgin, *The Theory of Free Banking*, p. 55.

rates. As the adjustment process proceeds, however, the entrepreneurs and owners of specific resources in the industries first affected by the increase in the demand for money are eventually driven to cut their expenditures and, therefore, their demands for the products of other industries in order to arrest and reverse the depletion of their cash balances. The result is a spreading decline in product prices which further restricts entrepreneurial profit and demand on resource markets and thus induces cuts in the prices of a growing range of specific resources and encourages more laborers to invest their services in job prospecting. Thus, as time goes on, the number of firms whose selling prices have not yet been reduced in response to the increased demand for money progressively declines, while the pool of laborers actively seeking alternative employment opportunities is continually being replenished and even expanded, resulting in an increasingly rapid fall in nominal wage rates.

When the overall price structure is in the last stages of adjusting to heightened liquidity preferences, there finally occurs a reduction in the product prices of those firms which, because their selling prices have held up the longest, have undertaken the greatest expansions of their labor forces. The result is a collapse of these firms' marginal revenue product of labor schedules and their nominal wage-rate offers. This effects a sudden reversal (disequilibrium) of wage-rate differentials, with the relatively highest wage rates now being offered by those firms that were first to experience the effects of the altered demand for money and that are now relatively undermanned. With this development, it finally becomes apparent that labor has been malinvested in job prospecting and misallocated in expanding those industries and firms whose product prices were the last to fall.

Hence it has been demonstrated that a rise in liquidity preferences which is completely unanticipated and initially misinterpreted by market participants causes the available stocks of inputs to be utilized by entrepreneurs and resource owners in productive combinations which yield a nonoptimal output mix, including, most conspicuously, an overproduction of job prospecting services. This confirms, however, the Huttian insight that, as long as resource prices clear markets and adjust to the competitive bidding of entrepreneurs, however ill-informed or egregiously myopic the latter's expectations and appraisements, scarce means are always fully employed and coordinated with the forecast ends of the economic system. It is not the theory of coordination, therefore, but the theory of equilibration which is relevant to the question of whether entrepreneurs are predisposed to misforecasting and misinterpreting changes originating on the money side of the economy.

This analysis of the coordinative quality of the social appraisement process leads me to conclude my comment with a confirmation and reiteration of "the great praxeological truth" enunciated by Hutt:

> ... under competition, *there is never any obstacle to the self-consistent use of scarce resources in the satisfaction of any set of noncontradictory preferences....* The origin of ... "economic disturbances" [characterized by involuntary idleness of scarce resources] must be attributed ... solely to the factors which prevent the value system from performing its coordinative task. For *there are no economic ends, and no entrepreneurial means which are incompatible with "full employment."* Entrepreneurs will never fail to use the full flow of productive services if the price mechanism is allowed to work....[36]

Bibliography

Davenport, Herbert J. [1913] 1968. *The Economics of Enterprise.* New York: Augustus M. Kelley.

Garrison, Roger W. 1990. "Austrian Capital Theory and the Future of Macroeconomics." Paper presented at Conference on Austrian Economics: Perspectives on the Past and Prospects for the Future, Hillsdale College, Hillsdale, Mich., April 1990.

Gunning, J. Patrick. 1989. "Mises on the Evenly Rotating Economy." *The Review of Austrian Economics* 3: pp. 123–35.

Hayek, F.A. [1937] 1972. "Economics and Knowledge." In *Individualism and Economic Order.* Chicago: Henry Regnery Company.

_____. 1978. "Competition as a Discovery Procedure." In *New Studies in Philosophy, Politics, Economics and the History of Ideas.* Chicago: University of Chicago Press.

---

[36] Hutt, *The Keynesian Episode*, p. 338.

Hutt, William H. 1963. *Keynesianism-Retrospect and Prospect: A Critical Restatement of Basic Economic Principles*. Chicago: Henry Regnery Company.

_____. 1974. *A Rehabilitation of Say's Law*. Athens, Ohio: Ohio University Press.

_____. 1977. *The Theory of Idle Resources: A Study in Definition*, 2nd ed. Indianapolis: Liberty Press.

_____. 1979. *The Keynesian Episode: A Reassessment*. Indianapolis: Liberty Press.

Kirzner, Israel M. 1985. "The Primacy of Entrepreneurial Discovery." In *Discovery and the Capitalist Process*, pp. 15–39. Chicago: University of Chicago Press.

_____. 1987. "The Economic Calculation Debate: Lessons for Austrians." *The Review of Austrian Economics* 2: pp. 1–18.

Mises, Ludwig von. 1966. *Human Action: A Treatise on Economics*, 3rd ed. Chicago: Henry Regnery Company.

_____. 1978. *On the Manipulation of Money and Credit*, Percy L. Greaves, Jr. ed., Bettina Bien Greaves, trans. Dobbs Ferry, N.Y.: Free Market Books.

Rothbard, Murray N. 1970. *Man, Economy, and State: A Treatise on Economic Principles*, 2 vols. Los Angeles: Nash Publishing.

Salerno, Joseph T. 1990a. "Ludwig von Mises as Social Rationalist." *The Review of Austrian Economics* 4: pp. 26–54.

_____. 1990b. "Why a Socialist Economy Is 'Impossible.'" A postscript to *Economic Calculation in the Socialist Commonwealth* by Ludwig von Mises, pp. 53–71. Auburn, Ala.: Praxeology Press.

Selgin, George A. 1988. *The Theory of Free Banking: Money Supply under Competitive Note Issue*. Totowa, N.J.: Rowman & Littlefield.

Wicksteed, Phillip H. [1910] 1967. *The Common Sense of Political Economy* and *Selected Papers and Reviews on Economic Theory*, 2 vols. New York: Augustus M. Kelley.

CHAPTER 8

Ludwig Von Mises
on Inflation and Expectations

I. Introduction

Among Ludwig von Mises's most important contributions to monetary theory are his sophisticated analyses of the social consequences of inflation and of the formation and evolution of inflationary expectations.[1] Mises's explanation of the inflationary

From: "Ludwig von Mises on Inflation and Expectations," *Advances in Austrian Economics* 2 (1995): pp. 297–325.

[1] Mises's pathbreaking analysis of inflation developed out of his integration of Austrian marginal utility theory with Carl Menger's cash-balance approach to the demand for money and the monetary process analysis originated by eighteenth- and nineteenth-century economists such as Richard Cantillon, David Hume, and J. E. Cairnes. On Mises's contributions and doctrinal influences in the area of monetary theory, see Murray Rothbard, "The Austrian Theory of Money," in *Foundations of Modern Austrian Economics*, ed. E.G. Dolan (Kansas City: Sheed & Ward, Inc., 1976), pp. 168–84; idem, *The Essential Ludwig von Mises*, 2nd ed. (Auburn, Ala.: Ludwig von Mises Institute, 1980), pp. 14–23; Joseph Salerno, "Commentary: The Concept of Coordination in Austrian Macroeconomics," in *Austrian Economics: Perspectives on the Past and Prospects for the Future*, ed. R.B. Ebeling (Hillsdale, Mich.: Hillsdale College Press, 1991): pp. 367–75; J.R. Edwards, *The Economist of the Country: Ludwig von Mises in the History of Monetary Thought* (New York: Carlton Press, Inc. 1985); L. Robbins, *Money, Trade and International Relations* (London: Macmillan, [1952] 1971). In contrast to his analysis of the inflation adjustment process, which has gained substantial recognition, Mises's innovative approach to expectations has garnered little if any attention, even from Austrian-oriented economists.

process is characterized by an emphasis on the kind of relative price effects that are inconsistent with the long-run neutrality of money. Probably for this reason, modern proponents of the quantity theory of money have generally neglected Mises's theory. And although modern quantity theorists[2] recently have begun to address Mises's analysis, they have for the most part misconceived his view of the nature and durability of these effects.

Modern Austrian economists, for their part, generally ignore Mises's theory of inflationary expectations. Some have either denied that Mises proposed such a theory or denied that he succeeded in integrating it with his overall vision of the economic process. For example, the late Ludwig Lachmann strongly implied that Mises offered no theory of expectations.[3] And even such a careful Mises scholar as Richard M. Ebeling,[4] while admitting that Mises "did attempt to formulate a constructive theory of expectations and their formation in the market process," concluded that Mises failed to fully integrate his theory of expectations formation with his theories of money and of entrepreneurship.[5] However, at least one sympathetic neoclassical monetary theorist[6] has taken note of Mises's analysis of the development of expectations about the future purchasing power

[2] Edwards, *The Economist of the Country*; T.J. Humphrey, "On the Nonneutral Relative Price Effects in Monetarist Thought," Federal Reserve Bank of Richmond *Economic Review* 70 (May/June): pp. 13–19.

[3] L.M. Lachmann ("From Mises to Schackle: An Essay on Austrian Economics and the Kaleidic Society," *Journal of Economic Literature* 14 (March): p. 58) declares that "Mises hardly ever mentions expectations, though entrepreneurs and speculators often enough turn up in his pages. Thus from 1939 onward Schackle had to take on expectations more or less single-handedly, without much benefit of support from the Austrian side."

[4] R.M. Ebeling, "Expectations and Expectations Formation in Mises's Theory of the Market Process," *Market Process* 6 (Spring): pp. 12–18.

[5] According to Ebeling ("Expectations and Expectations Formation," p. 16), "Mises's writings on monetary theory ... [are] not integrated into his theory of expectations formation, not even in *Human Action*. His theory is incompletely developed and applied within his own system." This misinterpretation aside, Ebeling's article is a valuable overview of Mises's influences and method in developing his theory of expectations.

[6] Edwards, *The Economist of the Country*, p. 104.

of money during historical episodes of inflation, criticizing it as an inconsistent amalgam of elements of the rational and adaptive expectations theories.

In the next section of this paper, I briefly review Mises's distinctive "step-by-step," or sequential analysis of changes in the the supply of money and demonstrate how this analysis implies that money is nonneutral in the long run as well as in the short run In the third section I contrast Mises's description of the inflationary process and its effects with the account given by the modern quantity theorists. I argue that recent monetarist criticisms of Mises's description of the consequences of unanticipated monetary inflation are based on a failure to adequately appreciate the subtleties of Mises's analysis. I also describe how Mises's analytical method led him to an explanation of the positive employment effect typical of initially unanticipated inflation that differs markedly from the explanation derived from the Friedman-Phelps natural rate hypothesis. In the fourth section of the paper, I present a comprehensive account of Mises's theory of expectations, showing how it is integrated with his praxeological approach to economic theory and elucidating the crucial role it plays in his analysis of the effects of an ongoing monetary inflation.[7] I also address the attempt to interpret Mises's writings on inflationary expectations in terms of macroeconomic expectations-formation mechanisms. The

---

[7] It should be pointed out here that Murray N. Rothbard's approach to expectations is implicitly Misesian. Thus the fact that Rothbard does not provide a formal explication of Mises's approach to expectations does not mean Rothbard does not "take the problem of expectations formation seriously" as Ebeling ("Expectations and Expectations Formation," p. 12) asserts. Ebeling's implication is logically unwarranted and is easily shown to be in error, once we consider a few of the most notable doctrines expounded by Rothbard in *Man, Economy, and State: A Treatise on Economic Principles*, 2 vols. (Los angeles: Nash Publishing, [1962] 1970). In his analysis of the pricing process, Rothbard, like the great Austrian price theorists Böhm-Bawerk and Wicksteed, focuses on the determination of actual, moment-to-moment prices, whose determinants include the speculative reservation ("inventory") demands of sellers. Rothbard also provides explicit and extended treatments of the influence of speculative anticipations on the formation of market supply and demand curves, of the inherently speculative cash-balance demand for money, and of the determination of the purchasing power component of the nominal interest rate. Finally, Rothbard recognizes the key role of the promoting, uncertainty-bearing, price-appraising capitalist-entrepreneur in driving the market process.

fifth section reviews Mises's discussion of the German hyperinflation to illustrate how his theory of expectations is woven into his economic analysis. I conclude by summarizing the lessons that contemporary economists can learn from Mises's analysis of the inflation process.

II. Mises's Analytical Method and the Long-Run Nonneutrality of Money

In his autobiographical *Notes and Recollections*,[8] written in 1940 but not published until 1978, Mises gave the following description of the "step-by-step" method of analyzing monetary phenomena, which he had formulated in his 1912 work *The Theory of Money and Credit*:

> The step-by-step analysis must consider the lapse of time. In such an analysis the time-lag between cause and effect becomes a multitude of time differences between single successive consequences. Reflection on these time-lags leads to a precise theory of the social consequences of changes in the purchasing power of money.

As Mises[9] proceeded to point out, such an analysis yields a "theory of the inevitable nonneutrality of money," implying "... that changes in purchasing power of money causes prices of different commodities and services to change neither simultaneously nor evenly, and that it is incorrect to maintain that changes in the quantity of money bring about simultaneous and proportional changes in the 'level' of prices."

Mises thus conceived inflation as a time-spanning process in which an increase in the stock of money invariably results in a sequential adjustment of prices, which necessarily alters relative prices and brings about a reallocation of productive resources and a redistribution of real income and wealth. The specific temporal sequence in which prices are adjusted, and thus the identity of those market participants experiencing gains or losses, is not deducible from economic theory. Rather, it depends concretely on the specific point at which

---

[8] Ludwig von Mises, *Notes and Recollections* (South Holland, Ill.: Libertarian Press, 1978), p. 59.

[9] Ibid.

the new money is injected into the economy and on the marginal utility schedules of those who receive and spend the new money.

One sympathetic neoclassical economist, James Rolph Edwards, points out, "[Mises's] description of the inflationary process is more complex and realistic than the sort of 'airplane spreading analysis' (involving miraculous equiproportional additions to cash balances) that economists all too frequently indulge in."[10] Unfortunately, Edwards erroneously concludes that Mises imagined this "lagged price adjustment process" as reaching completion "only when the original price relations were restored." As I argued in chapter 2, however, Mises took great pains to deny that either the instantaneous demand curve or the Patinkinite market equilibrium curve for nominal cash balances can ever take on the shape of a rectangular hyperbola under dynamic real-world, conditions. Moreover, Edwards[11] commits a blunder in elementary price theory when he insists that the relative position of the group of sellers whose receipt of the new money occurs late in the inflationary process is restored at the end of the process, although their "losses suffered in the interim go uncompensated." Logically, it is just such uncompensated losses (and gains) that *permanently* alter the pattern of individual wealth holdings, market demands, and relative prices, and therefore result in a revolution and not a restoration of the relative positions of various groups of sellers in the new long-run equilibrium, or what Mises called the "final state of rest."

Thus, as Mises[12] stated, "Precisely because the price increases have not affected all commodities at one time, shifts in the relationships of wealth and income are effected which affect the supply and demand of individual goods and services differently. Thus, these shifts must lead to a new orientation of the market and of market prices." Moreover, as Mises contended in criticizing Irving Fisher's formulation of the quantity theory, Fisher was led to contrive his artificial dichotomy between

---

[10] Ibid., pp. 92–93.

[11] Ibid., p. 92.

[12] Ludwig von Mises, *On the Manipulation of Money and Credit*, Percy L. Greaves, ed., trans. B.B. Greaves (Dobbs Ferry, N.Y.: Free Market Books, 1978), p. 96.

monetary theory and value theory as a makeshift defense against just such a charge of elementary logical error. Wrote Mises:[13]

> One thing only can explain how Fisher is able to maintain his mechanical Quantity Theory. To him the Quantity Theory seems a doctrine peculiar to the value of money; in fact he contrasts it outright with the laws of value of other economic goods.... With as much justification as that of Fisher and Brown for their mechanical formula for the value of money, a similar formula could be set out for the value of any commodity, and similar conclusions drawn from it.[14]

In fact the efforts by neoclassical monetary theorists following Patinkin to "integrate monetary and value theory" missed the point, because they were aimed at repairing the Fisherian dichotomy without coming to terms with the value-theoretic error embodied in the neutral-money doctrine.

III. The Inflationary Process: Mises Versus the Quantity Theorists

In analyzing the social consequences of inflation, Mises recognized that unanticipated inflation modifies the relative wealth positions of creditors and debtors. He also endorsed Fisher's original analysis of the adjustment of the nominal interest rate to an anticipated fall in the purchasing power of money. In fact, Mises[15] considered the emphasis on the link between fluctuations in the value of money and the formation of the interest rate to be "Fisher's most important contribution to monetary theory." In addition, Mises originated[16] the argument that inflation causes a falsification of capital accounting that leads to an overstatement of profits and brings about unintended consumption of the social stock of capital. This

---

[13] Ludwig von Mises, *The Theory of Money and Credit*, 2nd ed. (Irvington-on-Hudson, N.Y.: The Foundation for Economic Education, [1952] 1971).

[14] Ibid., pp. 144–45.

[15] Mises, *On the Manipulation of Money and Credit*, p. 93.

[16] Ludwig von Mises, *Nation, State, and Economy: Contributions to the Politics and History of Our Time*, trans. L.B. Yeager (New York: New York University Press, 1983), pp. 160–63.

occurs because depreciation quotas for capital goods during inflation continue to be computed on the basis of their historical costs
rather than their (necessarily higher) replacement costs. The entrepreneurs may dispose of these "accounting" profits by increasing
their own consumption, by cutting prices to consumers, or by bidding up the wage rates of laborers. In the latter two cases, a one-time
redistribution of wealth from one group to another accompanies the
"consumption of capital."

What Mises clearly regarded as the most important effect of
inflation, however, is the permanent redistribution of income and
wealth that results from the sequential and uneven adjustment
of prices to an addition to the stock of money. For Mises,[17] "... the
social consequences of changes in the value of money are not limited to altering the content of future monetary obligations." In fact, as
Mises[18] argued, in a continuing inflation that comes to be more or less
correctly anticipated by the public, the effects on short-term credit
transactions are mitigated by the Fisherian inflation premium that
becomes incorporated into loan contracts. In the case of long-term
credit, where it is much more difficult to forecast the precise degree
of depreciation of the monetary unit, a commodity with a relatively
stable value, such as gold or foreign currency, is substituted for the
depreciating money as the "standard of deferred payments." Mises[19]
also suggested that adjusting accounting procedures for durable
equipment to reflect replacement rather than historical costs would
be a practicable method for greatly reducing or eliminating the unintended consumption of capital and the associated redistribution of
income from capitalist-entrepreneurs to other groups in society that
occurs during inflation.

Mises[20] therefore argued (in sharp contrast to modern quantity
theorists) that the most significant social consequence of the variation
in the purchasing power of money is the "uncompensatable changes"

---

[17] Mises, *On the Manipulation of Money and Credit*, p. 95.

[18] Ibid., p. 94.

[19] Ludwig von Mises, *Human Action: A Treatise on Economics*, 3rd ed. (Chicago:
Henry Regnery Company, 1966), pp. 425–26.

[20] Mises, *On the Manipulation of Money and Credit*, p. 97.

in income and wealth that occur "… because of the uneven timing of the price changes of the various goods and services." Thus every change in the quantity of money leaves indelible imprints on the relative-price structure and therefore on the pattern of wealth and income distribution.

Recently, Thomas J. Humphrey has argued[21] that "the Austrian School's contention that monetarists invariably ignore relative price and real output effects in the monetary mechanism" is based on a misconception. Humphrey then goes on to impressively demonstrate that monetarists, like Milton Friedman, as well as their forerunners, including Fisher and Clark Warburton, do indeed take into account "the *temporary* nonneutral real-sector effects of monetary changes" (emphasis added). But, of course, recognition only of short-term relative price and real output effects that are inexplicably and exactly reversed in the course of the monetary adjustment process to yield the long-run neutrality of money does not constitute the resolution but the very crux of the problem that Austrian monetary theorists identify with the Fisherian quantity theory.

Humphrey misunderstands the basis of the Misesian proposition that any explanation of the monetary adjustment process must proceed in terms consistent with general value theory and with the inescapable fact that prices adjust sequentially over time. Thus Humphrey[22] touts Fisher's allusions to "contractual restraints, legal prohibitions, and the inertia of custom [which] render individual prices sticky" as a complete and convincing explanation of the "real" effects that invariably accompany monetary changes.

Humphrey[23] further claims that Austrians ignore the effect of increased employment caused by inflation's temporary distortion of the relative price between labor and output, that is, the real wage rate, an effect which has been particularly stressed by Friedman.

---

[21] T.M. Humphrey, "On the Nonneutral Relative Price Effects in Monetarist Thought," Federal Reserve Bank of Richmond *Economic Review* 70 (May/June): pp. 13–19; p. 13.

[22] Ibid., p. 15.

[23] Ibid., p. 18.

This charge is uninformed at best. In an article published in 1958,[24] the same year A.W. Phillips's famous article[25] was published and a full decade before Friedman unveiled his "natural rate" hypothesis in his Presidential address to the American Economic Association, Mises anticipated the essential points of Friedman's article. According to Edwards,[26] Mises set forth "... virtually all of the essential arguments Friedman later made on the subject in his Presidential address. The existence of a natural rate of unemployment conditioned by the state of real wages is clearly implicit.... The existence of a short-run trade-off between inflation and unemployment and the nonexistence of a long-run tradeoff due to some sort of expectations adjustment are both explicit elements of the argument." Referring to an even earlier essay by Mises,[27] Edwards[28] states that "Mises even more clearly anticipated Phelps and the accelerationists."

More important, for Mises, in contrast to Friedman and the natural-rate theorists, the "real wage/employment effect" attributable to inflation does not depend on the conjecture that "selling prices of products typically respond to an unanticipated rise in nominal demand faster than prices of factors of production,"[29] combined with an ad hoc assumption regarding the relatively slow rate at which laborers adapt

---

[24] Ludwig von Mises, "Wages, Unemployment and Inflation," in *Planning for Freedom and Sixteen Other Essays and Addresses*, 4th ed. (South Holland, Ill.: Libertarian Press, [1958] 1980), pp. 150–61.

[25] A.W. Phillips, "The Relation between Unemployment and the Rate of Change of Money Wage Rates in the United Kingdom, 1861–1957," in *Macroeconomic Readings*, ed. J. Lindauer, pp. 107–19. (New York: The Free Press, [1958] 1968).

[26] Edwards, *The Economist of the Country*, p. 100.

[27] Ludwig von Mises, "Economic Aspects of the Pension Problem," in *Planning for Freedom and Sixteen Other Essays and Addresses*, 4th ed. (South Holland, Ill.: Libertarian Press, [1950] 1980), pp. 83–93.

[28] Edwards, *The Economist of the Country*, p. 100.

[29] M. Friedman, "The Role of Monetary Policy," in *The Essence of Friedman*, ed. K.R. Leube (Stanford, Calif.: Hoover Institution Press, [1968] 1987), p. 395. For a demonstration that the available historical evidence does not support the hypothesis that wages generally lag behind prices during inflation, see A.A. Alchian and R.A. Kessel, "The meaning and Validity of the Inflation-induced Lag of Wages behind Prices," in *Economic Forces at Work*, ed. A.A. Alchian (Indianapolis, Ind.: Liberty Press, [1960] 1977), pp. 413–50.

their expectations about money's future purchasing power to their experience of its depreciation. In fact, in Mises's step-by-step exposition of the inflation-adjustment process, an industry may find the real wage rates it must pay decreasing or increasing, depending on the specific point at which the additional quantity of money first impinges on individual value scales and the exact sequence of individual cash balance adjustments that is then set in train. Thus, for example, an inflation precipitated by an expansion of bank loans for purposes of business investment entails *rising*, not falling, real wage rates and, therefore, a negative employment effect for lower-order capital and consumer goods' industries, that is, those industries that are late in the chain of spending of the newly-created fiduciary media.

As Mises[30] explained "... in the regular course of banking operations the banks issue fiduciary media only as loans to producers and merchants.... [T]hese fiduciary media are used first of all for production, that is to buy factors of production and pay wages. The first prices to rise, therefore, as a result of an increase of the quantity of money ... caused by the issue of such fiduciary media, are those of raw materials, semimanufactured products, other goods of higher orders, and wage rates. Only later do the prices of goods of the first order [i.e., of consumers' goods] follow." In this case, which still regularly recurs in modern economies, because the rise in wage rates precedes the rise in consumer goods' prices, unanticipated inflation does not produce the paradigmatic Friedmanite real wage/employment effect.

Mises[31] did appreciate, moreover, that the issue of fresh fiduciary media via the expansion of bank credit to business ignites a process of monetary depreciation that will typically "follow a different path and have different accompanying social side effects from those produced by a new discovery of precious metals or by the issue of paper money." In the case of the latter two sources of new money, the ensuing process of depreciation may feature the phenomenon of wage rates generally lagging behind the rise in commodity prices, resulting in a general decline in real wage rates and the phenomenon of "forced

---

[30] Mises, *On the Manipulation of Money and Credit*, pp. 120–21.
[31] Ibid., pp. 121–22.

saving," that is, the redistribution of wealth and income from wage earners to entrepreneurs. Mises[32] even allowed that such an effect on real wage rates may occur "If monetary depreciation is brought about by an issue of fiduciary media, and if wage rates for some reason do not promptly follow the increase in commodity prices."

Thus Mises[33] was adamant in his conclusion that, in an economy with unhampered labor markets:

> ... forced saving can result from inflation but need not necessarily. It depends on the particular data of each instance of inflation whether or not the rise in wage rates lags behind the rise in commodity prices. A tendency for real wages to drop is not an inescapable consequence of a decline in the monetary unit's purchasing power. It could happen that nominal wage rates rise more or sooner than commodity prices.

Mises's analysis led him to seek in another direction for the explanation of the observed positive effect of inflation on the employment of labor. His explanation begins with initially-prevailing conditions of excess supply in labor markets that are hampered by minimum wage laws and by the restrictionist policies of legally privileged unions. It is under these conditions, which have prevailed in most industrial economies since the 1920s, that unanticipated inflation via bank credit expansion can lower real wage rates toward market-clearing levels and increase the employment of labor. As Mises[34] argued:

> Under conditions of [the inflationary] boom, nominal wage rates which before the credit expansion were too high for the state of the market and therefore created unemployment of a part of the potential labor force are no longer too high and the unemployed can get jobs again. However, this happens only because under the changed monetary and credit conditions prices are rising or, what is the same expressed in other words, the purchasing power of the monetary unit drops ... inflation can cure unemployment only by curtailing the wage earner's real wages.

---

[32] Ibid., p. 121

[33] Mises, *Human Action*, p. 549.

[34] Mises, "Wages, Unemployment, and Inflation," p. 154.

Both Mises and Friedman recognize that when the discovery is made by laborers that their real wage rates have been eroded by inflation, supply of labor curves in nominal wage space shift leftward, driving up real wage rates toward former levels. For Friedman, inflationary monetary forces have displaced the real economy and this countermovement therefore represents its return to the quasi-general equilibrium state of the "natural rate of unemployment," according to Friedman,[35] "the level that would be ground out by the Walrasian system of general equilibrium equations, provided there is imbedded within them the actual structural characteristics of the labor and commodity markets." In Mises's analysis, in contrast, the reversal of the drop in real wage rates occurs because "... the unions ask for a new increase in wages in order to keep pace with the rising cost of living and we are back where we were before, i.e., in a situation in which large scale unemployment can only be prevented by a further expansion of credit."[36]

Now, unlike the Chicago price theorists, Mises and the Misesian wing of the modern Austrian school do not believe that the market economy is ever at, or even within sight of, long-run general equilibrium.[37] Rather, the structure of realized market-clearing prices is seen by Austrians as functioning, despite its non-general-equilibrium character, to continuously coordinate the uses and technical combinations of available resources in light of entrepreneurial forecasts of constantly shifting future market conditions, including consumer preferences.[38] Hence, for Mises, in direct contrast to Friedman,

---

[35] Friedman, "The Role of Monetary Policy," p. 394.

[36] Mises, "Wages, Unemployment, and Inflation," pp. 154–55.

[37] As I have argued elsewhere (Joseph T. Salerno, "Mises and Hayek Dehomogenized," *The Review of Austrian Economics* 6 (2): pp. 113–46), contemporary Misesians differ sharply from contemporary Hayekians on this issue.

[38] Thus, Mises (*The Ultimate Foundation of Economic Science: An Essay on Method*, 2nd ed. [Kansas City: Sheed Andrews and McMeel, Inc., 1978], p. 65) described the market as "the essence of coordination of all elements of supply and demand." For a treatment of this concept of moment-to-moment "price coordination" as the foundation of Austrian macro theorizing, see Salerno ("Coordination in Austrian Macroeconomics"). Also see the pathbreaking discussions by William H. Hutt (*A Rehabilitation of Say's Law* (Athens: Ohio University Press, 1975); *The Keynesian Episode: A Reassessment* (Indianapolis, Ind.: Liberty Press, 1979), pp. 137–77). Hutt named and formalized the concept of "price coordination" and first

it is the decline in real wage rates toward their market-clearing levels brought about by unforeseen inflation that is equilibrating—albeit crudely and temporarily; the ensuing restoration of the former level of real wage rates by renewed union restrictionism, on the other hand, marks a reversion to a pervasive and chronic disequilibrium situation in which the labor market is precluded from establishing even a momentary equilibrium of supply and demand, while the market's long-run *tendency* to generate a structure of final equilibrium wage rates and optimal allocation of labor is permanently stifled.

In his critique of the monetarists for downplaying the role of labor unions in shaping the inflationary process, Gottfried Haberler[39] presents a Misesian analysis of what he identifies as a money-fueled "wage-push inflation,"[40] and contends that the monetarists implicitly assume "a few islands of monopoly in a vast competitive sea; where monopolies existed wages and prices would be higher, production and consumption lower, but unemployment would be transitory and moderate because

---

elaborated its relevance to macroeconomic themes, although it had long been an essential part of classical and Austrian microeconomics. Joseph T. Salerno ("William H. Hutt") provides a survey of Hutt's contributions to economic theory.

[39] Haberler, *Economic Growth & Stability*, p. 105.

[40] For Haberler (ibid., pp. 101–02) both "demand-pull" and "cost-push" inflation "... are monetary in the important sense that they require monetary expansion.... [T]here has never, literally never as far as I know, been a case of sustained inflation without a rise in M." For the continuing Austrian influences on and orientation of Haberler's later work as an American academic, see Joseph T. Salerno ("Gottfried Haberler"). A similar explanation of the relationship between unions, unemployment, and inflation is offered by F.A. Hayek ("The Use of Knowledge in Society," in *Individualism and Economic Order* (Chicago: Henry Regnery Company, [1945] 1972), pp. 53–97). The point of view that ascribes an important role to unions in promoting and conditioning the inflationary process has been described as "Haberlerian" by Friedman and "Pigovian/Hayekian/Haberlerian" by Lionel Robbins (Robbins, et al., *Inflation: Causes, Consequences, Cures: Discourses on the Debate between the Monetary and Trade Union Interpretations* [Levittown, N.Y.: Transatlantic Arts, Inc., 1974], p. 44). However both of these labels obscure Mises's contributions referred to above and the fact that Mises (*On the Manipulation of Money and Credit*, pp. 173–203) outlined the argument as early as 1931 in a German-language publication addressing the causes of the unprecedented depth and persistence of the Great Depression. For evidence supporting the Austrian as opposed to the Friedmanite view of the influence of unions on unemployment, see R.K. Vedder and L.E. Gallaway, *Out of Work: Unemployment and Government in Twentieth-Century America* (New York: Holmes & Meier, 1993).

the labor and other productive resources set free in the monopolized areas would find employment, at somewhat lower wages, in the large competitive sector." While Haberler[41] disputes the empirical validity of this assumption even for conditions prevailing in the U.S. economy in the early 1970s, the significant point for our discussion is that the monetarist analysis is applicable only to those situations where the assumption in question holds true. Eschewing the monetarist focus on general equilibrium, Mises[42] explicitly predicated his analysis of the modern inflation-adjustment process on the existence of what he called "institutional" unemployment of labor created by political policies that foster labor union "restrictionism" and rigid wages.

In propounding his novel theory of union activity, Mises[43] argued that labor unions are unconcerned with the configuration of the demand curve for their product because they "... do not aim at monopoly wage rates." Unions are "restrictionist," and not monopolistic, organizations, because they "... are not concerned with what may happen to the part of supply which they bar from access to the market." While a monopolistic pricing policy is advantageous only if total revenue earned at the monopoly price equals or exceeds the total revenue earned at the competitive price (or if total cost falls more rapidly than total revenue between the competitive and monopoly prices), "Restrictive action ... is always advantageous for the privileged group and disadvantageous for those whom it excludes from the market. It always raises the price per unit and therefore the total net proceeds of the privileged group. The losses of the excluded group are not taken into account by the privileged group."[44]

An important implication of Mises's analysis is that the ability of unions to restrict supply in labor markets is much greater and less predictable than would be the case if they were merely engaged

---

[41] Haberler, *Economic Growth & Stability*, p. 106.

[42] Ludwig von Mises, *Theory and History: An Interpretation of Social and Economic Evolution* (Auburn, Ala.: Ludwig von Mises Institute, [1957] 1985), pp. 76–81.

[43] Ibid., pp. 87–81.

[44] Mises, *Human Action,* pp. 376–77. An illuminating discussion of the "restrictionist pricing of labor" can be found in Rothbard (*Man, Economy, and State,* vol. 2, pp. 620–29).

in monopolistic pricing, because, in the case of restrictionism, the desired shift of the supply curve to the left cannot be explained solely on the basis of the configuration of the total revenue and total cost curves. Thus, if we accept Mises's explanation of union activity, real wage rates may not be determinate in a strictly catallactic general-equilibrium model from which the concept of a natural rate of unemployment is deduced. This means that economists would have to draw their assumptions regarding union goals and plans from outside the system of catallactic theorems, that is, from historical analysis. They then must be prepared to admit that these goals are apt to shift, possibly rapidly, producing corresponding shifts in the natural rate and thus undercutting the practical usefulness of this concept.

The Misesian position has been recognized and challenged by monetary disequilibrium theorists, Dan E. Birch, Alan A. Rabin, and Leland B. Yeager.[45] Although they also reject Friedman's explanation of the positive effect of inflation on employment and real output, they do not accept the explanation of the phenomenon offered by W.H. Hutt,[46] which is essentially the Mises-Haberler view presented above. Indeed, they dismiss it out of hand because it dares to suggest that "villainy" is afoot in the pricing process in form of restrictionist pricing of labor by unions and governments.[47]

Hutt rebutted an earlier article by Yeager that argued that the shrinkage of real output below its potential level is generally attributable to unanticipated changes in aggregate monetary expenditure,

---

[45] Dan E. Birch, Alan A. Rabin, and Leland B. Yeager, "Inflation, Output, and Employment: Some Clarifications," *Economic Inquiry* 20 (April): pp. 209–21.

[46] Hutt's analysis of cost-push or wage-push inflation can be found in W.H. Hutt, *The Strike-Threat System: The Economic Consequences of Collective Bargaining* (New Rochelle, N.Y.: Arlington House, 1973), pp. 252–70.

[47] Ibid., pp. 213–14. Hutt appears to have developed his own position on this issue independently of the direct influence of Mises and the Austrians, having been heavily influenced during his formative years as an economist in the 1920s and 1930s by his teacher Edwin Cannan and other economists at the London School of Economics. The LSE economists stressed the coordinative functioning of the market process as the solution to the persistence of depressionary levels of resource unemployment and aggregate real output. See Joseph T. Salerno, Reply to Leland Yeager on "Mises and Hayek on Calculation and Knowledge," *The Review of Austrian Economics* 7 (2): pp. 111–25.

which generate disequilibrium "income constraints" of the Clower-Leijonhufvud type. According to Hutt "... the crucial continuity [of the market-clearing process] is *always* dependent upon valuing and pricing, whether or not monetary policy is flexible, rigid, inflationary or deflationary—that is, independently of the factors which determine the purchasing power of the monetary unit."[48] Elsewhere, Hutt countered a similar argument by Leijonhufvud by pointing out, "... at wage rates equal to the 'marginal *prospective* product,' all labor is immediately employable."[49] (Emphasis is added.)

IV. Mises's Theory of Expectations

This brings us to the vexed question of Mises's approach to the theory of expectations formation and adjustment, and his view of the role that expectations play in the adjustment of real variables to monetary inflation. Edwards[50] argues, "Mises's statements on the adjustment and effects of expectations in *The Theory of Money and Credit* seem to contain two distinct and somewhat contradictory attitudes and associated mechanisms." He also adduces evidence that Mises shifted back and forth in this work between the adaptive-expectations and rational-expectations approaches. In fact, at some points in his writings, Mises also appeared to have employed the assumption that expectations regarding movements of the future purchasing power of money are "rigidly inelastic" with respect to current changes in realized prices, and that such movements are thus anticipated to be completely reversed in the course of the agent's planning horizon.[51] At other times, Mises[52] regarded expectations as apparently "unhinged" from recent experience of objective market conditions, so that a small increase in

---

[48] Hutt, *A Rehabilitation of Say's Law*, p. 64.

[49] Hutt, *The Keynesian Episode*, p. 284.

[50] Edwards, *The Economist of the Country*, p. 100.

[51] For Hick's analysis of the concept of elasticity of expectations, see J.R. Hicks, *Value and Capital: An Inquiry into Some Fundamental Principles of Economic Theory*, 2nd ed. (New York: Oxford University Press, [1946] 1968), pp. 206–40.

[52] Ludwig von Mises, "The Great German Inflation," in *Money, Method, and the Market Process*, ed. R.M. Ebeling (Norwell, Mass.: Kluwer Academic Publishers, [1932] 1990), p. 102–03.

the quantity of money following upon a long interlude of price stability can drive the demand for money rapidly toward zero and precipitate an explosive upward spiral of prices. Mises also characterized the simultaneous actions of different groups of individuals operating on different markets as often dominated by different kinds of inflationary expectations. Nonetheless, the "contradictions" that Edwards[53] detects among Mises's various statements on inflationary expectations are superficial only and are resolved within an integrated praxeologico-historical account of the nature and formation of expectations.

According to Mises, any human action is aimed at substituting a more satisfactory state of affairs (from the point of view of the actor) for the state that would emerge without the action. Because of the lapse of time between the inception and the outcome of every action, the future conditions that an action will impinge upon and transform can never be known with certainty but must be forecast by the agent. Thus human action is inherently entrepreneurial, or, as Mises[54] puts it, "Every action is a speculation, i.e., guided by a definite opinion concerning the uncertain conditions of the future."

However, although praxeology can indisputably establish expectations as a logical prerequisite of every act of choice, it cannot shed light on the content or temporal evolution of expectations. Praxeology deals with the logical structure and implications of action, and, as such, "… is not concerned with the events which within a man's soul or mind or brain produce a definite decision between an A and a B…. Its subject is not the content of these acts of choosing, but what results from them: action."[55] For insight into the concrete process of expectations formation, Mises[56] directs us to the method of "specific understanding" (*Verstehen*) as it is utilized in the historical disciplines and "as it is practiced by everybody in all his interhuman relations and actions."

The specific understanding that is brought to bear by the historian in explaining past events is a mental process which "… establishes,

---

[53] Edwards, *The Economist of the Country*, p. 104.

[54] Mises, *Foundation of Economic Science*, p. 51.

[55] Mises, *Theory and History*, p. 271.

[56] Ibid., p. 310.

on the one hand, the fact that, motivated by definite value judgments, people have engaged in definite actions and applied definite means to attain ends they seek. It tries, on the other hand, to evaluate the effects and intensity of the effects of an action, its bearing upon the further course of events."[57] This method of proceeding is based on the insights of what used to be referred to derisively by experimental psychologists as "literary psychology," a discipline which Mises[58] redubbed "thymology." The word thymology, is a derivative of the classical Greek term denoting the mental faculty that was believed to be the source of thought, volition, and emotion. According to Mises,[59] thymology is itself a historical discipline, which:

> … derives knowledge from historical experience [from] observation both of other people's choices and of the observer's own choosing.… It is what a man knows about the way in which people value different conditions, about their wishes and desires and their plans to realize these wishes and desires. It is the knowledge of the social environment in which a man lives and acts or, with historians, of a foreign milieu about which he has learned by studying special sources.

The thymological method allows the historian to "understand" a complex historical event, in the dual sense of enumerating its causes, as far as they proceed from human values and volitions, and weighting the contribution of each of the causes to the observed outcome. The weights of the various causal factors, of course, cannot be quantitatively and mechanically determined but are a matter of the historian's necessarily subjective "judgments of relevance."[60] Just as thymological experience serves as the basis for the historian's interpretive understanding of past events (so far as they depend on social and not natural causes), it also conditions the actor's "specific understanding of future events" or, in current terminology, his formation of expectations about the future.

---

[57] Ibid., pp. 264–65.

[58] Ibid., p. 265.

[59] Ibid., pp. 272, 266.

[60] Mises, *Human Action*, pp. 56–57.

Like the historian, the acting individual must base his forecast of future conditions on an understanding both of the factors operating or likely to operate in producing the future outcome and of the degree of influence exercised by each of these factors in the emergence of the final result. But these two problems, that is, of "enumeration" and of "weighting," are precisely the problems that must be solved by the historian who seeks to explain the emergence of the same situation in retrospect. Moreover, as Mises[61] pointed out, "'The precariousness of forecasting is mainly due to the intricacy of this second problem [of weighting]. It is not only a rather puzzling question in forecasting future events. It is no less puzzling in retrospect for the historian." It is to emphasize the fact that the historian and the acting individual both must use the thymological method in solving the same type of problems that Mises[62] referred to them, respectively, as "the historian of the past" and "the historian of the future."

As noted earlier, concerning expectations, all that can be logically inferred from the action axiom, (which states that individuals behave purposefully by using means to achieve ends) is that they are a universal category of action, because all actions necessarily are future-oriented and take place under uncertainty. Logical deduction from the action axiom yields no information to the economist about the content and adjustment of expectations; nor is it permissible, from Mises's point of view, for the economist to simply "assume" an expectations adjustment mechanism for the purposes of generating testable hypotheses about observed economic variables. Assumptions about expectations that are to be used to supplement the action axiom in deducing catallactic theorems, like many of the other subsidiary assumptions of praxeological reasoning, must be drawn from the general thymological experience of the theorist or from more formal historical research. Mises[63] stressed that the incorporation of such experience-based assumptions into the chains of praxeological deduction does not alter the rigidly formal and aprioristic character of economic theory, but renders it useful for comprehending specific

---

[61] Mises, *Theory and History*, p. 314.

[62] Ibid, p. 320.

[63] Mises, *Human Action*, pp. 65–66.

phenomena of real human life and action. Without such a strict delim-
itation of its assumptions, praxeology—and, therefore, economics
also—would lose its function as a science and become merely "mental
gymnastics or a logical pastime."

Thus, for example, an account of the inflation-adjustment process that is based on the rational expectations hypothesis that "the
unobservable subjective expectations of individuals are exactly the
true mathematical conditional expectations implied by the [simulta-
neous-equation macroeconomic] model itself"[64] may offer an interesting, if idle, praxeological exercise, but it offers no scientific truths
about real-world inflation processes. Such a hypothesis contradicts
one of the most general and important conclusions of thymology that
must be accepted as a datum of economic theorizing, namely, that
there exists a broad and unpredictably varying range of differences
between human beings in their abilities to anticipate and adjust to
change.[65] The rational expectations approach also rejects the thymological insight that false economic doctrines may powerfully condition the public's, including bankers' and entrepreneurs', forecasts of the
future. The influence of these doctrines on economic activity is particularly potent when they are fostered by popular political ideologies, as
was and still remains the case with the "cheap money fallacy" and the
"balance-of-payments theory" of exchange rates. Similarly, misleading economic doctrines also may be promoted by a layman's superficial reading of long catallactic experience. Consider, for example, the
doctrine that variations in the purchasing power of money are caused
solely by extraordinary events emanating from the commodity side
of the economy. This doctrine, which dominated economic writings
until the mid-sixteenth century and lay opinion up until the inflations
following the First World War and which continued to underlie conventional accounting procedures until the inflations of the 1970s, is a
precipitate of age-old experience with commodity money standards.

Because the very function of thymology is to provide the acting individual with information about the social factors that are or

---

[64] D.K.H. Begg, *The Rational Expectations Approach in Macroeconomics: Theories
and Evidence* (Baltimore: The Johns Hopkins University Press, 1982), p. 30.

[65] Mises, *Human Action*, p. 255.

will be operating to promote or obstruct the achievement of his goals, it is also inconsistent with the assumption of adaptive expectations, which envisages economic agents as eschewing all causal investigation and attempting to forecast future values of an economic variable by mechanically extrapolating from their past errors in forecasting the same variable. For Mises,[66] a being becomes "thymologically human" as soon as it begins to cast around for specific means to apply to attaining definite goals, and thus begins to investigate the causal relationships between the various elements in its social and physical environment. As a result all market participants, when formulating the specific understanding of the future that guides their catallactic activities, are to some degree, depending on their entrepreneurial abilities, alive to the causal factors that determine prospective economic quantities. In the marketplace, as in every department of social intercourse, therefore, "All are eager to get information about other people's valuations and plans and to appraise them correctly."[67]

The thymological method of dealing with expectations also stands in opposition to the position proclaimed by Lachmann,[68] the late exponent of Shacklian "radical subjectivism," that expectations are "autonomous" in the same sense as human preferences, and that, therefore, the economist is "unable to postulate any particular mode of change." In such a world of divergent and unpredictably changing expectations and the speculative shifts of supply and demand curves they continually evoke, according to Lachmann,[69] the fact that realized prices continually clear markets "has little meaning." Such a radically nihilistic view of the price coordinating feature of the market economy results from ignoring the fact that an individual's expectations are derived from thymological and catallactic experience. This view was long ago rebutted by Arthur W. Marget[70] in the following terms:

---

[66] Mises, *Ultimate Foundation of Economic Science*, p. 49.

[67] Mises, *Theory and History*, p. 265.

[68] Lachmann, "From Mises to Schackle," p. 129.

[69] Ibid., p. 130.

[70] A.W. Marget, *The Theory of Prices: A Re-Examination of the Central Problem of Monetary Theory*, 2 vols. (New York: Augustus M. Kelley, [1938–42] 1966), pp. 228–30, 238 fn. 34, 456.

For unless we are to make of the so-called 'method of expectations' the kind of *deus ex machina* which ... would lead
to "the complete liquidation of economics as a science," we
must proceed upon the assumption [which is supported by
thymology] that expectations are what they are largely as the
result of the experience of economic processes as they have
been actually realized in the past and as they are being currently realized in the present.

Thus, "expectations" help to determine "realized" prices. But
the prices thus "realized" *help to determine expectations with
respect to the future course of prices....* When, therefore, it
is said that "equilibrium" is "indeterminate" whenever "the
final position is dependent upon the route followed" all that
this can mean is that no account of the actual functioning of
the economic process can be regarded as complete until it
undertakes, *upon the basis of a study of the successive, actually realized steps in any economic process actually unfolding itself in time*, to establish the nature of the considerations
likely to determine the nature of entrepreneurial responses to
changes in the market situation, *including the possible changing nature of the goals whose attainment these responses are
designed to aid....* [W]e have insisted throughout upon the
necessity for accompanying any use of an emphasis upon
"expectation" by a tracing of realized processes in all possible
detail, in order that these *realized processes* may be related
with all possible precision to the expectations which condition them and to which they give rise. (All emphases in this
passage are Marget's.)

Contrary to Lachmann's contentions, then, the moment-to-
moment structure of realized prices can be explained as a coordinative
outcome of past and always fallible speculative anticipations, while yet
remaining a meaningful factor in the explanation of the current entrepreneurial forecasts and price appraisements that shape the future
course of the market process. Expectations are thus not "autonomous";
they are rigidly circumscribed by the actor's chosen goals, the experience of success and failure he has acquired in pursuing these and
earlier goals, and his entrepreneurial ability, that is, his aptitude for
culling information and deducing implications from his experience
that are relevant to his future actions. Nor is it "impossible to derive a

group's state of expectations from its state of knowledge";[71] as an integral element of the human choice process expectations are discoverable by the methods of thymology regularly deployed in everyday life and in historical research and thus accessible to the economist as well. Accordingly, in the final sentence of the preceding quotation, Marget perceptively argued that information about the expectations-formation process can only be derived from thymological experience or historical investigation of "realized" market processes.

Ironically, Lachmann,[72] despite his strongly avowed antipositivism and radical subjectivism, declared that an actor's thymological knowledge "... must always remain problematical in the sense in which [the actor's] knowledge of molecules, machines or the human body is not."[73] But as Mises stressed, while experience-based thymological knowledge is "categorically different" from the experimentally established "facts" of the natural sciences, it is real knowledge nonetheless and is just as indispensable for the planning of action. "To know the future reactions of other people is the first task of acting man."[74]

The knowledge about future events that thymology yields is not in terms of statistical or "class" probabilities, it is true, but in terms of ranked likelihoods or "case" probabilities.[75] For example, it is through thymological experience that I "know" (as I write this in 1993) that the likelihood of each of the following events occurring in 1994 is negligible and certainly much lower than the likelihood of, for example, the Clinton health plan passing Congress without significant modification: my being drafted to replace Prince Charles as heir to

---

[71] L.M. Lachmann, *The Meaning of the Market Process* (New York: Basil Blackwell Inc., 1986), p. 29.

[72] Ibid.

[73] Hans-Hermann Hoppe, (*Praxeology and Economic Science* (Auburn, Ala.: Ludwig von Mises Institute, 1988), p. 48 fn. 37) uncovers the logical error in Lachmann's oft repeated asseveration that the "future is unknowable," particularly future states of knowledge and actions.

[74] Mises, *Theory and History*, p. 311.

[75] In this particular respect, Mises's theory of risk and uncertainty resembles Keynes's. For a discussion of this aspect of Keynes's theory, see Joseph T. Salerno, "The Development of Keynes's Economics: From Marshall to Millennialism," *The Review of Austrian Economics* 6 (1): pp. 9–10, 46–47.

the English throne; the United States of America being reconstituted as a monarchy; or professional football being displaced in popularity by professional soccer in the United States. I and masses of others regularly and successfully take nonstatistical but thymologically knowable likelihoods such as these into account in planning future actions.

From a thymological standpoint, not only the Lachmannian position but also the Hayekian position on expectations, elaborated so ably in the writings of Israel M. Kirzner,[76] must be rejected. Expectations of profit gaps between future output prices and resource prices are not formed merely on the basis of "alertness" to information about past price structures; we learn nothing directly about the future by merely absorbing, whether passively or alertly, information about the outcomes of realized market processes.[77] Entrepreneurial appraisements of future price structures are the outcome of a specific understanding of future market conditions that must be actively produced by deliberately bringing one's thymological experiences and insights to bear on information about past prices. Such "knowledge" about future profit opportunities is, therefore, emphatically not embodied in the objective (disequilibrium) price signals of the immediate past; its source is rather internal, resting on thymological insight and impinging on external events only through the actions it motivates.

The knowledge that is yielded by thymological investigation of human activities carried out in the market or elsewhere is embodied in what Mises[78] referred to as "ideal types." For example, the theoretical explanation of the German hyperinflation of the early 1920s may employ the distinct ideal types "German industrial laborer," "German entrepreneur," "German foreign exchange speculator" and so forth,

---

[76] Israel M. Kirzner, *Competition and Entrepreneurship* (Chicago: The University of Chicago Press, 1973), idem, *Perception, Opportunity, and Profit: Studies in the Theory of Entrepreneurship* (Chicago: University of Chicago Press, 1979).

[77] Various aspects of this controversy are critically reviewed in Joseph T. Salerno ("Ludwig von Mises as Social Rationalist," *The Review of Austrian Economics* 4: pp. 26–54) and Salerno ("Mises and Hayek Dehomogenized," *The Review of Austrian Economics* 6 (2): pp. 113–46).

[78] L.v. Mises, *Theory and History: An Interpretation of Social and Economic Evolution* (Auburn, Ala.: Ludwig von Mises Institute, [1957] 1985), pp. 315–20; *Human Action*, pp. 59–64.

depending on the economic analyst's reading of the historical record, which includes his own direct experience if it is relevant. Each of these ideal types differs from the others in terms of the experiences, reactions, and appraisements it postulates with respect to the depreciation of the German mark. Only understanding based on experience and careful study of the historical record can decide whether the content and number of ideal types to be introduced at different points in the praxeological chain of theoretical deductions are appropriate. For instance, it may be helpful to distinguish between the "German entrepreneur of 1919" and the "German entrepreneur of 1922" or between the "Prussian civil servant" and "the Bavarian farmer" in order to take account of the impact of different experiences and ideologies on the formation of expectations in reaction to information about a given increase in the money supply. When theorizing about the effect of a new issue of paper money on the demand for money during the final stages of hyperinflation, the economist may register his awareness of the spread of inflationary expectations to even the least entrepreneurial and most ideologically blinkered among the populace by resorting to a single ideal-typical "German income earner."

This discussion points to the solution of the continuing controversy between Misesians and Hayekians over whether economic theory can yield knowledge about human learning and interindividual knowledge-diffusion processes. As a branch of praxeology, economic theory per se cannot and need not establish a single proposition about such processes; as in the case of human goals and values, it accepts as given data for its reasoning the concrete details of what participants are capable of learning from the historical market process (as encapsulated in ideal types). The learning processes by which participants in the market acquire and interpret information are not logically deducible from universal and timeless praxeological categories; they must be "understood" or thymologically reconstructed from historical experience and then employed among the supplementary premises of aprioristic praxeological analysis to yield economic theorems that possess both logical and substantive truth.[79]

---

[79] This contrasts with Kirzner's view that "alertness" or the ability to notice or "discover" those changes in one's environment that promise to redound to one's benefit

As Mises[80] pointed out, "this singular and logically somewhat strange procedure" of analyzing economic phenomena, "in which aprioristic theory and the interpretation of historical phenomena are intertwined," can lead to serious errors. Indeed, the unsatisfactory and seemingly irreconcilable approaches to expectations that dominate mainstream monetary theory are a result of this failure to appreciate and come to grips with the indispensable role of thymology and history in establishing the subsidiary assumptions of economic reasoning.

It is illuminating to briefly compare Mises's view of expectations with Hayek's. In "Economics and Knowledge," Hayek[81] issued a plea for making equilibrium analysis applicable to the real world by incorporating into it an "empirical element" consisting of "propositions about the acquisition of knowledge" that were adequate to explaining the tendency to equilibrium supposedly observable in the actual economy. He went on to argue in general terms that the solution lay in the introduction into formal economic theory of "ideal types," meaning "concrete hypotheses concerning the conditions under which people are supposed to acquire the relevant knowledge and the process by which they are supposed to acquire it."[82] At this stage of his thinking, and before he had made much progress in selecting the empirically relevant ideal types to serve as supplementary hypotheses, Hayek's project appeared similar to Mises's. Nine years later, however, in "The Use of Knowledge in Society," Hayek[83] specifically identified the overarching ideal type to be used in economic analysis as an economy whose prices always approximate their long-run equilibrium values and therefore convey accurate knowledge about the scattered data of the economic system to decentralized decision makers.[84] Hayek's assumption of

---

is a propensity inherent in human action and constitutes the essence of purposeful behavior (Kirzner, *Perception*, pp. 13–33). For a critique of Kirzner's view from a Misesian standpoint, see Salerno, "Mises and Hayek."

[80] Mises, *Human Action*, p. 66.

[81] Hayek, "Economics and Knowledge."

[82] Ibid., pp. 47–48.

[83] F.A. Hayek, "The Use of Knowledge in Society," in *Individualism and Economic Order* (Chicago: Henry Regnery Company, [1945] 1972), pp. 77–91.

[84] Whether this mental construct can be called an "ideal type" is another question; Hayek himself refrained from using the term in this later article.

what I have elsewhere called "proximal equilibrium" is a major departure from Mises's theory of expectations in two ways. First, it banishes genuine uncertainty and the necessity of entrepreneurial forecasting and appraisement of future prices from economic analysis because it implies that "current prices are fairly reliable indications of what future prices will probably be";[85] and, second, Mises explicitly denied that the actual economy harbors an empirical tendency to operate close to long-run equilibrium or even to temporally progress toward such a state.[86]

V. Inflationary Expectations and the German Hyperinflation

Mises's thymological approach to expectations is clearly illustrated in his analysis of historical episodes of inflation, particularly the German hyperinflation after World War One. For example, at the very beginning of the war inflation in Germany in 1914, the ideal-typical German mark holder included workers, entrepreneurs, and bankers. They confronted the general rise in prices with deep-seated inelastic expectations, grounded on their long experience of the gold standard and reinforced by general acceptance of Georg Knapp's doctrine that State power was the source of money's value. According to Mises:[87]

> When the war inflation came nobody understood what a change in the value of the money unit meant. The businessman and the worker both believed that a rising income in Marks was a real rise of income. They continued to reckon in Marks without any regard to its falling value. The rise of commodity prices they attributed to the scarcity of goods due to the blockade.[88]

---

[85] F.A. Hayek, *Denationalisation of Money—The Argument Refined: An Analysis of the Theory, and Practice of Concurrent Currencies*, 2nd ed. (London: The Institute of Economic Affairs, 1978), p. 82.

[86] On Hayek's notion of "proximal equilibrium" and its inconsistency with Mises's theory of entrepreneurship and appraisement, see Salerno ("Mises and Hayek") and Salerno (Reply to Leland Yeager on "Mises and Hayek on Calculation and Knowledge," *The Review of Austrian Economics* 7, no. 2 (1994): pp. 111–25).

[87] Mises, "The Great German Inflation."

[88] Ibid., pp. 101–02.

Expectations eventually began to adjust, but "it took years" even for German entrepreneurs to recognize and adapt their expectations to the true cause of price inflation, while workers were slower still to adjust.[89] Even on the loan market, expectations adjusted very slowly. In the early stages of the inflation, after people had disentangled themselves from the grip of their long pre-inflationary experience with commodity money, what may be loosely characterized as adaptive expectations replaced inelastic expectations. During this period, the inflation premium of the nominal interest rate lagged behind the inflation rate "... because what generates it is not the change in the supply of money ... but the-necessarily later occurring-effects of these changes upon the price structure.[90]

As the inflation progressed, it started to become clear to those possessing the greatest degree of entrepreneurial foresight that it was likely to persist and even accelerate in the future and that there were pecuniary gains to be reaped from such an occurrence. What may be termed, again very loosely, "rational expectations" began to develop first on the foreign exchange market and then later on the stock and commodity markets. Speculators on the foreign exchange market began to anticipate the effects of current and then future increases in the money supply on domestic prices and therefore on exchange rates, and there came into being a substantial "reverse" lag between the rise of domestic commodity prices and the rise in prices of foreign exchange. Meanwhile, the high profits being earned by speculators on the foreign exchange market drew into this market other speculators who had previously operated on stock and bond markets. Unfortunately the experience, knowledge, and techniques that served these latter speculators well on other markets were ill suited to the foreign exchange market. According to Mises,[91] the ideal-typical stock market speculator of this period was ignorant of "the principles underlying the formation of monetary value" and "look[ed] on the monetary unit as if it were a share of stock in the government." As a result, he was apt to buy the mark after sharp declines, believing that it was due to appreciate just as sharply because

---

[89] Mises, "The Great German Inflation," p. 100.

[90] Mises, *Human Action*, p. 545.

[91] Mises, *On the Manipulation of Money and Credit*, p. 20.

the government remained stable and the economy just as productive. Thus, until they had learned from experience, the actions of the transplanted stock speculators retarded and may even have temporarily arrested the decline on foreign exchange markets of the domestically depreciating currency.

However, as long as most earners of monetary incomes failed to shake loose their ideological blinders and to recognize that their past experience with a commodity money was irrelevant, they were unable to draw the correct conclusions from their current experiences. This caused domestic price inflation to lag behind the growth of the money supply and the decline in the external value of the mark. Eventually, however, after years of experience with inflation, the masses of wage earners and farmers learned that the rising prices were directly linked to increases in the supply of paper money and their faith in the long-run stability of the purchasing power of the mark was shaken to the core. Once the masses developed "rational expectations" based on their hard-won insight into the link between money and prices, they finally realized that monetary inflation was a deliberate policy of government unlikely to be soon reversed and hyperinflation was at hand.

Mises[92] described this experience-driven evolution of inflationary expectations and abrupt transition from inelastic to rational expectations on the part of the public in dramatic terms:

> The first stage of the inflationary process may last for many years. While it lasts, the prices of many goods and services are not yet adjusted to the altered money relation [i.e., the supply of money and demand for money]. There are still people in the country who have not yet become aware of the fact that they are confronted with a price revolution which will finally result in a considerable rise in all prices, although the extent of this rise will not be the same in the various commodities and services. These people still believe that prices one day will drop. Waiting for this day they restrict their purchases and concomitantly increase their cash holdings....

But then finally the masses wake up. They become suddenly aware of the fact that inflation is a deliberate policy and will go on

---

[92] Mises, *Human Action*, pp. 427–28.

endlessly. A breakdown occurs. The crack-up boom appears.... Within a very short time, within a few weeks or even days, the things which were used as money are no longer used as media of exchange. They become scrap paper....

> Once people have experienced firsthand a hyperinflationary currency collapse, their knowledge and expectations are permanently altered. Even the slightest increase in the money supply will now lead all strata of the populace to forecast that the political authorities are once again embarking on a policy of deliberate inflation that will culminate in another catastrophic monetary breakdown. The public's panic-driven attempts to reduce cash holdings, on the basis of expectations that have come "unhinged" from any reasonable appraisement of the objectively evolving economic situation, will quickly catapult the economy into runaway price inflation. As Mises[93] observed:

> A nation which has experienced inflation till its final breakdown will not submit to a second experiment of this type until the memory of the previous one his faded.... Made overcautious by what they suffered, at the very outset of the inflation they [i.e., victims and witnesses of the 1923 inflation] would start a panic. The rise of prices would be out of all proportion to the increase in the quantity of paper money....

It remains for us to reconcile Mises's discussion of the evolution of expectations in the course of a hyperinflation with the pivotal role he attributed to expectations in the context of his theory of the business cycle. Mises[94] himself realized that there is an important problem that must be resolved. Why is it, he asked, that while the public learns the lessons taught by their experience with hyperinflation sufficiently well to undertake actions that prevent the regular recurrence of this fiat-money phenomenon, "people are incorrigible" when it comes to learning how to avoid the cyclical ups and downs associated with bank credit expansion.[95] In Mises's words, "What calls for special explanation is why attempts are made again and again to

---

[93] Mises, "The Great German Inflation," p. 102.

[94] Mises, *On the Manipulation of Money and Credit*, pp. 132–36.

[95] Mises, *Human Action*, p. 578.

improve general economic conditions by the expansion of circulation credit [i.e., bank credit in the form of fiduciary media] in spite of the spectacular failure of such efforts in the past."[96]

The answer to this question, Mises suggested, is twofold. First, there is the ideological factor: deeply ingrained in the minds of bankers and entrepreneurs is the view, which has been long reinforced by erroneous economic doctrines, that rising prices and low interest rates are a prerequisite of favorable business conditions and economic prosperity and therefore should be a goal of economic policy.[97] Second, this ideological factor makes it even more difficult for entrepreneurs, untrained in technical economics, to perceive the links between interest rates lowered by bank credit expansion, the capital malinvestments of the boom, and the ensuing crisis and depression that are the consequence of the sudden revelation and liquidation of these malinvestments. As Mises[98] pointed out, moreover, comprehending these links requires much more recondite knowledge and a more rigorous intellectual effort than that required for grasping the connection between the running of the printing presses and rising prices. Mises's point is reinforced by the fact that, after the initial phase of the credit expansion, interest rates do not appear unusually low and may even appear high to the entrepreneur because of the rising inflation premium that progressively drives up the nominal rate. So, even if the entrepreneur learned the basic lesson of avoiding an expansion of his operation when interest rates drop to unusually low levels, he would still be enticed into malinvestments as the inflationary boom progressed and nominal rates increased.

Mises[99] concluded: "Nothing but a perfect familiarity with economic theory and a careful scrutiny of monetary and credit phenomena can save a man from being deceived and lured into malinvestments." Certainly, thymological analysis reveals to the economist that the assumption that entrepreneurs in the contemporary

---

[96] Mises, *On the Manipulation of Money and Credit*, p. 136.

[97] Ibid., pp. 138, 146.

[98] Ludwig von Mises, "'Elastic Expectations' and the Austrian Theory of the Trade Cycle," *Economica* 10 (August): pp. 251–52.

[99] Ibid., p. 252.

world possess a grasp of the Austrian theory of the business cycle is patently false and would lead to erroneous theoretical deductions. But Mises also chided the "many economists" who "take it for granted" in dealing with concrete instances of credit expansion that the future will be like the past and the theorist need not take into account the effect of learning on entrepreneurs' expectations. Thus, Mises[100] argued, "It may be that businessmen will in the future react to credit expansion in a manner other than they have in the past. It may be that they will avoid using for an expansion of their operations the easy money available because they will keep in mind the inevitable end of the boom. Some signs forebode such a change."

In the paragraph that immediately follows the one from which the foregoing quotation by Mises is drawn and which appeared in the third (1966) but not the first edition (1949) of *Human Action*, Mises[101] suggested that the the public as well as the financial press had learned the main lessons of the Austrian theory of the trade cycle, which are that the boom causes the ensuing depression and that the boom is engendered by the preceding expansion of bank credit. The formation of expectations on the basis of this knowledge now compelled the monetary authorities to restrict credit whenever the first signs of the boom appeared. And it is to these factors that Mises attributed the marked reduction in the observed duration and severity of cyclical fluctuations during the 1950s.

Mises's thymological approach to expectations appears to be well suited for guiding applied research on developments in the U.S. economy in the 1980s and early 1990s. For example, the apparently high real long-term interest rates during the so-called "Reagan recovery" may be partially or even mainly explained as a high inflation premium on the real interest rate, which reflects persistent inflationary expectations carried over from the public's, and especially the bond market's, experience with the double-digit inflation rates of the Carter years. This Misesian interpretation contradicts the explanation proposed by Keynesians and others which attributes the stubbornly high real interest rates to a

---

[100] Mises, *Human Action*, p. 797.
[101] Ibid., p. 798.

"loose fiscal, tight monetary" policy stance. Also, the continued slow recovery from the 1990–1991 recession even in the face of substantial declines in short-term interest rates and increasingly rapid money supply growth might be explained as resulting from the reluctance of entrepreneurs and investors to employ the additional bank credit to finance long-term capital projects, because they expect the rate of return on investment ("the natural rate of interest") to be eroded by Clinton's tax increases, increased regulations, and the costs of impending health care legislation.

From the standpoint of pure theory,the thymological approach to expectations, in conjunction with the Austrian theory of the business cycle, provides an account of cyclical fluctuations which, in contrast to the rational-expectations-based Real Business Cycle theory, rigorously maintains the assumption that markets clear instantaneously without having to invoke improbably large regressive technology shocks and intertemporal labor substitution models that rely on improbably elastic responses of the labor supply to transitory fluctuations in the real wage rate.

VI. Conclusion

Mises's theory of the inflationary process has been either neglected or misunderstood by mainstream monetary theorists, because it is grounded in Austrian price theory. This theory, which owes much more to the works of Böhm-Bawerk and Wicksteed than to those of Marshall and Walras, seeks to explain the determination and the function of the prices that are actually realized in the real world of constant change and disequilibrium. In this setting, money is not merely a numeraire but is a causal factor in the market's pricing process, and Mises's step-by-step method of analysis is the only method suited to analyzing such a dynamic economy.

Despite the economy's disequilibrium character, however, the market-clearing process has an important function to perform in the pricing and allocation of scarce resources, a function that Hutt[102] felicitously

---

[102] Hutt, *The Keynesian Episode*, p. 285.

described as "the dynamic coordinative consequences of price adjustment." According to Mises, the coordinative social appraisement process of the market insures that the current price of every scarce resource is equal to its expected marginal revenue product (discounted by the interest rate), and thus that all existing productive resources are always fully employed in those uses that entrepreneurs consider to be most valuable in light of their knowledge of the technological possibilities and their forecasts of future market conditions, including their appraisements of prospective output prices.

As I have argued elsewhere,[103] a Misesian conceives the market's coordinative process as extremely hardy and no more liable to be disrupted by market-produced changes in the money-spending stream, such as hoarding, dishoarding, and changes in the production costs of mining gold, than by changes in the "real" data of the economic system. As Mises argued, however, the process *can* be hampered and distorted by external intervention that undermines or nullifies its market-clearing property in resource markets, a property that may be crudely and temporarily restored by an episode of unanticipated inflation which lowers the real prices of labor and other resources toward equilibrium levels. Thus Mises's analysis explains the observed effect of inflation on employment and output in a way that is fully consistent with the microfoundations of Austrian monetary theory and does not invoke ad hoc and unrealistic assumptions about the behavior of market participants.

Mises developed a theory of inflationary expectations and of expectations in general that has been largely ignored by contemporary Austrians, mainly because of their tendency to conflate the views of Mises and Hayek. Under Hayek's assumption of "proximal equilibrium," which is a situation in which ex ante coordination of individual plans is nearly perfect and prices are normally near their long-run equilibrium values, expectations are a trivial byproduct of the knowledge culled from past prices. For Hayek then, expectations do not require independent explanation.

---

[103] Salerno, "Commentary: The Concept of Coordination in Austrian Macroeconomics."

Kirzner, who follows Hayek in some important respects, posits that alertness to the information conveyed by the price system is a propensity inherent in human action. In his view, entrepreneurs alertly discover gaps between resource and output prices of the immediate past and costlessly exploit these profit opportunites. Kirzner's procedure effectively transforms entrepreneur-producers into arbitrageurs who are focused on current market conditions and have little interest in the future. This procedure obviates any discussion of how entrepreneurs formulate expectations of the uncertain future on the basis of their thymological experience and knowledge.[104]

Perhaps the most valuable lesson economists can learn from Mises's approach to expectations is the crucial importance of realistic subsidiary assumptions for correctly deducing and applying the laws of praxeological economics to the analysis of real-world economic events and policies. More braodly, Mises's theory of expectations opens up an avenue to the understanding of the proper role for historical and thymological research in the elaboration of economic theory.

Bibliography

Alchian, A.A., and R.A. Kessel. [1960] 1977. "The Meaning and Validity of the Inflation-Induced Lag of Wages behind Prices." In *Economic Forces at Work*, A.A. Alchian, ed., pp. 413–50. Indianapolis, Ind.: Liberty Press.

Begg, D.K.H. 1982. *The Rational Expectations Approach in Macroeconomics: Theories and Evidence*. Baltimore: The Johns Hopkins University Press.

Birch, D.E., A.A. Rabin, and L.B. Yeager. 1982. "Inflation, Output, and Employment: Some Clarifications." *Economic Inquiry* 20 (April): pp. 209–21.

Davenport, H.J. [1913] 1968. *The Economics of Enterprise*. New York: Augustus M. Kelley.

Ebeling, R.M. 1988. "Expectations and Expectations Formation in Mises's Theory of the Market Process." *Market Process* 6 (Spring): pp. 12–18.

Edwards, J.R. 1985. *The Economist of the Country: Ludwig von Mises in the History of Monetary Thought*. New York: Carlton Press, Inc.

Ellis, H.S. 1934. *German Monetary Theory, 1905–1933*. Cambridge, Mass.: Harvard University Press.

---

[104] For a recent attempt at a thoroughgoing dehomogenization of the Misesian and Hayekian/ Kirznerian paradigms see Salerno, "Mises and Hayek."

Friedman, M. [1968] 1987. "The Role of Monetary Policy." In *The Essence of Friedman*, K.R. Leube, ed., pp. 387–403. Stanford, Calif.: Hoover Institution Press.

Haberler, G. 1974. *Economic Growth & Stability: An Analysis of Economic Change and Policies*. Los Angeles: Nash Publishing.

Hayek, F.A. [1937] 1972. "Economics and Knowledge." In *Individualism and economic Order*, pp. 33–56. Chicago: Henry Regnery Company.

_____. [1945] 1972. "The Use of Knowledge in Society." In *Individualism and Economic Order*, pp. 77–91. Chicago: Henry Regnery Company.

_____. 1972. *A Tiger by the Tail: A 40-Years' Running Commentary on Keynesianism by Hayek*. Sudah A Shenoy, comp. London: The Institute of Economic Affairs.

_____. 1978. *Denationalisation of Money—The Argument Refined: An Analysis of the Theory, and Practice of Concurrent Currencies*, 2nd ed. London: The Institute of Economic Affairs.

Hicks, J.R. [1946] 1968. *Value and Capital: An Inquiry into Some Fundamental Principles of Economic Theory*, 2nd ed. New York: Oxford University Press.

Hoppe, H. 1988. *Praxeology and Economic Science*. Auburn, Ala.: Ludwig von Mises Institute.

Humphrey, T.M. 1984. "On the Nonneutral Relative Price Effects in Monetarist Thought." Federal Reserve Bank of Richmond *Economic Review* 70 (May/June): pp. 13–19.

Hutt, W.H. 1973. *The Strike-Threat System: The Economic Consequences of Collective Bargaining*. New Rochelle, N.Y.: Arlington House.

_____. 1975. *A Rehabilitation of Say's Law*. Athens: Ohio University Press.

_____. 1979. *The Keynesian Episode: A Reassessment*. Indianapolis, Ind.: Liberty Press.

Kirzner, I.M. 1973. *Competition and Entrepreneurship*. Chicago: University of Chicago Press.

_____. 1979. *Perception, Opportunity, and Profit: Studies in the Theory of Entrepreneurship*. Chicago: University of Chicago Press.

Lachmann, L.M. 1976a. "From Mises to Schackle: An Essay on Austrian Economics and the Kaleidic Society." *Journal of Economic Literature* 14 (March): p. 58.

_____. 1976b. "On the Central Concept of Austrian Economics: Market Process." In *The Foundations of Modern Austrian Economics*, E.G. Dolan, ed. pp. 126–32. Kansas City: Sheed and Ward, Inc.

_____. 1986. *The Meaning of the Market Process*. New York: Basil Blackwell, Inc.

Marget, A.W. [1938–42] 1966. *The Theory of Prices: A Re-Examination of the Central Problem of Monetary Theory*, 2 vols. New York: Augustus M. Kelley.

Mises, L. von. 1943. "'Elastic Expectations' and the Austrian Theory of the Trade Cycle." *Economica* 10 (August): pp. 251–52.

_____. 1966. *Human Action: A Treatise on Economics*, 3rd ed. Chicago: Henry Regnery Company.

_____. [1953] 1971. *The Theory of Money and Credit*, 2nd ed. Irvington-on Hudson, N.Y.: The Foundation for Economic Education.

_____. 1978a. *Notes and Recollections*. South Holland, Ill.: Libertarian Press.

_____. 1978b. *On the Manipulation of Money and Credit*, B. B. Greaves, trans. Dobbs Ferry, N.Y.: Free Market Books.

_____. 1978c. *The Ultimate Foundation of Economic Science: An Essay on Method*, 2nd ed. Kansas City: Sheed Andrews and McMeel, Inc.

_____. [1950] 1980. "Economic Aspects of the Pension Problem." In *Planning for Freedom and Sixteen Other Essays and Addresses*, 4th ed., pp. 83–93. South Holland, Ill.: Libertarian Press.

_____. [1958] 1980. "Wages, Unemployment and Inflation." In *Planning for Freedom and Sixteen Other Essays and Addresses*, 4th ed. South Holland, Ill.: Libertarian Press.

_____. 1983. *Nation, State, and Economy: Contributions to the Politics and History of Our Time*, L.B. Yeager, trans. New York: New York University Press.

_____. [1957] 1985. *Theory and History: An Interpretation of Social and Economic Evolution*. Auburn, Ala.: Ludwig von Mises Institute.

_____. [1932] 1990. "The Great German Inflation." In *Money, Method, and the Market Process*, R.M. Ebeling, ed., pp. 96–103. Norwell, Mass.: Kluwer Academic Publishers.

Moss, L.S. 1976. "the Monetary Economics of Ludwig von Mises." In *The Economics of Ludwig von Mises: Toward a Critical Appraisal*, pp. 13–49. New York: New York University Press.

Patinkin, D. 1965. *Money, Interest, and Prices: An Integration of Monetary and Value Theory*, 2nd ed. New York: Harper and Row Publishers.

Phillips, A.W. [1958] 1968. "The Relation between Unemployment and the Rate of Change of Money Wage Rates in the United Kingdom, 1861–1957." In *Macroeconomic Readings*, J. Lindauer, ed., pp. 107–19. New York: The Free Press.

Robbins, Lord. [1952] 1971. *Money, Trade and International Relations*. London: Macmillan.

Robbins, L., S. Brittan, A.W. Coats, M. Friedman, F.A. Hayek, P. Jay, and D. Laidler. 1974. *Inflation: Causes, Consequences, Cures: Discourses on the Debate between the Monetary and Trade Union Interpretations*. Levittown, N.Y.: Transatlantic Arts, Inc.

Rothbard, M.N. [1962] 1970. *Man, Economy, and State: A Treatise on Economic Principles*, 2 vols. Los Angeles: Nash Publishing.

_____. 1976. "The Austrian Theory of Money." In *The Foundations of Modern Austrian Economics*, E.G. Dolan, ed., pp. 160–84. Kansas City: Sheed & Ward, Inc.

_____. 1980. *The Essential Ludwig von Mises*, 2nd ed. Auburn, Ala.: Ludwig von Mises Institute.

Rousseas, S.W. 1972. *Monetary Theory*. New York: Alfred A. Knopf.

Salerno, J.T. 1990. "Ludwig von Mises as Social Rationalist." *The Review of Austrian Economics* 4: pp. 26–54.

_____. 1991. "Commentary: The Concept of Coordination in Austrian Macroeconomics." In *Austrian Economics: Perspectives on the Past and Prospects for the Future*, R.B. Ebeling, ed., pp. 325–43. Hillsdale, Mich.: Hillsdale College Press.

_____. 1992. "The Development of Keynes's Economics: From Marshall to Millennialism." *The Review of Austrian Economics* 6 (1): pp. 3–64.

_____. 1993. "Mises and Hayek Dehomogenized." *The Review of Austrian Economics*, 6 (2): pp. 113–46.

_____. 1994. Reply to Leland Yeager on "Mises and Hayek on Calculation and Knowledge," *The Review of Austrian Economics* 7 (2): pp. 111–25.

_____. 1995a. "William H. Hutt." Available at http://mises.org/daily/3915.

_____. 1995b. "Gottfried Haberler." Available at http://mises.org/resources/3232.

Vedder, R.K., and L.E. Gallaway. 1993. *Out of Work: Unemployment and Government in Twentieth-Century America*. New York: Holmes and Meier.

CHAPTER 9

War and the Money Machine: Concealing the Costs of War Beneath the Veil of Inflation

In every great war monetary calculation was disrupted by inflation.... The economic behavior of the belligerents was thereby
led astray; the true consequences of the war were removed from
their view. One can say without exaggeration that inflation is an indispensable means of militarism. Without it, the repercussions of war on
welfare become obvious much more quickly and penetratingly; war
weariness would set in much earlier.[1]

> [Governments] know that their young men will readily sac-
> rifice their lives and limbs and that their old men will readily
> sacrifice the lives and limbs of their sons and grandsons, and
> that their women will readily sacrifice the lives and limbs of
> their husbands, their sons, and their brothers in what they
> believe to be a noble cause, but they have a deadly fear—
> sometimes, but not always, well founded—that women and
> old men will shrink from pinching the stomachs of them-
> selves and the young children, so that warlike enthusiasm
> will decay if it once gets about that the association of war

From: "War and the Money Machine: Concealing the Costs of War beneath the Veil
of Inflation," *Journal des Economistes et des Etudes Humaines* 6 (March 1995): pp.
153–73.

[1] Ludwig von Mises, *Nation, State, and Economy: Contributions to the Politics and
History of Our Time,* trans. Leland B. Yeager (New York: New York University Press,
1983), p. 163.

with abundance to eat, drink, and wear is delusive, and that there is still truth in the old motto of "Peace and plenty.".... True that to be pinched by high prices rather than by small money incomes and large taxes made the people rage in the first place against the persons who were supposed to profit and often did profit—most of them quite innocently—by the rise of prices instead of against Government.[2]

[T]he true costs of the war lie in the goods sphere: the used-up goods, the devastation of parts of the country, the loss of manpower, these are the real costs of war to the economies.... Like a huge conflagration the war has devoured a huge part of our national wealth, the economy has become poorer.... However, in money terms the economy has not become poorer. How is this possible? Simply ... claims on the state and money tokens have taken the place of stocks of goods in the private economy.[3]

"War, huh, what is it good for? Absolutely nothin'.

It ain't nothin' but a heartbreaker

It's got one friend, that's the undertaker....

War can't give life, it can only take it away."[4]

1. Introduction

The costs of war are enormous, as the above quotations trenchantly indicate, and inflation is a means by which governments attempt, more or less successfully, to hide these costs from their citizens. War not only destroys the lives and limbs of the soldiery, but, by progressively consuming the accumulated capital stock of the belligerent nations, eventually shortens and coarsens the lives and shrivels the limbs of the civilian population. The enormous destruction of

---

[2] E. Cannan, *An Economist's Protest* (New York: Adelphi Company, 1928), p. 100; idem, *Money: Its connexion with Rising and Falling Prices*, 6th ed. (Westminster: P.S. King & Son, Ltd., 1929), p. 99.

[3] J.A. Schumpeter, "The Crisis of the Tax State," in idem, *The Econmics and Sociology of Capitalism*, ed. Richard Swedberg (Princeton, N.J.: Princeton University Press, 1991), pp. 118–19.

[4] E. Starr, "Recording of 'War,'" written by N. Whitfield and B. Strong, from the album *War & Peace* (Detroit: Motown Record Corporation, 1970).

productive wealth that war entails would become immediately evident if governments had no recourse but to raise taxes immediately upon the advent of hostilities; their ability to inflate the money supply at will permits them to conceal such destruction behind a veil of rising prices, profits, and wages, stable interest rates, and a booming stock market.

In the following section I explain how war, completely apart from its physical destructiveness, brings about the economic destruction of capital and a consequent decline in labor productivity, real income, and living standards. The argument in this section draws on the Austrian theory of capital as expounded in the works of Ludwig von Mises and Murray N. Rothbard. Section 3 analyzes the reasons why different methods of war financing will have different effects on the public's perceptions of the costs attending economic mobilization for war. The analysis developed in this section owes much to the classic discussion of inflationary war financing by Mises.[5] Section 4 concludes the paper with a brief explanation of how inflation constitutes the first step on the road to the fascist economic planning that is typically foisted upon capitalist economies in the course of a large-scale war.

2. The Economics of War

The conduct of war requires that scarce resources previously allocated to the production of capital or consumer goods be reallocated to the raising, equipping, and sustaining of the nation's fighting forces. While the newly enlisted or inducted military personnel must abandon their jobs in the private economy, they still require food, clothing, and shelter, in addition to weapons and other accoutrements of war. In practice this means that "nonspecific" resources such as labor and "convertible" capital goods including steel, electrical power, trucks, etc., which are not specific to a single production process, must be diverted from civilian to military production. Given the reduction in the size of the civilian labor force and the conversion of substantial amounts of the remaining labor and capital to the manufacture of military hardware, the general result is a greater scarcity of consumer goods and a decline of real wages and civilian living standards.

---

[5] Mises, *Nation, State, and Economy*, pp. 151–71.

However, the transformation of the economy to a war footing implies much more than merely a "horizontal" reallocation of factors from consumer goods to military production. It also entails a "vertical" shift of resources from the "higher" stages of production to the "lower" stages of production, that is, from the production and maintenance of capital goods temporally remote from the service of the ultimate consumers to the production of war goods for present use. For, as Mises[6] points out, "War can be waged only with present goods." but, in substituting the production of tanks, bombs, and small arms destined for immediate use for the replacement and repair of mining and oil drilling equipment intended to maintain the flow of future consumer goods, the economy is shortening its time structure of production and thus "consuming" its capital. Initially, this capital consumption is manifested in the idleness of fixed capital goods that cannot be converted to immediate war production, e.g., plant and equipment producing oil drilling machinery, and the simultaneous over-utilization of fixed capital goods that can be so converted, e.g., auto assembly plants now used to produce military vehicles. In the short-run, then, the flow of present goods or "real income," in the form of war goods and consumer goods, may actually rise, even in the face of a loss of part of the labor force to military service. But as years pass, and industrial and agricultural equipment is worn out and not replaced, real income inevitably declines—possibly precipitously—below its previous peacetime level.

Schumpeter[7] has provided a graphic summary of the horizontal and vertical shifts of resources caused by the exigencies of a war economy, and the deleterious effect of the vertical shift on the capital stock:

> First, "war economy" essentially means switching the economy from production for the needs of a peaceful life to production for the needs of warfare. This means in the first place that the available means of production are used in some part to produce different final goods, chiefly of course war materials, and in the most part to produce the same products as before but for other customers than in peacetime. This means,

---

[6] Ibid., pp. 168.

[7] Schumpeter, "The Crisis of the Tax State," p. 127.

furthermore, that the available means of production are mainly used to produce as many goods for immediate consumption as possible to the detriment of the production of means of production-particularly machinery and industrial plant—so that that part of production that in peacetime takes up so much room, namely the production for the maintenance and expansion of the productive apparatus, decreases more and more. The possibility to do just this, that is to use for immediate consumption goods, labor, and capital which previously had made producer's goods and thus only indirectly contributed to the production of consumer's goods (i.e., which made "future" rather than "present" goods, to use the technical terminology), this possibility was our great reserve which has saved us so far and which has prevented the stream of consumer's goods from drying up completely.... Our poverty will be brought home to us to its full extent only after the war. Only then will the worn-out machines, the run-down buildings, the neglected land, the decimated livestock, the devastated forests, bear witness to the full depth of the effects of the war.

In commenting upon the effects of World War I on the British economy, Edwin Cannan[8] also drew attention to the crucial fact of the vertical shift of resources and the capital consumption it implies, observing that

... during the war addition to material equipment at home and foreign property abroad wholly ceased. The labor thus set free was made available for war production and for the production of immediately-consumable peace-goods.

[Moreover] everyone conversant with business knows that renewals, if not repairs, have been very seriously postponed in all branches of production and that stocks of everything have run down enormously. The labor which would in ordinary times have been keeping up the material equipment was diverted to war-production and the production of immediately consumable peace-goods.... It was chiefly the tapping of these resources that enabled the country as a whole to get through the war with so little privation.

---

[8] Cannan, *An Economist's Protest*, p. 183.

It may be objected that empirically, the vertical shift of resources is likely to be trivial, because "investment" constitutes such a small segment of real output and therefore the increase in the output of war goods must come mainly from resources diverted from the consumer goods industries combined with a reduction of the leisure of the civilian population, i.e., through increased overtime and labor participation rates. But this fallacious consumer-belt-tightening theory of war economy is based on the Keynesian national income accounting framework, according to which capital investment constitutes a small fraction of total GDP. For example, during the fourth quarter of 1994, the annual rate of real gross private investment in the U.S. totaled $939.7 billion or slightly more than 17 percent of real GDP while real personal consumption expenditures in the same quarter equaled $3629.6 billion or almost 67 percent of real GDP.[9]

Unfortunately, in this framework the investment in "intermediate inputs" is netted out to avoid "double counting." These intermediate inputs to a great extent comprise precisely those types of capital goods, namely, stocks of raw materials, semi finished products, and energy inputs, that can most readily be converted for use in the production of present goods, whether for military or consumption purposes. As Mises[10] observes, this is one form that capital consumption took in Germany during the First World War: "The German economy entered the war with an abundant stock of raw materials and semi-finished goods of all kinds. In peacetime, whatever of these stocks were devoted to use or consumption was regularly replaced. During the war the stocks were consumed without being able to be replaced. They disappeared out of the economy; the national wealth was reduced by their value." These future or higher-stage goods permanently "disappeared" because the resources previously invested in their reproduction had been withdrawn in order to augment the production of war materials.

In fact, in a modern capital-using economy, at any given moment during peacetime, the aggregate value of resources devoted

---

[9] Federal Reserve Bank of St. Louis, *National Economic Trends* (May 1995), pp. 4, 18–19.

[10] Mises, *Nation, State, and Economy*, p. 162.

to production and maintenance of capital goods in the higher stages of production far exceeds the value of resources working to directly serve consumers in the final stage of the production process. As an example, for the U.S. economy in 1982 total business expenditures on intermediate inputs plus gross private investment totaled $3,196.7 billion while personal consumer expenditures totaled $2,046.4 billion. Over 60 percent of the available productive resources, outside the government sector, was therefore devoted to the production of capital, or future, goods as opposed to consumer, or present, goods.[11, 12]

3. The Financing of War

Governments have at their disposal three methods for financing a war: taxation, borrowing from the public, and monetary inflation or the creation of new money. Governments may also resort to coercive requisitioning, that is, confiscating the material resources and conscripting the labor services they deem necessary for the war effort without compensation or in exchange for below-market prices and wage rates. Historically, a combination of these methods has generally been used to effect the transfer of resources from civilian to military uses during a large-scale war. From the viewpoint of technical economic theory, however, the government could always realize the funds necessary to carry out its war aims exclusively from increased taxation and noninflationary borrowing on capital markets. As Schumpeter[13] pointed out with regard to Austria, immediately after the First World War, "It is clear … that strictly speaking we could have squeezed the necessary money out of the private economy just as the goods were squeezed out of it. This could have been done by taxes which would have looked stifling, but which would in fact have been

---

[11] M. Skousen, *The Structure of Production* (New York: New York University Press, 1990), pp. 191–92.

[12] On the critical importance, for analyzing the capital structure, of using a concept of "gross investment" that includes both investment in fixed capital and investment in intermediate inputs in all stages of production, see M.N. Rothbard, *Man, Economy, and State: A Treatise on Economic Principles*, 2nd ed. (Auburn, Ala.: Ludwig von Mises Institute, [1962] 1993), vol. 1, pp. 339–45.

[13] Schumpeter, "The Crisis of the Tax State," p. 121.

no more oppressive than the devaluation of money which was their alternative.[14]

Why, then, if strictly fiscal measures are capable of yielding sufficient revenues to pay market prices for all the resources required to conduct war, have belligerent governments almost always had recourse to the methods of monetary inflation and the direct commandeering of commodities and services? The answer lies in the fact that war is an extremely costly enterprise and the latter two methods, although in very different ways, operate to partially conceal these costs from the public's view.[15] When the public is accurately apprised of its full costs,

---

[14] Despite his general stance against inflationary financing of war, Schumpeter ("The Crisis of the Tax State," p. 121), does concede that "... it is everywhere impossible completely to cover the cost of war by taxation, from the point of view both of politics and fiscal technique." Mises (*Nation, State, and Economy*, pp. 151–71) and Cannan (*Money: Its Connexion with Rising and Falling Prices*, pp. 93–102) are even firmer than Schumpeter in their views that inflation is not technically necessary to finance a major war. For the latter two, whatever quantity of resources can be extracted from the private economy by inflationary finance can also be appropriated via taxation and non-inflationary borrowing. It should be noted however that Mises (*Nation, State, and Economy*, p. 165) maintained that market incentives could never be rendered attractive enough in practice to attract sufficient manpower to serve in the the armed forces under war conditions and that, therefore, conscription was a necessary supplement to market transactions financed by taxes and borrowing. Mises here not only argues that the supply curve of enlistees is inelastic but also implicitly assumes that it is fixed under all circumstances, seemingly ignoring the possibility that a spontaneous shift to the right in the supply curve will occur in the case of a war fought in defense of hearth and home or for a cause that is widely and passionately believed to be just.

[15] Not all pre-Keynesian economics acceded to the view of Mises, Schumpeter, and Cannan that inflation is not theoretically or practically necessary for financing a major war. Two of their prominent contemporaries, A.C. Pigou (*The Political Economy of War*, 2nd ed. [New York: Macmillan, 1941]) and Lionel Robbins (*The Economic Problem in Peace and War: Some Reflections on Objectives and Mechanisms* [London: Macmillan, 1950]) insisted that inflationary finance and direct government controls are an inescapable part of a war economy. Beginning in the early post-World War II era, neo-Keynesian economists like Keynes himself totally innocent of capital theory, turned the older approach to war economics on its head, arguing that war spending, like any other kind of spending, operating through the multiplier process, automatically generates full employment and, therefore, economic prosperity and is likely to create an "inflationary gap" in the macroeconomy They therefore concluded that the conduct of war is inherently inflationary and necessitates extensive government controls over prices, production and labor markets to repress inflation and prevent it from undermining the war economy. For examples of the

war becomes increasingly unpopular, civilian enthusiasm and labor efforts flag, and unrest and even active resistance may ensue on the home front and spread to the front lines. The movement for "revolutionary defeatism" successfully fomented by Russia's Bolsheviks during World War I is just one example of such mass resistance.

As Robert Higgs[16] points out with regard to the tendency of governments to partially substitute a command-and-control economy for the regular fiscal mechanism during wartime and other so-called national emergencies:

> Obviously, citizens will not react to the costs they bear if they are unaware of them. The possibility of driving a wedge between the actual and the publicly perceived costs creates a strong temptation for governments pursuing high-cost policies during national emergencies. Except where lives are being sacrificed, no costs are so easily counted as pecuniary costs. Not only can each individual count them (his own tax bill); they can be easily aggregated for the whole society (the government's total tax revenue). It behooves a government wishing to sustain a policy that entails suddenly heightened costs to find ways of substituting non-pecuniary for pecuniary costs. The substitution may blunt the citizen's realization of how great their sacrifices really are and hence diminish their protests and resistance.

The direct expropriation of resources works best when the resources in question are non-reproducible, as in the case of labor. By legally compelling its citizen-subjects to serve a specified term in military service at wage rates far below market levels, the government significantly reduces the budgetary costs of war and thus the amount by which it must ratchet up taxes. The cost concealment this facilitates

---

neo-Keynesian approach to "defense" economics, see A.G. Hart (*Defense without Inflation* [New York: The Twentieth Century Fund, 1951]) and D.H. Wallace (*Economic Controls and Defense* [New York: The Twentieth Century Fund, 1953]). Robert Higgs ("Wartime Prosperity? A Reassessment of the U.S. Economy in the 1940s," *The Journal of Economic History* 52 [March]: pp. 41–60) provides a superb and long-overdue demolition of the Keynesian claim that World War II brought prosperity to the U.S. economy.

[16] Robert Higgs, *Crisis and Leviathan: Critical Episodes in the Growth of American Government* (New York: Oxford University, 1987), p. 65.

explains the widespread use of mass conscription especially by almost all modern mass democracies, beginning with revolutionary France. But uncompensated confiscation of reproducible resources confronts an insuperable difficulty: while it does yield access to existing stocks of resources, it destroys the incentive on the part of private individuals and firms to reproduce these resources.

Continuation of industrial production processes requires pecuniary compensation to the producers as determined by the market, unless the government is willing to completely abolish exchange and implement a totally moneyless (and particularly chaotic) form of socialism, in which resources are allocated and the products distributed by bureaucratic ukase. This was attempted by the Bolsheviks during the period known as War Communism in the U.S.S.R. from 1918 to 1921 and proved a miserable failure.[17] While governments of mass democracies in fact went a long way toward replacing market incentives and processes with substantial elements of the centrally-planned or command-and-control economy during the two great wars of the twentieth century, at least at the inception of hostilities they still required a cost-concealing device that would yield them the money revenues with which to purchase real resources from their still-operative money-exchange economies. For this purpose, they consolidated the power to issue money in the hands of their central banks. Thus it was, for example, that within days of the outbreak of World War I each and every one of the belligerent governments suspended the operation of the gold standard, effectively arrogating to itself the monopoly of the supply of money in its own national territory.

---

[17] E.H. Carr (*A History of Soviet Russia,* Vol. 2, *The Bolshevik Revolution, 1917–23* [Hammondsworth, Middlesex, England: Penguin Books Ltd., 1971], pp. 151–268) and Alec Nove (*An Economic History of the U.S.S.R.* [Baltimore: Penguin Books, Inc., 1972], pp. 46–82) provide comprehensive descriptions of the policies and events that marked the period of War communism. Paul Craig Roberts (*Alienation and the Soviet Economy: Toward a General Theory of Marxian Alienation, Organizational Principles and the Soviet Economy* [Albuquerque: University of New Mexico Press, 1971], pp. 20–47) convincingly argues the revisionist case that War Communism was not a wartime expedient adopted willy-nilly by hapless soviet authorities but the deliberate application of Marxian doctrine.

To grasp how the issuing of new money obscures and distorts the true costs of war, we first must analyze the case of financing a war exclusively through the imposition of increased taxes supplemented with borrowing from the public. Prior to the increase of taxes and issue of government securities to raise war revenues, the national economy is operating with an aggregate capital structure whose size is determined by the "time preferences" or inter-temporal consumption choices of the consumer-savers. The lower the public's time preferences, and therefore the more willing its members are to postpone consumption from the immediate to the more remote future, the greater is the proportion of current income that is saved and invested in building up an integrated stucture of capital goods. The greater the stock of capital goods, in turn, the greater the productivity of labor and the higher the real wage rate earned by all classes of workers.[18]

From the point of view of individual investors in the capital structure—business proprietors, stockholders, bondholders, insurance policyholders—the values of their titles and claims to capital goods are revealed by monetary calculation, specifically, capital accounting, and are therefore conceived as sums of monetary wealth.[19] The accumulation or consumption of capital will always be readily evident in the changing monetary wealth positions of at least some individuals, assuming the purchasing power of money is roughly stable.

---

[18] For detailed explications of the time-preference theory of interest, see Rothbard (*Man, Economy, and State*, vol. 1., pp. 313–86) and Ludwig von Mises (*Human Action: A Treatise on Economics*, 3rd ed. [Chicago: Henry Regnery Company, 1966], pp. 479–536. A recent defense and clarification of the theory is presented by by I.M. Kirzner ("The Pure Time-Preference Theory of Interest: An Attempt at Clarification," in *The Meaning of Ludwig von Mises: Contribution in Economics, Sociology, Epistemology, and Political Philosophy*, J.M. Herbener, ed. [Norwell, Mass.: Kluwer Academic Publishers, 1993], pp. 166–92) while R.W. Garrison ("Professor Rothbard and the Theory of Interest," in *Man, Economy, and Liberty: Essays in Honor of Murray N. Rothbard*, W. Block and L.H. Rockwell, Jr., eds. [Auburn, Ala.: Ludwig von Mises Institute, 1988], pp. 44–55) offers an illuminating and concise overview.

[19] As Mises (*Human Action*, p. 230) explains: "Monetary calculation reaches its full perfection in capital accounting. It establishes the money prices of the available means and confronts this total with changes brought about by action and by the operation of other factors. This confrontation shows what changes occurred in the state of the acting men's affairs and the magnitude of those changes; it makes success and failure, profit and loss ascertainable."

It will especially be manifested in movements in the stock and real estate markets, which are devoted largely to the exchange of titles to aggregates of capital goods.[20] In addition, enlargements or diminutions of the capital stock will be manifested in fluctuations in current incomes—in aggregate pecuniary profits in the economy and in the general levels of salaries and wages.

As pointed out above, large-scale war involves a marked increase in preferences for present goods and necessitates a thoroughgoing reorientation of society's productive apparatus away from future and toward present goods. To effectuate this temporal restructuring of production in a money-exchange economy, there must occur a radical alteration in the proportions of money expenditure, with consumption and military spending rising relative to saving-investment. Regardless of what technique is utilized to accomplish this shift in relative expenditure, it must give rise to a "retrogressing economy" during the transition to the war economy. The retrogressing economy is one characterized by a declining capital stock. Its onset is marked by a "crisis" involving aggregate business losses, rising interest rates, plunging stock, bond, and real estate markets, and a deflation of financial asset values.[21]

When taxes are raised to finance the war, the crisis is immediately evident. In order to pay their increased tax liabilities, citizens retrench on their saving as well as their consumption. In fact, they reduce their saving proportionally more than their consumption, for two reasons. First, assuming an increase in the income tax, the net interest return on investment is lowered, meaning that the investor can now expect less future consumption in exchange for a given amount of saving or abstinence from present consumption. If his time preference remains unchanged, the worsened terms of trade between present and future goods encourages the taxpayer to escape

---

[20] Thus, as M.N. Rothbard (*America's Great Depression* [Kansas City: Sheed and Ward, Inc., [1963] 1975], pp. 75, 316 fn. 29) points out, "Stocks ... are units of title to masses of capital goods" and "... real estate convey[s] units of title of capital in land."

[21] For an explanation of the concept of a retrogressing economy and the accompanying crisis, see Rothbard (*Man, Economy, and State*, vol. 1, pp. 483–86) and Mises (*Human Action*, pp. 250–51, pp. 298–300).

the tax by increasing spending on present consumption and reducing saving and, thereby, his prospects for future consumption. With all saver-investors responding in this manner, the aggregate supply of savings will decrease and the interest rate will be driven up to reflect the increased tax on investment income.

Second, moreover, because the incidence of the increased tax always falls on his *present* income and monetary assets, it leaves the taxpayer less well-provided with present goods. As his supply of present goods diminishes toward the bare subsistence level—at which point the premium he attaches to present over future consumption becomes approximately infinite—the individual experiences a progressive rise in his time preference, and the prevailing (after-tax) interest rate no longer suffices as adequate compensation for sustaining his current level of saving-investment. He accordingly further reduces the proportion of his income allocated to saving investment.[22]

Finally, as a means of quickly generating the enormous revenues typically required at the outset of a large-scale war, the government might seek to tap, in addition to current income, accumulated capital. This most likely would involve a wealth tax that is levied on each household in some proportion to the market value of the property it owns, including and especially its cash balances. The tax, if it were uniformly enforced on all categories of wealth, would force capitalist-entrepreneurs to liquidate or issue debt against their real assets in order to discharge their tax liability. By its very nature, then, a wealth tax results directly in the consumption of capital. Moreover, even though such a tax is levied on net wealth accumulated in the past, it operates to powerfully increase time preferences and reduce savings even further, because it must be paid out of present income and monetary assets and the prospect of its recurrence can easily be precluded by completely consuming income as it is received and by consuming whatever privately owned capital remains.[23]

---

[22] On these two effects of the income tax, see Rothbard, *Man, Economy, and State*, vol. 2, pp. 797–99.

[23] An analysis of taxes on accumulated capital or wealth can be found in M.N. Rothbard, *Power and Market: Government and the Economy* (Menlo Park, Calif.: Institute for Humane Studies, Inc., 1970), pp. 83–84, 87–88. As an important measure

While the incidence of war taxes falls disproportionately on private saving-investment and wealth, the tax revenues thus appropriated are expended by the belligerent government mainly on present goods in the form of military services and equipment for immediate use. As in the case of an increase in the consumption/saving ratio that would follow from an autonomous increase in the social time preference rate, the "pure" or "real" interest rate that underlies the structure of risk-adjusted loan rates and rates of return on investment is driven up. The higher loan rates and the attendant fall in the market appraisals of debt and equity securities operate to discourage business borrowing and dampen investment in maintaining and reproducing the existing capital structure. The result is a contraction of the demand for capital goods and the sudden onset of "crisis" conditions.

The consequent decline in the prices of capital goods relative to consumer/military goods reflects the greater discount on future vis-a-vis present goods that is revealed in the higher interest rate, and it results in losses for firms in the higher stages of the production structure. In the aggregate, the losses of firms producing capital goods exceed the profits gained by the firms favored by the enhanced military expenditures. The appearance of aggregate losses in the capital-consuming or retrogressing economy is ultimately attributable to the fact that labor productivity and real income is declining as resources are bid away from capital goods production by the increased military expenditures. These transitional, though highly visible, losses suffered by business firms are the first step in the process of imputing the

---

of war finance, Pigou (*The Political Economy of War*, 2nd ed. [New York: Macmillan, 1941], p. 84) advocates a progressive tax on personal wealth, defined broadly to include durable consumer goods and "the capitalised value of a man's mental and manual powers." Mises (*Nation, State, and Economy*, pp. 166–67) views short-term government borrowing as a preferable alternative to a tax on personal wealth. Pigou also considers borrowing as economically substitutable for a wealth tax, but prefers the latter on grounds of equity, viz., it compels "the rich" to bear a greater proportion of the burdens of war. By the way, Pigou's statement that "the costs of a war can[not] be paid out of capital.... The source of the funds raised must be the real income of the country" misses the point (Pigou, *The Political Economy of War*, p. 84, fn. 1). The result of capital consumption induced by the wealth tax is precisely an increase in present real income at the expense of future real income as convertible capital goods and labor are shifted toward the production of present goods.

decline of marginal productivities attendant upon the dissipation of the capital stock back to the incomes of labor and natural resources.[24]

The capital-decumulation crisis is also manifested in a crash of the the stock market, because, as noted above, stocks represent titles to *pro rata* shares of ownership in existing complements of capital goods known as "business firms." It is precisely the values of the prospective future outputs of a firm's productive assets, particularly its fixed capital goods, that are suddenly more heavily discounted in appraising the capital value of the firm. This is especially true of firms that are themselves producing durable capital goods or inputs into these goods. The overall decline in the market's estimation of the capitalized value of various business assets that is indicated by the fall in value of equity and debt securities, of course, not only reflects current business losses but is precisely how monetary calculation reveals the fact of capital decumulation. A drop in real estate markets would also occur at the inception of a tax-financed transition to a war economy, because industrial and commercial construction and land represent particularly durable resources whose capital values are therefore extremely sensitive to a higher rate of discount on future goods. Even if such capital goods may be converted to current military production, their values would still have to be written down to reflect the waste of capital involved in their construction. In other words, if the exigencies of war had been anticipated, labor and other nonspecific resources would not have been "locked up" in them for such lengthy periods of time.[25]

Similar to business cycle crises, war mobilization crises will also feature certain secondary, although highly visible, financial and monetary aspects. Many highly leveraged firms in higher-stage industries, confronted by slumping output prices, will attempt to fend off the prospect of defaulting on their debts by undertaking a "scramble

---

[24] On this process of imputation see Rothbard (*Man, Economy, and State*, vol. 2, pp. 483–84) and Mises (*Human Action*, pp. 294–300).

[25] As Mises (*Human Action*, p. 503) notes, some capital goods "… can be employed for the new process without any alteration; but if it had been known at the time they were produced that they would be used in the new way, it would have been possible to manufacture at smaller cost other goods which could render the same service."

for liquidity," which drives up short-term interest rates, raises the demand for money, and sharply lowers the prices of commodities that are dumped on the market for quick cash. This will precipitate a general fall in prices, which will intensify and extend the liquidity scramble. Actual and threatened defaults on bank loans and other securities also will begin to erode confidence in the soundness of the financial system. Even if the fractional-reserve banking system bears up under the strain, sparing the economy a collapse of the money supply and a "secondary depression," the conspicuous bankruptcies of banks and business firms, reinforced by the sharp decline in private financial wealth and after-tax incomes, will quickly disabuse the populace of any notion that war breeds prosperity.

The government will be unable to avoid, and may even exacerbate, the mobilization crisis by substituting borrowing for higher tax levies. The reason is that, in contrast to taxes, which must be paid out of present income and monetary assets and therefore reduce both private consumption and saving (in accordance with taxpayers' time preferences), government borrowing directly taps saving. When selling securities, the government competes with business for the public's saved funds, and, because it is capable of bidding up the interest rate that it is willing to pay practically without limit, it is in the position to obtain all the funds it needs. As Rothbard[26] concludes "Public borrowing strikes at individual savings more effectively even than taxation, for it specifically lures away *savings* rather than taxing income in general."

With a qualification to be mentioned shortly, by thus "crowding out" private investment to acquire the funds for war financing, government borrowing insures that the entire burden of adjustment to a war economy is borne solely by the capital goods industries. The adjustment is now exclusively vertical, because consumption is not diminished, obviating any horizontal reallocation of resources. Mises[27] thus compares government borrowing to a kind of tax on accumulated capital in its devastating effect on the capital structure: "If current expenditure, however beneficial it may be considered, is financed by taking

---

[26] Rothbard, *Man, Economy, and State*, p. 881.
[27] Mises, *Human Action*, p. 850.

away by inheritance taxes those parts of higher incomes which would have been employed for investment, or by borrowing, the government becomes a factor making for capital consumption."[28]

Because it brings about greater capital consumption than tax financing does, government borrowing promotes a more severe crisis. Thus, for example, on the eve of the outbreak of World War I, between July 23 and July 31, and before the would-be belligerent States had "gone off" the gold standard and began inflating their respective national money supplies, panic selling forced the closing of all major stock exchanges from St. Petersburg and Vienna to Toronto and New York. Certainly, this broad decline in the market value of stocks was partially attributable to general uncertainty of the future and an increased demand for liquidity.[29] But it also represented a response to expectations of heavy government borrowing to finance war mobilization under the non-inflationary conditions of the gold standard.

The British economist Ralph G. Hawtrey[30] aptly described the initial stages of this mobilization crisis and the frantic attempts of government to suppress it by swift resort to legal debt moratoria and bank credit inflation:

> The prospect of forced borrowing by the Government on a large scale will stifle the demand for existing stock exchange securities, and stock exchange operators and underwriters will find themselves loaded up with securities which are saleable, if at all, only at a great sacrifice. The disorganisation of business may be so great that an almost universal bankruptcy can only be staved off by special measures for suspending the obligations of debtors, like the crop of moratorium statutes with which Europe blossomed out in 1914.
>
> A Government, indeed, faced with a great war, cannot afford to let half the business of the country slip into bankruptcy,

---

[28] For an analysis of the inheritance tax as a pure tax on capital, see Rothbard, *Power and Market*, pp. 84–85.

[29] B.M. Anderson, *Economics and the Public Welfare: A Financial and Economic History of the United States, 1914–1946* (Indianapolis: Liberty Press, [1949] 1979), pp. 28–29.

[30] R.G. Hawtrey, *Currency and Credit* (New York: Arno Press, [1919] 1979), pp. 210–11.

and … the embarrassed traders are propped up, either by lav-
ish advances granted them by arrangement, or by a special
statutory moratorium.[31]

As noted, there is an important qualification to our conclusion
that the substitution of government borrowing for taxation will exacerbate the mobilization crisis. Even if the monetary costs of war are
paid for entirely by borrowing, the resulting adjustment of the real
economy will not be entirely vertical, because the supply of savings is
more or less "elastic" or sensitive with respect to changes in the interest rate.

Consequently, as the government's fiscal agent bids up interest rates, some members of the public will be induced to voluntarily reduce their present consumption to a greater or lesser extent,
in order to take advantage of the increased premium in terms of the
enhanced future consumption per dollar of foregone present consumption promised by the higher-yielding securities. In fact, if the
public's structure of time preferences makes them sufficiently sensitive to rising interest rates in determining their consumption/sav-
ing ratio, consumer-good industries may conceivably come to bear a
larger burden of adjustment than they would under tax financing.

---

[31] Michael A. Heilperin, the Misesian international monetary theorist, in his study of
post-World War One inflations, also hints at a link between deficit financing and the
war mobilization crisis, writing that "Deficit financing was closely connected with
the course of development of monetary circulation. The outbreak of the war resulted
not only in a need for deficit financing but also in widespread movements of panic
on the part of the public. In order to prevent the panic from undermining the internal monetary conditions and thereby adversely affecting the war effort, moratoria on
banks were declared almost immediately…. Also the gold standard was suspended.
Curiously, Heilperin's valuable study, carried out in 1943–44 under the auspices of
the National Bureau of Economic Research and "circulated to a large body of leading American experts of the day," was never published by the NBER. In fact, when
the NBER agreed to allow the copyright to revert back to Heilperin so that he could
include the article in a book of his essays (published in 1968), the institute stipulated
that it wished to remain unnamed in his acknowledgement (Heilperin, "Post-War
European Inflations, World War I: A Study of Selected Cases," in idem, *Aspects of the
Pathology of Money: Monetary Essays from Four Decades* [London: Michael Joseph
Limited, 1968], p. 97). I possess a copy of the article in original mimeographed form
and the cover page is marked "Preliminary and Confidential" and bears the imprint
of the "National Bureau of Economic Research, Financial Research Bureau."

In any case, we conclude that, when undistorted by monetary inflation, regardless of the fiscal technique or combination of techniques employed, economic calculation clearly and immediately reveals to market participants, individually and in the aggregate, the enormous destruction of real wealth and decline in real income entailed in mobilizing for a large-scale war. What insures this result is monetary calculation based on genuine market prices. Indeed, as Mises[37] points out, "The market economy is real because it can calculate.... Among the main tasks of economic calculation are those of establishing the magnitudes of income, saving, and capital consumption."

Individual capital goods, even so-called fixed capital equipment, wear out in production and, in a world of unceasing change, must be replaced by physically different goods. The capital structure is thus undergoing a physical transformation at every instant of time. This means that capitalist-entrepreneurs, who must continually adjust the production processes under their control to changing consumer preferences, technical innovations, and resource availabilities, must have recourse to a common denominator in order to determine the outcome of their past production decisions and to assess the resulting quantity of productive resources they currently can dispose of as a starting point for future decisions.

> In other words, only the market's pricing process provides the meaningful cardinal numbers needed by entrepreneurs to calculate their costs, revenues, profits, and quantity of capital. Given the continual change in market conditions that impels constant adjustment of the real capital structure and given the vast physical heterogeneity of the complementary capital goods that constitute this structure, in the absence of monetary calculation utilizing genuine market prices, it becomes impossible for a producer not only to quantitatively appraise his capital and income, but to meaningfully conceive a distinction between them. Thus, without the guidance of capital accounting, there would be no telling how much of the gross receipts from his business the entrepreneur could allocate to

---

[32] Mises, *Human Action*, p. 261.

his present consumption without dissipating his capital and therefore his ability to provide for future wants.[33]

As we have learned from the socialist calculation debate, in the absence of monetary calculation using genuine market prices, rational allocation of resources is impossible. By proscribing private property in the so-called "means of production," socialist central planning effectively eradicates markets and prices for capital goods, thereby bringing about the abolition of monetary calculation and the inevitable destruction of the existing capital structure.[34] While the effects of monetary inflation on economic calculation are not as manifestly devastating as outright socialization—at least initially—it, nonetheless, operates insidiously to falsify profit and capital calculations. One of the main reasons why inflation distorts monetary calculation is because accounting must assume a stability of the value of money which does not exist in reality. Nonetheless, where fluctuations in the purchasing power of money are minor, as is the case with market-based commodity moneys represented historically especially by the gold standard, this assumption does not practically affect entrepreneurs' monetary calculations and appraisements. A mighty and complex structure of capital goods was built up under the nineteenth-century gold standard using precisely such methods of calculation.

---

[33] As Mises (*Human Action*, pp. 210–11) writes, "Economic calculation is either an estimate of the expected outcome of future action or the establishment of the outcome of past action. But the latter does not serve merely historical and didactic aims. Its practical meaning is to show how much one is free to consume without impairing the future capacity to produce. It is with regard to this problem that the fundamental notions of economic calculation—capital and income, profit and loss, spending and saving, cost and yield—are developed." Also see ibid., pp. 230, 260–62, 491, and 514–17.

[34] For recent views of the socialist calculation debate that emphasize Mises's original thesis that socialism is "impossible" precisely because it lacks the means of economic calculation, see Joseph T. Salerno, "Ludwig von Mises as Social Rationalist," *The Review of Austrian Economics*, vol. 4: pp. 26–54; idem, "Why a Socialist Economy Is 'Impossible,'" Postscript to Ludwig von Mises, *Economic Calculation in the Socialist Commonwealth*, trans. S. Adler (Auburn, Ala.: Praxeology Press, 1990), pp. 51–71; idem, Reply to Leland B. Yeager on "Mises and Hayek on Calculation and Knowledge," *The Review of Austrian Economics*, vol. 6, no. 2: pp. 111–25 and Murray N. Rothbard, " The End of Socialism and the Calculation Debate Revisited," *The Review of Austrian Economics*, vol. 5, no. 2: pp. 51–76.

However, when government operating through a central bank deliberately orchestrates significant fiat money inflation to pay for a war or for any other purpose, matters are much different. The resulting large decrease in the purchasing power of money, to the extent that it is not recognized and immediately adapted to in accounting procedures, will inescapably falsify business calculations. Moreover, prices in general do not adjust instantaneously upward in response to the increase in the money supply; rather, the fall in the overall purchasing power of money is the final outcome of a time-consuming, sequential adjustment process involving a distortion of relative prices, including the interest rate, *i.e.,* or the price ratio between present and future goods.[35] Both of these effects operate to conceal the process of capital consumption during its early stages.

Under modern conditions, inflationary financing of war involves a government "monetizing" its debt by selling securities, directly or indirectly, to the central bank. The funds thus obtained are then spent on the items necessary to equip and sustain the armed forces of the nation. The result is a sudden expansion of demand for the products of the military and consumer-good industries, with no reduction in the monetary demand for the products of the capital-good industries. A boom is consequently precipitated, featuring rising prices, profits, and stock values in the former industries; The boom is particularly intense and dazzling in these industries because, during an inflation, prices rise in temporal sequence. Thus, prices and nominal incomes initially increase only for those sellers who receive the new money in the first round of spending and, therefore, before the prices of the productive inputs and consumer goods they themselves regularly purchase have had a chance to rise. As Mises[36] concludes, "The war suppliers ... have therefore gained not only from enjoying good business in the ordinary sense of the word but also from the fact that the additional quantity of money flowed first to them. The price rise of

---

[35] On the long-run non-neutrality of the monetary adjustment process, see Mises, *Theory of Money and Credit,* pp. 160–68 and Joseph T. Salerno, "Ludwig von Mises on Inflation and Expectations," *Advances in Austrian Economics,* vol. 2: pp. 297–325 [reprinted here as Chapter 8].

[36] Mises, *Nation, State and Economy,* p. 158.

the goods and services that they brought to market was a double one, it was caused first by the increased demand for their labor, but then too by the increased supply of money."

Because the increase in the demand for credit represented by the Treasury's issuance of securities is met by newly-created bank credit, on the one hand, market interest rates do not initially rise. On the other hand, the higher prices for consumer and war goods eventually spread up the ladder of the structure of production and result in higher prices for the capital-good inputs produced by the higher-stage firms. As Heilperin[37] states in reference to World War I inflations, "The wave of rising prices tends to generate profits for anyone who holds inventories of goods and increases existing profits for producers. Higher current profits, in turn, induce a reappraisal by the market of future profit prospects which, when discounted by the unchanged interest rate, results in a rise in the equity values of capital-good firms also. War appears to breed universal prosperity."

Nonetheless, capital consumption is proceeding apace, with aggregate real losses being suffered especially by higher-order firms. The reason why these firms do not discern their losses and progressive decapitalization is because of their accounting practices, which served them so well during the prewar period of roughly stable prices. Thus, despite the depreciating monetary unit, they continue to carry their fixed capital equipment on their books at historical cost, calculating their depreciation quotas accordingly. Even though some of their costs, especially wage rates, are continually driven up by the inflation-fueled bidding of the producers of military and selected consumer goods, capital-good firms, nevertheless, appear to be earning profits as their output prices continue ever upward with a lag.

It is only when it comes to replacing their plant and machinery—possibly years down the road—at the much higher "replacement cost" reflecting monetary depreciation that their decline in capital will at last become evident. Moreover, in many cases, the entrepreneurs will then discover that they themselves inadvertently exacerbated this capital consumption by spending their illusory pecuniary profits,

---

[37] Heilperin, "Post-War European Inflations," p. 105.

which were actually part of their depreciation quotas, on high living and other forms of present consumption.

The Austrian economist, Fritz Machlup[38] illustrates this process of capital consumption for working capital with a striking example drawn from the Austrian inflation initiated during the First World War:

> A dealer bought a thousand tons of copper. He sold them, as prices rose, with considerable profit. He consumed only half of the profit and saved the other half. He invested again in copper and got several hundred tons. Prices rose and rose. The dealer's profit was enormous; he could afford to travel and to buy cars, country houses, and what not. He also saved and invested again in copper. His money capital was now a high multiple of his initial one. After repeated transactions—he always could afford to live a luxurious life—he invested his whole capital, grown to an astronomical amount, in a few pounds of copper. While he and the public considered him a profiteer of the highest income, he had in reality eaten up his capital.

4. War Inflation and The Road to Economic Fascism

Even after the monetary inflation manifests itself in a general rise in prices, the public can still be misled into believing that these price increases are the result of temporary shortages of essential materials or the machinations of unscrupulous war profiteers and price-gougers. It is only a matter of time, however, before workers and investors outside the military-industrial complex come to recognize that a depreciating monetary unit is a permanent feature of the war economy and their eroding real wages and illusory profits are brought clearly and painfully into focus. To postpone the day of accurate reckoning of the costs of war yet again, the government implements price controls. As a result of the inevitable shortages and inefficiencies generated by price controls, the government frantically institutes and then rapidly expands controls over production, distribution, and labor, until very little is left of the market economy and its capital structure. The final

---

[38] F. Machlup, "The Consumption of Capital in Austria," *The Review of Economic Statistics* (January): pp. 13–19.

outcome of this process is an economy in which, although productive resources are still nominally privately owned, the State has effectively arrogated to itself the power to make all crucial production decisions. The all-encompassing war economy is, ultimately and inescapably, a fascist economy.[39]

Guenter Reiman[40] has fittingly entitled his book on the fascist economic system of Nazi Germany, *The Vampire Economy*, because, as a permanent war economy, it systematically and madly consumes the capital, the very lifeblood, of the host capitalist economy. And to enforce the compliance of its citizens in this painfully self-destructive course, an all-powerful state is indispensable. As Reiman[41] puts it: "[I]t is impossible to foretell when a military system will collapse as a result of a deficiency in foodstuffs, raw materials or other economic factors. As long as the state machine is in order, it has the power to cut down the consumption of the general public and to reduce— almost to eliminate—expenditures for the renewal of the industrial machine…. It is possible to increase production of arms and ammunition even with reduced supplies of raw materials. This can be done by drastically limiting production of consumption goods, by putting

---

[39] As Charlotte Twight, *America's Emerging Fascist Economy* (New Rochelle, N.Y.: Arlington House Publishers, 1975), pp. 16–17 perceptively argues, "Fascism is unique among collectivist systems in selecting capitalism as its nominal economic mate, but capitalism is turned inside out in this unlikely union…. [F]ascism tolerates the form of private ownership at the government's pleasure, but it eliminates any meaningful right of private property. Fascist capitalism is 'regulated' capitalism; it is government intervention in the economy on a massive scale. Avraham Barkai (*Nazi Economics: Ideology, Theory, and Policy*, trans. Ruth Hadass-Vashitz [New Haven, Conn.: Yale University Press, 1990], p. 248) characterizes the Nazi economy in similar terms: "The market still existed but was not a free market, and most decisions taken by the owners of enterprise were not 'free' either. The term 'organized capitalism' suits this economic method, subject only to the reservation that organization was imposed from above by extraeconomic, that is, political factors; it was these factors that were responsible for directing the economy in accordance with basically non-economic considerations. It was therefore a capitalist economy in which capitalists, like all other citizens, were not free even though they enjoyed a privileged status, had a limited measure of freedom in their activities, and were able to accumulate huge profits as long as they accepted the primacy of politics."

[40] G. Reimann, *The Vampire Economy: Doing Business under Fascism* (New York: The Vanguard Press, 1939).

[41] Ibid., p. xi

the population on starvation rations, and by letting vast sectors of the economy decay." In Germany, for example, despite the fact that total production had increased from prewar levels as a result of the plundering of the productive wealth of vanquished nations and the relocation and forced labor of conquered peoples, by 1944 the output of the vital construction industries had shrunk to 25 percent of its prewar level while consumer goods output had declined by only 15 percent.[42] The capital consumption that inflation brings about surreptitiously in the beginning, a repressive fascist State is required to sustain over the long run in the service of the war effort.

The American journalist, John T. Flynn,[43] wrote that "A bad fascism is a fascist regime which is against us in the war. A good fascist regime is one that is on our side." But, to repeat, all war economies are and must be in the end fascist economies. Higgs[44] vividly characterizes the process by which, in an effort to conceal the costs of World War II from its citizens, the U.S. government was driven by the iron logic of economic theory to blunder into draconian fascist economic planning:

> Huge military and naval forces required correspondingly large amounts of equipment, supplies, subsistence, and transportation. When the government's procurement officers, their pockets bulging with newly created purchasing power, set in motion a bidding war that could have driven prices up to spectacular levels, thereby revealing the full costs of the government's program and provoking political reaction and resistance, the government moved to conceal the costs by price controls.... But price controls on goods and services could not be effectively enforced while wages remained free to rise. Hence controls of labor compensation followed in due course. The market economy, a vast and delicately interdependent system of transactions, invariably surprised and confounded the administrators of partial controls. In response the government progressively expanded and tightened the command system until, during the final two years

---

[42] Barkai, *Nazi Economics*, p. 238.

[43] J.T. Flynn, *As We Go Marching* (Garden City, N.Y.: Doubleday, Doran and Co., Inc., 1944), p. 165.

[44] Higgs, *Crisis and Leviathan*, pp. 234–35.

of the war, a thoroughgoing garrison economy had been brought into operation. Fundamentally the authorities, not the market, determined what, how, and for whom the economy would produce under this regime.

We conclude, then, that monetary inflation is the crucial first step in the process by which government seeks to conceal from its citizen-subjects the enormous costs associated with war, particularly the progressive destruction of the nation's productive wealth. Specifically, the inflationary process is indispensable for masking the capital decumulation crisis precipitated by war mobilization, which would otherwise be swiftly revealed to one and all by monetary calculation. In the absence of the veil cast over real economic processes by inflation, the public's enthusiasm for the alleged glories of war would be rapidly and significantly dampened by skyrocketing interest rates, plummeting stock and bond markets, and pandemic business bankruptcies and bank runs—not to mention the levying of confiscatory kinds and levels of taxation. Ironically, it is not money itself that is a "veil"—as classical economists used to claim and many contemporary quantity theorists still affirm—because it is precisely monetary calculation that permits market participants to meaningfully assess their wealth and income and appraise the outcomes of alternative allocations of resources. Rather it is central bank manipulation of the money supply that falsifies the calculation of economic quantities and distorts the insight of the citizenry into the true economic sacrifices that they are making for the cause.

Finally, it is worth emphasizing that the characterization of monetary inflation as a means for obscuring the real costs of war is an inference from strictly value-free economic theory and, as such, does not logically imply the value judgment that war ought to be financed by noninflationary fiscal methods. How a war should be financed and whether it should even be waged are equally questions that can only be resolved in light of a politico-ethical theory. Of course, this is not to deny that such a theory should be "consequentialist" in a broad sense and take into account in its formulation the positive conclusions of economics as well as of all other relevant sciences regarding the outcomes of various governnent policies. Indeed, given the conclusions of Austrian economic theory that the very concept of a "public good" is untenable and that national defense can and will, be supplied most efficiently by the market, like any other desired good, the road has been cleared for the construction of a politico-ethical argument that defense of person and property from local criminals as well as from foreign invaders should be left to the free market.[45]

Bibliography

Anderson, B.M. [1949] 1979. *Economics and the Public Welfare: A Financial and Economic History of the United States, 1914–1946.* Indianapolis: Liberty Press.

Barkai, A. 1990. *Nazi Economics: Ideology, Theory, and Policy,* Ruth Hadass-Vashitz, trans. New Haven, Conn.: Yale University Press.

Cannan, E. 1928. *An Economist's Protest.* New York: Adelphi Company.

_____. 1919. *Money: Its Connexion with Rising and Falling Prices,* 6th ed. Westminster: P.S. King & Son, Ltd.

Carr, F.H. 1971. *A History of Soviet Russia,* Vol. 2, *The Bolshevik Revolution, 1917–23.* Hammondsworth, Middlesex, England: Penguin Books Ltd.

Federal Reserve Bank of St Louis. 1995, National *Economic Trends* (May).

Flynn, J.T. 1944. *As We Go Marching.* Garden City, N.Y.: Doubleday, Doran and Co., Inc.

Garrison, R.W. 1988. "Professor Rothbard and the Theory of Interest." In *Man, Economy, and Liberty: Essays in Honor of Murray N. Rothbard,* W. Block and L.H. Rockwell, Jr., eds., pp. 44–55. Auburn, Ala: Ludwig von Mises Institute.

---

[45] For Austrian critiques of the concept of a public good, see, for example, Rothbard, *Man, Economy, and State,* vol. 2, pp. 883–90 and H.H. Hoppe, *A Theory of Socialism and Capitalism: Economics, Politics and Ethics* (Boston: Kluwer Academic Publishers, 1989), pp. 187–210. For the classic article defending the competitive production of defense services by private enterprise, originally penned in 1848 by a leading economist of the French liberal school, see Gustave de Molinari, *The Production of Security,* trans. J. Huston McCulloch (New York: The Center for Libertarian Studies, 1977). For more recent expositions of how the free market would work to provide defense and other public goods, see Morris and Linda Tannehill, *The Market for Liberty* (Lansing, Mich.: Morris and Linda Tannehill, 1970), pp. 107; Rothbard, *Power and Market,* pp. 1–7; M.N. Rothbard, *For a New Liberty: The Libertarian Manifesto,* 2nd ed. (New York: Collier Books, 1978), pp. 215–41; J.R. Hummel, "National Goods Versus Public Goods: Defense, Disarmament and Free Riders," *The Review of Austrian Economics,* pp. 88–122; and J.R. Hummel and D. Lavoie, "National Defense and the Public-Goods Problem," *Journal des Economistes et des Etudes Humaines* 5, nos. 2/3 (June/September): pp. 353–77.

Hart, A.G. 1951. *Defense without Inflation*. New York: The Twentieth Century Fund.

Hawtrey, R.G. [1919] 1979. *Currency and Credit*. New York: Arno Press.

Heilperin, M.A. 1968. "Post-War European Inflations, World War I: A Study of Selected Cases." In idem, *Aspects of the Pathology of Money, Monetary Essays from Four Decades,* pp. 97–152. London: Michael Joseph Limited.

Higgs, R. 1987. *Crisis and Leviathan: Critical Episodes in the Growth of American Government*. New York: Oxford University.

_____. 1992. "Wartime Prosperity? A Reassessment of the U.S. Economy in the 1940s." *The Journal of Economic History*, 52 (March): pp. 41–60.

Hoppe, H.H. 1989. *A Theory of Socialism and Capitalism: Economics, Politics, and Ethics*. Boston: Kluwer Academic Publishers.

Hummel, J.R. 1990. "National Goods Versus Public Goods: Defense, Disarmament, and Free Riders." *The Review of Austrian Economics*: pp. 88–122.

Hummel, J.R. and D. Lavoie. 1994. "National Defense and the Public-Goods Problem." *Journal des Economistes et des Etudes Humaines*, 5, nos. 2/3 (June/September): pp. 353–77.

Kirzner, I.M. 1993. "The Pure Time-Preference Theory of Interest: An Attempt at Clarification." In *The Meaning of Ludwig von Mises: Contribution in Economics, Sociology, Epistemology, and Political Philosophy*, J.M. Herbener, ed., pp. 166–92. Norwell, Mass.: Kluwer Academic Publishers.

Machlup, F. 1935. "The Consumption of Capital in Austria." *The Review of Economic Statistics* (January): pp. 13–19.

Mises, L.von. 1966. *Human Action: A Treatise on Economics*, 3rd ed. Chicago: Henry Regnery Company.

_____. 1981. *The Theory of Money and Credit*, 3rd ed. H.E. Batson, trans. Indianapolis: Liberty Classics.

_____. 1983. *Nation, State, and Economy: Contributions to the Politics and History of Our Time,* Leland B. Yeager, trans. New York: New York University Press.

Molinari, G. de. 1977. *The Production of Security*, J. Huston McCulloch, trans. New York: The Center for Libertarian Studies.

Norwell, M.A., Kiuwer Academic Publishers. pp. 166–92.

Nove, A. 1972. *An Economic History of the U.S.S.R*. Baltimore: Penguin Books, Inc.

Pigou, A.C. 1941. *The Political Economy of War*, 2nd ed. New York: Macmillan.

Reimann, G. 1939. *The Vampire Economy: Doing Business under Fascism*. New York: The Vanguard Press.

Robbins, L. 1950. *The Economic Problem in Peace and War: Some Reflections on Objectives and Mechanisms*. London: Macmillan & Co., Ltd.

Roberts, P.C. 1971. *Alienation and the Soviet Economy. Toward a General Theory of Marxian Alienation, Organizational Principles and the Soviet Economy*. Albuquerque: University of New Mexico Press.

Rothbard, M.N. 1970. *Power and Market: Government and the Economy.* Menlo Park, Calif.: Institute for Humane Studies, Inc.

_____. [1963] 1975. *America's Great Depression.* Kansas City: Sheed and Ward, Inc.

_____. 1978. *For a New Liberty: The Libertarian Manifesto,* 2nd ed. New York: Collier Books.

_____. 1991. "The End of Socialism and the Calculation Debate Revisited." *The Review of Austrian Economics,* 5, no. 2: pp. 51–76.

_____. [1962] 1993. *Man, Economy, and State: A Treatise on Economic Principles,* 2nd ed. Auburn, Ala.: Ludwig von Mises Institute.

Salerno, J.T. 1990a, "Ludwig von Mises as Social Rationalist." *The Review of Austrian Economics* 4: pp. 26–54.

_____. 1990b. "Why a Socialist Economy Is 'Impossible.'" Postscript to Ludwig von Mises, *Economic Calculation in the Socialist Commonwealth,* S. Adler, trans., pp. 51–71. Auburn, Ala.: Ludwig von Mises Institute.

_____. 1994. Reply to Leland B. Yeager on "Mises and Hayek on Calculation and Knowledge." *The Review of Austrian Economics* 6, no. 2: pp. 111–25.

_____. 1995. "Ludwig von Mises on Inflation and Expectations." *Advances in Austrian Economics,* vol. 2: pp. 297–325.

Schumpeter, J.A. 1991. "The Crisis of the Tax State." In idem, *The Economics and Sociology of Capitalism,* Richard Swedberg, ed., pp. 99–140. Princeton, N.J.: Princeton University Press.

Skousen, M. 1990. *The Structure of Production.* New York: New York University Press.

Starr, E. 1970. "Recording of 'War'", written by N. Whitfield and B. Strong, from the album *War & Peace.* Detroit: Motown Record Corporation.

Tannehill, M. and L. Tannehill. 1970. *The Market for Liberty.* Lansing, Mich.: Morris and Linda Tannehill.

Twight, C. 1975. *America's Emerging Fascist Economy.* New Rochelle, N.Y.: Arlington House Publishers.

Wallace, D.H. 1953. *Economic Controls and Defense.* New York: The Twentieth Century Fund.

CHAPTER 10

An Austrian Taxonomy of Deflation— With Applications to the U.S.

D eflation has been all over the news for the last two years. Financial journalists, market pundits, business forecasters, economic columnists, Fed governors and mainstream macroeconomists are all spooked by the specter of price deflation in the U.S. During this time we have been inundated with dire warnings of the looming prospect of a possibly catastrophic deflation in the U.S. Articles bearing such grizzly and creepy titles as "The Deflation Monster Still Lives," "The Specter of Deflation," "Deflation Boogeyman Haunts Fed," "The Greatest Threat Facing the U.S. Economy: Deflation," "Why We Should Fear Deflation," and "Deflation: Making Sure 'It' Doesn't Happen Here" abounded in the financial press and among the publications of such august and stodgy economic think tanks as the American Enterprise Institute and the Brookings Institution.[1] Recently, the International Monetary Fund held an economic

From: "An Austrian Taxonomy of Deflation—With Applications to the U.S.," *The Quarterly Journal of Austrian Economics* 6, no. 4 (2003): 81–109.

[1] See, for example, John H. Makin, "The Deflation Monster Lives," *Economic Outlook* (December 2001); Robert J. Samuelson, "The Specter of Deflation," *Washington Post Online* (November 21, 2001); Donald L. Luskin, "The Greatest Threat Facing the U.S. Economy: Deflation," *Capitalism-Magazine.com* (November 23, 2001); J. Bradford DeLong, "Why We Should Fear Deflation," *Brookings Papers on Economic Activity* (Spring 1999). http://www.j-bradford-delong.net; Richard W. Rahn, "Defeating Deflation," *Wall Street Journal* (November 19, 2001); and Bruce Bartlett,

forum entitled "Should We Be Worried About 'Deflation'?" to discuss a report it commissioned on the global risks of deflation.[2]

As their titles suggest, these articles delineate chilling scenarios for the American economy. Not only do these and other articles contend that deflation is close at hand but many of them assert or imply two additional propositions: first, that the effects of deflation are an unmitigated disaster for economic activity and welfare; and, second, that the Federal Reserve System needs to take prompt action to head off such devastation to the economy. In particular, their authors argue that the Fed must dexterously shift gears and become a deflation fighter rather than the staunch and valiant inflation-fighter it supposedly has been for the last two decades. A few authors even question whether the Fed is now constitutionally capable of making such a shift—as if any central bank would be unwilling or unable to create massive quantities of new money, given even the lamest of excuses.

Most of the growing host of deflation-phobes prudently leave the precise details of the impending deflationary debacle to our imagination with vague and foreboding references to the Great Depression in the U.S. in the early 1930s or to the experience of Japan since 1998. However, others, such as market pundit Donald L. Luskin, a self-proclaimed "unreconstructed supply-sider," delight in conjuring up lurid deflationary scenarios. According to Luskin,[3] deflation is:

> going to be a world of hurt. If you thought inflation was a nightmare, wait till you live with a deflation. Prices of everything eventually go down—stocks, real estate, wages ... the whole thing. You're a little poorer every day.... And if you're in debt then you're really in trouble. You'll have to make those same mortgage payments even though the value of your house is going down every month.... But that doesn't mean that deflation is any bed of roses for lenders either. Sure, it's nice to have locked in a stream of payments in money that

---

"The Deflation Dilemma: To Be Concerned or Not to Be?" *National Review Online Financial* (November 20, 2001).

[2] Kenneth Rogoff, Manmohan S. Kumar, Laurance Ball, Vincent Reinhart, and Kim Scoenholtz, Transcript of an IMF Economic Forum: "Should We Be Worried About 'Deflation'?", Washington, D.C. (May 29, 2003). Available at: http://www.imf.org.

[3] Luskin, "The Greatest Threat."

will buy you more and more apples and paper clips and houses as prices collapse. But you'll never get the money, because the borrowers will all default.[4]

But regardless of whether they indulge in such rhetorical excesses or state their case dispassionately in formal academic jargon, contemporary deflation-phobes fail to distinguish between the several different phenomena that are commonly jumbled together under the rubric of "deflation." And because modern macroeconomics was born of John Maynard Keynes's obsessive deflation-phobia,[5] academic macroeconomists are the most likely of all to be muddled about deflation. They are not inclined or equipped to give a coherent account of the separate economic processes designated as "deflationary"; nor are they able to ascertain which kinds of deflationary processes are "benign" and represent an improvement of economic efficiency and welfare and which kinds are "malign" and impair economic productivity and well-being by distorting monetary calculation.

Fortunately, Austrian monetary theory, which was developed primarily by Ludwig von Mises and Murray N. Rothbard, provides us with the means to cut through the tangle of anti-deflationist fallacies that we have lately been bombarded with and to neatly sort out the different types of deflation.[6] The remainder of the paper is divided as follows. Deflation is defined in Section 2. Austrian monetary theory is utilized to identify and analyze the different kinds of

---

[4] Ibid.

[5] John Maynard Keynes, *The General Theory of Employment, Interest, and Money* (New York: Harcourt, Brace and World, [1936] 1964), p. 269.

[6] The seminal work on Austrian monetary theory is Mises's *Theory of Money and Credit*, 2nd ed., trans. H.E. Batson (Indianapolis, Ind.: Liberty Classics, [1953] 1980). Mises's more mature statement of monetary theory can be found in *Human Action: A Treatise on Economics*, Scholar's Edition (Auburn, Ala.: Ludwig von Mises Institute, [1953] 1980), pp. 395–475. Murray N. Rothbard's comprehensive restatement and elaboration of Misesian monetary theory is contained in his treatise *Man, Economy, and State: A Treatise on Economic Principles*, 2nd ed. (Auburn, Ala.: Ludwig von Mises Institute), pp. 160–200, 661–764. For two shorter and very lucid treatments of Austrian monetary theory, see Murray N. Rothbard, *What Has Government Done to Our Money?* 4th ed. (Auburn, Ala.: Ludwig von Mises Institute); idem, "The Austrian Theory of Money," in *The Logic of Action One: Method, Money, and the Austrian School* (Cheltenham, U.K.: Edward Elgar, 1997), pp. 297–320.

deflation in Section 3, distinguishing between deflations that are natural and benign tendencies of a progressing free-market economy and deflation that results from malign intervention in the economy by government and its central bank and cripples monetary exchange and calculation. Section 4 contains a critique of the most common fallacies perpetrated by contemporary deflation-phobes. We conclude with an analysis of the likelihood that the U.S. economy is or soon will be in the throes of a deflationary recession.

The Definition of Deflation

Before World War II, when the terms "inflation" and "deflation" were used in academic discourse or everyday speech, they generally meant an increase or a decrease in the stock of money, respectively. A general rise in prices was viewed as one of several consequences of inflation of the money supply; likewise, a decline in overall prices was viewed as one consequence of deflation of the money supply. Under the influence of the Keynesian Revolution of the mid-1930s, however, the meanings of these terms began to change radically. By the 1950s, the definition of inflation as a general rise in prices and of deflation as a general fall in prices became firmly entrenched in academic writings and popular speech. We can ignore here the question of whether or not this change in usage enhanced conceptual clarity and analytical precision in dealing with monetary problems.[7] The point is that today when professional economists and members of the lay public utter or write the term "deflation," they invariably mean a decline in the overall prices of commodities and services purchased by the "average" consumer as expressed in a price index such as the CPI. Movements in the prices of consumer goods are relevant for identifying the existence and degree of inflation or deflation because consumer goods are the final output and, hence, the rationale, of all economic activity. Moreover, as Carl Menger, the founder of Austrian economics has taught us, the

---

[7] For a discussion of how the meaning of the words inflation and deflation was progressively transformed, see Joseph T. Salerno, "Money and Gold in the 1920s and 1930s: An Austrian View," *Freeman* 49 (October, 1999), pp. 31–33 [reprinted here as Chapter 16]. Mises (*Human Action*, pp. 419–21) argues that the modern definition of these terms is inexpedient for the purposes of scientific discourse.

prices of the myriad of intermediate and original inputs into the production process, broadly categorized as capital goods, labor and natural resources, are ultimately "imputed" via an entrepreneurial market process from the prices of consumer goods. Thus when economists, business forecasters, and Alan Greenspan scrutinize indexes of input prices such as the PPI or indexes of raw commodity prices, they do so because they incorrectly believe that changes in these indexes are harbingers of future changes in general consumer prices, as if input prices determined product prices rather than the other way around.

Defined as a general fall in consumer prices, deflation implies an increase in the value or purchasing power of the monetary unit—in the U.S. an increase in the amount of consumer goods that can be purchased for a dollar. Now there are a number of factors that tend to increase the value of the dollar. These deflationary factors and the processes they initiate may be benign or malign in their effects on productive efficiency and consumer welfare, depending on whether they result from the voluntary choices of laborers, capitalists, entrepreneurs, and consumers or from the coercive intervention of a government central bank such as the Fed. As we shall see, while the deflation-phobes have bemoaned the imaginary evils of deflationary scenarios that have not occurred and that actually would produce net benefits for consumers if they did, they have completely ignored the one kind of deflation that has actually materialized repeatedly in the last two decades and is truly a malign influence on consumer sovereignty and welfare.

Deflation: Good and Bad

According to Austrian theory, the value of money, which is the inverse of overall consumer prices, is determined by supply and demand like the individual prices of its component consumer goods. An increase in the value of a dollar, and a corresponding decline in overall dollar prices, may thus proceed either from an expansion of the demand for money or a contraction of the supply of money or a combination of both. There are four basic causes of deflation—two operating on the demand side and two on the supply side of the "money relation."[8] The economic processes associated with these factors may be categorized as "growth deflation," "cash-building deflation," "bank credit deflation," and "confiscatory deflation." Each is analyzed in turn below and its effect on economic efficiency and consumer welfare is appraised.

Growth Deflation

Let us begin with the demand side. One component of the demand for money is the total quantity of the various commodities and services that sellers supply to the market in exchange for money. The aggregate supplies of goods therefore constitutes what Austrian economists call the "exchange demand" for money, because by selling goods, including their own labor services, people are exercising a demand to acquire and hold money.[9] Hence, if supplies of certain goods in the economy increase due, for example, to increased saving and investment in additional capital goods or to technological progress, as has typically occurred in the historical market economy, then, all other things equal, their producers will be induced by competition to offer more units of their product for a dollar. As we are assuming that the supply of dollars remains fixed, the exchange value of a dollar will thus be bid up. This means that buyers will need to give fewer dollars than previously to obtain a given good and prices will fall.

This is precisely the process that occurred in the past three decades in the consumer electronics and high-tech industries, such as hand calculators, video game systems, personal computers, and DVD players. As a consequence of rapid technological improvement and its embodiment in additional capital investments, labor productivity increased phenomenally in these industries, driving down unit costs of production and increasing profit margins. Since the resulting expansion of the supplies of goods forthcoming from these industries outstripped the expansion of the supply of dollars during this period, the effect was a spectacular drop in the prices of high-tech products

---

[8] This term was coined by Mises (*Human Action*, p. 408) as a shorthand expression for the relation between the supply of and the demand for money.

[9] For a discussion of the "exchange demand" as a component of the total demand for money, see Rothbard, *Man, Economy and State*, p. 662.

and a corresponding rise in the dollar's purchasing power in terms of these products. Thus, for example, a mainframe computer sold for $4.7 million in 1970; today one can purchase a PC that is 20 times faster for less than $1,000.[10] The substantial price deflation in the high-tech industries did not impair and, in fact, facilitated the enormous expansion of profits, productivity and outputs in these industries. This is reflected in the fact that in 1980, computer firms shipped a total of 490,000 PC's while in 1999 their shipments exceeded 43 million units despite the fact that quality-adjusted prices had declined by over 90 percent in the meantime.[11]

The price deflation that was observed in the past three decades in selected high-growth industries, however, was not unprecedented or even unusual. In fact, historically, the natural tendency in the industrial market economy under a commodity money such as gold was for general prices to persistently decline as accumulation of capital and advances in industrial techniques led to a continual expansion in the supplies of goods. Thus throughout the nineteenth century and up until World War I a mild deflationary trend prevailed in the industrialized nations as rapid growth in the supplies of goods outpaced the gradual growth in the money supply that occurred under the classical gold standard. For example, in the U.S. from 1880 to 1896, the wholesale price level fell by about 30 percent, or by 1.75 percent per year, while real income rose by about 85 percent, or around 5 percent per year.[12] Aside from infrequent discoveries of major new sources of gold, this deflationary trend was only interrupted during periods of major wars, such as the Napoleonic wars in Europe and the American Civil War, which the belligerent governments invariably financed by printing paper fiat money.

In recent years we have seen a continuing growth deflation in China. In the four years from 1998 to 2001, real GDP has increased

---

[10] W. Michael Cox and Richard Alm, *Myths of Rich and Poor: Why We're Better Off Than We Think* (New York: Basic Books, 1999), p. 45.

[11] W. Michael Cox and Richard Alm, "The New Paradigm," in Federal Reserve Bank of Dallas *1999 Annual Report*.

[12] Milton Friedman and Anna J. Schwartz, *A Monetary History of the United States: 1867–1960* (Princeton, N.J.: Princeton University Press, 1971), pp. 94–95.

at an annual average rate of 7.6 percent. The average of general retail prices declined in each of those years; the declines ranged from 0.8 percent to 3.0 percent.[13]

The fall in the sale prices and average production costs of consumer goods during the growth process does not necessarily entail a decline in the selling price of labor. If the supply of labor is fixed then money, or "nominal," wage rates will remain constant. while "real" wage rates rise to reflect the increase in the marginal productivity of and employers' demand for labor as the purchasing power of every dollar earned rises with the decline of consumer prices.

Needless to say, both sound economics and common sense tell us that the effect of growth deflation on economic activity and consumer welfare is entirely benign, because it is the result of the voluntary exchanges of property titles among resource-owners, capitalist-entrepreneurs, and consumers. These monetary transactions generate a natural increase in the value of money as a necessary complement to the growth of real wealth and income and the greater satisfaction of human wants that they yield.

Cash-Building Deflation

Although a handful of mainstream macroeconomists might be persuaded that price deflation associated with economic growth is benign, they would all scoff at the view that "hoarding," a second factor tending toward price deflation, enhances economic prosperity and well-being.[14] Hoarding occurs when an individual deliberately chooses to reduce his current spending on consumer goods and investment assets below his current income, preferring to add the unspent income to his cash balance held in the form of currency and checkable, or otherwise instantly accessible, bank deposits. Hoarding is nothing but an increase in the individual's "cash balance," that is, the

---

[13] Federal Reserve Bank of Cleveland, "Deflation," *2002 Annual Report*, p. 10. Available at http://www.clevelandfed.org/annual02/Essay.pdf.

[14] For example, in the 2002 Annual Report of the Federal Reserve Bank of Cleveland ("Deflation," p. 8) we find the following amazing statement: "[T]here are circumstances in which deflation can be a characteristic of a healthy economy—namely, during productivity-driven booms."

amount of money that the individual keeps on hand over a period of time. The behavior described as hoarding may be more aptly labeled "cash building," a term that has the additional virtue of freedom from the negative connotations that burden the word "hoarding."

Cash building usually stems from a more pessimistic or uncertain attitude toward the future, caused possibly by the onset of a recession, a natural disaster or the imminent prospect of war. It may even result from speculation on the happy prospect that prices may fall in the near future as a result of economic growth or for other reasons. Under such circumstances, market participants appraise the value of the services yielded by a dollar in hand more highly than before relative to the services of the consumer goods or interest yield on investment goods that currently can be purchased for that dollar. All other things equal, including the number of dollars in existence, this increase in the demand to hold money will result in the bidding up of the market value of the dollar in terms of all goods. A pervasive price deflation will result, causing shrinkage of the aggregate flow of dollars spent and received in income per period of time.

Despite the reduction in total dollar income, however, the deflationary process caused by cash building is also benign and productive of greater economic welfare. It is initiated by the voluntary and utility-enhancing choices of some money holders to refrain from exchanging titles to their money assets on the market in the same quantities as they had previously. However, with the supply of dollars fixed, the only way in which this increased demand to hold money can be satisfied is for each dollar to become more valuable, so that the total purchasing power represented by the existing supply of money increases. This is precisely what price deflation accomplishes: an increase in aggregate monetary wealth or the "real" supply of money in order to satisfy those who desire additional cash balances.

We should note here that the fall in money expenditure that accompanies this process implies a fall in nominal wage rates as well as in consumer goods' prices, although the real wage rate—the amount of goods and services the laborer can purchase with his money wages—remains roughly unchanged. Nevertheless, if there is interference with the free exchange of property titles on the labor market that renders the money price of labor downwardly inflexible, such as minimum wage laws or laws that grant unions exclusive privileges as bargaining agents in particular firms or industries, then unemployment and a decline in economic activity will result. However, the consequent recession or depression does not result from cash-building deflation per se, but from the coercive political attempt to impede the exchanges of property titles that bring about the increase in the value of money desired by consumers.

Bank Credit Deflation

1. Bank Runs

There are also two major factors that have historically operated on the supply of money to produce deflation. The first is a decline in the supply of money that results from a contraction of fractional-reserve bank credit. This may occur either because during a financial crisis the depositors call upon the banks en masse to redeem their demand deposits and notes in cash, or because the central bank undertakes a deliberate policy to contract bank credit in order to arrest an inflationary boom in progress or to undo the effects of a previous runaway inflation and restore a depreciated currency to a specie standard. Let us deal with bank runs first.

Before World War II, bank runs generally were associated with the onset of recessions and were mainly responsible for the "bank credit deflation" that almost always characterized these recessions. Bank runs typically occurred when depositors lost confidence that banks were able to continue redeeming the titles—represented by bank notes and demand deposits—to the property they had entrusted to the banks for safekeeping and which the banks were contractually obliged to redeem upon demand. This property was usually gold and silver money, and the fractional reserve banks were not in a position to discharge their contractual obligations to all its rightful owners at once because they had created multiple titles to this property in the course of their lending operations. This meant that the outstanding stock of instantaneously redeemable notes and checking and savings deposits was expanded to a large multiple of the commodity money reserves the banks kept on hand. During financial crises, bank runs caused many banks to fail completely and most of their notes and deposits to be revealed for what they essentially were: worthless titles to nonexistent property. In the case of other banks, the threat that their depositors would demand cash payment en bloc was sufficient reason to induce them to reduce their lending operations and build up their ratio of specie reserves to note and deposit liabilities in order to stave off failure. These two factors together resulted in a large contraction of the money supply and, given a constant demand for money, a concomitant increase in the value of money.

Once again our judgment must be that deflation, even when caused by a contraction of bank credit amidst numerous bank failures, has a salutary effect on the economy and enhances the welfare of market participants. For it is initiated by a voluntary and contractual redemption of property titles to money by bank depositors who perceive that fractional reserve banks are no longer functioning to safely and securely store their cash balances. When any firm that trades on its trustworthiness, be it a financial services firm, an armored car company, or a law firm, loses the confidence of its customers or clients that it is operating in their best interests, it will be rapidly purged from the market by an adjustment process that reallocates resources and improves the welfare of consumers. Bank credit deflation represents just such a benign and purgative market adjustment process.

In fact in the era before the 1930s when the natural flexibility of prices and wage rates prevailed and was not impeded by legal constraints, bank credit deflations in the U.S. were swift and did not cause severe economic dislocations. A brief review of one such episode is instructive.

In the fall of 1839 there occurred a financial crisis in the U.S. that resulted from a massive expansion of the money supply during the 1830s initiated by the legally privileged Second Bank of the United States. From the peak of the business cycle in 1839 to its trough in 1843, the money supply contracted by about one-third (34 percent), almost one-quarter of the nation's banks collapsed (23 percent), including the Bank of the United States, and wholesale prices fell by 42 percent. Despite—or rather because of—the massive deflation of prices, real GNP and real consumption actually increased during this period by 16 percent and 21 percent, respectively. However, real investment did decline during this period by 23 percent, which was a benign development, because the malinvestments of the previous inflationary boom needed to be liquidated.[15] Unfortunately such benign episodes of property retrieval have been forgotten in the wake of the Great Depression. Despite the fact that the bank credit deflation that occurred from 1929 to 1933 was roughly proportional in its impact on the nominal money supply to that of 1839–1843, the rigidity of prices and wage rates induced by the "stabilization" policies of the Hoover and early Roosevelt administrations prevented the deflationary adjustment process from operating to effect the reallocation of resources demanded by property owners. With the free exchange of property titles thus hampered, the economy contracted by roughly one third and consumption fell by one-fifth during the years from 1929 to 1933.[16]

2. Contractionary or Deflationary Monetary Policy

When national central banks eventually took legal custody of the public's gold deposits, they went beyond their original function of "lender of last resort" during financial crises and assumed discretionary power to manipulate the nation's money supply, that is, to "conduct monetary policy." This occurred in the United States in 1917.[17]

---

[15] The data in this paragraph can be found in Peter Temin, *The Jacksonian Economy* (New York: W.W. Norton, 1969), pp. 155–65.

[16] For a description of the policies of the Hoover administration that impeded the bank credit deflation and the recession-adjustment process in general, see Murray N. Rothbard, *America's Great Depression*, 5th ed. (Auburn, Ala.: Ludwig von Mises Institute, 2000), pp. 209–337.

[17] The Amendment to the Federal Reserve Act of June 21, 1917 mandated that only reserve deposits held at the Federal Reserve banks would be counted as legal reserves of member banks, resulting in a centralization of gold reserves at the Fed (C.A. Philips, T.F. McManus, and R.W. Nelson, *Banking and the Business Cycle: A Study of the Great Depression in the United States* [New York: Arno Press, [1937] 1972], pp. 24–25; and W.P.G. Harding, *The Formative Period of the Federal Reserve System: During the World Crisis* (New York: Houghton Mifflin, 1925), pp. 72–74. As Benjamin Anderson (*Economics and the Public Welfare: A Financial and Economic History of the United States, 1914–1946*, 2nd ed. [Indianapolis, Ind.: Liberty Press, 1979], p. 56) pointed out, the theory underlying this Amendment was "not very clear" but "in 1916 and in early 1917 there was a very definite practical consideration that we might be involved in war, and that it was important that the gold of

As the custodian of the nation's gold reserves, the central bank would on occasion deliberately engineer bank credit deflation in order to avert or mitigate an impending financial crisis provoked by its previous inflationary policy. This "contractionary" or "deflationary"[18] monetary policy was usually invoked after a bank credit expansion in order to arrest and reverse an outflow of the stock of nationalized gold reserves abroad and to forestall depositors' loss of faith in the banking system, which would inevitably have culminated in the dreaded bank runs discussed above. This policy was implemented at first by raising the discount rate on collateralized central bank loans to commercial banks and later by open market sales of government securities to the public. The result of this policy was a contraction in outstanding bank credit and deposits and a reduction in the overall money supply.

How are we to classify such a deliberate reduction in the money supply by a central bank? Superficially, it appears to be a malign and arbitrary interference in the functioning of the market process on a par with monetary expansion, which misallocates resources and reduces the welfare of property owners. However, in evaluating the policy one must bear in mind the concrete institutional circumstances. A central bank operating within the framework of a gold standard has in effect arrogated to itself the monopoly of warehousing the gold deposits of the public. Its so-called "liabilities" in the form of bank notes and reserve deposits are not money per se but merely instantaneously redeemable property titles to the money commodity housed within its vaults. By issuing deposits and notes in excess of its gold reserves, it is creating and multiplying fictitious claims to property that have no counterpart in real goods and that derange market processes and arbitrarily redistribute real wealth and income. The destruction of such pseudo titles to the money commodity is no less

---

the country be concentrated in a central reservoir as a basis for war finance." So the centralization of gold reserves in the Fed was undertaken with the definite intention of facilitating an inflationary monetary policy.

[18] In this context we will use these two terms interchangeably to describe a policy-induced reduction or "contraction" of the money supply that results in a fall, or "deflation," of prices. The two terms describe aspects of a single economic process that are related as cause and effect or as means and end.

a benign development than the eradication of counterfeit titles to any other type of nonexistent property.

Certainly, it is an uncontroversial conclusion of value-free economic analysis that markets work more efficiently in serving consumers when the creation and exchange of counterfeit property titles to stocks of nonmonetary commodities are suppressed. For example, a large and reputable land development and real estate management company may begin contracting for the sale of fully furnished vacation homes in remote locations to more than one buyer, confident that multiple buyers will never occupy the same home simultaneously. Nevertheless this practice would still alter prices in this and related markets and alter the distribution of income and wealth and the structure of consumer demands throughout the economy. The discovery and elimination of this scam would reorient prices and quantities to more accurately reflect the scarcities of concrete goods. Hence, the economist would remain strictly within the bounds of Wertfreiheit in appraising this new constellation of market outcomes as superior to the old in terms of social welfare. Similarly, in carrying out a contractionary monetary policy, the central bank is merely ceasing to violate its contractual obligation to maintain the integrity of its depositors' titles to their stored money balances, and, therefore, the consequent readjustment of the purchasing power of money to the real scarcity of the money commodity implies a value-neutral judgment that social welfare has been enhanced.

Some will object that the economic distortions caused by monetary expansion occur only while the new money is being injected into the economy, so that a subsequent monetary contraction is unnecessary and only burdens the economy with further distortions. However, this objection does not take into account the fact that deflationary monetary policy has generally been implemented while the economy is still undergoing an inflationary boom and, therefore, operates to counteract and reverse the tendencies towards malinvestment and arbitrary redistribution of wealth that have not yet been consummated. In addition, and more important, any economic dislocations that may occur during deflation are the inevitable concomitant of a transition process back toward the original regime of pure commodity money. Given the historical market process in which it evolved, this regime is demonstrably consistent with the preferences of property owners and the mutually beneficial exchanges of genuine property titles that improve (ex ante) social welfare. The ultimate cause of the inflationary problems and the transitional deflationary problems is the central bank's facilitating and encouragement of the creation of unbacked bank notes and deposits in the first place.

Moreover, the nature and severity of these transitional deflationary problems are too frequently taken for granted and bear closer scrutiny. While a contractionary monetary policy will result in a tendency for the value of money to increase as overall prices decline, this does not present a serious problem in economic theory or history as long as markets are permitted to clear without the interference of political authorities. A case in point is the post-World War I American depression of 1920–21. From 1915 through 1919, the Fed stimulated a massive inflationary bubble. This was partly the result of the reduction of reserve requirements mandated by the Federal Reserve Act of 1913 and partly due to the Fed's efforts to accommodate deficit financing of the huge expenditures associated with World War I and its aftermath.

During this five-year period the money supply (M2) was increased at an average annual rate of 15.5 percent. Prices as measured by the GNP price deflator rose from 1916 to 1920 by 15.4 percent per annum while the CPI increased by 14.1 percent per annum from 1917 to 1920. The Fed began to recognize the dangerously inflationary nature of its policies in 1919 and raised its discount rate from 4 percent to 4.75 percent in December 1919, to 6 percent in January 1920, and to 7 percent in June 1920, where it held fast until May 1921. The consequence was a steep decline in the annual rate of growth in the money supply to 2.9 percent in 1920 and to −7.5 percent in 1921, causing the GDP deflator to decline by 16.6 percent in 1921 and 8.1 percent in 1922, while the CPI dropped by 10.9 percent in 1921 and 6.3 percent in 1922. Wholesale prices dropped even more precipitously, diving by 36.8 percent in 1921 and plummeting by an incredible 56 percent from mid-1920 to mid-1921. The fall in nominal wage rates was more moderate, but, nonetheless, as one Keynesian

observer[19] noted, "wage decreases were both general and substantial"
and outside of agriculture wage rates fell by nearly 11 percent over
the two-year period 1921–1922. Despite—or because of—this massive and broad-based price deflation, however, the economy began to
recover by August 1921, eighteen months after the downswing had
started in January 1920.[20]

Modern commentators on the 1920–21 Depression, to the
extent that they have taken note of it, tend to be surprised by its brev-
ity, given the sharp, policy-induced deflation that accompanied it and
the extreme reluctance of political and monetary authorities to undertake stimulatory measures to mitigate its severity. One of the leading
Keynesian authorities on "business fluctuations," Robert A. Gordon
described this depression thusly:

> The downswing ... was severe ... but relatively short. Its
> outstanding feature was the extreme decline in prices....
> Government policy to moderate the depression and speed
> recovery was minimal. The Federal Reserve authorities were
> largely passive.... Nor was any use made of fiscal policy.... In
> short, the federal budget was deflationary while the down-
> swing was in progress.... Despite the absence of a stimulative
> government policy, however, recovery was not long delayed.[21]

The monetarist macroeconomic historian Kenneth Weiher[22] predictably blamed the Fed for the depression, arguing, "the Fed earned
all the criticism it has since received for inaction. In the face of such a
severe contraction, accompanied as it was by unprecedented deflation,

---

[19] Robert Aaron Gordon, *Economic Instability and Growth: The American Record*
(New York: Harper and Row, 1974), p. 22.

[20] Accounts of the Depression of 1920–21 and the preceding inflationary boom can
be found in in Kenneth Weiher, *America's Search for Monetary Stability: Monetary and Fiscal Policy Since 1913* (New York: Twayne Publishers, 1992), pp. 26–37;
Robert A. Degen, *The American Monetary system: A Concise Survey of Its Evolution Since 1896* (Lexington, Mass.: D.C. Heath, 1987), pp. 30–40; Gordon, *Economic
Instability and Growth*, pp. 21–22; and Anderson, *Economics and the Public Welfare*, pp. 61–89.

[21] Gordon, *Economic Instability and Growth*, pp. 21–22.

[22] Weiher, *America's Search for Monetary Stability*, p. 34.

the Fed did nothing." And yet Weiher[23] appeared to be baffled by the fact that such a Fed-engineered "contraction-deflation of historic proportions" did not lead to total financial and economic ruin and that the economy rapidly and smoothly returned to prosperity. As Weiher[24] was forced to admit: "The Fed was not really called on to act as a lender of last resort to the banking system, because the system never really faced a major liquidity crisis. Why such relative calm persisted compared with the situation in earlier contraction periods is unclear."

If contractionary monetary policy is benign when the central bank exists within the institutional framework of a classical gold standard, how would we evaluate such a policy implemented in a pure fiat money system? For example, the current U.S. dollar is a pure name with no functional link whatsoever to a specific weight of gold or any other market-produced commodity. Surely in this system a contraction of the money supply engineered by the Fed is purely arbitrary and cannot be remotely linked to an improvement in social welfare? But this situation is not as simple as it seems and it requires deeper analysis before we can arrive at an informed welfare judgment.

For purposes of argument, let us begin with the assumption that deflation is just as damaging in its economic effects as is inflation of equal magnitude. Then ceteris paribus, that is, in a "stationary" or no-growth economy with a constant demand for cash balances, a 3 percent per annum contraction in the stock of fiat dollars should cause no more concern than a 3 percent expansion of the stock of dollars. With economic effects thus placed temporarily to one side, political and psychological factors always operate to make monetary inflation much more dangerous than monetary deflation, as Hayek courageously warned at the height of the Keynesian era in 1960:

> It is, however, rather doubtful whether, from a long-term point of view, deflation is really more harmful than inflation. Indeed, there is a sense in which inflation is infinitely more dangerous and needs to be more carefully guarded against. Of the two errors, it is the one much more likely to be committed. The reason for this is that moderate inflation

---

[23] Ibid., p. 37.

[24] Ibid., p. 36.

is generally pleasant while it proceeds, whereas deflation is immediately and acutely painful.... The difference between inflation and deflation is that, with the former, the pleasant surprise comes first and the reaction later, while, with the latter, the first effect on business is depressing. There is little need to take precautions against any practice the bad effects of which will be immediately and strongly felt; but there is need for precautions wherever action which is immediately pleasant or relieves temporary difficulties involves much greater harm that will be felt only later.... It is particularly dangerous because the harmful aftereffects of even small doses of inflation can be staved off only by larger doses of inflation. Once it has continued for some time, even the prevention of further acceleration will create a situation in which it will be very difficult to avoid a spontaneous deflation.... Because inflation is psychologically and politically so much more difficult to prevent than deflation and because it is, at the same time, technically so much more easily prevented, the economist should always stress the dangers of inflation.[25]

Hayek's argument clearly explains why a monopoly central bank in a fiat money regime is never likely to choose a contractionary monetary policy and why, especially under current conditions, fear of deflation is completely groundless. Moreover, granting our premise that equal amounts of inflation and deflation have equally pernicious economic effects, a case can be made based on Hayek's argument that the central bank should err on the side of deflation, because a mildly deflationary monetary policy is far less dangerous in the long run than the mildly inflationary policy of "inflation targeting" recommended by a consensus of contemporary economists.[26] Of course, Hayek himself

---

[25] Friedrich A. Hayek, *The Constitution of Liberty* (Chicago: Henry Regnery, [1960] 1972), pp. 330, 332, 333.

[26] On inflation targeting, see Ben S. Bernanke, "A Perspective on Inflation Targeting," Presented at the Annual Washington Policy conference of the National Association of Business Economists. Washington, D.C. (March 25, 2003); Ben S. Bernanke and Frederic S. Mishkin, "Inflation Targeting: A New Framework for Monetary Policy?" *Journal of Economic Perspectives* 11 (Spring 1997); and Laurence H. Meyer, "Inflation Targets and Inflation Targeting," Federal Reserve Bank of St. Louis *Review* 83 (November/December 2001). At an IMF conference recently Laurence Ball (Kenneth Rogoff, et al., Transcript of an IMF Economic Forum: Should We Be Worried About 'Deflation'? Washington, D.C. [May 29, 2003], p. 14. http://www.imf.org.) advocated

was opposed to monetary deflation and referred to it as an "error" in the passage quoted above. It is not our aim here to construct a case for a particular fiat money policy based on its long-run costs and benefits. Rather it is to challenge the initial premise that the welfare effects of deflationary and inflationary monetary policies are symmetrical by elucidating the purely economic advantages yielded by a deliberate reduction of the supply of fiat money—advantages which have been overlooked even by leading Austrian monetary theorists.

Writing in *Human Action* in 1949, Mises[27] emphasized the psychological reasons underlying the broad popular appeal of "inflation and expansion" and the even more widespread and violent opposition to "deflation and contraction" in terms very similar to Hayek's. However, in his earlier *Theory of Money and Credit*, which was written before the dread of falling prices had been entrenched and universalized among the public by the Keynesian misinterpretation of the Great Depression, Mises attributed much greater weight in the resistance to monetary contraction to the narrow economic interests of the ruling class or "caste," whose members: (1) control or have access to the funds disbursed by the State; and (2) tend to be debtors rather than creditors. As Mises incisively noted:

> Restrictionism [or "deflationism"] demands positive sacrifices from the national exchequer when it is carried out by the withdrawal of notes from circulation (say through the issuance of interest-bearing bonds or through taxation) and their cancellation; and at the least it demands from it a renunciation of potential income by forbidding the issue of notes at a time when the demand for money is increasing. This alone would suffice to explain why restrictionism has never been able to compete with inflationism.... But furthermore ... an increase in the value of money has not been to the advantage

---

an inflation target in the 2 to 4 percent range, proclaiming, "there's absolutely no evidence that that level of inflation has any economic cost we need to worry about." It is noteworthy that in the 1960s "Old" Keynesians such as Paul Samuelson (*Economics: An Introductory Analysis*, 7th ed. [New York: McGraw-Hill, 1967], p. 135) considered rates of inflation of the magnitude aimed at in this New Keynesian monetary policy as "a new disease—a tendency for anything like an approach to full employment to lead to 'creeping inflation.'"

[27] Mises, *Human Action*, pp. 564–65.

of the ruling classes. Those who get an immediate benefit
from such an increase are all those who are entitled to receive
fixed sums of money. Creditors gain at the expense of debtors. Taxation, it is true, becomes more burdensome as the
value of money rises; but the greater part of the advantage of
this is secured, not by the state, but by its creditors. Now policies favoring creditors at the expense of debtors have never
been popular.... Generally speaking, the class of persons who
draw their income exclusively or largely from the interest on
capital lent to others has not been particularly numerous or
influential at any time in any country.[28]

Now, like Hayek, Mises[29] opposed a deflationist policy and went
on to argue that it was deeply erroneous even in the case in which a
country was attempting to revalue its depreciated currency in order
to return to the gold standard at the previous mint par, as Great Britain did after both the Napoleonic wars and World War I. To avoid
monetary contraction, Mises favored a restoration of gold parity at
or near the currently prevailing price of gold. Even Murray Rothbard, although he was an enthusiastic proponent of bank credit deflation that results from spontaneous bank runs, generally refrained
from advocating a deliberate contraction of the money supply engineered by the central bank under an existing fiat money regime.
Thus, he referred to "the crucial British error" and "fateful decision"
of returning to the gold standard in the 1920s at the prewar parity. For
Rothbard,[30] "The sensible thing to do would have been to recognize
the facts of reality, the fact of the depreciated pound, franc, mark, etc.,
and to return to the gold standard at a redefined rate: a rate that would
recognize the existing supply of money and price levels." Additionally, in his proposals for the restoration of a 100-percent gold standard
in the United States, he conspicuously eschewed a contraction of the
supply of fiat dollars as a transition policy.[31]

---

[28] Mises, *Theory of Money and Credit*, pp. 263–64.

[29] Ibid., pp. 265–68.

[30] Rothbard, *What Has Government Done to Our Money?*, pp. 94–95.

[31] Rothbard has presented two different proposals for transforming the present U.S.
fiat dollar into a 100 percent gold dollar, which are outlined, respectively, in Murray
N. Rothbard, *The Mystery of Banking* (New York: Richardson and Snyder, 1983), pp.

Nonetheless, when combined with Mises's explanation of the opposition of the ruling elites to monetary contraction, Rothbard's positive analysis of the distribution effects of deflation reveals the asymmetric welfare effects between monetary expansion and monetary contraction and suggests that the latter policy can indeed play a benign role in the transition back from a fiat money to a full-bodied commodity money. According to Rothbard deflationary bank credit contraction.

> in a broad sense, takes away from the original coercive gainers [from credit expansion] and benefits the original coerced losers. While this will certainly not be true in every case, in the broad sense much the same groups will benefit and lose, but in reverse order from that of the redistributive effects of credit expansion. Fixed-income groups, widows and orphans, will gain, and businesses and owners of original factors previously reaping gains from inflation will lose.[32]

Now, Rothbard was referring here to the consequences of a bank credit contraction induced by the bank runs that occur during the downswing of a business cycle. But his analysis may be generalized to the case described by Mises above in which the money supply is contracted by the liquidation of central bank notes composing a fiscal surplus. A modern Austrian welfare analysis of this case, which might be called "fiscal deflation," is interesting because it presents a potential route back to a 100-percent gold dollar from our present fiat dollar.

In order to analyze the case within the context of contemporary institutions, it is necessary to provide some technical details of the relationship between the U.S. Treasury and the Fed. The Treasury maintains deposit balances at the Fed and at the commercial banks. The latter are called "tax and loan accounts" and are the temporary abode of funds that it has borrowed and collected in taxes. The Treasury makes its disbursements from its general working balances held at the regional Fed banks. When it needs to replenish the latter, it transfers funds from its tax and loan accounts at the commercial banks.

263–69 and idem, *The Case Against the Fed* (Auburn Ala.: Ludwig von Mises Institute, 1994), pp. 145–51.

[32] Rothbard, *Man, Economy, and State*, p. 865.

All other things equal, this shifting of Treasury funds from commercial bank deposits to Fed deposits reduces reserves in the commercial banking system and exerts contractionary pressure on the money supply. To avoid this, the Treasury tries to coordinate expenditures from its general working balances at the Fed with drafts on its tax and loan accounts at commercial banks, since the recipients of the Treasury's spending quickly redeposit the funds in commercial banks, replenishing bank reserves.[33]

Now, fiscal deflation requires that a portion of the funds collected in tax and loan accounts be transferred to the Fed where they are either cancelled or "spent" on programmed increases in required reserves for commercial bank deposits by distributing them on a pro-rated basis among the reserve deposits held at the Fed by commercial banks. In either case, the money supply would decrease, but we are interested in analyzing the latter case as one possible method of restoring a 100-percent gold dollar.

Let us assume, for example, that the fiat money stock is $1,000, all held in commercial bank demand deposits, and that the required reserve ratio is 10 percent. If all banks are fully loaned out, they are holding $100 in required reserves in reserve deposits at the Fed. When the Treasury shifts a surplus of, say, $20 to its general account at the Fed, it will leave the commercial banks with only $80 in reserves and the money supply will eventually shrink by $200 to $800. The Fed will then mandate an increase in the required reserve ratio to 12.5 percent and simultaneously the Treasury will "spend" its surplus funds by transferring them to the reserve deposits of the commercial banks, permitting them to meet the new reserve requirement with total bank reserves once again equal to $100 but now supporting only $800 of demand deposits. In the following year, the Treasury again runs a surplus of $20 (which at the new higher purchasing power of money exceeds in real terms the prior year's surplus). Following the same procedure of disposing of the fiscal surplus, the money supply shrinks by another 20 percent, or by $160 to $640, and the Fed

---

[33] A very clear and comprehensive discussion of the effects of Treasury activities on the money supply can be found in John G. Ranlett, *Money and Banking: An Introduction to Analysis and Policy* (New York: John Wiley and Sons, 1977), pp. 218–34.

raises the required reserve ratio to 100/640 or 15.63 percent. In the next round, again assuming a surplus of $20, the money supply would be contracted by $128 or 20 percent to $512 and the required reserve ratio raised to 19.53 percent.[34] This fiscal deflation of the fiat money stock will continue until demand deposits are backed 100 percent by reserves, at which point the Fed would be abolished and the dollar rendered convertible into gold along the lines suggested by Rothbard[35] to yield a pure gold dollar.

The purpose of the foregoing exercise was not to present an optimal plan for restoring a pure commodity money, but to highlight certain features of a policy of monetary contraction and deflation that are crucial to distinguishing its welfare effects from those of a policy of expansion and inflation. To begin with, almost all current macroeconomics textbooks characterize "seignorage" or "the revenue raised through the printing of money" as an "inflation tax" on money holders that adds to the existing tax burden on the private sector.[36] In sharp contrast, because deflationary monetary policy has been considered beyond the pale at least since World War II, it would be difficult to find one modern macroeconomics textbook that recognizes, let alone applies a name to, the opposite effect, which results when the State destroys money via fiscal deflation. Mises and Rothbard, in their respective writings quoted above, generally recognized this effect but did not name it or elaborate its welfare implications.

We may identify this effect by the French term *rabattage*, which signifies a diminution or abatement—in this case, of the fiscal burden of government on the private economy. In the fanciful scenario

---

[34] The nominal constancy of the fiscal surplus is assumed only for purposes of illustration and is not crucial to the social welfare inferences drawn in the text below. In this case, it assures a 20 percent per annum contraction of the money supply. A much more realistic and mild contraction, say 2 or 3 percent per year, would not change the conclusions of the welfare analysis. It should be noted, however, that a fixed rate of monetary contraction requires a fixed nominal dollar surplus and therefore an increasing real surplus. In contrast, an annually recurring surplus that is constant in real terms will result in a continually declining rate of monetary contraction.

[35] Rothbard, *Mystery of Banking*, pp. 263–69.

[36] N. Gregory Mankiw, *Macroeconomics*, 5th ed. (New York: Worth Publishers, 2003), p. 88.

of fiscal deflation outlined above, the *rabattage* effect comes about in the following way. The Treasury is deprived of a part of the funds appropriated through taxation. As a result, government expenditures are reduced, in both nominal and real dollars, because the spending occurs before the increase in the purchasing power of money caused by the fiscal deflation has taken place. Likewise, the recipients of pure transfers from and the suppliers of resources to government suffer an immediate fall in their nominal subsidies and selling prices while the prices of the goods they purchase remain near pre-existing levels, thus causing a decline in their real incomes. Ceteris paribus, as these separate spending-and-income chains that emanate from government progress, intersect, and reinforce one another throughout the economy, the monetary demands for more and more goods decline and their prices progressively adjust to the reduced stock of money. The final outcome of this deflationary adjustment process is that real income is distributed from the net "tax consumers," that is, the political-bureaucratic establishment and its subsidized constituencies and privileged resource suppliers, back to the taxpayers who originally produced the income in voluntary market activities.

By way of contrast, the seignorage effect of inflationary finance operates to enlarge the real incomes of government and the direct recipients of government largesse and purchases, precisely because these groups gain access to the newly created money at the outset of the inflationary adjustment process. Those who "pay" the seignorage are the receivers of fixed incomes as well as entrepreneurs and resource owners who do not sell to government and are therefore forced to endure progressively rising buying prices until their selling prices rise much later in the process.[37]

In thus altering the income distribution in favor of taxpayers and to the disadvantage of political tax consumers, the *rabattage* effect of fiscal deflation results in a new structure of consumer demands and

---

[37] For Austrians, seignorage is simply the first link in the chain of distribution effects that characterize the inflationary adjustment process. See, for example, Mises, *Theory of Money and Credit*, pp. 153–68; idem, *Human Action*, pp. 408–11; Rothbard, *Mystery of Banking*, pp. 47–53; idem, *Man, Economy, and State*, pp. 709–12, 850–53.

pattern of resource pricing and allocation that more accurately reflect the preferences of those who earn income from the production and exchange of goods on the market. From the standpoint of Austrian welfare economics this result represents an improvement in social welfare and economic efficiency because, even if the precise pre-tax pattern of income and wealth distribution is not restored, fewer resources are siphoned off from producers in the social division of labor, mitigating the distortion of economic calculation inherent in all government activities.[38] To put it another way, all government interventions have direct effects on the utility of the targeted victim or victims and indirect effects on monetary calculation and the efficiency of the economy at large, and these effects are analytically separable.[39] Thus the *rabattage* effect, even though it may not restore the pre-intervention wealth and income positions of the original taxpayers, certainly does improve economic efficiency by forcing political tax consumers to disgorge some of the expropriated resources and permitting the market to reallocate productive resources to the service of consumers who earn their livelihood through production for voluntary exchange.[40]

In light of the *rabattage* effect, the monetary contraction associated with fiscal deflation therefore must be judged as socially benign. In contrast, all other things equal, the seignorage effect is

---

[38] The case that all government expenditures introduce calculational chaos and economic inefficiencies into the market process that are separate from, and superadded to, the effects of taxation is elaborated in in Murray N. Rothbard, *Power and Market: Government and the Economy* (Menlo Park, Calif.: Institute for Humane Studies, 1970), pp. 125–49. See Joseph T. Salerno, "Mises and Hayek Dehomogenized," *Review of Austrian Economics* 6(2): pp. 130–31 for the argument that the "preferences and demands" of the participants in the social division of labor "must serve as the sole and ultimate standard of socially efficient resource use" and that the market demands of tax consumers falsify monetary calculation and lead to "a socially inefficient reallocation of productive resources."

[39] For the formulation of this distinction between direct and indirect effects of government intervention and its application in a comprehensive analysis of a myriad of government interventions, see Rothbard, *Power and Market*.

[40] Mises's argument against monetary contraction because "those who are enriched by the increase in the value of money are not the same as those who were injured by the depreciation of money in the course of the inflation" thus fails because it only takes account of the direct utility effects and ignores the indirect *rabattage* effects (Mises, *Theory of Money and Credit*, p. 266).

socially malign and destructive of economic efficiency because inflationary finance permits a further appropriation of property by the nonproductive, tax-consuming political sector and a corresponding misallocation of resources. In short, at a given level of taxation, fiscal deflation lightens the fiscal burden on the market economy and diminishes the calculational chaos inevitably induced by government expenditures, whereas inflationary finance intensifies the fiscal burden and promotes the spread of calculational chaos.

There is another effect of fiscal deflation that is socially benign, which has an admittedly narrower application than the *rabattage* effect but is important nonetheless. In the example of fiscal deflation presented above, the monetary contraction involved an ongoing increase in the required reserve ratio toward 100 percent. This deflationary process effectively involves the extinguishing of pseudo property titles to the money commodity, in this case the paper currency embodying the fiat dollar. As argued above, the suppression of fictitious property titles to any commodity ends the distortion of economic calculation and realigns the pattern of productive activities with actual underlying resource scarcities.

It bears reiteration that deflationary monetary policy is not the only, or necessarily the best, route back from a fiat to a commodity-based currency. But it is one route and it has succeeded historically, e.g., in Great Britain after the Napoleonic wars and in the United States after the Civil War. The latter episode bears particular scrutiny. From the beginning of 1875 until specie payments were resumed on January 1, 1879, the U.S. money stock contracted by about 8.6 percent, as estimated by James Kindahl.[41] Yet from 1876 through 1879,

---

[41] It is true, as Friedman and Schwartz (*Monetary History*, p. 82) pointed out, that the decrease in the money stock was not attributable solely to the Treasury's fiscal deflation because both the deposit/reserve and deposit/currency ratios declined as a result of financial crises and bank failures during this period. Nonetheless the stock of "high-powered money" did shrink as the stock of inconvertible greenbacks held as reserves by the banks and currency by the public contracted from $414 million in 1874 to $382 million in 1878 (James K. Kindahl, "Economic Factors in Specie Resumption: The United States, 1865–1879," in *The Reinterpretation of American Economic History*, eds. Robert W. Fogel and Stanley L. Engerman [New York: Harper and Row, [1961] 1971], p. 475).

real GDP growth averaged a phenomenal 5.20 percent per year, a growth rate that exceeded the average annual growth rate for the period 1876–1913 by more than 25 percent.[42] As a result of the coexistence of monetary contraction and real output growth, during the period 1876–1879 the CPI declined by 3.96 percent per year while the GDP deflator fell at an annual rate of 3.82 percent.[43]

The remarkably high rate of real output growth during a period of monetary contraction and declining prices—a period that was identified by the NBER as the longest contraction in U.S. history—even led Friedman and Schwartz[44] to obliquely question the conventionally held relationship between falling prices and real output:

> The contraction [of 1873–1879] was long and it was severe—of that there is no doubt. But the sharp decline in financial magnitudes, so much more obvious and so much better documented than the behavior of a host of poorly measured physical magnitudes, may well have led contemporary observers and later students to overestimate the severity of the contraction and perhaps even its length. Observers of the business scene then, no less than their modern descendants, took it for granted that sharply declining prices were incompatible with sharply rising output. The period deserves much more study than it has received precisely because it seems to run sharply counter to such strongly held views.

We might suggest here that perhaps the *rabattage* effect associated with fiscal deflation and bank failures during this period contributed to this sharp growth spurt of real output. Real resources that had been absorbed in wasteful uses by government or in propping up business malinvestments precipitated by previous bank credit expansion were now released through deflationary *rabattage* to be more efficiently allocated by entrepreneurs responding to the anticipated demands of fellow producers in the social division of labor.

---

[42] James B. Bullard and Charles M. Hokayem, "Deflation, Corrosive and Otherwise," Federal Reserve Bank of St. Louis *National Economic Trends* (July 2003): p. 1.

[43] Ibid.

[44] Friedman and Schwartz, *Monetary History*, pp. 87–88.

Finally, although our hypothetical example of fiscal deflation above was constructed primarily to highlight the socially benign effects of *rabattage* and the suppression of pseudo-titles to money balances, it does point out another social advantage of State money destruction over money creation. Whereas inflationary finance never moves us closer to a commodity money (and risks hyperinflation and the abolition of money in the bargain should the State's hunger for seignorage revenues exceed certain bounds), fiscal deflation, if carried out properly, conceivably moves the fiat monetary regime back toward its original roots in a market commodity.

Confiscatory Deflation

As suggested above, not all types of deflation are the outcome of benign market processes. There does exist an emphatically malign form of deflation that is coercively imposed by governments and their central banks and that violates property rights, distorts monetary calculation and undermines monetary exchange. It may even catapult an economy back to a primitive state of barter if applied long and relentlessly enough. This form of deflation involves an outright confiscation of people's cash balances by the political and bureaucratic elites. Yet confiscatory deflation has been almost completely ignored by our current deflation-phobes, despite the fact that it has occurred quite a few times in the last two decades—in Brazil, the former Soviet Union, and Argentina in the 1980s, in Ecuador in the late 1990s, and recently again in Argentina. In fact, one of the only economists to identify and condemn confiscatory deflation as a malignant attack on economic efficiency, consumer welfare, and property rights was Murray Rothbard.[45]

Confiscatory deflation is generally inflicted on the economy by the political authorities as a means of obstructing an ongoing bank credit deflation that threatens to liquidate an unsound financial system built on fractional reserve banking. Its essence is an abrogation of bank depositors' property titles to their cash stored in immediately redeemable checking and savings deposits.

---

[45] Murray N. Rothbard, "Deflation: Free or Compulsory," in *Making Economic Sense* (Auburn, Ala.: Ludwig von Mises Institute, 1995).

A glaring example of confiscatory deflation occurred recently in Argentina. In 1992, after yet another bout of hyperinflation, Argentina pegged its new currency, the peso, to the U.S. dollar at the rate of 1 to 1. In order to maintain this fixed peso/dollar peg, the Argentine central bank pledged to freely exchange dollars for pesos on demand and to back its own liabilities, consisting of peso notes and commercial bank reserve deposits denominated in pesos, almost 100 percent by dollars. Unfortunately this arrangement—which inspired confidence in international lenders because it was approved by the IMF and therefore carried its implicit bailout guarantee—did not prevent a massive and inflationary bank credit expansion. As investment dollars flooded into the country, they found their way into the central bank, enabling it to expand the amount of reserves available to the commercial banks. As fractional-reserve institutions, the latter in turn were able to inflate bank credit in concert by multiplying bank deposits on top of each new dollar or peso of reserves. As a result, Argentina's money supply (M1) increased at an average rate of 60 percent per year from 1991 through 1994.[46] After declining to less than 5 percent in 1995, the growth rate of the money supply shot up to over 15 percent in 1996 and nearly 20 percent in 1997. (See Appendix 1 for a graph of the growth of Argentine monetary aggregates.) With the peso overvalued as a result of inflated domestic product prices and with foreign investors rapidly losing confidence that the peso would not be devalued, the influx of dollars ceased and the inflationary boom came to a screeching halt in 1998 as the money supply increased by about 1 percent and the economy went into recession. In 1999, money growth turned slightly negative, while in 2000 the money supply contracted by almost 20 percent.

The money supply continued to contract at a double-digit annual rate through June of 2001. In 2001, domestic depositors began to lose confidence in the banking system and a bank credit deflation began in earnest as the system lost 17 percent or $14.5 billion worth of deposits. On Friday, November 30, 2001 alone, between $700 million and $2 billion of deposits—reports varied—were withdrawn from Argentine banks. Even before the Friday bank run, the central bank only

---

[46] Data on Argentina's money supply are provided by Frank Shostak, Ord Minnett Jardine Fleming Futures Daily Report (July 20, 2001).

possessed $5.5 billion of reserves ultimately backing $70 billion worth of dollar and convertible peso deposits. President Fernando de la Rua and his economy minister, Domingo Cavallo, responded to this situation on Saturday, December 1, announcing a policy that amounted to confiscatory deflation to protect the financial system and maintain the fixed peg to the dollar. Specifically, cash withdrawals from banks were to be limited to $250 per depositor per week for the next 90 days and all overseas cash transfers exceeding $1,000 were to be strictly regulated. Anyone attempting to carry cash out of the country by ship or by plane was to be interdicted. Finally, banks were no longer permitted to issue loans in pesos, only in dollars, but as it turns out this was a futile and desperate ploy to restore confidence in the peso and prevent its depreciation by insinuating that an imminent "dollarization" of the economy was being contemplated. Depositors were still able to access their bank deposits by check or debit card in order to make payments. Still, this policy was a crushing blow to poorer Argentines, who did not possess debit or credit cards and who mainly held bank deposits not accessible by check.

Predictably, Cavallo's malign confiscatory deflation dealt a severe blow to cash businesses and, according to one report, "brought retail trade to a standstill."[47] This worsened the recession, and riots and looting soon broke out that ultimately cost 27 lives and millions of dollars of damage to private businesses. These events caused a state of siege to be declared and eventually forced President de la Rua to resign from his position two years early.

By January 6, 2002 the Argentine government, now under President Eduardo Duhalde and Economy Minister Jorge Remes Lenicov conceded that it could no longer keep the inflated and overvalued peso pegged to the dollar at the rate of 1 to 1 and it devalued the peso by 30 percent to a rate of 1.40 pesos per dollar. Even at this official rate of exchange, however, it appeared the peso was still overvalued because pesos were trading for dollars on the black market at far higher rates. The Argentine government recognized this and instead of permitting the exchange rate to depreciate to a realistic level reflecting the past

---

[47] Reuters, "Riots and Looting in Argentina as Austerity Plan Bites," *New York Times on the Web* (December 19, 2001). http://www.nytimes.com.

inflation and current lack of confidence in the peso, it intensified the confiscatory deflation imposed on the economy earlier. It froze all savings accounts above $3,000 for a year, a measure that affected at least one-third of the $67 billion of deposits remaining in the banking system, of which $43.5 billion were denominated in dollars and the remainder in pesos. Depositors who held dollar accounts not exceeding $5,000 would be able to withdraw their cash in 12 monthly installments starting one year in the future, while those maintaining larger dollar deposits would not be able to begin cashing out until September 2003 and then only in installments spread over two years. Peso deposits, which had already lost one-third of their dollar value since the first freeze had been mandated and faced possible further devaluation, would be treated more liberally. They would be paid out to their owners starting in two months but this repayment would also proceed in installments. In the meantime, as one observer put it, "bank transactions as simple as cashing a paycheck or paying a credit card bill remained out of reach of ordinary Argentines."[48]

Mr. Lenicov openly admitted that this latest round of confiscatory deflation was a device for protecting the inherently bankrupt fractional reserve system, declaring, "If the banks go bust nobody gets their deposits back. The money on hand is not enough to pay back all depositors."[49] Unlike the bank credit deflation that Lenicov was so eager to prevent, which would have permitted monetary exchange to proceed with a smaller number of more valuable pesos, confiscatory deflation tends to abolish monetary exchange and propels the economy back to grossly inefficient and primitive conditions of barter and self-sufficient production that undermine the social division of labor.

Indeed, the regime of confiscatory deflation was beginning to "demonetize" the Argentine economy by the end of 2002. Corn, soybeans, sunflowers, and wheat had "become a preferred legal tender in Argentina, often more welcome than cash, because they are priced in dollars." Automobile sales had fallen by 61 percent in 2002 and rural dealerships began bartering for grain contracts, called trueques, to

---

[48] Larry Rohter, "Argentina Is Still Shaky Despite Currency Measures," *New York Times on the Web* (January 11, 2002). http://wwwnytimes.com.
[49] Quoted in Ibid.

stay afloat. Ford Motor Company, General Motors, and Toyota Motor implemented countrywide sales pitches and programs to teach their employees how to trade vehicles for grain. In Rosario, the grain capital of Argentina, the Ford dealership swapped 50 cars for grain in a three-month period. Daimler Chrysler introduced a "Grain Plan" which permitted Argentine customers to use grain to purchase Mercedes-Benz, Chrysler, Jeep, and Dodge vehicles. A farm equipment maker swapped $9.5 million of farm machinery for corn, sorghum, soybeans, and wheat and bought Toyota pickup trucks for its fleet with some of the grain received. Even a few insurance companies were considering plans to accept premiums in grain. Predictably, farmers began withholding some of their product, in effect treating grain hoarded in their silos as cash balances. Thus 25 percent of the soybean crop went unsold in 2002 compared to only 10 percent the previous year.[50]

Interestingly, many of the deflation-phobes in academia, the media, and supranational bureaucracies hailed the Argentine confiscatory deflation as a responsible "austerity measure," turning a blind eye to its devastating economic effects. This is unfortunate because there exists an effective and benign deflationary remedy that would solve the problem. The solution is for the Argentine government to recognize and adjust its policy to the reality of property—and the reality is that bank deposits are no longer (and really never were) par value property titles to fixed quantities of pesos and dollars. These currencies do not exist in the fractional-reserve banking system in anywhere near the quantities needed to pay off depositors. In economic reality, a bank's deposits are a claim on its loan and investment portfolio, including its cash reserve. Therefore, every bank in Argentina should be immediately handed over to its depositors, that is, transformed into a managed mutual fund. The ownership titles or "equity shares" in each mutual fund would be prorated among the former depositors in accordance with their share of the predecessor institution's deposit balances. The result would be a bank credit deflation that would result in a one-shot, swift and sharp contraction of the money supply down to the level of

---

[50] The examples cited in this paragraph may be found in Leslie Moore, "For Wary Argentines, The Crops Are Cash," *New York Times on the Web* (December 1, 2002). http://www.nytimes.com.

the monetary base, which is equal to the amounts of peso and dollar currencies held by the public plus the peso and dollar reserves held by the banks. While nominal prices and wage rates would have to be readjusted sharply downward, the value of the peso would rise commensurately, monetary exchange and calculation would be restored, and the allocation of resources and distribution of property titles would once again be determined by market processes.[51]

Deflation Fallacies

While blithely ignoring coercive political expropriation of the public's bank deposits, deflation-phobes exhibit an obsessive and misplaced concern with voluntary, market-driven deflation. Although deflation-phobia ranges across the spectrum of current schools of macroeconomic thought, the most numerous and vociferous group of contemporary deflation-phobes consists of the financial journalists, economic consultants, market pundits and conservative think-tank policy wonks who are more or less closely linked with supply-side economics. Donald L. Luskin, Bruce Bartlett, Richard Rahn, and Larry Kudlow are some of the supply-siders who have weighed in with antideflationist articles. The supply-side anti-deflation program can be boiled down to three basic propositions, each of which rests on fallacious assumptions.

The first proposition is that the prices of gold and other raw commodities are extremely sensitive to changes in monetary conditions and are therefore they are good predictors of future movements of general consumer goods' prices, which tend to respond much more slowly to such changes. As Bruce Bartlett[52] wrote, "When one sees a sustained fall in sensitive commodity prices—those that lead changes in the general price level—one can predict that eventually this trend will work its way through the economy as a whole." According to

---

[51] For more detail on this proposal, see Joseph T. Salerno ("Understanding Argentina," Daily Article (May 28, 2002). http://www.mises.org). Michael S. Bernstam and Alvin Rabushka ("Capital Swap à la Russe for Argentina," Hoover Institution Public Policy Inquiry. *Russian Economy* (June 6, 2002). http://www.russianeconomy.org/comments/060602.html) propose a similar plan to reform Russia's banking system.

[52] Bartlett, "The Deflation Dilemma."

Rahn,[53] since all major commodity indexes had fallen by double-digit percentages during 2001 and many commodity prices had fallen well below their levels of 10 years earlier, a deflation, possibly as severe as Japan's, loomed. The declines in CPI and PPI indexes in the fourth quarter of 2001 supposedly represented the first whiff of this onrushing deflation.

The fallacious assumption underlying this proposition is that there always exists a positive relationship between movements in raw commodity prices and movements in consumer prices. However, as the Austrian theory of the business cycle teaches, consumer goods' prices and capital goods', including raw commodity, prices change relative to one another during the different phases of the cycle and may very well vary in absolutely opposite directions during a recession.

Since World War II recessions have generally been precipitated by the Fed reducing the rate of growth of bank reserves and hence of the money supply, rather than absolutely contracting bank reserves and money. All other things equal, the immediate result is a reduction in the creation of bank credit, which leads directly to a higher interest rate that discourages business borrowing for investment projects. The subsequent constriction of investment spending causes the prices of capital goods to begin to fall both absolutely and relative to consumer goods' prices. The latter are generally still increasing at the start of a recession under the pressure exerted by past injections of new money that reaches consumers only after it has been spent by business investors. As profits in the capital goods industries turn negative and profit prospects for planned and partly finished investment projects in these industries suddenly dim, the demand for raw industrial commodities and other inputs specific to the production of capital goods declines precipitously and their prices plunge even further. Shaky capital goods' firms also scramble to acquire cash and stave off financial default and bankruptcy by liquidating their inventories of highly marketable industrial commodities, and this puts additional downward pressure on industrial commodity prices.

---

[53] Rahn, "Defeating Deflation."

Meanwhile, because the Fed has typically continued to expand bank credit and money during postwar recessions (although at a slower pace), the prices of consumer goods never do stop rising as the persistent injections of new money from "monetized" government deficits and more slowly growing bank loans and investments work their way through the economy to consumers. This vital lesson has been illustrated time and again in the series of inflationary recessions or "stagflations" that the U.S. has suffered through since 1969, during which the prices of consumer goods rose without interruption right through the recession phase of the cycle despite plunging commodity prices.

Unfortunately the supply-siders have never learned this lesson taught by theory and history, although they might have had they paid more attention to Murray Rothbard. Writing in an earlier era of deflation-phobia, the mid-1980s, Rothbard gave a definitive response to those, including supply-siders, who claimed then that a fall in a handful of industrial commodity prices presaged a general deflation:

> The fact that industrial commodity prices have fallen sharply means precisely nothing for the reality or the prospect of inflation or deflation. Industrial commodity prices always fall in recessions. They fell in the steep 1973–74 recession and they fell very sharply throughout [the recessions of] 1980 and 1981.... What was the impact of commodity prices on inflation or deflation? Precisely zero. The point is that consumer prices kept rising anyway, throughout these recessions and through the generally depressed period from 1980 to 1983.... Most laymen and economists think of industrial commodity or wholesale prices as harbingers of the move of consumer prices, which are supposed to be "sticky" but moving in the same direction. But they are wrong. One of the most important and neglected truths of business cycle analysis is that consumer prices and capital goods or producer prices move in different directions. Specifically, in boom periods capital goods or producer prices rise relative to consumer prices, while in recessions, consumer prices rise relative to producer prices. As a result, the fact that industrial commodity prices have been falling in no sense presages a later fall in consumer prices. Quite the contrary.[54]

---

[54] Murray N. Rothbard, "What's Ahead: Resurging Inflation or Sudden Deflation," *Jerome Smith's Investment Perspectives* (November 1984).

The second proposal of the supply-side program relates to the proper role of the Fed in averting this deflation. As Luskin colorfully described this role,

> The job of the Fed is to play a monetary Goldilocks—to provide just the right amount of money in the economy. The right amount isn't some arbitrary level of M1 or M2 or some other so-called measure of the money supply. In fact the supply of money is like any other supply—the supply of apples or the supply of paper clips—the "right" amount is the amount that satisfies demand.... So as the demand for money fluctuates, and as the economy's need to use it for transactions fluctuates, the job of the Goldilocks Fed is to supply just the right amount of money to keep the price of money constant.[55]

Now, first of all Luskin has—quite inadvertently to be sure—hit on a perfect analogy for the Fed. In fact Goldilocks surreptitiously redistributed property from a hapless and unsuspecting family of bears to herself, offering no property in exchange for the food and shelter she wantonly expropriated. This is precisely what occurs when the Fed creates new fiat money for whatever reason: the first recipients of this newly-created money, whether they be the government and its subsidized constituencies or banks lending newly-created dollars and their client firms borrowing at artificially low interest rates, are able to acquire titles to real property without the necessity of having first produced and exchanged property on the market. The result is a concealed and arbitrary redistribution of real income and wealth in favor of those who receive and spend the new money before prices have risen at the expense of firms and laborers whose selling prices and wage rates rise only after a lapse of time during which most of the prices of the things they purchase have already risen. Even if the Fed were to create just enough additional money to offset a growth deflation and maintain consumer prices roughly unchanged, it would still be distorting the market's distribution of property in favor of those who were immediate recipients of the monetary injection and were able to take advantage of the falling prices. Belated recipients of the new money and, especially, people living on fixed money incomes would have to purchase at

---

[55] Luskin, "The Greatest Threat."

unchanged prices and would thereby be deprived of the share of extra real income that would have accrued to them had consumer prices been permitted to fall in line with increased productivity.

Another fallacy embedded in the Fed-as-Goldilocks analogy relates to Luskin's misconception of the role of the pricing process in ensuring that the optimal quantities of goods are produced. It is incorrect to assert, as Luskin does, that the "right" amount of any good, such as paper clips or apples, is the amount that satisfies demand at the previously existing price. In fact, as we saw above with respect to the computer industry, the optimal quantity of PC's is determined by the profit maximizing decisions of competing firms in the industry. When productivity is growing rapidly and per-unit costs are declining rapidly, the attempt to maximize prospective profit results in an excess supply of the good at the previous market price. The free market ensures that the price then falls to once again precisely adjust the quantity supplied to the quantity demanded. In other words, from moment to moment, it is the continual variation of prices that ensures that the "right" quantity of any good is always supplied; the market economy does not operate to assure that the supply will always vary to perfectly satisfy demand at a price that is previously fixed once and for all. And it is just so for the money supply: if an excess demand for money emerges as a result of economic growth, the market phenomenon of growth deflation will ensure that the purchasing power of money rises, producing an increase in aggregate monetary wealth that exactly satisfies the extra demand. A Goldilocks Fed continually varying the money supply in order to maintain the purchasing power of money forever constant—even if it could be trusted to do so—is just as nonoptimal as computer firms supplying only the number of PC's that pegs their price at, let us say, the 1980 level.

Finally, it should be pointed out that Hayek[56] brilliantly demolished the argument in favor of a Goldilocks central bank that was put forth by a much earlier and more distinguished generation of

---

[56] F.A. Hayek, "the Paradox of Saving," in *Profits, Interest, and Investment and Other Essays on the Theory of Industrial Fluctuations* (New York: Augustus M. Kelley, [1939] 1969).

deflation-phobes in the late 1920s.[57] Although Hayek[58] never used the
term "deflation-phobes," he did refer to "the victims of that uncriti-
cal fear of any kind of fall in prices which is so widespread today, and
which lends a cloak to all the more refined forms of inflationism"—
a perfect characterization of contemporary deflation-phobes. In his
critique, which was based on Austrian business cycle theory, Hayek
pointed out that any attempt by the central bank to stabilize the price
level of consumer goods by increasing the quantity of money during
a period of rapid technological progress and capital investment inevitably drives the interest rate down below the level that equates the
supply of voluntary savings with the business demand for investment
funds. This gap is filled by the evanescent "forced savings" embodied
in the newly created money that the central bank injects into credit
markets. Once the bank credit expansion ceases or slows down, however, the forced savings vanish and the interest rate re-attains the
higher level consistent with the intertemporal consumption preferences of consumers. In the meantime the artificial reduction of the
interest rate falsifies the profit calculations of entrepreneurs and distorts their investment decisions, generating an unsustainable real
investment boom—or "bubble" in contemporary jargon—followed
inevitably by a bust when the interest rate rises again. It is during the
recession that the cluster of malinvestments is revealed and liquidated
and the production of capital and consumer goods is readjusted to the
quantity of voluntary savings. Hayek concluded with the warning that
any attempt to obstruct the benign deflationary process that accompanies economic growth by manipulating the quantity of money paradoxically leads to the very economic collapse that deflation-phobes
of every era are so desperate to avoid:

> So long as the volume of money in circulation is continu-
> ally changing, we cannot get rid of industrial fluctuations. In
> particular, every monetary policy which aims at stabilizing
> the value of money and involves, therefore, an increase of its

---

[57] Hayek's seminal article, "The Paradox of Saving" (1969), was originally published in German in 1929 and first appeared in English in 1931, effectively refuting
Keynes's "deficiency of aggregate demand" and "paradox of thrift" arguments at least
half-a-decade in advance in the two most important scientific languages of the time.

[58] Hayek, "The Paradox of Saving," pp. 253–54.

supply with every increase of production, must bring about those very fluctuations which it is trying to prevent.[59]

The third and final component in the supply-siders' anti-deflation program is to formulate a rule to guide the Fed in performing its Goldilocks role. This rule is a price-level rule that focuses on—what else?—sensitive commodity prices. According to Rahn,

> the Fed needs to say explicitly that it is adopting price-level targeting again, and that it is going to look at sensitive commodity prices as the indicator of where prices are headed rather than the CPI and other lagging indicators. The Fed should look at a market basket of commodities; if prices in the basket rise above a predetermined range, the Fed reduces the money supply and vice versa.[60]

Unfortunately, this rule may at times operate to promote a massive inflation because, as we saw above, industrial commodity prices and consumer prices move in opposite directions during periods of recession and financial crisis. By following this rule the Fed may very well accelerate an already high growth rate of the money supply and intensify inflation in the U.S. while reacting to a precipitous decline in industrial commodity prices caused, for example, by foreign financial crises like those that struck in Asia in 1997 and 1998. For example, the DJ-AIG Commodity Index in early February 2002 stood 10 percent below its level in 1991, and nearly 20 percent below its level of one year before, despite the fact that the monetary aggregate MZM (for "money of zero maturity") grew by 15.8 percent and AMS (for Austrian money supply) grew by 12.3 percent in 2001.[61] In these circumstances, if the Fed had heeded the advice of the supply-siders, who all purport to be

---

[59] Ibid., pp. 262–63.

[60] Rahn, "Defeating Deflation."

[61] Unless otherwise noted the statistics cited in this paper have been computed from data available in the Federal Reserve Economic Data (FRED) database on the Internet at www.stls.frb.org/fred2. The DJ-AIG Commodity Index can be found in Dow Jones and Company, Inc. 2002. The AMS aggregate is computed by Frank Shostak. For a description and justification of the AMS aggregate see Joseph T. Salerno, "The 'True' Money Supply: A Measure of the Supply of the Medium of Exchange in the U.S. Economy," *Austrian Economics Newsletter* 6 (Spring 1987). This article can be downloaded from www.mises.org.

unconcerned by the rate of growth of the money supply, by immediately ratcheting up money growth from its already high rate to a rate sufficient to rapidly increase commodity prices by 10 to 20 percent, they would have set the stage for a hyperinflation. And this would all have been in the name of averting a deflation whose only evidence was a small isolated decline in the fourth quarter 2001 CPI (−0.6 percent on an annualized basis) during a year in which the CPI rose 1.8 percent and the median CPI increased 3.9 percent.[62] Of course the feared deflation never materialized as the CPI climbed by 2.2 percent and the median CPI by 3.0 percent in 2002.

As noted above the supply-siders are by no means the only current macroeconomists afflicted with deflation-phobia. Recently, the doyen of monetarism, Milton Friedman,[63] wrote "the current rate of monetary growth of more than 10% is sustainable and perhaps even desirable as a defense against contraction and in reaction to the events of Sept. 11."[64] Also, the moderate Keynesian John H. Makin,[65] an economist associated with the establishment Republican think tank, the American Enterprise Institute, recently referred to the current recession as a "deflationary one" on the basis of the substantial fall in the October 2001 PPI index and the decline in one-year inflation expectations from September to November 2001. Makin went on to argue,

---

[62] The median CPI was developed by economists Michael F. Bryan and Stephen G. Cecchetti and is calculated by the Federal Reserve Bank of Cleveland. A short description of the aggregate and its rationale and its time series can be found in Federal Reserve Bank of Cleveland (2003). From the Austrian perspective, this statistic gives a far better "understanding" of fluctuations in the purchasing power of money because it is less aggregative than the standard CPI index and is more consistent with the Austrian notion of a "swarm" of individual and particular prices rising and falling together while constantly changing positions relative to one another. The metaphor of a bee swarm whose overall variations in altitude are reflected to different degrees in each of its individual members is sharply opposed to the metaphor of a "price level" uniformly changing like the level of a body of water, a misleading metaphor that has been entrenched in mainstream monetary thought at least since Irving Fisher's writings in the early twentieth century.

[63] Milton Friedman, "The 1990s Boom Went Bust. What's Next?" wsj.com (January 22, 2002).

[64] To be fair, Friedman (ibid.) did add the caveat, "continuation of anything like that rate of monetary growth will ensure that inflation rears its ugly head once again."

[65] Makin, "The Deflation Monster Lives."

> the Fed has no choice but to race to cut short-term interest rates
> faster than inflation and inflation expectations are falling.…
> After all, combating recession, especially this deflationary one,
> requires a real Fed funds rate of zero, and with expected infla-
> tion of 1 percent or below, a 1 percent nominal Fed funds rate
> is necessary to push real rates down to zero.[66]

So fearful was Makin that even zero short-term real rates alone would be insufficient to arrest and reverse this imagined deflationary recession that he also advocated that President Bush's fiscal stimulus package be increased in size and that the Democrats be invited in on the spending boondoggle. According to Makin,[67] the President "should suggest that the package be enlarged to $200 billion, with the Demo-crats allowed to specify $100 billion worth of their favorite spending increases while Republicans can specify $100 billion worth of their favorite tax cuts." Deflation fallacies are legion and in this section we have dealt only with some of the grosser fallacies that are current in order to illustrate the relevance of the Austrian taxonomy of deflation. A much more subtle, but no less specious, argument for fearing defla-tion, specifically anticipated deflation, is a staple of almost all recent writings on deflation by academic macroeconomists and is implicit in Makin's remarks quoted in the preceding paragraph. According to this argument, "The root reason to fear deflation is that the nomi-nal interest rate is bounded below by zero."[68] It would take us too far afield to address this argument in detail here. Suffice it to say, however, that this argument involves a fundamental misfocus on the "loanable funds" market as the basic determinant of the real rate of interest and completely ignores the fact that the loan rate is a mere epiphenome-non of the "natural" rate of interest or the uniform rate of price spreads between inputs and outputs. The latter constitutes the time-preference return to capitalist investment in all processes and stages of the inte-grated production structure. Ceteris paribus, any general anticipation of a rise in the purchasing power of money will therefore be reflected immediately in lowered entrepreneurial bids for, and prices of, inputs,

---

[66] Ibid.

[67] Ibid.

[68] DeLong, "Why We Should Fear Deflation."

and these lowered prices will instantaneously re-establish the pre-existing nominal (and real) rate of return on investment and therefore on funds loaned to investing capitalist-entrepreneurs.[69]

Conclusion:
The Prospect for Deflation in the U.S.

So what is the prospect for an imminent deflation in the U.S.—for an actual sustained fall in consumer prices—that so terrifies so many contemporary macroeconomic analysts and forecasters? The answer derived from our theoretical analysis of deflation above is: practically none. Year-over-year growth in real GDP for 2001 was a measly 0.1 percent, not surprising for a recession year, and 2.9 percent for 2002. The recovery has slowed down substantially the last quarter of 2002 and first quarter of 2003, with real GDP growing at an annualized rate of 1.4 percent in both quarters. As a slow recovery is widely expected to continue through 2003, this implies that the factor of growth deflation will be negligible for a while.

There does exist some evidence that a cash-building deflation process is operating. The ratio of total nominal income from current production as quantified in the nominal GDP aggregate (NGDP) to the money supply as defined by AMS, fell by 6.5 percent, from 6.48 in the 4th quarter of 2000 to 6.06 in the 4th quarter of 2001. The NGDP/AMS ratio fell by a further 2.3 percent in 2002 before increasing slightly by 0.7 percent in the first quarter of 2003. The NGDP/MZM ratio fell by 15.7 percent in 2001, followed by a 3.9 percent decline in 2002. The ratio stabilized in the first quarter of 2003. This indicates that during the recession and early stages of the halting recovery people were devoting a greater part of their income to holding cash balances, which generally occurs as a result of the greater uncertainty and pessimism that a recession and related financial collapses, such as the Enron debacle, introduce into their future income prospects. The higher value placed on ready cash relative to other opportunities for

---

[69] For a critique of the argument that a premium (discount) on the nominal interest rate results from anticipated inflation (deflation) in order to maintain the real rate, see Rothbard, *Man, Economy, and State*, pp. 693–98.

disposing of money places a downward pressure on the prices of consumer goods. This is a short-term phenomenon, however, and tends to reverse itself as recession nears an end and perceived income prospects brighten, as appears to be happening in 2003.

This brings us to the supply side of the money relation. During 2000, the AMS aggregate actually contracted by 1.29 percent after having risen by an annual average rate of 6.47 percent in the previous three years. After growing by an average of 12 percent per year in 1998 and 1999, the MZM grew by 8 percent in 2000. (See Appendix 2 for graphs of the growth of U.S. monetary aggregates.) There is no doubt that this sudden decline in monetary growth precipitated the current recession. However, the Fed's aggressive rate cutting in 2001 resulted in explosive growth in the money supply in 2001, with AMS growing by 12.33 percent and MZM by 15.78 percent. Monetary expansion slowed somewhat in 2002 but still continued at a rapid pace with AMS increasing by 6.38 percent and MZM by 12.78 percent. In the first six months of 2003, AMS has grown at an annual rate of 4.22 percent—but at a 12 percent annual rate in the final four months of this period—while MZM has risen at an annual rate of 6.56 percent, and by nearly 8 percent per year in the final four months. So any deflationary tendency proceeding from the relatively tight monetary policy in 2000 and the large increase in the demand for money during 2001 has since been swamped by the Fed's reversion to a massively expansionary money policy.

Finally there is no evidence that Americans are losing confidence in the banking system and poised to set off a much-needed purgative bank credit deflation à la Argentina. The currency/checkable deposit ratio rose very slightly in 2001 from 0.96 to 0.98, implying that there was a slight net withdrawal of currency from the banks by depositors. And even if a bank run did develop in the event that the fragile recovery failed and the economy plunged into a double-dip recession featuring additional high profile collapses among American corporations and financial institutions, there is very little probability that the Greenspan Fed would allow it to run its natural course. The Fed would sooner impose a "bank holiday," that is, an Argentine-style confiscatory deflation, to buy time in order to orchestrate a massive inflationary bailout of the financial system.

Whether the current recovery strengthens, which appears to be the current consensus, or whether unforeseen events in the financial arena abort it, we will see a hefty rise in consumer prices in the next few years. In other words, an existing or imminent deflation in the U.S. is a chimera conjured up by those unfamiliar with sound, Austrian monetary theory.

Appendix A

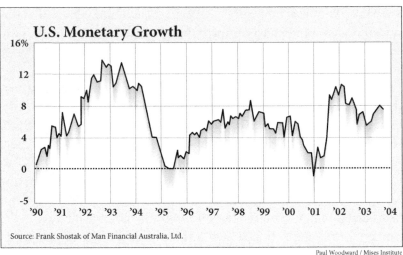

Source: Frank Shostak of Man Financial Australia, Ltd.

Paul Woodward / Mises Institute

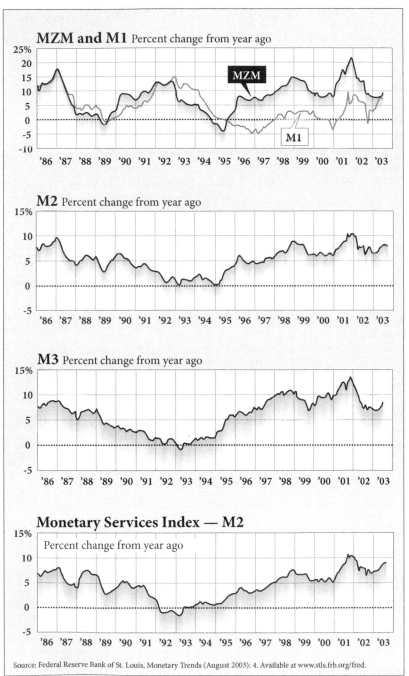

Source: Federal Reserve Bank of St. Louis, Monetary Trends (August 2003): 4. Available at www.stls.frb.org/fred.

Bibliography

Anderson, Benjamin M. 1979. *Economics and the Public Welfare: A Financial and Economic History of the United States, 1949–1946*, 2nd ed. Indianapolis, Ind.: Liberty Press.

Bartlett, Bruce. 2001. "The Deflation Dilemma: To Be Concerned or Not to Be?" *National Review Online Financial* (November 20).

Bernanke, Ben S. 2003. "A Perspective on Inflation Targeting." Presented at the Annual Washington Policy Conference of the National Association of Business Economists. Washington, D.C. (March 25).

Bernanke, Ben S., and Frederic S. Mishkin. 1997. "Inflation Targeting: A New Framework for Monetary Policy?" *Journal of Economic Perspectives* 11 (Spring).

Bernstam, Michael S., and Alvin Rabushka. 2002. "Capital Swap à la Russe for Argentina." Hoover Institution Public Policy Inquiry. Russian Economy (June 6). Http://www.russianeconomy.org./comments/060602.html.

Bullard, James B. and Charles M. Hokayem. 2003. "Deflation, Corrosive and Otherwise." Federal Reserve Bank of St. Louis *National Economic Trends* (July): p. 1.

Cox, W. Michael, and Richard Alm. 1999a. *Myths of Rich and Poor: Why We're Better Off Than We Think*. New York: Basic Books.

_____. 1999b. "The New Paradigm." In Federal Reserve Bank of Dallas *1999 Annual Report*.

Degen, Robert A. 1987. *The American Monetary System: A Concise Survey of Its Evolution Since 1896*. Lexington, Mass.: D.C. Heath.

DeLong, J. Bradford. 1999. "Why We Should Fear Deflation." *Brookings Papers on Economic Activity* (Spring). http://www.j-bradford-delong.net.

Dow Jones and Company. 2002. "Markets Diary." *Wall Street Journal* (February 5): p. C1.

Federal Reserve Bank of Cleveland. 2002. "Deflation." *2002 Annual Report*. http://www.clevelandfed.org/Annual02/Essay.pdf.

_____. 2003. Economic Research and Data. http://www.clevelandfed.org.

Friedman, Milton. 2002. "The 1990s Boom Went Bust. What's Next?" wsj.com (January 22).

Friedman, Milton, and Anna J. Schwartz. 1971. *A Monetary History of the United States: 1867–1960*. Princeton, N.J.: Princeton University Press.

Gordon, Robert Aaron. 1974. *Economic Instability and Growth: The American Record*. New York: Harper and Row.

Harding, W.P.G. 1925. *The Formative Period of the Federal Reserve System: During the World Crisis*. New York: Houghton Mifflin.

Hayek, Friedrich A. [1939] 1969. "The Paradox of Saving." In *Profits, Interest, and Investment and Other Essays on the Theory of Industrial Fluctuations*. New York: Augustus M. Kelley.

_____. [1960] 1972. *The Constitution of Liberty*. Chicago: Henry Regnery.

Keynes, John Maynard. [1936] 1964. *The General Theory of Employment, Interest, and Money.* New York: Harcourt, Brace and World.

Kindahl, James K. [1961] 1971. "Economic Factors in Specie Resumption: The United States, 1865–1879." In *The Reinterpretation of American Economic History*, Robert W. Fogel and Stanley L. Engerman, eds. New York: Harper and Row.

Luskin, Donald L. 2001. "The Greatest Threat Facing the U.S. Economy: Deflation." *Capitalism-Magazine.com* (November 23).

Makin, John H. 2001. "The Deflation Monster Lives." *Economic Outlook* (December).

Mankiw, N. Gregory. 2003. *Macroeconomics*, 5th ed. New York: Worth Publishers.

Meyer, Laurence H. 2001. "Inflation Targets and Inflation Targeting." Federal Reserve Bank of St. Louis *Review* 83 (November/December).

Mises, Ludwig von. [1953] 1980. *The Theory of Money and Credit*, 2nd ed., H.E. Batson, trans. Indianapolis, Ind.: Liberty Classics.

____. 1998. *Human Action: A Treatise on Economics*, Scholar's Edition. Auburn, Ala.: Ludwig von Mises Institute.

____. 1993. *Man, Economy, and State: A Treatise on Economic Principles*, 2nd ed. Auburn, Ala.: Ludwig von Mises Institute.

Moore, Leslie. 2002. "For Wary Argentines, The Crops Are Cash." *New York Times on the Web* (December 1). http://www.nytimes.com.

Philips, C.A, T.F. McManus, and R.W. Nelson. [1937] 1972. *Banking and the Business Cycle: A Study of the Great Depression in the United States*. New York: Arno Press.

Rahn, Richard W. 2001. "Defeating Deflation." *Wall Street Journal* (November 19).

Ranlett, John G. 1977. *Money and Banking: An Introduction to Analysis and Policy.* New York: John Wiley and Sons.

Reuters. 2001. "Riots and Looting in Argentina as Austerity Plan Bites." *New York Times on the Web* (December 19). http://www.nytimes.com.

Rogoff, Kenneth, Manmohan S. Kumar, Laurance Ball, Vincent Reinhart, and Kim Scoenholtz. 2003. Transcript of an IMF Economic Forum: Should We Be Worried About 'Deflation'? Washington, D.C. (May 29). http://www.imf.org.

Rohter, Larry. 2002. "Argentina Is Still Shaky Despite Currency Measures." *New York Times on the Web* (January 11). Http://www.nytimes.com.

Rothbard, Murray N. 1970. *Power and Market: Government and the Economy.* Menlo Park, Calif.: Institute for Humane Studies.

____. 1983. *The Mystery of Banking.* New York: Richardson and Snyder.

____. 1984. "What's Ahead: Resurging Inflation or Sudden Deflation." *Jerome Smith's Investment Perspectives* (November).

____. 1990. *What Has Government Done to Our Money?* 4th ed. Auburn, Ala.: Ludwig von Mises Institute.

_____. 1993. *Man, Economy, and State: A Treatise on Economic Principles.* 2nd ed. Auburn, Ala.: Ludwig von Mises Institute.

_____. 1994. *The Case Against the Fed.* Auburn, Ala.: Ludwig von Mises Institute.

_____. 1995. "Deflation: Free or Compulsory." In *Making Economic Sense.* Auburn, Ala.: Ludwig von Mises Institute.

_____. 1997. "The Austrian Theory of Money." In *The Logic Of Action One: Method, Money, and the Austrian School.* Cheltenham, U.K.: Edward Elgar.

_____. 2000. *America's Great Depression.* 5th ed. Auburn, Ala.: Ludwig von Mises Institute.

Salerno, Joseph T. 1987. "The 'True' Money Supply: A Measure of the Supply of the Medium of Exchange in the U.S. Economy." *Austrian Economics Newsletter* 6 (Spring). This article can be downloaded from www.mises.org.

_____. 1993. "Mises and Hayek Dehomogenized." *Review of Austrian Economics* 6 (2).

_____. 1999. "Money and Gold in the 1920s and 1930s: An Austrian View." *Freeman* 49 (October).

_____. 2002. "Understanding Argentina." Daily Article (May 28). http://www. mises. org.

Samuelson, Paul A. 1967. *Economics: An Introductory Analysis,* 7th ed. New York: McGraw-Hill.

Samuelson, Robert J. 2001. "The Specter of Deflation." *Washington Post Online* (November 21).

Shostak, Frank. 2001. *Ord Minnett Jardine Fleming Futures Daily Report* (July 20).

Temin, Peter. 1969. *The Jacksonian Economy.* New York: W.W. Norton.

Weiher, Kenneth. 1992. *America's Search for Monetary Stability: Monetary and Fiscal Policy Since 1913.* New York: Twayne Publishers.

CHAPTER 11

Comment on Tullock's "Why Austrians Are Wrong About Depressions"

Let me preface my comment with the following caveat: I am skeptical of the value of a scholarly journal article that attempts to critically evaluate the "canonical version" of an economic theory, particularly when the theory in question deals with a phenomenon as complex as the business cycle. Added to this is my uneasiness over the fact that the version that is chosen for criticism[1] was intended as a popular exposition of the theory. This hardly does justice to the profundity of the Austrian theory of the business cycle or to the scholarship of Murray N. Rothbard. If one wishes to pen a brief critique of the general thrust of Austrian cycle theory, it is more appropriately done as an explicit book review, say, of an anthology such as Mises et al.[2] Having expressed these reservations, I proceed with my comment.

From: Comment on Gordon Tullock, "Why Austrians Are Wrong about Depressions," *The Review of Austrian Economics* 3 (1988): pp. 141–45.

[1] Murray Rothbard, *Depressions: Their Cause and Cure* (Lansing, Mich.: Constitution Alliance, 1969).

[2] Ludwig von Mises, Gottfried Haberler, Murray N. Rothbard, abd Friedrich A Hayek, *The Austrian Theory of the Trade Cycle and Other Essays*, ed. Richard M. Ebeling (Auburn, Ala.: Ludwig von Mises Institute, 1983).

The three nits that Tullock picks at the beginning of his article[3] deserve comment because they bear out the concerns I mentioned in the preceding paragraph. First, the author correctly notes that, in the particular pamphlet under review, "Rothbard never explains why the inflation which is part of his theory cannot simply be continued or even accelerated." But, of course, this question is dealt with in many advanced expositions of Austrian cycle theory. As one of numerous examples, Rothbard,[4] himself, addresses the issue under the heading of "The Ultimate Limit: The Runaway Boom."

Moreover, Tullock's personal testimony that hyperinflation "is undeniably unpleasant, but not really a disaster,"[5] while certainly provocative, is irrelevant with respect to this issue. It is sufficient that the political and monetary authorities who orchestrate the inflationary boom fear the eventuality of hyperinflation and act to prevent it. Thus, for instance, the proximate cause of the 1980–82 U.S. depression was the well-publicized decision of the Volcker Fed to "disinflate" the economy from highly unpopular double-digit inflation levels by reining in the growth of money and bank credit.

The author's second nit[6] concerns Rothbard's alleged failure to come to grips with the question of why entrepreneurs do not eventually learn about, correctly forecast, and adjust their investment activities to the business cycle. In current jargon, the author is questioning why Austrian cycle theorists do not assume that market participants are capable of formulating "rational expectations," which incorporate a correct theory of economic relationships and preclude systematic forecasting errors. Without attempting to provide an answer to this question here, suffice it to say that the issue has been discussed by a

---

[3] Gordon Tullock, "Why Austrians Are Wrong About Depressions," in *The Review of Austrian Economics* 2 (1987).

[4] Murray Rothbard, Man, Economy, and State (Los Angeles: Nash Publishing, 1970), vol. 2, pp. 875–77.

[5] Tullock, "Why Austrians Are Wrong About Depressions," p. 73.

[6] Ibid., p. 73.

number of Austrian cycle theorists, including Mises,[7] O'Driscoll,[8] and Garrison.[9] Once again, the author's decision to avoid grappling with the extensive literature on the theory has led him to suggest a lacuna in the theory that simply does not exist.

The final nit Tullock picked out[10] stems from his apparent misunderstanding of the methodological context of the Austrian business cycle theory. Thus the author faults Rothbard for ignoring the results of statistical tests that suggest that depressions and booms do not follow a cycle but, instead, follow a so-called "random walk." This is beside the point, however, since Austrians do not construe the term *business cycle* as a mechanistic or statistical regularity that openly manifests itself in history, but as a recurring qualitative sequence of abstract economic phenomena that can only be detected in the historical data by the application of theory. In an early contribution, Mises [11] wrote: "Neither the connection between boom and bust nor the cyclical change of business conditions is a fact that can be established independent of theory. Only theory, business cycle theory, permits us to detect the wavy outline of a cycle in the tangled confusion of events." The author could have found a concise and lucid discussion of the methodological foundations of Austrian cycle theory in Rothbard.[12]

---

[7] Ludwig von Mises, "'Elastic Expectations' and the Austrian Theory of the Trade Cycle," *Economica* 10 (August): pp. 251–52.

[8] Gerald P. O'Driscoll, Jr. *Economics as a Coordination Problem: The Contributions of Friedrich A. Hayek* (Kansas City, Kan.: Sheed, Andrews and McMeel, 1977), pp. 106-08 and "Rational Expectations, Politics and Stagflation," in *Time, Uncertainty, and Disequilibrium: Exploration of Austrian Themes*, ed. Mario J. Rizzo (Lexington, Mass.: Lexington Books, 1979), pp. 166–68.

[9] Roger W. Garrison, "Hayekian Trade Cycle Theory: A Reapprisal," The Cato Journal 6 (Fall 1986): pp. 445–47.

[10] Tullock, "Why Austrians Are Wrong About Depressions," 1987, p. 74.

[11] Ludwig von Mises, *On the Manipulation of Money and Credit*, ed. Percy L. Greaves, Jr., Bettina Bien Greaves, trans. (Dobbs Ferry, N.Y.: Free Market Books, 1978) p. 117.

[12] Murray Rothbard, *America's Great Depression*, 3rd ed. (Kansas City: Sheed and Ward), pp. 1–7.

With regard to Tullock's "major objection" to the theory, his argument[13] is likewise marred by an apparent unfamiliarity with advanced expositions of the theory. I shall not attempt here to give a point-by-point critique of the author's main argument that, during a typical Austrian business cycle, "there would be only minor transitional unemployment [and] measured GNP would be higher as a result."[14] It is enough to point out that the author's conclusion rests on basic misconceptions about Austrian capital theory and structure-of-production analysis.

First, the author appears to ignore the important notion of intertemporal complementarity in the structure of production. Thus, even if the higher-stage investment projects and production processes induced by the artificially depressed interest rate are eventually completed in the technological sense, they still may be underutilized or wholly abandoned during the depression-adjustment phase. The reason is that the products yielded by these higher-order processes confront greatly contracted market demands, resulting from the suddenly revealed increased scarcity (and hence money costs) of the temporally "nonspecific" inputs with which they must be combined in lower-order production processes.

For example, a newly completed iron ore mine may be abandoned because, at any technically feasible rate of output, the price of the ore has fallen below the "marginal costs" of the mine's operation, including wage rates, prices of fuels, and the rents of power generators and hauling vehicles. Higher prices for the services of labor and of the other relatively nonspecific inputs or "convertible" capital goods are due, in turn, to the fact that too great a proportion of the available stock of these resources was erroneously invested in the production of "inconvertible" or "specific" higher-order goods, such as the iron mine shaft and related "fixed" investments. The higher monetary costs of nonspecific resources, which make their continued employment in certain higher-stage processes uneconomic, simply reflect the fact that such resources have higher-marginal-revenue

---

[13] Tullock, "Why Austrians Are Wrong About Depressions," pp. 3–10.
[14] Ibid., p. 74.

products in the lower-stage processes from which they were originally diverted during the inflationary boom. The bankruptcies and resource unemployment occurring in the mining and mining-equipment industries during the depression-adjustment phase are thus part and parcel of the process by which labor and other nonspecific factor inputs are reallocated to finished-goods production and to the wholesale and retail industries. It is the metaphorical "structure of production" itself—not necessarily particular factories or other construction—that cannot be completed, due to the unanticipated scarcity of capital that is suddenly revealed during the depression-adjustment phase.

A second basic confusion of the author involves his apparent belief that Austrian cycle theory indicates that an interest rate temporarily lowered by monetary inflation will lead to general overinvestment in capital and consumer goods industries.[15] But the main insight of Austrian cycle theory is that the inflationary boom induces "malinvestment," which denotes a diversion of scarce factors and money capital away from consumer-goods industries into capital-goods or, more generally, "higher-stage" industries, including, for example, investments in specially designed computers and software for specific R&D projects, expanding facilities supplying wildcat oil drillers, site planning for new hydroelectric plants, and so on. With scarce resources thus reallocated higher up the ladder of the structure of production, there necessarily occurs at least a temporary reduction in the quantities of final consumer goods produced.

Moreover, the uneconomic commitment of labor services and other nonspecific resources to the expansion of the production of relatively inconvertible higher-stage goods such as industrial construction and equipment will ultimately be revealed in an unforeseen bidding up of wage rates initiated in the lower stages, when it is discovered that available stocks of labor inputs are insufficient to complement the full array of products beginning to flow forth from the overbuilt higher stages. Such intertemporal price variations result in a shifting of labor as well as convertible capital goods into the rela-

---

15 Ibid., pp. 75–77.

tively undermanned and underequipped lower-stage industries, and account for the corresponding bankruptcies and retrenchments of overcapitalized higher-stage firms. As a result, many investments in inconvertible higher-order capital goods are abandoned, whether they are technologically completed or not. Even where the latter constitute completely sunk costs, they still may be entirely abandoned, because their continued utilization at any level of output does not generate an income sufficient to cover the "opportunity costs" of their complementary nonspecific factors, such as labor.

It is precisely the abandoned or underutilized factories, equipment, power generating sites, mines, and R&D projects that represent the "malinvested" capital of the boom period characterized by artificially lowered interest rates. In view of this wasted capital investment, the aggregate capital/labor ratio for the economy and, therefore, marginal productivity of labor and real wage rates can be expected to be lower than if investment of scarce productive resources and the "length" of the production structure had been determined by genuine market time preferences, which are reflected in the unmanipulated or "natural" interest rate. Thus, contrary to Tullock's contentions,[16] Austrian Cycle theory *does* explain the observed drop in "measured GNP" and in laborers' living standards during the depression.

At the end of his article,[17] Tullock rehearses his earlier objection regarding the explanatory power of the Austrian theory when confronted with rational expectations. This is an important and timely issue and the author could have provided a valuable service by formulating his objection in a manner that speaks to what Austrian theorists have already written on this subject. (The relevant contributions are cited in the third paragraph of this comment.) Having chosen not to do this, however, the author's discussion fails to provoke any new or interesting thoughts on the matter.

---

[16] Ibid., p. 74.
[17] Ibid., pp. 76–77.

Bibliography

Garrison, Roger W. 1986. "Hayekian Trade Cycle Theory: A Reappraisal." *The Cato Journal* 6 (Fall): pp. 437–53.

Mises, Ludwig von. 1943. " 'Elastic Expectations' and the Austrian Theory of the Trade Cycle." *Economica* 10 (August): pp. 251–52.

_____. 1978. *On the Manipulation of Money and Credit*, Percy L. Greaves, Jr., ed., Bettina B., Greaves, trans., Dobbs Ferry, N.Y.: Free Market Books.

Mises, Ludwig von, Gottfried Haberler, Murray N. Rothbard and Friedrich A. Hayek. 1983. *The Austrian Theory of the Trade Cycle and Other Essays*, Richard M. Ebeling, ed. Auburn, Ala.: Ludwig von Mises Institute.

O'Driscoll, Gerald P., Jr. 1977. *Economics as a Coordination Problem: The Contributions of Friedrich A. Hayek*. Kansas City, Kans.: Sheed Andrews and McMeel.

_____. 1979. "Rational Expectations, Politics and Stagflation." In *Time, Uncertainty, and Disequilibrium: Exploration of Austrian Themes*, Mario J. Rizzo, ed. pp. 153–76. Lexington, Mass.: Lexington Books.

Rothbard, Murray. 1969. *Depressions: Their Cause and Cure*. Lansing, Mich.: Constitutional Alliance.

_____. 1970. *Man, Economy, and State: A Treatise on Economic Principles*, 2 vols. Los Angeles: Nash.

_____. 1975. *America's Great Depression*, 3rd ed. Kansas City: Sheed and Ward.

Tullock, Gordon. 1987. "Why the Austrians Are Wrong About Depressions." In *The Review of Austrian Economics*, vol. 2. Lexington, Mass.: Lexington Books.

CHAPTER 12

The 100 Percent Gold Standard: A Proposal for Monetary Reform

Introduction: The Current Debate on Gold

On October 26, 1981, the Federal Gold Commission held its third meeting since its formation on June 22, 1981 under the aegis of the U.S. Treasury Department.[1] The commission, which consists of seventeen prominent economists, legislators, businessmen, and Reagan administration officials, is charged with studying and reporting upon the feasibility of according a larger role to gold in the monetary system of the U.S. Professor Paul McCracken, one of the commission's leading members and an adviser to three previous Republican Presidents, observed at its first meeting on July 16 that the commission is conducting the first serious governmental monetary study in over seventy-five years. Much more significant, of course, is the fact that the subject of the commission's study is the gold standard.[2]

From: "The 100 Percent Gold Standard: A Proposal for Monetary Reform," in *Supply-Side Economics: A Critical Appraisal*, ed. Richard H. Fink (Frederick, Md.: University Publications of America, 1982), pp. 454–88.

[1] *See* "Return to an International Gold Standard Opposed by U.S. Panel Majority at Debate," *Wall Street Journal*, October 27, 1981, p. 16.

[2] McCracken's remarks are reported in Rowland Evans and Robert Novak, "Gold Standard Rears Its Head Again," *New York Post*, August 5, 1981, p. 29.

As recently as the early 1970s, the prospect of a governmental body seriously deliberating the merits of reinstituting the gold standard would have been considered unthinkable. In the years following World War II, the overwhelming majority of economists and economic policymakers as well as the population at large came increasingly to consider gold as a relic of a barbarous and bygone age, unfit to perform the functions of money in a modern industrial economy. The tiny handful of gold standard advocates, both inside and outside the economics profession, were then regarded as hopelessly benighted economic Neanderthals or thralls to a peculiar fetish.

Recent developments in the world economy, however, have conspired to effect a profound rethinking of the prevailing view on gold. In particular, there was the cold reality of the chronic stagflation which began to engulf the market-oriented economies of North America, Western Europe, and Japan in the early 1970s and which has since proved unresponsive to the orthodox Keynesian demand-management policies of fiscal and monetary fine tuning. Moreover, the unprecedented and agonizing combination of double-digit inflation and recession-level unemployment which characterizes stagflation could not be explained within the theoretical framework of textbook Keynesianism. Not surprisingly, there has recently emerged a thoroughgoing disenchantment with the Keynesian approach to macroeconomic stabilization policy and a search for alternatives. One such alternative is offered by Milton Friedman and the "monetarists," who argue that the monetary authority should adopt "a stable and predictable monetary growth rule." However, in Great Britain, Margaret Thatcher's much ballyhooed attempt to implement the monetarist program has produced wildly erratic monetary growth accompanied by a continued and relentless upward spiral in prices and an unemployment rate which has not been exceeded since the Great Depression. For example, during 1980, money supply growth underwent spectacular swings, with the quantity of money growing at annual rates of 10 percent in the first quarter, −4.1 percent in the second quarter, 11 percent in the third quarter, and 17.8 percent in the last quarter, to yield an average growth rate of 8.4 percent for the year.[3] The effect of this monetary inflation was a 12.7 percent increase in consumer prices and a 10.9 percent rise in industrial wholesale pric- es.[4] In the meanwhile, the British economy was plunged deeper into recession as real gross domestic product and employment declined at annual rates of 3.4 percent and 4.1 percent respectively during the first three quarters of 1980.[5]

The story has been much the same in the U.S. where, in October 1979, the Federal Reserve publicly proclaimed its intention of eschew- ing all further attempts to control interest rates in favor of implement- ing the monetarist prescription of maintaining a steady rate of growth of the money supply. While its efforts in this direction have not led to a significant abatement of the symptoms of stagflation, the Fed has found its task impossibly complicated of late by the divergent signals being conveyed by alternative gauges of money supply growth. For example, while both M1A and M1B indicated that monetary growth was grossly deficient and, in fact, negative during the four months beginning April 1, 1981, M2 was growing at an annual rate of 7.2 percent over the same period—well within the Federal Reserve's tar- get range of growth for this monetary aggregate.[6] In fact, during July and August, when the growth rate of M1B (shift adjusted) was below its target range, the rate of growth of M2 actually exceeded its target range.[7] Consequently, while monetarists such as Milton Friedman who focus on M2 have urged the Federal Reserve to hold the line or even pull the reins in on money supply growth, others such as Under- secretary of the Treasury Beryl Sprinkel have pointed to M1B and chided the Fed for an overly stringent monetary policy which threat- ens to precipitate a recession.[8]

---

[3] Federal Reserve Bank of St. Louis, *International Economic Conditions* (August 15, 1981), p. 50.

[4] Ibid., p. 51.

[5] Ibid., pp. 52, 53.

[6] Federal Reserve Bank of St. Louis, *Monetary Trends* (September 25, 1981), pp. 2, 5.

[7] Editorial, "Blaming Volcker," *Wall Street Journal*, October 14, 1981, p. 28.

[8] Ibid.

It is this perceived failure of both the Keynesian and monetarist alternatives to provide any relief from our current economic malaise that accounts for the growing wave of support for gold and the sympathetic hearing it is being accorded in the renewed debate over macroeconomic stabilization policy. Although the new advocates of the gold standard are by no means a unified school of thought, the most prominent among them tend to be associated with "supply-side economics." These include Arthur Laffer, Jude Wanniski, George Gilder, Irving Kristol, Representatives Jack Kemp and Ron Paul, Senators Jesse Helms and Roger W. Jepsen, and even President Reagan himself in the early stages of his presidential campaign. Others who have been involved, though less intimately, with the supply-side movement are the eminent monetary economist Robert Mundell and Lewis Lehrman, a businessman and writer.

Support for the gold standard, however, has not been confined to the adherents of supply-side economics. A gold-based monetary standard has also elicited favorable comments from a number of "mainstream" academic economists. For example, the respected monetary theorist, Robert J. Barro, in a recent study, concluded that:

> In relation to a fiat currency regime, the key element of a commodity standard is its potential for automaticity and consequent absence of political control over the quantity of money and the absolute price level.... The choice among different monetary constitutions—such as the gold standard, a commodity reserve standard, or a fiat standard with fixed rules for setting the quantity of money—may be less important than the decision to adopt *some* monetary constitution. On the other hand, the gold standard actually prevailed for a substantial period (even if from an "historical accident," rather than a constitutional choice process), whereas the world has yet to see a fiat currency system that has obvious "stability" properties.[9]

---

[9] Robert J. Barro, "Money and the Price Level under the Gold Standard," *Economic Journal* 89 (March 1979): p. 31.

Another noteworthy contribution is an historical study of the gold standard by Professor Roy W. Jastram.[10] Quite recently, Jastram summarized the findings of this study for the *Wall Street Journal*:

> From 1792 into the 1930s Britain was on a gold standard and the United States was on either a bimetallic standard or one of gold alone. During all those years, in both countries, price inflations and subsequent deflations average sensibly to zero. The result: for both the U.K. and the U.S. the wholesale price index numbers at the end of the gold standard were at just the level of 1800.[11]

Jastram goes on to suggest that this is "not unpredictable because the gold standard discipline was at work." Thus he concludes that "With the money supply showing ominous signs of being out of control, serious thought must be given to a new form of monetary discipline, one which might be suggested by age-old experience."[12]

A further indication that proposals for a restoration of the gold standard are not being taken lightly can be seen in the growing number of prominent opponents of gold that have been induced to break their silence and join the controversy. For example, under the aegis of the prestigious and neo-Keynesian-oriented Brookings Institution, Edward M. Bernstein, a leading authority on the international monetary system, has taken up his pen against the gold standard.[13] Recently, an historical study of the classical gold standard appeared in the monthly review of the St. Louis Federal Reserve Bank,[14] a widely recognized bastion of monetarism. A critical analysis of the gold standard was contributed by William Fellner to the latest volume of the annual survey of contemporary economic problems published by the

---

[10] Roy W. Jastram, *The Golden Constant: The English and American Experience, 1560–1976* (New York: John Wiley & Sons, 1976).

[11] Roy W. Jastram, "The Gold Standard: You Can't Trust Politics," *Wall Street Journal,* May 15, 1981, p. 32.

[12] Ibid.

[13] Edward M. Bernstein, "Back to the Gold Standard?" *Brookings Bulletin* 17 (Fall 1980): pp. 8–12.

[14] Michael David Bordo, "The Classical Gold Standard: Some Lessons for Today," Federal Reserve Bank of St. Louis *Review* 63 (May 1981): pp. 2–17.

influential American Enterprise Institute,[15] an institution generally sympathetic to monetarist policy prescriptions. Finally, some former and current high-ranking economic policymakers including Herbert Stein,[16] William Nordhaus,[17] and Henry Wallich[18] have made their cases against gold in the popular press.

Despite its newfound respectability, however, the gold standard remains shrouded in an almost impenetrable fog of myths, which were concocted during the Keynesian revolution and the era of the "new economics" that it ushered in. For the most part, these myths have gone unchallenged to this day. As a consequence, the gold standard still remains for most people—and especially for most economists schooled in the current orthodoxy—beyond the pale of rational discussion. Indeed, if questioned on the issue, many laymen as well as economists are capable of reciting a seemingly formidable litany of objections to the gold standard. The result is that gold is usually peremptorily dismissed at the outset of any discussion of monetary policy. This places the gold standard advocate at a severe disadvantage since he must undertake to demythologize an institution before a rational consideration of his policy prescriptions can even begin.

The monetary reformer intent upon presenting the case for the gold standard confronts another problem created by the very ambiguity attaching to the term *gold standard*. This stems from the fact that the term has been used very loosely to denote a number of diverse historical monetary systems and monetary reform proposals in which gold is a key element. Since these gold-based monetary systems differ in much more than minor details, it behooves the monetary reformer—in order to avoid misinterpretation and misplaced

---

[15] William Fellner, "Gold and the Uneasy Case for Responsibly Managed Fiat Money" in idem, ed., *Essays in Contemporary Economic Problems: Demand, Productivity, and Population* (Washington, D.C.: American Enterprise Institute for Public Policy Research, 1981), pp. 92–97.

[16] Herbert Stein, "Professor Knight's Law of Talk," *Wall Street Journal*, October 14, 1981, p. 28.

[17] William Nordhaus, "Gold in the Year of the Quack," *New York Times*, October 4, 1981, section F, p. 3.

[18] Henry C. Wallich, "Should We (and Could We) Return to the Gold Standard?" *New York Times*, September 6, 1981, section E, p. 4.

criticism—to carefully specify the precise nature of the "gold standard" he is proposing.

In what follows, I shall present the main argument for the private, market-chosen, pure-commodity-money standard as represented by the 100 percent gold standard. After briefly delineating its
nature and operation, I shall address the most common objections to
such a standard and to the gold standard in general.

Why a Commodity Money

The case for a free market commodity money such as gold was
trenchantly and succinctly stated by Ludwig von Mises nearly sixty
years ago:

> The reason for using a *commodity* money is precisely to pre-
> vent political influence from affecting directly the value of
> the monetary unit....Gold is the standard money primar-
> ily because an increase or decrease in the available quantity
> is independent of the orders issued by political authorities.
> The distinctive feature of the gold standard is that it makes
> changes in the quantity of money dependent on the profit-
> ability of gold production.[19]

Almost one-half century later, with the government-manip-
ulated, pseudo-gold standard of the Bretton Woods system racked
by inflationary spasms and on the verge of collapse, von Mises elo-
quently restated his argument:

> The quantity of money is the decisive problem. The quality
> that makes gold fit for service as money is precisely the fact
> that the quantity of gold cannot be manipulated by govern-
> ments. The gold standard has one quality, one virtue. It is
> that the quantity of gold cannot be increased in the way that
> paper notes can be increased. The usefulness of the gold stan-
> dard consists in the fact that it makes the supply of money
> depend on the profitability of mining gold, and thus checks
> large-scale inflationary ventures on the part of governments.

---

[19] Ludwig von Mises, *On the Manipulation of Money and Credit*, ed. Percy L.
Greaves, Jr. and trans. Bettina Bien Greaves (Dobbs Ferry, N.Y.: Free Market Books,
1978), p. 22.

Gold cannot be produced in a cheaper way by any governmental bureau, committee, institution, office, international agency, or so on. This is the only justification of the gold standard. One has tried again and again to find some method to substitute these qualities of gold in some other way. But all these methods have failed.

The eminence of the gold standard is to be seen in the fact that the gold standard alone makes determination of the monetary unit's purchasing power independent of the ambitions and activities of dictators, political parties, and pressure groups.[20]

In short, the case for commodity money rests on the fact that it furnishes the only effective bulwark against inflation.

The 100 Percent Gold Standard

Under a pure commodity standard, the monetary unit would be a unit of weight of the commodity chosen by the market as the general medium of exchange. Assuming that the market chose gold—and this need not be the case—the monetary unit would be, e.g., an ounce or a gram of gold. The transformation of the money-commodity into those shapes such as coins which are deemed most useful by buyers and sellers for mediating their exchanges would be performed by private mints competing for profits in a free market. Whatever the various forms in which market participants might prefer to hold gold in their money balances, the total quantity of money in the economy would be rigidly fixed at any moment by the total weight of gold owned by all individuals in the economy. This is true despite the likely development under a pure commodity standard of money substitutes, i.e., claims to money which are tendered and accepted in monetary exchanges in place of the actual money-commodity.

Such claims to money arise when people choose to store a portion of their money holdings in private money warehouses, or "banks," receiving in exchange warehouse receipts, whether in the form of paper tickets or deposits subject to draft by check, entitling them to

---

[20] Ludwig von Mises, *On Current Monetary Problems* (Lansing, Mich.: Constitutional Alliance, Inc., 1969), pp. 29–30.

redeem their gold upon demand. If the money warehouses are generally viewed as reputable firms, then the notes and demand deposits which they issue would begin to function as money substitutes because, under certain circumstances, individual transactors would find it less costly to consummate exchanges without the money-commodity being physically present. The use of money substitutes would, however, have no effect on the quantity of money since, as actual warehouse receipts, they are and legally must be fully "covered" by the gold to which they are instantly redeemable claims. Rather than being a net addition to the money supply, the money substitutes would literally substitute for an equal amount of gold in circulation, with the gold so displaced now locked away in the vaults of the various money warehouses. In less apt but more familiar terminology, the banks would be legally required to maintain 100 percent reserves against all demand liabilities.[21]

The fundamental reason for preferring the 100 percent gold standard to other gold-based proposals for monetary reform is that it is the only monetary system which effects the *complete* separation of the government from the supply of money. Under this system, the money supply process is totally privatized: the mining, minting, certification, and storage of the money-commodity as well as the issuance of fully covered notes and deposits are carried out by private firms operating in a free market. In thus removing all vestiges of the government monopoly over money, the pure commodity standard provides

---

[21] For works detailing the nature and operation of a pure commodity money, see Murray N. Rothbard, *The Case for a 100 Per Cent Gold Dollar* (Washington, D.C.: Libertarian Review Press, 1974), reprinted from idem, "The Case for a 100 Per Cent Gold Dollar," in *In Search of a Monetary Constitution*, ed. Leland Yeager (Cambridge, Mass.: Harvard University Press, 1962), pp. 94–136; Murray N. Rothbard, *What Has Government Done to Our Money?* (Novato, Calif.: Libertarian Publishers, 1978); Milton Friedman, *Essays in Positive Economics* (Chicago: University of Chicago Press, 1970), pp. 206–10; idem, *A Program for Monetary Stability* (New York: Fordham University Press, 1959), pp. 4–8; idem, "Should There Be an Independent Monetary Authority," in Yeager, *In Search of a Monetary Constitution*, pp. 220–24; Jacques Rueff, "The Fallacies of Lord Keynes's General Theory," in *The Critics of Keynesian Economics*, ed. Henry Hazlitt (Princeton, N.J.: D. Van Nostrand Company, Inc., 1960), pp. 242–46; Mark Skousen, *The 100 Percent Gold Standard: Economics of a Pure Money Commodity* (Lanham, Md.: University Press of America, Inc., 1980).

a practically inflation-proof currency. This becomes clearer once it is realized that inflation occurs for no other reason than that it benefits that group or institution—in almost every case the national government—which succeeds in arrogating to itself the legal monopoly over money creation. This requires a few words of explanation.

In a money economy, an individual or organization can obtain a money income in one of two ideal typical ways: via the "economic means" or the "political means." The economic means refers to the voluntary production and exchange of useful goods on the market. The political means, on the other hand, denotes the expropriation of income from the producers—that is, those individuals who have obtained their incomes through the economic means."[22] Taxation, a levy on the incomes of the producers, is an example of the political means and is the method regularly employed by all governments to secure the bulk of their revenues. However, whatever the moral or practical justification of taxation, by virtue of the fact that it is essentially coercive, tax increases have historically found little favor with the citizenry. Fearful of arousing political unrest, governments through the ages have cast about for alternative methods of augmenting their revenues. Having secured the legal monopoly of the supply of money precisely for this reason, it is no wonder that almost all governments have resorted to inflation. For inflation provides its practitioners with a relatively simple, costless, and secure "political" avenue to amassing money assets, one which circumvents the unpopularity connected with the imposition of higher taxes. In substance, all government need do to increase its real income is slap some ink on paper and spend the proceeds on commodities and services produced by the private market. Actually, in the world of modem banking, inflation becomes a much more arcane process little understood by the population at large. This fact serves well to obscure the true cause of inflation and permits the government to shift the blame for the shrinking purchasing power of the monetary

---

[22] This important distinction between the "economic means" and the "political means" of acquiring income was drawn by the German sociologist and economist Franz Oppenheimer. See Franz Oppenheimer, *The State*, trans. John Gitterman (New York: Free Life Editions, Inc., 1975).

unit and the other undesirable consequences of inflation from itself to other groups, e.g., OPEC, monopolistic corporations, powerful nations, spendthrift consumers, etc.

It should be no cause for surprise, then, that all government-monopolized paper fiat currencies exhibit symptoms of inflationary disorder—just as it is no surprise when other groups in the economy exploit political means to augment their money incomes, e.g., via tariffs, occupational licensure, exclusive public franchises, etc. Indeed, it is a frequent observation of sociology as well as a rule of common sense that an individual or group endowed with a legal monopoly over *any* area of the economy will use it to its own best advantage. To put it rather bluntly, government is an inherently inflationary institution and will ever remain so until it is dispossessed of its monopoly of the supply of money.

Indeed, F. A. Hayek, Nobel Laureate in economics, has recently and forcefully argued that the recurring bouts of macroeconomic instability which have always afflicted market economies are "a consequence of the age-old government monopoly of the issue of money."[23] According to Hayek, furthermore:

> There is no justification in history for the existing position of a government monopoly of issuing money. It has never been proposed on the ground that government will give us better money than anybody else could. It has always, since the privilege of issuing money was first explicitly represented as a Royal prerogative, been advocated because the power to issue money was essential for the finance of government—not in order to give us good money, but in order to give to government access to the tap where it can draw money it needs by manufacturing it. That, ladies and gentlemen, is not a method by which we can hope ever to get good money. To put it into the hands of an institution which is protected against competition, which can force us to accept the money, which is subject to incessant

---

[23] F.A. Hayek, *Denationalization of Money—The Argument Refined: An Analysis of the Theory and Practice of Concurrent Currencies*, 2nd enl. ed. (London: The Institute of Economic Affairs, 1978).

political pressure, such an authority will not ever again give us good money.[24]

Certainly, Hayek's insight is amply illustrated in the history of government involvement with money which is, for all practical purposes, the history of inflation. Even a staunch proponent of fiat money and government monetary policy, such as William Fellner, has been reluctantly forced to admit recently that there is a "substantial element of truth involved in the assertion that fiat money has been misused in *all* history—has *always* led to the corruption of the currency."[25] (Emphases are mine.)

And therein lies the fatal flaw in the monetarist program. Aside from any theoretical objections to monetarism, its policy prescriptions completely fail to address the radical (in the etymological sense of "root") cause of inflation in the modern world, viz., the governmental monopolies of the money-supply process which exist in every nation. The monetarist "quantity rule" is not an anti-inflation *policy* at all, but merely the enunciation of a request that the political authorities exercise restraint in exploiting their monopoly, which, under the monetarist program, would remain virtually intact. Such a request, I might add, is incredibly naive in the light of theory and history.

The virtue of the 100 percent gold standard, in contrast, is precisely that it establishes a free market in the supply of money and brings about a complete abolition of the governmental monopoly in this most sensitive and vital area of the market economy. Indeed, although he regards a pure commodity standard as ultimately undesirable because of its high resource cost, Milton Friedman is essentially in agreement with this point. According to Friedman:

> If money consisted wholly of a physical commodity ... in principle there would be no need for control by the government at all....
>
> If an automatic commodity standard were feasible, it would provide an excellent solution to the liberal dilemma of how

---

[24] F.A. Hayek, "Toward a Free Market Monetary System," *Journal of Libertarian Studies* 3, no. 1 (1979): p. 7.

[25] Fellner, "Gold and the Uneasy Case for Responsibly Managed Fiat Money," p. 99.

to get a stable monetary framework without the danger of irresponsible exercise of monetary powers. A full commodity standard, for example, an honest-to-goodness gold standard in which 100 percent of the money consisted literally of gold, widely supported by a public imbued with the mythology of a gold standard and the belief that it is immoral and improper for government to interfere with its operation, would provide an effective control against government tinkering with the currency and against irresponsible monetary action. Under such a standard, any monetary powers of government would be very minor in scope.[26]

It should be emphasized that, while almost any type of a gold standard will yield a far less inflationary monetary system than the present regime of national fiat currencies, all but the 100 percent gold standard ascribe a greater or lesser role to the political authorities in their operation. As I shall argue in greater detail below, these watered-down versions of the gold standard are, as a consequence, dynamically unstable because the government can be expected to take every opportunity to use its predominant position in the system to further water down and undermine the barriers to its inevitably inflationary predilections. Historically, this is borne out by the key role played by the governments of the Western nations in the step-by-step transformation of the relatively noninflationary classical gold standard into the nominally gold-based and highly inflationary Bretton Woods system. This travesty of the gold standard was administered a merciful death in 1971 and, shortly thereafter, a regime of fluctuating national fiat currencies was foisted upon the world economy. It is no coincidence that inflation in most capitalist nations began to accelerate significantly at about the same time.

Although it is, of course, *possible* for the government to engineer an inflationary transformation of the 100 percent gold standard, it is much more difficult than in the case of other gold-based systems. The reason is that under a pure commodity standard every stage of the money-supply process from mining to banking is in private hands. Any steps taken by the state to achieve an initial position of power in this process could not be camouflaged as merely innocuous tinkering

---

[26] Friedman, "Should There Be an Independent Monetary Authority?" pp. 220–22.

with the "rules of the game." Such actions would be easily recognized for what they in fact were—a self-serving assault on private property rights by the government which would more than likely provoke stiff resistance on the part of the populace.

Having made my case for the desirability of the 100 percent gold standard, I shall now attempt to briefly delineate its workings. This will aid in detecting and dispelling the myths underlying a number of the more pervasive and persistent objections to the gold standard.

In order to grasp the functioning of a free market in money, all that is required is a basic understanding of the operation of the venerable supply-and-demand mechanism supplemented by insight into the unique position occupied by money in the sphere of economic goods. To begin with, the function of money is, by definition, to mediate the exchanges of all other goods. People acquire money in exchange for the goods and services which they themselves produce with a view to re-exchanging it for more desired goods and services at some time in the future. The performance of this medium-of-exchange function does not necessitate the physical destruction of the money-commodity. This fact differentiates money from consumers' goods and producers' goods—i.e., capital goods and natural resources, since the latter two are used up in performing their respective functions.

On the other hand, money, like other scarce goods, has a price which at any moment is determined by its supply and demand. Money's price is its purchasing power or command over all other goods for which it exchanges on the market. For example, if the demand for money increases while the supply of money remains unchanged, the purchasing power of money will rise. That is to say, the alternative quantities of other goods for which a given unit of money, such as a gold ounce, exchanges on the market will increase as money prices in the economy undergo a general fall. A rise in the purchasing power of money will also result from a decrease in the supply of money in the face of an unchanged monetary demand. Conversely, a decline in the demand for money or an augmentation of its supply, other things remaining equal, will bring about a decrease in the purchasing power of the monetary unit manifested in a general rise of money prices in the economy.

This brings us to the fundamental respect in which money differs from other economic goods. While increases in the supplies of the various nonmonetary goods in the economy augment the satisfaction of human wants—directly in the case of consumers' goods and indirectly in the case of producers' goods—the same cannot be said of an increase in the supply of money. An addition to the physical number of units of money in the economy will not permit money to discharge its medium-of-exchange function any more fully or expeditiously. The existing quantity of money is always sufficient to yield society the full utility of a medium of exchange. The sole effect of an increase in the supply of money will be a dilution of the purchasing power of the monetary unit or, what is the same thing, a general increase of money prices.

The foregoing analysis equips us to address some of the more common objections to the gold standard and to bare the myths upon which they stand.

One of the charges most frequently brought against the gold standard is that it cannot provide for the monetary needs of a growing economy. Increases in the supply of money, it is said, are necessary to finance the purchases of the increasing quantities of goods and services resulting from economic growth. The gold standard cannot be depended upon to produce the required additions to the money supply at the right times or in the right proportions. The consequence of such monetary deficiency is a stunting of economic growth or possibly even a precipitous depression. It is this reasoning which underlies a popular explanation of the Great Depression as stemming from a worldwide shortage of gold. It has also served as the rationale of governments for their implementation of policies which led to the progressive debilitation and eventual collapse of the classical gold standard in the 1930s. The view that the relative insufficiency of gold constitutes a barrier to economic growth was summed up in the oft-quoted statement of Keynes that, "at periods when gold is available at suitable depths experience shows that the real wealth of the world increases rapidly; and when but little of it is so available, our wealth suffers stagnation or decline."[27]

However plausible, this line of reasoning is untenable because it ignores the supply-and-demand mechanism operative in a free market for money. The market insures that any quantity of money is capable of performing all the work required of a medium of exchange by adjusting its purchasing power to the underlying conditions of supply and demand. The increasing stocks of goods which sellers seek to exchange for money in a growing economy represent an overall increase in the demand for money. Thus, if the quantity of money remains unchanged in the face of a growth in real output, the result will be a general bidding down of prices in the economy and, *pari passu,* an increase in the purchasing power of money. With each unit of money now capable of doing more work in exchange, the same quantity of money will suffice to finance the increased volume of transactions.

It might be added that it is precisely through falling prices that the fruits of increased productivity and economic growth are spread throughout the market economy. For example, if prices in general fall due to a growth in real output, all other things equal, all individuals in the economy will experience a growth in their real incomes despite the fact that their money incomes remain unchanged. If the government, acting under the false belief that a growth in real output necessitates an increase in the money supply, injects new money into the economy, it will counteract the free-market forces leading to a fall in prices, and consequently frustrate the natural market process by which productivity gains are distributed throughout society. The result will be that some groups, especially those who receive the new money first, such as stockholders and workers in defense firms working on government contracts, will appropriate a disproportionate share of the gains at the expense of other groups—pensioners, annuitants, and others whose money incomes are fixed.

The same considerations apply to the objection that the gold standard is not flexible enough to withstand the bouts of hoarding

---

[27] John Maynard Keynes, *The General Theory of Employment, Interest, and Money* (New York: Harcourt, Brace & World, Inc., 1964), p. 132.

which, it is alleged, may spontaneously take hold among consumers and investors in the economy. If not offset by timely injections of new money in the economy, it is argued, such hoarding threatens a shrinkage of expenditure, income, and output which may plunge the economy into a downward spiral of deflation and depression. These fears are groundless, however, because the term "hoarding" denotes nothing more or less than the voluntary decisions of individuals in the economy to reduce their rate of spending in order to increase their money holdings. The result of these decisions is an increase in the aggregate demand for money on the market. If the supply of money is fixed, the increased demand for money will effect a general fall in money prices. Lower prices will translate into a greater purchasing power of the monetary unit, a development which allows the same quantity of money to fulfill people's desires for increased money holdings. Thus "hoarding"—or more properly, an increase in the social demand for money—far from being economically disruptive, is in fact a boon to society. It is the means by which the free market adjusts the purchasing power of individuals' money balances to suit their voluntarily expressed preferences. Once again, any government intervention designed to offset the effects of hoarding merely hampers this market adjustment process and frustrates the desires of money-holders.

This brings us to the criticism that, under the gold standard, the "price level" is unstable. Among other things, this allegedly reduces money's effectiveness as a "measure of value," introducing widespread inefficiency and instability into the economy. For example, unforeseen changes in money's value or purchasing power cause businessmen to err in their anticipations of future costs and prices and in their subsequent allocation of scarce resources. Moreover, such changes effect an unforeseen redistribution of wealth between debtors and creditors.

This objection rests on a basic confusion regarding the nature of money. Simply put, money is not some sort of measuring device whose value is or should be eternally fixed. Money is, in fact, a commodity chosen by the market as a medium of exchange. Like other goods on the market it has a price which fluctuates according to changes in its supply and demand. There is no more justification for government to take steps to render the free market supply-and-demand mechanism inoperative in the case of money than there is in the case of other commodities. In fact, changes in the purchasing power of money have important functions on the market. As we saw above, these include the distribution of the fruits of a growing economy to all the public and the satisfaction of people's desires for changes in their money balances. If the government were to succeed in freezing the purchasing power of money—i.e., in "stabilizing the price level"—money would be rendered incapable of performing these vital functions. In practice, of course, the attempts of modern governments to achieve a stable price level through manipulations of the money supply have succeeded only in seriously destabilizing the economy (witness our present stagflation) while, at the same time, rendering the purchasing power of money much more volatile than it ever was under the classical gold standard.

Furthermore, the desire for a stable "price level" betrays a fundamental misconception of the value of money. As noted above, the value or purchasing power of the monetary unit, say an ounce of gold, is a vast array of alternative quantities of goods and services for which a gold ounce exchanges on the market, e.g., one color television set or four men's suits or one-twentieth of a new automobile, etc. Since the array consists of specific and heterogeneous quantities, it cannot be mathematically manipulated to yield a unitary value such as a "price level." In other words, the value of money is embedded in the specific prices of particular goods and services—e.g., 1 oz. per color television, 1/4 oz. per men's suit, 20 oz. per automobile, etc.

If the value of money cannot be expressed apart from the reality of specific prices paid in specific market transactions, then stabilizing the value of money logically implies freezing all market prices both absolutely and in relation to one another. For it is precisely through the interaction of the supplies and demands for particular goods as expressed in sales and purchases for money that there emerges, at one and the same time and as part of the same process, the exchange value of each good in terms of every other—"relative prices"—and of each good in terms of money—the so-called price level or purchasing power of money. As a result, the "value of money" is inextricably intertwined with *particular money prices* and the two cannot be even conceptually separated. It is therefore meaningless to advocate, as proponents of price level stabilization do, that on the one hand, the value of money or the general level of prices be held constant while, on the other hand, particular prices be left free to vary in relation to one another according to supply and demand.

Of course, those who favor stabilizing the value of money have no desire to see the price of every single good eternally fixed. Instead, they advocate that some arbitrarily chosen statistical index of the prices of selected goods—the consumer price index, the GNP deflator, etc.—be maintained constant through political manipulation of the money supply. Unfortunately, this presents yet another problem. For even if the government possessed the inclination and the ability to implement such a monetary policy, their success in doing so would not suppress fluctuations in the value of money; it would merely alter and distort the structure of particular prices which emerges on the market and through which is reflected the purchasing power of the monetary unit. These distortions in relative prices, furthermore, effect an allocation of investments and resources which is not in accord with the true preferences of consumers and savers in the economy. The result of the continued pursuit of this monetary policy is the piling up of unsustainable malinvestments and resource misallocations which will eventually precipitate a painful but necessary period of liquidation and readjustment for the economy. In sum, every attempt to "stabilize the price level" through governmental monetary policy *inevitably distorts* the free-market pattern of relative prices and *leads to a destabilization* of the entire economy through business cycles, or, in more modern parlance, fluctuations in macroeconomic activity.

Finally, under a free market commodity-money standard, if debtors and creditors truly wished to rid themselves of the uncertainty born of unanticipated changes in the value of money, they could voluntarily avail themselves of the indexing techniques provided by a tabular standard. Under the voluntary tabular standard, the money payments called for in a credit or loan contract would be adjusted according to an agreed-upon index number registering changes in the prices of a selected group of commodities and services. The fact that these voluntary indexing schemes have never been widely resorted to

(except, perhaps, during hyperinflation) should indicate to the stabili-
zationists that, in Murray Rothbard's words:

> Businessmen apparently prefer to take their chances in a
> speculative world rather than agree on some sort of arbitrary
> hedging device. Stock exchange speculators and commodity
> speculators are continually attempting to forecast future prices,
> and, indeed all entrepreneurs are engaged in anticipating the
> uncertain conditions of the market. Apparently, businessmen
> are willing to be entrepreneurs in anticipating future changes
> in purchasing power as well as other changes.[28]

Another oft-repeated criticism of the gold standard is that the
supply of gold, and therefore of money, is determined "arbitrarily,"
depending as it does on such fortuitous factors as discoveries of new
mines and technological improvements in the methods of extraction.
This is surely a curious, if not vacuous, use of the term "arbitrary,"
however, since the supplies of oil and of apples and, for that matter, of
every good produced on the market are influenced by changes in the
availability of resources specific to their production and by improvements in technology. In truth, what these critics are really objecting
to is precisely the greatest virtue of the gold standard: the determination of the supply of money solely by market forces and independently of political considerations. In this context, an examination of
the money-supply process operative under a pure commodity standard will serve to illustrate further the superiority of the gold standard
over a government-monopolized fiat money.

Under the gold standard, the supply of the money-commodity
depends entirely upon the demand for it in monetary and nonmonetary uses and the money costs involved in its production. A change
in either factor brings about a change in the supply of money in the
economy. To delineate the process involved, let us begin from a position of equilibrium in which the supply of and demand for money
and, hence, its purchasing power are constant. In this situation, gold

---

[28] Murray N. Rothbard, *Man, Economy, and State: A Treatise on Economic Principles*, 2 vols. (Los Angeles: Nash Publishing, 1970), Vol. 2, p. 742. For a description
and critique of the tabular standard, see also Edwin W. Kemmerer, *Money: The Principles of Money and Their Exemplification in Outstanding Chapters of Monetary
History* (New York: Macmillan, 1937), pp. 103–07.

mining firms maximize monetary profits by producing a quantity of gold per year just equal to the annual amount allocated to nonmonetary uses plus the amount used up or destroyed in monetary employment during the course of a year as a result of wear and tear.

An improvement in the technology of mining gold or the discovery of new, more accessible sources of gold destroys this initial equilibrium by lowering the costs and, thereby, increasing the profitability of gold production, resulting in an increased annual supply of gold on the market. With an unchanged demand for money, the larger supply of the money-commodity exerts an upward pressure on prices which reduces the purchasing power of money, as each gold ounce now purchases fewer goods and services on the market. Happily, the dilution of the purchasing power of the monetary unit is not the only effect of the augmentation of the supply of gold. A fall in the monetary value of gold also reduces the opportunity costs of employing it in alternative nonmonetary uses like jewelry, dental filling, raw material in industrial processes, etc. As a result, a portion of the additional supply of gold is employed in expanding the supplies of producers' and consumers' goods on the market, thus facilitating an increased satisfaction of human wants.

An increase of the supply of the money-commodity under the gold standard yields net benefits to society assuming there is still a nonmonetary demand for gold. But a government fiat currency, by definition, has no alternative nonmonetary uses. An increase in the supply of a fiat currency, as in the case of counterfeiting, benefits primarily those who create the new money, as well as the initial recipients of their largesse or expenditures, at the expense of the rest of society. Most importantly however, even in the case in which gold has completely lost its value in nonmonetary uses—certainly a theoretical possibility, if not an empirical likelihood—the money-commodity would still involve the use of scarce, and therefore costly, resources. As a result, the 100 percent gold standard provides a natural market brake on the supply of money which is practically immune to tampering by the political authorities.

Furthermore, since gold is an extremely scarce as well as highly durable commodity its annual production tends to be a tiny proportion of the existing stock. Consequently, even relatively large reductions or increases in its costs of production will not cause great fluctuations in the annual supply of money. The significance of the scarcity and durability of gold for the stability of the money supply has been vividly expressed by the monetary theorist, Edwin Kemmerer:

> Largely by reason of its beauty, gold very early in the history of the human race became an object of keen and widespread demand for ornament. The fact, however, that, although gold is found almost everywhere throughout the world, both on land and sea, it usually can be obtained in substantial quantity only by much effort and that nature is very niggardly in her offering of gold to man, except in a few limited parts of the world, makes gold a very scarce commodity. The entire twelve billion dollars of monetary gold in the world today [1935] would represent a cube only about 42.1 feet on a side. A universal demand for gold for ornament and a widespread demand for gold for monetary uses, coupled with this very limited supply, spell scarcity and high values.

> Gold is a very durable metal, especially when alloyed with a baser metal like copper, as it usually is. There is gold in the world today that men extracted from nature thousands of years before Christ. Ancient gold ornaments and coins may be seen in almost any of the world's leading museums. Gold in one form is continually being melted down to reappear in another form. Doubtless there are modern gold coins and gold watches in the world today that contain gold that was dug out of the earth thousands of years ago. Although the permanent losses of gold through abrasion, shipwreck and similar causes, are substantial, it should be remembered that, because of their high value, one's gold possessions are usually guarded carefully. The world's present total known supply of gold, therefore, is the accumulation of the ages. Gold being such a durable object and the world's present stock being the accumulation of the ages, the production of any one year is a small percentage of the total stock. Furthermore, since a large part of the world's known stock of gold—much more than half—is in relatively unspecialized forms, such as coins and bars, forms into which very little labor has been wrought, the major part of the world's accumulated gold at any time is a potential supply on the market. It therefore takes a relatively

long time for changes in the amount of gold produced annually to affect materially the market supply.[29]

Under a pure commodity standard, the supply of money also responds to forces operating on the demand side. For instance, an increase in the demand for money, *ceteris paribus*, effects a general lowering of prices in the economy, including lower prices for the resources employed in mining gold. As a result, the production of gold is rendered more profitable relative to the production of other goods and services. Entrepreneurs respond by increasing the rate of production from currently operational mines, by reopening old mines, and by exploiting for the first time previously known but submarginal sources of gold. They also increase investment in the search for new sources of gold and in the development of new and less costly methods of extraction. In addition, the higher monetary value of gold gives individuals an incentive to shift additional amounts of existing gold from nonmonetary to monetary employments. Thus, an increase in the market demand for money, which is initially satisfied by an increase in the purchasing power of the monetary unit, calls forth a gradual expansion of the supply of money that tends, in the long run, to offset the initial decline in prices and to restore the purchasing power of money to its original level.

Conversely, a fall in the demand for money causes a general rise in prices, and in the process drives up the costs associated with digging up gold. As higher costs reduce the profit margins of gold-mining firms, the production of the metal tends to fall off. Additionally, the lower monetary value of gold induces people to shift some units out of their money balances and into nonmonetary uses, the products of which are now, in effect, purchased more cheaply. The operation of these actors results eventually in a contraction of the supply of money on the market, which tends to reverse the initial rise of prices and re-establish the original purchasing power of the monetary unit.

In summary, under a gold standard, the supply of money does not change arbitrarily but varies directly with monetary demand, resulting in a tendency to long-run stability in the purchasing power

---

[29] Kemmerer, *Money*, pp. 76–77.

of gold. Moreover, in the short term, large fluctuations in the supply of money are precluded by the natural scarcity and durability of gold. Of course, this is not to argue that the gold standard would, or even should, insure perfect stability in the value of money. In fact, as I have argued above, such a goal is chimerical, and all attempts to achieve it in the real world will only create widespread maladjustments and instability in the economy. The point to be made, however, is that the market, when left to its own devices, has chosen and will choose a commodity money whose qualities render its purchasing power sufficiently stable over time to permit market participants to realize the tremendous benefits of indirect exchange and economic calculation which accrue in the form of a tremendously broadened scope for division of labor and specialization and for capital accumulation. As von Mises has noted in this regard:

> The free market has succeeded in developing a currency system which well served all the requirements both of indirect exchange and of economic calculation. The aims of monetary calculation are such that they cannot be frustrated by the inaccuracies which stem from slow and comparatively slight movements in purchasing power. Cash-induced changes in purchasing power of the extent to which they occurred in the last two centuries with metallic money, especially with gold money, cannot influence the result of the businessmen's economic calculations so considerably as to render such calculations useless. Historical experience shows that one could, for all practical purposes of the conduct of business, manage very well with these methods of calculation.[30]

Indeed, the historical record clearly shows that a gold money, even when adulterated with elements of fiduciary media—uncovered bank notes and deposits and government fiat currency—and subject to a variety of government interventions, has maintained great stability in its purchasing power over the long run.[31] Furthermore, it must be realized that any attempt to improve upon the money

---

[30] Ludwig von Mises, *Human Action: A Treatise on Economics*, 3rd rev. ed. (Chicago: Henry Regnery Company, 1966), p. 425.

[31] For abundant evidence of the long-run stability of the purchasing power of gold in English and American monetary experience, see Jastram, *The Golden Constant*.

which emerges spontaneously on the market involves the enormous presumption that the myriad of individual transactors whose decisions and actions have conditioned the market's choice of a money over the ages have consistently and repeatedly erred in assessing the relative benefits and costs of alternative media of exchange. In fact, it is much more likely that the age-old political interference with money, far from improving it, has severely hindered the evolution and improvement of money and monetary institutions which would have occurred naturally on the free market. We cannot even presume to know the direction which such improvement would have taken precisely because, like the institution of money itself, it is the unintended result of a free and spontaneous process of interaction among a multitude of human minds. In Hayek's words:

> The monopoly of government of issuing money has not only deprived us of good money but has also deprived us of the only process by which we can find out what would be good money. We do not even quite know what exact qualities we want because in the two thousand years in which we have used coins and other money, we have never been allowed to experiment with it, we have never been given a chance to find out what the best kind of money would be.[32]

This brings us to the most serious objection to the gold standard. Milton Friedman, among others, has argued that the gold standard "is not desirable because it would involve a large cost in the form of resources used to produce the monetary commodity."[33] Surprisingly, many staunch defenders of the gold standard, from Adam Smith to Ludwig von Mises, have conceded the point to their opponents that the scarce resources expended in the provision of a commodity money represent a pure economic loss to society because these resources are diverted from the satisfaction of human wants. Advocates of the gold standard like von Mises go on to contend, however, that "if one looks at the catastrophic consequences of the great paper money inflations, one must admit that the expensiveness of gold production is the minor

---

[32] Hayek, "Toward a Free Market Monetary System," p. 5.
[33] Friedman, "Should There Be an Independent Monetary Authority?" pp. 223–24.

evil."[34] On the other hand, Opponents of gold urge that the substitution of a "practically costless" and "well-managed" paper fiat currency would yield substantial benefits to society because the productive resources previously tied up in gold mining as well as the monetary stock of gold itself could now be allocated to the production of producers' and consumers' goods, leading to a net increase in human want-satisfaction.

The foregoing is a most persuasive argument which has seduced many good economists out of sound habits of thought. Setting aside for the moment the sociological insight that a legal monopoly of money is inherently inflationary and will never be "well-managed," the flaw in the argument is that it proves too much. Thus, it could be argued, per analogiam, that the enormous diversity in clothing styles and colors on the free market involves a wasteful expenditure of scarce resources which curtails human want satisfaction in other areas. If only a more "rational," i.e., government-monopolized production and distribution system for clothing could be organized, the cost of providing the populace with clothing would be drastically cut. And no doubt the outfitting of the whole population with, say, gray Mao pajamas, would diminish the physical amount of resources devoted to producing clothing in the economy. But any economist worth his salt would reject this preposterous proposal out of hand as hardly optimal from an economic standpoint. Why so? Because he understands that, from the point of view of consumers, gray pajamas are a lower-*quality* clothing than the clothing array available on the market. In other words, the higher level of resource expenditure associated with clothing diversity is economically justified because the increased quality of clothing which results is more highly valued by consumers than the products yielded by alternative employments of the extra resources.

But the same chain of reasoning holds, link for link, in the case of money, which is itself a tangible economic good necessarily possessing qualitative dimensions. The choice of gold by the market, therefore, was not arbitrary but crucially dependent upon its possession

---

[34] Mises, *Human Action*, p. 422.

of certain qualities: general acceptability, natural scarcity, durability, portability, etc., which well suit it to function as the general medium of exchange. On the other hand, since the market has never deemed inconvertible paper tickets issued by one agency to be fit for monetary use, we are forced to conclude that a paper currency is not more efficient than a gold currency in discharging the functions of money *in the relevant economic sense which must necessarily take into account quality considerations.* As a consequence, the substitution of government-monopolized paper money for a free market commodity money must bring about a misallocation of resources which, ipso facto, raises costs in the economy—and this apart from the misallocations caused by the inflation which will almost inevitably follow.

Although the objection to the gold standard on the grounds of its high resource cost was probably first introduced into economics by Adam Smith, it holds a particular allure for modem economists, who tend to theorize in a general equilibrium framework. Since general equilibrium involves the conceptualization of an economy in which the interrelated phenomena of time and economic change are assumed absent, it in effect assumes away the basic reason why people desire to hold money—the uncertainty of the future bred by ceaseless and unforeseen economic change. Needless to say, what is called "money" in this system "is not a medium of exchange; it is not money at all; it is merely a numeraire, an ethereal and undetermined unit of accounting of … vague and undefinable character…."[35] For someone who conceives of money in this way, as an insubstantial accounting fiction, it is quite easy to downplay or altogether ignore the qualitative aspects of the tangible economic good which constitutes the general medium of exchange in the real world.[36] The resource-cost argument

---

[35] Ibid., p. 249.

[36] Very few economists have taken issue with the resource-cost argument against a commodity money. Two who have come to my attention are the nineteenth-century American monetary economist and 100 percent gold standard advocate, Francis Amasa Walker, and the eminent French monetary theorist Charles Rist. Both explicitly attacked the argument on the grounds that it ignores the qualitative aspects of money. See Francis Amasa Walker, *Money* (New York: Augustus M. Kelley Publishers, 1968), pp. 521–28; and Charles Rist, *History of Monetary and Credit Theory: From John Law to the Present Day*, trans. Jane Degras (New York: Augustus M. Kelley Publishers, 1966), pp. 80–90.

against a commodity money thus only has validity in the context of a highly unrealistic theoretical construct where the very conditions of money's existence have been assumed away!

There is one other criticism of the gold standard which, because of its apparently wide acceptance by free-market-oriented economists, also warrants brief mention and response. This criticism, generally leveled by proponents of freely floating exchange rates between national fiat currencies, invokes the prestige of the free market against the international gold standard. Thus, it is alleged by these critics that the gold standard is a fixed-exchange-rate system which requires governments to intervene in the market to "fix" the prices of gold and foreign currencies in terms of the domestic currency. Such governmental price fixing, it is said, disrupts the smooth and efficient operation of the free market in foreign exchange and inevitably results in surpluses and shortages of the various national currencies. Government policies, such as tariffs, quotas, exchange controls, etc., designed to suppress the symptoms of these foreign-exchange disequilibria only breed further distortions and inefficiencies in international trade and investment.

While superficially quite plausible, this argument is based on a fundamental conceptual confusion. For, under a genuine gold standard, national currencies do not exist as separate and distinct entities apart from gold. For example, during the era of the classical gold standard prior to 1914, governments did not "fix" the price of gold in terms of their national currencies; the national currency units, such as the "dollar," "pound," "franc," etc., were themselves merely names for a specific weight of the money-commodity, gold. Thus the dollar was *defined* as $\frac{1}{20}$ ounces of gold, the pound as slightly less than $\frac{1}{4}$ ounces of gold, and so forth. The "rate of exchange" between dollars and pounds was therefore five to one, not as a consequence of government "price fixing," but simply because, by the rules of arithmetic, $\frac{5}{20}$ ounces of gold (five dollars) equals $\frac{1}{4}$ ounces of gold (one pound). In fact, strictly speaking, it is inappropriate to use the concept of an exchange rate when describing the relationship of equivalence between dollars and pounds. The reason is that an exchange rate or price designates a ratio of quantities of two different goods, whereas pounds and dollars denote different weights of the same good, i.e., gold.

Thus, the argument that the international gold standard involves fixed exchange rates between different national currencies is akin to arguing that the present U.S. monetary system involves fixed exchange rates between, say, nickels, dimes, and dollars. That this is not immediately apparent is the unfortunate result of certain peculiarities of the classical gold standard. Under this system, as already noted, the gold currency unit came to bear different names in different nations rather than being denominated by standard weight units such as the gram or ounce, a development which was actively fostered by governments who stood to benefit thereby.[37] Furthermore, monopolization of the note issue and the centralization of gold reserves were achieved by government-controlled central banks. These developments gave rise to the fiction that the notes issued by the central bank and the deposits of private banks denominated in these notes were not merely claims to the actual money-commodity, gold, but were themselves money. As a result, gold came to be viewed as "reserves" or "backing" for the nation's money supply which was "bought" and "sold" by the central bank at a "fixed price" in terms of the national currency unit.

It should be noted that such confusion could not have arisen under a fully private 100 percent gold standard because, in this system standard names of weight are used to designate the currency unit, with the consequence that the absurdity of speaking of an "exchange rate" between a gram of gold and an ounce of gold becomes immediately apparent. Furthermore, since bank notes and deposits are issued solely by private, profit-making institutions, which are not invested with the high authority and prestige of a government central bank, there is little likelihood that people will think that these warehouse receipts for gold are a money that is separate and distinct from gold.

---

[37] On government actions which helped foster the supercession of standard units of weight by national currency names, see Rothbard, *The 100 Percent Gold Dollar*, pp. 12–19.

Bibliography

Barro, Robert J. 1979. "Money and the Price Level under the Gold Standard." *Economic Journal* 89 (March).

Bernstein, Edward M. 1980. "Back to the Gold Standard?" *Brookings Bulletin* 17 (Fall): pp. 8–12.

Bordo, Michael David. 1981. "The Classical Gold Standard: Some Lessons for Today." Federal Reserve Bank of St. Louis *Review* 63 (May): pp. 2–17.

Evans, Rowland and Robert Novak. 1981. "Gold Standard Rears Its Head Again." *New York Post* (August 5): p. 29.

Federal Reserve Bank of St. Louis. 1981. *International Economic Conditions* (August 15).

_____. 1981. *Monetary Trends* (September 25).

Fellner, William. 1981. "Gold and the Uneasy Case for Responsibly Managed Fiat Money." In idem, ed., *Essays in Contemporary Economic Problems: Demand, Productivity, and Population*. Washington, D.C.: American Enterprise Institute for Public Policy Research.

Friedman, Milton. 1959. *A Program for Monetary Stability*. New York: Fordham University Press.

_____. 1970. *Essays in Positive Economics*. Chicago: University of Chicago Press.

Hayek, F.A. 1978. *Denationalization of Money—The Argument Refined: An Analysis of the Theory and Practice of Concurrent Currencies*, 2nd enl. ed. London: The Institute of Economic Affairs.

_____. 1979. "Toward a Free Market Monetary System." *Journal of Libertarian Studies* 3, no. 1.

Jastram, Roy W. 1976. *The Golden Constant: The English and American Experience, 1560–1976*. New York: John Wiley & Sons.

_____. 1981. "The Gold Standard: You Can't Trust Politics." *Wall Street Journal* (May 15).

Kemmerer, Edwin W. 1937. *Money: The Principles of Money and their Exemplification in Outstanding Chapters of Monetary History*. New York: Macmillan.

Keynes, John Maynard. 1964. *The General Theory of Employment, Interest, and Money*. New York: Harcourt, Brace & World, Inc.

Mises, Ludwig von. 1966. *Human Action: A Treatise on Economics*, 3rd rev. ed. Chicago: Henry Regnery Company.

_____. 1969. *On Current Monetary Problems*. Lansing, Mich.: Constitutional Alliance, Inc.

_____. 1978. *On the Manipulation of Money and Credit*, Percy L. Greaves, Jr., ed., Bettina Bien Greaves, trans. Dobbs Ferry, N.Y.: Free Market Books.

Nordhaus, William. 1981. "Gold in the Year of the Quack." *New York Times* (October 4): section F, p. 3.

Oppenheimer, Franz. 1975. *The State*, John Gitterman, trans. New York: Free Life Editions, Inc.

Reuff, Jacques. 1960. "The Fallacies of Lord Keynes's General Theory." In *The Critics of Keynesian Economics*, Henry Hazlitt, ed. Princeton, N.J.: D. Van Nostrand Company, Inc.

Rist, Charles. 1966. *History of Monetary and Credit Theory: From John Law to the Present Day*, Jane Degras, trans. New York: Augustus M. Kelley.

Rothbard, Murray N. 1970. *Man, Economy, and State: A Treatise on Economic Principles*, 2 vols. Los Angeles: Nash Publishing.

_____. 1974. *The Case for a 100 Per Cent Gold Dollar.* Washington, D.C.: Libertarian Review Press. Reprinted from idem, 1962. "The Case for a 100 Per Cent Gold dollar." In *In Search of a Monetary Constitution,* Leland Yeager, ed., pp. 94–136. Cambridge, Mass.: Harvard University Press.

_____. 1978. *What Has Government Done to Our Money?* Novato, Calif.: Libertarian Publishers.

Skousen, Mark. 1980. *The 100 Percent Gold Standard: Economics of a Pure Money Commodity*. Lanham, Md.: University Press of America, Inc.

Stein, Herbert. 1981. "Professor Knight's Law of Talk." *Wall Street Journal* (October 4): p. 28.

Walker, Francis Amasa. 1968. *Money.* New York: Augustus M. Kelley.

Wallich, Henry C. 1981. "Should We (and Could We) Return to the Gold Standard?" *New York Times* (September 6): section E, p. 4.

Wall Street Journal Article. 1981. "Return to an International Gold Standard Opposed by U.S. Panel Majority at Debate." *Wall Street Journal* (October 27): p. 16.

Wall Street Journal Editorial. 1981. "Blaming Volcker." *Wall Street Journal* (October 14).

CHAPTER 13

Gold Standards: True and False[1]

The Basic Characteristics of a Genuine Gold Standard

Expressions of sympathy for gold as a potentially useful device for restraining the more flagrant excesses of the political control of money hardly constitute an endorsement of the overall traditional case for the gold standard. For implicit in the case for gold is a vision of an ideal monetary system in which *government is totally and permanently debarred from manipulating the supply of money.* Under the ideal hard-money regime, the composition, quantity, and value of the commodity used as money is determined exclusively by market forces. In fact, strictly speaking, the advocate of hard money does not favor a gold standard per se, but endorses whatever commodity is chosen by the market as the general medium of exchange. The hard-money program tends to be couched in terms of the gold standard because gold represents the money that emerged in the past from a natural selection process of the free market that spanned centuries.

With this caveat, I now turn to the characteristics of a "real" or "genuine" gold standard as this is construed within the context of the

---

From: "Gold Standards: True and False," in *The Search for Stable Money: Essays on Monetary Reform*, eds. James A. Dorn and Anna J. Schwartz (Chicago: University of Chicago Press, 1987), pp. 241–55.

[1] Reprinted from *Cato Journal* 3 (Spring 1983): pp. 239–67, with revisions.

traditional, or hard-money, case for gold. The defining characteristic of such a monetary system has been incisively identified by Milton Friedman. In his words, "A real, honest-to-God gold standard ... would be one in which gold was literally money, and money literally gold, under which transactions would literally be made in terms either of the yellow metal itself, or of pieces of paper that were 100 per cent warehouse certificates for gold."[2]

Thus, under a genuine gold standard, the monetary unit is, in fact as well as in law, a unit of weight of gold. This is the case whether the monetary unit bears the name of a standard unit of weight, such as a "gram" or "ounce," or whether it bears a special name, like "dollar" or "franc," that designates specifically a standard weight of the commodity used as money.

While it is true that certain types of government intervention in the monetary system are consistent with the basic criterion of a genuine gold standard, it is equally true that no particular government policy is essential to the operation of this monetary standard. Indeed, as Friedman notes, "If a domestic money consists of a commodity, a pure gold standard or cowrie bead standard, the principles of monetary policy are very simple. There aren't any. The commodity money takes care of itself."[3]

---

[2] M. Friedman, "Has Gold Lost Its Monetary Role?" in *Milton Friedman in South Africa*, ed. M. Feldberg, K. Jowell, and S. Mulholland (Johannesburg: University of Cape Town Graduate School of Business and *The Sunday Times*, 1976), p. 34. (Friedman's address was given at the University of Cape Town, 2 April 1976.)

[3] M. Friedman, "Monetary Policy: Theory and Practice," *Journal of Money, Credit, and Banking* 14 (February 1982): p. 99. For works detailing the nature and operation of a pure commodity money, see Murray N. Rothbard, "The Case for a 100 Per Cent Gold Dollar," in *In Search of a Monetary Constitution*, ed. Leland B. Yeager (Cambridge, Mass.: Harvard University Press, 1962), pp. 94–136; idem, *Man, Economy, and State: A Treatise on Economic Principles*, 2 vols. (Los Angeles: Nash Publishing, 1970), vol. 2, pp. 66–764; idem, *What Has Government Done to Our Money?* (Novato, Calif.: Libertarian Publishers, 1978); Milton Friedman, "Real and Pseudo Gold Standards," in *Dollars and Deficits* (Englewood Cliffs, N.J.: Prentice-Hall, 1968), pp. 247–65; idem, *Essays in Positive Economics* (Chicago: University of Chicago Press, 1970), pp. 206–10; idem, *A Program for Monetary Stability* (New York: Fordham University Press, 1959), pp. 4–9; idem "Should There Be an Independent Monetary Authority," in *In Search of a Monetary Constitution*, pp. 220–24; Mark Skousen, *The 100 Percent Gold Standard: Economics of a Pure Money Commodity*

Under the quintessential hard-money regime, therefore, the money-supply process is totally privatized. The mining, minting, certification, and warehousing of the commodity money are undertaken by private firms competing for profits in an entirely unrestricted and unregulated market. The money supply consists of gold in various shapes and weight denominations and claims to gold, in the form of paper notes or checkable demand deposits, that are accepted in monetary transactions as a substitute for the physical commodity money. These money substitutes are literally warehouse receipts that are redeemable for gold on demand at the issuing institutions, which hold a specifically earmarked reserve of gold exactly equal in amount to their demand liabilities. Barring fraud or counterfeiting, the total supply of money in the economy is therefore always equal to the total weight of gold held in the money balances of the nonbank public and in the reserves of the banks.

The total supply of money and the total demand of the public for money balances determine the value or purchasing power of money in terms of other goods and services on the market. Thus, for example, if the demand for money increases while the supply of money remains unchanged, the purchasing power of money rises. That is to say, the alternative quantities of goods and services for which a given unit of money, such as an ounce of gold, can be exchanged increase; or, obversely, the money prices of goods and services undergo a general fall. A rise in the purchasing power of money also results from a decrease in the supply of money in the face of an unchanged demand for money. On the other hand, a decline in the demand for money or an augmentation of its supply, other things remaining equal, brings about a decrease in the purchasing power of the monetary unit manifested in a general rise of money prices in the economy.

Like the purchasing power of money, the quantity of money itself is governed purely by the market conditions affecting the overall demand for and supply of gold. These include the total demand

---

(Lanham, Md.: University Press of America, 1980); and Joseph T. Salerno, "The 100 Percent Gold Standard: A Proposal for Monetary Reform," in *Supply-side Economics: A Critical Appraisal*, ed. Richard H. Fink (Frederick, Md.: University Publications of America, 1982), pp. 458–74 [reprinted here as Chapter 12].

for gold for monetary and nonmonetary uses and the monetary costs involved in producing gold. A change in either factor brings about a change in the quantity of money in the economy.

To see how this occurs, let us begin from a position of equilibrium, in which the supply of and demand for money, and hence its purchasing power, are constant. In this situation, gold-mining firms maximize monetary profits by producing a quantity of gold per year just equal to the annual amount allocated to nonmonetary uses plus the amount used up or destroyed in monetary employment during the course of the year. In this equilibrium situation the net return to a unit of gold, say an ounce, employed in industrial production processes tends to be equal to an equivalent weight of monetary gold.

An improvement in the technology of mining gold or the discovery of new, more accessible sources of gold destroys this initial equilibrium by lowering the costs and thereby increasing the profitability of gold production, resulting in an increased annual output of gold. With an unchanged demand for money, the larger supply of the commodity money exerts an upward pressure on prices that reduces the purchasing power of money, as each gold ounce now purchases fewer goods and services on the market.

The general rise of prices in the economy includes the prices of goods in whose production gold enters as an input, such as jewelry, dental filling, and various electronic products. The result is that a unit of gold employed in industrial processes now yields a net return in terms of monetary gold that is greater than its own weight, and this encourages entrepreneurs to allocate additional quantities of the metal to the production of various consumer and capital goods. The resulting increase in the supplies of these gold products eventually drives their prices down and eliminates the discrepancy between the value of gold in monetary and nonmonetary uses. The absorption of part of the new gold in nonmonetary uses thus serves to temper the effect of the increased output of gold on the money supply. Nonetheless, in the new equilibrium, the supply of monetary gold will have risen, producing a general increase in prices or a reduction in the purchasing power of money.

In the opposite case, in which the costs of producing the monetary metal increase, due for instance to a depletion of the most accessible old ore deposits, the result is a reduction in the annual rate of production of gold. In the long run, this reduction entails a contraction of the industrial uses of gold as well as a decline in the money supply and, hence, a general fall in prices or rise in the purchasing power of money.

While changes in the monetary costs of producing gold, therefore, do have an effect on the money supply, this effect tends to be minimal. The reason is that gold is an extremely scarce as well as a highly durable commodity, and its annual production tends to be a tiny proportion of the existing stock. As a result, even relatively large reductions or increases in the costs of producing gold will not cause great short-term fluctuations in the supply of money.

The quantity of money also responds to forces operating on the demand side. For instance, an increase in the demand for money, other things constant, effects a general lowering of prices in the economy, including the prices of the resources employed in mining gold. Consequently, the production of gold is rendered more profitable relative to the production of other goods and services. Entrepreneurs respond by increasing the rate of production from currently operational mines, by reopening old mines whose continued operation had become unprofitable, and by initiating the exploitation of known but previously submarginal deposits of gold. They also increase investment in the search for new sources of gold and in the development of new and less costly methods of extraction. Furthermore, the higher monetary value of gold gives individuals an incentive to shift additional amounts of existing gold from industrial and consumption uses to monetary employments. Thus, an increase in the market demand for money, which is initially satisfied by an increase in the purchasing power of the monetary unit, calls forth a gradual expansion of the supply of money that tends, in the long run, to offset the initial decline in prices and to restore the purchasing power of money.

Conversely, a fall in the demand for money causes a general rise in prices and, in the process, drives up the costs associated with mining gold. As higher costs reduce the profit margins of gold-mining firms, the production of the metal tends to fall off. Also, the general price rise in the economy spreads to all industrial inputs, including gold, and this stimulates a shift of some units of gold out of money balances and into industrial employments. The operation of these forces eventually results in a contraction of the supply of money that tends to reverse the initial rise of prices and reestablish the original purchasing power of the monetary unit.

The foregoing analysis of the factors governing the quantity and purchasing power of money under a pure commodity standard permits us to lay to rest two persistent and related objections to the gold standard.

The first criticism is that the supply of gold and, therefore, of money is determined "arbitrarily," since it depends on such fortuitous factors as discoveries of new mines and technological improvements in the methods of extraction. This is surely a curious, if not vacuous, use of the term "arbitrary" since the supplies of oil, copper, wheat, and, for that matter, of all goods produced on the market are influenced by changes in the availability of the natural resources required in their production as well as by advances in technology. Moreover, in the specific case of gold, purely fortuitous discoveries of new gold deposits and of improved methods of extraction have long ceased to have a significant effect on the annual output of gold. The regularization of gold production has resulted from the operation of the market itself. In a pathbreaking but unduly neglected article on "Causes of Changes in Gold Supply," Frank W. Paish observed:

> [T]he power of economic forces to accelerate or delay the exhaustion of existing deposits, and to promote or discourage the discovery of new ones, is now so great that changes in the output of gold are now much less "accidental" and much more "induced" than they were half a century ago. Today, indeed, there is no reason to assume that the output of gold is less sensitive to changes in costs than is the output of other commodities.[4]

The second charge frequently brought against the gold standard is that it cannot provide for the monetary needs of a growing

---

[4] Frank W. Paish, *The Post-War Financial Problem and Other Essays* (London: Macmillan, 1950), p. 151.

economy. Increases in the supply of money, it is alleged, are necessary to finance the purchases of the increasing quantities of goods and
services resulting from economic growth. The gold standard cannot
be depended on to produce the required additions to the money supply at the right times or in the right proportions. The consequence of
such monetary deficiency is a stunting of economic growth or possibly even a precipitous depression.

However plausible it may be, this line of reasoning is untenable
because it ignores the mechanism of demand and supply operative
in a free market for money. The market ensures that *any* quantity of
money is capable of performing all the work required of a medium of
exchange by adjusting its purchasing power to the underlying conditions of demand and supply. The increasing stocks of goods that sellers
seek to exchange for money in a growing economy represent an overall increase in the demand for money. Thus, if the quantity of money
remains unchanged while real output grows, then overall prices are
bid down and the purchasing power of money increases. With each
unit of money now capable of doing more work in exchange, the
same quantity of money suffices to finance the increased volume of
transactions.

But this is by no means the end of the process. The general
decline in prices brought about by the increased demand for money
directly stimulates growth in the money supply. On the one hand, it
renders gold mining more profitable. On the other, it causes a fall in
the value of gold in industrial uses. The result is a flow of additional
gold into the money balances of the public from these two sources.
This expansion of the money supply tends to mitigate the fall of prices
in the economy. Under a genuine gold standard, then, the growth in
real output tends to naturally call forth additions to the money supply.

Finally, let me turn my attention to an objection raised specifically against the 100 percent gold standard, usually by proponents
of a gold-based private fractional reserve, or "free," banking system.
It is alleged by these critics that the 100 percent reserve requirement
for banks represents an arbitrary interference with a truly free-market banking system, wherein considerations of profit and loss would

dictate the fraction of its demand liabilities that a bank keeps on hand in gold.

The basic problem with this allegation is that it confuses two very different types of institutions. The first type, let us call it a "bank," operates directly on the money supply. The second, which I shall call a "money market mutual fund" for lack of a better term, influences the money supply only indirectly through its impact on monetary demand. Both of these institutions could and probably would exist as the product of purely private contractual arrangements consistent with a free-market monetary regime. It is the identification of the precise nature of these contractual arrangements that is the key issue here.

In the case of a bank, the 100 percent reserve requirement is not arbitrarily imposed from outside the market, but is dictated by the very nature of the bank's function as a money warehouse. Now, we may not wish to use the name "bank" to designate such an institution, but that is beside the point.

What is important is that if people generally perceived a need, for whatever reason, to store a portion of their money balances outside their own households or businesses, entrepreneurs would invest in the establishment of money warehouses on the free market. For a competitively determined price, such a firm would accept gold deposits and store them under conditions stipulated in the contractual agreement entered into with the depositors. This transaction is not a credit transaction. The depositors' gold is not *loaned* to the money warehouse to dispose of as it sees fit (for a stipulated period of time) but rather is *bailed* to it for the specific purpose of safekeeping. Under the terms of a bailment, the bailor surrenders physical possession of his property to the bailee for a stipulated purpose. Should the bailee use or dispose of the property for any but the specific purposes stipulated in the bailment contract, he would be violating the contract and committing fraud against the bailor.

Thus, a money warehouse operating on the free market is contractually obligated to always maintain in its vaults the entire amount of its depositors' gold. Loaning part of it out at interest to a third party obviously constitutes an infringement of its contractual agreements.

Now things do not change just because the warehouse receipts or money certificates issued by the firm to its depositors, which entitle them to take physical possession of their gold as per terms of the contract, come to be used as money substitutes in exchange. Should the money warehouse print up and loan out additional quantities of (pseudo-) receipts and then honor them by paying out its depositors' gold, it would still be defrauding them even if it took due care to always maintain a reserve of gold more than adequate to meet all their calls for redemption. In the same way, a tailor would be defrauding a customer who left a tuxedo with him to be altered if he rented it out to a third party, even though the tailor took special precautions to insure the tuxedo's availability when the owner showed up with his claim check.

In short, under a free-market monetary regime, banks are required to hold a 100 percent gold reserve for their notes and demand deposits, precisely because these are the contractual terms on which such money substitutes are issued. In this respect, free-market banks would have the same legal obligations as armored car companies do in today's economy. Money is bailed to the latter for the performance of the specific tasks of transportation and temporary storage. I doubt if anyone would seriously suggest that the laws requiring these companies retain in their physical possession the full amount of money for which they have issued receipts constitutes an arbitrary intervention into the free market.

But there is a second type of nonbank institution that would very likely develop and flourish in an unrestricted market for monetary and financial services and that could have a significant, although indirect, effect on the supply of money. The prototype of this institution is the current money market mutual fund.

Unlike banks qua money warehouses, money market funds are not in the business of storing money. Their contractually specified function is to manage a short-term, fixed-income asset portfolio for their investors or shareholders. In effect, each shareholder has title not to a specific sum of money but to a pro rata share of the asset portfolio. Money market fund shares, therefore, are not ownership claims to money but to nonmonetary financial assets that are, for all intents and purposes, maturing daily. Checks written on money market funds are simply orders to the fund's managers to liquidate a specified portion of the investor's share of the portfolio and to pay a third party according to the terms of the contractual agreement between the fund's managers and shareholders.

Under a free-market monetary system, money market funds would not be legally obliged to maintain 100 percent gold reserves or any reserves at all because of the specific contractual arrangements under which they exist and operate. It might be the case, however, that some funds, possibly to appeal to the more risk-averse members of the public, would offer investment portfolios containing a significant proportion of money or warehouse receipts for money. For example, a fund might feature a portfolio that is 20 percent invested in monetary gold. The managers of the fund would then be contractually obligated to always maintain 20 percent of the fund's assets in the form of gold. Whether or not one wishes to refer to such an institution as a "fractional-reserve" bank is not the crucial issue. The important thing for the advocate of a genuine, 100 percent gold standard is that this financial arrangement is, in fact, purely the product of a private contractual agreement and therefore consistent with a free market in money.

If a money market fund's assets are partially in the form of money, its shares represent ownership claims to money balances as well as to nonmonetary financial assets. The fund, in effect, is a hybrid institution operating partly as a money warehouse or bank. Its money assets should therefore be imputed on a pro rata basis to the money balances of its individual shareholders and the total counted in the aggregate money supply.

Not only are money market funds, of the pure or hybrid type, fully in accord with the principles of a genuine gold standard, but, in a denationalized monetary regime, it is not difficult to envision their shares becoming the predominant means of payment in the economy. This would bring about a precipitous fall in the demand for money, and hence for gold in monetary use, and the eventual reallocation of most of the monetary gold stock to nonmonetary employments. Taken to its extreme, this development would result in only a minute fraction of the existing gold stock remaining in monetary employment, solely as a means for clearing balances between money market funds, whose shares would be the only means of payment utilized by the general public.

While I would not expect this extreme scenario to play itself out, it illustrates how market forces might operate to reduce the much-lamented "resource cost" of a genuine gold standard. But in this case, as opposed to that of a government-monopolized paper fiat currency, the cost saving is genuine, because it is produced by the voluntary choices of market participants.

The Gold Price Rule: A Pseudo Gold Standard

In sharp contrast to the proponents of a genuine gold standard, who seek to put an end to government monetary policy by completely denationalizing the money-supply process, the advocates of a gold price rule seek to integrate gold into existing fiat money arrangements in such a way as to improve the conduct of government monetary policy.

For example, economist Alan Reynolds, a staunch supporter of a monetary policy based on a gold price rule, argues: "The purpose of the gold standard is to improve the efficiency and predictability of monetary policy by providing a flexible signal and mechanism for balancing the supply of money with the demand for money at stable prices."[5] Elsewhere Reynolds writes: "The central issue, however, is whether monetary policy is to be judged by clumsy tools, like M1 or by results. When sensitive prices [such as the price of gold] are falling, money is too tight; when prices are rising, money is too loose."[6]

Two other prominent supporters of a gold price rule, Arthur Laffer and Charles Kadlec state that "The purpose of a gold standard is not to turn every dollar bill into a warehouse receipt for an equivalent

---

[5] Alan Reynolds, *Testimony before the United States Gold Policy Commission*, Political and Economic Communications (Morristown, N.J.: Polyconomics, Inc., 1981), p. 15.

[6] Alan Reynolds, "The Monetary Debate: Stabilize Prices, Not Money," *Wall Street Journal* (29 June 1982): p. 26.

amount of gold, but to provide the central bank with an operating rule that will facilitate the maintenance of a stable price level."[7]

What is of overriding significance in the foregoing passages is the explicit or implicit characterization of the gold standard as a mechanism deliberately designed to implement specified policy goals, such as a stable price level, that are aimed at by the government money managers. For it is the underlying conception of the nature and role of money that is implied in this portrayal of the gold standard that ultimately and irreparably divides the modern from the traditional advocates of a gold-based monetary regime. I shall make this point in greater depth after I spell out why the gold price rule is not a genuine gold standard.

Friedman has aptly characterized a pseudo gold standard as "a system in which, instead of gold being money and thereby determining the policy of the country, gold was a commodity whose price was fixed by governments."[8] While Friedman is referring here to the international monetary system between 1934 and 1971, his characterization applies to the various proposals for a monetary regime based on a gold price rule. In fact, proponents of the gold price rule have themselves pointed to the Bretton Woods system as the historical embodiment of the essence of their proposal.[9]

Basically, under a gold price rule, the Fed is charged with fixing the dollar price of gold. However, gold itself is not money but the "external standard" whose price the Fed is to fix in terms of the existing fiat dollar. Nor is it necessary that the Fed itself directly buy and sell dollars for gold to maintain the fixed gold price. The "intervention asset," that is, the asset which the Fed trades on the market for gold, may just as well be U.S. government securities or foreign exchange or any commodity. All that is required of the Fed is that it sell some assets for dollars on the open market when the price of gold rises,

---

[7] Arthur B. Laffer and Charles W. Kadlec, "The Point of Linking the Dollar to Gold," *Wall Street Journal* (13 October 1981): p. 32.

[8] Friedman, "Has Gold Lost Its Monetary Role?" p. 36.

[9] See, for example, Robert A. Mundell, "Gold Would Serve into the 21st Century," *Wall Street Journal* (30 September 1981): p. 32.

thus deflating the supply of money and bringing the gold price back to its "target" level. If the price of gold begins to fall, the Fed is to purchase gold or other assets on the market, creating an inflation of the supply of dollars that drives the price of gold back up to its target level.

By using the gold price as a proxy for the general price level, the advocates of a price-rule regime thus hope to stabilize the purchasing power of the fiat dollar. While some of its supporters have made vague references to the desirability of getting gold coin into circulation,[10] it is clear that the gold price rule is not meant to provide a genuine gold money.

In fact, gold itself need not play any role at all in the price-rule regime. As Arthur Laffer and Marc Miles point out, the external standard "could be a single commodity or a basket of commodities (a price index)."[11] Indeed, recently there have been calls for the Fed to institute a price rule targeting an index of spot commodity prices.[12]

Stripped of its gold-standard terminology, the price rule can be seen as a technique designed to guide the monetary authorities in managing the supply of fiat currency. It is thus very similar in nature, if not in technical detail, to the quantity rule advocated by the monetarists. This is clearly evident in Laffer and Miles's admission that "in an unchanging world where all information is freely available, there of course would be a 'quantity rule' which would correspond to a given 'price rule.'"[13]

What may be called "price-rule monetarism," then, is vulnerable to criticism on precisely the same grounds as the more conventional quantity-rule monetarism. The most serious criticism of both varieties of monetarism is that they fail to come to grips with the root cause of inflation, namely, the government monopoly of the

---

[10] Mundell, "Gold Would Serve," p. 32; Arthur B. Laffer, *Reinstatement of the Dollar: The Blueprint* (Rolling Hills Estates, Calif.: A.B. Laffer Associates, 1980), p. 7.

[11] Arthur B. Laffer and Marc A. Miles, *International Economics in an Integrated World* (Oakland, N.J.: Scott, Foresman and Co., 1982), p. 399.

[12] See Reynolds, "The Monetary Debate," p. 26; and Laffer and Kadlec, "Has the Fed Already Put Itself on a Price Rule?" *Wall Street Journal* (28 October 1982): p. 30.

[13] Laffer and Miles, *International Economics*, p. 401.

supply of money. The built-in inflationary bias of the political process virtually guarantees that both quantity and price rule targets will be ignored or revised when they become inconvenient to the government money managers.

We may appeal to history for evidence regarding the success of the gold price rule in stanching the flow of government fiat currency. We need look no further than the late, unlamented Bretton Woods system (1946–71). Under this "fixed-exchange-rate" system, the U.S. monetary authority followed a gold price rule, buying and selling gold at an officially fixed price of $35 per ounce. Foreign monetary authorities, on the other hand, pursued a dollar price rule, maintaining their respective national currencies convertible into dollars at a fixed price. According to Laffer and Miles, "as long as the rules of the system were being followed, the supplies of all currencies were constricted to a strict price relationship among one another and to gold."[14]

Unfortunately, "the rules of the system" were subjected to numerous and repeated violations and evasions, including frequent outright readjustment of the price rules, i.e., exchange-rate devaluations, when they became inconvenient restraints on the inflationary policies pursued by particular national governments. Needless to say, the Bretton Woods system did not prevent the development of a worldwide inflation which brought the system to its knees in 1968 and led to its final collapse in 1971.

Money: Policy Tool or Social Institution?

From this brief overview of the gold price rule, it is evident that its proponents accept the currently prevailing view of money as a "tool" of government policy. According to this view, the monetary system is or ought to be deliberately and rationally constructed so as to promote as efficiently as possible the attainment of the various macro-policy goals sought by government planners. These policy goals are formulated and ranked in accordance with criteria that are developed independently of, and often in conflict with, the valuations and

---

[14] Ibid., p. 260.

choices of market participants as these are expressed in the pattern of prices and quantities that spontaneously emerge in the free-market economy. From this standpoint, the degree to which a particular monetary policy is judged to be "optimal" depends on the extent to which it succeeds in altering the spontaneous microeconomic processes of the economy to yield macro-statistical outcomes that are consistent with the planners' chosen policy goals.

Thus, those who defend the gold standard on the basis of its superiority or optimality as a technique of monetary policy differ little from the supporters of fiat money in their mode of argumentation. Both sides direct their arguments almost exclusively to the question of what means, that is, what monetary policy, is best suited to achieve certain identifiable and quantifiable macro-policy goals whose desirability—except for possible differences regarding weighting and statistical expression—is not subject to dispute.

The widely accepted goals that a successful monetary policy is supposed to achieve include: a stable value of the monetary unit or, more accurately, constancy of some selected price index, e.g., the CPI, the GNP deflator, or an index of spot commodity prices; the mitigation of cyclical fluctuations via the stabilization of various statistical aggregates and averages, such as the unemployment rate, the GNP index, the index of industrial production, and others; the maintenance of a high rate of secular growth in real output, once more as gauged by the behavior of selected statistical indicators; and stability of "real" interest rates.

Whether or not free-market processes should be modified in the service of such extra-market macro-policy goals by government manipulation of the supply of money—that is, whether or not government should conduct a monetary policy at all—is a question never addressed by those who regard money as a political tool deliberately and specifically fashioned for such a use.

In sum, the arguments of the policy-oriented advocates of gold are founded upon a presumption which they share in common with their anti-gold opponents and which hard-money advocates emphatically reject. This presumption is that money is a mechanism consciously designed and constructed to serve certain known purposes.

These purposes are those of a small group of individuals acting in concert, namely government planners, and are therefore limited in number, subject to a unitary and consistent ranking and capable of being readily communicated to those undertaking the design of the monetary system. Following Hayek, the attitude toward monetary institutions to which this presumption gives rise may be designated "constructivism."[15]

The constructivist approach to the nature and function of money is logically bound up with a particular view of the origin of money. According to this view, money originated in an extra-market social agreement or legal fiat as a useful convention consciously designed to overcome the perceived problems and inefficiencies of direct exchange.

It should be emphasized here that the basic point at issue between the monetary constructivists and those advocates of the gold standard who adopt a Mengerian perspective[16] is not the normative one of whether money *ought* to be a tool of policy or an integral element of the market process but the existential one of whether money *is* one or the other. In affirming that money is in fact a market institution, hard-money advocates do not mean to deny that money can be subjected to political control, just as they would not wish to deny that market prices and interest rates can be controlled by the political authorities. Indeed, Menger himself pointed out that "legislative compulsion not infrequently encroaches upon this 'organic' developmental process [of money's emergence] and thus accelerates or modifies

---

[15] For illuminating critiques of the constructivist approach to social phenomena, see Hayek, "Kinds of Rationalism," in idem, *Studies in Philosophy, Politics and Economics* (New York: Simon and Schuster, 1969), pp. 82–95; and idem, "The Errors of Constructivism," in idem, *New Studies in Philosophy, Politics, Economics and the History of Ideas* (Chicago: University of Chicago Press, 1978), pp. 3–22.

[16] Carl Menger demonstrated that money is an "organic" or "unintentionally created" social institution that is "the unintended result of innumerable efforts of economic subjects pursuing individual interests." Menger, *Problems of Economics and Sociology*, ed. Louis Schneider, trans., Francis J. Nock (Urbana: University of Illinois Press, 1963), p. 158. For a detailed account of the Mengerian perspective on money, see Gerald P. O'Driscoll, Jr., "Money: Menger's Evolutionary Theory," *History of Political Economy* 18 (Winter 1986): pp. 601–16.

the results."[17] But this is precisely the crux of the hard-money, or traditional, case for gold.

In the same way that price controls alter the "quality" of the affected prices, government monetary policy impinges on the "quality" of the institution of money. A price that is set by bureaucratic fiat ceases to provide market participants with relatively quick and accurate information regarding changes in present and future economic conditions, and also ceases to provide the incentives needed to induce actions in accordance with this information. Such a controlled price introduces an element of discoordination into the market economy. The most obvious manifestation of this discoordination is the failure of the plans of buyers and sellers to match, as reflected in surpluses or shortages of the good in question.

Now, it may well be that the state of affairs that develops under the stimulus of the price control is, at least temporarily, consistent with government policy goals, as was the case in the United States during the "gasoline shortages" of the 1970s. Nevertheless, in terms of its social coordinating function, as opposed to its function as a policy tool, it is also quite clear that the controlled price is qualitatively inferior to its free-market counterpart. In other words, in attempting to deliberately transform a spontaneous market price into a tool for realizing their own extra-market objectives, government planners render that price much less fit to serve the diverse and multitudinous ends pursued by market participants.

Analogously, when the political authorities arrogate to themselves a legal monopoly of issuing money, the character of the money supply process undergoes a radical transformation. The government fiat-money managers are not in a position to receive the same information as free-market money suppliers pertaining to changes in the conditions affecting the demand for and production of the commodity money. Nor, as de facto monopolists, do they confront the incentives that would induce them to respond appropriately to such knowledge even if they could somehow miraculously obtain it. The upshot is that market participants receive an inferior-quality, and

---

[17] Menger, *Problems of Economics*, p. 157.

inexorably inflated, medium of exchange that tends to greatly impair the coordination, and hence achievement, of their individual purposes. This is the case even if, in contradiction to the lessons of theory and history, we assume that government money managers foreswear inflation and succeed in achieving their announced macro-statistical policy objectives, such as a stable price level and "full employment." The reason is that money and monetary policy are not "neutral" to the constituent macroeconomic processes and quantities of the overall economy. Manipulating the supply of money to insure a particular aggregate statistical outcome, therefore, inevitably has an impact on these processes and quantities, diverting resources from those uses that are in accordance with consumers' preferences.

Bibliography

Friedman, Milton. 1959. *A Program for Monetary Stability.* New York: Fordham University Press.

_____. 1968. "Real and Pseudo Gold Standards." In *Dollars and Deficits.* Englewood Cliffs, N.J.: Prentice-Hall.

_____. 1970. *Essays in Positive Economics.* Chicago: University of Chicago Press.

_____. 1976. "Has Gold Lost Its Monetary Role?" In *Milton Friedman in South Africa*, M. Feldberg, K. Jowell, and S. Mulholland, eds. Johannesburg: University of Cape Town Graduate School of Business and *The Sunday Times.* (Friedman's address was given at the University of Cape Town, 2 April 1976.)

_____. 1982. "Monetary Policy: Theory and Practice." *Journal of Money, Credit, and Banking* 14 (February).

_____. 1962. "Should There Be an Independent Monetary Authority?" In *In Search of a Monetary Constitution*, L.B. Yeager, ed. Cambridge, Mass.: Harvard University Press.

Hayek, A.K. 1969. "Kinds of Rationalism." In idem, *Studies in Philosophy, Politics, and Economics.* New York: Simon and Schuster.

_____. 1978. "The Errors of Constructivism." In idem, *New Studies in Philosophy, Politics, Economics and the History of Ideas.* Chicago: University of Chicago Press.

Laffer, Arthur B. 1980. *Reinstatement of the Dollar: The Blueprint.* Rolling Hills Estates, Calif.: A.B. Laffer Associates.

Laffer, Arthur B., and Charles W. Kadlec. 1981. "The Point of Linking the Dollar to Gold." *Wall Street Journal* (13 October): p. 32.

_____. 1982. "Has the Fed Already Put Itself on a Price Rule?" *Wall Street Journal* (28 October): p. 30.

Laffer, Arthur B., and Marc A. Miles. 1982. *International Economics in an Integrated World.* Oakland, N.J.: Scott, Foresman and Co.

Menger, Carl. 1963. *Problems of Economics and Sociology*, Louis Schneider, ed., Francis J. Nock, trans. Urbana: University of Illinois Press.

Mundell, Robert A. 1981. "Gold Would Serve into the 21st Century." *Wall Street Journal* (30 September): p. 32.

O'Driscoll, Gerald P. 1986. "Money: Menger's Evolutionary Theory." *History Of Political Economy* 18 (Winter): pp. 601–16.

Paish, Frank W. 1950. *The Post-War Financial Problem and Other Essays.* London: Macmillan.

Reynolds, Alan. 1981. *Testimony before the United States Gold Policy Commission*, Political and Economic Communications. Morristown, N.J.: Polyconomics, Inc.

_____. 1982. "The Monetary Debate: Stabilize Prices, Not Money." *Wall Street Journal* (29 June): p. 26.

Rothbard, Murray N. 1962. "The Case for a 100 Per Cent Gold Dollar." In *In Search of a Monetary Constitution*, Leland B. Yeager, ed. Cambridge, Mass.: Harvard University Press.

_____. 1970. *Man, Economy, and State: A Treatise on Economic Principles*, 2 vols. Los Angeles: Nash Publishing.

_____. 1978. *What Has Government Done to Our Money?* Novato, Calif.: Libertarian Publishers.

Salerno, Joseph T. 1982. "The 100 Percent Gold Standard: A Proposal for Monetary Reform." In *Supply-Side Economics: A Critical Appraisal*, Richard H. Fink, ed. Frederick, Md.: University Publications of America.

_____. 1983. "Gold Standards: True and False." Reprinted, with revisions, from *Cato Journal* 3 (Spring): pp. 239–67.

Skousen, Mark. 1980. *The 100 Percent Gold Standard: Economics of a Pure Money Commodity.* Lanham, Md.: University Press of America.

CHAPTER 14

The Gold Standard:
An Analysis of
Some Recent Proposals

Introduction

The case for a free-market commodity money as provided by a genuine gold standard is simple yet decisive. It is based on the insight that the root cause of inflation in the modern world is the almost absolute monopoly over the supply of money which all national governments possess within their respective political jurisdictions. That such an arrangement necessarily produces inflation is not difficult to explain.

To begin with, almost all governments obtain the bulk of their revenues through taxation, which, regardless of its particular form, ultimately involves—indeed, is definable as—a coerced levy upon the monetary incomes or assets of its citizens, i.e., the net taxpayers. Whatever ethical or practical considerations may be brought forward to justify taxation, tax increases have always found little favor among the citizenry since they are essentially coercive. So, ever fearful of arousing popular unrest, governments have naturally sought alternative means for augmenting their revenues from taxation. It was

From: The Gold Standard: An Analysis of Some Recent Proposals, Policy Analysis Occasional Paper (Washington, D.C.: Cato Institute, 1982), 28 pages.

for this purpose that all national governments eventually secured for themselves a legal monopoly of issuing money, which empowered them to inflate, i.e., to create new money, virtually at will.

Especially under today's various national fiat-money standards, inflation provides a relatively simple, costless, and secure means for amassing money assets. In substance, all a government needs to do to increase its real income is slap some ink on paper and spend the proceeds on commodities and services produced by the private market. In this way, the national government is able to divert scarce resources from private uses and utilize them for its own purposes, while circumventing the popular discontent which invariably accompanies an overt imposition of higher taxes. Actually, in the world of modern monetary and financial institutions and practices, inflation entails a much more arcane process than the mere printing and spending of new units of currency. This fact obscures the true cause of inflation from the public and permits the government to shift the blame for the monetary unit's shrinking purchasing power and other undesirable consequences of inflation from itself to other groups or to circumstances beyond its control: OPEC, monopolistic corporations, powerful labor unions, spendthrift consumers, unfavorable weather conditions, etc.

In a nutshell, those who advocate a gold standard argue that governments are inherently inflationary institutions and, therefore, the only realistic and lasting solution to the problem of inflation is to completely separate the government from money and return the latter institution to the free market whence it originally emerged. Recently a number of mainstream economists have begun to re-evaluate the gold standard as a means of restraining the inflationary propensity of governments. Some have even proposed that gold once again be given a role in the U.S. monetary system.

Proposals for a Gold Standard

We now turn to a critical examination of several of these proposals. Although the plans to be considered vary significantly in basic conception as well as in the details, all but one suffer, to a greater or lesser degree, from the same fundamental flaw: they leave intact the current government monopoly of money. For purposes of discussion, these monetary reform proposals may be grouped under four headings: the gold-certificate reserve, the gold "price rule," the classical gold standard, and the parallel private gold standard.

The Gold-Certificate Reserve

Robert E. Weintraub, senior economist for the Joint Economic Committee, has proposed the reinstatement of the gold-certificate reserve requirement for Federal Reserve notes.[1] Under Weintraub's plan, the Fed would be legally required, as it was prior to 1968, to maintain a reserve of gold certificates whose value, at a stipulated legal price of gold, would be a fixed proportion of its outstanding note liabilities. Before 1968, when the legal or "par" value of gold was $35 per ounce, the reserve requirement was 25 percent, and so, in effect, each dollar of currency in circulation was "backed" by 25 cents in gold. Weintraub's plan "would require that the Federal Reserve banks hold at least 9 cents in gold certificates at their legal value [$42.22 per ounce since 1973] behind each dollar of note liabilities in perpetuity."[2] The nine percent reserve requirement reflects the ratio of par value gold certificates held by the Fed to its note liabilities prevailing at the end of 1980.

According to Weintraub:

> Legislation to keep the percent of legal value gold certificates behind Federal Reserve notes what it was at the end of 1980 in perpetuity would prevent any future currency growth. And, unless the public wanted to hold an increasing part of its total transactions balances (currency plus checking deposits in depository institutions) in the form of checking deposits,

---

[1] U.S. Congress, Joint Economic Committee, The Gold Standard: Its History and Record Against Inflation, by Roy W. Jastram, with an Appendix on "Restoring the Gold Certificate Reserve," by Robert E. Weintraub (Washington, D.C.: Government Printing Office, 1981), pp. 21–24. Weintraub's plan is also described in Lindley H. Clark, Jr., "What Kind of a Gold Standard is Needed?" Wall Street Journal (August 18, 1981): p. 33.

[2] Weintraub, "Restoring the Gold Certificate Reserve," p. 21.

preventing currency growth would prevent any future growth
in the transactions or exchange media measure of money.[3]

However, Weintraub finds such a result undesirable because
he believes that some growth in the money supply is necessary "to
accommodate our economy's long-term growth potential."[4] His proposal, therefore, includes a provision for increasing the legal value of
gold, which would initially be set at the current $42.22 per ounce, at
a stipulated monthly rate. This would bring about an effective expansion in the Fed's reserve of gold certificates and permit a corresponding increase in the currency in circulation and, hence, in the overall
money supply. Weintraub favors an annual rate of increase in the par
value of gold which would ultimately facilitate a three percent per
annum rate of growth in the supply of money.

Weintraub expresses the belief, moreover, that "the plan should
prove attractive to both monetarists and gold standard advocates."[5] In
fact, it should appeal to neither group and for good reason.

To begin with, Weintraub's plan is essentially an attempt to realize through legislation the monetarist goal of a steady and predictable rate of growth of the money supply within the existing fiat-money
framework. Its main drawback, from the monetarist perspective, is
that it involves a needlessly complicated and cumbersome technique
to achieve the desired goal. Why not simply legally mandate the Fed
to pursue a straightforward "quantity rule," as the monetarists have
always argued? Weintraub does not provide an answer to this question.

Advocates of a gold standard, on the other hand, also should
find little to be pleased about in this proposal because a gold-certificate reserve requirement is not a genuine gold standard at all. Under
the gold standard, the monetary unit is a weight unit of gold; under
Weintraub's plan, gold is not money but a reserve commodity which is
supposed to restrain the creation of government fiat money. Furthermore, since Weintraub's proposal leaves untouched the government
monopoly of the money supply, it is unreasonable to expect that the

---

[3] Ibid., p. 22.

[4] Ibid.

[5] Ibid., p. 24.

gold-certificate reserve requirement, even if enacted, would long serve as a bulwark against inflation. The most likely prospect is that it would be gradually reduced and finally eliminated altogether, no doubt in the wake of a series of "emergencies." Indeed, Weintraub fully recognizes and is prepared for such a prospect, arguing that his plan "could be amended if the constraint proved to be harmful, and probably it could be changed or repealed in a day or two in such unlikely case."[6] Needless to say, this hardly recommends it as a durable barrier against inflation.

Moreover, past experience with the gold certificate reserve also leads to the expectation that it would provide a weak and easily manipulated restraint on inflation. Thus, up until World War II, the Fed was legally required to hold a 35 percent gold certificate reserve for its deposit liabilities and a 40 percent reserve for its note liabilities. To facilitate the wartime inflation, the reserve requirement was reduced to 25 percent for both the Fed's note and deposit liabilities. As a result of persistent, inflation-induced balance-of-payments deficits, the gold-certificate reserve requirement for the Fed's deposit liabilities was abolished in 1965, while the reserve requirement for its note liabilities was finally eliminated in 1968.

In conclusion, what Weintraub proposes is not a gold standard but an unwieldy and historically ineffective expedient designed to mitigate the inflationary tendencies of a government fiat money.

The Gold "Price Rule"

The gold "price rule" denotes the monetary reform proposal put forth in various forms by a number of supply-siders, including Arthur Laffer,[7] Robert Mundell,[8] and Jude Wanniski.[9] Laffer's

---

[6] Clark, "What Kind of a Gold Standard Is Needed?"

[7] Arthur Laffer, *Reinstatement of the Dollar: The Blueprint* (Rolling Hill Estates, Calif.: A.B. Laffer Associates, 1980). Also see Arthur B. Laffer and Charles W. Kadlec, "The Point of Linking the Dollar to Gold," *Wall Street Journal* (October 13, 1982): p. 32.

[8] Robert A. Mundell, "Gold Would Serve into the 21st Century," *Wall Street Journal* (September 30, 1981): p. 33.

[9] Jude Wanniski, *The Way the World Works* (New York: Simon and Schuster, 1978), especially pp. 161–67. See Wanniski, "A Job Only Gold Can Do," *New York Times* (August 27, 1981): p. A31.

detailed formulation of the proposal has also served as the basis of the Gold Reserve bill, introduced in the Senate by Jesse Helms in January 1981.[10]

According to Laffer's blueprint, at the end of a previously announced transition period of three months, the Federal Reserve would establish an official dollar price of gold "at that day's average transaction price in the London gold market."[11] From that date onward, the Fed would stand ready to freely convert dollars into gold and gold into dollars at the official price. In addition, "when valued at the official price, the Federal Reserve will attempt over time to establish an average dollar value of gold reserves equal to 40 percent of the dollar value of its liabilities."[12] This level of gold reserves Laffer designates the "Target Reserve Quantity."

Once Laffer's plan was fully operational, the Fed would have full discretion in conducting monetary policy through discounting, open market operations, etc., provided that: the dollar remains fully convertible into gold at the official price; and the quantity of actual gold reserves does not deviate from the Target Reserve Quantity by more than 25 percent in either direction, i.e., actual gold reserves do not fall below 30 percent or rise above 50 percent of the Fed's liabilities, which are also known as the "monetary base." However, should gold reserves decline to a level between 20 percent and 30 percent of its liabilities, the Fed would lose all discretion in determining the monetary base which, as a result, would be completely frozen at the existing level. If, in spite of this, gold reserves continued to decline to between 10 percent and 20 percent of the Fed's liabilities, the Fed would be legally constrained to reduce the monetary base at the rate of one percent per month.

> Should these measures prove incapable of arresting the decline in the dollar value of gold reserves before it reaches less than 10 percent of Fed liabilities, then:

---

[10] The text of Helms' bill is reproduced in Ernest P. Welker, "Plans to Revive the Gold Standard," *Economic Education Bulletin* 20, no. 10 (Great Barrington, Mass.: American Institute for Economic Research, 1980), pp. 7–9.

[11] Laffer, *Reinstatement of the Dollar*, p. 4.

[12] Ibid.

> The dollar's convertibility will be temporarily suspended and the dollar price of gold will be set free for a three month adjustment period.
>
> During this temporary period of inconvertibility, the monetary authorities will be required to suspend all actions that would affect the monetary base. Again, the price of gold would be reset as before and convertibility would be reinstated.[13]

Laffer's plan also includes "a symmetric set of policy dicta" which are to be implemented in the case in which actual gold reserves exceed the Target Reserve Quantity.

It must first be pointed out that Laffer's monetary reform proposal, whatever its merits or drawbacks, is not a blueprint for the gold standard. Rather, it is an outline of an elaborate scheme for legally constraining the monetary authority to adhere to a "price rule" in determining the supply of fiat money in the economy. In fact, as Laffer himself has made clear recently, gold has no necessary role in the implementation of such a price rule. According to Laffer and Miles:

> ... the Fed would institute its dollar "price rule" by stabilizing the value of the dollar in terms of an external standard. This standard would be a single commodity or a basket of commodities (a price index)....
>
> Regardless of precisely which external standard is chosen, there are two basic rules of Fed behavior under the price rule. First, if the dollar price of the standard starts to rise (the dollar starts to fall in value), the Fed must reduce the quantity of dollars through open market sales of bonds, foreign exchange, gold, or other commodities. Second, if the dollar price starts to fall (the dollar rises in value), the Fed must increase the quantity of dollars through open market purchases of bonds, foreign exchange, gold or other commodities. The Fed is charged with keeping the value or price of the dollar stable in terms of the external standard.[14]

---

[13] Ibid., p. 5.

[14] Arthur B. Laffer and Marc A. Miles, *International Economics in an Integrated World* (Glenview, Ill.: Scott, Foresman and Co., 1982), pp. 399–400.

Even if gold is chosen as the "external standard" in the price-rule regime, it is not itself money, as in the case of a genuine gold standard, but merely "the intervention asset" or "the item for which dollars are exchanged."[15]

When we strip away its gold plating, Laffer's price rule appears as a technique designed to control inflation under the current fiat-money standard. It is thus differs only in technical detail from the quantity rule advocated by the monetarists. Laffer and Miles admit as much when they state, "in an unchanging world where all information is freely available, there of course would be a 'quantity rule' which would correspond to a given 'price rule.'"[16] In fact, Miles and Laffer prefer a price rule to a quantity rule because they believe that, under the current monetary system, the former is technically superior to the latter in "restraining the supply of dollars."[17]

Under close examination, Laffer's plan thus turns out to be, in essence, a kind of "price-rule monetarism," the references to gold notwithstanding. The most serious defect in both variants of monetarism is that they fail to address the underlying cause of inflation, namely, the government monopoly of the supply of money. This is true of Laffer's plan despite the elaborate set of legal sanctions which would be invoked against the monetary authorities for their violations of the price rule. For, in the end, such sanctions, even if rigorously applied, do not prevent inflation but merely respond to a fait accompli. This point is implicitly recognized by Laffer, who includes in his plan a provision for "temporary periods" of dollar inconvertibility. These would readjust the official gold price following sustained bouts of monetary inflation which cause gold reserves to fall below the legally permissible lower limit.

Furthermore, as in the case of the gold certificate reserve, we may appeal to history for evidence regarding the success of the gold price rule in stanching the flow of government fiat currency. We need look no further than the late, unlamented Bretton Woods System

---

[15] Ibid., p. 400.

[16] Ibid., p. 401.

[17] Ibid.

(1946–1971). Under this "fixed-exchange-rate" system, the U.S. monetary authority followed a gold price rule, buying and selling gold at an officially fixed price of $35 per ounce. Foreign monetary authorities, on the other hand, pursued a dollar price rule, maintaining their respective national currencies convertible into dollars at a fixed price. According to Laffer and Miles, "as long as the rules of the system were being followed, the supplies of all currencies were constricted to a strict price relationship among one another and to gold."[18]

Unfortunately, "the rules of the system" were subjected to numerous and repeated government violations and evasions, including frequent outright "readjustment" of the price rules, i.e., exchange-rate devaluations, when they became inconvenient restraints on the inflationary policies pursued by particular governments.[19] Needless to say, the Bretton Woods System did not prevent the development of a worldwide inflation which brought the system to its knees in 1968 and led to its final collapse in 1971.

After duly noting the political manipulations involved in the destruction of the Bretton Woods System,[20] Laffer and Miles clearly delineate the reasons why governments prefer and benefit from the removal of any and all checks on their power to inflate the money supply:

> Why should governments be biased toward increasing the money supply at a faster rate? There are essentially two incentives—a political incentive and a financial one. The political incentive is political survival. Many politicians, especially those up for reelection, are familiar with the theory that increases in the money supply promote expenditure, increase GNP, and reduce unemployment. These changes in turn are assumed to make the citizens of the country look more kindly upon the incumbent government. While there may be some validity in this theory, unfortunately it is often implemented

---

[18] Ibid., p. 260.

[19] For accounts of the breakdown of the Bretton Woods System see Jacques Rueff, *The Monetary Sin of the West*, trans. Roger Glémet (New York: Macmillan Co., 1972); and Guillaume Guindey, *The International Monetary Tangle: Myths and Realities*, trans. Michael L. Hoffman (White Plains, N.Y.: M.E. Sharpe, Inc., 1977).

[20] Laffer and Miles, *International Economics*, pp. 259–62.

under the notion that if a little money creation is good, a lot must be even better.

The financial motive for printing money is the fact that while money is practically costless to produce, it can be used for purchasing goods and services. The resulting seignorage represents revenue to the government. Revenue gathered in this way means less revenue must be gathered in another way, say, through direct taxation.

Given these incentives to print money, it can be seen why removal of the monetary constraints on governments tends to create inflation rather than deflation.[21]

Given his recognition of the powerful inflationary bias built into the political process and of the historical failure of monetary price rules to hold such a bias in check, Laffer's advocacy of a renewed gold price rule is something of a mystery.

The Classical Gold Standard

Over the past few years, the case for reinstituting the "classical" gold standard has been propounded with great vigor and insight by Lewis Lehrman, a businessman and scholar whose views were influential in formulating the economic policy agenda of the Reagan administration and who is now a candidate for governor of New York.[22] Lehrman's writings are heavily influenced by the ideas of his former teacher, the late French economist and longtime gold-standard advocate, Jacques Rueff.[23]

---

[21] Ibid., pp. 397–98.

[22] Lehrman has stated his view on the gold standard in a number of publications, including: Lewis E. Lehrman, *The Case for the Gold Standard: Reflections on the Struggle for Financial Order* (New York: Morgan Stanley & Co., Inc., 1981); idem, *Monetary Policy, the Federal Reserve and Gold* (New York: Morgan Stanley & Co., Inc., 1980); idem, "The Case for the Gold Standard," *Wall Street Journal* (July 30, 1981): p. 33; idem, "Should We (and Could We) Return to the Gold Standard?" *New York Times* (September 6, 1981): p. 4E.

[23] For Rueff's views on the gold standard, see Jacques Rueff, *The Age of Inflation*, trans. A.H. Meeus and F.G. Clarke (Chicago: Henry Regnery Co., 1964); and Rueff, *Balance of Payments: Proposals for the Resolution of the Most Pressing World Economic Problem of Our Time*, trans. Jean Clément (New York: Macmillan, 1967).

Like his mentor, Lehrman advocates a genuine gold standard which "would establish the dollar as a weight unit of gold."[24] As Lehrman explains:

> Under the gold standard there is no price for gold. The dollar is the monetary standard, set by law equal to a weight of gold. The price of gold does not exist.... Under the gold standard, the paper dollar is a promissory note. It is a claim to a real article of wealth defined by law as the standard.[25]

In Lehrman's proposal, Federal Reserve notes as well as dollar-denominated demand deposits at commercial banks and other depository institutions would once more become (as they were prior to 1933) warehouse receipts for gold, instantly redeemable for gold dollars at face value upon the demand of the bearer or depositor. Legal reserve requirements for bank deposits would be superfluous since "the failure to redeem ... excess dollars for gold would, under convertibility rules, threaten the bankruptcy and dissolution of a commercial bank."[26] The monetary authority, for its part, would be "constrained ... by law to redeem excess dollars with specified weight units of gold...."[27] Or, in other words, it must stand ready "... to buy and sell at the official rate all the gold offered or all the gold demanded."[28] The Fed would furthermore be restrained from carrying out any open-market operations, although it would be permitted to lend reserves to commercial banks at an "unsubsidized" discount rate, i.e., a rate at or slightly above the market rate.

Without going into further detail, it is clear that Lehrman proposes a monetary system which very closely approximates the classical gold standard with all its strengths and weaknesses. The most serious weakness of the classical gold standard, and of Lehrman's proposal, is the predominant role played by what Lehrman himself calls,

---

[24] Lehrman, *The Case for the Gold Standard*, p. 21.

[25] Lehrman, "Should We (and Could We) Return to the Gold Standard?"

[26] Lehrman, *Monetary Policy, the Federal Reserve System, and Gold*, p. 41.

[27] Ibid.

[28] Lehrman, *The Case for the Gold Standard*, p. 20.

"a monopoly central bank."[29] Lehrman is willing to countenance the existence of such an institution and, indeed, to cede significant powers to it so long as it adopts "reasonable self-denying ordinances."[30] Thus, for example, the Fed would be expected to abstain from manipulating the gold content of the dollar or from directly purchasing assets on the open market. On the other hand, under Lehrman's plan, it would still retain its monopoly of the note issue and its position as the central warehouse and clearinghouse for commercial bank reserves. Moreover, its discretion with regard to discount-rate policy would still permit it to function as a "lender of last resort."

With so much power over the monetary system thus concentrated in the hands of a government institution, it is no wonder that Lehrman refers to the gold standard repeatedly as a "political institution"[31] and not once as a "free-market institution." In fact, at one point Lehrman comes perilously close to conceiving the gold standard as price-rule monetarism, that is, as merely an efficient political technique for controlling the government monopoly of the money supply. Thus, he writes:

> To be sure, Monetarists would claim to fix the total quantity of money, through a specified money stock rule, in order to regulate the government monopoly (the Federal Reserve Board) which supplies cash balances to the market. Yet the simpler, market-related technique would be to make the value of a unit of money equal to a weight unit of gold, in order to regulate the same monopoly.[32]

In any case, since government is an inherently inflationary institution, it can be expected to be an implacable enemy of the gold standard. Under these circumstances, to grant to a government institution, such as a central bank, a powerful influence over the operation of the gold standard is not unlike proffering the fox an invitation to guard the chicken coop. This is surely the lesson taught by the broad sweep of monetary history, especially in more recent times as we witness Western

---

[29] Ibid., p. 6.

[30] Ibid.

[31] Ibid., pp. 8, 10, 17, 18.

[32] Lehrman, *Monetary Policy, the Federal Reserve System, and Gold*, p. 40.

governments employing every means at their disposal to progressively transmogrify the classical gold standard into our current, highly inflationary system of fluctuating national fiat currencies. Von Mises does not exaggerate when he states:

> ... the gold standard did not collapse. Governments abolished it in order to pave the way for inflation. The whole grim apparatus of oppression and coercion—policemen, customs guards, penal courts, prisons, in some countries even executioners—had to be put into action in order to destroy the gold standard. Solemn pledges were broken, retroactive laws were promulgated, provisions of constitutions and bills of rights were openly defied.[33]

Von Mises proceeds to demolish the deeply entrenched myth, which Lehrman appears to accept, that likens the gold standard to a political "game" wherein the government players must adhere to some vaguely specified "rules of the game." Writes von Mises:

> But the gold standard is not a game; it is a market phenomenon, and as such a social institution. Its preservation does not depend on the observation of some specific rules. It requires nothing else than that the government abstain from deliberately sabotaging it. To refer to this condition as a rule of an alleged game is no more reasonable than to declare that the preservation of Paul's life depends on compliance with the rules of Paul's-life game because Paul must die if somebody stabs him to death.[34]

In summary, there is no compelling reason to believe that the classical gold standard will prove to be a more durable barrier to political manipulation of the money supply the second time around than it was the first time.

Aside from its overriding political flaw, Lehrman's proposal is characterized by serious economic shortcomings. These are ultimately related to the fact that the type of gold standard that Lehrman

---

[33] Ludwig von Mises, *The Theory of Money and Credit*, trans. H.E. Batson, new enl. ed. (Irvington-on-Hudson, N.Y.: The Foundation for Economic Education, Inc., 1971), p. 420.

[34] Ibid.

proposes is what Hayek has termed a "national reserve system."[35] The
essential feature of such a system is fractional-reserve banking, combined with the concentration of the ultimate cash reserves of all the
nation's banks in the nation's financial center or, more likely, in the
government central bank.

An historical example of the operation of the national reserve
system is provided by the classical gold standard. Under this system,
the central bank generally holds the ultimate cash reserve—in this
case, gold—for the entire national banking system. The gold reserve
serves as immediate backing for the central bank's note and deposit
liabilities which, in turn, constitute the reserve base for the notes and
deposits of commercial banks. The latter are held, along with central bank notes and gold itself, in the money balances of the public.
Since both the central bank and the commercial banks hold fractional
reserves against their liabilities, the money and credit structure of the
economy resembles an inverted pyramid, with a relatively narrow
base of gold reserves supporting a much larger superstructure of bank
notes and deposits ultimately convertible into gold.

As a result, the classical gold standard was and is extremely vulnerable to monetary deflations and inflations, due to balance-of-payments disequilibria, changes in the public's preferences for holding
gold vis-à-vis bank notes and deposits, financial crises, etc. The reason for this is that any loss or gain of gold reserves by the banking
system causes a multiple expansion or contraction of bank notes and
deposits, which constitute a large proportion of the money supply.
These frequent bouts of monetary inflation and deflation, moreover,
are likely to be aggravated by the fact that the very mechanism by
which the banking system adjusts to changes in the gold reserve base
involves an artificial alteration in the entire structure of interest rates
in the economy. This leads to a distortion in productive activity.

A brief example will suffice to illustrate this point. Suppose that the
central bank is faced with an influx of gold reverses due to a balance-of-

---

[35] For a discussion of the nature and operation of the national reserve system, see
F.A. Hayek, *Monetary Nationalism and International Stability* (New York: Augustus
M. Kelley, 1971), pp. 1–34 passim.

payments surplus. In order to arrest and reverse this inflow, it will lower the discount rate and thus expand its loans to commercial banks. Commercial bank reserves will, as a result, increase, and, while maintaining their accustomed or legally required ratio between reserves and liabilities, the banks will be able to profitably increase their loans by lowering the interest rate they charge. Since the bulk of these loans are taken up for investment purposes, investment spending in the economy will rise relative to consumption spending. This will naturally induce a shift of productive resources and monetary investment out of consumer goods industries and into capital goods industries.

Unfortunately, this outcome, the fall of interest rates and the decline of consumption relative to investment, does not reflect a genuine and voluntary shift in the time preferences of the public, i.e., deliberate choices to save more of their income and spend less on consumption. Consequently, the expansion of capital goods industries at the expense of consumer goods industries will eventually prove to be unsustainable, resulting in widespread unemployment and business failures when economic activity is finally readjusted to more faithfully reflect the time preferences of consumer-savers in the economy. As a matter of fact, the day of reckoning will come when the monetary inflation engineered by the central bank has raised prices and incomes in the country sufficiently so that the balance-of-payments surplus is transformed into a deficit and gold begins to flow out of the country. In order to stanch the outflow of gold reserves, the central bank is constrained to raise its discount rate, which in turn drains reserves out of the banking system and causes a rise in bank loan rates and a corresponding contraction in bank loans and, ultimately, in the money supply. As the structure of interest rates in the economy begins to readjust to reflect the voluntary social allocation of income between consumption and saving, the numerous malinvestments and resource misallocation engendered by the previous inflationary boom are revealed and corrected amidst conditions of economic depression.

In light of the foregoing analysis, it is my belief that Lehrman's plan for restoring the classical gold standard, while it will undeniably provide greater long-run stability in the value of money than the present fiat-money regime, will not rid us of the recurring fluctuations in macroeconomic activity which have plagued the market economy for the past two centuries. I hasten to stress that this is not a defect of the gold standard itself but of its organization along the lines of the national reserve system described above. In fact, most of the oft-noted defects in the classical gold standard lie in precisely those areas where its operation diverges from that of a fully free-market, 100 percent gold standard. This point has been cogently argued by Leland Yeager:

> National fractional reserve systems are the real source of most of the difficulties blamed on the gold standard.... The difficulties arise because the mixed national currencies— currencies which are largely paper, only partly gold—are insufficiently international. The main defect of the histori- cal gold standard is a necessity of "protecting" national gold reserves.... In short, whether a Central Bank amplifies the effects of gold flows, remains passive in the face of gold flows, or "offsets" gold flows, its behavior is incompatible with the principles of the full-fledged gold standard.... Indeed, any kind of monetary management runs counter to the principles of the pure gold standard.[36]

On the other hand, notes Yeager:

> Under a 100 percent hard-money international gold standard, the currency of each country would consist exclusively of gold (or of gold plus fully-backed warehouse receipts for gold in the form of paper money and token coins). The government and its agencies would not have to worry about any drain on their reserves. The gold warehouses would never be embarrassed by requests to redeem paper money in gold, since each dol- lar of paper money in circulation would represent a dollar of gold actually in a warehouse. There would be no such thing as independent national monetary policies; the volume of money in each country would be determined by market forces. The world's gold supply would be distributed among the various countries according to the demands for cash balances of the individuals in the various countries. There would be no danger

---

[36] Leland B. Yeager, "An Evaluation of Freely-Fluctuating Exchange Rates" (Ph.D. dis- sertation, Columbia University, 1952), quoted in M.N. Rothbard, "The Case for a 100 Percent Gold Dollar," in *In Search of a Monetary Constitution*, ed. Leland Yeager, pp. 94–136 (Cambridge, Mass.: Harvard University Press, 1962), rep. in *Case for a 100 Percent Gold Dollar* (Washington, D.C.: Libertarian Review Press, 1974), p. 30.

of gold deserting some countries and piling up excessively in others, for each individual would take care not to let his cash balance shrink or expand to a size which he considered inappropriate in view of his income and wealth.

Under a 100 percent gold standard ... the various countries would have a common monetary system, just as the various states of the United States now have a common monetary system. There would be no more reason to worry about disequilibrium in the balance of payments of any particular country than there is now reason to worry about disequilibrium in the balance of payments of New York City. If each individual (and institution) took care to avoid persistent disequilibrium in his personal balance of payments, that would be enough.... The actions of individuals in maintaining their cash balances at appropriate levels would "automatically" take care of the adequacy of each country's money supply.[37]

The Parallel Private Gold Standard

The most innovative scheme for establishing a gold money involves a wholly private, "parallel" gold standard which would exist side by side with the already established government fiat money standard. Variations on this plan have been proposed by Henry Hazlitt[38] and Professor R.H. Timberlake.[39] Although I shall focus primarily on Timberlake's proposal because it is worked out in greater detail, reference will be made to Hazlitt's proposal in order to highlight several substantive differences between the two.

Timberlake's plan holds forth great initial promise because, unlike the preceding three plans that have been examined, it is predicated on

---

[37] Yeager, "Evaluation of Freely-Fluctuating Exchange Rates," quoted in ibid., pp. 30–31.

[38] Henry Hazlitt, "The Search for an Ideal Money," *The Freeman* 25 (November 1975): pp. 660–72; Hazlitt, *Inflation Crisis, and How to Resolve It* (New Rochelle, N.Y.: Arlington House, 1978).

[39] R.H. Timberlake, Jr., "Solving the Monetary Crisis," *Policy Report* 3 (October 1981): p. 9. See also Timberlake, "Monetization Practices and the Political Structure of the Federal Reserve System," *Policy Analysis* (Washington, D.C.: Cato Institute, August 12, 1981).

the recognition that inflation "will be stopped only by fundamental changes in the Fed."[40] Thus, Timberlake's plan "would begin with the abolition of the Federal Reserve System as a policy-making central bank."[41]

Timberlake foresees no technically insurmountable barriers to such a course of action. He argues that the regulatory functions of the Fed can easily be dispensed with since "banks have no more reason to be regulated than grocery stores" and "should be left alone to justify their existence in a free-market system."[42] Regarding the check-clearing services provided by the Fed to its member banks, Timberlake points to privatization as the simple and sensible solution. Writes Timberlake:

> The technical check-clearing operations of the Federal Reserve Bank could still be handled by the existing physical facilities. Federal Reserve Banks could be reorganized as regional bank clearing houses. Since the Fed banks are already legally owned by commercial banks that exercise no control or ownership, the solution is simple: Turn the Federal Reserve Banks over to the legitimate owners and let the member banks operate them. This change would probably result in many interesting innovations and economies in bank management and checking facilities.[43]

This leaves the Fed's functions of executing monetary policy. According to Timberlake, they are at best superfluous and at worst highly inflationary. In the case of reserve requirements, Timberlake contends that "banks can manage their own reserve necessities," noting that "no other system in the world employs reserve requirement laws to regulate commercial banks."[44] The discounting function, Timberlake holds to be "both unnecessary and undesirable." Not only does it play a minor role in the Fed's execution of monetary policy, but commercial banks are able to fulfill their needs for reserves by borrowing from

---

[40] Timberlake, "Solving the Monetary Crisis.".

[41] Ibid.

[42] Ibid.

[43] Ibid., p. 10.

[44] Ibid.

one another on the well-organized and private Federal Funds market. "Ending Federal Reserve discounting," writes Timberlake, "therefore, would simply be ending something that is largely an advertising gimmick for promoting the image of the Fed as a banker's welfare agency."[45]

But what of open-market operations, "the process that keeps the money stock growing at inflationary rates"? It is in answering this question that Timberlake introduces his proposal for a parallel gold standard. First, the U.S. Treasury would sell its entire gold stock (260 million ounces) or distribute a pro rata share to every U.S. citizen either in coin or in redeemable certificates. Second, the "policy-making structure of the Federal Reserve System" would be abolished. Finally, the outstanding note liabilities of the Fed, the currency in circulation, would be frozen and the member-bank reserve accounts converted into Federal Reserve notes. The commercial banks would have the option of holding the latter in their own vaults or leaving them on deposit in the "new" regional clearinghouses.

Timberlake expects that the gold, once in private hands, would soon find its way into private depository institutions, thus giving rise to gold-based demand deposits and notes redeemable upon demand in gold or Federal Reserve notes, at the option of the depositor. According to Timberlake:

> This new system would not be a gold standard because the government would not declare gold or anything else legal tender....

> Gold-based deposits and currency would circulate side by side with the frozen stock of existing federal reserve notes. Prices of gold in terms of other moneys would be quickly determined by market factors.[46]

Timberlake's proposal includes two elements that are absolutely essential to the establishment of a stable commodity money: the complete liquidation of the government central bank; and the return of the gold stock to private hands. In this respect, it is far superior to the first three proposals which I have analyzed because all of them

---

[45] Ibid.

[46] Ibid.

leave the existing structure of the Federal Reserve system, for the most part, untouched. Moreover, under the plans of Laffer and Lehrman, even though the public can convert dollars into gold, the Fed still retains strategic control over the nation's gold stock by virtue of its position as a monopoly "banker's bank."

Unfortunately, Timberlake's proposal involves two drawbacks. First, by stipulating only that depository institutions are legally required to redeem their notes and demand deposits for gold upon demand, Timberlake is opening the door to a system of "free banking" based on fractional reserves. Although this system would, in fact, produce a much sounder and "harder" money than even the classical gold standard, there would still be potential, albeit severely limited, for inflation. More important than the direct economic effects of such inflation, however, there looms the distinct possibility that the political authority may use the occasional, but highly visible, financial crises and bank failures which follow the inflationary boom as a pretext for regulation of the banks "in the public interest." Having thus regained its first crucial foothold, the government would be well on its way to reimposing its monopoly over money.

There is a much more serious shortcoming in this plan, however. It is obscured by Timberlake's overly optimistic assumption that once the gold stock has been retrieved from government control, gold will be automatically and as a matter of course remonetized by the market, thus serving as the basis for a parallel private currency. But the sad fact is that the public, who ultimately determines what is and what is not money, has grown accustomed to governmental fiat money and, as a result, is unlikely to undertake spontaneously the actions necessary to create de novo a parallel commodity money. This is so despite the fact that the existing fiat money, e.g., the dollar, was at one time merely a name for a specific weight of gold, and despite the more general fact that money always initially emerges as a useful commodity produced on the free market. For once the government succeeds in severing the name of the monetary unit, which the public has grown accustomed to over the years, from the free-market money-commodity, a government-monopolized fiat money becomes entrenched among the public and the money-commodity is effectively demonetized. This is certainly borne out, for example, by the history of the dollar. Originally the name for approximately one-twentieth of an ounce of gold money (from 1834 to 1933), the dollar is today a purely nominal entity and, consequently, whatever is legally designated as a "dollar" is accepted by the public as money. Gold is now one among many nonmonetary commodities for which the fiat dollars are exchanged.

It follows from what has been said that, once a fiat money has gained currency in the economy, the only sure method for restoring a free-market commodity money necessarily involves once again legally defining the monetary name already in use as some definite unit of weight of the former money-commodity. Of course, considerations of the prevailing economic reality—namely, the enormous inflation of the supply of fiat dollars that has occurred since the severing of the gold dollar link—would determine the exact ratio at which the redemption of dollars for gold could be initiated and maintained without precipitating severe economic dislocations. But this is a complex issue which cannot be addressed here.

In light of the foregoing discussion, the most that could reasonably be expected from Timberlake's proposal is not the spontaneous emergence of a parallel gold standard at all, but the existing unitary fiat-dollar standard in which the monetary base, as embodied in the frozen stock of Federal Reserve notes, remains constant. Two important points can be made regarding the inflationary potential of the reformed fiat-money regime which is actually likely to emerge under Timberlake's proposal.

First, even if we assume that the monetary base (equal to the total quantity of Federal Reserve notes held in the money balances of the public and in private bank reserves) remains rigidly fixed, there is still room for monetary inflation and deflation so long as fractional reserve banking exists (as it apparently would under Timberlake's proposal). Thus, for example, increased public preference for holding money balances in the form of demand deposits or private bank notes, as opposed to Federal Reserve notes, would result in an influx of Fed notes into private bank reserves, leading to the familiar process of a multiple expansion of bank credit for the system as a whole. The final result of this process would be an inflationary expansion of private bank notes and demand deposits. On the other hand, a contraction of the money supply would occur due to the public's shifting some of its money holdings from, e.g., checking accounts to Fed notes in hand.

Second, and more important in the long run, although Timberlake's program laudably envisions the dismantling of the Federal Reserve system and the complete privatization of banking, the dollar, which constitutes the "high-powered" money or the ultimate reserves of the banking system, still remains an essentially nominal entity subject to inflationary creation by government fiat. Given its inflationary proclivity, it is highly improbable that the government will forever resist the opportunity to increase its revenues by expanding the supply of dollars.

In sum, Timberlake's proposal does not live up to its initial promise, either as a blueprint for achieving a free-market gold money or as a long-run cure for inflation. The reason underlying both shortcomings is that the proposal does not even address the most crucial issue of meaningful monetary reform: the denationalization of the existing fiat moneys.

Henry Hazlitt's proposal for a private parallel gold standard is much more modest in conception than Timberlake's, although he too wishes "to get government, as far as possible, out of the monetary sphere."[47] The first and most crucial step in Hazlitt's plan "is to get our government and the courts not only to permit, but to enforce, voluntary private contracts providing for payment in gold or in terms of gold value."[48]

The full plan would be implemented as follows:

> Governments should be deprived of their monopoly of the currency-issuing power. The private citizens of every country should be allowed, by mutual agreement, to do business with each other in the currency of any country. In addition, they should be allowed to mint privately gold or silver coins and to do business with each other in such coins.... Still further,

---

[47] Hazlitt, *The Inflation Crisis*, p. 176.
[48] Ibid.

> private institutions should be allowed to issue notes payable
> in such metals. But these should be only gold or silver certifi-
> cates, redeemable on demand in the respective quantities of
> the metals specified. The issuers should be required to hold
> at all times the full amount in metal of the notes they have
> issued, as a warehouse owner is required to hold at all times
> everything against which he has issued an outstanding ware-
> house receipt, on penalty of being prosecuted for fraud. And
> the courts should enforce all contracts made in good faith in
> such private currencies.[49]

Hazlitt's proposal is at once less ambitious but more realistic than
the proposal put forth by Timberlake. Thus, Hazlitt does not propose
the immediate abolition of the Federal Reserve system or the return
of the government gold hoard to private hands. Instead, recognizing
that a private gold standard would not emerge immediately and automatically alongside the well entrenched fiat-dollar standard, Hazlitt
believes that, given the legal framework he has set out, a private, 100
percent gold standard would slowly but surely evolve in step with
the inevitable inflationary destruction of the fiat dollar. According to
Hazlitt:

> As the rate of inflation increased, or became more uncer-
> tain, Americans would tend increasingly to make long-term
> contracts payable in gold. This is because sellers and lend-
> ers would become increasingly reluctant to make long-term
> contracts payable in paper dollars or in irredeemable money-
> units of any other kind.
>
> This preference for making long-term contracts in gold
> would apply particularly to international contracts. The buyer
> or debtor would then either have to keep a certain amount
> of gold in reserve, or make a forward contract to buy gold,
> or depend on buying gold in the open spot market with his
> paper money on the date that his contract fell due. In time, if
> inflation continued, even current transactions would increas-
> ingly be made in gold.
>
> Thus, there would grow up, side by side with fiat paper
> money, a private domestic and international gold standard.

---

[49] Ibid., pp. 187–88.

> Each country that permitted this would then be on a dual
> monetary system, with a daily-changing market relation
> between the two monies. And there would be a private gold
> system ready to take over completely on the very day that the
> government's paper money became absolutely worthless—as
> it did in Germany in November, 1923, and in scores of other
> countries at various times.[50]

As described by Hazlitt, the process of transition to a private gold
standard amidst the hyperinflationary breakdown of the fiat currency
is certainly realistic enough. Moreover, it must be admitted that the
economy would suffer much less devastation from the consequences
of hyperinflation if, upon the demise of the primary fiat-money standard, people did not have to resort to barter but were able to take
advantage of an already developing commodity-money standard. Still,
Hazlitt's plan leaves one naturally wondering why meaningful monetary reform must await the catastrophe of a hyperinflation, while the
economy continues in the throes of an ever worsening stagflation.

In fact, Hazlitt himself expects that the implementation of his
proposal will serve to avert a hyperinflationary Armageddon by constraining the government to surrender its fiat money monopoly and
restore a genuine gold standard. Unfortunately, Hazlitt is not very
clear on exactly how this would come to pass. He writes:

> I should perhaps make one point clear. I do not expect that
> allowing citizens to do business in the currencies of for-
> eign nations or in private gold coins will in the long run in
> most countries mean that these citizens will do most of their
> business in these foreign or private currencies. I am assum-
> ing that practically all governments will continue to issue
> an official currency and that, when they have ceased inflat-
> ing, they will issue their own gold coins and certificates. And
> I assume that most of their citizens will then use their own
> governments' money and coins. But this is because I expect
> that once freedom of choice in currencies is permitted, each
> government will begin to reform its own monetary practices.
> What will count is not only the actual competition of foreign

---

[50] Ibid., p. 177.

money or private coins, but the ever-present possibility of the
competition of foreign or private money.[51]

In this passage, Hazlitt alludes to the potential competition from
a private gold standard as the key factor which will induce government to abandon its inflationary ways and embrace the gold standard.
However, this contradicts his earlier analysis of the transition from
a hyperinflated fiat money to a free-market gold money. As Hazlitt
points out, it is only after hyperinflation is well under way that the
public will even contemplate incurring the substantial costs of completely abandoning the existing medium of exchange in current transactions as well as credit transactions. In short, inflation will have to
progress a long way before the parallel gold standard, as conceived
in Hazlitt's plan, presents serious competition to the government fiat
money. In the meanwhile, the economy will still be left to suffer the
ravages of a hyperinflation.

Conclusion

The road to long-term monetary stability leads ultimately to the
complete abolition of the government monopoly of issuing money
and, concomitantly, to the return of the function of supplying money
to the free market. The most crucial and difficult step along this road
involves reconstituting the dollar, the existing fiat money, as a commodity money. This would be done by restoring it to its original status
as a legally redeemable claim to a fixed weight of the former money-
commodity, gold. Only if and when this step is taken is there hope of
ever achieving the ultimate aim of a wholly "denationalized" money
whose supply and value are at long last free from the arbitrary manipulations of a nonmarket monopolist.

---

[51] Ibid., pp. 189–90.

Bibliography

Clark, Lindley H., Jr. 1981. "What Kind of a Gold Standard Is Needed?" *Wall Street Journal* (August 18): p. 33.

Guindey, Guillaume. 1977. *The International Monetary Tangle: Myths and Realities*, Michael L. Hoffman, trans. White Plains, N.Y.: M.E.Sharpe, Inc.

Hayek, F.A. 1971. *Monetary Nationalism and Internation Stability*. New York: Augustus M. Kelley.

Hazlitt, Henry. 1975. "The Search for an Ideal Money." *The Freeman* 25 (November): pp. 660–72.

_____. 1978. *Inflation Crisis, and How to Resolve It*. New Rochelle, N.Y.: Arlington House.

Laffer, Arthur. 1980. *Reinstatement of the Dollar: The Blueprint*. Rolling Hill Estates, Calif.: A.B. Laffer Associates.

Laffer, Arthur, and Charles W. Kadlec. 1982. "The Point of Linking the Dollar to Gold." *Wall Street Journal* (October 13): p. 32.

Laffer, Arthur B. and Marc A. Miles. 1982. *International Economics in an Integrated World*. Glenview, Ill.: Scott, Foresman and Co.

Lehrman, Lewis E. 1980. *Monetary Policy, the Federal Reserve, and Gold*. New York: Morgan Stanley & Co., Inc.

_____. 1981a. *The Case for the Gold Standard: Reflections on the Struggle for Financial Order*. New York: Morgan Stanley & Co., Inc.

_____. 1981b. "The Case for the Gold Standard." *Wall Street Journal* (July 30): p. 33.

_____. 1981c. "Should We (and Could We) Return to the Gold Standard?" *New York Times* (September 6): p. 4E.

Mises, Ludwig von. 1971. *The Theory of Money and Credit*, H.E. Batson, trans., new enl. ed. Irvington-on-Hudson, N.Y.: The Foundation for Economic Education, Inc.

Mundell, Robert A. 1981. "Gold Would Serve into the 21st Century." *Wall Street Journal* (September 30): p. 33.

Rothbard, Murray N. 1962. "The Case for a 100 Percent Gold Dollar." In *In Search of a Monetary Constitution*, Leland Yeager, ed., pp. 94–136. Cambridge, Mass.: Harvard University Press, rep. In *The Case for a 100 Percent Gold Dollar*. Washington, D.C.: Libertarian Review Press.

Rueff, Jacques. 1964. *The Age of Inflation*, A.H. Meeus and F.G. Clarke, trans. Chicago: Henry Regnery Co.

_____. 1967. *Balance of Payments: Proposals for the Resolution of the Most Pressing World Economic Problem of Our Time*. Jean Clément, trans. New York: Macmillan.

_____. 1972. *The Monetary Sin of the West*, Roger Glémet, trans. New York: Macmillan.

Timberlake, R.H., Jr. 1981a. "Solving the Monetary Crisis," *Policy Report* 3 (October): p. 9.

_____. 1981b. "Monetization Practices and the Political Structure of the Federal Reserve System." *Policy Analysis* (August 12). Washington, D.C.: Cato Institute.

Wanniski, Jude. 1978. *The Way the World Works*. New York: Simon and Schuster.

_____. 1981. "A Job Only Gold Can Do." *New York Times* (August 27): p. A31.

Weintraub, Robert E. 1981. Appendix on "Restoring the Gold Certificate Reserve." In *The Gold Standard: Its History and Record Against Inflation*, by Roy W. Jastram. Washington, D.C.: Government Printing Office.

Welker, Ernest P. 1980. "Plans to Revive the Gold Standard," *Economic Education Bulletin* 20, no. 10. Great Barrington, Mass.: American Institute for Economic Research.

Yeager, Leland B. 1952. "An Evaluation of Freely-Fluctuating Exchange Rates." Ph.D. dissertation, Columbia University.

CHAPTER 15

The International
Gold Standard:
A New Perspective

1. Introduction

As early as 1923, John Maynard Keynes declared that the choice of an international monetary regime involved an unpleasant dilemma. Keynes argued that "If ... the external price-level lies outside our control, we must submit either to our own internal price-level or to our exchange being pulled about by external influences. If the external price-level is unstable, we cannot keep *both* our own price level *and* our exchanges stable. And we are compelled to choose."[1]

The most significant practical implication of Keynes's contention is, of course, that a nation must choose either to maintain 'fixed' exchange rates between its own and foreign currencies by participating in the international gold standard or to maintain reasonable stability in domestic levels of prices, output, and employment. Following Keynes, most economists today are inclined to accept the view that the operation of the gold standard tends to be inconsistent with the

---

From: "The International Gold Standard: A New Perspective," *Eastern Economic Journal* 10, (October/December 1984): pp. 488–98.

[1] John Maynard Keynes *A Tract on Monetary Reform*, (London: Macmillan, 1923), pp. 154–55.

maintenance of domestic macroeconomic stability. Indeed, this is one of the major considerations that led many economists and informed economic policymakers during the Bretton Woods era to conclude that a regime of fluctuating exchange rates is superior to a fixed exchange-rate system.

In this paper, I shall suggest that the generally accepted explanation of the impact of the international gold standard on the stability of an individual nation's domestic economy rests on an overly aggregative approach to monetary and balance-of-payments theory. This approach tends to obscure rather than elucidate important issues whose understanding is vital in assessing the relative merits of competing international monetary systems. The issues in question include: 1. The type of price variations that are necessary to adjust balance-of-payments disequilibria under the gold standard; 2. The meaning of the terms "inflation" and "deflation" in the context of an "open" national economy; and 3. The international transmission of business cycles or "macroeconomic instability" under fluctuating exchange rates.

In addressing these issues below, I shall attempt to rehabilitate and extend the approach of a number of economists writing in the 1930s who pioneered the development of a micro-oriented "process analysis" of monetary and balance-of-payments phenomena.[2] These writers include the prominent monetary economists Ralph Hawtrey,[3] Friedrich A. Hayek,[4] and Lionel (later Lord)

---

[2] For an overview of the development of monetary process analysis through the 1930s, see Arthur W. Marget, *The Theory of Prices: A Re-Examination of the Central Problems of Monetary Theory.* vol. 2, (New York: Augustus M. Kelley, 1966), pp. 346–403. For a recent study that focuses exclusively on the Swedish school's contributions, see Björn A. Hansson, *The Stockholm School and the Development of Dynamic Method* (London: Croom Helm, Ltd., 1982).

[3] R.G. Hawtrey, *Currency and Credit* (New York: Longmans, Green and Co., 1919); idem, "The Gold Standard and the Balance of Payments," *The Economic Journal* 36 (March 1926): pp. 50–68.

[4] F.A. Hayek, *Monetary Nationalism and International Stability* (New York: Augustus M. Kelley Publishers, 1971).

Robbins,[5] and the less well known Michael A. Heilperin[6] and F.W. Paish.[7]

2. Price Changes and Balance-of-Payments Adjustment under the Gold Standard

The belief that there exists a dilemmatic tradeoff between fixity of exchange rates and stability of domestic economic activity can be traced partly to the conventional explanation of how disequilibria in the balance of payments are normally adjusted under the gold standard. According to this explanation, the normal operation of the balance-of-payments adjustment mechanism necessarily subjects a participating nation to recurrent bouts of inflation and deflation of its money supply and, therefore, of its price level.

To illustrate this, let us suppose that there occurs a decline in the foreign demand for an important export product of a particular nation. Starting from an initial position of balance-of-payments equilibrium, the immediate effect of the falling off of the nation's exports is a deficit in its external payments and an associated outflow of gold. The loss of gold results in an overall decrease in the national money stock, because, under the gold standard, gold serves both as hand-to-hand currency and as reserves for bank notes and checkable deposits. The contraction in the domestic money supply, ceteris paribus, causes a deflation of the price level in the deficit nation. With domestic prices now lower relative to prices generally prevailing in the rest of the world economy, the nation's exports are stimulated while its imports decline, resulting in the eventual restoration of equilibrium in its balance of payments.

---

[5] Lionel Robbins, *Economic Planning and International Order* (New York: Macmillan, 1937); and idem, *Money, Trade and International Relations* (New York: St. Martin's Press, 1971).

[6] Michael A. Heilperin, *International Monetary Economics* (London: Longmans, Green and Co., 1939); and idem, *Aspects of the Pathology of Money: Monetary Essays from Four Decades* (London: Michael Joseph Limited, 1968).

[7] F.W. Paish, "Banking Policy and the Balance of Payments" *Economica* 3 (November 1936), pp. 404–22 rep. in Howard S. Ellis and Lloyd A. Metzler, *Readings in the Theory of International Trade* (Homewood, Ill.: Richard d. Irwin, 1950): pp. 35–55.

During the course of the equilibration process, however, the required deflation of domestic money and prices may severely depress domestic economic activity, occasioning substantial unemployment of productive resources and losses of real output. This is especially likely to be the outcome in modern economies, characterized, as they are, by prices and wage rates that tend to be "sticky downward."

Now, it is widely admitted that this textbook description of the "price-specie-flow" adjustment mechanism gives a highly oversimplified picture of the balance-of-payments adjustment process under the gold standard and must be considerably augmented to approach a realistic explanation of the process. But what is not generally understood is that it is positively misleading. The source of the problem is the tendency to use the concept of a "national price level" when theorizing about the balance of payments.

As Heilperin points out, such "statistical constructions" seem

> ... to provide a comfortable way out of the perplexing multiplicity and heterogeneity presented by the economic world and the processes that are taking place therein.... But the multiplicity *does* exist and by ignoring it one falls into erroneous or meaningless statements about the world and about economic processes. Averages more often conceal reality than reveal it and have to be used cautiously, even in homogeneous collections; but they are simply without meaning in collections that are not homogeneous. There is no such thing in the real economic world as the "general price level"; but what exists are prices, and it is the movements of prices and the changes in the structure of money values (including prices, incomes, debts) that are of real interest and of intense importance for the understanding of economic phenomena.[8]

By focusing analysis on national price levels, one is naturally led to conclude that what is required in the case of a deficit (surplus) is a general deflation (inflation) of domestic prices. But this hides the fact that what is really needed to restore balance-of-payments equilibrium, for example, in a deficit situation is a relative decline of particular prices, which hardly qualifies as a "deflation" in the usual sense of the term.

----

[8] Heilperin, *International Monetary Economics,* p. 13.

As an example, let us suppose that there develops a world-wide decline in the demand for U.S. wheat, precipitating a deficit in the U.S. balance of payments. This development will initiate a fall in specific prices, incomes, and cash balances in the U.S. Certainly the first effects will include a decline in the price of wheat and a contraction of the incomes and cash balances of wheat farmers. And there will later emerge secondary effects on prices and incomes in the farm machinery and other industries that directly supply wheat farmers with capital or consumers' goods. Thus, if, as a result of the decline in their incomes, American wheat farmers substantially reduce their consumption of domestic beer, its price will fall and the incomes and money holdings of workers and stockholders in the domestic beer industry will begin to shrink. Without going into more detail, there will occur tertiary and further effects of the deficit on the domestic economy.

Now, it is this sequential process of declining prices and incomes that serves to provide individuals with the incentives to undertake those actions necessary to adjust the deficit. For example, foreigners will be induced to increase their purchases of wheat, farm equipment, and beer by the lower prices of these goods, thereby expanding U.S. exports. On the other hand, there will occur a shrinkage of U.S. imports as lower incomes and the threat of insufficient money balances stimulate those in American industry experiencing adverse shifts in demand to cut their spending on foreign products. Imports will contract further as U.S. residents begin to substitute relatively cheaper domestic products for foreign products, e.g., domestic beer for imported brews.

It is important to realize that these equilibrating processes of sequential price and income variations operate without respect to national borders. The magnitude and even the direction of the change of a particular good's price does not depend, therefore, upon the nation in which the good is offered for sale. In the foregoing example, foreign barley growers, who, let us assume, were favored by the initial shift in demand away from U.S. wheat, may have a sufficiently high "income elasticity of demand" for California wines (and other U.S. products) so that one of the more immediate responses to the balance-of-payments disequilibrium is a rise in the demands for and prices of these goods. Moreover, as these equilibrating processes proceed to work their way throughout the world economy, further redistributions of income and redirections of expenditures occur that may very well cause the prices of many other goods produced in the deficit nation to rise.[9]

In general, as Hayek explains:

> The important point in all this is that what incomes and what prices will have to be altered in consequence of the initial change will depend on whether and to what extent the value of a particular factor or service, directly or indirectly, depends on the particular change in demand which has occurred, and not whether it is inside or outside the same "currency area." We can see this more clearly if we picture the series of successive changes of money incomes, which will follow on the initial shift of demand, as single chains, neglecting for the moment the successive ramifications which will occur at every link. Such a chain may either very soon lead to the other country or first run through a great many links at home. But whether any particular individual in the country will be affected will depend on whether he is a link in that particular chain, that is whether he has more or less immediately been serving the individuals whose income has first been affected, and not simply on whether he is in the same country or not.[10]

Hayek concludes that this disaggregated approach to balance-of-payments analysis reveals "... how superficial and misleading the kind of argument is which runs in terms of *the* prices and *the* incomes of the country, as if they would necessarily move in unison or even in the same direction. It will be prices and incomes of particular industries which will be affected and the effects will not be essentially different from those which will follow any shifts of demand between different industries or localities."[11]

---

[9] On the conditions under which this would occur, see Paish, "Banking Policy," pp. 45–48.

[10] Hayek, *Monetary Nationalism*, pp. 21–22.

[11] Ibid., p. 23.

In fact, it is the unwarranted concentration upon aggregates and averages in conjunction with a quirk of statistical compilation that has prevented economists from grasping the simple truth that all prices in a given nation need not move in the same direction to equilibrate the balance of payments. As Hayek points out, "it is 'the purely accidental fact' that price levels are constructed for prices in a national area that leads to the mistaken belief ... that in some sense all prices of a country could be said to move together relatively to prices in other countries." Needless to say, "The fact that the averages of (more or less arbitrarily selected) groups of prices move differently in different countries does of course in no way prove that there is any tendency of the price structure of a country to move as a whole relatively to prices in other countries."[12]

To sum up, the variations of particular prices, incomes, and cash balances that are the essence of the balance-of-payments adjustment mechanism under the gold standard do not constitute a general deflation of money and prices, such as that which accompanied the retirement of the Greenbacks in the U.S. in the 1870s or the collapse of the U.S. banking system in the early 1930s. In fact, the effects on prices and incomes that result from a decline in foreign demand for a domestic product are qualitatively no different from the effects that would be produced by a decline in demand for the same product which originates domestically. Both cases reflect the usual response of the market to diminished relative demand for a particular good on the part of market participants, wherever they reside. To label this market process "deflationary" in the one case and not in the other is confusing and serves no useful purpose.

3. The Meaning of the Terms "Inflation" and "Deflation" in an Open Economy

This brings me to the second issue, regarding the applicability of the terms "inflation" and "deflation" in describing the effects of money

---

[12] Ibid., p. 45.

flows that normally take place between nations participating in the international gold standard.

Under the gold standard, gold serves in effect as a homogeneous international currency. Each member nation, therefore, does not constitute an independent "currency area" but is merely a constituent of a larger currency area, comprising the nations that employ gold as the general medium of exchange. A most important, although often ignored, implication of this fact is that changes in the quantity of money in a particular nation on the gold standard have no more and no less significance than changes in the quantity of money in a particular state, city, or even household existing within a purely national fiat-currency area.

Barring a change in the world's supply of gold, a long-run net transfer of money from one gold-standard nation to another will occur only in response to a relative change in the aggregate demands for money between the two regions. But the same is true today of a net transfer of dollar balances from one region to another within the U.S., or dollar, currency area. In the latter case, we would hardly refer, let us say, to the loss of dollars in New Jersey and the acquisition of these currency units by New York residents as constituting a monetary deflation and inflation respectively. Thus to assert that the fluctuations in national stocks of money under the international gold standard constitute deflation or inflation is to confuse "redistributions of money between areas" that are components of a unified currency area with changes in "the quantity of money in a closed system."[13]

Lord Robbins gives a particularly incisive illustration of this point.[14] He considers a closed economy with a unified monetary system in which a shift in conditions of supply or demand, e.g., a discovery of valuable mineral resources or a changed fashion in tourism, produces an increase in the relative value of product and factor services in a particular area. In these circumstances, it is natural to expect a general rise of prices and incomes in the area. And it would

---

[13] Ibid., p. 24.

[14] Lord Robbins, "Inflation: An International Problem," in *Inflation as Global Problem*, ed. Randall Hinshaw (Baltimore: Johns Hopkins University Press, 1972), pp. 16–17.

prove inconvenient and confusing to label this phenomenon "inflationary." "You only have to carry the thing to its limit and consider the rise of prices and the accompanying rise of incomes of a single industry, due to any of the causes I have mentioned, to see how very odd that would be."[15]

But the same reasoning is applicable to the effects of international movements of money under the gold standard. As Robbins explains:

> "... exactly the same thing can occur in national areas which are parts of the world economy. If the demand for their product rises in comparison with the demand for the products of other areas, or if the volume of these products forthcoming in markets of elastic demand increases, then, in a regime of fixed exchange rates, the way in which the workers and owners of productive resources situated there can receive the increased share of world production which is awarded to them by the market is just this: that domestic incomes and prices of home products rise pari passu, and the increase of real incomes comes via increased power to buy import goods, goods with import ingredients, or various kinds of foreign services.... Movements of this sort therefore can be conceived in a world in which the movements of price levels in the world as a whole are not inflationary."[16]

There is a plausible objection to the foregoing discussion which notes that, in contrast to redistributions of money balances between regions within a national currency area, transshipments of monetary gold reserves between national sovereignties generally involve multiple expansion and contraction of national money stocks. In other words, the nation losing gold experiences a reduction in its money stock that is greater in absolute amount than the gold outflow. Conversely, the money stock of the nation gaining gold expands by a multiple of the gold influx.

While this is certainly an accurate description of the way in which international gold flows affected national money supplies

---

[15] Robbins, "Inflation," p. 16.
[16] Ibid., pp. 16–17.

under the "classical" gold standard, it by no means follows that this is an inherent feature of the operation of the gold standard itself. Rather, it is a direct consequence of the fact that, in the nineteenth century, the banking systems of most nations were organized along the lines of what has been called the "national reserve system."[17]

Under this system, the ultimate cash reserves, gold, for all the nation's banks were centralized in the hands of the central bank. The gold reserves served as immediate backing for central bank note and deposit liabilities, which, in turn, constituted the reserve base for the notes and deposits of the commercial banks. The latter were held, along with central bank notes and gold itself, in the money balances of the public. Since both the central bank and the commercial banks generally held cash reserves against only a fraction of their liabilities, the money and credit structure of each national economy resembled an inverted pyramid, with a relatively narrow base of gold support-ing a much larger superstructure of bank notes and deposits con-vertible into gold. As a result, whenever gold began to leave its vaults to finance a balance-of-payments deficit, the central bank would be compelled to respond by applying measures designed to halt the out-flow in order to maintain its accustomed or required ratio of gold reserves to liabilities. It generally accomplished this goal by rais-ing the discount rate and thereby discouraging the discounting and borrowing of the commercial banks. The central bank was thus able to contract its outstanding note and deposit liabilities. This, in turn, placed pressure on the commercial banks to reduce their own note and deposit liabilities, since the supply of reserve assets in the system had fallen. Eventually, the general deflation of money engineered by the central bank would affect domestic prices, causing a cessation and reversal of the deficit and the associated gold outflow.

---

[17] For a description of the operation of the international gold standard in a world of national reserve banking systems, see Hayek, *Monetary Nationalism*, pp. 25–32. Also see Joseph T. Salerno, "The 100 Percent Gold Standard: A Proposal for Mon-etary Reform," in *Supply-Side Economics: A Critical Appraisal*, ed. Richard H. Fink (Frederick, Md.: University Publications of America, Inc., 1982), pp. 481–82 [reprinted here as Chapter 12].

This "secondary" and artificial monetary contraction, piled on top of the natural monetary effect of the original gold outflow, was only necessary because, under the national reserve system, the central bank generally held only a small gold reserve relative to the total stock of bank liabilities convertible on demand into gold. Obviously, no such secondary deflation would have to occur in a system where the money supply consisted solely of full-bodied gold coin and notes and demand deposits backed 100 percent by gold. Nor would it be likely to take place in a competitive free banking system where there existed no political lender of last resort. In this case the strivings for profit amidst the rivalry of competitor banks would lead each bank to identify and maintain the minimum stock of reserves sufficient to meet temporary disequilibria in the regional balance of payments without having to resort to drastic alterations of its supply of notes and deposits to the public.[18]

To conclude this section, the international gold standard is not necessarily incompatible with domestic macroeconomic stability. The flows of gold that regularly occur through a nation's balance of payments are not exogenous causes of inflation or deflation. They are, rather, an endogenous response to relative shifts in the aggregate demands for money between different nations within the gold-standard currency area and are therefore explicable on the same principles as intranational flows of fiat currency.

This is not to deny that a system-wide variation in the value of money could develop in which every member nation was compelled to participate. In the most likely case, inflation or deflation would occur when the augmentation of the world's monetary gold stock during a given period exceeded or fell short of the increase in world output in the same period. In the long run, however, such overall movements in world prices tend to be self-reversing since gold production is directly related to the purchasing power of money.[19]

---

[18] For a modern explication of free banking theory, including a discussion of the market forces that determine the individual bank's optimal reserve position, see Lawrence H. White, *Free Banking in Britain: Theory, Experience, and Debate, 1800–1845* (New York: Cambridge University Press, 1984), especially chapters 1 and 5.

[19] Theoretical elaborations of this point are provided by Milton Friedman, "Commodity-Reserve Currency," in idem, *Essays in Positive Economics* (Chicago: University of

4. Fluctuating Exchange Rates and the Autonomy of National Monetary Policy

This brings us to the objection to the international gold standard on the grounds of its alleged incompatibility with domestic macroeconomic stability. Granted that the "normal" operation of the gold standard secures tolerable long-run price stability in the world economy, is it not still the case that it facilitates the domestic importation of random shocks or monetary policy errors originating abroad? For example, a rise in prices generated by an abnormally expansionary monetary policy in a large nation will result in a balance-of-payments surplus and influx of gold for a nation pursuing a relatively non-inflationary monetary policy. If it strictly adheres to the gold standard, the latter nation will be denied recourse to an "autonomous" or "independent" monetary policy designed to dampen the inflationary impact on domestic prices. Conversely, a contraction of economic activity abroad will generate a balance-of-payments deficit and loss of gold reserves for the nation in question, due to a falling off of demand for its products on depressed world markets. The resulting contraction of its money stock will create excess supply in the domestic goods' market, thus depressing domestic prices, employment, and real income.

All this, it is generally held, can be avoided at very little cost by the simple instrumentality of a freely floating national fiat currency. Under this monetary regime, when expansionary pressure is exerted on a nation from abroad, the exchange rate will simply float upward, obviating the need for balance-of-payments adjustment via inflation of domestic money and prices. Contrariwise, foreign depressions will be stopped dead at the nation's borders by a painless depreciation of the exchange rate, which substitutes for the grinding shrinkage of money, prices, and economic activity imposed by the gold standard.[20]

Chicago Press, 1953), pp. 206–08; and Joseph T. Salerno, "Gold Standards: True and False," *The Cato Journal* 3, (Spring 1983): pp. 251–55 [reprinted here as Chapter 13]. An empirical illustration can be found in Michael David Bardo, "The Classical Gold Standard: Some Lessons for Today," Federal Reserve Bank of St. Louis, *Review* 63 (May 1981): pp. 2–17.

[20] See the classic article, Milton Friedman, "The Case for Flexible Exchange Rates," in Friedman, *Positive Economics*, pp. 157–203.

While this argument is very plausible, it is open to challenge on the grounds that it ignores the effects of inflation and deflation on relative prices. It is true that some advocates of floating exchange rates have recognized this issue and attempted to deal with it.

For instance, Gottfried Haberler has admitted that "… floating does not provide complete protection from recession abroad, because it shields a country only from purely monetary disturbances from abroad, which can be defined as foreign-induced changes in the money supply. But floating does not protect a country from real disturbances. And the effects of recessions are not purely monetary in nature. Nonmonetary (real) aspects of recessions are their differential impact on different commodities and industries (for example, on raw materials versus manufactured goods and, often overlapping, export versus import goods).…"[21]

The foregoing is a significant qualification, which opens the door for the development of a much more fundamental criticism of the case for fluctuating exchange rates.

This development was begun by Heilperin in the 1930s. He argued that complete insulation from the destabilizing effects of foreign monetary policies can never be successfully achieved as long as the nation's residents are free to carry on any international economic relations at all. Fluctuating exchange rates cannot insure internal stability—although they may indeed stabilize some arbitrarily selected price index—because a country's internal "price structure" or actual pattern of relative prices is primarily determined by world market forces.

According to Heilperin:

> The very *fact* of international trade ought to convey a warning to advocates of a choice (between internal and external stability)! Fluctuating exchanges *must* affect the formation of prices within any one country, and do so to an increasing degree as foreign trade plays a more important part in

[21] Gottfried Haberler, "The International Monetary System after Jamaica and Manila," in William Fellner, *Contemporary Economic Problems 1977* (Washington, D.C.: American Enterprise Institute for Public Policy Research, 1977), p. 273.

the economy of a country. Countries which are working with imported raw materials could hardly maintain stable internal prices when exchanges of the countries from which they import raw materials fall or rise. If advocates of internal stability, as opposed to international stability, would state their case in terms of the structure of prices and not in terms of average price levels, they would see at once that their case is very weak, unless, of course, they go on to condemn the whole of foreign trade as a disturbing factor and proceed to advocate a policy of autarchy.[22]

On this basis, Heilperin objects to the view that economic disturbances and fluctuations are an imported evil, against which a country can insulate itself through fluctuating exchange. The main body of the theory of business cycles is worked out on the assumption of a closed economy. International relations spread and synchronize economic fluctuations...."[23]

As a proponent of the "Austrian" or "monetary overinvestment" theory of the business cycle developed by Ludwig von Mises and Hayek, Heilperin emphasizes the key role of relative changes between the prices of capital goods and the prices of consumers' goods, which are wrought by monetary inflation, in precipitating business fluctuations.[24] But a system of fluctuating exchange rates does not interfere with the international transmission of changes in relative prices; it merely neutralizes the external forces acting upon a given nation's absolute level of prices. Indeed, the free-market proponents of freely-floating exchange rates tirelessly proclaim that one of the greatest virtues of their scheme is that it does not preclude the international changes in relative prices which are needed to induce a rearrangement of productive activities according to the ever-changing dictates of comparative advantage.

---

[22] Heilperin, *International Monetary Economics*, p. 12

[23] Heilperin, *Pathology of Money*, p. 71.

[24] For a sympathetic discussion of the Austrian theory of the business cycle, see Heilperin, *Pathology of Money*, 153–62. A detailed explication and critique of the theory can be found in Gottfried Haberler, *Prosperity and Depression: A Theoretical Analysis of Cyclical Movements* (New York: Atheneum, 1963), pp. 33–72.

This is precisely the reason why fluctuating exchange rates cannot successfully insulate a nation from macroeconomic fluctuations generated abroad. Although Heilperin himself never extended his analysis this far, this point can be illustrated by using the Austrian business-cycle theory to develop a model sequence of the effects that follow from the initiation of a purely national inflation in a world of fluctuating exchange rates.

When the monetary authorities of a foreign nation of significant size inflate their national fiat money stock, typically via the expansion of bank loans to business borrowers in their own nation, the prices of capital, or "higher-order," goods are bid up—not just in the inflating nation but throughout the world economy, since commodity markets are internationally integrated. The increase of capital goods' prices relative to consumer goods' prices signals business firms in the relevant industries *in all nations* to expand the output of capital goods and contract the output of consumer goods. The stimulus to capital goods' production will continue until the inflation is brought to a halt. At that time, a reverse movement of inflation-distorted relative prices occurs and businessmen finally realize that many of the long-term investments made in the capital goods industries during the inflationary boom are unprofitable and must be liquidated. The revelation of these malinvestments and misallocations of productive factors coincides with the onset of a worldwide recession or depression.

Internationally integrated capital markets provide a further mechanism for transmitting the business cycle from country to country. Thus the impulse to (artificially) lowered interest rates on the money and capital markets of the country experiencing bank credit expansion will swiftly spread throughout the world economy, as domestic and foreign investors are induced by the developing interest-rate differential to shift their funds to higher-yielding investments abroad. In addition, foreign business firms will find it profitable to expand their sales of their securities in that market where security prices have begun to rise above world levels due to declining interest rates, while restricting their borrowings and security offerings on their respective domestic credit markets. Such equilibrating shifts in the supply of and demand for savings between national capital markets (actually submarkets) insure that a strictly national bank credit inflation will tend to uniformly drive down interest rates throughout the world economy. This fall in interest rates will give further impetus to the worldwide boom in capital goods' prices and production described above, since lower interest rates promote an increase in the capital values of long-lived plant and equipment. On the other hand, when the inflating nation calls a halt to further bank credit creation, an impulse to rising interest rates travels throughout international capital markets, precipitating a world-embracing collapse of the capital values of investment goods and the onset of recession.

As long as it engages in international trade, therefore, a country may undergo a boom-and-bust cycle with a perfectly 'stable' national price level, protected by floating exchange rates, when there occur reversible relative-price and interest-rate changes in world commodity and capital markets that are the result of an inflationary boom engineered by foreign monetary authorities.

The alleged benefits of a system of fluctuating exchange rates, purchased at the substantial cost of the demolition of an international money, thus turn out to be only a mirage of macroeconomic theorizing.

Bibliography

Bardo, Michael David. 1981. "The Classical Gold Standard: Some Lessons for Today." Federal Reserve Bank of St. Louis, *Review* 63 (May): pp. 2–17.

Friedman, Milton. 1953. "Commodity-Reserve Currency." In idem, *Essays in Positive Economics.* Chicago: The University of Chicago Press.

_____. 1953. "The Case for Flexible Exchange Rates." In Friedman, *Essays in Positive Economics.* Chicago: University of Chicago Press.

Haberler, Gottfried. 1963. *Prosperity and Depression: A Theoretical Analysis of Cyclical Movements.* New York: Atheneum.

_____. 1977. "The International Monetary System after Jamaica and Manila." In William Fellner, *Contemporary Economic Problems, 1977.* Washington, D.C.: American Enterprise Institute for Public Policy Research.

Hawtrey, R.G. 1919. *Currency and Credit.* New York: Longmans, Green and Co.

_____. 1926. "The Gold Standard and the Balance of Payments." *The Economic Journal* 36 (March): pp. 50–68.

Hayek, F.A. 1971. *Monetary Nationalism and International Stability.* New York: Augustus M. Kelley.

Heilperin, Michael A. 1939. *International Monetary Economics.* London: Longmans, Green and Co.

_____. 1968. *Aspects of the Pathology of Money: Monetary Essays from Four Decades.* London: Michael Joseph Limited.

Keynes, John Maynard. 1923. *A Tract on Monetary Reform.* London: Macmillen.

Marget, Arthur W. 1966. *The Theory of Prices: A Re-Examination of the Central Problems of Monetary Theory,* 2 vols. New York: Augustus M. Kelley.

Paish, F.W. 1936. "Banking Policy and the Balance of Payments." *Economica* 3 (November): pp. 404–22, rep. in Howard S. Ellis and Lloyd A. Metzler, 1950. *Readings in the Theory of International Trade,* pp. 35–55. Homewood, Ill.: Richard D. Irwin.

Robbins, Lionel. 1937. *Economic Planning and International Order.* New York: Macmillan.

_____. 1971. *Money, Trade and International Relations.* New York: St. Martin's Press.

_____. 1972. "Inflation: an International Problem." In *Inflation as Global Problem,* Randall Hinshaw, ed. Baltimore: Johns Hopkins University Press.

Salerno, Joseph T. 1982. "The 100 Percent Gold Standard: A Proposal for Monetary Reform." In *Supply-Side Economics: A Critical Appraisal.* Richard H. Fink, ed., Frederick, Md.: University Publications of America, Inc.

_____. 1983. "Gold Standards: True and False." *The Cato Journal* 3 (Spring): pp. 251–55.

White, Lawrence H. 1984. *Free Banking in Britain: Theory, Experience, and Debate, 1800–1845.* New York: Cambridge University Press.

CHAPTER 16

Money and Gold
in the 1920s and 1930s:
An Austrian View

In consecutive issues of *The Freeman*, Richard Timberlake has contributed an interesting trilogy of articles advancing a monetarist critique of the conduct of U.S. monetary policy during the 1920s and 1930s.[1] In the first of these articles, Timberlake disputes the late Murray Rothbard's "Austrian" account of the boom-bust cycle of the 1920s and 1930s. Timberlake contends that Rothbard proceeds on the basis of a "new and unacceptable meaning" for the term "inflation" and a contrived definition of the money supply to "invent" a Fed-orchestrated inflation of the 1920s that, in fact, never occurred. Moreover, Timberlake alleges, Rothbard's account was marred by a "mismeasurement of the central bank's monetary data" as well as by a misunderstanding of the nature and operation of the Fed-controlled pseudo-gold standard by which U.S. dollars were created during this period.

In the two subsequent articles, Timberlake takes issue, respectively, with the U.S. Treasury's policy of neutralizing gold inflows and

---

From: "Money and Gold in the 1920s and 1930s: An Austrian View," *The Freeman: Ideas on Liberty* 49 (October 1999). Available at thefreemanonline.org [reprinted here as Chapter 16].

[1] Richard H. Timberlake, "Money in the 1920s and 1930s," *The Freeman* (April 1999): pp. 37–42; "Gold Policy in the 1930s," *The Freeman* (May 1999): pp. 36–41; and "The Reserve Requirement Debacle of 1935–1938," *The Freeman* (June 1999): pp. 23–29.

the Fed's policy of sharply raising reserve requirements in the mid-1930s, arguing that these complementary policies aborted an incipient economic recovery and brought on the recession of 1937–38. In what follows I will address the weighty charges brought against Rothbard and, in the process, offer an evaluation of the Federal Reserve System's culpability for the economic events of these tragic years that diverges radically from Timberlake's.

The Meaning of "Inflation"

Let me begin with Timberlake's contention that Rothbard imputes a meaning to the word "inflation" that is both new and unacceptable. In fact Rothbard's definition of inflation as "the increase in money supply[2] not consisting in, i.e., not covered by, an increase in gold," is an old and venerable one. It was the definition that was forged in the theoretical debate between the hard-money British Currency School and the inflationist British Banking School in the mid-nineteenth century. According to the proto-Austrian Currency School, which triumphed in the debate, the gold standard was not sufficient to prevent the booms and busts of the business cycle, which had continued to plague Great Britain despite its restoration of the gold standard in 1821.[3]

In brief, according to the Currency School if commercial banks were permitted to issue bank notes via lending or investment operations in excess of the gold deposited with them this would increase the money supply and precipitate an inflationary boom. The resulting increase in domestic money prices and incomes would eventually cause a balance-of-payments deficit financed by an outflow of gold. This external drain of their gold reserves and the impending threat of internal drains due to domestic bank runs would then induce the banks to sharply restrict their loans and investments, resulting in a

---

[2] For a review of this debate, see Murray N. Rothbard, *Classical Economics: An Austrian Perspective on the History of Economic Thought* (Brookfield, Vt.: Edward Elgar Publishing Company, 1995), vol. 2, pp. 225–74.

[3] Charles Holt Carroll, *Organization of Debt into Currency and Other Papers*, ed. Edward C. Simmons (Princeton, N.J.: D. Van Nostrand Company, Inc., 1964), p. 333.

severe contraction of their uncovered notes or "fiduciary media" and a decline in the domestic money supply accompanied by economy-wide depression.

To avoid the recurrence of this cycle, the Currency School recommended that all further issues of fiduciary media be rigorously suppressed and that, henceforth, the money supply change strictly in accordance with the Inflows and outflows of gold through the nation's balance of payments. The latter provided a natural, non-cycle-generating mechanism for distributing the world's money supply strictly in accordance with the international pattern of monetary demands.

Following the triumph of the Currency School doctrine and the implementation of its policy prescription by the Bank of England, its definition of inflation became accepted in the English-speaking world, especially in the United States, where there existed a much more radical and analytically insightful American branch of the School. The term "inflation" was now used strictly to denote an increase in the supply of money that consisted in the creation of currency and bank deposits unbacked by gold. Thus for example, the American financial writer Charles Holt Carroll wrote in 1868 that "The source of inflation, and of the commercial crisis, is in the nature of the system which pretends to lend money, but creates currency by discounting such bills when there is no such money in existence." Even earlier, in 1858, Carroll had written, "Instead of using gold and silver for currency they are merely used as the basis of the greatest possible inflation by the banks," and that "we should prevent any artificial increase of currency to prevent a future … catastrophe."[4] So it was the "artificial increase of currency" only—through the creation of unbacked bank notes and deposits—that constituted inflation.

The leading monetary theorist in the United States in the last quarter of the nineteenth century was Francis A. Walker. According to Walker, writing in 1888, "A permanent excess of the circulating money of a country, over that country's distributive share of the money of

---

[4] Ibid., p. 91.

the commercial world is called inflation."[5] While this version of the definition is applicable to inconvertible paper fiat currency, Walker also believed that inflation was an inherent feature of the issuance of convertible bank notes and deposits that lacked gold backing. In Walker's words, "there resides in bank money, even under the most stringent provisions for convertibility, the capability of local and temporary inflation."[6]

Unfortunately, however, because the writers of the British Currency School, unlike their American cousins, neglected to consider bank deposits as part of the money supply, their policies as adopted in Great Britain failed to prevent inflation and the business cycle. Consequently, and tragically, the School's doctrines and policies fell into profound disrepute by the late nineteenth century, and its definition of inflation was replaced by that of the opposing Banking School, which saw inflation as a state in which the money supply exceeds the needs of trade.

Early American quantity theorists following the proto-monetarist Irving Fisher, in particular, seized upon and adapted this definition to their peculiar analytical perspective. Thus, Edwin Kemmerer wrote in 1920 that, "Although the term inflation in current discussion is used in a variety of meanings, there is one idea common to most uses of the word, namely, the idea of a supply of circulating media in excess of trade needs."[7] Kemmerer went on to define inflation as a state in which, "at a given price level, a country's circulating media—money and deposit currency—increase relatively to trade needs." From here it was a short step to the currently prevailing definition of inflation as an increase in the price level.[8]

So Rothbard's theory is surely not new and to say that it is "unacceptable" is simply to express one's agreement with the long-entrenched

---

[5] Francis A. Walker, *Political Economy* (New York: Henry Holt and Company, 1888), p. 151.

[6] Ibid., p. 171.

[7] Edwin Walter Kemmerer, *High Prices and Deflation* (Princeton, N.J.: Princeton University Press, 1920), p. 3.

[8] Ibid., p. 4.

preference among orthodox quantity theorists, including contemporary monetarists, for the Banking School over the Currency School.

Defining Money

Timberlake also challenges Rothbard's statistical definition of the money supply for including savings and loan share capital and life insurance net policy reserves, alleging that Rothbard contrived this definition in order to make the rate of monetary growth appear larger than it actually was during the 1920s. Timberlake argues that the two items in question are not money because "they cannot be spent on ordinary goods and services. To spend them, one needs to cash them in for other money—currency or bank drafts."[9] Let us take these items one at time.

In the case of savings and loan share capital, there are two responses to Timberlake. First, the "share accounts" offered by savings and loan associations are and always have been economically indistinguishable from the savings deposits offered by commercial banks, included in the older (pre-1980) definition of M2 that Timberlake apparently upholds as the appropriate definition of the money supply.[10] In practice, depositors could withdraw their savings deposits from commercial banks on demand, because the law that permitted the banks to insist on a waiting period was rarely if ever invoked. Similarly, while savings and loan associations were contractually obligated to "repurchase" their "shares" at par on request of the shareholder, they could legally delay such repurchase for shorter or longer periods depending on their individual bylaws. Nonetheless such delays

---

[9] Timberlake, "Money in the 1920s and 1930s," p. 38. For Rothbard's explanation and defense of his broader definition of the money supply, see Murray N. Rothbard, *America's Great Depression* (Los Angeles: Nash Publishing Corporation, [1963] 1972), pp. 83–86.

[10] I say "apparently," because he states that "No basis exists for a more inclusive money stock than M2" (Ibid., p. 42, fn. 3). It should be pointed out that, since February 1980, savings accounts of savings and loan associations and credit unions have been included, along with savings deposits of commercial and mutual savings banks in the new M2, an official Fed statistic that is today considered to be the most reliable indicator of movements in the money supply by many economists.

rarely occurred and "for many years savings and loan associations have made the proud boast 'every withdrawal paid upon demand' or some similar statement."[11]

Moreover, while Timberlake is right that "shareholders" had to trade their share accounts in for currency or bank drafts (at par and on demand) before they could spend them on goods and services, this was equally true of savings depositors at commercial banks. Thus the public has always considered dollars held in savings and loan share accounts or savings accounts as readily spendable as dollars held in commercial bank savings deposits.

Second, Timberlake curiously does not object to Rothbard's inclusion of the savings deposits of mutual savings banks in the money supply, although they also are not included in the M2 definition he favors.[12] What makes Timberlake's position even more puzzling is that mutual savings banks were practically identical in economic function to savings and loan associations and were also technically "mutually" owned by their depositors.[13] So why, then, does Timberlake insist so vehemently on treating the liabilities of these two institutions differently?

A resolution of this mystery can perhaps be found in the work of Milton Friedman and Anna Schwartz, who excluded the share accounts of savings and loans (and of credit unions) from their definition of the money supply on the grounds that these institutions are technically not banks as defined "in accordance with the definition of banks agreed upon by federal bank supervisory agencies" since "holders of funds in these institutions are for the most part technically shareholders, not depositors." Despite this legal technicality, however, even Friedman and Schwartz were forced to admit that those who

---

[11] John G. Ranlett, *Money and Banking: An Introduction to Analysis and Policy* (New York: John Wiley & Sons, Inc., 1969), p. 251.

[12] Paul A. Meyer, *Monetary Economics and Financial Markets* (Homewood, Ill.: Richard D. Irwin, Inc., 1982), pp. 31–32.

[13] Walter A. Haines, *Money, Prices, and Policy* (New York: McGraw-Hill Book Company, Inc., 1961), pp. 249–50.

place funds with these institutions "clearly ... may regard such funds as close substitutes for bank deposits, as we define them."[14]

Life Insurance Reserves

This brings us to the issue of the net policy reserves of life insurance companies. Rothbard claimed that the cash surrender values of life insurance companies, that is, the immediately cashable claims possessed by policyholders against life insurance companies, statistically approximated by the companies' net policy reserves, represent a source of currently spendable dollars and should be included in the money supply. Once again the question is not whether insurance companies superficially resemble banks or can be technically classified as such according to some arbitrary regulatory definition. It is whether they essentially function like depository institutions, receiving funds from the public with which to make loans and investments, while contractually promising that such funds are available for withdrawal on demand by the policyholder. In Rothbard's view, the policyholder is economically in precisely the same position as a bank depositor (and thrift institution shareholder) in holding an immediately cashable par-value claim to dollars.

Now admittedly, Rothbard's inclusion of this item in the money supply is controversial, much more so than his inclusion of savings and loan share accounts. However, he was hardly alone in maintaining this position. A number of mainstream writers of money and banking textbooks in the 1960s and 1970s recognized that cashable life insurance reserves possessed some of the characteristics of money. For example, Walter W. Haines characterized insurance companies as "savings institutions" and noted that these savings "can be withdrawn

---

[14] Milton Friedman and Anna Jacobson Schwartz, *A Monetary History of the United States, 1867–1960* (Princeton, N.J.: Princeton University Press, 1963), p. 4, fn. 4. The essential economic—as opposed to the technical legal—identity between commercial bank deposits and all kinds of instantaneously cashable savings accounts held at the various nondepository or thrift institutions was established many years before Friedman and Schwartz wrote, in 1937, in a brilliant but neglected article by Lin Lin ("Are Time Deposits Money?" *American Economic Review* [March 1937]: pp. 76–86). This article was not cited by Friedman and Schwartz but greatly influenced Rothbard.

at any time" simply by allowing the policy to lapse, a feature that marks them as a "near-money" on a par with savings accounts.[15] M.L. Burstein maintained that the cash value of a life insurance policy offered "ready convertibility" into cash, was "almost as liquid as a mattressful of currency," and satisfied the "precautionary motive" for holding liquid assets no less than savings and loan accounts and savings bonds.[16] Albert Hart and Peter Kenen included the "net cash values of life insurance" in the broadest class of financial assets possessing the attribute of "moneyness," while Thomas F. Cargill ranked them on a liquidity spectrum immediately below large certificates of deposit, which are included in the current M3 definition of the money supply.[17]

More important, however, even if we grant for the sake of argument that net life insurance reserves should be excluded from the money supply, we find that it makes very little difference to Rothbard's characterization of the 1920s as an inflationary decade. With this item included, the increase in Rothbard's M between mid-1921 and the end of 1928 totaled about 61 percent, yielding an annual rate of monetary inflation of 8.1 percent a year; with this item left out (but savings and loan share accounts included), the money supply increased by about 55 percent over the period or at an annual rate of 7.3 percent.[18] Mirabile dictu, by using a definition of the money stock that arbitrarily excludes savings and loan share accounts while including mutual savings bank deposits on the basis of an inexplicable adherence to a legalistic regulatory definition of banks, it turns out that it is Timberlake (and Friedman and Schwartz) who have mismeasured money supply growth during the 1920s.

---

[15] Haines, *Money, Prices and Policy*, pp. 253–54, 31–32.

[16] M.L. Burstein, *Money* (Cambridge, Mass.: Schenkman Publishing Company, Inc., 1963), p. 111.

[17] Albert Gaylord Hart and Peter B. Kenen, *Money, Debt, and Economic Activity* (Englewood Cliffs, N.J.: Prentice-Hall, Inc., 1961), pp. 4–6; Thomas F. Cargill, *Money, the Financial System and Monetary Policy* (Englewood Cliffs, N.J.: Prentice-Hall, Inc., 1979), p. 11.

[18] I have based this calculation on Rothbard's data. See Rothbard, *America's Great Depression*, p. 88.

Flawed Institutions

Timberlake also criticizes Rothbard for "ignorance of the flawed institutional framework within which the gold standard and the central bank generated money" and also of "mismeasurement of the central bank's monetary data."[19] But this is surely a curious charge to level against Rothbard, steeped as he was in Currency School doctrine. In fact, Rothbard was quite cognizant that the U.S. monetary regime of the 1920s and 1930s was not a genuine gold standard in which the supply of money was determined exclusively by market forces, that is, by the balance of payments and the mining of gold, but a hybrid system in which the Fed possessed substantial power to manipulate the money supply by pyramiding paper bank reserves atop its stock of gold reserves. Indeed, Rothbard went much further than Timberlake in rigorously and completely separating those factors affecting the money supply that were subject to Fed control from those that the Fed had no control over.[20]

In analyzing the central bank monetary data, Timberlake starts with the monetary base or "Total Fed," which is equal to currency in circulation plus member bank reserves. From this aggregate he properly subtracts the Fed's legal-tender reserves, mainly the gold stock, whose size depends on balance-of-payments flows and is not under the immediate control of the Fed. What remains is the "net monetary obligations" of the Fed or "Net Fed," which, according to Timberlake, "faithfully indicates the intent of Fed policy."[21] From 1921 to 1929, this aggregate declined by 8 percent per year, leading Timberlake to conclude that the intent of Fed policy was decidedly deflationary during this period. The motive for this deflationary policy bias was, Timberlake suggests, to aid Great Britain in re-establishing and maintaining gold convertibility for the pound sterling.

However, as important as it is, the gold stock is not the only factor that lay beyond the Fed's control. For as Rothbard points out, currency in circulation, which improperly remains in Timberlake's Net

---

[19] Timberlake, "Money in the 1920s and 1930s," p. 38.
[20] Rothbard, *America's Great Depression*, pp. 94–100.
[21] Timberlake, "Money in the 1920s and 1930s," p. 40.

Fed aggregate, is not controlled by the Fed at all but by the banking public. Any time a depositor withdraws cash from a bank, currency in circulation increases and bank reserves decline, dollar for dollar. Under a fractional-reserve banking system, this loss of reserves causes a multiple contraction of bank deposits that far exceeds the original increase in currency in circulation that induced it and therefore results in a net deflation of the money supply. Conversely, a decline in the amount of currency held by the public causes an overall increase in bank reserves and an overall inflation of the money supply.

This is not all, however—Timberlake also ignores the fact that under the prevailing policy regime the banks themselves could autonomously reduce the amount of bank reserves and thus the quantity of money in existence by deliberately reducing their indebtedness to the Fed. During this period, it was the chosen policy of the Fed to lend liberally and continuously to all banks at an interest, or "discount," rate below the market rate. While the Fed was legally authorized to make such loans to its member banks, it was not mandated to do so. Furthermore, it also retained complete power to set the "discount rate" it charged on these loans. Hence, if it had chosen to, the Fed could have restricted its lending to emergency situations and charged a penalty rate substantially above the market rate, so as to discourage all but the most seriously troubled banks from applying for loans. In short, it could have almost completely neutralized the inflationary impact of its discounting operations. This "emergency lending" policy had been urged by some prominent officials within the Fed establishment itself.[22]

The fact that the Fed chose instead to pursue a "continuous lending" policy meant that the increase in bank reserves that resulted from the origination of new Fed loans to member banks via the rediscounting of business bills or advances on collateralized bank promissory notes was under the exclusive control of the Fed. But it also meant that the reduction in bank reserves entailed by the net repayment of discounted bills was uncontrolled by the Fed, because it depended solely on the decisions of the banks. Given the Fed's indiscriminate, below-market rate discount policy, the banks were always in a position to

---

[22] On the Fed's discount policy in the 1920s, see Rothbard, *America's Great Depression*, pp. 111–16.

maintain or augment their debts to the Fed if they so desired simply by discounting additional bills with the Fed. Thus, as Rothbard concluded, when "Bills Repaid" exceeded "New Bills Discounted," banks were deliberately and autonomously diminishing their level of indebtedness to the Fed and this must be counted as an uncontrolled deflationary influence on bank reserves.

Real Fed Intent

If we follow Rothbard, then, in identifying currency in circulation and the reduction of bank indebtedness to the Fed along with the gold stock as the main "uncontrolled" factors affecting bank reserves, we get a picture of the Fed's intent during the 1920s and early 1930s that is poles apart from the one suggested by Timberlake. Indeed, we find that from the inception of the monetary inflation in mid-1921 to its termination at the end of 1928, "uncontrolled reserves" decreased by $1.430 billion while controlled reserves increased by $2.217 billion. Since member bank reserves totaled $1.604 billion at the beginning of this period, this means that controlled reserves shot up by 138 percent or 18.4 percent per year during this seven-and-one-half year period, while uncontrolled reserves fell by 89 percent or 11.9 percent per year. Thus Rothbard correctly concluded that the 1920s were an inflationary decade and that it was indeed the intention of the Federal Reserve System that it be so.[23]

The Fed's inflationary intent is perfectly consistent, moreover, with its motive of helping Great Britain re-establish and maintain the pre-war parity between gold and the British pound. While Timberlake properly recognizes this motive underlying Fed policy, he is incorrect in suggesting that it necessitates a deflationary policy on the part of the Fed. In fact, the precise opposite is required. The British pound in the mid-1920s was overvalued vis-à-vis gold and the U.S. dollar, causing British products to appear relatively overpriced in world markets. As a result, Great Britain experienced imports chronically in excess of exports accompanied by persistent balance-of-payments deficits and

---

[23] For an analysis of the factors involved in the development of the monetary inflation of the 1920s, see ibid., pp. 101–25.

outflows of gold reserves. Had the Fed deflated the U.S. money supply, thus lowering U.S. prices even more relative to British prices as Timberlake claims was its intention, it would have exacerbated, and not resolved, Great Britain's gold drain. Clearly, then, the Fed's desire to aid Britain in reversing its balance-of-payments deficits and rebuilding its gold stocks called for an inflationary policy intended to pump up U.S. prices, thereby rendering British products relatively cheap and enhancing the demand for them on world markets.[24]

This point about the motive for the Fed's easy-money policy in the 1920s was not only advanced by Rothbard, but by other economists, including monetarists such as Kenneth Weiher. According to Weiher:

> Great Britain was calling for help [in 1924] and Benjamin Strong [president of the New York Fed] heard the call. Expansionary monetary policy in the U. S. would drive prices up and interest rates down in this country, which would tend to send gold flowing toward Great Britain, where prices were lower and interest rates higher. These changes would help America's ally build up its stock of gold.... [T]here can be no question that the Fed would not have moved when it did were it not for concern over the gold standard and the plight of Great Britain.... By 1927, the stagnant British economy needed help from the United States and the rest of Europe.... Just as had been the case in 1924, monetary policy was shifted to an expansionary program in an effort to aid Great Britain's struggles to return to the gold standard.[25]

Rothbard's reinterpretation of the monetary data also cuts against Timberlake's claim that the Fed "monetarily starved the country into the worst economic crisis it has ever experienced."[26] On the contrary, the factors controlled by the Fed continued to exercise a

---

[24] On the desire to help Great Britain restore the gold standard at an overvalued gold parity without having to endure the consequences of deflating its economy as an important motive driving the Fed's inflationary monetary policy in the 1920s, see ibid., pp. 131–45.

[25] Kenneth Weiher, *America's Search for Economic Stability: Monetary and Fiscal Policy Since 1913* (New York: Twayne Publishers, 1992), pp. 48–49.

[26] Timberlake, "Gold Policy in the 1930s," p. 36.

highly inflationary impact on bank reserves and the money supply from late 1929 through 1932, as the Fed attempted desperately to ward off the depression precipitated by the termination of the bank credit inflation that it had orchestrated in the 1920s.

The deflation of the money supply, therefore, was caused wholly by factors beyond the control of the Fed. First, there was a loss of confidence in the Fed-dominated phony gold standard among the domestic public and foreign investors. As a result there occurred an increase in currency in circulation and a decline in the Fed's gold stock, both of which caused bank reserves to decline. Second, U.S. banks prudently attempted to save themselves and their depositors by restricting their loans to overcapitalized and failing businesses and instead using these funds to pay down their indebtedness to the Fed, which gave further impetus to the "uncontrolled" reduction of bank reserves. Third, in the second quarter of 1932, the banks also began to increase their liquid reserves beyond the legal minimum. The accumulation of "excess reserves," as they were called, constituted a separate uncontrolled factor that reinforced the deflationary influence of the uncontrolled decline in bank reserves on the money supply.

From the end of December 1929 to the end of December 1931, bank reserves fell from $2.36 billion to $1.96 billion causing RM (for Rothbard's money supply) to drop from $73.52 billion to $68.25 billion or at an annual rate of 3.6 percent. But this monetary deflation was not caused by the Fed, which pumped up controlled reserves by $672 million or at an annual rate of 17 percent during the period, while uncontrolled reserves declined by $1,063 million or by 27 percent per year. During 1932, RM continued to decline, falling to $64.72 billion or by 5.2 percent. But bank reserves increased sharply during the year from $1.96 billion to $2.51 billion, as the Fed furiously inflated controlled reserves. In the last ten months of the year, controlled reserves rose by a staggering $1,165 million, or at an annual rate of 76 percent. Fortunately, this attempted massive inflation of the money supply was undone by the domestic public, foreign investors, and the banks as uncontrolled reserves dwindled by $495 million and banks began to accumulate substantial excess reserves.

The story was much the same in 1933 as a determined inflationary campaign conducted by the Fed in the early part of the year—controlled reserves rose by $785 million in February alone—was defeated by the public and the banks, and RM declined by over $3 billion, or by almost 5 percent.[27]

So once the data have been properly arranged and interpreted, it becomes clear that the Fed does not deserve praise for the bank credit deflation of 1930–1933. This honor goes to private dollar-holders, domestic and foreign, who attempted to reclaim their rightful property from a central bank-manipulated and inflationary financial system masquerading as a gold standard that had repeatedly betrayed their trust.

"Sterilizing" Gold

In two follow-up articles, Timberlake extends his attack on what he considers to be the "deflationary" monetary policies pursued by the Treasury and Fed in the mid-1930s. In particular, he criticizes the Treasury's policy of "neutralizing," or "sterilizing," the effect of the inflow of gold on bank reserves from late 1936 to early 1938 and the Fed's policy of increasing reserve requirements in 1936 and 1937. But neither of these policies caused a contraction of the money supply. They merely temporarily interrupted a massive monetary inflation caused by the abolition of the gold standard and subsequent devaluation of the dollar engineered by the Roosevelt administration.

It is important to recognize that this influx of gold was not a result of the "uncontrolled" operation of the gold standard, which had been abolished in 1933. Rather, it was the result of the deliberate and steady increase in the price at which gold was purchased by the U.S. Treasury and the Reconstruction Finance Corporation. By January 1934, the price of gold had risen from $20.67 to $35.00 per ounce, or by almost 70 percent, where it was officially pegged by the Gold Reserve Act of 1934. The Treasury was now legally mandated to maintain this

---

[27] On the factors responsible for the monetary deflation of the early 1930s, see Rothbard, *America's Great Depression*, pp. 186–295 passim.

devalued exchange rate between gold and the dollar by freely purchasing all the gold offered to it at this price. In effect, then, Treasury gold purchases were now economically identical to inflationary Fed open market purchases, substituting demonetized gold for government securities. Consequently, in response to this unilateral increase in the price of gold above its world price, there occurred a prodigious influx of gold into the United States—a "golden avalanche" it was called at the time—which vastly increased bank reserves. The result was an unprecedented inflation of the money supply (M2) during 1934, 1935, and 1936 at annual rates of 14 percent, 14.8 percent, and 11.4 percent, respectively.[28]

With respect to its influence on the supplies of bank reserves and money, the demonetized gold stock thus had been transformed into a factor "controlled" by monetary—in this case Treasury—policy. Given that the use and ownership of gold money by the public had been legally suppressed, gold was effectively demonetized and its continued purchase by the Treasury was purely a matter of discretionary monetary policy. Accordingly—and contrary to Timberlake's assertion— when during 1937 the Treasury began to finance its purchases of gold in a manner that neutralized their effect on bank reserves, it was not engaging in deflation. The simultaneous sales of government securities to finance these purchases were simply and properly eliminating any extraneous effects of a demonetized asset on the money supply.

Even if gold were permitted to continue in its monetary function, however, Timberlake would still be wrong in criticizing the policy of neutralizing its effect on bank reserves. For under a genuine, Currency School-type gold standard, a country's money supply would increase by exactly the amount of the gold inflow from abroad. This is not inflationary and represents precisely the proper amount by which the money supply should expand, because it is the outcome of the deliberate actions of the country's residents who are decreasing their purchases of foreign imports and increasing their sales of exports in order to satisfy their desires for greater money holdings. This balance-of-payments mechanism is a natural part of the market

---

[28] Weiher, *America's Search for Economic Stability,* pp. 75, 79–82.

economy and works continually on all levels—including the region, state, town, and even household—to efficiently adapt money supply to relative changes in money demand.

A problem arises, however, when these benign, money demand-driven gold inflows are used, as they were in the 1920s and early 1930s, as bank reserves to create unbacked notes and deposits. In this case, as F. A. Hayek has so aptly described, international gold flows will regularly cause a serious distortion of the free-market interest rate and investment pattern in the affected countries, leading to a business cycle.[29] The reason is that the needed adjustment in national money supplies upward or downward now entails creating or destroying fiduciary media by expanding or contracting bank loans in defiance of the preferences of the economy's consumers and savers. Thus, a policy of neutralizing the effect of gold flows on bank reserves in the context of a fractional-reserve banking system dominated by a central bank does not constitute a gross violation of the rules of the gold standard; to the contrary, it tends to facilitate the operation of the natural money-supply mechanism that prevails under a genuine gold standard.

Not surprisingly, in the third article of the trilogy, Timberlake also objects to the Fed's policy of raising reserve requirements in 1936 and 1937, which was undertaken to mop up the massive amounts of excess reserves held by the banking system. Timberlake advances two criticisms against this policy. First, the policy was unnecessary because, even if all the excess reserves that existed on the eve of its implementation were subsequently fully loaned out by the banks, the inflationary potential was relatively minor. Appealing to the Banking School definition of inflation, Timberlake pronounces the 52 percent increase in the money supply that would have resulted as only mildly inflationary because the larger money supply would have exceeded the needs of trade of a fully employed economy by 5.6 percent at 1929 prices, which were about 25 percent higher than prices prevailing in June 1936.[30] In plain language, Timberlake is literally defining

---

[29] F.A. Hayek, *Monetary Nationalism and International Stability* (New York: Augustus M. Kelley, [1937] 1971), pp. 25–32.

[30] These figures are calculated from Timberlake's data. See Timberlake, "The Reserve Requirement Debacle," p. 27.

away a potential money and price inflation of gargantuan proportions because of its perceived expedience in expanding employment
and output and extricating the economy from a depression. But as
Timberlake himself admits in a footnote—and as Rothbard and other
Austrians have never ceased to argue—what impeded the economy's
natural and noninflationary recovery from the depression was the
existence of "government programs [that] had actively worked against
money price declines for ten years."[31]

Growing Money Supply

In his second criticism, Timberlake contends that the increase
in reserve requirements went beyond closing off a potential avenue
of recovery for the economy and "turned what had been an ongoing recovery into another cyclical disaster." But if we once again turn
to Timberlake's data we find that the money supply (M2) continued
to grow, from \$43.3 to \$45.2 billion or by 4.4 percent, between June
30, 1936, and June 30, 1937, the year in which this policy was implemented. Even if we focus on the last six months of the period, there
was hardly a wrenching deflation, as the money supply increased at
an annual rate of 0.8 percent.[32] Even from Timberlake's monetarist
standpoint, then, it is difficult to blame the "recession within a depression" of 1937–1938 on deflationary Fed policy.

Unfortunately Timberlake's strained and narrow emphasis on
Fed deflationism as the cause of all the woes of the 1930s causes him
to ignore a plausible "Austrian" explanation of the relapse of 1937. As a
result of a spurt of union activity due to the Supreme Court's uphold-
ing of the National Labor Relations Act of 1935, money wages jumped
13.7 percent in the first three quarters of 1937. This sudden jump in
the price of labor far outstripped the rise in output prices and, with
labor productivity substantially unchanged, brought about a sharp
decline in employment beginning in late 1937.[33] The large upward

---

[31] Ibid., p. 29, fn. 11.

[32] Ibid., p. 27.

[33] Richard K. Vedder and Lowell E. Gallaway, *Out of Work: Unemployment and Government in Twentieth-Century America* (New York: Holmes and Meier, Publishers,

spurt in excess reserves and the accompanying decrease in the money supply that we observe in Timberlake's data between June 30, 1937, and June 30, 1938, therefore, can be explained as the result, and not the cause, of the recession.[34] As business profits were squeezed by the run-up of labor costs and the economy slipped into recession, banks prudently began to contract their loans and pile up liquid reserves to protect themselves against prospective loan defaults and bank runs. To offset this uncontrolled decline of the money supply, beginning in mid-1938 the Fed (and the Treasury) once again resorted to an inflationary policy, reversing the reserve requirement increase and allowing gold inflows to once again pump up bank reserves. As a result, M2 increased by 5.9 percent, 10.1 percent, and 12.5 percent in 1938, 1939, and 1940, respectively.[35]

Our conclusion, then, is that the Fed's monetary policy, except for very brief periods in 1929 and 1936–1937 when it turned mildly disinflationist, was consistently and unremittingly inflationist in the 1920s and 1930s. This inflationism was the cause of the Great Depression and one of the reasons why it was so protracted.

Bibliography

Anderson, Benjamin M. [1949] 1979. *Economics and the Public Welfare: A Financial and Economic History of the United States, 1914–1946*. Indianapolis: Liberty Press.

Burstein, M.L. 1963. *Money*. Cambridge, Mass.: Schenkman Publishing Company, Inc.

Cargill, Thomas F. 1979. *Money, the Financial System and Monetary Policy*. Englewood Cliffs, N.J.: Prentice-Hall, Inc.

Carroll, Charles Holt. 1964. *Organization of Debt into Currency and Other Papers*, Edward C. Simmons, ed. Princeton, N.J.: D. Van Nostrand Company, Inc.

Inc., 1993), pp. 129–36. For a similar explanation of the 1937 slump, see Benjamin M. Anderson, *Economics and the Public Welfare: A Financial and Economic History of the United States, 1914–1946* (Indianapolis: LibertyPress, [1949] 1979), pp. 432–38.

[34] Timberlake, "The Reserve Requirement Debacle," p. 27.

[35] Weiher, *America's Search for Economic Stability*, pp. 75–86.

Friedman, Milton and Anna Jacobson Schwartz. 1963. *A Monetary History of the United States, 1867–1960*. Princeton, N.J.: Princeton University Press.

Haines, Walter A. 1961. *Money, Prices, and Policy*. New York: McGraw-Hill Book Company, Inc.

Hart, Albert Gaylord, and Peter B. Kenen. 1961. *Money, Debt, and Economic Activity*. Englewood Cliffs, N.J.: Prentice-Hall, Inc.

Kemmerer, Edwin Walter. 1920. *High Prices and Deflation*. Princeton, N.J.: Princeton University Press.

Lin, Lin. 1937. "Are Time Deposits Money?" *American Economic Review* (March): pp. 78–86.

Meyer, Paul A. 1982. *Monetary Economics and Financial Markets*. Homewood, Ill.: Richard D. Irwin, Inc.

Ranlett, John G. 1969. *Money and Banking: An Introduction to Analysis and Policy*. New York: John Wiley & Sons, Inc.

Rothbard, Murray N. [1963] 1972. *America's Great Depression*. Los Angeles: Nash Publishing Corporation.

_____. 1995. *Classical Economics: An Austrian Perspective on the History of Economic Thought*, vol. 2. Brookfield, Vt.: Edward Elgar Publishing Company.

Timberlake, Richard H. 1999a. "Money in the 1920s and 1930s." *The Freeman* (April): pp. 37–42.

_____. 1999b. "Gold Policy in the 1930s." *The Freeman* (May): pp. 36–41.

_____. 1999c. "The Reserve Requirement Debacle of 1935–1938." *The Freeman* (June): pp. 23–29.

Vedder, Richard K., and Lowell E. Gallaway. 1993. *Out of Work: Unemployment and Government in Twentieth-Century America*. New York: Homes and Meier, Publishers, Inc.

Walker, Francis A. 1888. *Political Economy*. New York: Henry Holt and Company.

Weiher, Kenneth. 1992. *America's Search for Economic Stability: Monetary and Fiscal Policy Since 1913*. New York: Twayne Publishers.

CHAPTER 17

Inflation and Money:
A Reply to Timberlake

In his reply to my October 1999 *Freeman: Ideas on Liberty* article, Richard Timberlake fails to address or misconstrues most of the substantive issues I raised in my comment on his earlier three articles. Space constraints, however, permit me to respond only to a few of his more important arguments. These involve the evolution of the word "inflation" and the definition of money.

Evolution of the Word "Inflation"

The reader should recall that it was Timberlake himself who, in his first article, described Rothbard as "endowing inflation with a *new* and unacceptable meaning" (my emphasis) in order to "discover" a nonexistent inflation in the 1920s. I spent a substantial part of my article responding to his erroneous claim and documenting that inflation in Rothbard's sense has a long and venerable history in monetary thinking.

Now Timberlake shifts ground and argues that the pedigree of a definition of "inflation" is "largely irrelevant to substantive issues." Whether or not this latter claim is true, he is arguing to a conclusion that does not bear on the issue at hand, an issue that Timberlake himself first raised. But a few sentences later Timberlake shifts ground yet

From: "Inflation and Money: A Reply to Timberlake," *The Freeman: Ideas on Liberty* 50 (September 2000). Available at thefreemanonline.org.

again, now linking Rothbard's definition with that of some nameless "ancient economists" who he alleges "used the term 'inflation' to mean an increase in the stock of paper money together with an increase in prices." Is Rothbard's definition of inflation a newly invented ploy or an ancient fallacy? Timberlake cannot have it both ways.

Timberlake is also incorrect in asserting that it was only after the invention of price indices in the mid-nineteenth century that economists were able to "describe the value of money as the inverse of money prices" or to "properly distinguish between increases in the stock of money and general increases in money prices." In fact, the earlier British classical economists whom Timberlake cites, namely, Thornton, Ricardo, and Mill, accomplished precisely these things without recourse to a price index. As Jacob Viner, the great historian of classical economic thought, pointed out long ago, "When [the classical economists] speak of the value of money or the level of prices without explicit qualification, they mean the array of prices, of both commodities and services, in all its particularity and without conscious implication of any kind of statistical average."[1] In other words, the classical economists recognized that the value of money consisted of the "array" of alternative quantities of particular goods purchasable by the monetary unit, for example, two candy bars or one frozen yogurt cone or one-tenth of a baseball cap, and so on. If we assume that the monetary unit is the dollar, then each of these quantities of goods represents the inverse of the respective good's dollar price—$.50 per candy bar, $1.00 per frozen yogurt cone, $10.00 per baseball cap. Furthermore, the leading classical economists were insightful enough to recognize that the individual elements constituting the value of money, that is, the reciprocals of particular money prices, were heterogeneous and continually varying in relation to one another. This led some of them to deliberately shun or explicitly criticize the use of a price index, the first of which was developed in England in 1798.[2]

This brings me to Timberlake's mischaracterization of the modern Austrian case against price indices. According to Timberlake, the

---

[1] Jacob Viner, *Studies in the Theory of International Trade* (New York: Harper & Brothers Publishers, 1937), p. 314.

[2] Ibid., pp. 312–14.

thrust of the Austrian case is that price indices are "non-subjective." But this is not the Austrian objection at all. Quite to the contrary, Austrian economists, like classical monetary theorists, argue that what exists in objective reality at any moment, and what market participants therefore use in their economic calculations, are particular money prices actually paid or expected to be actually paid in the future. As noted above, the value of money is embedded in the structure of individual money prices, and cannot be conceived of apart from it. Any attempt to average this structure into a unitary price level is completely arbitrary because it entails a subjective choice by the statistician among the variety of available methods for constructing indexes. Nor is such a unitary index for measuring changes in the value of money needed by households and businesses in planning their everyday transactions. For as Ludwig von Mises pointed out:

> A judicious housewife knows much more about price changes as far as they affect her own household than the statistical averages can tell. She has little use for computations disregarding changes both in quality and the amount of goods which she is able or permitted to buy at the prices entering into the computation. If she "measures" the changes for her personal appreciation by taking the prices of only two or three commodities as a yardstick, she is no less "scientific" and no more arbitrary than the sophisticated mathematicians in choosing their methods for the manipulation of the data of the market.[3]

Thus from a substantive standpoint, Rothbard and the Austrians object to the definition of inflation as a general rise in the CPI or GDP deflator because this definition obscures the relative changes within the price structure caused by an expansion of the money supply. In other words, an increase in the money supply will cause prices to rise unevenly, with some rising earlier and to a greater extent than others.

---

[3] Ludwig von Mises, *Human Action: A Treatise on Economics*, Scholar's Edition (Auburn, Ala.: Ludwig von Mises Institute, 1999), pp. 223–24. Mises's point is most recently illustrated in the discussion of how to change the CPI to improve its "measurement" of inflation. Needless to say, the suggested changes, just as the earlier exclusion of food and energy prices on the grounds of their alleged "volatility," are themselves based on the subjective preferences of economists and statisticians. Of course, it is absurd to suggest that American households and businesses discount the recent run-up in gasoline prices in allocating their expenditures just because they are volatile.

Indeed, the very notion of a "price level" is a profoundly misleading metaphor, because it suggests the level of a body of water rising and falling uniformly and instantaneously. The more instructive metaphor is that of a swarm of bees, in which the individual bees are never lost sight of as they continually alter their relative positions within the swarm as it changes altitude. In the same manner, as the "price swarm" rises or falls as a result of a change in the supply of money, the relative positions of the individual prices, and therefore of the distribution of individual incomes and demands, undergo continual alteration and remain permanently altered even after the price swarm adjusts to its new height.[4]

The revolution in the price structure that inevitably accompanies any change in the purchasing power of money is instructively illustrated by the experience of the 1920s. As Timberlake recognizes, consumer and wholesale prices gradually declined during this decade due to a productivity-driven increase in the supplies of goods and services that outstripped the increase in the supply of money. However, what he fails to mention is that this expansion of the money supply, as a consequence of its initial injection into credit markets, also increased the prices of capital goods relative to the prices of consumer goods. The relative increase in the prices of capital goods was manifested in the boom in real estate and stock markets, in which titles to aggregates of capital goods are exchanged. In addition, long-term and short-term interest rates, which reflect the differential between capital and consumer good prices, were driven down from 1921 through 1928.[5] Owing to their reliance on a definition of "inflation" that mandates exclusive attention to a nonexistent price level, Timberlake and the monetarists are oblivious to movements in real money prices that crucially affect the economic calculations and plans of entrepreneurs and, therefore, the real production processes of the economy.

---

[4] The suggestion that the concept of a price swarm is superior to that of a price level is due to the brilliant but neglected monetary theorist Arthur W. Marget, *The Theory of Prices: A Re-examination of the Central Problem of Monetary Theory*, 2 vols. (New York: Augustus M. Kelley Publishers [1938–1942] 1966), vol. 2, pp. 330–36.

[5] Sidney Homer, *A History of Interest Rates*, 2nd ed. (New Brunswick, N.J.: Rutgers University Press, 1977), pp. 354, 372.

Finally, Timberlake invokes a strangely irrelevant "thought experiment" to disprove Rothbard's claim that a major inflation occurred
during the 1920s. According to Timberlake, an inflation could not
have occurred between 1921 and 1929 because anyone would prefer
$2,000 of income in 1929 dollars to the same income in 1921 dollars,
given that prices were lower in 1929 than in 1921. While this is true,
it is a textbook case of begging the question by assuming what is to be
proved.[6] Obviously, if Rothbard's definition is assumed to be wrong
from the outset and, therefore, inflation is defined as a general rise in
prices, and prices have indeed fallen, then it can be validly inferred
that no inflation has occurred. But Timberlake's argument proves
nothing against the usefulness of Rothbard's definition of inflation. I
could just as easily argue that if the Fed had not "inflated" the money
supply during the 1920s, the value of money would have been even
higher in 1929 than it actually was and people would prefer $2,000 of
income in the 1929 dollars of this counterfactual world to the same
nominal income in actual 1929 dollars. This would hardly prove that
Timberlake's definition of inflation is useless, though I believe it is for
the reasons stated above.

The Definition of Money

In discussing the issue of which items to include in the definition of the money supply, Timberlake refers to Leland Yeager's
empirical test for identifying those assets that function as a general
medium of exchange. According to this test, when people feel that
they are holding too much money they attempt to rid themselves of
the excess by spending it on various goods and services, thus causing money prices in these markets to begin to rise. The extra spending and rising prices spread throughout the economy will continue
until the value of money has been driven down to the point at which
people are satisfied with holding the entire existing stock of money
because their anticipated transactions will now require greater sums
of the less-valuable money. Thus for Yeager the money supply consists

---

[6] Antony Flew, *Thinking Straight* (Amherst, N.Y.: Prometheus Books, 1977), pp.
65–66.

of those things, such as currency and demand deposits, that are routinely spent and accepted as final payment in all markets.

However, demand deposits do not pass Yeager's test just because checks drawn on them are spendable or because they operate as an independent medium of exchange alongside currency. Rather, demand deposits can be considered part of the money supply because they are interchangeable at par and on demand into currency, that is, Fed notes, which in our present system is the ultimate embodiment of the general medium of exchange. But once this is realized, it becomes immediately clear that noncheckable savings deposits at commercial and savings banks as well as the share accounts of savings and loan associations operate likewise as instantaneously redeemable, par-value claims to definite quantities of currency.[7] The fact that the owner of a savings deposit in the 1920s could not spend by directly transferring a portion of his deposit balance to a third party via check but had to walk or drive to the bank to redeem it before making his expenditure is a technical detail that does not affect the essence of the economic transaction. Savings deposits and savings and loan share accounts, no less than demand deposits, therefore, offer unconditional access to immediately spendable dollars and thus meet Yeager's criterion for inclusion in the money supply.

Rothbard clarified this point with the following example. Let us assume that as a result of the development of a sudden and widespread cultural aversion to the number 5 among the nonbank public, five-dollar bills are no longer accepted in exchange. When someone now wishes to exchange some of his five-dollar bills, he must first travel to the bank to convert them into dollar bills of other denominations. Now as long as these bills remain interchangeable at par and on demand into dollar bills of other denominations, no one would have reason to object to their inclusion in the money supply. Indeed, they

---

[7] As I pointed out in my previous article, savings deposits and S&L share accounts were, for all intents and purposes, effectively convertible into currency on demand. Moreover, just as in the case of demand deposits, after 1934 the par-value interchangeability between savings deposits and S&L share accounts on the one hand and currency on the other was insured by an agency of the federal government. This occurred for credit unions only after 1971.

would pass Yeager's test: thus, if a helicopter were sent forth by the Fed to shower the country with additional billions of dollars in five-dollar bills, money prices and incomes would soon begin a general rise as the populace scrambled to spend their surplus cash balances. But as Rothbard pointed out, savings deposits are in precisely the same situation as the five-dollar bills in this example: other things equal, an increase in their total would create an excess supply of spendable dollars in the economy initiating an adjustment process that lowers the value of money. In fact, in the 1920s bank credit expansion resulted in a disproportionate growth in "time," or savings, deposits vis-à-vis demand deposits, because businessmen were induced by the payment of interest on savings deposits to hold the less active portion of their balances in this type of bank account.[8]

Timberlake offers a second test that allegedly supports his narrower definition of the money supply. According to this econometric test, a particular type of asset is to be included in the definition of the money supply if its inclusion improves the positive correlation between the empirical monetary aggregate and total dollar spending on final goods and services or gross national product. The logic of this test implies that if the addition of the supply of peanut butter to the monetary aggregate being tested improved its "explanation" of total spending, then peanut butter would be considered part of the money supply. But this positivist test is in direct conflict with Yeager's test, which is designed to identify only those assets as money that function essentially as a general medium of exchange, that is, which are purchased in anticipation of being resold for other goods in the future. Thus Yeager's essentialist test would exclude peanut butter because, in our economy at least, it is a consumer's good, an excess supply of which results in a fall in its own money price and not directly in an increase in the money prices of other goods. In fact, in the same article

---

[8] On this neglected aspect of the 1920s inflation, see C.A. Phillips, T.F. McManus, and R.W. Nelson, *Banking and the Business Cycle: A Study of the Great Depression in the United States* (New York: Arno Press, [1937] 1972), pp. 95–101; Benjamin M. Anderson, *Economics and the Public Welfare: A Financial and Economic History of the United States, 1914–1946*, 2nd ed. (Indianapolis: Liberty Press, 1979), pp. 139–43. Not coincidentally, the authors of these two volumes were heavily influenced by Austrian monetary and business-cycle theory.

that Timberlake quotes from, Yeager strongly criticizes precisely the very positivist approach to defining money that Timberlake defends.

Bibliography

Anderson, Benjamin M. 1979. *Economics and the Public Welfare: A Financial and Economic History of the united States, 1914–1946,* 2nd ed. Indianapolis: Liberty Press.

Flew, Antony. 1977. *Thinking Straight.* Amherst, N.Y.: Prometheus Books.

Homer, Sidney. 1977. *A History of Interest Rates,* 2nd ed. New Brunswick, N.J.: Rutgers University Press.

Marget, Arthur W. [1938–1942] 1966. *The Theory of Prices: A Re-Examination of the Central Problem of Monetary Theory,* 2 vols. New York: Augustus M. Kelley.

Mises, Ludwig von. 1999. *Human Action: A Treatise on Economics,* Scholar's Edition. Auburn, Ala.: Ludwig von Mises Institute.

Phillips, C.A., T.F. McManus, and R.W. Nelson. [1937] 1972. *Banking and the Business cycle: A Study of the Great Depression in the United States.* New York: Arno Press.

Viner, Jacob. 1937. *Studies in the Theory of International Trade.* New York: Harper & Brothers Publishers.

CHAPTER 18

A Monetary Explanation of the October Stock Market Crash: An Essay In Applied Austrian Economics

This article will attempt to place the events of "Black Monday," October 19, 1987, in perspective by explaining how they fit into the broader boom-bust cycle, as this sequence of phenomena is conceived by the Austrian theory of the business cycle. The monetary aggregate known as TMS, initially outlined in the works of Murray Rothbard, plays a central role in my explanation.[1] In particular, I will argue that the October stock market crash was the inevitable consequence, not of newfangled computer trading programs, but of an old-fashioned inflationary boom. Like all inflations, the Great Inflation of 1982–87 was fundamentally a monetary phenomenon. It was orchestrated by the Federal Reserve System and financed by a massive and prolonged increase in the money supply.

Setting the Stage: The Inflationary Boom of 1982–1987

In analyzing the development of the inflationary boom, I focus in turn on developments in the supply of money, the market for consumer goods, capital markets, and foreign exchange markets.

From: "A Monetary Explanation of the October Stock Market Crash: An Essay in Applied Austrian Economics," *Austrian Economics Newsletter* 9 (Spring/Summer 1988): pp. 2–6.

[1] TMS stands for "true money supply"—in the sense of true to the theoretical definition of money as athe general medium of exchange. For a discussion of TMS and its components, see Chapter 3.

The Supply of Money

The Penn Square bank failure and the threat of default by Mexico and then other LDCs (less developed countries) on their international loans in the summer of 1982 underscored the precarious stability of the world financial system, including and especially U.S. money-center banks. These events in conjunction with the continuing recession in the U.S. economy—whose persistence had repeatedly defied official forecasts—prompted the Federal Reserve System, in July of that year, to initiate a policy of vigorous monetary expansion.

The dimensions of this inflation of money, which propelled the U.S. economy on a rapid recovery from the recession of 1981–1982, can be seen in the sharp acceleration of the growth of adjusted bank reserves.[2] From 3Q-82 (third quarter, 1982) to 4Q-83, adjusted reserves increased from $49.3 to $54.2 billion, or at an annual rate of 9.94 percent, which represents a tripling of the 3.31percent annualized rate of reserve growth occurring over the seven quarters from 4Q-80 to 3Q-82.[3] To supplement its reserve-creating open market operations and to emphatically signal the markets of its resolve to reinflate the economy, the Fed cut the discount rate seven times just in the last two quarters of 1982. Fueled by this rapid increase in bank reserves and by the introduction of MMDA's, TMS shot up from an average of $929.8 billion in 3Q-82 to an average of $1,355.2 billion in 3Q-83, equivalent to a 45.76 percent (uncompounded) annual rate of growth. It is true that much of the enormous increase in TMS coincided with an anomalous one-shot increase in the overall demand to

---

[2] I focus on adjusted reserves to gauge the intended thrust of Fed policy, because variations in adjusted reserves are directly related to variations in the aggregate money stock and because the Fed possesses the means for controlling the rate of growth of total reserves, if not in the short run then certainly in the intermediate run (quarter to quarter). In addition, since 1979 the Fed's policy-making arm has been using reserve targets to guide its actions toward policy objectives. To ascertain short-run changes in monetary policy, I resort to month-to-month changes in the Fed's stock of government securities, which are determined solely by Fed open market operations, although changes in Federal Reserve credit or even in the adjusted monetary base could also be used for this purpose.

[3] All statistics relating to adjusted reserves and the Fed stock of government securities are drawn from *Monetary Trends*, published monthly by the Federal Reserve Bank of St. Louis.

hold money by a public eager to add high interest-earning and feder-ally-insured dollars in checkable MMDAs to its cash balances. Since (personal) MMDAs require no legal reserve backing, their expansion did not absorb the existing bank reserves, and it was therefore possible for the banking system to meet this demand without a net contraction of other components of TMS. Nonetheless, TMS net of MMDAs and saving deposits still expanded over the period under consideration at the dramatically inflationary rate of 14.17 percent per year. During the same period, the reserve absorbing aggregate of demand deposits plus other checkable deposits grew at an average annual rate of 14.45 percent.[4]

By the fourth quarter of 1983 the Fed had switched to a more restrictive monetary policy, signaled by a freezing of adjusted reserves at a level of $54.2 billion from 3Q-83 to 4Q-83. The restriction of reserve growth constricted TMS growth over the same quarter to a per annum rate of 2.7 percent. The Fed's less expansionary policy remained in force through the fourth quarter of 1984. Over the five quarters from 3Q-83 through 4Q-84, adjusted reserves expanded at an annual rate of 6.05 percent, from $54.2 to $58.3 billion, a reduction of more than 3.5 percentage points in its annual growth rate when compared to the previous four quarters. In the same period, TMS was inflated at an annual rate of 4.27 percent or from $1,355.2 to $1,427.6 billion.

The third quarter of 1984 saw the reduction of the rate of money creation begin to "bite" in the real economy, causing a "growth slow-down" and precipitating fears of an imminent recession. By 4Q-84, real GNP growth had slowed to an annual rate of 1.7 percent, compared to 10.7 percent and 5.5 percent in 1Q-84 and 2Q-84, respectively.[5] In addition to the looming specter of an economy-wide recession, the Fed also confronted localized depression in particular

---

[4] For a discussion of the effects on the money supply of the new structure of reserve requirements for different kinds of bank deposits introduced in 1980 , see R. Alton Gilbert, "A Revision in the Monetary Base," Federal Reserve Bank of St. Louis *Review* 69 (August/September): pp. 24–29.

[5] Federal Reserve Bank of St. Louis, *National Economic Trends* (December 1987), p. 12.

U.S. export and import-competing industries, attributable to ongoing international shifts in comparative advantage and the relentless strengthening of the dollar on foreign exchange markets. Thus, as early as August 1984, some members of the policy-setting Fed Open Market Committee (FOMC) were advocating a return to vigorous monetary stimulation, referred todescribed as "a lessening in the degree of reserve restraint."[6] Between the FOMC's November and December meetings, open market operations were ". . . directed at achieving some reduction in pressures on bank reserves against the background of lagging growth in the narrow money supply, generally sluggish expansion in the economy, subdued inflation, and continued strength of the dollar in the foreign exchange markets."[7] Finally, at the December 1984 meeting, an imminent renewal of the inflationary boom was declared in euphemistic terms, as "… most of the members expressed a preference for directing open market operations toward some further easing of reserve conditions to encourage satisfactory growth in M1 and to improve the prospects for economic expansion in 1985."[8]

Thus the third and final phase of the boom was ushered in at the beginning of 1985 when the Fed unleashed a new and sustained burst of monetary inflation on the U.S. economy with the aim of forestalling the impending recession and driving down the value of the dollar on world currency markets. From December 1984 to the end of the boom in May 1987, adjusted reserves grew by over 24 percent (from $58.4 to $73 billion) or at an uncompounded rate of slightly more than 10 percent per annum. The result was an explosion in TMS, which increased by almost 34 percent in this period (from $1,452 to $1,942.2 billion) or at an annualized rate of about 14 percent.

Prices of Consumer Goods

What enabled the Fed to stoke the fires of monetary inflation as vigorously and as long as it did was the fact that the effects of this

---

[6] Hafer, 1985, p. 27.

[7] Ibid., p. 28.

[8] Ibid.

inflation were obscured in U.S. consumer-goods markets, especially in 1985 and 1986. For example, in the years 1983–1986, consumer prices, as represented by the CPI, increased at annual rates of 3.8 percent, 4.0 percent, 3.8 percent, and 1.1 percent, respectively. In the same four years, the fourth quarter-to-fourth quarter rates of increase for TMS were: 38.8 percent; 4.62 percent; 13.44 percent; and 12.7 percent

The large discrepancy between money inflation and price inflation is attributable to the simultaneous operation of a number of adventitious factors. These include the prolonged appreciation of the dollar on foreign exchange markets, which began in 1980 and propelled the dollar to postwar peaks against the German mark and a trade-weighted basket of foreign currencies in February 1985. The downward pressure that this exerted on the dollar prices of internationally traded goods, and thus on the overall U.S. price level, was reinforced by concurrent developments affecting supplies on various world commodity markets.

For example, the spread of technological advances in food-grain production to developing countries resulted in increased supplies and reduced prices of food products on the U.S. market. The collapse of OPEC and ITA cartel agreements led to supply gluts and sharply lower prices for oil and tin, as well as for substitute fuels and metals. Moreover, the belated and sluggish recovery of Western Europe from recession dampened the world demand for imports of primary commodities at the same time that the supply of these products to world markets was being stepped up by producing nations desperate for foreign exchange, especially dollars, to finance debt repayments.

These exchange-rate and supply factors heavily influenced domestic input prices, as exemplified in annual rates of change of the U.S. producer price index for crude materials for the four years 1983–1986. After a 4.7 percent increase in 1983, changes in the index for the next three years were: −1.6 percent; −5.6 percent; and −9 percent.[9] To use Mises's terminology, the tendency to higher consumer prices emanating from the "money-side" of the economy was partially offset by temporary price-reducing factors operating concurrently on

---

[9] Federal Reserve Bank of Cleveland 1988.

the "goods-side" of the economy. We may gain some perspective on the moderating effect of goods-side factors on the overall rate of U.S. price inflation by comparing the GNP deflator for service-producing industries with the GNP deflator for manufacturing industries, whose product costs and prices tend to be directly affected by developments on world currency and commodity markets. In 1982–85, the former index rose at an average annual rate of 5.4 percent, while the latter was rising at a 1.9 percent average annual rate. Alternatively, we note that, for the years 1983–1986, the average annual rate of increase of the CPI computed for all items except food and energy exceeded that of the CPI for all items by 1.3 points (4.5 percent vs. 3.2 percent).[10]

Another deflationary influence on prices of consumer goods was the increase in the total demand to hold U.S. dollars, which, ceteris paribus, tends to increase the purchasing power of the dollar in goods markets. One component of this increased demand can be traced to the enormous expansion of the volume of transactions in U.S. financial markets, which, for a variety of reasons, has been under way in the 1980s. To finance this growth in transactions, both domestic and foreign investors were required to acquire and hold larger dollar balances. In addition, capital fleeing from hyperinflationary and collapsing currencies abroad, e.g., Mexico and Argentina, found a "safe haven" in U.S. bank deposits and currency. Indeed, as Murray Rothbard has pointed out, there has occurred a substantial but un-measurable leakage of dollar currency out of the U.S. into foreign hoards and to finance transactions in the subterranean economies of foreign nations, especially in Latin America and Asia. There is also evidence that the ever-growing, worldwide drug trade, now estimated at $100 billion per year, absorbed substantial quantities of U.S. currency and thereby contributed to a rise in the global demand for dollars.

Capital Markets

Austrian business-cycle theory leads us to expect that monetary inflation will have an earlier and more intense impact on capital

---

[10] Federal Reserve Bank of Cleveland, *Economic Trends* (February 1987).

markets than on markets for consumer goods for two reasons. First, in the modern economy, most newly-created money initially enters the economy via increased commercial bank lending to business firms, which directly tends to lower interest rates. The additional loan funds are used by borrowing firms to increase investment in productive assets, especially fixed investment in long-lived capital goods such as producers' durable equipment and business structures. The increased investment spending, in turn, leads to higher prices for capital goods (relative to consumer goods), and higher earnings and capital values for firms producing these goods. Furthermore, the lowering of interest rates produced by the inflow of new money through the credit markets tends to increase the capital values and market prices of existing capital goods and of productive land factors, and this is reflected in increased market values for the firms which own these productive assets. Stock, credit (bond, commercial paper, commercial bank loan), and real estate markets, therefore, react most sensitively to monetary expansion, because these are the markets in which ownership titles to capital goods are exchanged.

The second reason why price inflation in consumer goods markets is generally presaged by boom conditions in capital markets involves the nature and formation of inflationary expectations. As Mises points out, during a progressing monetary inflation, inflationary expectations do not abruptly take hold of all market participants at once, but spread gradually through the ranks of those who are most keenly attuned to developments affecting the future state of market prices, and subsequently to the public-at-large. In particular, the premium on interest rates which reflects generally prevailing expectations of inflation in credit markets ". . . comes into existence step by step as soon as first a few and then successively more and more actors become aware of the fact that the market is faced with cash-induced changes in the money relation [i.e., the supply of and demand for money] and consequently with a trend oriented in a definite direction."[11]

---

[11] Ludwig von Mises, *Human Action: A Treatise on Economics* (Chicago: Henry Regnery, 1966), p. 544.

Empirically, those who are first to anticipate a decline in the purchasing power of the monetary unit and to adjust their buying and selling decisions accordingly tend to be the "entrepreneur-promoters," who regularly and successfully operate on capital markets and whose livelihood depends on rapidly and correctly adjusting their current activities to anticipated changes in future market conditions.

Thus the "promoter" concept is central to the theory of inflationary expectations,

> for it refers to a datum that is a general characteristic of human nature, that is present in all market transactions and marks them profoundly. This is the fact that various individuals do not react to a change in conditions with the same quickness and in the same way. The inequality of men, which is due to differences both in their inborn qualities, and in the vicissitudes of their lives, manifests itself in this way too. There are in the market pacemakers and others who only imitate the procedures of their more agile fellow citizens.... The driving force of the market, the element tending toward unceasing innovation and improvement, is provided by the restlessness of the promoter and his eagerness to make profits as large as possible....[12]

Moreover, in the modern economy, the main locus of entrepreneurial activities tends to transcend the narrow confines of the organization of the business firm and to center in markets in titles to capital goods, that is, in capital markets. As Mises explains:

> The entrepreneurs and capitalists ... perform all those acts the totality of which is called the capital and money market. It is these financial transactions of promoters and speculators that direct production.... These transactions constitute the market as such. If one eliminates them, one does not preserve any part of the market.... The speculators, promoters, investors and moneylenders [determine] the structure of the stock and commodity exchanges and of the money market....[13]

---

[12] Mises, *Human Action*, p. 255.

[13] Ibid., p. 708.

These theoretical considerations account for the accelerated price inflation evidenced in capital markets during the inflationary boom of 1982–1987.

For example, the bond market rallied and short-term interest rates fell steadily from the inception of the inflationary boom in mid-1982 and reached a plateau in 1983. After trendless fluctuations through the period of slower monetary growth ending in early 1985, rates trended sharply downward during the renewed burst of monetary expansion of the next two years. The three-month commercial paper rate fell almost three percentage points, from 8.77 percent to 5.87 percent, from March 15, 1985 to January 23, 1987. Over approximately the same period, the yield on Corporate Triple A bonds declined from 12.64 percent to 8.31 percent and the prime rate fell from 10.5 percent to 7.5 percent. One bond price index, the Dow Jones Index for 10 Industrials, rose from an intrayear low of 57.36 for 1982 to a yearly high of 93.10 for 1987, an increase of about 62 percent.

In the case of the stock market, the great bull market(s) of the 1980s coincided almost exactly with the accelerated monetary inflations of 1982–83 and 1985–1986. In the fifteen months from the end of August 1982 through October 1983, the broad-based Standard & Poor's Index of 400 Industrial stocks increased by about 54 percent, from 122.49 to 189.00. After a period, of stagnation, decline, and recovery, which lingered through 1984, the bull market resumed in 1985, propelling the index upward to 334.65 by March 1987. Over the entire period, the index rose by 173 percent. Concomitantly, the annual yield on stocks (the inverse of the P/E ratio), averaged over the same 400 stocks, was driven down from 5.91 percent in July 1982 to 2.51 percent in March 1987.

Foreign Exchange Markets

The latest approach to foreign exchange markets, which was clearly formulated by Mises as early as 1912, treats them as efficient asset markets, wherein current prices or exchange rates quickly adjust to take account of changes in expectations regarding the future development of the relative purchasing powers of the various currencies. Mises's statement of the approach, however, is more realistic than the modern approach. Whereas the latter assumes "rational expectations," Mises bases his statement of the approach on a realistic theory of expectations formation and revision which that focuses on the entrepreneur-promoter described above. An important implication of this asset market approach to exchange rates, in both its Misesian and rational-expectations variants, is that exchange rates adjust to monetary inflation very rapidly and certainly before consumer prices and the internal purchasing power of the currency fully adjust. As Mises explained in 1919:

> Price increases, which are called into existence by an increase in the quantity of money, do not appear overnight. A certain amount of time passes before they appear. The additional quantity of money enters the economy at a certain point. It is only from there, step by step, that it is dispersed. It goes first to certain individuals in the economy only and to certain branches of production. As a result, in the beginning it raises the demand for certain goods and services only, not for all of them. Only later do the prices of other goods and services also rise. Foreign exchange quotations, however, are speculative rates of exchange—that is they arise out of the transactions of business people, who, in their operations, consider not only the present but also potential future developments. Thus, the depreciation of the money becomes apparent relatively soon in the foreign exchange quotations on the Bourse—long before the prices of other goods and services are affected....[14]

In the first part of the boom, the dollar continued to appreciate against foreign currencies generally, including the Japanese yen and the German mark, reaching its peak in February 1985. The dollar appreciation was due to the fact that the price inflation rate in the U.S. before 1985 was not significantly higher than in Germany and Japan, while relatively high U.S. interest rates resulting from heavy government borrowing to finance federal budget deficits attracted

---

[14] Ludwig von Mises, "Balance of Payments and Foreign Exchange Rates," in idem, *On the Manipulation of Money and Credit*, ed. Percy L. Greaves, trans. Bettina Bien Greaves (Dobbs Ferry, N.Y.: Free Market Books, 1978), p. 51.

a substantial influx of foreign capital. In early 1985, however, symptoms of the ongoing dollar inflation finally began to appear in world currency markets as inflationary expectations were kindled by the ballyhoo and publicity surrounding the decision of the Fed to cure the yawning U.S. trade gap by deliberately driving down the foreign-exchange value of the dollar.

As a consequence, the dollar price of a German mark was bid steadily upward from approximately $.31 at its all time low in February 1985 to around $.55 at the end of the boom in April-May 1987, representing a price increase of 7.42 percent. Over the same period, the dollar exchange rate for the yen rose from just under $.004 to just over $.007 per yen, a price inflation of 75 percent.[15] Against a trade-weighted basket of foreign currencies, the dollar lost about 40 percent of its market value during the period.

Monetary Deflation and Crash

The monetary deflation of 1987 was motivated by the Fed's desire to arrest the two-year decline in the external value of the dollar. In late January, the U.S. and Japan undertook "coordinated intervention" into the foreign exchange markets to support the dollar. Under the terms of the Louvre accord, concluded in late February, monetary authorities of six industrial countries including the U.S. agreed "…to cooperate closely to foster stability of exchange rates around current levels."[16]

The decision to prevent further depreciation of the dollar on foreign exchange markets and to stabilize its exchange rates with the mark and yen within "narrow bands" established by the Louvre accord brought monetary inflation to a screeching, if only temporary, halt in February 1987. During the six months prior to this date, the annualized growth rates of adjusted reserves and TMS were 18.27 percent and 19.59 percent, respectively. Suddenly, monetary

---

[15] Federal Reserve Bank of St. Louis, *International Economic Conditions* (January 1988): pp. 2–3.

[16] Federal Reserve Bank of St. Louis, *National Economic Trends* (December 1987): p. 58.

policy was thrown into reverse as the Fed sold $8.4 billion of government securities, disgorging almost 4 percent of its entire stock in one month. This produced a virtual halt in the growth of bank reserves and a collapse of TMS, which fell from $1,920.4 to $1,873.3 to yield an annual growth rate of −29.4 percent for February. The result was that from late January to early March, dollar exchange rates held firm.

Despite the fact that the Fed's actions continued to lean toward a policy of monetary tightness in March (open-market operations were slightly expansionary and adjusted reserves grew negligibly), TMS continued to spiral upward at an annual rate of 13.8 percent, fueled by a mammoth 9 percent expansion of the nonreservable savings deposit component that swamped a net decline in other elements of TMS. With the onset of the bond market collapse in April, however, the Fed turned expansionary with a vengeance, swelling its stock of government securities by 4 percent and driving up adjusted reserves and TMS at annual rates of 24.6 percent and 27.7 percent, respectively. Predictably, the dollar once again depreciated sharply on foreign exchange markets from mid-March through April despite active and strong intervention by the U.S. and foreign central banks. From its levels in mid-March, the dollar had depreciated 8.38 percent against the yen and 4.38 percent against the mark by the end of April.[17]

Alarmed at the accelerating free fall of the dollar, Paul Volcker announced in late April that the Fed had "snugged up" monetary policy to counteract exchange rate pressure.[18] Thus in May, reserve growth virtually ceased and TMS increased at an annual rate of 2.2 percent, with the dollar falling to nearly a 40-year low against the yen and to a seven-year low against the mark before beginning to sharply appreciate in late May. The Fed continued efforts to bolster the external value of the dollar through the next three months by contractionary open market operations, which saw it shrink its government securities portfolio by 4.2 percent. The result was a three-month monetary deflation, with TMS contracting by a total of about $21 billion or at annual rates of −4.6 percent, −1.0 percent, and −7.0 percent

---

[17] Ibid, p. 62.
[18] Ibid.

for June, July, and August, respectively. The deflationary policy came to an end in September when the Fed reinstituted expansionary open market operations (although adjusted reserves declined for the month) and TMS increased at a 6.3 percent annual rate, fueled mainly by a large increase in U.S. Government Deposits.

As noted above, the bond market began a steep fall in early April that persisted through May. The interest rate on Triple A corporate bonds rose more than one percentage point, from 8.36 percent to 9.49 percent, between March 27 and May 22. Other credit markets followed, as the commercial paper and prime rates increased, respectively, from 6.29 percent to 6.96 percent and from 7.5 percent to over 8 percent. After relative stability through June, July, and most of August, credit markets became firmly convinced that the monetary inflation was at an end and interest rates resumed their steep ascent, which continued until the October crash. By October 16, the AAA corporate bond rate had reached 10.73 percent, over one percentage point higher than its rate on August 28. Likewise, short-term interest rates rose rapidly between these two dates, with the commercial paper rate jumping from 6.64 percent to 7.86 percent and the prime rising from 8.25 percent to 9.25 percent.

Equities markets followed a different pattern than credit markets in 1987. During the steep run-up in interest rates that occurred during March-May, the stock market experienced only a temporary pause, with the S & P 400 Industrials averaging 334.65 in March and 336.10 in May. While conditions stabilized in credit markets during the summer months, the stock market resumed its boom, the S & P index averaging 14.53 percent higher in August than in May. The deflationary monetary policy of the summer months finally brought the stock market boom to an end in August. However, it took another month and one-half and a series of further events to fully break the back of inflationary expectations in the stock market. The renewed depreciation of the dollar on the foreign exchange markets, which had begun in early August, provoked a discount rate hike in early September, which failed to more than momentarily strengthen the dollar. Against the background of further weakening of the dollar in early October, Treasury Secretary James Baker's desperate bashing of and threats against West Germany for raising the discount rate in the week before the crash at long last galvanized investors into the realization that tight monetary policy was here to stay and that the Fed was not about to reignite boom conditions.

The result of the divergent movements in credit and equities markets during April-September 1987 was to create a growing differential between bond and stock yields. Thus, between 1981 and Spring 1987 stock and bond prices and yields tracked one another quite closely.[19] However, from April to September 1987, the average yield for S & P's 400 Industrial stocks fell from 2.52 percent to 2.33 percent, while the yield on Triple A bonds rose from 8.85 percent to 10.18 percent. With inflationary expectations no longer operative in the stock market, this unprecedented yield differential became unsustainable. During the boom—but especially from early 1985 onward—stock P/E ratios were driven to dizzying heights by investors' expectations of a continuation of low interest rates and of the imminent arrival of price inflation and inflated corporate earnings. The Fed's volte-face on monetary policy eventually compelled a wrenching revision of expectations among bull-market investors, who now were convinced that interest rates would remain high for the foreseeable future and began to use these higher rates to discount their lowered estimates of future corporate earnings.

The precipitous fall of stock prices on Meltdown Monday thus represented a fundamentally rational, if belated, adjustment of the market to the termination of the Fed-induced inflationary boom. The remedy for stock-market volatility therefore does not lie in the proposals offered by the new Luddites on the Brady commission, who seek to seriously impede, if not destroy, the new productive machinery of stock index trading, portfolio insurance, and computer program trading. No, the aim of preventing stock-market crashes can be attained only by successfully preventing monetary inflation. And this can be achieved only by restoring the ultra-hard money of a genuine gold standard and putting a definitive end to political manipulation of the supply of dollars.

---

[19] Federal Reserve Bank of Cleveland, *Economic Trends* (December 1987).

Epilogue: After the Crash[20]

Since the October stock market crash and especially since the beginning of 1988 the Federal Reserve System has pursued a vigorously inflationary monetary policy and this has succeeded in rekindling the boom and postponing the recession-readjustment which had just begun to take hold in 4Q-88. The fact that interest rates have risen steadily since March has misled financial writers and some economists into proclaiming that the Fed has been progressively tightening monetary policy during this period. But let us examine the money supply figures.

From December 1987 to March 1988 adjusted reserves increased at an annual rate of 7.36 percent, while M1 expanded at a 6.5 percent annual rate and TMS by a 2.78 percent annual rate. The period March 1988 to June 1988 witnessed a speed-up of monetary inflation, as the annual growth rates of adjusted reserves, M1, and TMS accelerated to 10.56 percent, 7.05 percent, and 7.36 percent, respectively. In response to the inflationary monetary policy, the U.S. economy experienced a significant increase in the rate of price inflation in 2Q-88, as the CPI rose at a 4.8 percent annual rate in this period after increasing at a 3.4 percent annual rate in 1Q-88. Credit markets responded to the expansionary monetary policy with steadily declining interest rates from the beginning of 1988 through early March. The sharp reversal of this downward trend during March, especially with respect to short-term rates, was due not to any alleged tightening of monetary policy by the Fed but to the growing realization and conviction among market participants that inflation rather than recession was the most likely prospect for the near future. While the trauma of the October crash kept a jittery stock market on a roller coaster during the first five months of 1988, inflationary expectations finally took hold at the end of May and drove the market (as measured by the Dow Jones Average for 30 Industrial Stocks) to post-crash highs by late June. The real sector of the economy, particularly in the area of investment, also

---

[20] This Epilogue is an excerpt from an article (Joseph T. Salerno, "The October Stock Market Crash: Causes and Consequences," *The University of Baltimore Business Review*, 8, no. 5 [September/October 1988]: pp. 1–3, 6–8) published one year after the October stock market crash of 1987.

regained substantial momentum in the first half of 1988 under the stimulus of inflationary credit creation by the commercial banking system. From December 1987 to June 1988, commercial bank loans to business expanded at a 10.22 percent annual rate, with the rate exceeding 17 percent over the final three months of the period. The explosive growth of new bank deposits in the hands of business firms succeeded in rekindling the investment boom that had all but died out in 4Q-87. Business fixed investment, which had grown at a paltry 1.7 percent per annum year during 4Q-87, increased by annual rates of 7.6 percent in 1Q-88 and 15.65 percent in 2Q-88. The investment boom also manifested itself during 2Q-88 in a dramatic surge in the after-tax "profits" (net incomes) of corporations operating in basic or "higher-stage" industries such as autos and equipment, forest products, industrial and farm gear, nonferrous metals, petroleum, pipelines, railroads, and steelmaking. Throughout the third quarter, evidence has continued to mount that the American economy is in the midst of a renewed inflationary boom. For example, price inflation, as measured by the CPI, exceeded 5 percent per annum for July and August. Inflationary expectations have driven short term interest rates up between 100 and 150 basis points since March. Whether and for how long this boom can be prolonged and the inevitable recession delayed depends crucially on the actions of U.S. policymakers, particularly the Federal Reserve System.

The Fed signaled its concern with inflation by raising the discount rate from 6.0 percent to 6.5 percent in early August. The minutes of the mid-August meeting of the FOMC reveal that many of the members "saw substantial risks that inflationary pressures would intensify" and "thought that some further firming was likely to be necessary, perhaps relatively soon." So far, however, the Fed has refrained from significantly tightening monetary policy. Nor is the Fed likely to tighten and risk panicking financial markets before the Presidential election.

In the months after the election, however, the Fed's hand will be forced. In response to the rapid increase of the money supply in 1988, consumer price inflation will worsen and will head into the range of 6 percent to 8 percent per year This will intensify inflationary expectations and cause interest rates to rise more steeply. The new president, whoever he turns out to be, will be eager to get the accelerating inflation under control in the first year or two of his administration in order to avoid the prospect of the consequent recession dragging on into the year leading up to the 1992 election.

But the greatest pressure moving the Fed to slow monetary growth will not come from the speed-up of domestic price inflation. As inflationary expectations take hold in the foreign exchange markets, the recent appreciation of the dollar, which has been due to the operation of several temporary factors, will be reversed. As the dollar heads downward to the lower end of its "official" trading ranges with the yen and mark, U.S. policymakers may importune the Germans and Japanese to lend support to the dollar by accelerating the inflation of their own currencies. It is highly unlikely, however, that the U.S. will obtain more than rhetoric and token support from this quarter. Foreign capital will begin to leak and then run out of U.S. financial markets, putting additional upward pressure on interest rates and causing the long-term bond market to begin to crumble.

At this point, there will be enormous pressure brought to bear on the Fed to provide increased "liquidity" to financial markets and to bring down interest rates, in order to avert defaults of LDC debtors and a new rash of failures among still-weak U.S. thrift and banking institutions. Should the Fed succumb to this pressure and increase the rate of monetary growth, it will only succeed in intensifying inflationary expectations, accelerating the depreciation of the dollar, and precipitating a full-fledged capital flight out of the U.S. economy.

If the Fed did not already realize it, then it would quickly discover that the only viable option for restoring confidence in the future purchasing power of the dollar and arresting its decline on currency markets is to significantly restrict or even halt the growth of money and credit. When this occurs, the expansion of the 1980s will come to a definitive end and recession will set in. One optimistic note in this scenario regards the stock market. Since the stock market has already discounted the next recession in its October crash, the downtown in real economic activity should not be accompanied by a large drop of overall stock prices.

Based on Austrian cycle theory, my summary outlook for the U.S. economy for the next year therefore includes accelerating price inflation coinciding with rising interest rates and a declining dollar during the first two or three quarters of 1989. While these trends of interest rates and exchange rates may be temporarily interrupted by well-publicized attempts by the U.S. and foreign governments to coordinate support of the dollar on currency markets, the Fed will be compelled to substantially tighten monetary policy before the end of the year. This will usher in a recession in late 1989 or early 1990, which should strike the U.S. economy with a particularly heavy impact on the thrift and banking industries.

Bibliography

Federal Reserve Bank of Cleveland. 1987a. *Economic Trends* (February).

Federal Reserve Bank of Cleveland. 1987b. *Economic Trends* (December).

Federal Reserve Bank of Cleveland. 1988. *Economic Trends* (January).

Federal Reserve Bank of New York. 1987. "Treasury and Federal Reserve Foreign Exchange Operations: February-April 1987." *Quarterly Review* 12 (Spring 1987). Available at http://www.newyorkfed.org/research/quarterly_review/1987v12/v12n1article5.pdf.

Federal Reserve Bank of St. Louis. 1987. *National Economic Trends* (December).

_____. 1988. *International Economic Conditions* (January).

Gilbert, R. Alton. 1987. "A Revision in the Monetary Base," Federal Reserve Bank of St. Louis *Review* 69 (August/September): pp. 24–29.

Hafer, R. W. "The FOMC in 1983–84: Setting Policy in an Uncertain World." Federal Reserve Bank of St. Louis *Review* 68 (April): pp. 15–37. Available at http://research.stlouisfed.org/publications/review/85/04/FOMC_Apr1985.pdf

Mises, Ludwig von. 1966. *Human Action: A Treatise on Economics*. Chicago: Henry Regnery.

_____. 1978. "Balance of Payments and Foreign Exchange Rates." In idem, *On the Manipulation of Money and Credit*, Percy L Greaves, ed., Bettina Bien Greaves, trans. Dobbs Ferry, N.Y.: Free Market Books.

Salerno, Joseph T. 1988. "The October Stock Market Crash: Causes and Consequences." *The University of Baltimore Business Review* 8, no. 5 (September/October): pp. 1–3, 6–8.

CHAPTER 19

Beyond Calculational Chaos: Sound Money and the Quest for Capitalism and Freedom in Ex-Communist Europe

1. Introduction: The Lesson of the Socialist Calculation Debate

A lthough the argumentation in the papers collected in this volume may sometimes be complex, the lesson they teach is simple and direct: any hope for the successful transformation of ex-Communist economies into full and productive market economies depends crucially on the implementation of institutional reforms that establish the prerequisites of economic calculation. These include: 1. full private property rights in all categories of goods and services, including, and especially, capital goods; 2. freedom to exchange these property titles at prices established on unhampered markets; and 3. sound money. The absence of even one of these preconditions results in what Murray Rothbard[1] has called "calculational chaos," which imposes a pervasive and irremediable misallocation of

From: "Beyond Calculational Chaos: Sound Money and the Quest for Capitalism and Freedom in Ex-Communist Europe," *Polis* 5, no. 1 (1998): pp. 114–33.

[1] Murray N. Rothbard, *Man, Economy, and State: A Treatise on Economic Principles,* 2nd ed. (Auburn, Ala.: Ludwig von Mises Institute), p. 825.

resources on the economy. When private property in "the means of production" is abolished, as it is under socialist central planning, markets for capital goods and natural resources cannot come into being and it is impossible for the planners to calculate production costs. Economic irrationality and chaos also reign where the freedom to exchange is impaired by universal price controls, a central feature of national socialist and state capitalist war economies.[2] Where prices are arbitrarily fixed by government decree, the profit calculations of capitalist-entrepreneurs are meaningless and give absolutely no indication of the most valuable uses for scarce resources. Finally, arbitrary manipulation of the money supply by central banks or governments distorts monetary calculation and, in the latter stages of hyperinflation, renders it completely useless for planning production processes of more than a few days duration.

The collapse of the Soviet and other Communist economies has compelled even mainstream economists to begin to absorb this lesson after they have insisted for decades that the problem of economic calculation could be solved without the institutions of private property, free markets, and sound money. Thus, articles in leading mainstream economic journals now recognize "privatization," "marketization," and "monetary restraint" as indispensable steps on the road to economic reform.[3] But, while there is now basic recognition by economists that rational allocation of resources necessitates institutional reforms that return resources to private hands and restore genuine markets for productive inputs, there is no such comprehension of the importance of sound money to the processes of economic calculation or of the thoroughgoing institutional reconstruction necessary to attain it. Programs for enforcing "monetary discipline" or "monetary restraint" by

---

[2] George Reiman, *The Government against the Economy* (Thornwood, N.Y.: Caroline House Publishers, 1979); Guenter Reimann, *The Vampire Economy: Doing Business under Fascism* (New York: The Vanguard Press, 1939).

[3] Samantha Carrington, "The Remonetization of the Commonwealth of Independent States," *AEA Papers and Proceedings* 82 (May) : pp. 22–26; Jeffrey Sachs, "Privatization in Russia: Some Lessons from Eastern Europe," in *AEA Papers and Proceedings* 82 (May): pp. 43–48; Ronald I. McKinnon, "Financial Control in the Transition from Classical Socialism to a market Economy," in *Journal of Economic Perspectives* 5 (Fall): pp. 107–22.

reorganizing the existing central bank along Western lines—the preferred solution of most Western economist-advisers to governments of former Communist countries[4]—is hardly a substitute for a regime of sound money.

The reason for the continuing failure of the majority of Western economists to absorb the complete lesson of the calculation debate has to do with the yawning gulf between Austrian and mainstream monetary theory.[5] While Austrian and neoclassical microeconomics share a common heritage in the marginal revolution of the 1870s, Austrian and neoclassical monetary theory, despite a brief period of cross-fertilization during the debates of the 1930s on capital, saving and investment, and business cycles—the fruits of which were subsequently aborted by the Keynesian Revolution—developed in isolation from one another. Given this situation, a few words on the nature of sound money, its role in economic calculation, and the means by it which might be achieved is hopefully not out of place in this Postscript.

2. Sound Money and Monetary Calculation

Economic calculation requires homogeneous units that can be manipulated in arithmetic operations. Because money is the general medium of exchange and, as such, the one good that is universally and routinely accepted by market participants, it always constitutes one of the two goods that are exchanged in every market. Consequently, money is the item in which all economic quantities—cost and revenue, profit and loss, and capital and income—are expressed and computed. Economic calculation, therefore, always is and must be monetary calculation, i.e., calculation employing money prices that result, or are expected to result, from actual exchanges. Thus, the

---

[4] Jeffrey Sachs, *Poland's Jump to the Market Economy* (Cambridge, Mass.: The MIT Press, 1993), pp. 49–54.

[5] Joseph T. Salerno, "Two Traditions in Modern Monetary Theory: John Law and A.R.J. Turgot," in *Journal des Economistes et des Etudes Humaines* 2 (June/September): pp. 337–80 [reprinted here as Chapter 1]; idem, "Ludwig von Mises's Monetary Theory in Light of Modern Monetary Thought," in *The Review of Austrian Economics* 8, no. 1 (1994): pp. 71–115 [reprinted here as Chapter 2].

primitive production processes of household or barter economies are driven by subjective valuations of collections of heterogeneous goods, not by objective calculations of profit and loss. Moreover, while capital goods may exist in these economies, there is no way of ascertaining their capital values singly or in combination. Without such an aggregate expression for his productive wealth, an individual agent producing in autarky or for direct exchange would never be able to precisely determine if a particular action would (or did) result in an expansion or diminution of his sources of future production, that is, in capital accumulation or capital consumption. All he would be able to anticipate (or record) is the collection of heterogeneous and non-commensurable goods and services used as inputs in the production process and the different variety of goods composing or received in exchange for the output of the process. It would also be impossible, without monetary exchange, to identify a uniform interest or social time-preference rate to be utilized in capital accounting.[6] In short, in the absence of money, there are no economic quantities and no economic calculation. This insight is the foundation of the classical doctrine of sound money, as reformulated by Ludwig von Mises.

Mises[7] stated this doctrine in the following terms:

> What economic calculation requires is a monetary system whose functioning is not sabotaged by government interference. The endeavors to expand the quantity of money in circulation in order to increase the government's capacity to spend or in order to bring about a temporary lowering of the rate of interest disintegrate all currency matters and derange economic calculation. The first aim of monetary policy must be to prevent governments from embarking upon inflation and from creating conditions which encourage credit expansion on the part of banks.

---

[6] Joseph T. Salerno, "Monetary Neutrality vs. Monetary Calculation: The Problem of Deflation," 1997 Austrian Scholars Conference Working Paper 27 (Auburn, Ala.: Ludwig von Mises Institute), pp. 21–23; Ludwig von Mises, *Economic Calculation in the Socialist Commonwealth*, trans. S. Adler (Auburn Ala.: Praxeology Press, 1990), p. 65; Ludwig von Mises, *Human Action: A Treatise on Economics*, 3rd ed. (Chicago: Henry Regnery Company, 1966), pp. 210–11.

[7] Mises, *Human Action*, p. 224.

Money is thus unsound to the extent that it promotes calculational chaos by falsifying entrepreneurial price appraisements and
profit calculations and causing a systematic misallocation of monetary investment and production factors. Let us take the extreme
case of hyperinflation, in which "the price level," i.e., overall prices,
begins to rise at rapidly and unpredictably accelerating rates. With no
prospect of reasonably appraising output prices for more than a few
weeks or days in advance, entrepreneurs' bids on factor markets come
to exclusively reflect the value of resource uses in production processes geared to serve consumer demand in the immediate future, for
instance, in consumer services, in the wholesale and retail trades, and
in enterprises involved in various kinds of commodity speculation.
When the entrepreneurial appraisement process has been rendered
incapable of taking account of the value of resource contributions to
time-consuming production processes, the economy's structure of
production is radically "shortened" and ceases to be coordinated with
the underlying structure of consumer preferences for consumption
in the present and future. As calculational chaos begins to prevail,
industrial processes, especially those involving production of business
structures, durable capital goods, and raw materials grind to a halt,
unemployment skyrockets, and a full-blown depression takes shape
in the very midst of the raging hyperinflation.[8] When hyperinflation reaches its final stage, there is a headlong "flight into real values,"
during which market participants are eager to rid themselves of the
continuously depreciating and nearly worthless currency by immediately spending it, although there is scarcely anyone to be found who is
willing to accept it in exchange for "real" goods on any terms. At this

---

[8] As Costantino Bresciani-Turroni (*The Economics of Inflation: A Study of Currency Depreciation in Post-War Germany*, trans. Millicent E. Savers [London:
George Allen & Unwin Ltd., (1937) 1968], p. 220) observed regarding the German
hyperinflation, ". . . the continual and very great fluctuations in the value of money
made it very difficult to calculate the costs of production and prices, and therefore
also made difficult any rational planning of production.

The entrepreneur, instead of concentrating his attention on improving the product
and reducing his costs, often became a speculator in goods and foreign exchanges."
Bresciani-Turroni (ibid., pp. 222–23) went on to describe the widespread stoppage of
sales and mass unemployment that developed in October and November of 1923 at
the height of the hyperinflation.

point, barring the ready availability of either a relatively sound foreign currency or a commodity money, monetary calculation is completely nullified and the economy is plunged into the calculational chaos of barter.[9]

But we need not wait until the hyperinflationary "crack-up boom" and the abolition of monetary exchange in order to see the onset of calculational chaos. As Murray N. Rothbard[10] has pointed out, ". . . each governmental firm introduces its own island of chaos into the economy; there is no need to wait for full socialism for chaos to begin its work.... [A]ny governmental operation injects a point of chaos into the economy; and since all markets are interconnected in the economy, every governmental activity disrupts and distorts pricing, the allocation of factors, consumption/investment ratios, etc." But if this is true for the economy in general, it is true a fortiori in the monetary sphere. The function of money as a general medium of exchange and tool of economic calculation insures that, even at the outset of an inflationary monetary regime, its distortive effects on pricing, calculation, and resource allocation are transmitted swiftly and directly to all markets.

A case in point is the situation in which inflation of the money supply occurs via the emission of unbacked notes and deposits, known as "fiduciary media," by a fractional-reserve banking system.

Today, this usually occurs when a central bank creates additional reserves for its national banking system in order to drive down domestic interest rates. When the commercial banks receive these new reserves they loan them out by creating new checking deposits, in the process temporarily increasing the supply of credit and lowering the structure of interest rates. Unfortunately, this decline in interest rates does not reflect a change in the underlying intertemporal consumption, or "time," preferences of market participants. Moreover, this movement of interest rates will reverse itself just as soon as the inflation of bank credit ceases. Nevertheless, entrepreneurs, should

---

[9] Ludwig von Mises, *On the Manipulation of Money and Credit*, ed. Percy L. Greaves, trans. Bettina Bien Grieves (Dobbs Ferry, N.Y.: Free Market Books, 1978), pp. 5–16.

[10] Rothbard, *Man, Economy, and State*, p. 826.

they misperceive the initial fall in rates as a long-term development, are induced to borrow the additional credit and invest it in adding to their stocks of capital goods. They act in this way because their calculations using the lower interest rate indicate that the present discounted value of the future output attributable to a specific capital good now exceeds its current purchase price, despite the fact that overall consumer preferences for consumption in the more remote future have in reality not intensified. The increase in demand for capital goods that results will lead to broad-ranging increases in the prices of capital goods relative to prices of consumer goods. This relative-price movement, to the extent that it is expected to persist and even strengthen, will further falsify profit calculations and mislead capitalist-entrepreneurs into increasing the allocation of monetary investment and productive inputs to capital goods' industries in order to expand output.

The apparent prosperity in the real economy will be mirrored in the financial sector, as the artificially-depressed interest rates in conjunction with higher earnings of firms producing capital goods precipitate a boom in the stock, bond and real estate markets. The calculational chaos produced by the unsound bank credit inflation will only be revealed when fears of price inflation compel the central bank to constrict or arrest the flow of new money through credit markets. At this point the distortion of the pricing process ceases and monetary calculation once again comes to accurately and sensitively reflect the most highly valued uses of scarce resources. There generally ensues a sharp upward movement of interest rates and a financial collapse, followed sooner or later by a depression of real economic activity and higher rates of unemployment and business bankruptcies centered in the capital goods industries. The so-called "depression" or "recession" is the period during which the errors and malinvestments committed during the calculational chaos fostered by bank-credit inflation are exposed and corrected, and the economy painfully re-coordinates the relative outputs of consumer and capital goods with the demonstrated consumption/saving preferences of the public.

A sound money, then, is simply one that does not lead to systematic falsification or nullification of economic calculation. In Mises's words, "[f]or the sake of economic calculation all that is needed is to avoid great and abrupt fluctuations in the supply of money." The sound money program, therefore, is not an unattainable ideal but one that can be realized by totally separating the money supply process from the State. This involves abolishing central banking and paper fiat money and restoring a commodity money chosen by and totally subject to the market. Historically, the classical gold coin standard provided a sound money: the natural and unalterable scarcity of gold completely precluded hyperinflation as well as rigidly limiting the extent to which fractional-reserve banks could expand fiduciary media. As Mises[11] explained:

> Gold and, up to the middle of the nineteenth century, silver served very well all the purposes of economic calculation. Changes in the relation between the supply of and demand for the precious metals and the resulting alterations in purchasing power went on so slowly that the entrepreneur's economic calculation could disregard them without going too far afield.

But the classical gold standard, especially in those countries where a central bank sat atop the commercial banking system as an acknowledged "lender of last resort" or provider of "emergency liquidity," still permitted some scope for credit expansion and the systemic calculational chaos manifested in business cycles. Mises himself recognized that "The first aim of monetary policy must be to prevent governments from embarking on inflation and from creating conditions which encourage credit expansion on the part of banks." So a completely sound monetary policy would require not only the abolition of fiat currency and central banking, but also the strict prohibition of fractional-reserve banking. In other words, sound money necessitates that all demand liabilities incurred by banks, whether in the form of notes or demand deposits, be "backed" 100 percent by reserves of the money commodity. More accurately sound money requires that, both legally and economically, bank notes and deposits be made to function as genuine property titles to the money commodity, standing in the same relation to gold deposits at banks as

---

[11] Mises, *Human Action*, p. 224.

warehouse receipts for wheat stand to the wheat deposited for storage in grain elevators. This means that the creation and exchange of titles to nonexistent property, which is the essence of fractional reserve banking[12] and is considered fraudulent if undertaken by any other business enterprise, must be diligently suppressed. Only under these conditions would the banking system cease to operate as a source of calculational chaos.

3. Sound Money versus "Stable Money" and "Neutral Money"

To reiterate, sound money is a praxeologically attainable and historically attained ideal; it requires only that the government be restrained from intervening in the market's money supply process and that standard contract law be rigorously applied to the banking sphere. The sole aim of the sound money program is the preservation of monetary calculation from distortion by extra-market forces; it does not aim at "stabilizing" a specific economic quantity, such as the purchasing power of money, much less "neutralizing" the influence of money on real economic quantities. These latter goals are impossible of achievement because, as noted above, calculability in economic processes only exists by virtue of monetary exchange, so that the very notion of purely real economic quantities, wholly uninfluenced by money, is contradictory. Consequently, in the sound money program, the terms "inflation" and "deflation" do not apply to fluctuations in the value of money, as they do in current usage; rather, the terms denote changes in the money supply that do not rigidly and exactly correspond to changes in the stock of the market-chosen money commodity, which is to say that they apply exclusively to changes in the supply of money that distort the processes of monetary calculation and price

---

[12] For the elaboration of this view of fractional reserve banking, see Hans-Hermann Hoppe, with Jörg Guido Hülsmann and Walter Block, "Against Fiduciary Media," in *The Review of Austrian Economics* 11, no. 1 (1998): pp. 15–20. For a juridical characterization of the demand deposit contract which is founded on a similar conception of fractional-reserve banking, see Jesús Huerta de Soto, "Critical Note on Fractional/Reserve Free Banking," unpublished manuscript, pp. 29–39.

appraisement.[13] And this is precisely the reason for the practicability of the sound money program: it seeks only to liberate the purchasing power of money from government manipulation and control so that it can fluctuate freely in response to market demand and supply. As Mises[14] emphasized, "[The sound money] program is very different from the confused and self-contradictory program of stabilizing purchasing power."

Because money is a tangible commodity that is traded on the market, it is endowed with its own variable supply and demand, and therefore its "price" or purchasing power can never be rendered constant or stable. Unlike a nonmonetary good, however, whose price is almost always determined and expressed as a unitary quantity of money, the purchasing power of money itself is embodied in an exhaustive and heterogeneous array of the alternative quantities of nonmonetary goods for which the money unit exchanges at a given moment. In other words, the purchasing power of money is simply the unaveraged series of exchange ratios constituted by the reciprocals of all realized money prices in the economy. Thus money's purchasing power is unavoidably entwined with the economy's structure of relative prices, which is constantly in flux. To stabilize purchasing power in the strict sense, then, means to freeze relative prices permanently, effectively abolishing monetary calculation and the market economy.

---

[13] In defending this use of the terms "inflation" and "deflation" as the only one that is praxeologically meaningful, Rothbard (*Man, Economy, and State*, p. 878) writes: "Movements in the supply-of-goods and in the demand-for-money schedules are all the results of voluntary changes of preferences on the market. The same is true for increases in the supply of gold or silver on the market. But increases in fiduciary or fiat media are acts of fraudulent intervention into the market, distorting voluntary preferences and the voluntarily-determined pattern of income and wealth. Therefore, the most expedient definition of 'inflation' is one we have set forth above: an increase in the supply of money beyond any increase in specie." Mises (*Human Action*, p. 422; Ludwig von Mises, "Summary Statement," in *Defense, Controls, and Inflation: A Conference Sponsored by the University of Chicago Law School*, ed. Aaron Director, [Chicago: University of Chicago Press, 1952], p. 333), too, maintained that "inflation" and "deflation," defined as variations in the purchasing power of money, "are not praxeological concepts," and argued for restricting the term "inflation" to mean "increasing the quantity of money and bank notes in circulation and of bank deposits subject to check."

[14] Mises, *Human Action*, p. 224.

Some contemporary macroeconomists, such as those associated with either the monetarist or the modern free banking schools, find fault with the sound money program precisely because it makes no attempt to stabilize one or another macroeconomic statistical construct. For example, Milton Friedman and other monetarists argue that the long-run appreciation of the purchasing power of money, or "price deflation," is likely to occur under a sound money regime because the secular growth of real output tends to outstrip the increase in the supply of gold, thereby discouraging investment and producing a suboptimal rate of economic growth. In addition, they claim, the purchasing power of money is subject to unpredictable variations as a result of changes in the stock of money due to alterations in the costs of producing gold and in the demand for gold for nonmonetary uses. These sudden changes in the money supply are likely to bring about short-run fluctuations in real output during the transition to the altered purchasing power of money. The monetarists therefore prescribe a program of stabilizing the purchasing power of money, or "stable money" for short, but they do not actually intend to freeze all prices in the economy. Rather their goal is stabilization of "the price level," an average of particular prices arrived at by some arbitrarily selected statistical method.[15] They rightly perceive that any political interference with the structure of relative prices produces calculational chaos. However, in an attempt to circumvent this insight, they posit the "long-run neutrality" of money, meaning that the general level of prices is ultimately determined by a monetary process operating in a macroeconomic realm separate and distinct from the real or microeconomic processes that determine the system of relative prices.

---

[15] On the impossibility of measuring changes in the purchasing power of money and on the arbitrary nature and analytical meaninglessness of all statistically constructed price indexes, see Mises, *Human Action*, pp. 219–23 and Michael A. Heilperin, *International Monetary Economics* (Philadelphia: Porcupine Press, [1939] 1978), pp. 259–69. As Mises concluded: "A judicious housewife knows much more about price changes as far as they affect her own household than the statistical averages can tell.... If she 'measures' the changes for her personal appreciation by taking the prices of only two or three commodities as a yardstick, she is no less 'scientific' and no more arbitrary than the sophisticated mathematicians in choosing their methods for the manipulation of the data of the market." (*Human Action*, pp. 222-23).

Thus, in terms of the Equation of Exchange, i.e., MV=PQ, the monetarists advocate that the central bank be legally bound to pursue a "quantity" rule," which involves attempting to stabilize P, some statistical average of prices, by increasing the stock of money, M, at a steady rate that roughly matches the long-run rate of growth of real output, Q, minus the presumably stable secular growth rate of V, which denotes the velocity of circulation of money. The monetarists would implement their program via a central bank with absolute, monopolistic control over a money supply consisting of its own fiat currency and bank-issued fiduciary media.[16]

A variant of this stable money program is offered by the supply-side school, an offshoot of monetarism founded by Arthur Laffer and Robert Mundell in the 1970s. Supply-siders also uphold the stability of the price level as the overarching goal of monetary policy, but quibble with the monetarist presumption of long-run stability of the growth rate of money's velocity. If V is subject to sudden and unpredictable variations, they argue, a quantity rule fixing the growth rate of M would give rise to cyclical instability in P and Q. Supply-siders would thus bind the central bank to follow a "price rule." Under this rule, the central bank would fix the money price of some widely-traded commodity (or basket of commodities), within narrow limits. The commodity selected to serve as the external standard—let us assume it is gold—would be a sensitive indicator of impending fluctuations of the price level. Thus, when V increases, causing total spending (MV) in the economy to increase, there would quickly ensue an

---

[16] For brief overviews of monetarism, see Phillip Cagan, "Monetarism," in *The New Palgrave: Money*, eds. John Eatwell, Murray Milgate, and Peter Newman, (New York: W.W. Norton & Company, Inc., 1989) pp. 195–205 and Allan H. Meltzer, "Monetarism," in *The Fortune Encyclopedia of Economics*, ed. David R. Henderson, (New York: Warner Books, Inc., 1993) pp. 128–34; detailed expositions of the monetarist reform program can be found in Michael D. Bordo and Anna J. Schwartz, "The Importance of Stable Money: Theory and Evidence," in *The Search for Stable Money: Essays on Monetary Reform*, eds. James A. Dorn and Anna J. Schwartz, (Chicago: University of Chicago Press, 1987) pp. 53–72 and Allan H. Meltzer, "Monetary Reform in an Uncertain Environment," in *The Search for Stable Money: Essays in Monetary Reform*, eds. James A. Dorn and Anna J. Schwartz, (Chicago: University of Chicago Press, 1987) pp. 201–20. For a critique of monetarism from the perspective of Austrian monetary theory, see Salerno, "Two Traditions in Modern Monetary Theory."

upward movement of the gold price, and the central bank, by engaging in open market sales to reduce M and prevent the gold price from exceeding its upper limit, would head off the imminent rise in the general price level. Conversely, a fall in the price of gold toward its lower limit would indicate an incipient price-level deflation, which would signal the central bank to buy securities and increase M. Despite their gold-standard rhetoric, then, the supply-siders do not advocate a genuine gold standard, but a pseudo-gold standard of the Bretton Woods type. In effect, what they are proposing is " price-rule monetarism." Under this system: gold is not actually utilized as a circulating medium of exchange by the public; the central bank still enjoys a virtual monopoly of the money supply; and the ability of the commercial banking system to create fiduciary media at the behest of the central bank remains intact.[17]

Unlike monetarists, whether of the quantity-rule or price-rule variety, the modern free banking school does not propose a money of stable purchasing power. Instead it prescribes a money whose purchasing power appreciates (depreciates) at a rate equal to the rate of growth (decline) of factor productivity in the economy. Of course, the proponents of this "productivity norm" do not actually call for an equiproportional change in each and every element of the really existing purchasing-power array of money, which would be tantamount to freezing relative prices. Rather, their program, like the monetarists'

---

[17] The classic proposal for a gold price rule is presented in Arthur Laffer, *Reinstatement of the Dollar, The Blueprint* (Rolling Hill Estates, Calif.: A.B. Laffer Associates, 1980). Marc A. Miles (*Beyond Monetarism: Finding the Road to Stable Money* (New York: Basic Books, Inc., 1984) provides a book-length exposition of supply-side monetary theory and policy. Unlike Laffer, Miles would dispense with gold altogether and advocates a combination of a "forward index price rule" based on a basket of selected commodities and an "interest-rate price rule" targeting long-term interest rates. Under this proposal, the central bank would retain its virtual monopoly over the money supply process, buying and selling both commodity index futures contracts and long-term government bonds. For a critique of supply-side proposals for monetary reform, see Joseph T. Salerno, "The Gold Standard: An Analysis of Some Recent Proposals," Cato Institute *Policy Analysis* (September 9) pp. 7–11 and idem, "Gold Standards: True and False," in *The Search for Stable Money: Essays on Monetary Reform*, eds James A. Dorn and Anna J. Schwartz (Chicago: University of Chicago Press, 1987), pp. 249–52 [reprinted here as Chapter 13].

program, focuses on optimal movements in an arbitrarily selected average of prices representing some fictional general price level.[18]

If the productivity norm were operative, an increase in labor productivity, for example, would cause a fall in P equal in percentage terms to the rise in Q resulting from this "productivity innovation." With nominal wage rates maintained constant, labor would reap the fruits of the productivity enhancement as real wage rates increased pari passu with the drop in P. Without going too deeply into the rationale of the productivity norm, the superiority of a price level that varies inversely with productivity innovations over a stable price level supposedly lies in the greater success of the former in neutralizing "unwarranted," i.e., purely money-induced changes in relative prices. To implement such a neutral money, it is necessary only that the monetary system operate to maintain constancy in the total flow of spending, MV, in the economy. Stabilizing MV is equivalent to stabilizing nominal income or PQ and insuring that productivity-driven increases in Q always elicit an inverse and equiproportonal change in P. Actually, stability of nominal income results in only an approximation of the productivity norm, which, strictly speaking, dictates that variations in Q that are not caused by productivity changes but by changes in factor supplies be fully accommodated by an increase or decrease in MV rather than a fall or rise in P. This would prevent a fall in the nominal price level of labor and capital services in the case where their supplies have expanded. The productivity norm is thus also consistent with stability of nominal wage rates and rents.

What is the connection between the neutral-money doctrine and free banking? According to George Selgin,[19] a leading free-banking theorist,

---

[18] For discussions of the productivity norm, see George Selgin, *Praxeology and Understanding: An Analysis of the Controversy in Austrian Economics* (Auburn, Ala.: Ludwig von Mises Institute, 1991); idem, "The 'Productivity Norm' vs. Zero Inflation in the History of Economic Thought," *History of Political Economy* 27 (1995): pp. 705–35; and idem, *Less Than Zero: The Case for a Falling Price Level in a Growing Economy* (London: The Institute of Economic Affairs, 1997).

[19] Selgin, *Less Than Zero*, pp. 67–69.

> ... a comprehensively deregulated or "free" banking system [makes] for a relatively stable relationship between the volume of aggregate spending (the one thing the central bank needs to control) and the quantity of central-bank-created base money (the one thing it definitely can control).... In short, a free banking system, given some fixed quantity of base money to work with, tends automatically to stabilise nominal income. Getting nominal income to grow at some predetermined rate then becomes a relatively simple matter of having the central bank expand the stock of base money by that rate.

What both the money stabilizers (monetarists) and neutralizers (free bankers) have in common, then, is their strongly-held, but profoundly erroneous, belief that money, when it is functioning properly, exists in hermetically-sealed isolation from real economic processes. This is the reason that both of their approaches to monetary reform involve stabilizing elements, such as P or PQ, of the macroeconomic Equation of Exchange. The use of this analytical device obscures the unavoidable microeconomic implications of the formation of money's purchasing power. Thus the proponents of stable and of neutral money fail to comprehend that the market determines both the general level of prices and the complex structure of their interrelationships as part of one and the same pricing process. Any change in the supply of or demand for money originates at a specific point in the system, precipitating a sequential and uneven adjustment process that alters individual selling prices, incomes, cash balances, and demand schedules for goods at each and every step of the way. As this monetary adjustment process unfolds over time, real income and wealth are therefore necessarily redistributed between individuals, depending on their position in the process and the nature of its initiating cause, e.g., whether it is an increase or decrease in the supply of money. Consequently, at the end of this process, not only has the scale of nominal prices and incomes been raised or lowered but, more importantly, the structure of relative prices and incomes has been completely and permanently revolutionized. The proper metaphor to aid in conceptualizing changes in the purchasing power of money, therefore, is not a homogeneous body of water smoothly changing its level but of a bee swarm rising and falling, even as the relative positions of the individual bees are continually being modified.[20]

If we consider further that fresh changes in real monetary demand are taking place at each succeeding moment and, simultaneously, at a multitude of different points in the system, both autonomously and induced by ceaseless shifts in the distribution of incomes and wealth attributable to prior changes in the real data, we cannot escape the conclusion that money's effect on relative prices and the allocation of resources can never be neutralized by stabilizing a macroeconomic aggregate or average. As Mises explained:

> It may happen that the effects of a change in the demand for or supply of money encounter the effects of opposite changes occurring by and large at the same time and to the same extent; it may happen that the resultant of the two opposite movements is such that no conspicuous changes in the price structure emerge. But even then the effects on the conditions of the various individuals are not absent. Each change in the money relation takes it own course and produces its own particular effects. If an inflationary movement and a deflationary one occur at the same time or if an inflation is temporally followed by a deflation in such a way that prices are not very much changed the social consequences of each of the two movements do not cancel each other. To the social consequences of an inflation those of a deflation are added.[21]

The terms "neutral money" and "stable money," strictly speaking, are both oxymorons.

Money, by its very nature as the general medium of exchange, is bought and sold on all markets and is therefore subject to continual

---

[20] The metaphor of a "price swarm," I believe, is due to the American monetary theorist, Arthur W. Marget (*The Theory of Prices: A Re-Examination of the Central Problems of Monetary Theory*, 2 vols. (New York: Arthur M. Kelley Publishers, [1938–42] 1996), although I cannot seem to find the exact location of its use.

[21] Mises, *Human Action*, pp. 417–18. F.A. Hayek (*Prices and Production*, 2nd ed. [New York: Augustus M. Kelley, (1935) 1967], p. 124) too, recognized this crucial point, writing, "… in order to eliminate all monetary influences on the formation of prices and the structure of production, it would not be sufficient merely quantitatively to adapt the supply of money to these changes in demand [for money], it would be necessary to see that it came into the hands of those who actually desire it.…"

and ineradicable fluctuations of its value. These constant changes in purchasing power undeniably do generate "apparent" profits and losses that cannot be distinguished from those "genuine" profits and losses that reflect alterations in supply and demand in the "real" economy. Nonetheless, this does not affect the case for a market-evolved money, because every conceivable kind of money is subject to changes in its purchasing power. Moreover, the sound money that has been developed by the market embodies those qualities that optimally suit it to serve both as a medium of exchange and a tool of economic calculation. Thus, for the purposes served by monetary calculation, entrepreneurs could—and in fact, always did—safely ignore the comparatively slight changes in purchasing power that have historically characterized a sound money. For instance, the variations in the value of gold that occurred in the course of the nineteenth century and up until 1914 did not prevent private individuals and firms from building an intricate and mighty capital structure in the West. The financial panics and depressions that periodically racked the nascent industrial economies of Western Europe and the U.S. during this era were attributable to the sharp, recurrent bursts of inflationary credit expansion undertaken by the national fractional-reserve banking systems that had been superimposed on the international gold standard.[22]

In sharp contrast to sound money, monetary regimes that aim at stabilizing the absolute level of some macroeconomic construct such as the price level or nominal income in a vain effort to negate the purely monetary influences on economic calculation end up seriously deranging the structure of relative prices and falsifying real-world monetary calculation. As demonstrated above, when a fractional-reserve banking system, either as a result of its alleged own inner workings or in responding to the stimulus of a net inflow

---

[22] As Nobel Laureate Maurice Allais ("The Credit Mechanism and Its Implications," in *Arrow and the Foundations of the Theory of Economic Policy*, ed. George R. Feiwel [New York: New York University Press, 1987] pp. 491–561) puts it: "In the final analysis, the only effect of the [fractional-reserve banking] system is to create morally indefensible 'false claims' and 'unearned income,' despoiling one part of the population in favor of another.... The system generates economic imbalance, an unhealthy concentration on financial rewards, and unbridled speculation.... All the major crises of the eighteenth, nineteenth, and twentieth century were the result of the proliferation of promises to pay and their monetization."

of cash reserves created by a stabilizationist central bank, expands its credit by creating fiduciary media, it causes a reduction of interest rates not warranted by a change in social time preferences. This results in a pervasive misdirection of entrepreneurs' intertemporal price appraisements and economic calculations, and promotes systemic capital malinvestment and resource misallocation. There are many other criticisms that could be made of macroeconomic stabilization, but, for our purposes, here the important point is that the goals of stable money and neutral money are both fundamentally inconsistent with the preservation of the integrity of monetary calculation. Only the implementation of a sound money program, in conjunction with full and unfettered private property and free exchange, provides an escape for ex-Communist countries from their lingering calculational chaos.

4. The Road to Sound Money

What Mises said in 1953 is still valid: "Sound money still means today what it meant in the nineteenth century: the gold standard. The eminence of the gold standard consists in the fact that it makes the determination of the monetary unit's purchasing power independent of the measures of government. It wrests from the hands of the 'economic tsars' their most redoubtable instrument. It makes it impossible for them to inflate." The sound money ideal is thus a full-bodied gold standard that is completely separated from the State. Unfortunately, unlike the implementation of the other two prerequisites of economic calculation, private property and free markets, which can and should be accomplished swiftly—in one day if possible—the establishment of a sound money regime will require a somewhat longer transition period.[23] But this does not mean that rapid and meaningful strides cannot be taken toward the ideal immediately.

----

[23] Ludwig von Mises, *The Theory of Money and Credit* (Indianapolis, Ind.: Liberty Classics, [1952] 1981), p. 480. On this point, see Murray N. Rothbard, "How and How Not to Desocialize," in *The Review of Austrian Economics* 6, no. 1 (1992): pp. 70–71. Otherwise, Rothbard supports the "One-Day Plan" for desocialization put forward by Yuri N. Maltsev, "The Maltsev One-Day Plan," in *The Free Market* 8 (November 1990): p. 7.

In fact, Mises[24] suggested a transition program for the monetary reconstruction of postwar Europe in the early 1950s that can be readily adapted to the case of contemporary ex-Communist Europe today. Indeed, the Currency Board option that has been proposed by a number of proponents of stable money in recent years represents nothing but a flawed variation of Mises's program.[25] The Misesian reform is driven by two aims: to debar the national government from financing any future budget deficits by means of debt monetization and to preclude the systematic distortion of the interest-rate structure and the intertemporal price system that inevitably results from bank credit expansion. As Mises[26] explained, "The main thing is that the government should no longer be in a position to increase the quantity of money in circulation and the amount of checkbook money not fully—that is, 100 percent—covered by deposits paid in by the public. No back door must be left open where inflation can slip in."

The first step in this reform is to prohibit the existing central bank or the government itself from engaging in any future transactions that expand the supply of money. This includes open-market operations and loans by the central bank and "emergency" currency issues by the finance ministry. Second, commercial banks and other financial institutions must also be forbidden from loaning any portion of new demand deposits; in other words all demand deposits—including noncheckable "savings" deposits redeemable on

---

[24] Mises, *Theory of Money and Credit*, pp. 485–90.

[25] An especially good discussion of the nature and functioning of currency boards, which includes references to the recent literature, is Owen F. Humpage and Jean M. McIntire, "An Introduction to Currency Boards," Federal Reserve Bank of Cleveland *Economic Review* 31 (2nd Quarter 1995): pp. 2–11. Currency boards have been suggested for countries such as Lithuania (Kurt Schuler, George Selgin and Joseph Sinkey, Jr., "Replacing the Ruble in Lithuania: Real Change versus Pseudoreform," in *Policy Analysis* 163 [October 28, 1991], Washington D.C.: The Cato Institute), Russia (Steve H. Hanke and Kurt Schuler, "Currency Boards and Currency Convertibility," in *The Cato Journal* 12 [Winter 1993]: pp. 687–705 and Steve H. Hanke, Lars Jonung and Kurt Schuler, *Russian Currency and Finance: A Currency Board Approach to Reform* [New York: Routledge, 1993], and Mexico (Owen F. Humpage, "A Mexican Currency Board?" Federal Reserve Bank of Cleveland *Economic Commentary* [March 15, 1995]).

[26] Mises, *Theory of Money and Credit*, p. 481.

demand—made after the start of the monetary reform are to be rig-idly subject to 100 percent reserves. To insure observance of this rule banks would be legally obliged to split themselves into "deposit" and "savings" departments, and the former would be strictly prohibited from expanding its noncash assets beyond the total of its uncovered demand liabilities as they stood on the date of the implementation of the reform. In other words, all new issues of fiduciary media would be strictly precluded. The savings department would be free to issue bona fide time deposits, such as certificates of deposit with contractu-ally fixed maturities, and these liabilities would not be subject to any law regarding reserve requirements; banks' savings departments and other institutions would also be free to offer equity shares in money-market and other types of mutual funds entirely unencumbered by legal reserve requirements, since these too are vehicles for genuine savings and investment. These two measures taken together would succeed in freezing the domestic money supply.

A third step, undertaken simultaneously with the first two, is the freeing of the foreign exchange market so that the domestic currency becomes fully and effectively convertible into historically "harder," i.e., less inflationary, fiat currencies, such as the U.S. dollar, the Ger-man mark, and the Swiss franc. As dealers and speculators on foreign exchange markets become increasingly convinced of the credibility and durability of these reform measures the depreciation of domes-tic currency—let us assume it is the Romanian leu—will eventually cease; an appreciation will set in as the purchasing power of the leu, whose stock is now rigidly frozen, begins to rise relative to that of for-eign currencies, even the hardest of which is likely to have its quantity continually increased by its central bank. As soon as the leu's broad-ranging appreciation becomes manifest, the existing exchange rate between the leu and a selected hard currency, for example, the dollar, is to be established as the new legal parity. This parity is to be effec-tively maintained by full and unconditional convertibility between the two currencies.

To implement the convertibility between the leu and the dol-lar, a fourth step is necessary: the creation of a Conversion Agency charged with the sole function of buying and selling leus in exchange

for dollars at the legal parity (and only at the legal parity). In order
to achieve its purpose of establishing the legal parity as the effective
market exchange rate, the agency would be legally empowered to create leus that are backed 100 percent by dollars. The agency would also
require an initial stock of dollar reserves with which to redeem any
and all leus offered to it at the legal parity rate. These reserves are to
be lent to it by the central bank or the fiscal arm of the government,
in perpetuity and at a zero interest rate. It must be emphasized that
the Conversion Agency will have no further dealings with the central
bank or the finance ministry after the receipt of the initial loan of foreign exchange reserves. Moreover, the strict legal prohibition against
the central bank creating leus through loans or asset purchases will
continue in force until the transition to a classical gold coin standard
is completed and the central bank is abolished.[27] Nor will the government be permitted ever again to issue leus, with the exception of the
minting of subsidiary coins. However, to forestall any attempt by the
government to finance its deficits by flooding the market with small
change, the minting of coins will be subject to two legal conditions:
first, the coins will have full legal-tender power against no payee but
the government itself; second, the government will be obliged to
redeem all coins offered in leu notes or deposits without delay or cost
to the bearer. And finally, the Conversion Agency will not be granted
any monopoly privileges in its dealings in foreign exchange; it will
operate as any other agent in the foreign exchange market, buying
and selling on an unhampered market.

Once these four steps have been taken the country will effectively be on a dollar-exchange standard. Under this monetary regime,

---

[27] The central bank may be permitted to remain in existence during the course of
the transition period, continuing to collect and dispose of the interest on its assets
and to provide check-clearing services to the commercial banks (if it had performed
this function in the past). Under no circumstances, however, should the central bank
be permitted to retain its function of regulating the banking system and, in particular, of monitoring and enforcing the system's adherence to the new 100 percent-
reserve rule for demand deposits. The very rationale of central banking is to foster
and support fractional-reserve banks in their natural desire to expand credit, and
this has been its historical function as well. Thus, it would be the height of folly to
permit officials whose very jobs consisted in undermining sound money to exercise
any influence over the emerging sound money regime.

so long as the dollar-leu exchange rate remains fixed, arbitrage will ensure that the purchasing power of the leu continually and rapidly adjusts so as to maintain "purchasing power parity" with the dollar. Thus, both the rate of overall price inflation and the configuration of relative prices in terms of leus and of dollars will tend to be identical. This means that it will be impossible for a given commodity to be purchased more cheaply in terms of one currency than the other anywhere in the world.

This also implies that there is no necessity for a domestic monetary policy: the supply of leus will fluctuate automatically in response to variations in the balance of payments as an essential part of the process of preserving purchasing power parity. Thus if there is an increase in the demand for leus in the economy, the attempts by households and businesses to increase their holdings of the currency will cause a reduction in the demand for nonmonetary commodities and services. As leu prices begin to decline, the purchasing power of the leu will rise above parity with the dollar, making it cheaper to buy with leus than with dollars. This will lead to an increase in exports and fall in imports for Romania, resulting in a balance of payments surplus and a net influx of dollars. These excess dollars will then be brought to the Conversion Agency and redeemed for leus at the par exchange rate. As the supply of leus in circulation thus expands, leu prices will be bid back up until purchasing power parity and, consequently, balance of payments equilibrium are restored.

While the money supply is thus spontaneously adjusted to the demand for money through changes in the balance of payments, it is also the case that this system facilitates the "importation" of the U.S. inflation rate, whatever it may be. To see how this might occur, consider an expansion of the supply of dollars generated by the Federal Reserve System that does not correspond to an increased demand to hold dollars. This will initially drive up prices in the U.S., causing the ratio between the purchasing powers of the dollar and the leu to decline below the fixed leu-dollar exchange rate. Since it will now be cheaper to purchase goods with leus, there will develop a surplus of dollars at the legally fixed exchange rate, which the Conversion Agency will be called upon to redeem in leus. As these newly-issued

leus swell the stock of money, general prices in Romania will be bid
up to reestablish parity with U.S. prices. And as long as the U.S. continues to inflate its domestic money stock, the operation of the dollar-exchange system will insure that the leu loses purchasing power
at roughly the same rate as the dollar. Additionally, as this inflation
adjustment process runs its course, real income and wealth will be
redistributed from Romanians, who tend to receive the new dollars
late in the process, i.e., after most prices in the U.S. have already risen,
to U.S. residents and organizations, especially the U.S. government
and other initial recipients of the new money.[28] This transfer of real
income and wealth from leu users to dollar users is manifested in the
balance of payments surplus that Romania experiences with the U.S.
during the process, as there emerges a balance of Romanian products
sold to the U.S. that is compensated not by imports of real goods and
services from the U.S. but by paper dollars. It should be noted that
the specific effects on domestic income and wealth distribution of
imported dollar inflation would not be altered just because the Conversion Agency might hold its dollar reserves in the form of interest-
bearing assets.[29]

Not only will Romania import whatever price inflation the U.S.
experiences, however; arbitrage will also insure that the distortion of
the structure of interest rates and relative prices produced by the creation of fiduciary media in the U.S. is rapidly and fully transmitted
to Romania. This means that Romania will experience the ups and
downs of the U.S. business cycle in the same manner as any other

---

[28] This is only true to the extent that Romanians actually do receive the newly-created dollars late in the process. However, although this would generally be the case, it
need not be so. Should the initial recipients of the new money, e.g., the U.S. government or U.S. import firms, spend most of their newly-acquired dollars directly on
Romanian exports, and the Romanian exporters in turn spend this windfall mainly
on domestic products, causing prices in Romania to rise in advance of the rise in
U.S. prices, the redistribution of real income caused by the dollar inflation would
generally benefit Romanians at the expense of Americans.

[29] In other words, even though the Romanian Conversion Agency would capture
the "seignorage" from issuing leus by investing its dollar reserves in interest-bearing
securities, this would not negate the likelihood that the seignorage appropriated by
the Fed's dollar creation would take a separate toll on the income and wealth of individual Romanians.

integral component of the dollar "currency area," e.g., Texas or Maine. At least temporarily, then, the economic fate of Romania will rest to a great degree on the policy of the U.S. Federal Reserve System (or some other foreign central bank, as the case may be).

I dwell on these disadvantages of a system that involves fixing the exchange rate between the domestic currency and a historically "harder"—yet still central-bank-issued—fiat currency in order to emphasize the point that it is to be viewed strictly as a transitional expedient. Yet, in this function it does have several substantial virtues. First, and most important, it takes control over the quantity of money out of the hands of the domestic government and its central bank, thereby providing immediate relief from the danger of the extreme calculational chaos caused by hyperinflation, which is a threat under the current regime of unrestrained debt monetization. Second, by rigorously suppressing all further domestic emissions of fiduciary media, it removes the temptation for government to reestablish control over the banking system as a means of intervening in credit markets to lower interest rates and to provide a short-run boost to employment and real output during (imported) cyclical downturns.[30] Simultaneously, it roots out the underlying cause of financial panics: the mismatching of the term structure of assets and liabilities that is an inherent feature of fractional-reserve banking. With the ever-impending threat of financial collapse removed, the government can no longer seize on the need to inject "emergency liquidity" into

---

[30] Of course, such a domestic "cheap money" policy is completely ineffective in dealing with the temporary upsurge in unemployment that normally accompanies a cyclical downturn. This unemployment is inherently speculative and self-liquidating, as workers whose labor services have previously been misallocated invest their time and other resources in "job prospecting" for their best employment opportunities in an economy whose production structure and pattern of resource allocation is being radically reshaped to reflect consumers' genuine time preferences. As long as the freedom to exchange is rigorously enforced in the labor market, however, this process will operate expeditiously and efficiently, and no permanent mass unemployment will result. Laborers will quickly find that they have no recourse but to accept the lower real wage rates necessitated by the malinvestment and destruction of capital that follows in the wake of imported credit inflation. An expansionary domestic monetary policy will only delay the needed labor market adjustments and pile new capital malinvestments atop the old.

the financial system as an excuse for once again unleashing the central bank to inflate the money supply.

This last quality of Mises's transition program is absent from the currency board solution favored by free bankers and some monetarists. Under the currency board system, although the currency board notes themselves would be backed one hundred percent (or more) by debt claims denominated in the foreign reserve currency, much as the notes of Mises's Conversion Agency are, commercial banks would be free to issue deposits and even notes only fractionally backed by the currency board notes.[31] This would leave the system vulnerable to financial panics, especially those initiated by or involving "capital flight" into foreign currency.[32] In this situation a broad movement by foreign and domestic investors in Romanian enterprises and securities to liquidate their investments and convert their leus into dollars for investment abroad would first bring about a wholesale conversion of leu deposits into currency board leu notes. This would threaten to break the fractional-reserve banking system and undoubtedly bring irresistible pressure on the currency board to assume the central banking function of a "lender of last resort."[33]

---

[31] Schuler et al., "Replacing the Ruble," p. 17; and George Selgin, "The ECU Could Stabilize Eastern Currencies," in *The Wall Street Journal* (January 9, 1992): p. A12.

[32] This is recognized by by Allan H. Meltzer ("The Benefits and Costs of Currency Boards," *The Cato Journal* 12 [Winter 1993]: p. 709), a lukewarm proponent of currency boards. On the key role of fractional-reserve banking in precipitating the capital flight of the 1930s, see Mises, *Economic Calculation*, pp. 107–09.

[33] This scenario appears to be developing in Hong Kong as I write this in September 1997. A general—but not yet headlong—exodus of capital from Southeast Asia is beginning to cause a credit crunch, resulting in a sharp increase in the Hong Kong interbank, or Hibor, rate and the drawing down of dollar reserves by Hong Kong's currency-board-like Monetary Authority to defend the fixed exchange rate between the Hong Kong and U.S. dollars. Should large lenders to the region, such as the Japanese banks, lose confidence in the stability of the indigenous currencies, a pell-mell flight of capital would ensue, the Hibor would climb to stratospheric heights and weaker Hong Kong banks would be unable to borrow on the market to finance the continuing redemption of their demand liabilities. At this point the Hong Kong Monetary Authority would forsake its role as a strict currency board and begin to lend to the failing banks to ward off bank runs and widespread financial panic. On the developing financial crisis in Southeast Asia, see Erik Guyot ("Hong Kong's Rates Rise, Prompting Fears of Slowdown," in *The Wall Street Journal* 230 [September 10, 1997]: p. A16)

A final virtue of Mises's proposed transition regime is that the last step to a completely sound money, a 100 percent gold standard, would be simple and painless. Unfortunately, this final step could only take place after the U.S. itself had decided to restore the gold basis of the dollar.[34] But once the U.S. dollar was again defined as a specific weight of gold, say one-two thousandth of an ounce, the Romanian Conversion Agency would then be in a position both to convert its paper dollar reserves into gold at the rate of $2,000 per ounce and to calculate the gold content of the new gold leu.[35] It would then use the gold obtained to immediately redeem its leu notes and close its doors. Since the Romanian public thinks and calculates in leus, it might be wise for the Conversion Agency to mint the gold reserve into coins denominated in leus, before paying them out to the public. This once-and-for-all coinage operation could be paid for by a special fund built up from the interest earned on the Agency's dollar reserves. But whether it does this or pays out gold in the form of bullion and dollar-denominated coins, leaving it to the payees to engage private mints to transform the gold

---

and Jathon Sapsford ("Japan's Banks Will Keep Asian Spigot Flowing and Help Avoid Credit Crunch," in *The Wall Street Journal* 230 [September 8, 1997]: p. A15).

[34] If a small country like Romania attempted to unilaterally reestablish gold convertibility for its currency, it would face the problem of sudden and unpredictable fluctuations of its price level. This would result not from any innate feature of gold but from the actions of governmental monetary authorities abroad. If the latter begin to substantially increase the rates of growth of their national fiat money supplies, this could precipitate panic buying of gold by their citizens as a hedge against inflation. This would drive up the value of gold relative to other goods, thereby causing a sudden deflation of prices in terms of Romania's gold currency. Or foreign governments might decide to dump part of their accumulated gold stocks to temporarily prop up the exchange rate for their depreciating fiat currencies, to increase their current revenues, or to punish gold speculators. This sell-off would depress the value of gold and cause leu prices to surge upward. But the risks associated with unilaterally establishing a gold convertible currency must, of course, be compared with the inflationary risks posed by tying on to a "harder" fiat currency such as the dollar, whose stock may be inflated at double-digit rates at any time as the result of an arbitrary political decision. If, in assessing these risks, Romanians decide that a gold-convertible currency is the safer course for the transition period, then the proposal in the text is readily adaptable to this decision by simply substituting "gold" and "gold market" for "dollar" and "foreign exchange market" wherever these terms appear.

[35] If the par rate between the leu and the dollar had been fixed at 7,000 leus per dollar, then, given the definition of the dollar as $\frac{1}{2,000}$ oz. of gold, each gold leu would contain $\frac{1}{14}$ millionth oz. of gold (= $\frac{1}{2,000}$ oz. of gold per dollar x $\frac{1}{7,000}$ dollars per leu).

at their own expense into coins of their preferred sizes and denominations, it is indispensable for the public to take physical possession of and become familiar with gold money. In either case, individual leu holders would then decide what portion of their cash balances to retain in the form of gold coin and what portion to hold in the form of instantaneously redeemable claims to gold, such as bank notes and demand deposits. The latter would be literal money certificates, which would function as substitutes for the actual gold in exchange and would certify that those who receive them in exchange are getting de facto title to the ownership of the precise quantity of gold specified on their face. In order for these notes and deposits to operate as the bona fide property titles to gold that they purport to be, their issuing institutions would be legally obliged to hold 100-percent gold reserves against all demand liabilities.[36]

Of course, as critics of sound money tirelessly remind us, even the gold standard may be undone if a government decides not to continue to abide by "the rules of the game." But, of course, this objection is

---

[36] The enforcement of one hundred percent reserves would not require the continuation of the administrative mandate of the transition regime that banks be split into deposit and saving departments. Presumably, by the time the government of the U.S. and possibly other G-7 governments have decided to restore the gold standard, Romania will have formulated a body of property law that includes recognition of the true economic nature of bank notes and demand deposits, i.e., as nothing more or less than property titles to the money commodity, gold. In fact, it would not be difficult to incorporate a legal principle requiring 100 percent reserves for demand deposits into a system of property law adopted from Western market economies, because, as de Soto ("A Critical Analysis of Central Banks," pp. 29–30) has pointed out, such a general legal principle was contained in the continental European juridical tradition which extends from old Roman Law to the French and Spanish legal codes of the early twentieth century. A second problem that would need to be resolved upon the transition to a completely sound money is the disposition of the fiduciary media that were issued by the banks prior to the transition period and whose stock has been since frozen. While the continued existence of these media would not necessarily disrupt monetary calculation, they would remain a source of weakness—and, therefore, of never-ending temptation for government intervention—in the financial system. One possible method of liquidating them is to transfer to the commercial banks the proceeds from the sale of the central bank's assets upon its dissolution. The commercial banks would then use these assets to purchase the gold reserves necessary to transform their margin of unbacked demand liabilities into 100-percent gold-backed money certificates. This would mean of course a windfall capital gain for the shareholders of these banks.

completely vacuous, because it applies just as fully to any of the reforms aimed at restoring the market economy and economic calculation. The government may in the future choose to institute all-around price controls or to once again collectivize the means of production. And these violations of "the rules of the game," or, more properly, of the rights to private property and freedom of exchange, would undoubtedly plunge the economy once again into calculational chaos. The point is that sound money is also a fundamental institutional requirement of economic calculation that can be wrecked by government destruction of property rights. But this means that its restoration and preservation is imperative if a nation wishes to survive and flourish.

Bibliography

Allais, Maurice, 1987. "The Credit Mechanism and Its Implications." In *Arrow and the Foundations of the Theory of Economic Policy*, George R. Feiwel, ed., pp. 491–561. New York: New York University Press.

Bordo, Michael D., and Anna J. Schwartz. 1987. "The Importance of Stable Money: Theory and Evidence." In *The Search for Stable Money: Essays on Monetary Reform*, James A. Dorn and Anna J. Schwartz, eds., pp. 53–72. Chicago: University of Chicago Press.

Bresciani-Turroni, Costantino. [1937] 1968. *The Economics of Inflation: A Study of Currency Depreciation in Post-War Germany*, Millicent E. Savers, trans. London: George Allen & Unwin, Ltd.

Cagan, Phillip. 1989. "Monetarism." In *The New Palgrave: Money*, John Eatwell, Murray Milgate, and Peter Newman, eds., pp. 195–205. New York: W.W. Norton & Company, Inc.

Carrington, Samantha. 1992. "The Remonetization of the Commonwealth of Independent States." *AEA Papers and Proceedings* 82 (May): pp. 22–26.

De Soto, Jesús Huerta. 1995. "A Critical Analysis of Central Banks and Fractional/Reserve Free banking from the Austrian Perspective." *The Review of Austrian Economics* 8, no. 2: pp. 25–38.

_____. 1997. *A Critical Note on Fractional/Reserve Free banking*, unpublished MS.

Guyot, Erik. 1997. "Hong Kong's Rates Rise, Prompting Fears of Slowdown." In *The Wall Street Journal* 230 (September 10), p. A16.

Hanke, Steve H., and Kurt Schuler. 1993. "Currency Boards and Currency Convertibility." In *The Cato Journal* 12 (Winter): pp. 687–705.

_____, and Kurt Schuler. 1993. "Currency Boards and Currency Convertibility." *The Cato Journal* 12 (Winter): pp. 687–705.

Hayek, F.A. [1935] 1967. *Prices and Production*, 2nd ed. New York: Augustus M. Kelley.

_____. 1978. *Denationalisation of Money — The Argument Refined*. London: The Institute of Economic Affairs.

Heilperin, Michael A. [1939] 1978. *International Monetary Economics*. Philadelphia: Porcupine Press.

Hoppe, Hans-Hermann, Jörg Guido Hülsmann, and Walter Block. 1998. "Against Fiduciary Media." *The Review of Austrian Economics* 11, no. 1: pp. 15–50.

Humpage, Owen F. 1995. "A Mexican Currency Board?" Federal Reserve Bank of Cleveland *Economic Commentary* (March 15).

_____, and Jean M. McIntire. 1995. "An Introduction to Currency Boards," Federal Reserve Bank of Cleveland *Economic Review* 31 (2nd Quarter): pp. 2–11.

Laffer, Arthur. 1980, *Reinstatement of the Dollar: The Blueprint*. Rolling Hill Estates, Calif.: A.B. Laffer Associates.

Maltsev, Yuri N. 1990. "The Maltsev One-Day Plan." *The Free Market* 8 (November): p. 7.

Marget, Arthur W. [1938–42] 1996. *The Theory of Prices: A Re-Examination of the Central Problems of Monetary Theory*, 2 vols. New York: Augustus M. Kelley.

McKinnon, Ronald I. 1991. "Financial Control in the Transition from Classical Socialism to a Market Economy." *Journal of Economic Perspectives* 5 (Fall): pp. 107–22.

Meltzer, Allan H. 1987. "Monetary Reform in an Uncertain Environment." In *The Search for Stable Money: Essays in Monetary Reform*, James A. Dorn and Anna J. Schwartz, eds., pp. 201–20. Chicago: University of Chicago Press.

_____. 1993a. "The Benefits and Costs of Currency Boards." *The Cato Journal* 12 (Winter): pp. 707–10.

_____. 1993b. "Monetarism." In *The Fortune Encyclopedia of Economics*, David R. Henderson, ed., pp. 128–34. New York: Warner Books, Inc.

Miles, Marc A. 1984. *Beyond Monetarism: Finding the Road to Stable Money*. New York: Basic Books.

Mises, Ludwig von. 1952. "Summary Statement." In *Defense, Controls, and Inflation: A Conference Sponsored by the University of Chicago Law School*, Aaron Director, ed., pp. 331–35. Chicago: University of Chicago Press.

_____. 1966. *Human Action: A Treatise on Economics*, 3rd ed. Chicago: Henry Regnery Company.

_____. 1978. *On the Manipulation of Money and Credit*, Percy L. Greaves, ed., Bettina Bien Greaves, trans. Dobbs Ferry, N.Y.: Free Market Books.

_____. [1952] 1981. *The Theory of Money and Credit*. Indianapolis, Ind.: Liberty Classics.

_____. 1990. *Economic Calculation in the Socialist Commonwealth*, S. Adler, trans. Auburn, Ala.: Ludwig von Mises Institute.

Reimann, Guenter. 1939. *The Vampire Economy: Doing Business under Fascism*. New York: The Vanguard Press.

Reisman, George. 1979. *The Government against the Economy*. Thornwood, N.Y.: Caroline House Publishers, Inc.

Rothbard, Murray N. 1992. "How and How Not to Desocialize." *The Review of Austrian Economics* 6, no. 1: pp. 65–77.

_____. 1993. *Man, Economy and State: A Treatise on Economic Principles*, 2nd ed. Auburn, Ala.: Ludwig von Mises Institute.

Sachs, Jeffrey. 1992. "Privatization in Russia: Some Lessons from Eastern Europe." *AEA Papers and Proceedings* 82 (May): pp. 43–48.

_____. 1993. *Poland's Jump to the Market Economy*. Cambridge, Mass.: The MIT Press.

Salerno, Joseph T. 1982. "The Gold Standard: An Analysis of Some Recent Proposals." Cato Institute *Policy Analysis* (September 9).

_____. 1987. "Gold Standards: True and False." In *The Search for Stable Money: Essays on Monetary Reform*, James A. Dorn and Anna J. Schwartz, eds., pp. 241–55. Chicago: University of Chicago Press.

_____. 1991. "Two Traditions in Modern Monetary Theory: John Law and A.R.J. Turgot." In *Journal des Economistes et des Etudes Humaines* 2 (June/September): pp. 337–80.

_____. 1994. "Ludwig von Mises's Monetary Theory in Light of Modern Monetary Thought." *The Review of Austrian Economics* 8, no. 1: pp. 71–115.

_____. 1997. "Monetary Neutrality vs. Monetary Calculation: The Problem of Deflation." Austrian Scholars Conference Working Paper, 27. Auburn, Ala.: Ludwig von Mises Institute.

Sapsford, Jathon. 1997. "Japan's Banks Will Keep Asian Spigot Flowing and Help Avoid Credit Crunch." *The Wall Street Journal* 230 (September 8): p. A15.

Schuler, Kurt. 1996. *Should Developing Countries Have Central Banks? Currency Quality and Monetary Systems in 155 Countries*. London: Institute of Economic Affairs.

_____, George Selgin, and Joseph Sinkey, Jr. 1991. "Replacing the Ruble in Lithuania: Real Change Versus Pseudoreform." *Policy Analysis* 163 (October 28). Washington, D.C.: The Cato Institute.

Selgin, George. 1991. *Praxeology and Understanding: An Analysis of the Controversy in Austrian Economics*. Auburn, Ala.: Ludwig von Mises Institute.

_____. 1992. "The ECU Could Stabilize Eastern Currencies." *The Wall Street Journal* (January 9), p. A12.

_____. 1995. "The 'Productivity Norm' vs. Zero Inflation in the History of Economic Thought." *History of Political Economy* 27 (1995): pp. 705–35.

_____1997. *Less Than Zero: The Case for a Falling Price Level in a Growing Economy*. London: The Institute of Economic Affairs.

Walters, Allan. 1992. "A Hard Ruble for the New Republics." *National Review* (February 3): pp. 34–36.

CHAPTER 20

Preventing Currency Crises: The Currency Board Versus the Currency Principle

Introduction

The institution of the currency board began to gain increasing favor among mainstream economists in the mid-1990s because of its apparent success in taming hyperinflation in Argentina, restoring orderly monetary conditions to Estonia and Lithuania, and restraining inflation in Hong Kong. Eventually, the IMF, which had bitterly opposed the implementation of currency boards in Argentina, Indonesia and the Baltic countries in the early 1990s did an abrupt about face and purportedly even mandated the establishment of a currency board in Bulgaria as a precondition of granting credit.[1]

A backlash against currency boards began to build when the repercussions of the Southeast Asian currency crisis of 1997 shook the foundations of Hong Kong's currency board and financial system later that year and then again in 1998. Argentina's currency crisis of 2001, which resulted in the total collapse of its currency board, solidified the

---

From: "Preventing Currency Crises: The Currency Board Versus the Currency Principle," *Indian Journal of Economics and Business* 6, no. 1 (2007): pp. 161–83.

[1] Nikolay Gertchev, "The Case Against Currency Boards," *The Quarterly Journal of Austrian Economics* 5 (Winter 2002): p. 66.

case against this monetary regime and stimulated a renewed faith in central banking and orthodox IMF policies for emerging market economies. Since then, criticism of so-called "hard peg" currency arrangements for developing nations has grown steadily and has recently even penetrated to the college textbook literature.[2]

Instead of a currency board, mainstream critics advocate that governments of emerging market economies implement conventional flexible exchange-rate regimes dominated by central banks. This type of arrangement, they claim, will forestall currency crises and provide scope for activist monetary stabilization policy. A small but vocal group of economists and international policymakers even proposes the restriction of international capital movements where emerging market economies are involved. However, these are precisely the policies that have repeatedly failed in the past, plunging developing countries into recurrent cycles of hyperinflation and recession, suppressing capital accumulation and hampering long-term progress toward material prosperity.

It is argued in this paper that the currency board does indeed suffer from an inherent flaw that renders it susceptible to currency crises, but that this defect has been incorrectly identified by mainstream critics because they have misinterpreted the nature and causes of such crises. It is also contended that a "hard-peg" arrangement based on the "currency principle" does not share the currency board's vulnerability to recurrent crises. The "currency principle" was initially, but imperfectly, formulated in the mid-nineteenth century by the British Currency school. It had long since fallen into disrepute by the time Ludwig von Mises reformulated it in the early twentieth century. This principle served as the point of departure for the development of a comprehensive theory of currency crises by Mises and other monetary theorists in the 1930s. Mises[3] also used this principle in formulating a proposal for postwar monetary reform for small countries

---

[2] Stephen G. Cecchetti, *Money, Banking, and Financial Markets* (New York: McGraw-Hill Irwin, 2006).

[3] Ludwig von Mises, *The Theory of Money and Credit*, 3rd ed. (Indianapolis, Ind.: Liberty Classics, 1981), pp. 485–90.

whose currencies had been wrecked by the breakdown of the international monetary order during the 1930s.[4]

Section 2 of the paper presents what may be called the neo-Currency school theory of currency crisis, a theory that was developed as an explanation of the breakdown of the international gold standard in the interwar period. The structure and operation of the currency board system is explained in section 3 and the systemic flaw that predisposes it to currency crises is identified. In section 4, the neo-Currency school (NUS) theory of currency crises is applied to elucidate the financial perturbations that engulfed Hong Kong at the end of the 1990s. Hong Kong is chosen for analysis because its currency board is generally touted as the most orthodox and successful by proponents.[5]

The Neo-Currency School Theory of Currency Crises

The NCS theory of currency crises was formulated in the 1930s to explain an unprecedented event in monetary history: the nearly contemporaneous abandonment of the gold standard during peacetime by all major industrialized nations. The NCS approach to currency crises was developed and expounded by economists whose theoretical perspective on money and finance had been shaped by Mises's path-breaking work, *The Theory of Money and Credit*,[6] which had been initially published in German in 1912. Besides Mises,[7] other

---

[4] For a modern application of Mises's proposal to Eastern European transition economies see Joseph T. Salerno, "Beyond Calculational Chaos: Sound Money and the Quest for Capitalism and Freedom in Ex-Communist Europe," *Polis: Revistă de "tinke Politice*," 5, no. 1: pp. 114–33 [reprinted here as Chapter 19].

[5] Steve H. Hanke, Lars Jonung and Kurt Schuler, *Russian Currency and Finance: A Currency Board Approach to Reform* (New York: Routledge, 1993), p. 82.

[6] Mises, *Theory of Money and Credit*.

[7] Ludwig von Mises, "Senior's Lectures on Monetary Problems," in *Money, Method, and the Market Process: Essays by Ludwig von Mises,* ed. Richard M. Ebeling, pp. 104–09 (Norwell, Mass.: Kluwer Academic Publishers, 1990); idem, *Human Action: A Treatise on Economics*, Scholar's Edition, Introduction by Jeffrey M. Herbener, Hans-Hermann Hoppe, and Joseph T. Salerno (Auburn, Ala.: Ludwig von Mises Institute, 1998); idem, "A Noninflationary Proposal for Postwar Monetary Reconstruction," in *Selected Writings of Ludwig von Mises: The Political Economy of Inter-*

notable proponents of the NCS theory included Friedrich Hayek,[8] Lionel Robbins,[9] Gottfried von Haberler,[10] Fritz Machlup[11] and Michael A. Heilperin.[12]

The Neo-Currency School that emerged in the 1930s derived from the British Currency school (BCS) of the mid-nineteenth century.[13] The latter had recognized that Great Britain's return to the gold standard in 1821, after a hiatus of almost a quarter of a century, had not rid the economy of recurring inflationary booms that culminated in financial crises. The BCS theorized that the financial crises and ensuing deflationary busts that had struck the British economy in 1825, 1836 and 1839 were the result of prior inflationary "overissue" of currency by

---

national Reform and Reconstruction, ed. Richard M. Ebeling (Indianapolis, Ind.: Liberty Classics, 2000), pp. 71–118.

[8] Friedrich Hayek, *Monetary Nationalism and International Stability* (New York: Augustus M. Kelley, [1937] 1971).

[9] Lionel Robbins, *Economic Planning and International Order* (London: Macmillan, 1937).

[10] Gottfried von Haberler, *Theory of International Trade,* trans. Alfred Stonier and Frederic Benham (Clifton, N.J.: Augustus M. Kelley, [1936] 1968).

[11] Fritz Machlup, "Foreign Debts, Reparations, and the Transfer Problem," in *International Payments, Debts, and Gold: Collected Essays by Fritz Machlup* (New York: Charles Scribner's Sons, 1964), pp. 396–416; idem, "My Early Work on International Monetary Problems," *Banca Nazionale Del Lavoro Quarterly Review* 133 (June 1980): pp. 115–46.

[12] Michael A. Heilperin, "Economics of Banking Reform," *Political Science Quarterly* 50 (September 1935): pp. 359–76; idem, *Aspects of the Pathology of Money: Monetary Essays from Four Decades* (London: Michael Joseph Limited, 1968); idem, *International Monetary Economics* (Philadelphia: Porcupine Press, [1939] 1978). Heilperin is nearly forgotten today, but he was a prolific writer and an important thinker on international monetary economics whose career extended from the early 1930s to the early 1960s. He published books and articles in three languages, his native Polish, French, and English and was a colleague of Mises's at the Graduate Institute of International Studies in Geneva. For an overview and evaluation of his work, see Joseph T. Salerno, "Gold and the International Monetary System: The Contribution of Michael A. Heilperin," in *The Gold Standard: Perspectives in the Austrian School,* 2nd ed., ed. Llewellyn H. Rockwell, Jr. (Auburn, Ala.: Ludwig von Mises Institute, 1992), pp. 81–111.

[13] Murray N. Rothbard, *Classical Economics: An Austrian Perspective on the History of Economic Thought,* vol. 2 (Brookfield, Vt.: Edward Elgar Publishing Company, 1995), pp. 225–74 provides a comprehensive discussion of the British Currency School and its origins, doctrines, and opponents.

the fractional-reserve banking system whose gold reserves were concentrated in the Bank of England, a privileged private bank that effectively operated as a central bank. The BCS theorists recognized that the gold standard was capable of moderating and reining in such overissue, but that it would do so only after a time lag during which regional or national prices would rise relative to world prices, causing a balance-of-payments deficit and an external drain of gold reserves. This in turn set the stage for panic among domestic bank note holders and depositors resulting in the threat of bank runs inducing the central bank to raise the discount rate and contract the supply of money and bank credit to reverse the loss of reserves. This deflationary policy resulted in financial crisis and recession.

The BCS developed its famed "currency principle" as the solution to the problem. According to this principle, variations in the quantity and value of the British "mixed" currency, defined to include gold in circulation plus bank notes, were to conform precisely to the variations that would occur if the money supply consisted exclusively of gold coin. In practice, the principle dictated that changes in the supply of bank notes be rigidly linked, pound for pound, with changes in the supply of gold, with additional bank notes issued only in exchange for deposits of gold of equal denomination. With the money supply thus varying in accordance with the state of the balance of payments, currency overissue would be totally suppressed and domestic prices would vary in lockstep with world prices.

Unfortunately, there were two fateful flaws in the BCS theory that resulted in a failure to correctly apply the currency principle on the policy level. First, the currency principle was not applied to bank deposits because the latter were not included in the BCS's definition of the money supply. And second the BCS did not realize the implication of implementing a policy based on this principle under a monetary regime in which the gold reserves of the entire system were concentrated in the central bank. Thus the enactment of the BCS program into law as the Bank Act of 1844, also known as Peel's Act, failed in its stated purpose of abolishing currency crises and by the late nineteenth century the BCS and its currency principle had been discredited.

In resurrecting the currency principle, Mises[14] identified and corrected the most important defect in the BCS formulation of the principle by extending its coverage to bank deposits. Furthermore, all the NCS theorists more or less recognized the inconsistency between the currency principle and a system of nationally centralized reserves, a position that was stated most clearly by Hayek as we shall see in the next section. Emerging in a much different politico-economic environment, however, the NCS went far beyond the BCS in another respect. NCS theorists characterized the currency principle as more than merely a technical recipe for monetary policy. Rather, they viewed it as a method of re-integrating and anchoring the money supply process in the regime of private property rights and the rule of contract. The NCS theory thus characterized currency crises as the inevitable outcome of a series of *interventions* by governments aimed at circumventing or abolishing the relatively rigid limits on credit expansion imposed by the classical gold standard. In effect, the theory represented the logical extension of Menger's theory of the origin of commodity money as a general medium of exchange to the explanation of money's progressive transformation into a government "policy tool." Following Menger's historico-logical approach, the NCS theorists of the 1930s gave a rich or "thick" explanation of currency crises as the logical outcome of hampered market processes operating under specific political, ideological and institutional conditions.

A. The National Reserve System: Origin and Effects

According to the NCS theory, currency crises occur within the institutional framework of a fractional-reserve banking system in which the cash reserves of the private commercial banks have been nationalized and concentrated in the central bank. This system was generally referred to as the "one-reserve system",[15] however Hayek

---

[14] Ludwig von Mises, "The 'Austrian' Theory of the Trade Cycle," in Richard M. Ebeling, *The Austrian Theory of the Trade Cycle and Other Essays*, 2nd ed. (Auburn, Ala.: Ludwig von Mises Institute, [1978] 1996), pp. 25–27.

[15] Mises, *Human Action*, p. 462; Hayek, *Monetary Nationalism*, p. 12.

suggested a more descriptive name for it, "the system of national reserves." This system was not the outcome of market forces, but rather was superimposed on the commercial banks by governments "in order to make it easier for the central banks to embark upon credit expansion."[16] The United States, for example, effectively nationalized bank reserves in 1917. The Amendment to the Federal Reserve Act of June 21, 1917 mandated that only reserve deposits held at the Federal Reserve Banks would be counted as legal reserves of member banks, resulting in a centralization of gold reserves at the Fed.[17]

In European countries, where central banks began to emerge as early as the late seventeenth century, the nationalization of reserves began even earlier, under the classical gold standard.[18] Other countries arrived at the national reserve system by adopting the gold exchange standard after World War I in order to economize on their gold holdings which yielded no return. This attenuated version of the gold standard naturally centralized reserves in the form of interest-bearing foreign securities in the central bank and thus placed "in the hands of governments the power to manipulate their nations' currency easily."[19] Another postwar device for "economizing gold," the gold bullion standard, under which currencies were only convertible into large and expensive bars of gold, also served to concentrate

---

[16] Mises, *Human Action*, p. 262.

[17] C.A. Phillips, T.F. McManus, and R.W. Nelson, *Banking and the Business Cycle: A Study of the Great Depression in the United States* (New York: Arno Press & The New York Times, [1937] 1972), pp. 24–25; W.P.G. Harding, *The Formative Period of the Federal System (During the World Crisis)* (New York: Houghton Mifflin Company, 1925), pp. 72–74. As Benjamin Anderson (*Economics and the Public Welfare: A Financial and Economic History of the United States, 1914–1946*, 2nd ed. [Indianapolis, Ind.: Liberty Press, 1979], p. 56) pointed out, the theory underlying this Amendment was "not very clear" but "in 1916 and in early 1917 there was a very definite practical consideration that we might be involved in war, and that it was important that the gold of the country be concentrated in a central reservoir as a basis for war finance." So the centralization of gold reserves in the Fed was undertaken with the definite intention of facilitating an inflationary monetary policy.

[18] According to Mises, "In order to make it easier for the central banks to embark upon credit expansion, the European governments aimed long ago at a concentration of their countries' gold reserves with the central banks (Mises, *Human Action*, p. 462).

[19] Ibid., p. 780.

gold reserves in the hands of the central bank and "made possible an increase in circulating media out of all proportion to the current production of gold."[20]

The national reserve system brought about two momentous changes in the institutional framework of financial markets. The first was a radical alteration of the way in which the commercial banks conducted business. When a central bank was granted the legal or de facto monopoly of warehousing the gold deposits of the public, its notes and deposits were no longer treated as instantaneously redeemable *property titles* to the actual money commodity housed within its vaults. The gold now became subsumed under the general category of central bank "assets" serving as "reserves" against its issue of instantly maturing "liabilities," i.e., notes and deposits. These notes and deposits in time came to be generally accepted by the public as money itself rather than what they actually were: titles to money or "money certificates" that conveniently substituted in trade for the money commodity.

This development in turn led the commercial banks to hold the minimum amount of reserves—now in the form of central bank notes and deposits—necessary to meet the day-to-day net redemptions of their own instantaneous liabilities. These included not only their demand deposits but also their interest-bearing savings deposits, upon which notice of withdrawal was increasingly waived, despite the fact that the funds for both of these categories of deposits had been invested by business borrowers for shorter or longer periods in the economy's structure of production.[21] This mismatching of the maturity structure of the commercial banks' assets and liabilities, which had always existed to a limited extent when fractional reserves banks were responsible for holding their own gold reserves, was thus greatly

---

[20] Phillips et al., *Banking and the Business Cycle*, p. 49.

[21] For discussion of the changes in the legal and institutional conditions that led to the transformation of time deposits into instantaneous liabilities and their role in generating bank credit inflation and financial instability in the 1920s and 1930s, see Heilperin, *Aspects of the Pathology of Money*, pp. 267–68 and idem, *International Monetary Economics*, pp. 92–93; Mises, "Senior's Lectures on Monetary Problems," pp. 107–08; Phillips et al., *Banking and the Business Cycle*, pp. 29, 95–101.

promoted by the practically unlimited access granted to banks under the national reserve system to loans from the central bank when they found themselves short of reserves.

Mises[22] concisely summed up the revolution in banking practice that resulted from the national reserve system:

> [The banks] no longer keep a reserve against their daily maturing liabilities. They do not consider it necessary to balance the maturity dates of their liabilities and assets in such a way as to be any day ready to comply unaided with their obligations to their creditors. They rely upon the central bank. When the creditors want to withdraw more than the 'normal' amount, the private banks borrow the funds needed from the central bank. A private bank considers itself liquid if it owns a sufficient amount either of collateral against which the central bank will lend or of bills of exchange which the central bank will rediscount.

The national reserve system effected a second revolutionary alteration in the financial system of the interwar period. This was the layering of different moneys—more properly, money substitutes—of a progressively narrower range of acceptability atop one another so that the monetary structure of a nation came to resemble an inverted pyramid resting upon a narrow base of gold, the universally accepted money. As Hayek,[23] who was the first to fully elaborate the implications of this institutional structure, explained:

> The ordinary individual will hold only a sort of money which can be used directly for payments of clients of the same bank; he relies upon the assumption that his bank will hold for all its clients a reserve which can be used for other payments. The commercial banks in turn will only hold reserves of such more liquid or more widely acceptable sort of money as can be used for inter-bank payments within the country. But for the holding of the reserves of the kind which can be used for payments abroad, or even those which are required if the public would want to convert a considerable part of its deposits into cash, the banks rely largely on the central bank.... It was only

---

22 Mises, *Human Action*, p. 462.
23 Hayek, *Monetary Nationalism*, pp. 10, 12.

> with the growth of centralized national banking systems that
> all inhabitants of a country came ... to be dependent on the
> same amount of more liquid assets held for them collectively
> as a national reserve.[24]

Hayek's analysis of the national reserve system sheds important light on the effects of international monetary flows under alternative institutional arrangements. Within the national currency area, inter-local transfers of money, no matter how large or abrupt, put no strain on the overall financial system because they do not entail any disturbance of the gold base of the national monetary pyramid. In particular, they do not necessitate that the central bank raise its discount rate to "protect" its "gold reserves," because the monetary transfers were accomplished wholly though changes in the assets and liabilities of banks within the same national reserve system. This is especially important because, as Hayek[25] pointed out, "not every movement of money ... is a transfer of capital."[26] That is, not every net flow of money between regions is a response to a shift of supply and demand on the investible funds market. Some movements of money result either from a temporary and reversible discrepancy between the imports and exports of a given region or from a more permanent reconfiguration of the interregional pattern of the demand for money. In both cases,

---

[24] Two minor mistakes marred Hayek's analysis. It ignored Mises's crucial distinction between "money" and "money substitutes" and it confounded the Mengerian concept of "acceptability" or "marketability" and the Keynesian notion of "liquidity." Different kinds of money substitutes can be more or less widely acceptable, but as soon as any kind comes to be considered as less than perfectly "liquid," it will be deprived of its monetary function. For an enlightening discussion of the difference between the two concepts from a slightly different perspective, see Heilperin, *International Monetary Economics*, pp. 93–94. For an explanation of Mises's taxonomy of money and a defense of his distinction between money and money substitutes, see Joseph T. Salerno, "Ludwig von Mises's Monetary Theory in Light of Modern Monetary Thought," *The Review of Austrian Economics* 8, no. 1: pp. 75–77 [reprinted here as Chapter 2].

[25] Hayek, *Monetary Nationalism*, p. 31.

[26] Heilperin (*International Monetary Economics*, pp. 92–93) made a similar distinction: " '[C]apital' is the fund of purchasing power made available for investment. It is to be distinguished from monetary funds whose destination has not yet been decided upon by the owners. One has to note that the organization of credit does not make possible a sharp distinction between the two types of funds—which is one of the great factors in economic instability."

therefore, no change of the discount rate or of interest rates in general is warranted, since no transfer of real capital is involved.

When we consider purely monetary transfers between two regions that are parts of different national reserve systems, matters are not much different as long as these transfers are the result of normal fluctuations in the balance of trade or occasional changes in the relative demands for money. In these cases, the accompanying movements of gold from one country to another would be relatively minor and would be rapidly ended or reversed by relative changes in the price structures of the two countries as described by the classical price-specie-flow mechanism. In order for this mechanism to function central banks need do no more than honor their contractual obligations to redeem at par and on demand the titles to gold they issued and to strictly limit the new receipts issued to the actual amount of new gold that is brought to them for storage, i.e., to operate as honest and simple bailees in warehousing the money commodity. If central banks operated in this manner, the expansion of the money supply in the surplus country and the contraction of money supply in the deficit country would be precisely equal to each other and to the net transfer of gold through the balance of payments. This outcome is precisely the same economically as it would be if the transfer of money occurred between two regions that were constituents of the same system of national reserves.

The (Mis)Behavior of the Central Bank

According to the NCS analysis, then, when central banks behaved according to the "currency principle"—ensuring that the national money supply varies on a one-to-one basis with gold flows to and from abroad—the nation's currency was unlikely to encounter crisis conditions. Things were radically different, however, when a central bank attempted to lower domestic interest rates by unilaterally expanding bank credit. This caused the pyramided layers of money substitutes to expand relative to the national reserve of gold, resulting in a progressive rise of domestic prices. The rise in domestic prices and the decline of domestic interest rates relative to levels prevailing abroad would precipitate a deficit on both current and capital accounts.[27] This overall deficit in the balance of payments would persist until the cheap money policy was brought to an end. In the meantime, the deficit was financed by the steadily dwindling "gold reserves" of the expansionist central bank. This "external drain" of gold would eventually inspire a loss of confidence in the domestic currency, precipitating an "internal drain" of gold as domestic and foreign investors and the public at large rushed to convert into gold the ever-growing mass of money substitutes issued by the central bank and the commercial banks. As this crisis point approached, the central bank, if it wished to maintain the gold standard, would be compelled to sharply raise its discount rate in order to contract bank credit and replenish its depleted stock of gold.[28]

The outflow of gold reserves and the rise of the discount rate marked the turning point in the business cycle, when it was revealed that domestic interest rates could not be permanently reduced by central bank credit expansion below their natural level as determined on international capital markets by the quantity of voluntary savings. The rise of the discount rate was therefore not an exogenous cause of the ensuing recession, but rather a necessary step in the corrective process which revealed to entrepreneurs that there were not sufficient savings and real capital goods available to sustain the investment projects they had initiated under the stimulus of cheap money.

The NCS theorists emphasized that the inapt rhetoric of war used to describe the sequence of events leading up to the loss of reserves led to serious misconceptions among economists and the public about the causal process involved as well as the role of central banks in this process. Mises[29] cut through this rhetoric and identified the true cause as the violation of contract:

---

[27] Of course, if the country in question is experiencing relatively rapid growth in real output, the credit expansion may not manifest itself in rising prices of consumer goods, but solely in declining interest rates and swelling bubbles in financial and real estate markets. This occurred in the U.S. in the 1920s and 1990s.

[28] After the discovery of open market operations in the 1920s, the central bank could also initiate monetary contraction and avoid a currency crisis by selling securities to the commercial banks and the public.

[29] Mises, *Human Action*, pp. 456–57.

The truth is that all that a central bank does lest its gold reserves evaporate is done for the sake of the preservation of its own solvency. It has jeopardized its financial position by embarking upon credit expansion and must now undo its previous action in order to avoid its disastrous consequences.... No "defender" is needed to "protect" a nation's currency system.... When the Bank of England redeemed a bank note issued according to the terms of the contract ... [i]t simply did what every housewife does in paying the grocer's bill. The idea that there is some special merit in a central bank's fulfillment of its voluntarily assumed responsibilities could originate only because again and again governments granted to these banks the privilege of denying to their clients the payments to which they had a legal title.

In particular, the central bank in the deficit (surplus) nation did not need to increase (decrease) the discount rate and bring about a contraction (expansion) of the national money supply that was a multiple of the loss (gain) of gold through the balance of payments. The raising of the discount rate by the central bank of a deficit nation thus was not one of the "the rules of the game" of the gold standard.[30] It was merely a byproduct of the cessation of credit expansion by a central bank that had been vainly attempting to maintain the domestic interest-rate structure below that prevailing on the global capital market. In other words, the fundamental rule of contract, not arbitrary and changeable rules of the game, dictated the central bank's decision to preserve the redeemability of its demand liabilities at par.

Indeed, to the proponents of the NCS theory, the gold standard emerged in defiance of the arbitrary rules of the bimetallic standard adhered to by governments for centuries in a futile attempt to stabilize the exchange ratio between gold and silver.[31] In the their view, then, the international gold standard was not a creation of policy rules but rather an organic product of the market economy, and its functioning, like

---

[30] As Mises (*Human Action*, p. 459) explained: "it has been asserted that the 'orthodox' methods of fighting an external drain by raising the rate of discount no longer work because nations are no longer prepared to comply with 'the rules of the game.' Now the gold standard is not a game, but a social institution. Its working does not depend on the preparedness of any people to observe some arbitrary rules."

[31] Mises, *Human Action*, pp. 468–70.

that of all market institutions, was "controlled by the operation of inexorable economic law.[32]

Anti-Deflation Policy and the Problem of "Hot Money"

Under the attenuated gold standard that arose in the 1920s, most central banks sought to evade the inevitable deflation of the domestic money pyramid entailed by external payments deficits. They began to treat money as a tool of policy rather than as simply the property of their depositors and note-holders who had been contractually assured complete and unimpeded disposal of their gold for domestic or foreign transactions. The NCS theorists pointed out that the efforts of central banks in the postwar period to deliberately implement anti-deflation policy not only conflicted with their contractual obligations but disabled the balance of payments adjustment process that had operated under the gold standard to continually adapt the spatial distribution of money to the ever changing conditions of international monetary equilibrium.

In a retrospective on his early contributions to international monetary theory, Machlup[33] emphasized that equilibrating money flows were an inherent feature of the international gold standard and that the policy of creating domestic credit to replace gold and foreign exchange reserves lost through payments deficits only recreated monetary disequilibrium and caused further outflows of gold:

> Under a gold standard ... any excess stock of money leads to a deficit in the balance of payments which in turn leads to an outflow of gold reserves and to a concomitant contraction of the money stock, restoring the balance ... But all this presupposes that domestic credit creation does not recreate the excess money stock and rising prices.... I tried to make it clear that these policies of offsetting the contractionary effects of official sales of foreign exchange by expansions of domestic credit were sabotaging the adjustment mechanism.

---

[32] Ibid., p. 459.
[33] Machlup, "My Early work on International Money Problems," pp. 118–19.

> The automatic contraction of the money supply in the course
> of financing the payments deficit was the very essence of the
> adjustment process, and to offset this contraction was to pre-
> vent the adjustment and to make the deficit chronic.[34]

Robbins recognized that the classical gold standard was essentially in conflict with and destined to be undermined by the political
institution of central banking that had grown up concurrently with it
but separately from it. Central banks had been set up specifically to
make loans to governments, that is, to expand credit. They were thus
deliberately designed to replace the general rule of property and contract with arbitrary policy rules. As noted above, the national reserve
system was imposed by governments precisely as a method of promoting central bank expansionism by neutralizing internal drains of
gold to competing domestic banks. But this system could not prevent
the external drain of gold to less expansionary central banks abroad
and the emergence of so-called "balance-of-payments problems." As
Robbins[35] stressed:

> [When] governments have been inclined to use [central
> banks] as instruments of positive policy, they have become
> the most potent cause of general economic nationalism. If
> the government of a certain area imposes upon the banks
> under its jurisdiction a policy of expansion at a time when
> the local position offers no scope for such expansion, then
> ... the international equilibrium is ruptured. The "problem"
> of maintaining international equilibrium at once arises—and
> with it all the policies designed to solve such a problem.

One of the manifestations of this institutional disruption of
international monetary equilibrium was the sudden emergence of
"hot money" in the early 1930s. NCS theorists perceived that this
phenomenon was caused by the behavior of the central bank, which,
when operating under the national reserve system, produced a peculiar incentive structure for commercial banks that encouraged abrupt
movements of deposited funds. A country that incurred persistent
deficits in its balance of payments as a consequence of a relatively

---

[34] In this passage Machlup combines passages from his 1923 text with his commentary on this text in 1980. I have suppressed the brackets that he inserted.

[35] Robbins, *Economic Planning*, p. 302.

inflationary monetary policy would eventually encounter growing skepticism regarding its ability to maintain the gold parity of its currency. This was because in the interwar period it eventually came to be expected that central banks would no longer impose orthodox discount rate policy, as they had before World War I, in response to the serious gold/foreign exchange outflow inevitably precipitated by their attempt to unilaterally depress domestic interest rates. Instead, it was anticipated, they would now engage in further inflationary credit expansion to prevent the necessary contraction of the domestic money stock, and this would only intensify the gold drain.[36]

Foreign-exchange speculators and foreign investors were the first to formulate and manifest these pessimistic expectations by selling the currency short and withdrawing their short-term capital from domestic banks and sending it to safe havens abroad. These flows of hot money through the capital account would further exacerbate the overall deficit and put "pressure" on the currency's exchange rate. If the central bank continued its policy of recreating the excess supply of money, the hot money flows would worsen and the government would soon be confronted with a full-blown currency crisis. The only way out would be either devaluing the currency, imposing foreign exchange controls, or abandoning the gold standard altogether.

One of the key insights of the NCS theory was that the phenomenon of hot money was not generated by the normal operation of the gold standard. In fact its emergence signaled the breakdown of the inflationary national reserve system that was instituted to neutralize the adjustment mechanism of the gold standard. "Capital flight," as it was often labeled, did not embody genuine movements of capital that occur under a sound international monetary system.

---

[36] For an insightful discussion of the historical, political, intellectual, and ideological factors responsible for this radical transformation of central banks' view of the role they played in the operation of the gold standard after 1914, see Melchior Palyi, *The Twilight of Gold, 1914–1936: Myths and Realities* (Chicago: Henry Regnery Company, 1972), pp. 45–60, 101–06. Also see Anderson, *Economics and the Public Welfare*, pp. 182–89.

As Heilperin[37] pointed out; most international movements of short-term funds during the 1930s were "operations with cash and with demand deposits ... result[ing]from purely financial transactions disconnected in their origin from any other international economic operations." Heilperin[38] went on to explain, "when anticipations of the future are uncertain and when pessimism prevails home investments are deferred and cash balances increase. Funds of purchasing power wait for an appropriate moment to be invested, and as that moment gets postponed the non-invested savings (or hoards) keep accumulating. It is those funds which are easily induced into more or less panicky movements from country to country, from currency to currency."

The root of the hot-money problem lay in the national reserve system. Under this system, the commercial banks came to treat the accumulation of speculative cash balances as genuine savings and loaned them out to domestic business, maintaining only minimal cash reserves against them. They operated in this manner because, as noted above, each individual bank regarded itself as sufficiently liquid as long as it owned securities that the central bank was normally willing to rediscount or accept as loan collateral. But the quantity of gold and foreign exchange reserves concentrated in the central bank—the ultimate cash upon which the financial system rested—was grossly insufficient to cover the sight deposits of all commercial banks, rendering the overall system at all times illiquid. Institutionally, these sight deposits took the form mainly of savings or time deposits upon which interest was paid and whose mandatory "notice of withdrawal" was progressively shortened and then effectively waived altogether as banks responded to the perverse incentives generated by the national reserve system.[39]

---

[37] Heilperin, *International Monetary Economics*, pp. 97–98.

[38] Ibid., p. 100.

[39] For a recent analysis of the general effects of the mishandling of speculative cash balances as genuine savings by the banking system see John P. Cochran and Steven T. Call, "The role of Fractional-Reserve Banking and Financial Intermediation in the Money Supply Process: Keynes and the Austrians," *The Quarterly Journal of Economics* 1 (Fall 1998): pp. 29–40; also see Jesús Huerta De Soto, *Money, Credit and*

Mises[40] summarized the interrelated roles of the system of national reserves, the cheap-money policy of the central bank and the conditions of moral hazard that these two institutional factors created for the commercial banks in generating currency crises. He pointed out that "short-term debt," specifically saving deposits, had come to play a dominant role in the banking system of the 1930s. Banks of creditor countries had invested an enormous amount of funds in interest-bearing deposits in banks located in debtor countries, with the understanding that they would be able to withdraw such "saving deposits" at a moment's notice. But it was impossible for all or most of the lending banks to retrieve their credits all at once since these funds had been, in turn, lent to businesses for capital investment in the debtor country. Thus "international credit relations were based on a fallacious assumption of liquidity" and banks in debtor countries "became exposed to the dangers of a panic." It was not therefore the "flight of capital" proper that endangered monetary stability. Savings invested in industrial plants, corporate shares, and real estate could not literally flee to another country; in the absence of bank credit expansion, every seller of such titles to real capital assets must be replaced by a buyer, either foreign or domestic, in order for the seller to realize his proceeds and invest them abroad. The result is that the withdrawal of capital from a country "can never be a mass movement."

For Mises, the "one apparent exception" to this rule was "the saving deposit which can be withdrawn from the bank at once or at short notice." Even in this case, a "hot money" problem would not have ensued, had the central bank refrained from expanding credit to assist the errant banks. Without inflationary credits from the central bank, the commercial banks would have been forced to negotiate generalized "Standstill Agreements" with their domestic and foreign creditors that acknowledged the reality of the distinction between cash balances and invested savings and "adjusted payments due to payments receivable."

Mises[41] concluded:

Economic cycles, trans. Melinda A. Stroup (Auburn, Ala.: Ludwig von Mises Institute, 2006), pp. 167–295.

[40] Mises, "Senior's Lectures on Monetary Problems," pp. 107–09.

[41] Ibid., p. 109.

> It is obvious that not the flight of capital but the credit expansion in favor of the saving banks is the root of the evil.... The pith of the problem lies in the deposit policy. Banks which promise no more than they can fulfill without extraordinary assistance from the central bank never jeopardize the stability of the country's currency. And even the other banks who [sic] have been imprudent enough to assume liabilities which they cannot meet are only a danger when the central bank tries to assist them. If the Central Bank were to leave them to their fate, their peculiar embarrassment would not have any effect on the foreign exchanges.[42]

Mises[43] also contended that had the central banks not tacitly assumed the role of lender of last resort entailed by the national reserve system, then commercial banks would have been forced to deal prudently with the hot money influx by keeping "a reserve of gold and foreign exchange big enough to pay back the whole amount in case of a sudden withdrawal." Of course this would have entailed their "charging their customers a fee to keep their funds safe" instead of paying interest on them.

Mises[44] applied the theory of currency crises to explaining the devaluation of the Swiss franc in 1936. In late September of that year the French franc had been devalued, causing a widespread expectation that Switzerland would follow suit and devalue the Swiss franc.

---

[42] Reporting on his own research on capital flight in the 1930s, Machlup ("My Early Work on International Monetary Problems," p. 133) appears to have reached a similar conclusion regarding its nature and necessary precondition: "I found that there were 'natural' limits to the possible flight of capital—except if the central bank permits an expansion of domestic credit and thereby finances the capital exports. In this case the central bank provides or replenishes the domestic funds that seek conversion into foreign currencies, with the result that no capital export takes place (since the loss of monetary reserves constitutes an official capital import) and, of course, no transfer of real resources takes place." Interestingly, Machlup (ibid.) confided that he resisted including his article on capital flight in the English-language collection of his essays "chiefly because of its implied policy recommendation for central banks never to come to the aid of commercial banks confronted with sudden withdrawals of foreign loans." While he conceded that such "a tough position" may have been "justified" in the case in question, "as a general principle," he feared his "1932 position appears unduly dogmatic and insensitive."

[43] Mises, *Human Action*, p. 462.

[44] Ibid., pp. 462–63.

During the early 1930s Swiss commercial banks had accumulated a large fund of hot money deposits which they had pledged to redeem on demand, while lending them out to business. A large part of these loans had gone to firms in foreign countries which had since implemented foreign exchange controls that effectively blocked repayment of these loans. The only recourse for the Swiss banks would have been to seek emergency loans from the Swiss National Bank in order to pay their depositors. But the depositors would have immediately demanded that the National Bank redeem the notes paid out in gold and foreign exchange in order to transfer their funds to Great Britain, the U.S. or even to France which had already devalued and so did not pose a threat of a second devaluation in the short term. The National Bank would have thus lost most of its reserves. This in turn would have generated a domestic panic and the remainder of its reserves would have drained out into the cash balances of Swiss depositors, effecting a collapse of the monetary system. However, if the National Bank had resisted the requests of the private banks for aid, then the country's leading financial institutions would have become insolvent. So the Swiss government solved the crisis by immediately devaluing the Swiss franc by 30 percent and suspending domestic gold payments, thereby relieving the pressure on its reserves.[45]

So, according to the NCS theory, a currency crisis is not a mysterious scourge that suddenly strikes from out of the blue but is the predictable pattern of events that is caused by a combination of identifiable politico-economic institutions and policies.

The Currency Board As a National Reserve System

The contemporary currency board is in effect, if not by design, a national reserve system only formally distinct from the gold exchange system of the interwar years. As pointed out by the NCS theory of currency crises, the national reserve system is a self-liquidating system. It

---

[45] On the Swiss devaluation, see Palyi, *The Twilight of Gold*, pp. 290–91 and Leland B. Yeager, *International Monetary Relations: Theory, History, and Policy*, 2nd ed. (New York: Harper & Row Publishers, 1976), pp. 258–63.

is foredoomed by an inherent flaw to degenerate into either a system of "flexible" exchange rates or a system of rigid exchange controls.

Under the currency board system, although currency board notes and deposit liabilities themselves are backed one hundred percent (or more) by debt claims denominated in the foreign reserve currency, commercial banks are free to issue demand deposits and instantly maturing "saving" deposits that are only fractionally backed by the notes and deposits issued by the currency board. In other words, the currency board system provides for one hundred percent reserves only for the domestic monetary base, sometimes referred to as "high-powered money."[46] Furthermore, just as under the interwar gold exchange standard, the ultimate cash reserves of the entire banking system are centralized in the hands of a government agency. In consequence, the domestic money supply under the currency board resembles Hayek's inverted pyramid of different kinds of money substitutes of progressively narrower range of acceptability, i.e., currency board notes and commercial bank deposits, which is perched atop a slender base of the foreign currency that serves as the ultimate cash reserves of the system.

This renders the system vulnerable to financial panics, initiated by or involving "capital flight" into foreign currency. This is especially true in emerging market economies where large inflows of foreign

---

[46] On the design and operation of currency boards: see Steve H. Hanke and Kurt Schuler, *Currency Boards for Eastern Europe*. The Heritage Lectures 355 (Washington, D.C.: The Heritage Foundation, 1991); idem, "Currency Boards and Currency Convertibility," *The Cato Journal* 12 (Winter): pp. 687–705; Hanke et al., *Russian Currency and Finance*; Anna J. Schwartz, *Do Currency Boards Have a Future?* (London: Institute of Economic Affairs, 1992); Owen F. Humpage and Jean M. McIntire, "An Introduction to Currency Boards," Federal Reserve Bank of Cleveland *Economic Review* 31 (Quarter 2): pp. 2–11; Charles Enoch and Anne-Marie Guide, "Making a Currency Board Operational," *Paper on Policy Analysis and Assessment of the International Monetary Fund* (November 1997); Richard W. Kopcke, "Currency Boards: Once and Future Monetary Regimes," *New England Economic Review* (May/June 1999): pp. 21–37, and the literature cited therein. For the most thorough critical analysis of the currency board from the perspective of the NCS, see Gertchev, "The Case Against Currency Boards." Some of the above as well as additional articles discussing various aspects of the currency board can be found on the "Currency Board" Homepage at *http://politics.ankara.edu.tr/~kibritci/cur-board.html*.

capital can rapidly expand the domestic monetary base and money supply, thereby raising domestic prices to a level that renders the domestic currency overvalued at the prevailing exchange rate. As Hayek argued, in the absence of a relative increase in the demand for money in the receiving country, a capital inflow does not necessitate a permanent expansion of the domestic money supply. The initial inflow of money capital is merely the first step of the process by which the capital transfer is effected in real terms. Once this process has been completed, balance of payment equilibrium is re-established and the distribution of the common money between the two countries is returned to its original pattern.

The outcome is much different, however, where the expansion of the domestic money supply is a multiple of the initial capital inflow—where, in Machlup's terms, new money is issued on the basis of "domestic credit"—which is the case under the currency board. The persistent decline in the purchasing power of money and loss of foreign exchange reserves under such circumstances stimulate a movement by foreign speculators and investors to withdraw their deposits from domestic banks and liquidate their holdings of domestic securities, converting their proceeds into the reserve currency for investment abroad. This exacerbates the loss of the reserve currency and threatens to precipitate a full-blown banking panic among domestic depositors, accompanied by an "internal" drain of foreign currency reserves. Recently, Nouriel Roubini[47] has argued in a similar vein:

> The argument that currency boards cannot collapse because the monetary base is fully backed by the foreign reserves of the country is patently incorrect. If an attack on the currency occurs, domestic residents may try to get rid of domestic financial assets and buy foreign assets by running down the foreign reserves … of the central bank. The domestic financial assets that may be used to buy foreign currency are not limited to the monetary base (that is fully backed by foreign reserves in a CB [central bank] but rather the entire stock of

---

[47] Nouriel Roubini, "The Case Against Currency Boards: Debunking 10 Myths about the Benefits of Currency Boards," Working Paper. Stern School of Business, New York University. Available at http://www.geocities.com/Eureka/Concourse/8751/jurus/vs-cbs.htm.

liquid monetary assets that is usually a large multiple of the monetary base.

These events, if left unchecked, would not only exhaust foreign reserves but would break the fractional-reserve banking system. Clearly, then, at the first sign of a flight from the currency, there would be an almost irresistible pressure on the currency board to assume the central banking function of "lender of last resort" in order to avert a banking panic. The massive injection of credit and liquidity into the financial system, even if not immediately followed by a currency devaluation, transforms the currency board into a central bank and clearly undermines the credibility of its commitment to maintain a rigidly fixed exchange rate in the future.

The recent case of Hong Kong, recounted in the next section, illustrates the inherent instability of the currency board that is manifested in national currency crises and its natural tendency to devolve into a central bank during such crises.

Recent Experience With the Currency Board in Hong Kong

Hong Kong's Currency Board System

Hong Kong's currency board, known officially as the Linked Exchange Rate System, began operation in October 1983 and implemented a fixed exchange rate between the Hong Kong dollar and the U.S. dollar of HK$7.80 per US$1.00. Under this system, which is administered by the Hong Kong Monetary Authority (HKMA), the monetary base, including, among other items, all currency in circulation (most of which is issued by three private note-issuing banks) and commercial bank clearing accounts held with the HKMA is fully backed by foreign exchange reserves in the form of short-term debt instruments denominated in U.S. dollars.[48] Thus any change in the monetary

---

[48] For details of the history and operation of the Hong Kong currency board, see Hong Kong Monetary Authority, *HKMA Background Brief No. 1: Hong Kong's Linked Exchange Rate System* (November). Available at http://www.info.gov.hk/hkma/eng/public/hkmalin/index.htm. It should be noted that there is no deposit

base is fully matched by a change in the stock of foreign reserves at the prevailing exchange rate and fluctuations of the monetary base are completely and solely dependent on the net flow of dollars to and from Hong Kong. This means that the flow as well the stock of the monetary base is fully backed by dollar reserves. For example, from December 1998 to November 2005, the stock monetary base increased from HK$193,718 million to HK$276,859 million while the stock of currency board "backing assets" increased from HK$209,684 million to $HK308,989 million. The "backing ratio" of U.S. dollar reserves to the monetary base thus increased slightly from 108.24 percent to 111.61 percent. The monetary base flow of HK$83,141 million during this period was therefore more than matched by the influx of US$ backing assets equal to HK$99,305 million.[49]

According to the neo-Currency theory, however, the important stock and flow ratios for analyzing currency crises relate foreign exchange reserves to a broader measure of the money supply that encompasses the total stock of the medium of exchange.[50] If we calculate the backing ratio of US$ assets to the HK$ M3 over the same period we find that this ratio stood at 11.4 percent in December 1998 when M3 was HK$1,840,824 million and rose to 13.2 percent in November 2005 when M3 totaled HK$2,331,578 million.[51] Thus

---

reserve requirement in Hong Kong and that banks need only maintain a clearing balance with the HKMA sufficient to cover their interbank settlements (Tsang Shu-ki, "Is a Currency Board System Optimal for Hong Kong," [May 18, 1998]. Available at http://www.hkbu.edu.hi/~econ/web986.html).

[49] Unless otherwise noted, all statistics relating to the Hong Kong currency board system are available on the HKMA website at http://www.info.gov.hk/hkma/index.htm.

[50] Some contemporary critics of currency boards also suggest that it is the ratio of a broad measure of the money supply to foreign reserves that is appropriate in gauging the adequacy of reserves in the face of a currency crisis. See Roubini, "The Case Against Currency Boards," for references.

[51] M3 is a particularly appropriate measure of the money supply in Hong Kong, because, in contrast to the M3 aggregate calculated for most other developed countries, Hong Kong M3 excludes repos and money market mutual funds which are not general media of exchange on a par with currency and bank deposits. Furthermore, unlike U.S. monetary statistics, for example, which exclude bank deposits held by foreign official institutions, monetary aggregates in Hong Kong properly do not differentiate between deposits held by resident and non-resident entities (Hong Kong Monetary Authority, "Definition of Money Supply," *Quarterly Bulletin* [May 2002]:

M3 flow was HK$490,763 million during the same period, almost five times as large as the backing asset inflow of HK$99,305 million. Since most items included in M3 are instantaneously redeemable in US$ at par, the currency board system in Hong Kong is just as vulnerable to a currency crisis as the national reserve systems of the 1930s based on the gold exchange standard. The fact that the monetary base is more than 100 percent backed by foreign exchange is completely irrelevant, since under the national reserve system the monetary base itself is generally exceeded by the total supply of monetary assets of lesser degrees of acceptability by orders of magnitude.

Now, an argument can be, and has been, made that the foreign exchange assets backing HK$ M3 is much greater than the backing assets recorded on the HKMA balance sheet. The reason is that, since the mid-1970s the Hong Kong political authority has been accumulating its fiscal reserves in foreign exchange and transferring them to the Exchange Fund, which also holds the backing assets of the HKMA.[52] If we include these cumulative fiscal surpluses along with the backing assets held by the HKMA, the ratios of foreign currency reserves to the monetary base and to MS increase dramatically. For instance, the ratio of foreign currency reserves to the monetary base stood at 3.61 in December 1998 and 3.45 in November 2005. However for the same two months, the foreign currency reserves/M3 ratio equaled .53 and .41, respectively. Also flow M3 during this period was HK$490,763 million compared to HK$255,856 million for the flow of foreign currency reserves, or about two times as great. Thus even with this dubious broadening of the definition of "backing assets," the stock and flow ratios of foreign currency reserves to M3, still violate the currency principle and reflect a systemic flaw in Hong Kong's currency board system that leaves it vulnerable to currency crises.

---

pp. 16–23. Available at http://www.info.gov.hk/hkma/eng/public/index.htm, p. 16). For a critique of U.S. monetary aggregates including M3, see Robert Batemarco and Joseph T. Salerno, "SME: A new Measurement of the U.S. Money Supply," *The Mid Atlantic Journal of Business* 29 (March 1993): pp. 109–31. Available at http://www. highbeam.com/librarydocFree.asp?drjcid=1G1:14332205&key=0C177A56741C146 0120D001A026A06087D07740B74ZR7aUG72on.

[52] Shu-ki, "Is a Currency Board System Optimal for Hong Kong."

Moreover, there are a number of reasons why this inclusion of foreign currency reserves generated by the fiscal operations of government in the backing assets of the money supply should be rejected. First, precisely because they are not the result of private commercial operations, they are not a component of the balance sheet of the HKMA and have no direct causal connection to the determination of the money supply, movements in the structure of interest rates, and fluctuations in the purchasing power of money. These exchange reserves, therefore, do not have a direct role in generating the economic conditions that lead up to currency crises. Second, as the backing assets of the HKMA near exhaustion during a currency crisis, the probability of a substantial domestic currency devaluation would increase along with a corresponding appreciation of foreign currency reserves. It is at least a matter of reasonable doubt whether the government would expend its imminently more valuable fiscal reserves in an attempt to quell a currency crisis already in progress.[53]

The NCS theory thus implies that a monetary system structured like that of Hong Kong, especially given the great degree of "openness" of its economy, would be subject to cycles of inflation and depression, of booms and busts, brought on by flows of reserves through its balance of payments. A net inflow, for example, resulting from an external payments surplus generates both equilibrating and disequilibrating expansion in the total money stock. The part of the increase in the money stock that exactly matched the net increase of foreign exchange reserves would be necessary to increase prices to a level that would tend to bring both the purchasing power of the local currency and the domestic structure of interest rates into alignment with prices and interest rates in the reserve-currency country. The outcome would be balance-of-payments equilibrium. However, the

---

[53] David F. DeRosa (*In Defense of Free Capital Markets: The Case Against a New International Financial Architecture* (Princeton, N.J.: Bloomberg Press, 2001), p. 120) makes a similar point in his discussion of Hong Kong's currency crisis of 1997:

[T]he continued operation of the [currency] board under conditions of duress is a function of the country's willingness to sacrifice hard currency reserves. At some time or other, the country might decide that enough is enough and that keeping its foreign reserves is more important than maintaining its currency peg.

additional enlargement of the money stock produced by the multiplication and pyramiding of domestic bank credit atop the new reserves of foreign exchange would elevate domestic prices to a level that was inconsistent with balance of payments equilibrium. The structure of domestic interest rates would also be depressed below the level compatible with the overall quantity of voluntary savings, foreign and domestic, that were available for domestic investment. As long as net foreign exchange inflows continued, as they did in Hong Kong during the 1990s up until the last quarter of 1997, the underlying disequilibrium both in the financial sector and in the real structure of production would be masked and exacerbated.

This disequilibrium is only sustainable until a headline event, typically a currency crisis in a similarly situated economy abroad, suddenly awakens investors, currency speculators, and the public at large to the fact that the domestic currency is overvalued. Then despite—or because of—the existence of the currency board system, it is recognized that the currency peg may not be sustainable and there is an imminent threat of depreciation of the domestic currency. At this point there is the characteristic "capital flight" into foreign currencies and financial assets. In accordance with the theories of the NCS, the capital flight takes the form of an outflow of hot money rather than of actual capital funds invested in the real sector of the economy. With this mass withdrawal of unbacked domestic bank deposits convertible on demand at the fixed exchange rate into foreign currency reserves, the national reserve system is thus put under pressure, interest rates skyrocket, bank credit shrinks, and the national money stock contracts rapidly. The first effect on the real sector is a precipitous drop in investment and the liquidation of malinvested capital projects undertaken on the basis of mistaken anticipations of the continuation of artificially lowered interest rates. The drop in investment results in an unexpected decline in demand for new capital goods construction and a time-consuming reallocation of labor to less capital-intensive lines of production. Thus, a fall in real GDP and rise in unemployment accompanies the decline in investment. Moreover, the revelation of capital malinvestment and collapse of capital goods' prices brings in its wake a fall in financial asset markets on which titles to aggregates of capital goods are traded, such as stock, bond, and real estate markets.

The Hong Kong Currency Crises of 1997–1998

During the 1990s Hong Kong experienced a financial boom that was accompanied by strong if not overwhelming growth in real output.[54] From 1990 to 1996 "broad monetary growth" averaged 13.8 percent per year while the annual growth in CR1 averaged 9.1 percent.[55] During this period the annual average of stock prices on the Hang Seng Index, using 1984 as the base year, more than quadrupled from 300.18 in 1990 to 1,406.6 in 1997.[56] Even more starkly, on the first trading day of 1990 the Hang Seng Index closed at 2,838.1 and nearly sextupled to its peak at 16,673 at the market's close on August 7, 1997. A real investment boom stimulated the bubble in financial markets, with gross fixed investment as a percent of GDP rising by over 7 percentage points from 26.4 percent in 1990 to a peak of 33.6 percent in 1997.[57]

The unraveling of the Hong Kong boom and the run-up to a full blown currency crisis began in October 1997.[58] The Southeast Asian crisis had begun when the Thai baht was devalued on July 2 1997. Hong Kong was unscathed by the crisis. Then, on October 20 the Central Bank of Taiwan abruptly discontinued its program of supporting

---

[54] Real GDP growth per year averaged 5.0 percent in 1990–1997 versus 6.8, 8.9, and 7.9 percent in the 1980s, 1970s and 1960s respectively. This has led Shu-ki ("Is a Currency Board System Optimal for Hong Kong") to comment, "The fall in the real growth rate of per capita GDP has been particularly disappointing, as Hong Kong should not have 'matured' so quickly."

[55] These statistics were computed from the electronic databases accompanying Atish R. Ghosh, Anne-Marie Gulde, and Holger C. Wolf, *Exchange Rate Regimes: Choices and Consequences* (Cambridge, Mass.: The MIT Press, 2003). Data on monetary aggregates are not published by the HKJVIA for the years before 1997. Thus it is difficult to gauge the degree to which the operation of the Hong Kong currency board violated the currency principle in the years leading up to the currency crises of 1997 and 1998.

[56] Shu-ki, "Is a Currency Board System Optimal for Hong Kong."

[57] Ghosh et al., *Exchange Rate Regimes.*

[58] The following account is drawn from DeRosa, *In Defense of Free Capital Markets.*

the New Taiwan dollar, which immediately depreciated by 9 percent. At the beginning of the summer, the Taiwanese central bank had accumulated a massive stock of foreign reserves that exceeded by orders of magnitude the stocks held by the Southeast Asian countries engulfed in crisis. Although there was no close connection between the Hong Kong and Taiwanese economies, the inability of the Taiwanese central bank to "defend" its currency even with its huge stock of reserves immediately raised questions about the HK$. Hong Kong was almost immediately swept up in a rapidly intensifying currency crisis of its own. In the following two days local residents as well as foreigners began panic sales of the HK$ and Hong Kong stocks. By October 23, hedgers and speculative short-sellers had driven the short-term interest rates to 280 percent and stock prices plunged by 23.3 percent, as the Hang Seng Index dropped from 13,601 on October 17 (the last trading day before the depreciation of the New Taiwanese dollar) to 10,426.3 on October 23. After partially recovering and languishing in the 11,000 range after a number of months, the stock market spiraled slowly downward with the Hang Seng Index breaking below 8,000 in late July 1998 and continuing downward.

Hong Kong survived the crisis with its currency board and currency peg intact, only to confront a more serious "attack" on its currency following on the heels of the Russian default of August 1998. Sounding like any conventional central banker trying to evade responsibility for an overvalued currency, Joseph Yam, Chief Executive of the HKMA, spoke of "a much more complicated situation, in which speculators launched coordinated and well planned attacks across our financial markets."[59] This time the currency board system broke in the face of a second stock market collapse and the HKMA used its assets to purchase shares in the market. It is estimated that in a two week period the currency board used US$15 billion of its US$96.5 billion foreign reserve holdings (including the government fiscal surplus). While a second meltdown of the stock market was averted by these operations, the government absorbed 5 percent of the total stock market float.[60] For July 1998, the month immediately preceding the crisis,

---

[59] Quoted in DeRosa, *In Defense of Free Capital Markets.*
[60] Ibid., p. 144.

total foreign currency reserves had equaled US$96.5 billion but dwindled to a total of US$88.4 billion in September 1998.

The financial crises of 1997 and 1998 set in motion the purgative recession-adjustment process in the real sector. Investment as a percentage of GDP, which had reached a peak of 33.6 percent in 1997 plummeted to 30.2 percent in 1998 and 25.6 percent in 1999.[61] This latter figure was below the investment/GDP ratio of 26.4 percent at the beginning of the inflationary boom in 1990. The liquidation of the malinvestments of the boom was also reflected in the annual growth of real GDP, which fell from 4.9 percent in 1997 to –0.5 percent and 0.3 percent in 1998 and 1999 respectively.

With its intervention to provide "liquidity" to the stock market in the 1998 crisis it appears that Hong Kong's currency board has shown its true stripes as a conventional central bank. Several measures taken since then to re-establish and enhance its credibility as a currency board actually reveal the fatal flaw in the currency board system. For example, under the Convertibility Undertaking, the HKMA announced that it would guarantee the US$ value of clearing accounts (reserves) of the licensed banks. Basically this means that, in the event of the abandonment of the peg and depreciation of the HK$, the banks would have a legally enforceable claim on the government for losses suffered on some of their HK$-denominated assets. In 2005 a Convertibility Zone of plus or minus HK$.05 was established around the fixed peg of HK$7.80 to US$1.00, within which "the HKMA may choose to conduct open market operations consistent with Currency Board principles with the aim of promoting smooth functioning of the money and foreign exchange markets."[62] In addition "a cushion of liquidity" is provided by a Discount Window facility that permits banks to borrow from the HKMA via repurchase agreements using as collateral Exchange Fund bills and notes, which are claims on foreign exchange reserves held by banks as backing for currency issues.

---

[61] Ghosh et al., *Exchange Rate Regimes.*
[62] Hong Kong Monetary Authority, *HKMA Background Brief,* p. 38.

In effect, this permits a doubling of the monetary base in the case of a financial crisis.[63]

Conclusion

After the outright collapse of the Argentine currency board system and the subtle transformation of the Hong Kong currency board, contemporary opinion remains an odd mixture of insight and confusion regarding the true nature of this peculiar monetary regime. On the one hand, some economists have identified the flaw in the system as the bank credit creation it permits without appreciating its full implications. For example DeRosa[64] has written:

> [R]egardless of the size of the reserves held by the currency board, external shocks may be big enough to damage confidence in the currency board. This happened to Hong Kong in October 1997 ... and again in August 1998 despite there being a massive stock of reserves.

The Achilles heel of a currency board is that the public's perception of its permanence can vanish in a moment. If the integrity of the board or the intention of the government to maintain the board comes into doubt, then something akin to a bank panic can ensue when local citizens, foreign investors, and foreign exchange traders try to sell the local currency.

Unfortunately, DeRosa does not put his finger on the ultimate cause of the system's vulnerability to bank panics: the fact that domestic credit creation by commercial banks produces a national reserve system.[65] Indeed some observers explicitly deny that domestic credit creation takes place under a currency board at all. Thus

---

[63] Ibid., p. 39; Kenneth Kasa, "Why Attack a Currency Board?" Federal Reserve Bank of San Francisco *Economic Letter* (November 26, 1999), p. 4. Available at http://www.frbsf.org/econrsrch/wklyltr/wklyltr99/el99-36.html.

[64] DeRosa, *In Defense of Free Capital Markets*, pp. 162, 163–64.

[65] See Carlos E. Zarazaga, "Can Currency Boards Prevent Devaluations and Financial Meltdowns?" Federal Reserve Bank of Dallas *Southwest Economy* (July/August 1995): p. 9 for an earlier and clearer statement of the problem.

Guillermo Calvo[66] contends, "A common feature in recent crisis is a large expansion of domestic credit from the central bank.... Actually, as illustrated by the tequila crisis [that afflicted Mexico in 1994–1995], in most cases (Argentina and Hong Kong SAR are exceptions) the loss of international reserves is almost entirely driven by international reserves." While Calvo's diagnosis of modern financial crises is in accordance with the NCS theory of currency crises with respect to most traditionally pegged exchange-rate regimes, his parenthetical exception of the Argentine and Hong Kong currency boards is seen to be unjustified in light of the argument of this paper. In fact, national reserve systems absent a central bank are perfectly capable of continually expanding domestic credit and re-creating an excess supply of money. Eventually this ongoing process of bank credit expansion leads to a severely overvalued monetary unit that precipitates a bank panic and financial crisis.

Finally we might note the revealing response of two leading currency board proponents to the earlier Argentine currency crisis of 1995. Hanke and Schuler[67] initially frankly recognized that the currency board was in effect a national reserve system. They nonetheless dismissed the currency principle as a guide to sound money and argued that even inverse movements of the money supply and the balance of payments were completely consistent with stability of the currency board regime:

> It is even possible for changes in the money supply under a currency board system to move opposite from balance-of-payment changes. However that is perfectly acceptable. There is no reason why the money supply in a modern fractional-reserve bank banking system should have a rigid relation with the balance of payments, if other factors simultaneously move the money supply in the other direction. Hong Kong and Singapore experienced balance-of-payments deficits for decades at a time, yet their money supplies steadily increased because they were attracting large inflows of foreign investment.

---

[66] Guillermo A. Calvo, *Emerging Capital Markets in Turmoil: Bad Luck or Bad Policy?* (Cambridge, Mass.: The MIT Press, 2005), p. 341.

[67] Hanke and Schuler, *Currency Boards for Eastern Europe*, p. 15.

Hanke and Schuler went on to contend that "market forces of profit and loss" would determine the appropriate variations in the money supply as long as the currency board remained "entirely passive" and converted "notes and coins into and out of the reserve currency as the public and banks demand." In this case, when the rate of return on investment (adjusted for risks and net of transactions costs) in the currency board country exceeded interest rates abroad, foreign investment would flow in increasing bank reserves and causing a multiple expansion of bank loans and the money supply. The money supply would stop expanding when further expansion of bank loans "would be less profitable than investing the funds abroad." The money supply would thus be endogenously determined by a vaguely specified interest-rate arbitrage mechanism.

Hanke,[68] at least, seemed to abandon this argument for the stability of the money supply process under the currency board when he was forced to address the Argentine currency crisis of 1995, which was marked by domestic bank runs. Now, Hanke[69] distinguished between "a sound currency" and "a sound credit system," and claimed that the crisis reflected on the soundness of the latter, not the former. Contradicting his earlier view of an optimal money supply determined by market forces, Hanke arbitrarily dichotomized the money supply process into the efficient provision of currency by the currency board and the unruly behavior of private bank deposits. Hanke[70] thus blamed Argentina's plight on the fact that it lacked any of the four "classic policies" for preventing "internal drains" or domestic bank runs: deposit insurance; the existence of a lender of last resort; the ability to suspend the convertibility of bank deposits into currency; or 100 percent-reserve banking. He thus supported a proposed deposit insurance system funded by compulsory contributions from the banks themselves, with each bank's premium based on an asset risk assessment conducted by the Argentine central bank.

---

[68] Steve H. Hanke, "Argentina, the 'Germany' of South America?" in *The Contributions of Murray Rothbard to Monetary Economics,* ed. Clifford F. Thies (Winchester, Va.: Durell Institute at Shenandoah University, 1996), pp. 19–30.

[69] Ibid., p. 28.

[70] Ibid., p. 29.

Perhaps perceiving the advantages of the currency principle he also recommended, "One avenue worth further exploration is 100 percent banking." In any case, Hanke has in effect conceded the point of the NSC theory: that a pure currency board system, lacking additional restraints on commercial bank credit creation, is incapable of preventing currency crises.

The conclusions of this paper are twofold. First, the Neo-Currency School theory of currency crises developed in the 1930s sheds valuable light on the likely performance of currency boards in emerging market economies. Second, the case of Hong Kong, when interpreted in the light of this theory, reveals a vital structural flaw even in the most rigid currency board system.

Bibliography

Anderson, Benjamin M. 1979. *Economics and the Public Welfare: A Financial and Economic History of the United States, 1914–1946.* 2nd ed. Indianapolis, Ind.: Liberty Press.

Batemarco, Robert and Joseph T. Salerno. 1993. "SME: A New Measurement of the U.S. Money Supply." *The Mid-Atlantic Journal of Business* 29 (March): pp. 109–31. Available at http://www.highbeam.com/doc/1G1-14332205.html

Cochran, John P., and Steven T. Call. 1998. "The Role of Fractional-Reserve Banking and Financial Intermediation in the Money Supply Process: Keynes and the Austrians." *The Quarterly Journal of Economics* 1 (Fall): pp. 29–40.

Calvo, Guillermo A. 2005. *Emerging Capital Markets in Turmoil: Bad Luck or Bad Policy?* Cambridge, Mass.: The MIT Press.

Cecchetti, Stephen G. 2006. *Money, Banking, and Financial Markets.* New York: McGraw-Hill Irwin.

Currency Board Homepage at http://kisisel.cc.ankara.edu.tr/politics.ankara.edu.tr/kibritci/curboard. html

DeRosa, David F. 2001. *In Defense of Free Capital Markets: The Case Against a New International Financial Architecture.* Princeton, N.J.: Bloomberg Press.

De Soto, Jesús Huerta. 2006. *Money, Credit and Economic Cycles*, Melinda A. Stroup, trans. Auburn, Ala.: Ludwig von Mises Institute.

Enoch, Charles and Anne-Marie Gulde. 1997. "Making a Currency Board Operational." *Paper on Policy Analysis and Assessment of the International Monetary Fund* (November).

Gertchev, Nikolay. 2002. "The Case Against Currency Boards." *The Quarterly Journal of Austrian Economics* 5 (Winter): pp. 57–75.

Ghosh, Atish R., Anne-Marie Gulde, and Holger C. Wolf. (2003). *Exchange Rate Regimes: Choices and Consequences.* Cambridge, Mass.: The MIT Press.

Haberler, Gottfried von. [1936] 1968. *Theory of International Trade.* Alfred Stonier and Frederic Benham, trans. Clifton, N.J.: Augustus M. Kelley Publishers.

Hanke, Steve H. 1996. "Argentina, the 'Germany' of South America?" In *The Contributions of Murray Rothbard to Monetary Economics*, Clifford F. Thies, ed., pp. 19–30. Winchester, Va.: Durell Institute at Shenandoah University.

Hanke, Steve H., Lars Jonung, and Kurt Schuler. 1993. *Russian Currency and Finance: A Currency Board Approach to Reform.* New York: Routledge.

_____, and Kurt Schuler. 1991. *Currency Boards for Eastern Europe.* The Heritage Lectures 355. Washington, D.C.: The Heritage Foundation.

_____, and Kurt Schuler. 1993. "Currency Boards and Currency Convertibility." *The Cato Journal* 12 (Winter): 687–705.

Harding, W.P.G. 1925. *The Formative Period of the Federal System (During the World Crisis).* New York: Houghton Mifflin Company.

Hayek, F.A. [1937] 1971. *Monetary Nationalism and International Stability.* New York: Augustus M. Kelley Publishers.

Heilperin, Michael A. 1935. "Economics of Banking *Reform.*" *Political Science Quarterly* 50 (September): pp. 359–76.

_____. 1968. *Aspects of the Pathology of Money: Monetary Essays from Four Decades.* London: Michael Joseph Limited.

_____. [1939] 1978. *International Monetary Economics.* Philadelphia: Porcupine Press.

Hong Kong Monetary Authority. 2002. "Definition of Money Supply." *Quarterly Bulletin* (May). pp. 16–23. Available at http://www.info.gov.hk/hkma/eng/public/index. htm.

_____. 2005. *HKMA Background Brief No. I: Hong Kong's Linked Exchange Rate System* (November). Available at http://www.info.gov.hk/hkma/eng/public/hkmalin/index.htm.

Humpage, Owen F. and Jean M. McIntire. 1995. "An Introduction to Currency Boards." Federal Reserve Bank of Cleveland *Economic Review* 31 (Quarter 2): pp. 2–11.

Kasa, Kenneth. 1999. "Why Attack a Currency Board?" Federal Reserve Bank of San Francisco *Economic Letter* (November 26). Available at *http://www.frbsf.org/econrsrch/wklyltr/wklyltr99/el99-36.html.*

Kopcke, Richard W. 1999. "Currency Boards: Once and Future Monetary Regimes." *New England Economic Review* (May/June): pp. 21–37.

Machlup, Fritz. 1964. "Foreign Debts, Reparations, and the Transfer Problem." In *International Payments, Debts, and Gold: Collected Essays by Fritz Machlup.* pp. 396–416. New York: Charles Scribner's Sons.

_____. 1980. "My Early Work on International Monetary Problems." *Banca Nazionale Del Lavoro Quarterly Review* 133 (June): pp. 115–46.

Mises, Ludwig von. 1981. *The Theory of Money and Credit*. 3rd ed. Indianapolis, Ind.: Liberty Classics.

_____. 1990. "Senior's Lectures on Monetary Problems." In *Money, Method, and the Market Process: Essays by Ludwig von Mises*, Richard M. Ebeling, ed., pp. 104–09. Norwell, Mass.: Kluwer Academic Publishers.

_____. [1978] 1996. "The 'Austrian' Theory of the Trade Cycle." In *The Austrian Theory of the Trade Cycle and Other Essays*, 2nd ed. Richard M. Ebeling, ed., pp. 25–35. Auburn, Ala.: Ludwig von Mises Institute.

_____. 1998. *Human Action: A Treatise on Economics*, Scholar's Edition, Introduction by Jeffrey M. Herbener, Hans-Hermann Hoppe, and Joseph T. Salerno, Auburn, Ala.: Ludwig von Mises Institute.

_____. 2000. "A Noninflationary Proposal for Postwar Monetary Reconstruction." In *Selected Writings of Ludwig von Mises: The Political Economy of International Reform and Reconstruction*, Richard M. Ebeling, ed., pp. 71–118. Indianapolis, Ind.: Liberty Classics.

Mishkin, Frederic S. 2004. *The Economics of Money, Banking, and Financial Markets*, 7th ed. New York: Pearson Addison Wesley.

Palyi, Melchior. 1972. *The Twilight of Gold, 1914–1936: Myths and Realities*. Chicago: Henry Regnery Company.

Phillips, C.A., T.F. McManus, and R.W. Nelson. [1937] 1972. *Banking and the Business Cycle: A Study of the Great Depression in the United States*. New York: Arno Press & *The New York Times*.

Robbins, Lionel. 1937. *Economic Planning and International Order*. London: Macmillan.

Rothbard, Murray N. 1995. *Classical Economics: An Austrian Perspective on the History of Economic Thought*, vol. 2. Brookfield, Vt.: Edward Elgar Publishing Company.

Roubini, Nouriel. 1998. "The Case Against Currency Boards: Debunking 10 Myths about the Benefits of Currency Boards." Working Paper. Stern School of Business, New York University. Available at http://www.dse.unive.it/summer-school/papers/rubini.htm.

Salerno, Joseph T. 1992. "Gold and the International Monetary System: The Contribution of Michael A. Heilperin." In *The Gold Standard: Perspectives in the Austrian School*, 2nd ed., Llewellyn H. Rockwell, Jr., ed., pp. 81–111. Auburn, Ala.: Ludwig von Mises Institute.

_____. 1994. "Ludwig von Mises's Monetary Theory in Light of Modern Monetary Thought." *The Review of Austrian Economics*, vol. 8, no. 1: pp. 71–115.

_____. 1998. "Beyond Calculational Chaos: Sound Money and the Quest for Capitalism and Freedom in Ex-Communist Europe." *Polis: Revistă "tinke Politice,"* 5, no. 1: pp. 114–33.

Schwartz, Anna J. 1992. *Do Currency Boards have a Future?* London: Institute of Economic Affairs.

Shu-ki, Tsang. 1998a. 'The Hong Kong Government's Review Report: An Interpretation and a Response" (May 4). Available at http://sktsang.computancy.com/attrachment/web985.html.

_____. 1998b. "Is a Currency Board System Optimal for Hong Kong" (May 18). Available at http://sktsang.computancy.com/attrachment/web986.html.

_____. 1998c. "Handling Credit Crunch under Hong Kong's Currency Board System" (August 6). Available at http://sktsang.com/ArchiveI/web987.html.

Yeager, Leland B. 1976. *International Monetary Relations: Theory, History, and Policy*, 2nd ed. New York: Harper & Row Publishers.

Yu, George. 1998. "Is Hong Kong Ready to Delink the Currency?" Reprinted from *HKCER Letters* (March). Available at http://www.hku.hk/hkcer/articles/v49/george.htm.

Zarazaga, Carlos E. 1995. "Can Currency Boards Prevent Devaluations and Financial Meltdowns?" Federal Reserve Bank of Dallas *Southwest Economy* (July/August): pp. 2–9. Available at www.dallasfed.org/research/swe/1995/swe9504.pdf.

CHAPTER 21

Greenspan's Empty Talk

On February 1, 2001, the day after the Federal Open Market Committee (hereafter, FOMC) cut the target Fed funds rate by ½ percentage point, The Wall Street Journal published a front-page article under the headline "Psychology Test: Latest Fed Rate Cut Combats a Contagion of Low Confidence." The opening sentence reads: "With yesterday's half-point interest rate cut, Federal Reserve Board Chairman Alan Greenspan is hoping to lift the nation's spirits before they pull the economy into recession."[1] The article reports that, in the statement accompanying the announcement of its rate cut, the FOMC referred to "consumer and business confidence" that had "eroded further."[2]

The article observes that "More than usual, the Fed chief appears to be engaged in a game of psychology, struggling less to revive a moribund economy than to restore a sense of confidence to the nation's consumers and businesses. He remains convinced that the New Economy is for real and that it promises above-average economic growth in the years ahead. But recent surveys have lost that faith."[3]

The article goes on to solemnly warn that "Fear of a recession can quickly bring on the real thing. 'Animal spirits,' the British economist

From: "Greenspan's Empty Talk," *Mises Daily* (February 28, 2001). Available at Mises.org.

[1] Greg Ip and Nicholas Kulish, "Psychology Test: Latest Fed Rate Cut Combats a Contagion of Low Confidence," *The Wall Street Journal* (February 1, 2001): p. A1
[2] Ibid.
[3] Ibid.

John Maynard Keynes wrote, can hold the key to important economic variables, such as business investment."[4] The article also quotes eminences in the Wall Street and academic communities supporting the latest move by the Greenspan Fed on similar grounds. William Dudley, head of U.S. economic research at Goldman Sachs in New York argues "that maintaining confidence is the key to keeping a temporary slowdown from snowballing into a more serious recession."

Former Fed Vice Chairman and leading Keynesian macroeconomist Alan Blinder offers that one of the reasons Greenspan moved so aggressively in cutting rates was because "the market has gotten better at thinking ahead to what the Fed is going to do. The result is that his previous worry—that if you move too much at once you'll unsettle the markets—isn't a worry anymore."[5] In its concluding paragraph the article leaves readers to ponder whether the Fed's move will achieve its goal of alleviating the collective angst of the nation's households and business firms: "Whether the Fed's action will be sufficient to revive the economy's sagging spirits remains to be seen." The article, however, closes with a hint of optimism, quoting Jerry Jasinowski, president of the National Association of Manufacturers, who proclaims that "The astute timing of the Fed's last two interest-rate moves … probably has prevented an economy-wide recession."

This article illustrates just how completely Alan Greenspan, in his tenure as Fed Chairman, has succeeded in misleading almost everyone, including many economic journalists and professional economists, into accepting a bizarre and idiosyncratic view of the business cycle. Throughout his career as Fed chairman, Greenspan has relentlessly propagated the view that the business cycle is a mysterious phenomenon, the result of imponderable forces operating deep within the market economy and inaccessible to human reason.

Hence, for Greenspan, business cycles are a source of wonderment rather than a subject for rigorous logical analysis: "There is always something different; something that does not look like all the previous ones. There is never anything identical and it is always

---

[4] Ibid.

[5] Ibid., p. A8

a puzzlement."[6] The implications of this view, of course, are not at all uncongenial to Greenspan's position as Chairman of the Federal Reserve System. For the Fed is cast in the role of a vigilant and indispensable protector of the market economy, continually operating to monitor and contain the unruly forces of inflation and recession that constantly threaten to emerge from the economy's dark-side. Moreover, the very mystery that Greenspan claims enshrouds the workings of the business cycle provides a ready-made excuse to absolve the Fed from all blame on the occasions when its best efforts at containment go awry and the business cycle is loosed upon the economy.

A troubling question immediately suggests itself, however: If indeed the business cycle is beyond rational analysis, how then can we depend on the Fed to control or mitigate it? The answer, according to Greenspan, is to completely ignore economic theory and to pore over the economic data on a daily or even hourly basis, trusting to his own intuition to discern the future movements of the economy from the signals that are secreted deep within the ceaseless flood of data.

In his very revealing book on Greenspan, *Maestro: Greenspan's Fed and the American Boom*, Bob Woodward describes what he calls Greenspan's "near obsession with the economic data."[7] For example, on a calm day Greenspan checked 50 different real-time charts on his computer once every half hour.[8] When Greenspan began as Fed chairman he spent an inordinate amount of time regularly contacting friends and acquaintances within the business community, eagerly seeking bits of current industry-level and even firm-level data. In fact he was elated when he found that his position as Fed chairman gave him ready access even to information from the competitors of his consulting firm's clients, information that he was previously barred from obtaining as a private citizen.

Eventually, Woodward tells us, Greenspan was compelled to "set up a system in which Fed staff members would formally call a long list

---

[6] Alan Greenspan, quoted in Bob Woodward, *Maestro: Greenspan's Fed and the American Boom* (New York: Simon & Schuster, 2000), pp. 35–36.

[7] Ibid., p. 54.

[8] Ibid., p. 102.

of companies each week to get their real time numbers."[9] Revealing the extent of his obsessive concern with the data, Greenspan once jubilantly remarked to President Clinton in 1998: "This is the best economy I've ever seen in fifty years of studying it every day."[10] Woodward pithily sums up Greenspan's hyper-empirical and profoundly anti-theoretical approach in the following terms: "Unlike many economists, he has never been rule driven or theory driven. The data drive."[11]

Without the aid of logical-deductive economic theory, however, it would appear to be impossible for the raw data of past history to drive Greenspan, or anyone else, to any conclusions regarding the future movements of the economy. According to Greenspan, however, a lifetime of intimate engagement with the data has caused him to develop a non-rational and almost visceral capacity for intuiting a body of generalized knowledge about economic relationships. This knowledge, he claims, while it cannot be completely articulated, serves him in forecasting the economy. Woodward vividly describes one instance in which Greenspan appealed to this intuitive knowledge in an attempt to persuade the FOMC to moderate a prospective increase in the fed funds rate:

> "Were we to go the ½ percent with the announcement effect and the shock effect, I am telling you that these markets will not hold still." Then, pulling out all the stops, he said, "I've been in the economic forecasting business since 1948, and I've been on Wall Street since 1948, and I am telling you I have a pain in the pit of my stomach".... This pain in the stomach was a physical awareness Greenspan had experienced many times. He felt he had a deeper understanding of the issue—a whole body of knowledge in his head and a whole value system—than he was capable of stating at that moment.... "I am telling you," the chairman continued, "and I've seen these markets, this is not the time to do this.... I really request that we not do this."[12]

---

[9] Ibid., pp. 60–61.

[10] Ibid., p. 195.

[11] Ibid., p. 227.

[12] Ibid., p. 120.

(Amazingly, the Committee was swayed by Greenspan's stomachache and voted unanimously in favor of the ¼ percent rate increase that he urged.) So it turns out that, despite his pronouncements that the causes of the business cycle are unknowable, Greenspan is really not an agnostic at all. He is actually a Gnostic when it comes to business cycles, or one who claims to be blessed with an internal, esoteric source of knowledge that permits him to mystically intuit the inner meaning of the business cycle and to divine its future course.

But despite his visceral certitude about his own intuitive knowledge of the business cycle, when it comes to practical knowledge about everyday matters that is seemingly accessible to everyone, Greenspan is a radical epistemological skeptic who maintains that nothing can be known with certainty. Thus, as an insider in the Ayn Rand circle in the 1950s, Greenspan argued, according to Woodward, "that his own existence could not be proven beyond doubt. Absolute certainty was impossible. All that one could count on were degrees of probability." When Greenspan later relented from this absurd and nihilistic position, he triumphantly declared to Rand: "Guess who exists?"[13]

Nonetheless, despite his epiphany with regard to his own existence, in his economic consulting business Greenspan persistently repeated "the future is unknowable" while "[h]e spoke in terms of most likely outcomes and probabilities."[14] But if almost nothing can be known with certainty and yet all relationships between real-world events are probabilistic, then on what basis are these probabilities to be assigned? In answering this question, it becomes clear that Greenspan's gnosticism and his radical epistemological skepticism are not contradictory at all.

For Greenspan the logically deduced propositions of economic theory, with their pretence to universality and absolute certainty, are useless in providing knowledge about the future consequences of current events and policies, because they take no account of hidden forces that may suddenly begin to operate, revolutionizing seemingly

---

[13] Ibid., p. 56.
[14] Ibid., p. 34.

established economic relationships and falsifying economic laws. These new forces, however, will generate previously unseen and unexpected patterns or wrinkles in the data that, if one possesses the ability to discern and interpret them, will suggest new and more accurate generalizations about economic relationships. In Greenspan's analogy, the planet Pluto was discovered because Neptune's movement was not strictly following the law of gravity. Woodward reports that Greenspan used this analogy to explain to President Clinton why rapid economic growth and the accompanying decline in the rate of unemployment in the late 1990s had defied the expectations of economists and had not precipitated price inflation. Woodward summarizes Greenspan's argument as follows:

> In a similar way [to Neptune], the economy was not following the laws of economics. He did not have any hard evidence why this was happening—hard in the sense of being provable to economists. He really only had anecdotal evidence. Technology, global competition from our own open markets and the competitive environment within the United States were all keeping prices down.[15]

With economic science thus supposedly discredited by anecdotal empiricism, Greenspan's private stock of intuitive knowledge becomes the exclusive means available for the interpretation and forecasting of economic events. Putting it starkly, this means that it is Alan Greenspan himself who alone is capable of weighing and assigning the probabilities of the prospective outcomes of the economic process. And Woodward recounts a number of instances in which Greenspan indeed blithely assigns numerical probabilities to uncertain future events apparently on a basis no more substantial than his own intuition. For example, with respect to his own career, when Greenspan learned that he was being considered by the Reagan administration as a candidate for the Fed chairmanship in 1987, Woodward reports that he estimated the probability of his own appointment as follows: "The chance that he would get the appointment was not in the low range, 1 out of 10. It was high probability, Greenspan figured, maybe 3 out of 4."[16]

---

[15] Ibid., p. 196.
[16] Ibid., p. 22.

After he became Fed chairman, Greenspan's often demonstrated this penchant for assigning numerical probabilities to genuinely uncertain future events. Thus, when Greenspan detected signs of an inflationary resurgence in May 1993, he informed the FOMC "history tells us the chances of [choking off inflation in the prevailing circumstances] are zero short of a 2 or 3 or 4 percent rise in interest rates."[17] In an FOMC meeting in 1994, Greenspan argued that if the committee raised the Fed Funds rate ½ percent now, "the chances were better than 50–50" that it would not have to raise them before the end of the year.[18] When Long Term Capital Management (LTCM) hedge fund wound up on the verge of collapse in 1998, Greenspan calculated that "the probability that LTCM's collapse would unravel the entire world financial system was significantly less than 50 percent."[19] Also, Greenspan considered "about 95 percent accurate" his computations that indicated that labor productivity in the American economy in the 1990s had increased more than previously thought.[20]

Given his peculiar view of the economic universe in which everyone is beset by utter ignorance of the future except himself, Greenspan takes a highly unconventional view of the Fed's role in the economy. To begin with, as Woodward tells us, by the early 1990s Greenspan was arguing that "the Fed had been unable to control or even accurately measure the money supply for years." Greenspan even maintained that the very notion that it was possible to measure and control money was "outdated."[21] In fact, Greenspan had been radically de-emphasizing the role of the money supply in guiding the Fed's policy decisions almost from the moment he assumed the position of chairman in 1987. Finally in February 1993, he formally announced that the Fed was giving "less weight to the monetary aggregates as guides to policy."[22] Characterizing this announcement as a "magnificent understatement," Alan Blinder,

---

[17] Ibid., pp. 105–06.

[18] Ibid., p. 130.

[19] Ibid., p. 206.

[20] Ibid., p. 170.

[21] Ibid., p. 88.

[22] Alan Greenspan, quoted in Alan S. Blinder, *Central Banking in Theory and Practice* (Cambridge, Mass.: The MIT Press, 1999), p. 29.

former Fed vice chairman under Greenspan, recently remarked: "Less? How about zero? Greenspan's remarks were greeted with yawns in both academia and the financial markets because it was old news."[23]

So, for Greenspan, the primary task of the Fed is not to manage the money supply, which it could not control or even measure, but to manage the unruly and ill-informed perceptions and expectations of market participants. This task requires that the Fed, particularly, the Fed chairman, anticipate unexpected changes in the economy and carefully mold the public's perceptions and expectations to take account of these impending changes without disturbing their confidence. Allowing the public to fall victim to "irrational exuberance" on the one hand or "a contagion of low confidence" on the other would call forth the hidden forces of inflation or recession roiling beneath the surface of market phenomena.

Woodward recounts a number of incidents that exemplify Greenspan's belief that the Fed's overriding purpose in manipulating the fed funds rate is not to directly and systematically operate on economic variables like the money supply, investment, or total spending but to massage and mold the public's and, particularly, the capital market's perceptions of the Fed's performance in containing inflation or recession. For example, in August 1990, in the midst of the uncertainties engendered by an incipient recession and the Persian Gulf crisis, Greenspan declared to the FOMC, "I don't think it is within our power to create a boom or prevent a recession. I would suggest that perhaps the greatest positive force that we could add to this particular state of turmoil is not to be acting but to be perceived as providing a degree of stability [by refraining from lowering interest rates]."[24]

In the November meeting of the FOMC, Greenspan observed, "Slowing inflation is now finally becoming credible." However, he continued, "It's very clear to me that if we are perceived as responding excessively easily to all the other signs that would induce central bank ease, that the risks of the system cracking on us are much too

---

[23] Ibid.

[24] Greenspan, quoted in ibid., p. 69.

dangerous."[25] Prior to the scheduled February 1991 meeting of the FOMC, Greenspan convened a conference call of the committee to inform the members that he was unilaterally lowering the fed funds rate by ½ percent. He preferred the unilateral action to one voted by the committee because, according to Woodward, Greenspan feared that "a formal FOMC vote ... would have more of an impact than a quiet unilateral action by the chairman."[26] Speaking at an FOMC meeting in 1993, Greenspan urged "we ought to try first to find a means by which to separate what policy is and then to discuss the issue of how we wish to be perceived."[27]

Indeed, at times it seems that the real, brick-and-mortar economy where people produce and exchange tangible property to achieve their ends is completely lost sight of in Greenspan's policy considerations. Addressing an FOMC meeting in February 1994, Greenspan stated his preference for a smaller rather than larger increase in the fed funds rate, reasoning that "it may be very helpful to have anticipations in the market now that we are going to move rates higher because it will subdue speculation in the stock market; at this particular stage, having expectations hanging in the market that we may move again, and reasonably soon, could have a very useful effect. If we have the capability of having a sword of Damocles over the market, we can prevent it from running away."[28] By the November 1994 FOMC meeting, Greenspan noted that the markets had already factored in a prospective rate increase in excess of ½ percentage point, cautioning that "we have to be very careful at this stage that we are ahead of general expectations. I think we can do that with ¾ of a point."[29]

Woodward reports that Greenspan came progressively to believe that his job as Fed chairman "was to anticipate the unexpected. He was increasingly convinced that the unexpected, in one form or another, would occur. He knew that what seemed impossible at first

---

[25] Ibid., p. 72.

[26] Ibid., p. 76.

[27] Ibid., p. 167.

[28] Ibid., p. 119.

[29] Ibid., p. 136.

was often what happened, so preparation for dealing with the inconceivable was a necessary part of his job." In particular, Greenspan was referring to the long dormant inflationary forces that had wrecked the economy in the 1970s and that he feared could emerge without warning at any time to wreak havoc on the fragile and sluggish economic recovery of the early 1990s.

Greenspan was especially fearful of the hangover of inflationary expectations from the 1970s that he believed were still built into long-term interest rates in 1992 and would be immediately aroused at the first sign of inflation, driving up long-term interest rates further and precipitating a vicious wage-price spiral.[30] However, Greenspan reasoned, if the public could be led to perceive that the Fed was taking a strong anti-inflationary stance by a pre-emptive and sustained rise in short-term interest rates, inflationary expectations would be quelled and long-term rates would begin to fall, thus strengthening the economic recovery. This was the rationale behind the Fed's strategy of pushing up short-term interest rates by 3 percentage points over the course of twelve months in 1994–1995.

Even "hard-headed" academic economists like Alan Blinder have apparently come to partially accept Greenspan's quirky view that monetary policy consists of managing the public's perceptions of the economy's prospective performance, particularly as manifested in the bond market. Referring to a statement that Greenspan made in February 1995 vaguely hinting at a future loosening of monetary policy after the year-long rise in the fed funds rate, Blinder declared: "In fact, the statement itself amounted to a monetary easing, since it fueled a bond-market rally well before the Fed started cutting interest rates [in July 1995]."[31]

Greenspan recognizes, however, that the root causes of inflation, or, what he refers to as "inflationary forces," extend beyond the meta-economy of impressions, anxieties, perceptions and anticipations— that these subjective states themselves are ultimately derived from and expressed through market exchanges of real goods and services. The

---

[30] Ibid., p. 102.
[31] Blinder, *Central Banking*, p. 19.

problem is that Greenspan, with his anti-theoretical and ultra-empiricist bent, has a very weak grasp of the causal laws governing the operation of the real-world market process, whose outcomes households and businesses are continually reacting to and trying to anticipate. His "theory" of the causes of inflation consists of a hodgepodge of impressionistic generalizations inferred from history. Not surprisingly, these generalizations hardly constitute a logically coherent theoretical system and may be summed up in four words: "Anything But the Fed."

While Greenspan views excessive government spending and budget deficits as a potential cause of inflation,[32] it is the private economy that he perceives as a hotbed of inflationary forces. Thus when housing prices began to skyrocket in the mid-1970s, he inferred that increased housing prices were a source of inflation because he noted that the sellers of these houses were spending their profits on consumer goods.[33] But of course this is nonsense.

First, the run-up in housing prices was itself initiated by the rapid increase in the money supply that began in the mid-1960s and which the public increasingly came to anticipate would continue. These spreading inflationary expectations caused consumers to further increase their demand for houses and other durable consumer goods as a hedge against future price inflation.

Second, had the rise in housing prices been initiated purely by a shift in the relative demands for consumer goods, unaccompanied by an inflation of the supply of dollars and a fall in demand to hold the depreciating dollar, then the prices of other consumer goods and services would have fallen and not risen. In this case the profits that Greenspan observed the sellers of houses expending on consumer goods would have been roughly offset by the restriction in consumer spending that losses imposed on the sellers of goods whose demand had originally declined due to the alteration in relative demands. Thus, contrary to Greenspan's empirical observations, sound economic theory informs us with absolute certainty that increased housing prices per se cannot initiate general price inflation.

---

[32] Woodward, *Maestro*, pp. 56, 99–100.

[33] Ibid., pp. 60–61.

Greenspan also was concerned that the rise in stock prices in the 1990s had made people feel wealthier, and that this "wealth effect" might induce an increase in consumer spending and attendant price inflation.[34] But, once again, it is a firm conclusion of economic theory that rising stock prices are not, in and of themselves, a source of inflationary pressure. For, assuming that the supply of and demand for money are constant, an increase in the price of stocks can only occur as a result of people's decisions to save and invest a greater proportion of their incomes, which reflects a relative shift in their preferences away from present consumer goods and toward future consumer goods. This "fall in time preferences," as it is called, lowers current spending on consumer goods. Thus, a rise in the stock market, all other things equal, is accompanied by a deflation of consumer prices.

Perhaps the inflationary force that Greenspan feared most, however, was economic growth, at least until recently. According to Greenspan, when firms wish to invest in new and more productive capital goods and technological processes, they demand additional credit from banks and when this new credit is expended on the planned investment projects, input prices, including wages, begin to increase. In response to their rising costs of production, businesses begin to raise their product prices, pushing up the cost of living and stimulating workers to demand further wage increases. This in turn drives up production costs and product prices even further, precipitating a potentially explosive wage-price spiral leading to runaway inflation.[35]

The foregoing theory is profoundly and thoroughly flawed and has been refuted time and again by Austrian, as well as monetarist, economists.[36] To begin with, the very first step of the explanation is wrong. If some firms demand more credit to invest in new technology—barring for the moment any increase in the supply of genuine savings in the economy—interest rates will rise and other firms will be

---

[34] Ibid., pp. 28, 195.

[35] Ibid., pp. 51, 104–05.

[36] See, for example, Henry Hazlitt, *The Inflation Crisis and How to Resolve It* (New Rochelle, N.Y.: Arlington House Publishers, 1978), pp. 23–26; and J. Huston McCulloch, *Money and Inflation: A Monetarist Approach*, 2nd ed. (New York: Academic Press, 1982), pp. 34–36.

induced to borrow less. Now if the Fed decides to "accommodate" this increase in the demand for credit, it can only do so by injecting additional bank reserves into the system and expanding the money supply. In other words, there can be no inflationary increase in the supply of credit in the absence of an increase in the money supply. Secondly, the process of economic growth is generally actuated when households choose to save a greater proportion of their current incomes than previously. These additional savings provide businesses with the funds to invest in the construction of additional capital goods, including the new and different capital goods needed to implement innovative and more productive technological processes. Eventually, after these capital investments are completed and the new technological processes are in place, labor productivity rises, thus permitting businesses to supply a greater output of consumer goods at lower per-unit costs.

The expansion in the supplies of various types of consumer goods pouring forth onto the market during periods of economic growth results in a fall in prices. But profits remain high and business firms flourish in the growing industries despite declining selling prices because of the declining average costs of production induced by the accumulation of additional capital goods and enhanced labor productivity. This is precisely what has occurred in the high tech industries in the past thirty years. In 1970 a mainframe computer sold for $4.7 million while today one can purchase a PC that is 20 times faster for less than $1,000.[37] In 1980, computer firms shipped a total of 490,000 PCs while in 1999 they shipped 43 million units despite the fact that quality-adjusted PC prices had fallen by well over 90 percent in the meantime.[38] Thus Greenspan is once again exactly wrong: economic growth is a deflationary force and not an inflationary force.

Between 1996 and 1999, the growth rate of the U. S. economy was extremely high by historical standards; meanwhile stock market and housing prices rose into the stratosphere. Yet, despite these

---

[37] W. Michael Cox and Richard Alm, *Myths of Rich & Poor: Why We're Better Off Than We Think* (New York: Basic Books, 1999), p. 45.

[38] Idem, "The New Paradigm," in the Federal Reserve Bank of Dallas 1999 *Annual Report*, p. 22.

occurrences, the rate of price inflation in the U. S. actually declined to levels not seen since the early 1960s, with the CPI rising by 1.6 percent and 2.2 percent in 1998 and 1999, respectively.[39] Now this seems to imply that Greenspan's pet theories of inflation have been proved wrong by the very economic data that he knows and loves so well. Or so you would think. However, in the late 1990s Greenspan shifted ground and began to promote the view that the laws of economics had changed as a result of the rapid technological progress that brought the New Economy into being.

The first law of the New Economy is that rapid technological change has substantially lessened job security for laborers. As a result, there has abruptly materialized what Greenspan calls the "traumatized worker" who is reluctant to demand large wage increases and whose docility has kept inflation from following its natural upward course during the growth process.[40] But this is hardly a new economic law; rather it is a species of the old and oft-refuted economic fallacy noted above, i.e., that costs of production drive the price level. Secondly, Greenspan has suddenly discovered a truth that Austrian economists have known all along and that scarcely qualifies as a new law of economics: that labor productivity increases and per-unit costs diminish during periods of economic growth, leading to an expansion of the supplies of consumer goods that exercises a deflationary influence on overall prices.[41]

Unfortunately, what Greenspan has not learned from the data, but what Austrian business cycle theorists from Ludwig von Mises to Murray Rothbard have known all along, is that the deflationary influence of economic growth on prices can disguise the distortional effect of a rapid expansion of the money supply on the economy. This occurred during the 1920s when, in a misguided attempt to stabilize the price level, the Fed inflated the money supply at a rapid rate.

---

[39] The Federal Reserve Bank of St. Louis National *Economic Trends* (January 2001): p. 26.

[40] Woodward, *Maestro*, pp. 168–69.

[41] Ibid., pp. 167, 172–74, 195, 223.

Despite the fact that the ongoing expansion of the money supply did not manifest itself in a rise in consumer prices because of the decade's rapid capital accumulation and technological progress, the monetary inflation did artificially lower interest rates and distort capital markets, precipitating unsustainable stock market investment, and real estate booms.

At the time, most people, including most economists, were fooled by the stable prices that accompanied the apparently robust growth of the real economy into believing that the Fed had averted an inflationary boom and that the business cycle had been abolished and a new "Era of Perpetual Prosperity" was at hand.[42] Just as today, and for similar reasons, most pundits and business leaders as well as many economists tout the emergence of the New Economy in which the Fed with the Maestro at the helm will deftly pilot a rapidly growing economy safely past the shoals of inflation and recession into a "soft landing."

One school of economists that has not been fooled then or now is the Austrian School. Economists, investors, and financial writers who have learned the lessons taught by Mises, Hayek and Rothbard today understand that inflation is not caused by economic growth or high stock prices; they also know that the underlying causes of recessions are neither "a contagion of low confidence" nor "a loss of faith in the New Economy." They realize that the only institution that can

----

[42] The story of this era is well told in Murray N. Rothbard, *America's Great Depression*, 5th ed. (Auburn, Ala.: Ludwig von Mises Institute, 2000). For a recent exchange between a monetarist and an Austrian economist on the interpretation of the events of the 1920s and 1930s, see the following series of articles: Richard H. Timberlake, "Money in the 1920s and 1930s," *The Freeman: Ideas on Liberty* 49 (April 1999): pp. 37–42; Richard H. Timberlake, "Gold Policy in the 1930s," *The Freeman: Ideas on Liberty* 49 (May 1999): pp. 36–41; Richard H. Timberlake, "The Reserve Requirement Debacle of 1935–1938," *The Freeman: Ideas on Liberty* 49 (June 1999): pp. 36–41; Joseph T. Salerno, "Money and Gold in the 1920s and 1930s: An Austrian View," *The Freeman: Ideas on Liberty* 49 (October 1999): pp. 31–40 [reprinted here as Chapter 16]; Richard H. Timberlake, "Austrian 'Inflation,' Austrian 'Money,' and Federal Reserve Policy," *Ideas on Liberty* 50 (September 2000): pp. 38–43; Joseph T. Salerno, "Inflation and Money: A Reply to Timberlake," *Ideas on Liberty* 50 (September 2000): pp. 43–47 [reprinted here as Chapter 17]; Richard H. Timberlake, "Final Comment on Salerno's Monetary Program," *Ideas on Liberty* 50 (September 2000): pp. 47–48.

initiate inflation in the U.S. is the Fed—the Maestro himself—because it is the only institution legally entitled to create money. The Austrian theory of the business cycle teaches us that the Fed's injection of newly created reserves into the banking system via open market operations pumps up bank credit and the money supply, distorts the interest-rate structure, and ignites an unsustainable investment boom that culminates inevitably in recession or depression. In fact the Austrian explanation of the boom-and-bust, or business, cycle fits to a tee the experience of the U.S. economy in the 1990s.

In the early 1990s the U.S. was mired in a recession followed by a sluggish recovery that ultimately cost the elder George Bush re-election to the Presidency. In 1992 and 1993, the Fed gunned the money supply, increasing it at double-digit annual rates in an attempt to propel the economy into a more expeditious recovery.[43] In 1994, the Fed reversed course and held the monetary growth rate at low levels through 1995. In 1996 it did another about-face and substantially increased the pace of monetary inflation through 1999. Just as the Austrian business cycle theory predicted, real private investment soared from a low of 12 percent of GDP in 1991 to an unprecedented high of 20 percent of GDP by mid-2000 with a pause in the tight money years 1994–1995. It should be noted that this ratio never exceeded 16 percent in the inflationary 1970s and hovered around 14 percent in the boom years of the late 1980s before falling to 12 percent at the trough of the 1990–1991 recession.[44]

---

[43] The monetary aggregate I am using is one originally formulated by Murray N. Rothbard and myself. It is equal to the Fed's MZM (for "money of zero maturity") minus traveler's checks and money market mutual funds plus the deposits of the U.S. government and foreign governments and official institutions. Today the aggregate is called AMS (for "Austrian money supply") and tracked by financial economist Frank Shostak (shostak@one.net.au). The movements in AMS and MZM have been reasonably close during the 1990s. For an explanation and defense of AMS see Joseph T. Salerno, "The 'True' Money Supply: A Measure of the Supply of the Medium of Exchange in the U.S. Economy," *Austrian Economics Newsletter* 6 (Spring 1987): 1–6 [reprinted here as Chapter 3]. For the definition of and data on MZM, see The Federal Reserve Bank of St. Louis *Monetary Trends* (available electronically at http//www.stls.frb.org/publications/mt).

[44] The Federal Reserve Bank of St. Louis National *Economic Trends* (January 2001): p. 14.

Although this phenomenal investment boom has been almost completely ignored until very recently, it represents the real counterpart of the nineties' bull market in stocks. And like the stock bubble, the investment bubble was driven by monetary inflation and doomed to collapse whenever Greenspan decided that the economic data were signaling impending price inflation and slammed on the monetary brake. This occurred last year when consumer price inflation shot up to nearly 4 percent per year and jolted Greenspan and the FOMC into raising short-term interest rates. Indeed the money supply actually shrunk by $20 billion and its annual rate of growth (year over year) plummeted from an average of 6.23 percent for the period 1996–1999 to −1.24 percent in 2000.[45]

This monetary tightening devastated the New Economy and the NASDAQ tanked, falling by over 50 percent from its high in March 2000. But even more importantly, it also brought the investment boom in the real sector of the economy to a screeching halt. This momentous news was duly noted in the Wall Street Journal article I quoted earlier: "And new numbers out yesterday [January 31, 2001] show that investment did drop in last year's fourth quarter ... business investment on equipment and software actually fell at a 5% rate—a dramatic reversal from 21% growth in the first quarter of 2000. A big drop reported last week in orders for capital goods, excluding aircraft and defense, suggest that capital retrenchment isn't over."[46]

This news should give Greenspan a great pain in the pit of his stomach. Unfortunately, it is unlikely to do the economy any good, because Greenspan and the legion of economists, journalists and business leaders that he has misled with his empty talk believe that the slowdown is a simple matter of sagging spirits and lost faith and that this malaise can be cured by the psychological hocus pocus of reducing short-term interest rates—i.e., turning on the monetary spigot full

---

[45] This refers to the AMS aggregate (see footnote 39 above). The MZM aggregate dropped from an average annual rate of growth of 12 percent for the years 1998–1999 to 7.86 percent in 2000 (The Federal Reserve Bank of St. Louis *Monetary Trends* [February 2001], p. 18).

[46] Ip and Kulish, "Psychology Test: Latest Fed Rate Cut Combats a Contagion of Low Confidence," p. A1.

blast again. This does not appear to be working however. Although Greenspan's first interest-rate cut on January 3 appeared to give the NASDAQ a boost, despite a second cut in interest rates on January 31 the index has fallen back into the doldrums where it began the year. So I hold out great hope that before the end of this year, with the arrival of a full-blown recession, all will finally see that the Maestro has no clothes—and absolutely no real knowledge of how the economy works. I wonder what the probability would be of his resigning in that case?

Bibliography

Cox, W. Michael, and Richard Alm. 1999. *Myths of Rich & Poor: Why We're Better Off Than We Think.* New York: Basic Books.

Federal Reserve Bank of Dallas. 1999. "The New Paradigm." *Annual Report.*

Federal Reserve Bank of St. Louis. 2001. *Economic Trends* (January 2001).

_____. 2001. *Monetary Trends* (February).

_____. *Monetary Trends.* Available at http://www.stls.frb.org/publications/mt.

Greenspan, Alan. 1999. Quoted in Alan S. Blinder, *Central Banking in Theory and Practice.* Cambridge, Mass.: The MIT Press.

_____. 2000. Quoted in Bob Woodward, *Maestro: Greenspan's Fed and the American Boom.* New York: Simon & Schuster.

Hazlitt, Henry. 1978. *The Inflation Crisis and How to Resolve It.* New Rochelle, N.Y.: Arlington House Publishers.

Ip, Greg, and Nicholas Kulish. 2001. "Psychology Test: Latest Fed rate Cut Combats a Contagion of Low Confidence." *The Wall Street Journal* (February 1): p. A1.

McCulloch, J. Huston. 1982. *Money and Inflation: A Monetarist Approach,* 2nd ed. New York: Academic Press.

Rothbard, Murray N. 2000. *America's Great Depression,* 5th ed. Auburn, Ala.: Ludwig von Mises Institute.

Salerno, Joseph T. 1999. "Money and Gold in the 1920s and 1930s: An Austrian View." *The Freeman: Ideas on Liberty* 49 (October): pp. 31–40.

_____. 1987. "The 'True' Money Supply: A Measure of the Supply of the Medium of Exchange in the U.S. Economy." *Austrian Economics Newsletter* 7 (Spring): pp. 1–6.

Timberlake, Richard H. 1999a. "Money in the 1920s and 1930s." *The Freeman: Ideas on Liberty* 49 (April): pp. 37–42.

_____. 1999b. "Gold Policy in the 1930s." *The Freeman: Ideas on Liberty* 49 (May): pp. 36–41.

_____. 1999c. "The Reserve Requirement Debacle of 1935–1938." *The Freeman: Ideas on Liberty* 49 (June): pp. 36–41.

_____. 2000. "Austrian 'Inflation,' Austrian 'Money,' and Federal Reserve Policy." *Ideas on Liberty* 50 (September): pp. 43–47.

_____. 2000. "Final Comment on Salerno's Monetary Program." *Ideas on Liberty* 50 (September): pp. 47–48.

CHAPTER 22

Did Greenspan Deserve Support for Another Term?

On April 22, 2003, President George W. Bush declared in response to a reporter's question, "I think Alan Greenspan should get another term."[1] Bush's expression of support for Greenspan's reappointment for another four-year term as chairman of the Federal Reserve System (the Fed) came more than a year in advance of the expiration of the chairman's term in June 2004. Regardless of his decision to accept or decline reappointment, the question of whether Greenspan deserved support for another term merits consideration for the light it sheds on the performance of the U.S. economy in the dawning years of the twenty-first century.

To begin with, my answer to the question posed is a resounding "No!" I have two reasons for this negative response. First, the Fed's performance has been astoundingly bad throughout Greenspan's tenure as chairman. Second, and perhaps worse, Greenspan has been a relentless purveyor of economic fallacies designed to obscure and justify this egregious performance. Unfortunately, his exalted position, combined with his unrivaled facility for circumlocution and obfuscation, has led

From: "Did Greenspan Deserve Support for Another Term?" *The Independent Review: A Journal of Political Economy* 9 no. 1 (2004): pp. 117–26.

[1] Peter Maer and Associated Press, "Greenspan Gets Bush's Blessing," CBSNEWS. com, April 22. Available at: www.cbsnews.com/stories/2003/04/23/politics/printable550803.shtml.

the media, the markets, and even many professional economists to treat his fallacious dicta as profound insights into the economic process. Astonishingly, the media-fueled cult of Chairman Greenspan continued throughout the 1990s even though some of the most celebrated pseudo-profundities that he uttered represented blatant reversals of views he had expressed just months earlier. For example, Greenspan's famous "discovery" that the productivity growth of the New Economy was causing the stock-market boom of the late 1990s came hard on the heels of his contradictory and equally famous declaration that "irrational exuberance" was driving the stock-market run-up.[2]

An Austrian Perspective on the Recession

In an address a few years ago, I gave a detailed analysis and critique of Greenspan's public utterances on money and the economy. I concluded that they added up to little more than empty rhetoric that served as a cover for the Fed's cheap-money policy of the Clinton years, which had caused massive and unsustainable malinvestments in the real economy and an inflationary bubble in financial markets.[3] I need not repeat this analysis here. However, I quote the concluding paragraphs of my address because they bear on Greenspan's more recent words and deeds at issue in this article. In February 2001, I wrote:

> This monetary tightening [of 2000] devastated the New Economy and the NASDAQ tanked, falling by over 50 percent from its high in March 2000. But, even more importantly, it also brought the investment boom in the real sector of the economy to a screeching halt. This momentous news was duly noted in the Wall Street Journal.... "And new numbers out yesterday [January 31, 2001] show that investment did drop in last year's fourth quarter.... [B]usiness investment on equipment and software actually fell at a 5% rate—a dramatic reversal from

---

[2] Bob Woodward, *Maestro: Greenspan's Fed and the American Boom* (New York: Simon and Schuster, 2000), pp. 172–74, 179–82, 195–96, 223.

[3] Joseph T. Salerno, Greenspan's Empty Talk. Speech given February 3, 2001. Published as Mises.org Daily Article, February 29, 2001. Available at: www.mises.org/fullarticle.asp?record=620&month=29 [reprinted here as Chapter 21].

21% growth in the first quarter of 2000. A big drop reported last week in orders for capital goods, excluding aircraft and defense, suggest that capital retrenchment isn't over."

This news should give Greenspan a great pain in the pit of his stomach.[4] Unfortunately, it is unlikely to do the economy any good, because Greenspan and the legion of economists, journalists, and business leaders that he has misled with his empty talk believe that the slowdown is a simple matter of sagging spirits and lost faith and that this malaise can be cured by the psychological hocus pocus of reducing short-term interest rates—i.e., turning on the monetary spigot full blast again. This does not appear to be working, however. Although Greenspan's first interest-rate cut on January 3 appeared to give the NASDAQ a boost, despite a second cut in interest rates on January 31, the index has fallen back into the doldrums where it began the year. So I hold out great hope that before the end of this year, with the arrival of a full-blown recession, all will finally see that the Maestro has no clothes—and absolutely no real knowledge of how the economy works. I wonder what the probability would be of his resigning in that case?

Permit me to boast of my prowess as a contrarian economic forecaster for a moment. One month after I wrote those words, the U.S. economy plunged into recession, according to the official definition of the National Bureau of Economic Research (NBER). Actually, my forecast that the economy stood on the precipice of recession, when almost everyone else was misled by Greenspan's talk of a "soft landing," was based squarely on the Austrian theory of the business cycle. This theory informs us that a fall in real investment resulting from a reversal of inflationary monetary policy, which occurred in 2000, presages the inevitable onset of economic recession. Moreover, the theory focuses our attention on the pattern of real investments in the economy, which is distorted by the Fed's persistent manipulation of interest rates. Once such distortions have built up over time and have been embodied in the economy's structure of physical capital goods, a long period of readjustment, which non-Austrians call a "recession,"

---

[4] This passage refers to Greenspan's belief that the visceral discomfort he experienced when poring over economic data was a good predictor of the economy's going sour (Woodward, *Maestro*, p. 120).

is required for their correction. Most economists and market pundits unfortunately ignored this insight and focused exclusively on financial markets rather than on the underlying entrepreneurial combinations of concrete capital goods to which stocks and bonds are mere property titles. Thus, they were taken in by Greenspan's assertion that the Fed could pilot the economy safely in for a "soft landing" by slowly letting the air out of the stock market bubble.

The prevailing consensus overlooked that a cessation or even a slowing in the growth of the money supply precipitates a rise in interest rates back toward levels that reflect voluntary saving and risk preferences in the economy and, in the process, reveals to entrepreneurs the unsustainability of many capital investments. This revelation induces a time-consuming process of liquidation and destruction of various capital-labor combinations and the reallocation of the more versatile of these resources, especially labor, to more valuable uses. Thus, for example, when interest rates suddenly rise, investment in the continued construction and utilization of new plants manufacturing oil-drilling equipment may be abandoned as unprofitable. Construction and factory workers are laid off from these projects and must then search for employment opportunities in plants producing consumer goods or in the retail sector, while the idled raw-material stocks, power-generating capacity, and transportation equipment are also diverted back toward consumer-goods production and distribution.

Deflation Phobia and the Fed

Now let us return to Greenspan. As 2003 dawned, the economy had been mired in recession and "jobless recovery" for two years, and Greenspan's tattered reputation was threatening to disintegrate along with the New Economy he had trumpeted for so long. His convoluted and banal pronouncements were increasingly met with skepticism, if not with outright incredulity, by the media and the markets. His cherished serioso image as the profound Maestro of Money was giving way to the perception of a cunning but clueless Master of Illusion who has suddenly run out of tricks. Greenspan did have one more trick up his sleeve, however, and so he played the deflation card—and he did so with all the guile at his command.

Deflation phobia had been ignited earlier in the United States by a few isolated monthly declines in consumer and producer prices that occurred in the latter half of 2001. Almost immediately a deluge of articles gushed forth to warn of the looming prospect of a catastrophic, Japanese-style deflationary depression in the United States if the Fed did not promptly and drastically cut interest rates. The authors of the first wave of these articles were mainly financial columnists and think-tank economists associated with the supply-side school, although a few Keynesian academic economists also issued dire warnings. The deflation hysteria abated somewhat after the Consumer Price Index (CPI) and Producer Price Index (PPI) finished 2001 at levels 2.8 percent and 2.0 percent higher, respectively, than their levels of a year earlier. The Fed, to its credit, ignored this initial wave of deflation phobia.

As the recession/jobless recovery lingered, relentlessly dragging down Greenspan's prestige along with the number of jobs, the Fed's tune began to change. Thus, in November 2002, Fed governor Ben Bernanke,[5] a former Princeton University professor and prominent macroeconomic theorist, delivered remarks to the prestigious National Economists Club in Washington, D.C., titled "Deflation: Making Sure 'It' Doesn't Happen Here." Now, given Bernanke's status as a Fed governor, the topic, content, and venue of his remarks would have required Greenspan's clearance; indeed, Greenspan might even have actively suggested them.

Bernanke began his speech by affirming his belief "that the chance of significant deflation in the United States in the foreseeable future is extremely small." He further expressed confidence "that the Fed would take whatever means necessary to prevent significant deflation in the United States and, moreover, that the U.S. central bank in cooperation with other parts of the government as needed, has sufficient policy instruments to ensure that any deflation that might occur would be both mild and brief." In a Greenspan-like equivocation, Bernanke added: "So having said that deflation in the

---

[5] Ben S. Bernanke, Deflation: Making Sure "It" Doesn't Happen Here. Speech before the national Economics Club, Washington, D.C., November 21, 2002. Available at: http://www.federalreserve.gov.

United States is highly unlikely, I would be imprudent to rule out the possibility altogether." He then went on to identify the cause of deflation in standard Keynesian terms as "in almost all cases a side effect of a collapse of aggregate demand—a drop in spending so severe that producers must cut their prices on an ongoing basis in order to find buyers."[6] Bernanke devoted the rest of his remarks to detailing the measures available to the Fed to prevent deflation from occurring and to cure it if such preventative measures somehow failed. Not surprisingly, all of these preventive and remedial measures amounted to little more than conventional and unconventional guidelines and techniques for creating money.

For example, Bernanke suggested that to prevent an unanticipated fall in aggregate demand from initiating a deflation, the Fed needed to establish "a buffer zone for the inflation rate," which means that it should deliberately aim at inflating prices in the United States from 1 to 3 percent per year. In addition, the Fed should remain continually on the alert for any sign of weakness in financial institutions and markets and stand ready to flood the financial system with inflationary credit in case of, for example, a stock-market crash or even a shock to confidence caused by a terrorist attack. Finally, even with the inflation rate safely within the buffer zone, if the Fed were to observe a sudden deterioration of the fundamentals of the macroeconomy, such as a fall in investment or consumption spending, it must act "more preemptively and more aggressively than usual" to forestall deflation.

In the unlikely event that these tried and true precautionary measures fail to stave off the dreaded fall in prices and the Fed has already reduced the fed funds rate to zero, Bernanke assured us that the Fed has an arsenal full of additional weapons at its disposal capable of generating the desired positive inflation. These unconventional techniques for money creation include:

1. Reducing and capping yields on medium- and long-term Treasury debt by committing itself to making unlimited purchases of these securities at a fixed price consistent with the targeted yields.

---

[6] Ibid.

2. Following the same strategy in the market for foreign government debt, which the Fed has been legally empowered to purchase since 1980 and the outstanding stock of which is several times the size of U.S. government debt.

3. To circumvent the restrictions on Fed purchases of private securities by extending zero-interest-rate loans to banks, accepting commercial paper, corporate bonds, and even mortgages as collateral, thus effectively driving down the yields on these debt instruments.

4. Financing a massive Treasury tax cut dollar for dollar by monetizing the resulting deficit to the full extent of the lost tax revenues or by monetizing direct Treasury purchases of current goods and services or of private financial and physical assets.[7]

As Bernanke pointed out, this last alternative is tantamount to showering the country with money à la Milton Friedman's famous hypothetical helicopter. Make no mistake about it, the Fed governor was proposing inflation pure and simple—and plenty of it—as the panacea for an economy beset by a falling price level. Bernanke made this fact explicit in the following passage:

> The conclusion that deflation is always reversible under a fiat money system follows from basic economic reasoning. A little parable may prove useful: Today an ounce of gold sells for $300, more or less. Now suppose that a modern alchemist solves his subject's oldest problem by finding a way to produce unlimited amounts of new gold at essentially no cost. Moreover his invention is widely publicized and scientifically verified, and he announces his intention to begin massive production of gold within days.

> What would happen to the price of gold? Presumably, the potentially unlimited supply of cheap gold would cause the market price of gold to plummet. Indeed, if the market for gold is to any degree efficient, the price of gold would collapse immediately after the announcement of the invention, before the alchemist had produced and marketed a single ounce of yellow metal.

---

[7] Ibid.

> What has this got to do with monetary policy? Like gold,
> U.S. dollars have value only to the extent that they are strictly
> limited in supply. But the U.S. government has a technology,
> called a printing press (or, today, its electronic equivalent),
> that allows it to produce as many U.S. dollars as it wishes at
> essentially no cost. By increasing the number of U.S. dollars
> in circulation, or even credibly threatening to do so, the U.S.
> government can also reduce the value of a dollar in terms of
> goods and services, which is equivalent to raising the prices
> in dollars of those goods and services. We conclude then that,
> under a paper-money system, a determined government can
> always generate higher spending and hence positive inflation.

This passage is both true and chilling. Bernanke's analogy is based on correct economic analysis: the Fed indeed does have the power to bring about a collapse in the value of the dollar. What is so frightening is that Fed governor Bernanke, an allegedly moderate free-market macroeconomist who was appointed by a Republican administration, dares to propose the use of such power as the remedy for a minor rise in the value of money. After all, the deflation of consumer prices in Japan, which Bernanke is so determined to avoid here in the United States, has averaged less than a paltry 1 percent per year since it began in mid-1999.[8]

Now one might plausibly object that I have misinterpreted Bernanke's remarks, that they were meant to apply only in the realm of theoretical conjecture, and that no one in full possession of his senses really expects a Japanese-style deflationary recession to take hold in the United States. This objection, however, ignores the context of the remarks, for Bernanke was only setting the stage for the latest performance by the Master of Illusion himself. The very fact that a prominent member of the Fed would focus on deflation in his remarks

---

[8] According to the Fed's own publications, the annual declines in the Japanese Consumer Price Index from 1999 through 2002 have been 0.3 percent, 0.7 percent, 0.8 percent and 0.9 percent, respectively (Federal Reserve Bank of Cleveland, "Deflation," in *2002 Annual Report* (May 9, 2003): pp. 6–14. Available at: www.clevelandfed.org/Annual02/Essay.pdf). Also see James B. Bullard and John Seiffert, "Japanese Deflation Loses Something in the Translation," Federal Reserve Bank of St. Louis *National Economic Trends* (September 2003): p. 1. Available at: research.stlouisfed.org.

before a business group on such a highly visible occasion signaled the unfolding of a new strategic tack by the beleaguered Fed chairman.

Sure enough, a few months later, when Greenspan testified before Congress in April 2003, he shocked the markets by proclaiming that a further drop in inflation was "an unwelcome development,"[9] slyly stoking the still smoldering fears of deflation. A few weeks later the Fed Open Market Committee (FOMC) followed up Greenspan's bombshell by releasing a typically ambiguous, Greenspan-era statement indicating a "minor" probability that "an unwelcome substantial fall in inflation" outweighed the risk of higher inflation.[10] The FOMC's oblique warning appeared to be confirmed a week later when data were released showing small declines in April's CPI and retail sales, although these developments were owing for the most part to falling oil prices as the U.S. invasion of Iraq wound down. Nonetheless, deflation fears were running high once again. These fears were at fever pitch when Greenspan valiantly leaped into the breach a few days later, solemnly declaring before a Congressional panel, "we see no credible possibility that we will at any point … run out of monetary ammunition to address problems of deflation."[11] Although May's data did not bear out the threat of the imminent onset of deflation widely perceived in April's numbers, the FOMC subsequently cut the fed funds rate in late June to its lowest level since 1958.

Despite the rate cut and the Maestro's soothing words, payrolls continued to shrink, the unemployment rate was stuck at its highest level in nine years, and industrial production continued to grow at a snail's pace—fully twenty months after the NBER declared the official end of the recession. Moreover, doubts began to spread among

---

[9] U.S. House of Representatives, Committee on Financial Services. Testimony of Chairman Alan Greenspan, Follow-up to the Semiannual Monetary Report to the Congress, before the Committee on Financial Services. 108th Congress, 1st session, April 30, 2003. Available at: http://www.federalreserve.gov/boarddocs/hh/2003/april/testimony.html.

[10] John M. Berry. "Fed Fears a Spiral of Falling Prices: Deflation Risk May Prompt Rate Cuts," *Washington Post* (May 7, 2003). Available at: http://www.washington-post.com.

[11] Quoted in Martin Wolk, "Fed Ready to Fight Deflation," *MSNBC News* (May 21, 2003). Available at: www.msnbc.com/news.

economists about the wisdom of the Fed's inexplicably sudden concern with deflation. Stated Chicago economist David Hale, "They let themselves get swept up in the deflation delirium and it's locked them into a rate cut that they may not want or need to make right now."[12]

Nonetheless, Greenspan would not be deterred from reinventing the Fed as an antideflationary crusader that could be depended upon to pump progressively cheaper money into the economy for as long as necessary to slay the fictitious deflation monster. Indeed, Vincent Reinhart, the Fed's director of monetary affairs, laid out the rationale for Greenspan's strategy in a little noted speech the month before the June 2003 rate cut. Reinhart suggested that the central bank conduct monetary policy to bolster markets and revive the economy by "shaping expectations" without necessarily cutting rates. According to Reinhart, "A central bank can provide impetus to the economy at an unchanged short-term interest rate by encouraging investors to expect short term interest rates to be lower in the future than they currently anticipate."[13] In other words, Greenspan's strategy was deliberately to mislead the markets regarding the future course of interest rates. Thus, Greenspan himself again transparently played the deflation card in his semiannual monetary policy report to Congress in mid-July, alluding to the "especially pernicious, albeit remote, scenario in which inflation turns negative against a backdrop of weak aggregate demand" and avowing that "the FOMC stands ready to maintain a highly accommodative stance of policy for as long as it takes to achieve a satisfactory economic performance."[14] The desperate Maestro also let slip—and the media breathlessly reported—that at its June meeting the FOMC had discussed at some length the possibility of utilizing "alternative"

---

[12] Quoted in Peter G. Gosselin, "Confusion as Fed Talks Up Deflation," latimes.com (June 23, 2003).

[13] Vincent Reinhart, Conducting Monetary Policy at Very Low Short-Term Interest Rates. Speech given May 29, 2003. Available at: www.imf.org/external/np/tr/2003/pdf/tr030529.pdf.

[14] U.S. Senate, Committee on Banking, Housing and Urban Affairs. Statement of Alan Greenspan, Chairman Board of Governors of the Federal Reserve System, Before the Committee on Banking, Housing and Urban Affairs. 108th Cong., 1st sess., July 16, 2003. Available at http://wwwbanking.senate.gov/_files/greenspan2.pdf.

methods of reducing interest rates, including the purchase of longer-term securities, but the committee had concluded that it was "unlikely" that these unconventional measures would be necessary. So it was a short jump from Governor Bernanke's theoretical ruminations about cures for potential deflation to Chairman Greenspan's reference to them as "alternative" practical policies in a prospective but supposedly "remote" war against deflation.

If we look more closely at Greenspan's testimony, we find that in his cynical attempt to manipulate markets he has profoundly contradicted himself. While he was pointing to the "remote" probability of deflation with one hand, he was encouraging the housing bubble with the other. Thus, he noted "a solid advance in the value of the owner-occupied housing stock," noting "changes in technology and mortgage markets that have dramatically transformed accumulated home equity from a very illiquid asset into one that is now an integral part of households' ongoing balance-sheet management and spending decisions."[15] In plain English, this statement means that the ready availability of cheap mortgages via Internet shopping has fueled consumption spending as people cash out some of the gains realized in the ever-expanding housing bubble.

Unfortunately for Greenspan, the media and the markets have finally begun to catch on to his verbal legerdemain and are no longer diverted by his invocation of the specter of deflation. Greenspan hoped to stimulate investment spending and economic recovery by solemnly talking up the threat of prospective deflation and the Fed's determination to fight it, and thus duping the markets into expectations of aggressive rate cutting. The Fed then proceeded to disappoint market expectations by reducing the federal funds rate by a measly one-quarter of a point in June. Hence, the strategy backfired, and, as one journalist noted in late August, "Greenspan now finds himself the subject of derision and doubt in the bond market. Investors, stung by the wide swings in bond prices over the past few months, blame Greenspan and the Fed for misleading the markets about the threat

---

[15] Quoted in Ian Campbell, "Analysis: Greenspan's New Paradigm," *United Press International* (July 15, 2003). Available at: http://www.upi.com.

of deflation and the central bank's likely response to it."[16] Even some regional Federal Reserve Banks, such as the relatively "hard money" St. Louis and Cleveland Feds, sought to disassociate themselves subtly from Greenspan's deflation hysteria by attempting to distinguish between benign and malignant deflation.[17]

By the end of September 2003, the yield on ten-year Treasury bonds and the rate on conventional mortgages had risen by nearly one percentage point, indicating spreading anticipations of future inflation as the Fed continued to expand the money supply rapidly to get the economy back on track.[18] Indeed, one perceptive journalist, Ian Campbell, pinpointed the real and present danger to the economy: unrestrained money creation to maintain low interest rates in the face of an exploding federal budget deficit. Wrote Campbell:

> The danger, to our mind, is that Greenspan's "solid advance" is not solid at all. It is all based on flooding the markets with liquidity, forcing down mortgage rates to indecently low levels, cutting rates on savings deposits, encouraging the creation of more and more debt—while friend George racks up the government debt—and encouraging spending based on extracting equity from an asset, housing, whose price is inflating recklessly and which subsequently, like the equity market is likely to fall.

Conclusion

Thus, we have yet another in a string of performances by the Master of Illusion that has flopped badly and should have disqualified him from consideration for another term. Unfortunately, Greenspan's departure from the stage would not be cause for unalloyed joy among

---

[16] Rich Miller, "Greenspan's Credibility Gap," *Business Week Online* (August 29, 2003). Available at: http://www.businessweek.com/bwdaily/dnflash/aug23/nf20030829_9263_db016.htm.

[17] See, for example, Federal Reserve Bank of Cleveland, "Deflation" as well as James B. Bullard and Charles M. Hokayem, "Deflation, Corrosive and Otherwise," *National Economic Trends* (July 2003): p. 1. Available at: research.stlouisfed.org.

[18] For current monetary and interest-rate data, see the Federal Reserve Bank of St. Louis' *Monetary Trends*, available at http://www.research.stlouisfed.org.

proponents of sound money, for although his personal style may be uniquely irritating and egregious, his inflationary "conduct" and "performance" are ultimately determined by the monopolistic structure of the institution he heads. In other words, because the Fed possesses a legal monopoly to create money, the chairman always faces overwhelming incentives to employ his position and power to benefit the constituencies that directly or indirectly enable the continuation of the Fed's "independence," or monopoly power. These constituencies include, in roughly descending order of importance, the incumbent administration, Congress, banks and other financial firms, and the capital-goods and consumer-durable-goods sectors of the U.S. economy dominated by large corporations and unions. The one thing that all these disparate groups agree and thrive on is "cheap money"—the cheaper the better. So it is no surprise that the Fed chairman, whoever that individual happens to be and whatever his style, strives more or less successfully to deliver a low-interest-rate policy, employing any argument that is plausible and ready-to-hand in order to deny or downplay that policy's inflationary consequences.

Finally, consider again the conduct of Governor Bernanke, a low-key and straightforward academic who has done some very respectable work in macroeconomic history and has in the past been rumored to be Greenspan's heir apparent. Although Bernanke's manner could not be more different than Greenspan's, this highly trained technical economist, since joining the governing body of the Fed, has expressed views more and more indistinguishable from the untutored Maestro's intuitive and ad hoc effusions. In January 2004, although conceding to the growing chorus of anti-inflationary critics that the Fed's interest-rate policy was "unusually accommodative in historical terms" for the then-current stage of the business cycle, Bernanke maintained: "That accommodation is justified, I believe, by the current very low level of inflation, and by the productivity gains and the weakness in the labor markets, both of which suggest that inflation is likely to remain subdued."[19] Thus, it is likely that, with or without

---

[19] Quoted in Louis Uchitelle, "Fed Governor Defends Call to Hold Rates at Low Level," nytimes.com (January 5, 2004). Available at: www.nytimes.com/2004/01/05/business/05fed.html.

Greenspan as Fed chairman, the long-run prospect for the U.S. economy is a persistent war against the phantom of deflation waged by misleading rhetoric and cheap money. This policy runs the serious risk of re-creating the financial and real-investment bubbles of the late 1990s, rekindling the smoldering embers of consumer-price inflation, and eventually precipitating global investors' full-blown flight from the U.S. dollar.

Bibliography

Bernanke, Ben S. 2002. Deflation: Making Sure "It" Doesn't Happen Here. Speech before the National Economics Club, Washington, D.C., November 21. Available at: http://www.federalreserve.gov.

Berry, John M. 2003. "Fed Fears a Spiral of Falling Prices: Deflation Risk May Prompt Rate Cuts." *Washington Post* (May 7). Available at: http://www.washingtonpost.com.

Bullard, James B., and Charles M. Hokayem. 2003. "Deflation, Corrosive and Otherwise." *National Economic Trends* (July): 1. Available at: research.stlouisfed.org.

Bullard, James B., and John Seiffert. 2003. "Japanese Deflation Loses Something in the Translation." Federal Reserve Bank of St. Louis *National Economic Trends* (September): p. 1. Available at: research.stlouisfed.org.

Campbell, Ian. 2003. "Analysis: Greenspan's New Paradigm." *United Press International* (July 15). Available at: http://www.upi.com.

Federal Reserve Bank of Cleveland. 2003. "Deflation." In *2002 Annual Report* (May 9), pp. 6–14. Available at : www.clevelandfed.org/Annual02/Essay.pdf.

Gosselin, Peter G. 2003. "Confusion as Fed Talks Up Deflation." latimes.com, June 23.

Hill, Patrice. 2003. "Bush Endorses Reappointment of Greenspan." *Washington Times*, April 23. Available at: www.moralgroup.com/NewsItems/Economy/p4.htm.

Maer, Peter and Associated Press. 2003. "Greenspan Gets Bush's Blessing." CBSNEWS.com, April 22. Available at: www.cbsnews.com/stories/2003/04/23/politics/printable550803.shtml.

Miller, Rich. 2003. "Greenspan's Credibility Gap." *BusinessWeek Online*, August 29. Available at: http://www.businessweek.com/bwdaily/dnflash/aug23/nf20030829_9263_db016.htm.

Reinhart, Vincent. 2003. Conducting Monetary Policy at Very Low Short-Term Interest Rates. Speech given May 29. Available at: www. imf.org/external/np/tr/2003/ pdf/tr030529.pdf.

Salerno, Joseph T. 2001. Greenspan's Empty Talk. Speech given February 3. Published as Mises.org Daily Article, February 29. Available at: www.mises.org/fullarticle.asp? record=620&month=29.

Uchitelle, Louis. 2004. "Fed Governor Defends Call to Hold Rates at Low Level." nytimes.com, January 5. Available at: www.nytimes.com/2004/01/05/business/05fed.html.

U.S. House of Representatives. Committee on Financial Services. 2003. Testimony of Chairman Alan Greenspan, Follow-up to the Semiannual Monetary Report to the Congress, Before the Committee on Financial Services. 108th Cong., 1st sess., April 30. Available at: http://www.federalreserve.gov/boarddocs/hh/2003/april/testimony.html.

U.S. Senate. Committee on Banking, Housing, and Urban Affairs. 2003. Statement of Alan Greenspan, Chairman Board of Governors of the Federal Reserve System, Before the Committee on Banking, Housing, and Urban Affairs. 108th Cong., 1st sess., July 16. Available at: http://www.banking.senate.gov/_files/greenspan2.pdf.

Wolk, Martin. 2003. "Fed Ready to Fight Deflation." *MSNBC News* (May 21). Available at: www.msnbc.com/news.

Woodward, Bob. 2000. *Maestro: Greenspan's Fed and the American Boom.* New York: Simon and Schuster.

CHAPTER 23

The Role of Gold in the Great Depression: A Critique of Monetarists and Keynesians

The historical embodiment of monetary freedom is the gold standard. The era of its greatest flourishing was, not coincidentally, the nineteenth century, the century in which classical liberal ideology reigned, a century of unprecedented material progress and peaceful relations between nations. Unfortunately, the monetary freedom represented by the gold standard, along with many other freedoms of the classical liberal era, was brought to a calamitous end by World War One.

Also, and not so coincidentally, this was the "War to Make the World Safe for Mass Democracy," a political system which we have all learned by now is the great enemy of freedom in all its social and economic manifestations.

Now, it is true that the gold standard did not disappear overnight, but limped along in weakened form into the early 1930s. But this was not the pre-1914 classical gold standard, in which the actions of private citizens operating on free markets ultimately controlled the supply and value of money and governments had very little influence.

From: "The Role of Gold in the Great Depression: A Critique of Monetarists and Keynesians," presented at the History of Liberty Conference, Ludwig von Mises Institute, Auburn, Ala., 1999. Published as "Money and Freedom," *Mises Daily* (February 2, 2000).

Under the classical gold standard, if people in one nation demanded more money to carry out more transactions or because they were more uncertain of the future, they would export more goods and financial assets to the rest of the world, while importing less. As a result, additional gold would flow in through a surplus in the balance of payments, increasing the nation's money supply.

Sometimes, private banks tried to inflate the money supply by issuing additional bank notes and deposits, called "fiduciary media," promising to pay gold but unbacked by gold reserves. They lent these notes and deposits to either businesses or the government. However, as soon as the borrowers spent these additional fractional-reserve notes and deposits, domestic incomes and prices would begin to rise.

As a result, foreigners would reduce their purchases of the nation's exports, and domestic residents would increase their spending on the relatively cheap foreign imports. Gold would flow out of the coffers of the nation's banks to finance the resulting trade deficit, as the excess paper notes and checks were returned to their issuers for redemption in gold.

To check this outflow of gold reserves, which made their depositors very nervous, the banks would contract the supply of fiduciary media, bringing about a monetary deflation and an ensuing depression.

Temporarily chastened by the experience, banks would refrain from again expanding credit for a while. If the Treasury tried to issue convertible notes only partially backed by gold, as it occasionally did, it too would face these consequences and be forced to restrain its note issue within narrow bounds.

Thus, governments and commercial banks under the gold standard did not have much influence over the money supply in the long run. The only sizable inflations that occurred during the nineteenth century did so during wartime when almost all belligerent nations would "go off the gold standard." They did so in order to conceal the staggering costs of war from their citizens by printing money rather than raising taxes to pay for it.

For example, Great Britain experienced a substantial inflation at the beginning of the nineteenth century during the period of the Napoleonic Wars, when it had suspended the convertibility of the British pound into gold. Likewise, the United States and the Confederate States of America both suffered a devastating hyperinflation during the War for Southern Independence, because both sides issued inconvertible Treasury notes to finance budget deficits. It is because politicians and their privileged banks were unable to tamper with and inflate a gold money that prices in the U. S. and in Great Britain at the close of the nineteenth century were roughly the same as they were at the beginning of the century.

Within weeks of the outbreak of World War One, all belligerent nations departed from the gold standard. Needless to say, by the war's end the paper fiat currencies of all these nations were in the throes of inflations of varying degrees of severity, with the German hyperinflation that culminated in 1923 being the worst. To put their currencies back in order and to restore the public's confidence in them, one country after another re-instituted the gold standard during the 1920s.

Unfortunately, the new gold standard of the 1920s was fundamentally different from the classical gold standard. For one thing, under this latter version, gold coin was not used in daily transactions. In Great Britain, for example, the Bank of England would only redeem pounds in large and expensive bars of gold bullion. But gold bullion was mainly useful for financing international trade transactions.

Other countries such as Germany and the smaller countries of Central and Eastern Europe used gold-convertible foreign currencies such as the U.S. dollar or the pound sterling as reserves for their own domestic currencies. This was called the gold-exchange standard.

While the U.S. dollar was technically redeemable in honest-to-goodness gold coin, banks no longer held reserves in gold coin but in Federal Reserve notes. All gold reserves were centralized, by law, in the hands of the Fed and banks were encouraged to use Fed notes to cash checks and pay for checking and savings deposit withdrawals. This meant that very little gold coin circulated among the public in the 1920s, and residents of all nations came increasingly to view the paper IOUs of their central banks as the ultimate embodiment of the dollar, franc, pound, etc.

This state of affairs gave governments and their central banks much greater leeway for manipulating their national money supplies. The Bank of England, for example, could expand the amount of paper claims to gold pounds through the banking system without fearing a run on its gold reserves, for two reasons.

Foreign countries on the gold exchange standard would be willing to pile up the paper pounds that flowed out of Great Britain through its balance of payments deficit and not demand immediate conversion into gold. In fact by issuing their own currency to tourists and exporters in exchange for the increasing quantities of inflated paper pounds, foreign central banks were in effect inflating their own money supplies in lock-step with the Bank of England. This drove up prices in their own countries to the inflated level attained by British prices and put an end to the British deficits.

In effect, this system enabled countries such as Great Britain and the United States to export monetary inflation and to run "a deficit without tears"—that is, a balance-of-payments deficit that does not involve a loss of gold.

But even if gold reserves had drained out of the vaults of the Bank of England or the Fed to foreign nations, British and U.S. citizens would have been deterred, either by law or by custom, from going to the banks to rid themselves of their depreciating notes and retrieve their rightful property left with the banks for safekeeping. Without the threat of bank runs, the central banks were under little pressure to stop inflating the currency.

Unfortunately, contemporary economists and economic historians do not grasp the fundamental difference between the hard-money classical gold standard of the nineteenth century and the inflationary phony gold standard of the 1920s.

Thus many admit, if somewhat grudgingly, that the gold standard worked exceedingly well in the nineteenth century. However, at the same time, they maintain that the gold standard suddenly broke down in the 1920s and 1930s and that this breakdown triggered the

Great Depression. Monetary freedom in their minds is forever discredited by the tragic events of the 1930s. The gold standard, whatever its merits in an earlier era, is seen by them as a quaint and outmoded monetary system that has proved it cannot survive the rigors and stresses of a modern economy.

Those who implicate the gold standard as the main culprit in precipitating the events of the 1930s generally fall into two groups. One group argues that it was an inherent flaw in the gold standard itself that led to a collapse of the financial system, which in turn dragged the real economy down into depression. Writers in the second group maintain that governments, for social and political reasons, stopped adhering to the so-called "rules of the gold standard," and that this initiated the downward spiral into the abyss of the Great Depression.

From either perspective, however, it is clear that the gold standard can never again be trusted to serve as the basis of the world's monetary system. On the one hand, if it is true that the gold standard is fundamentally flawed, that in itself is a crushing practical argument against the principle of monetary freedom. On the other hand, if the gold standard is in fact a creature of rules contrived by governments, and it is politically impossible for them to follow those rules, then monetary freedom is simply irrelevant from the outset. The first argument is the Keynesian argument and the second the monetarist argument against the gold standard. Two recent books have elaborated these arguments against the gold standard.

The Keynesian economic historian Barry Eichengreen published a book in 1992 entitled *Golden Fetters: The Gold Standard and the Great Depression, 1919–1939*. Eichengreen summarized the argument of this book in the following words:

> The gold standard of the 1920s set the stage for the Depression of the 1930s by heightening the fragility of the international financial system. The gold standard was the mechanism transmitting the destabilizing impulse from the United States to the rest of the world. The gold standard magnified that initial destabilizing shock. It was the principal obstacle to offsetting action. It was the binding constraint

> preventing policymakers from averting the failure of banks
> and containing the spread of financial panic. For all these
> reason the international gold standard was a central factor
> in the worldwide Depression. Recovery proved possible, for
> these same reasons, only after abandoning the gold standard.

According to Eichengreen, then, not only was the gold standard responsible for initiating and internationally propagating the Great Depression, it was also the primary reason why the recovery was delayed for so long.

It was only after governments one after another in the 1930s severed the link between their national currencies and gold that their national economies finally began to recover. This was because, unbound by the rules of the gold standard, governments were now able to bail out their banking systems and run budget deficits financed by bank credit inflation without the constraining fear of losing their gold reserves.

Thus, the phrase "golden fetters" in the title of Eichengreen's book is a reference to Keynes's statement in 1931, "There are few Englishman who do not rejoice at the breaking of our gold fetters."

Of course, what Keynes and Eichengreen fail to understand is that the end of the classical liberal era in 1914 caused the removal from government central banks of the "golden handcuffs" of the genuine gold standard. Had these "golden handcuffs" still been in place in the 1920s, central banks would have been restrained from inflating their money supplies in the first place and the business cycle that culminated in the Great Depression would not have taken place.

A second book that inculpates the gold standard as a leading cause of the Great Depression was published in 1998 and is entitled *The Great Depression: An International Disaster of Perverse Economic Policies*. According to its monetarist authors, Thomas E. Hall and J. David Ferguson, one of the most perverse and destabilizing economic policies of the 1920s was the Fed's alleged policy of violating the rules of the gold standard by "sterilizing" the inflow of gold from Great Britain.

This means that the Fed refused to pyramid inflated paper dollars on top of these newly-acquired gold reserves in quantities sufficient to drive U.S. prices up to the inflated level of British prices. Such pyramiding would have made U.S. products more expensive relative to British products on world markets and would have helped mitigate Great Britain's ongoing loss of gold reserves, which resulted from Britain's balance-of-payments deficits.

These deficits were the result of the fact that Great Britain had returned to the gold standard after its wartime inflation at the prewar gold parity, which, given the inflated level of domestic prices, significantly overvalued the British pound in terms of the dollar.

These deficits could have been avoided if the British government had either deflated its price level sufficiently or chosen to return to gold at a devalued exchange rate reflecting the true extent of its previous inflation.

Hall and Ferguson, however, ignore these considerations, arguing that when the U.S. sterilizes gold:

> The impact on the system is that Britain bears the brunt of the adjustment. Since the money supply in the United States did not rise, neither did U.S. incomes and prices as they were supposed to, which would have helped Britain eliminate their payments deficit. Since Britain was not aided by rising exports to the United States, Britain must experience a more severe decline in incomes and prices than would have been the case if the U.S. money supply had gone up. In this way Britain would bear the brunt of the adjustment in the form of a more severe recession than would have occurred if the United States had been playing by the rules. Thus it was critical that each country play fair.

Thus, in Hall and Ferguson's view, the rules of the gold standard dictate that when one central bank irresponsibly engages in monetary inflation and subsequently attempts to maintain an overvalued exchange rate, less inflationary central banks must rush to its aid and expand their own nations' money supplies in order to prevent it from losing its gold reserves.

But if a nation losing gold due to inept or irresponsible monetary policy can always count on those gaining gold to share "the brunt of the adjustment" by expanding their own money supplies, this is surely a recipe for worldwide inflation.

Now, this line of argument indicates that Hall and Ferguson completely misunderstand the true purpose and function of the gold standard. To begin with, a gold standard functions much better without a central bank, because these institutions, as creatures of politics, are inherently inflationary and tend to promote rather than restrain the inflationary propensities of the fractional-reserve commercial banks.

But, second, under a genuine gold coin standard, the choices of private households and firms effectively control the money supply. As I explained above, if the residents of one nation demand to hold more money for whatever reason, they can obtain the precise quantity of gold coin they require through the balance of payments by temporarily selling more exports and buying fewer imports.

This implies that, if a central bank does exist and it wishes to act in accordance with a genuine gold standard, it should always "sterilize" gold inflows by issuing additional notes and deposits only on the basis of 100 percent gold reserves and insisting that the commercial banks do the same. It should not permit these gold reserves to be used as the basis of a multiple credit expansion by the banking system.

In this way, a nation's money supply would be completely subject to market forces. By the way, this is precisely how the distribution of the supply of dollars between the different states of the U.S. is determined today. There is no government agency charged with monitoring and controlling New Jersey's or Alabama's money supply.

Hall and Ferguson reveal their uneasiness with and lack of insight into the operation of the money supply process under a genuine gold standard with the following example:

> Suppose a fad had swept the nation in 1927 because Calvin Coolidge appeared in public wearing one gold earring. Then every teenager in America wanted to wear a gold earring "just like silent Cal".... The result would be an [increase] in the commercial demand for gold. Since more gold would

> be used in earrings less would be available for money.... It
> would be beyond the power of government to do anything
> about this fact. What a scary thought, the teenagers of Amer-
> ica would have caused the U. S. money supply to decline.

While it is true that the commercial demand for gold does play a role in determining the supply and value of money under a gold standard, it is hardly cause for alarm. Rather, it highlights the important fact that the gold standard evolved on the market from a useful commodity with a pre-existing supply and demand and was not the product of a set of arbitrary rules promulgated by governments.

Now, Hall and Ferguson conclude that by breaking the rules of the game and persisting in sterilizing the gold inflows from 1929 to 1933, the Fed caused a monetary deflation in Great Britain and throughout Europe. The nations losing gold were forced to contract their money supplies and this contributed to a financial collapse and a precipitous decline in real economic activity that marked the onset of the Great Depression.

While the authors thus blame the start of the Great Depression on Fed sterilization policies, they attribute its length and severity to the gold standard. According to the authors: As long as European countries remained on the gold standard and U.S. sterilization continued, there could be no end of the Depression in sight. The U.S. gold stock would become a huge pile of sterilized and useless gold. Starting with the British in 1931, our trading partners began to recognize this fact, and one by one they left the gold standard. The Germans and ironically the U.S. were among the last to leave gold and so were hurt the worst, experiencing the longest and deepest forms of the Depression.

So although Eichengreen emphasizes the gold standard as a restraint on government monetary policy and Hall and Ferguson emphasize the failure of governments to play by its rules, in effect, they reach the same conclusion: the gold standard, and with it monetary freedom, stands indicted as a primary cause of the greatest economic catastrophe in history.

In the face of the historical evidence they adduce, can any defense be mounted in favor of the gold standard? The answer is a resounding "yes," and the defense is as simple as it is impregnable. As I have tried to indicate above, the case against the gold standard is from beginning to end a case of mistaken identity. The genuine gold standard did not fail in the 1920s, because it had already been destroyed by government policies after 1914.

The monetary system that sowed the seeds of the Great Depression in the 1920s was a central-bank-manipulated and inflationary pseudo-gold standard. It was central banking that failed in the 1920s and should stand discredited today as the cause of the Great Depression.

A detailed case in support of this view can be found in the works of Murray N. Rothbard, particularly in his books *America's Great Depression* and *A History of Money and Banking in the United States: The Colonial Era to World War II.*

In these works you will read that the U.S. money supply, properly defined, increased from 1921 to 1928 at the annual rate of 7 percent per year, a rate of monetary inflation that was unseen under the classical gold standard. You will also learn that during the 1920s the Fed, far from operating as the deflationary force on the money supply portrayed by some monetarists, increased the categories of bank reserves within its control at the annual rate of 18 percent per year.

Finally you will read that from 1929 to 1932 the Fed continued to exert a highly inflationary influence on the money supply, as it feverishly pumped new reserves into the banking system in a vain attempt to ward off the cyclical downturn entailed by its own earlier inflation of the money supply. The Fed was defeated in this endeavor to pump up the money supply and reinflate prices in the early 1930s by domestic and foreign depositors who reclaimed their rightful property from an inherently bankrupt U.S. banking system. They had suddenly lost confidence in the Fed-controlled monetary system masquerading as a gold standard when they perceived at last the dwindling prospect of ever redeeming the rapidly expanding mountain of inflated paper claims for their gold dollars.

CHAPTER 24

Comment on
A Tale of Two Dollars:
Currency Competition and the
Return to Gold, 1865–1879

By Robert L. Greenfield and Hugh Rockoff

T he stated purpose of the paper by Robert L. Greenfield and Hugh Rockoff[1] is to attempt to derive a lesson for public policy from a less-than-dramatic monetary experiment which was initiated in the United States in 1870. This experiment concerns the attempt by the U.S. Congress to establish national gold banks throughout the country in order to assist in the resumption of the gold standard after the Civil War. In contrast to an ordinary national bank, which could satisfy the 25-percent reserve requirement by holding fiat-currency greenbacks the notes they issued, a national gold bank was required to hold its reserves exclusively in gold (or silver) coin.

From: Comment on "A Tale of Two Dollars: Currency Competition and the Return to Gold, 1865–1879," by R.L. Greenfield and Hugh Rockoff, in The George Edward Durell Foundation, ed., *Money and Banking: The American Experience* (Fairfax, Va.: George Mason University Press, 1995), pp. 221–28.

[1] Robert L. Greenfield and Hugh Rockoff, "A Tale of Two Dollars: Currency Competition and the Return to Gold, 1865–79," in The George Edward Durell Foundation, *Money and Banking: The American Experience* (Fairfax, Va.: George Mason University Press, 1995), pp. 207–19.

While I believe that Greenfield and Rockoff have identified a potentially fruitful experiment, I have questions about their interpretation of the factual background of the experiment and the conclusions they draw from it. Most significantly, I question their main thesis that the national gold banks authorized by the amendment to the National Currency Act of July 12, 1870 represented an attempt by the U.S. government to "launch an alternative monetary unit." Despite my reservation on this crucial point, however, I do consider the period during which the experiment occurred to hold valuable lessons concerning the possibilities and the institutional preconditions of currency competition.

Before we are able to determine whether national gold bank notes or "yellowbacks," as they were called, can be classified as an independent alternative to existing monies in the United States, we must be clear about what those monies were. From the breakdown of bimetallism in 1853 until the U.S. Treasury and state bank suspensions of specie payment on December 30, 1861, the gold dollar, legally defined as 23.22 grains of pure gold, effectively served as the uniform medium of exchange for the entire United States.[2]

In the states east of the Rocky Mountains, these dollars circulated in the form of gold coins as well as of state bank notes and deposits redeemable in gold coin upon demand. In the Pacific states, the medium of exchange was embodied almost exclusively in gold coin. In California and Oregon, for example, banks of issue were expressly prohibited by the state constitutions and there were only a few banks of deposit. Also in circulation were the U.S. Treasury notes redeemable in gold and fractional silver coins.[3]

After the first Legal Tender Act of February 25, 1862, United States notes or "greenbacks" swiftly became the "domestic currency,"

---

[2] Ron Paul and Lewis Lehrman, *The Case for Gold: A Minority Report of the U.S. Gold Commission* (Washington, D.C.: Cato Institute, 1982), pp. 63–66.

[3] Richard A. Lester, *Monetary Experiments: Early American and Recent Scandinavian* (Devon, Great Britain: David and Charles Reprints, 1970), p. 163; Wesley Clair Mitchell, *A History of Greenbacks: With Special Reference to the Economic Consequences of Their Issue: 1862–65* (Chicago: University of Chicago Press, 1903), pp. 141–42.

that is, the medium of exchange used in everyday transactions, of the Eastern states. Although gold coins disappeared from circulation as a result of the operation of Gresham's Law, gold continued as a parallel currency in the East, because of its use in foreign trade. In fact, in order to accommodate foreign exchange dealers, New York national banks among others offered demand deposits denominated and payable in gold dollars as an alternative to greenback-denominated deposits.[4] In addition, the federal government continued to pay interest on a large portion of its debts in gold and to require import duties to be paid in gold.[5] There is evidence that uncoined gold was used as the medium of exchange in large domestic transactions.[6]

The extensive employment of the gold dollar as an alternative currency in the East naturally led to its use alongside the greenback dollar as a unit of pricing and of economic calculation. Thus Benjamin M. Anderson[7] concluded that, during the greenback era, "People *thought* in both standards." Circumstances differed considerably west of the Rockies during this era. By all accounts residents of the Pacific states made little or no use of greenbacks in exchanges or in cash balances.[8] Merchants refused to accept the greenback dollar at par in current transactions and deposit banks in California and Oregon refused to accept greenback deposits under any circumstances. Instead, people clung tenaciously to the gold dollar as their domestic currency. Thus gold continued to be used for everyday purchases of consumer goods and wage payments, and as the stipulated means of repayment in credit transactions.

There was, however, a foreign-exchange demand for greenbacks on the part of those importing goods from the East. Technically,

---

[4] Milton Friedman and Anna Jacobson Schwartz, *A Monetary History of the United States, 1867–1960* (Princeton, N.J.: Princeton University Press, 1963), pp. 28–29 fn. 17; Mitchell, *A History of Greenbacks*, p. 142.

[5] Mitchell, *A History of Greenbacks*, p. 142.

[6] Benjamin M. Anderson, Jr., *The Value of Money* (New York: Richard R. Smith, [1917] 1936), pp. 148–49.

[7] Ibid., p. 422.

[8] Bernard Moses, "Legal Tender Notes in California," *The Quarterly Journal of Economics* 7 (October 1892): pp. 1–25; Mitchell, *A History of Greenbacks*, p. 142; Lester, *Monetary Experiments*, pp. 164–65.

therefore, a regime of parallel currencies also existed in the Pacific states, with greenback dollars exchanging for gold dollars at a market-determined exchange rate. It is doubtful, however, that, outside of a narrow circle of currency speculators, money brokers, and those directly involved in trade with the Eastern states, economic calculation took place in terms of both dollars to the same extent as it did in the East.

My account of the facts is substantially in agreement with the account given by Greenfield and Rockoff. However, Greenfield and Rockoff draw an important inference from these facts which appears to me to be questionable although it is the main prop upon which much of their argument rests. The questionable inference is embodied in the authors' statement, "No particular medium of exchange *defined* California's unit of account. Instead, the standard weight of gold served as a kind of independently-defined unit of account."[9] This is a startling conclusion given the facts as the authors present them, because they clearly recognize that, in the Pacific states, the gold dollar was not only the standard pricing unit, but, in the form of gold coin, was physically present in almost every domestic exchange. Indeed, there was an estimated $25 million of gold and silver coin in circulation on the Pacific Coast during the greenback era.[10] Moreover, there was no bank note circulation and, with very few banks of deposit, presumably little use of checks.

Of course, the authors do not intend to deny that gold coin was used almost exclusively as the medium of exchange in California. Their point is that no particular *brand* of gold dollar had achieved dominance in circulation in California, where the issuance of exchange media denominated in the gold dollar was undertaken by a number of competing institutions, including private mints. Moreover, none of these institutions was responsible for originating the standard weight of gold as the unit of account. This contrasted with the situation in the East, where the greenback dollar, which was solely the creation of the U.S. Treasury, dominated as medium of exchange and defined the accounting unit. From these facts the authors' conclude

---

[9] Greenfield and Rockoff, "A Tale of Two Dollars," pp. 216–17.

[10] Lester, *Monetary Experiments*, p. 162.

that, in California, media of exchange were denominated in, but did not define, the gold dollar, which therefore existed as an "independently-defined unit of account."

While plausible, Greenfield and Rockoff's argument is based on an apparent confusion, which could have been avoided had they addressed the issue of the evolution of the gold and greenback dollars. Contrary to what the authors seem to imply, a thing does not attain the position of a general medium of exchange by virtue of its brand name but by virtue of its qualities as a specific commodity.

Without going into great depth, the theory of the evolution of money as formulated by Carl Menger[11] and later refined by Ludwig von Mises[12] and Murray Rothbard[13] tells us that the general medium of exchange originated on the market as the most saleable commodity in the pre-existing state of barter. Money thus initially circulated as a generic and unbranded commodity. The unit of account then naturally emerged as a standard weight unit of the money commodity that is most convenient for calculation, for example, pound, ounce, or gram. It is only later with the advent of coinage that the money commodity was branded to certify weight and purity and to distinguish between different issuers. It was only then that coins of particular weights came to be designated by distinctive names.

But regardless of the emergence of special currency names and the proliferation or dominance of specific currency brands, the generic money commodity itself retained the position of the general medium of exchange, and the unit of account continued to be rigidly defined as a weight of this commodity. Thus, contrary to Greenfield and Rockoff, the medium of exchange and unit of account in California were inextricably linked together and embodied in gold. In its various shapes and forms gold functioned as the "dominant" medium

---

[11] Carl Menger, *Principles of Economics,* trans. Dames Dingwall and Bert F. Hoselitz (New York: New York University Press, [1950] 1981), pp. 257–85.

[12] Ludwig von Mises, *The Theory of Money and Credit*, 2nd ed. (Irvington-on-Hudson, N.Y.: The Foundation of Economic Education, Inc., [1952] 1971), pp. 30–37, 108–24.

[13] Murray Rothbard, *What Has Government Done to Our Money?* 2nd ed. (Novato, Calif.: Libertarian Publishers, 1974).

of exchange and the unit of account "defined" as a "dollar," which was another name for the standard weight of gold.

This analysis also sheds light on the evolution of the greenback dollar. Whether it was a credit money, for which the public from the first entertained reasonable expectations of an eventual resumption of specie redeemability, or whether it was a pure fiat currency, for which such expectations were entirely absent, the greenback dollar could only emerge as a general medium of exchange and accounting unit by virtue of its previous link with gold. Indeed the forerunners of the irredeemable greenbacks were U.S. Treasury notes redeemable on demand in specie, whose issue was authorized by the act of July 17, 1861 and even "... these notes were acceptable with reluctance" by banks and the public.[14] It was only after state banks had suspended specie payments on December 31, 1861, in effect forcibly shaking gold loose from its dominant position as a medium of exchange, that the Treasury suspended specie payments and the greenback dollar came into being as an independent entity. The passage of the first Legal Tender Act on February 26, 1862, which authorized a fresh issue of the irredeemable notes, cemented the greenback's standing as the dominant medium of exchange east of the Rockies.

The point is that the greenback dollar never could have attained its standing by political fiat alone, independently of a pre-existing relationship with market-chosen commodity money. The greenback dollar did not emerge *ex nihilo* as a pure brand name.

Moreover, it is clear that, as a medium of exchange, the generic gold dollar was more dominant on the Pacific Coast than the greenback dollar was in the rest of the Union. The gold dollar was well entrenched as a medium of exchange and unit of account in the East, since it did function as an intermediary in some types of domestic exchanges and was held in business cash balances and as part of the monetary reserves of banks. In contrast, greenbacks in California played almost no role in domestic exchanges and were not held in cash balances by the public. As Greenfield and Rockoff[15] themselves point

---

[14] Mitchell, *A History of the Greenbacks*, p. 26.
[15] Greenfield and Rockoff, "A Tale of Two Dollars," p. 15.

out, even Californians who were bullish on the prospects for resumption and inclined to speculate on the long-term appreciation of the greenback did not need to hold greenbacks, since speculative gains could have been secured by acquiring and holding any interest-bearing greenback-denominated asset.

Once we recognize that the generic gold dollar was a medium-of-exchange as well as a unit-of-account dollar in California and in the East, we are able to evaluate Greenfield and Rockoff's main thesis: that the bank notes issued by the national gold banks constituted a new and independent currency.

The national gold bank notes were redeemable upon demand in gold coin and the issuing institution was required to maintain a reserve of gold and silver coin equal to twenty-five percent of the notes in circulation.[16] In drafting this legislation, the government intended that the gold notes would displace the full-bodied gold coin circulation of the Pacific Coast and perhaps also would be used in foreign-exchange transactions in the East in place of Treasury gold certificates and gold deposits of New York banks, both of which were effectively if not legally backed by one hundred percent gold reserves.[17] It was thus the hope of the government that the fractional-reserve yellowbacks would help to facilitate resumption of the gold standard by economizing on the gold in circulation and in the monetary reserves of financial institutions, thereby reducing the premium on gold and permitting the Treasury to lay in the needed stock of gold at a lower cost. However, this hope was never realized, because only ten national gold banks were organized, one in Boston, which never issued any gold notes, and nine in California.[18]

Greenfield and Rockoff's attempt to square the absence of gold note circulation in the East with its development, albeit limited, in California rests on their thesis that the national gold bank note was

---

[16] William H. Dillistin, "National Gold Banks and Bank Notes," *The Numismatist* (March 1950): pp. 133–34.

[17] Friedman and Schwartz, *A Monetary History of the United States*, p. 25 fn. 11, pp. 28–29 fn. 17.

[18] W.A. Philpott, Jr., "National Gold Bank Notes," *The Numismatist* (November 1934): pp. 717–18; Dillistin, "National Gold Banks," pp. 134–35.

an independent and self-subsisting medium of exchange. Thus they argue that, in California, which lacked a "dominant" medium of exchange, the gold note was able to easily "hitch onto" the independently-defined unit of account, that is, the standard weight of gold. Conversely, they attribute the failure of gold notes to gain currency in the East to the fact that there the greenback already dominated as the medium of exchange. Somewhat inconsistently, the authors attribute the inability of the greenback to catch on in the West and of the gold note to catch on in the East to the fact that each "lacked a connection to the established unit of account," rather than to the lack of a connection to the dominant medium of exchange.[19]

In any case, Greenfield and Rockoff conclude that the general lesson to be learned from the national gold bank episode is that for an item to gain acceptance as a medium of exchange, it must be denominated in units of the dominant medium of exchange, where one exists. This implies that, from the standpoint of current U.S. monetary policy, the issue of an alternative medium of exchange denominated in something other than Federal Reserve notes would fail to gain currency among the American public.[20]

The essential problem with Greenfield and Rockoff's explanation of the varying fortunes of the gold note on the opposite sides of the Rocky Mountains is based on what I have just argued above is a misinterpretation of the facts. Once it is recognized that the generic gold dollar was both the medium of exchange and the unit of account in California during the greenback era, there ceases to be mystery about why the gold note achieved acceptability. The gold note was accepted in exchange and held in cash balances precisely because it was redeemable in gold coin, the general and exclusive medium of exchange The gold note therefore was not a newly issued medium of exchange. Given confidence in the issuing institution's ability to maintain convertibility of the gold notes, market forces insured a rigidly uniform purchasing power for gold coins and gold notes of equal denominations. The gold notes therefore substituted to some extent for gold coin in people's cash

---

[19] Greenfield and Rockoff, "A Tale of Two Dollars," p. 16.

[20] Ibid., p. 17.

balances because they represented a more convenient way to hold and pay gold dollars.

Regarding the status of greenbacks in California, it is not quite correct to say, as the authors do, that they did not "catch on." Despite the fact that they were not denominated in units of the dominant medium of exchange (or in the established unit of account), the greenback dollar did emerge as a parallel currency by virtue of the interlocal trade relations existing between California and the Eastern states. As Ludwig von Mises[21] was the first to note, from the point of view of the theory of exchange-rate determination, there is no difference between two currencies used side by side in the same region and two currencies each of which is considered to be the domestic currency of one region and the foreign exchange of the other.

The same general analysis can be applied to explain the failure of the gold note to catch on in the East. The explanation does not lie, as Greenfield and Rockoff claim, in the fact that gold notes were not denominated in terms of the dominant greenback dollar—after all, Treasury gold certificates and gold deposits at national banks also had no link with the greenback dollar and yet each achieved circulation. Rather, it is probable that the absence of national gold bank notes in the East was due to the fact that, for certain transactions, these notes were considered less convenient than checks drawn on a national bank gold deposit and that, for transactions better served by gold-backed currency, Treasury gold certificates were preferred because they were perceived to have a lower default risk.

Despite this criticism, I believe that the policy lesson which Greenfield and Rockoff uphold is both true and important. Currency competition can only emerge out of an evolutionary market process and cannot be implemented in one fell swoop by legal fiat or by a private entrepreneurial scheme. Certainly, this is the lesson we learn from the extreme reluctance of the residents of the bankless Pacific states to accept the greenback as their domestic currency, while the greenback gained swift acceptance among the residents of

---

[21] Mises, *Theory of Money and Credit*, pp. 179–80; Lord Robbins, *Money, Trade and International Relations* (London: Macmillan, 1971), p. 22.

the remaining (loyal) states whose attachment to the gold dollar had long been attenuated by their repeated subjection to depreciated and inconvertible state bank notes.

Bibliography

Anderson, Benjamin M., Jr. [1917] 1936. *The Value of Money.* New York: Richard R. Smith.

Dillistin, William H. 1950. "National Gold Banks and Bank Notes." *The Numismatist* (March): pp. 133–39.

Friedman, Milton, and Anna Jacobson Schwartz. 1963. *A Monetary History of the United States, 1867–1960.* Princeton: Princeton University Press.

Greenfleld, Robert L., and Hugh Rockoff. 1995. "A Tale of Two Dollars: Currency Competition and the Return to Gold, 1865–79." In The George Edward Durell Foundation, *Money and Banking: The American Experience.* Fairfax, Va.: George Mason University Press. pp. 207–19.

Lester, Richard A. [1939] 1970. *Monetary Experiments: Early American and Recent Scandinavian.* Devon, Great Britain: David and Charles Reprints.

Menger, Carl. [1950] 1981. *Principles of Economics.* James Dingwall and Bert F. Hoselitz, trans. New York: New York University Press.

Mises, Ludwig von. [1952] 1971. *The Theory of Money and Credit,* 2nd ed. Irvington-on-Hudson, N.Y.: The Foundation of Economic Education, Inc.

Mitchell, Wesley Clair. 1903. *A History of the Greenbacks: With Special Reference to the Economic Consequences of Their Issue 1862–65.* Chicago: The University of Chicago Press.

Moses, Bernard. 1892. "Legal Tender Notes in California." *The Quarterly Journal of Economics* 7 (October): pp. 1–25.

Paul, Ron, and Lewis Lehrman. 1982. *The Case for Gold: A Minority Report of the U.S. Gold Commission.* Washington, D.C.: Cato Institute.

Philpott, W.A., Jr. 1934. "National Gold Bank Notes." *The Numismatist* (November): pp. 717–19.

Robbins, Lord. 1971. *Money, Trade and International Relations.* London: The Macmillan Press Ltd.

Rothbard, Murray N. 1974. *What Has Government Done to Our Money?* 2nd ed. Novato, Cal.: Libertarian Publishers.

CHAPTER 25

Money Matters No More?

Although there are deep and abiding differences between Chicago School monetarists and Austrian monetary theorists, there has always been strong agreement among them on one thing: the central importance of the money supply in explaining the purchasing power of money, or "price level," in the economy.

This does not appear to be the case any longer. The June 2004 cover article of *Monetary Trends,* a publication of the St. Louis Federal Reserve Bank, long a staunch bastion of monetarism, is entitled "How Money Matters."[1] A more accurate description of its contents is "Why Money Doesn't Matter Anymore." The author, William T. Gavin, emphasizes that "money still matters"—just not its quantity.

When economists such as Irving Fisher and other pre-Friedmanite quantity theorists used to conceive the medium of exchange as the central function of money, they focused on M1—basically currency and demand deposits—as the relevant empirical measure of the money supply. Later, under the influence of the Keynesian Revolution, Friedman "restated" the quantity theory, shifting its main focus to money's function as a "store of value" whose corresponding statistical aggregate

From: "Money Matters No More?" *Mises Daily* (June 29, 2004). Available at Mises.org.

[1] William T. Gavin, "How Money Matters," The Federal Reserve Bank of St. Louis *Monetary Trends* (June 2004): p. 1. Available at http://research.stlouisfed.org/publications/mt/20040601/cover.pdf.

M2 included interest-bearing financial assets in addition to the transaction balances included in M1.[2]

Austrians, beginning with Carl Menger in 1871,[3] considered the store-of-value function of money as secondary and derived from its primary function as the general medium of exchange. They therefore objected that some of the items included in the Friedman/Schwartz M2 aggregate did not fulfill this primary function while other assets excluded from M2 were in fact instantaneously interchangeable at par with currency or demand deposits and hence economically indistinguishable from the latter.[4]

This led to differences in the monetary aggregates emphasized by the two groups, but they remained united in a shared view of the tight link between the quantity of money and the height of prices, despite Friedman's formalization of the "inflation transmission mechanism" in terms of a Keynesian portfolio balance approach.

Now it appears that this last area of agreement between Austrians and monetarism, at least on the policy level, has gone by the boards.

Whereas Austrians since Menger have considered money's function as the unit of account as another derivative function of the general medium of exchange, Gavin now tells us, "The role of money as our unit of account … is at center stage in monetary policy today."

---

[2] Milton Friedman, "The Quantity Theory of Money—A Restatement," in idem, ed., *Studies in the Quantity Theory of Money* (Chicago: University of Chicago Press, 1973), pp. 3–21. For a description of the monetary aggregate preferred by monetarists, see Milton Friedman and Anna Jacobson Schwartz, *A Monetary History of the United States, 1867–1960* (Princeton, N.J.: University Press, 1963), pp. 4–5.

[3] Carl Menger, *Principles of Economics*, trans. James Dingwall and Bert F. Hoselitz (New York: New York University Press, 1981), pp. 258–80.

[4] For an explanation of the empirical definition of the money supply based on the Austrian theoretical emphasis on money as the general medium of exchange, see Murray N. Rothbard, "Austrian Definitions of the Supply of Money," in idem, *The Logic of Action One: Method, Money, and the Austrian School* (Lyme, N.H.: Edward Elgar Publishing, Inc., 1997), pp. 337–49; and Joseph T. Salerno, "The 'True' Money Supply: A Measure of the Supply of the Medium of Exchange in the U.S. Economy," *Austrian Economics Newsletter* 6 (Spring 1987): pp. 1–6 [reprinted here as Chapter 3].

The reason, according to Gavin, is "Our models and our discussions focus not on the quantity of money but on the purchasing power of the dollar." In other words the essential nature of money has changed merely because economists' models and Fed policy have been altered to "keep [the] federal funds rate fixed for months at a time," in which case "the short-term money supply is perfectly elastic with respect to the interest rate and all changes in money demand are perfectly accommodated."

Gavin goes on to conclude: "[A]n important channel by which the Federal Reserve stabilizes the value of a dollar is through expectations of future inflation, the main channel through which monetary policy affects the real economy. We do not have to pay attention to the quantity of money today because policymakers are paying attention to its price, by focusing on inflation and inflation expectations."

Gavin thus depicts the essential role of money in the economy today as a disembodied accounting unit whose value can be stabilized by a central bank that ignores the law of supply and demand while carefully molding the public's expectations of inflation through the hocus pocus of manipulating, or even just making "credible" threats to manipulate, a short-term interest rate. This is nonsense on stilts, and merely a sophisticated version of George Knapp's mystical State theory of money—demolished by Ludwig von Mises in 1912—according to which the value of money was not determined by market forces but directly imposed by State fiat regardless of its quantity.[5]

Hayek once commented to the effect, "God help us, if people ever forget the lessons taught by the naive quantity theory of money." Who would have thought that the St. Louis Fed would one day require such divine guidance?

---

[5] For Mises's critique of the several variants of the State theory of money, see Ludwig von Mises, *The Theory of Money and Credit*, trans. H.E. Batson, 3rd ed. (Indianapolis, Ind.: Liberty Classics, 1981), pp. 506–12.

Bibliography

Friedman, Milton and Anna Jacobson Schwartz. 1963. *A Monetary History of the United States, 1867–1960*. Princeton, N.J.: University Press.

Friedman, Milton. 1973. "The Quantity Theory of Money—A Restatement." In idem, ed., *Studies in the Quantity Theory of Money*, pp. 3–21. Chicago: University of Chicago Press.

Gavin, William T. 2004. "How Money Matters." The Federal Reserve Bank of St. Louis *Monetary Trends* (June): p. 1. Available at http://research.stlouisfed.org/publications/mt/20040601/cover.pdf.

Menger, Carl. 1981. *Principles of Economics*, James Dingwall and Bert F. Hoselitz, trans. New York: New York University Press.

Mises, Ludwig von. 1981. *The Theory of Money and Credit*, 3rd ed., H.E. Batson, trans. Indianapolis, Ind.: Liberty Classics.

Rothbard, Murray N. 1997. "Austrian Definitions of the Supply of Money." In idem, *The Logic of Action One: Method, Money, and the Austrian School*. Lyme, N.H.: Edward Elgar Publishing, Inc.

Salerno, Joseph T. 1987. "The 'True' Money Supply: A Measure of the Supply of the Medium of Exchange in the U.S. Economy." *Austrian Economics Newsletter* 6 (Spring): pp. 1–6.

CHAPTER 26

Deflation and Depression: Where's the Link?

R ecent events such as the "deflationary boom" in China have led a few mainstream macroeconomists to re-examine and revise their views on the phenomenon of deflation, conventionally defined as a general and persistent decline in prices. The long-held view that a general fall in prices, or increase in the value of money, whatever its origin, spells unmitigated disaster for overall economic activity and social welfare has begun slowly to give way to attempts to distinguish between "good" and "bad" deflation. The distinction between "corrosive" deflation and deflation that is compatible with healthy economic growth has even penetrated the publications of some of the more enlightened regional Federal Reserve Banks.[1]

These developments, while gratifying to Austrian economists, are hardly sufficient to undo nearly a century of myths about the pernicious effects of deflation that have been systematically perpetrated by professional economists beginning with the proto-monetarist Irving Fisher. But now comes a simple and straightforward empirical study published in the leading academic economics journal by two

From: "Deflation and Depression: Where's the Link?" *Mises Daily* (August 6, 2004). Available at Mises.org

[1] "Deflation," The Federal Reserve Bank of Cleveland *2002 Annual Report* (May 9, 2003); and James B. Bullard and Charles M. Hokayem, "Deflation, Corrosive and Otherwise," Federal Reserve Bank of St. Louis *National Economic Trends* (July 1, 2003): p. 1. Available at research.stlouisfed.org.

economists with impeccable mainstream credentials and affiliations successfully challenging the most widespread and deeply ingrained belief about deflation: that there is a well established empirical relationship between deflation and depression.[2]

Atkeson and Kehoe utilize panel data on inflation and real output growth for seventeen countries, including the United States, the United Kingdom, France, and Germany. The data set for each country encompasses at least 100 years. The authors focus on medium-term fluctuations by breaking the time series on inflation and on economic growth for each country into periods of five years and calculating the average annual rates of real output growth and inflation for each such period or "episode."

"Deflation" is then defined for each episode as "a negative average inflation rate" and "depression" as "a negative average real output growth rate." The five-year episodes are selected so as to begin and end with years ending in "9" or "4" so that, for example, the years of the Great Depression (1929–1933) and the depression of 1921–22 are grouped together in single episodes, 1929–1934 and 1919–1924, respectively.

The Great Depression Episode

Isolating the Great Depression episode, the authors do find a loose link between deflation and depression. All 16 countries for which data were available experienced deflation during this episode, while only 8 of the 16 experienced depression. Output growth was regressed on a constant and the inflation rate, and the estimated slope coefficient was .40 while the standard error was .28.

In other words, a one-percentage point reduction in inflation is associated with a .40 percentage point decline in real output growth during the Great Depression, although even during this episode

---

[2] Andrew Atkeson and Patrick J. Kehoe, "Deflation and Depression: Is There an Empirical Link," *American Economic Review Papers and Proceedings* 94 (May 2004): pp. 99–103. The first co-author is on the faculty of the Department of Economics of UCLA and the second works in the Research Department of the Federal Reserve Bank of Minneapolis.

the probability that there is no relationship between deflation and depression (the level of significance) exceeds 10 percent. In the jargon of statistical inference this means that the relationship between deflation and depression is not "statistically significant."

All Episodes Exclusive of the Great Depression Episode

When the authors leave the Great Depression aside, and plot average inflation and output growth rates for all countries for all five year episodes—which begin in 1820 for some countries in the sample—except 1929–1934 it turns out that 65 of 73 deflation episodes involved no depression while 21 of 29 depression episodes were not associated with deflation. In other words, 90 percent of deflation episodes did not culminate in depression. From this the authors conclude, "In a broader historical context, beyond the Great Depression, the notion that deflation and depression are linked virtually disappears." This conclusion is also supported by the slope coefficient and the standard error for the data excluding the Great Depression, which are 0.04 and 0.03 respectively.

All Episodes

When the regression is run for all episodes including the Great Depression, the result is that a 1-percentage point drop in inflation is associated with a piddling decline in the average growth of real output of .08 percentage points with a standard error of .03. While this result is statistically significant it is certainly not economically significant.

Thus, for example, assuming the value of money was initially constant and then began to appreciate by 1 percent per year, real output growth in the economy would fall from, say, 3.00 to 2.92 percent per year. This means that even a massive deflation of 30 percent per year visited upon an economy that was growing at 3.00 percent per year would not cause a depression—defined as negative growth of real output—since it would only lower the real growth rate by 2.4 percentage points to 0.60 percent per year. From a strictly empirical standpoint, then, the Great Depression can hardly be explained by a price level that declined by about 5 percent per year between 1929 and 1933.[3]

Pre- and Post-World War II Episodes

The study also finds that the relation between deflation and depression differs markedly before and after World War II. The regression using the prewar data yields a slope coefficient of 0.11 with a standard error of 0.04, indicating a weak link between deflation and depression. In contrast, the regression run with postwar data suggests no link between deflation and depression, with the slope coefficient of –0.03 and a standard error of 0.04. Indeed the negative slope coefficient suggests the possibility of a link between inflation and depression. Given this empirical result, you might hope that the large and growing contingent of mainstream economists who are clamoring for the Fed to implement "inflation targeting" of 2 to 3 percent per year—i.e., to deliberately dilute the purchasing power of the dollar by a fixed percentage every year—would now switch to prescribing deflation targeting of a few percent per year just to be on the safe side.[4]

Conclusion and Implications

As Atkeson and Kehoe conclude: "The data suggest that deflation is not closely related to depressions. A broad historical look finds more periods of deflation with reasonable growth than with depression, and many more periods of depression with inflation than with deflation. *Overall, the data show virtually no link between deflation and depression.*" (Emphases added.) The authors caution, however, that their study "characterizes the relation in the raw data between deflation and output growth, with no attempt to control for anything"

---

[3] This figure is computed from the data in Kenneth Weiher, *America's Search for Economic Stability: Monetary and Fiscal Policy since 1913* (New York: Twayne Publishers, 1992), pp. 39, 57.

[4] On the current status of the inflation targeting debate, see the articles in Inflation Targeting: Prospects and Problems, Proceedings of the Twenty-Eighth Annual Economic Policy Conference of the Federal Reserve Bank of St. Louis, Federal Reserve Bank of St. Louis *Review* 86 (June/August 2004).

and "perhaps a link between deflation and depression could be teased out of the data with a well-motivated set of controls."[5]

From the Austrian standpoint, it is precisely the virtue of the Atkeson-Kehoe study that it uses raw data that have not been subjected to arbitrary statistical manipulations. For it is unaveraged, unsmoothed, unadjusted data that are the direct and immediate outcome of unique and non-repeatable human choices in the marketplace. As such, these data are the most meaningful in applied theoretical analysis and for the interpretation of economic history.

As Murray Rothbard often emphasized: "Austrians realize that empirical reality is unique, particularly raw statistical data. Let that data be massaged, averaged, seasonals taken out, etc. and then the data necessarily falsify reality."[6]

Rothbard objected even to the seemingly innocuous practice of seasonally adjusting the data: "In our view the further one gets from the raw data the further one goes from reality, and therefore the more erroneous any concentration upon that figure. Seasonal adjustments in data are not as harmless as they seem, for seasonal patterns, even for such products as fruits and vegetables, are not set in concrete. Seasonal patterns change, and they change in unpredictable ways, and hence seasonal adjustments are likely to add distortions to the data."[7]

The Atkeson-Kehoe study has a number of important implications for competing schools of macroeconomics. First, from the point of view of "aprioristic" or logical-deductive Austrian economic theory, while it does not validate or "falsify" any particular theoretical approach to business cycle theory, it is certainly illustrative of the Mises-Rothbard argument that an increase in the value of money is neither a necessary cause of depression nor an impediment to healthy economic growth. Second, the monetary disequilibrium approach

---

[5] Atkeson and Kehoe, "Deflation and Depression," p. 102.

[6] Murray N. Rothbard, *Making Economic Sense* (Auburn, Ala.: Ludwig von Mises Institute, 1995), pp. 233–34.

[7] Murray N. Rothbard, *The Mystery of Banking* (New York: Richardson & Snyder, 1983), p. 259.

to depression, which has been embraced by many, but not all, of the "free banking" wing of Austrian macroeconomics, seems to now have a serious problem.[8] According to this approach, which was initiated in the writings of the proto-monetarist, FDIC official Clark Warburton in the 1940s, the primary cause of depression is the emergence of an excess demand for money in the economy whose effects are not instantaneously or rapidly neutralized by a corresponding increase in the supply of money.[9] The result is a tendency toward a general fall in prices (deflation) and, at least in the short run, in real output (depression).

The lack of a historical relation between deflation and depression found by Atkeson and Kehoe, however, seems to indicate that the monetary disequilibrium theory of depression, which is also a logical-deductive theory, is inapplicable to most, if not all, of empirical reality. Along the same lines, the study also demolishes one of the main props of the argument in favor of unregulated fractional-reserve banking. If there is no link between deflation and depression then there is no need for banking institutions that putatively respond to every change in the demand for money with an offsetting change in the supply of money.

Finally, the study is potentially devastating to the now widely accepted Friedman-Schwartz explanation of the Great Depression. In a recent symposium celebrating the fortieth anniversary of their famous work, A Monetary History of the United States, Milton Friedman correctly noted, "The most controversial of [our major themes]—our attribution to the Federal Reserve of a major share of

---

[8] Two works which are representative of this branch of Austrian macroeconomics are: George A. Selgin, *The Theory of Free Banking: Money Supply under Competitive Note Issue* (Totowa, N.J.: Rowman & Littlefield, Publishers 1988); and Steven Horwitz, *Microfoundations and Macroeconomics: An Austrian* Perspective (New York: Routledge, 2000).

[9] Clark Warburton, *Depression, Inflation, and Monetary Policy: Selected Papers, 1945–1953* (Baltimore: The Johns Hopkins Press, 1966). The most prominent contemporary proponent of this approach is Leland Yeager. (See Leland Yeager, *The Fluttering Veil: Essays on Monetary Disequilibrium*, ed. George Selgin [Indianapolis, Ind.: Liberty Fund, Inc., 1997]).

the responsibility for the 1929–1933 contraction—has become almost conventional wisdom."[10]

Friedman and Schwartz ascribed culpability to the Fed for what they called the "Great Contraction" because it allegedly pursued deflationary policies in the early 1930s.[11] Unfortunately, for Friedman and Schwartz the causal connection they posited between the deflation and depression of the early 1930s was purely empirical, based not on sound praxeological reasoning, but on statistical correlations using the data of a single country for the years 1857–1960.

With the validity of their correlations now called into serious question by a study using well over 100 years of data from seventeen different countries, we may yet see the deflation-depression link follow another supposedly ironclad empirical relation, the Phillips Curve, into well-deserved oblivion.

Bibliography

Atkeson, Andrew, and Patrick J. Kehoe. 2004. "Deflation and Depression: Is There an Empirical Link." *American Economic Review Papers and Proceedings* 94 (May): pp. 99–103.

Bernanke, Ben S. 2000. *Essays on the Great Depression.* Princeton: N.J.: Princeton University Press.

Bullard, James B. and Charles M. Hokayem. 2003. "Deflation, Corrosive and Otherwise." The Federal Reserve Bank of St. Louis *National Economic Trends* (July 1): p. 1. Available at research.stlouisfed.org.

Federal Reserve Bank of Cleveland. 2003. "Deflation." *2002 Annual Report* (May 9, 2003).

---

[10] Milton Friedman, "Reflections on a Monetary History," *The Cato Journal* 23 (Winter 2004): p. 349. For evidence that the Friedman-Schwartz view has indeed become the dominant explanation of the Great Depression among mainstream macroeconomists, see Ben S. Bernanke, *Essays on the Great Depression* (Princeton, N.J.: Princeton University Press, 2000), pp. 6–8.

[11] For a defense of Murray Rothbard's view that the Fed did not pursue a deflationary policy in the early 1930s and, indeed, tried desperately to inflate the money stock, see Joseph T. Salerno, "Money and Gold in the 1920s and 1930s: An Austrian View," *Ideas on Liberty* 49 (October 1999) [reprinted here as Chapter 16].

Federal Reserve Bank of St. Louis. 2004. Inflation Targeting: Prospects and Problems, Proceedings of the Twenty-Eighth annual Economic Policy Conference of the Federal Reserve Bank of St. Louis, Federal Reserve Bank of St. Louis *Review* 86 (June/August).

Friedman, Milton. 2004. "Reflections on a Monetary History." *The Cato Journal* 23 (Winter).

Horwitz, Steven. 2000. *Microfoundations and Macroeconomics: An Austrian Perspective*. New York: Routledge.

Rothbard, Murray N. 1983. *The Mystery of Banking*. New York: Richardson & Snyder.

_____. 1995. *Making Economic Sense*. Auburn, Ala.: Ludwig von Mises Institute.

Salerno, Joseph T. 1999. "Money and Gold in the 1920s and 1930s: An Austrian View." *Ideas on Liberty* 49 (October).

Selgin, George A. 1988. *The Theory of Free Banking: Money Supply under Competitive Note Issue*. Totowa, N.J.: Rowman & Littlefield, Publishers.

Warburton, Clark. 1966. *Depression, Inflation, and Monetary Policy: Selected Papers 1945–1953*. Baltimore: The Johns Hopkins University Press.

Weiher, Kenneth. 1992. *America's Search for Economic Stability: Monetary and Fiscal Policy since 1913*. New York: Twayne Publishers.

Yeager, Leland. 1977. *The Fluttering Veil: Essays on Monetary Disequilibrium*, George Selgin, ed. Indianapolis, Ind.: Liberty Fund, Inc.

INDEX

About the Author

Joseph Salerno is academic vice president of the Ludwig von Mises Institute, professor of economics at Pace University, and editor of the *Quarterly Journal of Austrian Economics*.

Printed in Great Britain
by Amazon

49517766R00366